Burgundy

Anthony Hanson is a Master of Wine who lived in Burgundy for three years. He has been studying, buying, selling and enjoying its wines for three decades.

BURGUNDY

ANTHONY HANSON, M.W.

new edition

faber and faber

LONDON · BOSTON

First published in 1982
This completely revised second edition
first published in 1995
by Faber and Faber Limited
3 Queen Square, London, WC1N 3AU

Phototypeset by Intype, London
Printed in England by Clays Ltd, St Ives plc

© Anthony Hanson 1995

Maps © John Flower 1995

Anthony Hanson is hereby identified as author of this work in
accordance with Section 77 of the Copyright, Designs and
Patents Act 1988.

A CIP record for this book
is available from the British Library

ISBN 0–571–153895 (cased)
0–571–151787 (pbk)

2 4 6 8 10 9 7 5 3 1

TO ROSI
with love

Contents

CONTENTS

Illustrations

MAPS

TABLES AND FIGURES

Figures

Tables

Acknowledgements

=====

'You are worse than the priest, with your questions,' said one vine-yard owner. Indeed, I have been very intrusive into matters of family history and private property, not to mention trade secrets. Burgundians were boundlessly generous with information; without their openness and co-operation this book would not have been possible.

For it to appear has required a cast of hundreds, and I am extremely grateful to all those who agreed to play a part. It would not be possible to name them all, but I hope they will accept my thanks for the time they gave, the books they lent, the corks they drew, and the information and advice which they passed on so freely.

In particular I would like to thank six Burgundy wine-brokers: Henri Meurgey, Tim Marshall (who has now retired from broking to tend his vineyards), Becky Wasserman, Maurice Vollot, Michel Gormand and, last but not least, Patrick Saulnier Blache. I am also greatly indebted to two 'new generation' négoçiants: Olivier Leflaive, who runs a family firm of that name in Puligny-Mont-rachet and Pierre Meurgey who runs the old firm of Champy Père & Co. in Beaune.

I shall always be grateful to the late Robert and Georges Bouchard, who, with the latter's son Paul, first most hospitably gave me a job in Burgundy, and to Dr P. Wallace, who checked early drafts of the geology chapter. Robert Joseph brought to light several errors in the first edition, and many readers wrote in with queries, corrections or findings. I am much indebted to them all. Any inaccuracies in this completely rewritten second edition are, of course, entirely my responsibility.

On a personal note, the Meurgey family in Beaune – Henri,

Marie-Thérèse, Pierre and Frédéric – have been exceptionally kind and helpful on many occasions. So have Patrick and Sachiko Saulnier Blache in Paris, to whom I owe a special debt for their hospitality and insights.

Particular thanks are also due to Becky Wasserman and her husband Russell Hone for their warm welcomes and encouragement. Their home in Bouilland has remained a hub around which numerous Burgundy enthusiasts circle, regularly drawn back in. Few foreigners can have done as much to spread knowledgeable enthusiasm for fine Burgundy overseas since the mid-1970s.

I offer special thanks to Bart Wasserman, now living in America, who introduced me to many of the best wine addresses when I was first in Burgundy. He has remained a precious sounding board.

I am indebted to many people for their writings on Burgundy since the mid 1980s, as will be seen in the 'new literature' section of the Bibliography.

I am especially grateful to all those who have invited me to judge or speak at non-European wine shows or conferences: Len Evans in respect of Canberra, John Hanley for Perth, John Comerford for Auckland and David Adelsheim in Oregon. Overseas wine judging is difficult, but immensely rewarding and enriching, allowing me to see Burgundy in its global context.

Particular thanks go to those people who steered me, sometimes no doubt obliviously, by a phrase, a bottle, an idea, a hint or a push – or several of these together. Although I owe them much, no one saw parts of the book in draft or final form, so they are responsible for none of it:

In France, to Guillaume d'Angerville, Jean-Pierre Auvigue, Xavier Barbet, Ghislaine Belicard, Jean-Claude Berrouet, Michel Bettane, Patrick Bize, M. et Mme Simon Bize, Nelly Blau, Michel Boss, Claude Bourguignon, Alain and Dominique Burguet, Charlois père et fils, Louis-Marc Chevignard, Jean-Paul Couillault, François Faiveley, Nancy and Alex Gambal, Etienne and Marielle Grivot, Jean Grivot, Franck Grux, Frédéric and Chantal Lafarge, Alix Marshall, Jean-François Mestre, Alix de Montille, Hubert de Montille, Christian Moueix, Michel Poitout, Jean-Marie, Bernard and Bernadette Raveneau, Olivier Ravier, Michel Rémon, Jacky Rigaux, Nicolas and Florence Rossignol-Trapet, Jean-Marc Roulot, Raoul Salama, Jean-Charles Servant, Nathalie Tollot, Pascal

Wagner, Jean-Claude Wallerand, Paul Wasserman and Peter Wasserman.

To Les Amis du Clos Vougeot for their help with the updating of the Clos Vougeot map, showing owners' plots, and to Noëlle and Jean François of Saint-Romain for arranging for me to visit stave-splitters in the Bertranges forest near Nevers, and watch coopers at work, I am exceptionally grateful.

In Japan, I offer thanks to John Bisazza, Professor Hiroshi Yama-moto, Asaichi Taguchi, Wataru Ohgari; in Singapore, to Laura Hwang and Alan Wong.

In Australia, special thanks go to James and Suzanne Halliday, to John and Toni Tate, and to Tony Devitt, as also to Paul de Burgh-Day, Vanya Cullen, John Durham, Ray Jordan, Terry Lee, Ian McKenzie, Tony Smith, John Wade and the Wignall family. In New Zealand, particular thanks go to John and Chris Comerford and Philip Gregan, as also to Alan McCorkindale, Larry McKenna, Rolfe and Lois Mills, Clive Paton and Richard Riddiford. I offer my thanks to Nils Dyvad in Denmark, and to Constantine Stergides in Greece.

In North America, I am indebted to Clayton Ruby, who regularly updated me on fine Burgundy as seen from north of the Canadian border; to Kermit Lynch for giving my hazy thoughts on wine clarity something of a filtration, and particularly to Mel Knox for speech-writing and pronunciation coaching, along with much else.

I also warmly thank Gerald Asher, Bob Good, Robert Haas, David Lett, George Michas, Ellen Nicot-Cartsonis, Rick Ostrand, David Ramey, Todd Ruby, David Schildknecht, and particularly Dick Ward.

In the United Kingdom I thank Adam Bancroft, Suzannah Beat-son-Hird, Hew Blair, Nick Clarke, Clive Coates, Simon Cock, David Cossart, David Dugdale, Sir Ewen Fergusson, Hilary Gibbs, Tim Hart, Mark Hopkins, Simon Loftus, Catherine Manac'h, Jasper Morris, Richard and Shelagh Nichols, Sebastian Payne, Margaret Rand, Roy Richards, Jancis Robinson, Anthony Rose, Guy Ruddle, Mark Savage, Michael Schuster, Steven Spurrier, John Surtees, Charles Taylor, and John Thorogood.

To Denis Haynes, Nicholas Clark and Bobby McAlpine, my original business partners on the setting up of wine merchants Haynes Hanson and Clark in 1978 (from which I resigned as a director in June 1991, but to which I have remained linked as a consultant) I am most grateful, as to Philip Rogers-Coltman, Rosie Buckley, Jim Eustace and Jamie Strutt for their skilful help.

Lisella Wilkinson gave me much help with the early research, as did Harriet Salisbury. First Carole McGlynn then Mary Dortch were constructive, painstaking copy-editors, and Ingrid Grimes's contributions were extremely valuable. The completely new maps bring far greater detail than I imagined was possible in a book of this size, and I am most grateful to John Flower for his meticulous pursuit of accuracy and clarity. At Faber and Faber, Justine Willett's careful coordination of the final stages of the book's production was much appreciated, while Belinda Matthews and Sarah Gleadell were towers of supportive insistency. The book owes a great deal to Julian Jeffs for his vision and patient editing, and I am extremely grateful to him.

My debt to my wife Rosi is immense. Without her inspiration and input the first edition would have had little value, and that is even more true of the second. To her, and to my son Christopher (for whom I have been either abroad or in front of a screen for too long) I offer special thanks.

For permission to quote from published sources my thanks are due to: Editions Montalba, for extracts from the section by Raymond Bernard in *Le Vin de Bourgogne*; Société Française d'Editions Vinicoles for a quotation from *Les Vins de Bourgogne* by Pierre Bréjoux; Mitchell Beazley Publishers for quotations from Hugh Johnson's *The Story of Wine*, and James Halliday's and Hugh Johnson's *The Art and Science of Wine*; Madame Rolande Gadille for much material from *Le Vignoble de la Côte bourguignonne* published by the Université de Dijon; the estate of the late Professor Roger Dion, author of *Histoire de la vigne et du vin en France des origines au XIXème siècle*; Les Presses Universitaires de France for a quotation from *Origines du vignoble bourguignon* by the late Pierre Forgeot; Flammarion for an extract from *La Bouillie bordelaise* by Bernard Ginestet; Dunod for quotations from *Connaissance et travail du vin* by Emile Peynaud; Penguin Books for a quotation from *Valois Burgundy* by Richard Vaughan and for permission to reproduce the geological time scale in *The Penguin Dictionary of Geology* by D. G. A. Whitten and J. R. V. Brooks; Madame Françoise Grivot for an extract from *Le Commerce des vins de Bourgogne*; Justin Dutraive for a quotation from *Jadis en Beaujolais*; Pierre Poupon for quotations from *Nouvelles Pensées d'un dégustateur*, published by the Confrérie des Chevaliers du Tastevin; the Comité National des Appellations d'Origine des Vins et Eaux-de-Vie and Louis Larmat for quotations from *L'Evolution de la législation sur les appellations d'origine – genèse des appellations contrôlées*; Jonathan Cape for a quotation from *A Book of French Wines* by P. Morton Shand (revised and edited by Cyril Ray): A. P. Watt Ltd for a quotation from *Champagne, the Wine, the Land and the People* by Patrick Forbes; Christie Manson & Woods for a quotation from a sale memorandum by Michael Broadbent of June 1979; Masson for permission to reproduce the diagram showing rock strata of the Côte de Beaune and Nuits from *Bourgogne Morvan* by Pierre Rat; Horizons de France for a quotation from *La Bourgogne, tastevin en main* by Georges Rozet; and Edition du Seuil for several quotations from *Les Bons Vins et les autres* by P. M. Doutrelant.

A.H.
June 1994

Quels sont . . . les caractères essentiels du critique?
Il faut que, sans parti pris, sans opinions précon-
çues, sans idées d'école, sans attaches avec aucune
famille d'artistes, il comprenne, distingue et
explique toutes les tendances les plus opposées, les
tempéraments les plus contraires, et admettent
les recherches d'art les plus diverses.

Guy de Maupassant, *Préface à Pierre et Jean*

PART ONE

I

Introducing Burgundy and Its Wines

Burgundy is one of the more difficult wines to buy: there are many growers, merchants and wine names. I hope this book will guide newcomers to Burgundy in their search for wines which are delicious and good value; and that it will also be valuable to those who are already enthusiasts.

Buying white Burgundy is easy; any Chardonnay lover can approach it. The red is more tricky, the rewards much greater.

I toyed with the idea of classifying every supplier numerically, or with stars, grape-bunches, *tastevins*, lop-sided berets or snails. The trouble is, within each cellar one finds disappointments as well as pleasures, and of course results change with each vintage. Most significantly, I might be qualified to rate one hundred or so growers (those I know quite well) but this book describes six times that number. A classification might appear to make the reader's work lighter, but it only *seems* to make things simpler.

There is only one way to buy Burgundy: you have to grapple with it personally. If you are not prepared to do that, then leave this book alone. But if you want to grapple, I hope the book will help you enjoy the wines more, and that it will also save you money.

If the text seems sparse or contradictory the thing to do is: draw a cork from the Burgundy being described, look, smell and taste – and all will become clearer, once you start talking about the wine.

In my own mind, I visualize suppliers in three broad groups: exciting, respectable and dull. But one often gets merely respectable wines from a cellar which is usually exciting, and all the other combinations. It is really difficult to be categorical.

BURGUNDY AND ITS WINES

For centuries Burgundy has produced some of the finest wines in the world, wines steeped in tradition and praised wherever wine is drunk. They are mainly dry white and red wines, though some rosé and sparkling wines of various colours are also made.

A glance at the map on p. 5 will show that the Burgundy area is found in central-eastern France, on the right bank of the Saône river, which runs into the Rhône at Lyon. It is divided into six main regions, which will be considered individually; from north to south they are: Chablis and the Auxerrois, the Côte de Nuits, the Côte de Beaune, the Côte Chalonnaise, the Mâconnais and the Beaujolais.

The naming of Burgundy is a little complicated, but can be quickly grasped. It is no worse than the naming of American roads, for instance. When a European first starts driving round the USA, she or he discovers that the same road may start with one number, then take on a second, then a third, then revert to just one; and that a road may be travelling east, yet be called South, or be going west, yet be named North. That European may be close to despair – but all that is needed is an atlas. If you know the idea, you can get along.

Figure 1 may help to explain Burgundy's wine names. As may be noticed, there are one or two booby traps. For instance, you might reasonably expect First Growth (*Premier Cru*) Burgundy to be the best, just as you might expect that you had the best seats, if someone gave you a ticket for No. 1 Court on Wimbledon tennis finals day. But no, the top classification in Burgundy is called Great Growth (*Grand Cru*). And the place to be for the last match in the men's singles is, of course, the Centre Court.

Another Burgundian booby trap is that certain villages have added the name of their most famous vineyard to their own, in order to benefit from its fame. The village of Gevrey became Gevrey-Chambertin; Morey became Morey-Saint-Denis; Chambolle became Chambolle-Musigny; Aloxe became Aloxe-Corton; and Puligny and Chassagne both tacked on Montrachet, the world-famous white wine vineyard approximately half of which is in each commune. So one should not imagine one is drinking Chambertin when one buys a bottle of Gevrey-Chambertin.

The best vineyards are very small indeed when compared with their peers in Bordeaux and they are usually split up between many

Wine areas of Burgundy

The Burgundy Pyramid
How the wines are named and classified

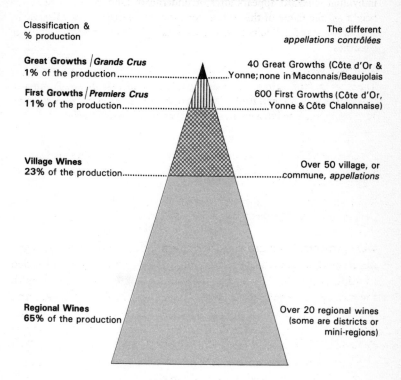

Classification &
% production

The different
appellations contrôlées

Great Growths / *Grands Crus*
1% of the production...

40 Great Growths (Côte d'Or &
.........Yonne; none in Maconnais/Beaujolais

First Growths / *Premiers Crus*
11% of the production.......................................

600 First Growths (Côte d'Or,
.......................Yonne & Côte Chalonnaise)

Village Wines
23% of the production................

Over 50 village, or
.................commune, *appellations*

Regional Wines
65% of the production

Over 20 regional wines
(some are districts or
mini-regions)

Examples
GREAT GROWTHS (Grands Crus)
These are in theory the finest wines of all and are labelled simply with the name of the vineyard, output being restricted. There are many red Great Growths on the Côte de Nuits, for instance Clos de Vougeot, Romanée-Saint-Vivant, Charmes-Chambertin, Musigny, and both red and white on the Côte de Beaune: Corton-Bressandes, Corton-Charlemagne, Bâtard-Montrachet, for instance. In Chablis there are seven: Chablis-Clos, Chablis-Vaudésir, etc.

1 Adapted from the pyramid diagrams in the Salle Olivier de Serres of the Musée du Vin in Beaune, and Pitiot and Servant's *Les Vins de Bourgogne*, Presses Universitaires de France, Paris, 1992.

FIRST GROWTHS (*Premiers Crus*)
These come from superior vineyards within a village. The name of the
individual vineyard appears after or underneath (and in letters the same
height as) the name of the village, for instance Mercurey Les Montaigus,
Beaune Bressandes, Nuits-Saint-Georges Les Vaucrains or Meursault Les
Charmes.

VILLAGE WINES
These carry the name of their own commune, such as Pommard,
Chassagne-Montrachet, Rully, Chablis or Morgon, the yield from the vine-
yard being restricted to a greater extent than with regional wines.

REGIONAL WINES
These are the least prestigious and carry names like Bourgogne *rouge*,
Beaujolais, Bourgogne Aligoté or Mâcon, being made on certain soils from
specified grape-types within a large area. Hautes Côtes-de-Beaune is a
mini-region behind the Côte de Beaune, Bourgogne Côte Chalonnaise or
Bourgogne Côtes d'Auxerre being other mini-regions.

wine-growers. Each grower cultivates his vines and makes his wine
differently, and much of the wine is then sold in barrels and bottled
by local shippers, so varying qualities appear on the market with
the same wine-name on the label. The names of the wine-maker and
bottler are more important in Burgundy than in any other wine-
producing area – indeed they are more important than the name of
the wine. That is why a significant part of this book (all of Part
Two) is devoted to an examination of who is responsible for what.

Chablis is an isolated pocket of vineyards in the Yonne *département*, barely two hours' drive down the motorway from Paris. Here
we first meet the Chardonnay vine, whose grapes are responsible
for all of Burgundy's best white wines. The vineyards are planted
on limestone hillsides and produce dry white wines which vary in
character from light and appetizing to rich (though without
sweetness) and long-flavoured. In a neighbouring valley near Auxerre, a little-known wine-producing area offers a variety of white
wines from other grapes (Aligoté and Sauvignon), some fine red
wines which used to be consumed locally (but now often get to
Paris, and beyond) and some very decent sparkling wine, called
Crémant de Bourgogne. In the wake of the world success of Champagne, many French vineyards have increased their productions of
sparkling wine. Burgundy has four main centres for the industry:

7

the Auxerrois, Nuits-Saint-Georges, Savigny-lès-Beaune and Rully, Champagne methods being used in the production, as we shall see.

The greatest Burgundy vineyards are to be found in the *département* to the south-east of the Yonne, the Côte d'Or. It takes its name from the narrow slope of vineyards fifty kilometres long, running approximately north–south from Dijon to Santenay. This is golden in the autumn when the leaves turn, and golden in the wealth it can bring to owners of its best plots – and now you need a pile of gold to buy land there. The hillside is divided into two vineyard areas, the Côte de Nuits centred on Nuits-Saint-Georges, and the Côte de Beaune on Beaune. The vineyards form an east-facing strip approximately 1,500 metres wide, but the slope is at varying angles, as is the orientation. The bedrock, soil and drainage change repeatedly, for the Alpine upheavals 35 million years ago caused faults in the many-layered limestone and marlstone. The wines of the villages along the hillside taste different, and there are major variations within each commune.

There is nothing else in France quite like this narrow vineyard escarpment, protected by woods on top of the hills, perfectly orientated and sloped to catch the first sun each day, and to retain moisture, yet allow excess rain to run off. The Champagne vineyards (Montagne de Reims and Côte des Blancs) are at first sight similar, and certainly more grandiose. But they do not have the subtle variations of soil and subsoil, due to the buckled, and varied, sedimentary Jurassic rocks which are the bedrock of the Côte. The Alsace vineyards, on the eastern flanks of the Vosges mountains, perhaps come nearest, but in Alsace there is no unifying limestone bedrock to bring harmony to the wine production. Alsace is frontier land, full of contrasts and surprises.

Almost all the wines of the Côte de Nuits are red and are produced from the Pinot Noir vine. The best are highly individual and their detailed origins can be identified to within a few hundred yards, or less, by people who are familiar with them. Nowhere else in the world has yet succeeded in producing Pinot Noir wines of the complexity and fascination of the best Côte d'Or bottles – but there is a catch. It requires exceptional skills in vineyard and vat-house to produce red Burgundy of decent quality in years when the summer or autumn weather is imperfect.

The reputation of the region was made by wines from long hot summers, which ripen the grapes naturally and allow the red pigments in the skins to develop exceptionally. In years of imperfect maturity, until recently a large proportion of the wine was sold to local *négociants* to be beefed up illegally, with deep-coloured, alcoholic blending-wines from outside the region. This rendered palatable a mass of wine which was otherwise unsaleable, but it falsified the consumer's notion of what red Burgundy tastes like. We are now caught in the middle of a historic shift in perceptions: half the world of Burgundy drinkers knows the smell and taste of authentic Pinot Noir, while the other half bemoans the rarity of the blended wine it first (thinking it was Burgundy) fell in love with.

We shall return to the problem of the off-vintages later, but for the moment, let us look at a glass of red Burgundy from a good vintage: wherein lies its fascination and complexity?

Maximum enjoyment is to be had from wine-drinking if one looks at a wine before smelling it, and smells it carefully before tasting it. One will look at it for purple tones which signify youth or the red-brown colour which comes (often all too rapidly) with age. Burgundy is not normally as deeply coloured as a fine claret or northern Rhône wine, and it should be limpid. Whether young or old, wines from the Pinot Noir have aromas about them which are hard to describe but wholly their own. In fact, they have at least two aromas: one when the wine is youthful, and quite another when it has aged. They are often slightly mouth-watering, because of the presence of natural acids in the grapes. When young, the aroma is not straightforwardly grapey, or plummy, or floral, but freshly fruity in a surprisingly complex way. When aged the perfume is much more spicy; it can sometimes be agreeably leathery, gamey, smoky, or like decaying undergrowth or leaves – both animal and vegetable, appetizing and intriguing.

Only four things are perceived by the sense of taste: sweetness, acidity, bitterness and saltiness, the last being of little significance in wine-tasting. A really fine wine has sufficient acidity, coming from natural grape acids, and astringency, from the tannins of the grape skins, to balance the sweetness of the grape-sugar, the latter having been completely or partially transformed into alcohol, which itself has a sweet taste, when the wine was made. The palate also notices the weight of the wine: its wateriness or richness. At the same time, the sense of smell continues to register the intensity and variety of its perfumes. Some wines make an immediate impact when tasted which may or may not persist while they are in the mouth. The very best coat the inside of the mouth with a layer of lingering flavour which is still noticeable half a minute or more after the wine has been swallowed.

One of the reasons Burgundy's fame has spread so far is that the Côte d'Or is easily accessible. A railway line, a *route nationale* and now an *autoroute* run along the foot of the slope in full view of the vineyards. Indeed, Burgundy's vineyards lie exactly at the hub of one of Europe's greatest *autoroute* crossroads, where motorways converge from all quarters of the compass: from Paris and north-west France, from the Channel and Low Countries, from the Rhine and all the countries to its north and east, and from the Rhône valley, leading up from the Mediterranean.

The slope is mostly wood-capped, with villages in the combes formed where streams run down. To the east, the flat plain of the Saône runs into the far distance where the Jura mountains rise. The Côte d'Or is scenically unremarkable (indeed marred between the Côte de Nuits and Côte de Beaune by pyramids of broken stones from the marble quarries) but its village names, nevertheless, bring one to a halt: Gevrey-Chambertin, Vougeot, Volnay, Puligny-Montrachet; these and their neighbours are capable of producing exceptional wines.

Broadly speaking, the red wines of the Côte de Nuits have more richness and length than those of the Côte de Beaune and they often take longer to mature. The Côte de Beaune is the less glamorous of the two Côtes, in terms of the fame of its red wines, but it is a marvellous source of large quantities of red Burgundy, and the produce of its four most famous villages – Volnay, Pommard, Beaune and Aloxe-Corton – often reach heights of dizzy-making quality. The white wines of the Côte de Beaune (Meursault, Puligny-Montrachet, Chassagne-Montrachet and Corton-Charle-magne, for instance) are thought by many to be, at their best, the most famous, perfectly balanced, and delicious dry white wines in the world.

In the hills to the west of the Côte d'Or, wine is produced in the Hautes Côtes de Nuits and Hautes Côtes de Beaune. The grapes ripen later than on the Côte, because of the altitude, and many vineyard owners also grow raspberries and blackcurrants, and keep goats or other animals. Pinot Noir and Chardonnay grapes are grown, along with the white Aligoté (its wine has higher acidity and less length, flavour and roundness than that of the Chardonnay).

The last wine-making village of the Côte de Beaune is Santenay. If one continues southwards, one crosses into the Saône-et-Loire *département* and a different wine region, the Côte Chalonnaise, otherwise known as the Région de Mercurey from its best-known red wine. There are five main wine villages in this region: Bouzeron, Rully, Mercurey, Givry and Montagny.

Rully is a centre for sparkling wine manufacture, which in the past was the best way of rendering saleable large quantities of Burgundies from the Aligoté and Gamay grapes which were too acid for sale as such. Improved wine-making methods and replanting in Rully with the noble Pinot and Chardonnay grapes have recently changed the village's main activity and one can now find good bottles of Burgundy there, in the style of Côte de Beaune wines. Mercurey has a large production of longer-lasting reds, Montagny specializes in whites and Givry makes a bit of both.

We are now approaching the Mâconnais, which supplies much of Burgundy's regional *appellations*, the Bourgogne *blanc* and *rouge*, the Bourgogne Aligoté and both red and white Mâcons. The vines are planted on chains of small hills, interspersed with meadows and fields of vegetables. Many of the growers have grouped themselves into co-operatives, and these produce large quantities of Mâcon-Villages from Chardonnay vines. It is an important source of fine white Burgundy which is still reasonably priced, though some of the quality is still pretty dreadful.

The countryside changes to the south of Mâcon, where the Beaujolais begins, for the rounded eroded forms of ancient granites are found at the surface, where previously we have travelled through still jagged limestone hillsides. The Gamay grape is here in its element, and its grapes give mouth-wateringly fresh red wine if picked just before complete ripeness, and vinified without being squashed. Over 150 million bottles of authentic Beaujolais are produced every year, varying in style from light quaffing wine such as Beaujolais Nouveau to purply-red, well-constituted wines from single communes such as Morgon or Brouilly. The region is highly prosperous, for it makes France's most immediately attractive red wine, and one which requires the minimum of ageing.

Something must be said of the characteristics of recent vintages, and details will be found in Appendix B on pp. 666–71. One should be cautious with generalizations about Burgundy vintages, for several reasons. Human brilliance or error produce successes or disasters from similar raw materials, and wines have sometimes been quite altered in character after sojourning in the cellars of *négociants*, as will be explained in Chapter 6. After bottling, the conditions in which wines are stored are of vital importance. Fine whites or light elegant reds can turn brown and oxidize irrevocably if stored at ground level without temperature control, or if exposed to light, or kept standing upright for long in a shop window or on a shelf. *There is absolutely no substitute for tasting what is in the bottle*, and no purchase of Burgundy should ever be made unless you have tried the wine or are buying from a properly qualified and trusted supplier.

I have not transcribed many of my tasting notes, for Burgundies often evolve quickly, and of course they develop unexpectedly according to how they are kept. Burgundy tasting notes between the covers of a book are almost immediately out of date. Because of the enormous number of different wines produced each year by the many owners of Burgundy's vineyards they would have little relevance. Tasting notes on individual Burgundies belong, it seems to me, in wine articles and reviews (with addresses of sources) and in merchants' lists (followed by a price) so that the reader may track down what appeals to her or him.

Instead, having lived behind the scenes in Burgundy and watched some of its best actors at work, and having traded its wines for thirty years, I have tried to describe how the best actors practise their art. We shall meet some charlatans who stage-manage pretentious and expensive illusions. But if you read on to the end you will know, I hope, how to tell the one from the other, and feel confident about tasting all Burgundies in a critical spirit.

In the tracking down of those bottles of Burgundy which make the pulse thump and the senses sway, for which this book is your guide, goad and tool, nothing matters except your *own* impression of the wine in the glass before you.

How to buy Burgundy

Many people (not just Americans) assume that if you pay top dollar, you will get top quality. With Burgundy, that is rarely valid. Top dollar often gets paid for wines which are fashionable, or rare, or both. To get top quality you have to be very determined, very focused, and not allow yourself to be waylaid by rarity or fashion.

This book does not claim to give all Burgundy's best addresses, but it will provide some jumping-off points, from which to start uncorking. One cannot grasp Burgundy except by drawing corks, and talking. *That is the only way.*

If possible, you must visit the place. For then, when you spend your money on its bottles, you find you also have the memory of the hillside, the family, and the mould-hung vaulted cellars along with the wine. You get the grower or merchant with the wine, and when that is thrown in (if you have been in good hands) the wines are not expensive after all.

Burgundy is for friends, I think, not for impressing people (deep-coloured Cabernet Sauvignons and Bordeaux château names do that). For wine traders, Burgundy is a brilliant place for small companies to operate, for that is the size of most of the best sources of supply. Even when planning to trade it, the best way to buy is still as a consumer, as if for one's own drinking, with best friends in mind. That way, it is hard to go wrong.

Visiting Côte d'Or

It is worth looking out for *De Vignes en Caves* signs – white rectangles, featuring a glass each of red and white wine – outside growers and merchants. Members of this group (launched in 1991, and numbering over 250 cellars) welcome visitors, may speak other languages than French, and are subject to spot tests to ensure that the welcome stays warm. You will be offered a visit, at least one wine to taste at no cost, and there is no obligation to purchase. Many of Burgundy's best domaines belong. From 1994, new signs read *Bourgognes Découverte – Visite & Degustation*.

Changing Burgundy

Between 1956 and 1958 France took stock of its viticultural areas, establishing a national register of its vineyards (known as the 'cadastre viticole'). This has never been completely updated, but thirty years later, in 1988, it was possible to make some interesting comparisons[2] in the three northerly *départements* of Yonne, Côte d'Or, and Saône-et-Loire. Beaujolais will be considered separately.

Production of table wine (including wine produced from hybrid vines) had fallen by 74 per cent in thirty years, while that of AC (*appellation contrôllée*) wine had risen by 34 per cent. The main *vinifera* vines (Aligoté, Gamay, Chardonnay and Pinot Noir) now represented 89 per cent of the planted area, against a mere 53 per cent thirty years previously.

Aligoté vineyards had fallen by more than a third in the Côte d'Or, and slipped in the Saône-et-Loire, but increased in the Yonne, perhaps reflecting the latter's position as an increasingly important white wine production area.

Gamay vineyards in the Côte d'Or had been cut by half (much of the wine had been used, blended with Pinot Noir, to make Bourgogne Passe-Tout-Grains), though its surfaces had held their own around Mâcon and in the northern Beaujolais.

Vineyards planted with Chardonnay had more than tripled in the Yonne, nearly doubled in the Côte d'Or, and increased by 70 per cent in the Saône-et-Loire (which covers the Côte Chalonnaise and Mâconnais).

If one took the three *départements* together, Pinot Noir vineyards had more than doubled in size in thirty years, just like Chardonnay. Plantings of Pinot Noir in the Côte d'Or (where many of the best sites had already been filled by 1958) went up by 73 per cent, in the Yonne by a factor of eight, though here it remained relatively small: 440 hectares. In the Saône-et-Loire Pinot Noir vineyards almost tripled in size, reflecting the extent to which Pinot had replaced table wine, and the old hybrid vines (Plantet, Baco and Oberlin, which are Franco-American crosses), dating from the phylloxera replantation.

So, by 1988 there were over 9,000 hectares of Pinot Noir and 8,000 hectares of Chardonnay in the three *départements*, in both cases twice the figure of thirty years previously. These are the largest planted areas of its two finest vines that Burgundy has ever seen, in 1,600 years of wine history.

Burgundy's enormous commercial asset – being easy of access,

---

2 'Commission "Recherche Progrès et Qualité" ', Michel Leguay, ONIVINS (Office National Interprofessionnel des Vins), Dijon, June 1989.

the crucial, north–south trading link between the Mediterranean and the countries of northern Europe – brings with it the disadvantages found at any crossroads. You see it in the food, for instance: tacky as a Leicester Square pizza bar, or a Champs Elysées tourist café, unless you choose carefully. It is no good a Burgundian restaurant owner holding *lettres patentes et épatantes* in the brotherhood of chitterling sausages, with half a dozen wine banquet certificates on his walls, if he does not care for the customer. The same protein-rich Burgundian fare is offered up endlessly: ham or terrines, followed by beef or chicken, followed by cheeses. Vegetarians can feel highly discouraged on the two Côtes. Such establishments can be very successful, and full of earnest travellers drinking red wine reverently from large balloon glasses on short stems. An example has been in the hills behind Beaune and Nuits, at the Maison des Hautes Côtes, supposedly the show-case for the products of this struggling area. Not only has the food been of the dreariest, they have been serving wine by the glass, without properly protecting it from oxidation. The wines are anonymous, sold under a committee label, no doubt to protect a grower from embarrassment, when the wine is poor, or to prevent a wine-maker from receiving due credit, when it is good. If only the growers of the Hautes Côtes would take a trip to Carneros and San Francisco Bay, for instance, to set up an exchange programme with some young Californian-Italian chef-cooks as they qualify from restaurant school, then let them loose in their kitchens and wine cellars, they could revitalize their menus at a stroke. One and a half million visitors pour through Beaune each year. To get them up to Mavilly-Mandelot or Marey-lès-Fussey requires some imaginative leaping.

Burgundy is the tube of a double-ended funnel, down which streams a constant flow of tourists and traders. More must be done to protect it from falling into crossroads' mediocrity, providing the sort of products and services we find at King's Cross concourse in the rush hour.

We need a Mediocrity-Out Campaign. Unexciting wines need hissing out of existence. It is no good waiting for the fraud inspectors, or the delegates of the INAO (Institut National des Appellations d'Origine des Vins et Eaux-de-Vie), or the presidents of the local growers' syndicates to push for further change; they are primarily holding the boat steady as she goes. They will surely, however, welcome input from consumers. Here is Jules Tourmeau,[3] the INAO's north-east regional division chief, defining quality: 'One may define quality as a combination of factors which make a product consumable – what one may call the threshold above which the consumer agrees to consume. For wines ... quality is good and one drinks, or it is bad and one rejects. No intermediate position is possible.'

A threshold in French is *un seuil*, and wines which do not reach the quality threshold, which are bad and should be rejected, might be said to be *sous-seuil*. *Ce vin est sous-seuil ... sss ... sss*, and this wine, I suggest, should be hissed out of existence. This is *l'action anti-sous-seuil*. Consumers should try hissing if a wine is not good enough for the name it carries, and the price being asked. At a tasting of Burgundies, such wines can be greeted appropriately, until those responsible are shamed out of releasing such suckers, and shamed into delivering what the region's reputation encourages us to expect.

This is not a problem of epic proportions, but a cleaning-up operation: piloting the wounded off the battlefield, filling in craters. Some corpses need burying now the guns have fallen silent, a few scared people need leading out of fox-holes and some vultures need shooing away.

What could the BIVB[4] do to start reducing mediocrity? It only needs one president of a Syndicat Viticole to address the problem, it seems to me. Twice yearly blind tastings could be organized, behind closed doors, at village level, tasting like-with-like wines by the growers of the *appellation*. The wines should be drawn by chance from bottled stocks, and tasted anonymously, the discussion to be open, with marks voiced by all present – the wines being identified only after the results had been handed out (no outsiders allowed in, of course). It would certainly be embarrassing for some, but isn't that preferable to some consumers continuing to be ripped off, albeit much less often than in the past? Producers *should* feel embarrassed sometimes, but it should happen in their own back-yards, at the heart of that communal property, the *appellation*, rather than on a wider stage.

3 He is Chef de Division Nord-Est so heads up the Institut National des Appellations d'Origine in Burgundy.
4 Bureau Interprofessionnel du Vin de Bourgogne, which defends and promotes the interests of the region's wines, growers, brokers and traders.

If the BIVB could just get this off the ground, the idea could roll like a snowball through the villages and the *Grands Crus* of both Côtes. If I ran the BIVB I should want to double the dues of any union which didn't introduce blind, internal tastings. Then double again the next year, and the next, and the next, until they did. Internal control would be much more effective than Paris snooping, or press sneering.

Burgundy and oriental rugs

There is another benefit that would accrue if blind discussion-tastings could take place within the circle of individual *appellations*: a defining, and honing, by the wine-makers of the style of wine represented by the owned-in-common name.

Oriental rugs and modern red Burgundies have much in common. Their histories go back many centuries, the origins of the vines (in the case of the Burgundies) and the designs (in the case of the rugs) being mysterious, and impossible to pin down. The productions have been handed down from one generation of skilled craftsmen to another. Traditional, immediately recognizable products come from individual villages, in both cases.

Modern techniques, and the demands of modern markets, put both at risk. As Jon Thompson has pointed out,[5] tribal and domestic rug weavings have a strong local, traditional character, and the designs having often been in use for many centuries. Rugs made for the home and special occasions would be functional and simple, but also lively and decorative. Market demand can soon become an influence of such importance that it overrides any considerations of communal tradition. Weavers are then at the mercy of market pressures, and soon they and their work are transformed into a cottage industry. The rugs lose their vigour and the clarity of their designs.

When I taste from village to village on the two main Côtes, finding cold-soaked wines, strongly oak-juiced (whatever the *appellation*) it is easy to start worrying that Burgundy is allowing market pressures to hijack its *terroirs*, and to gum up its traditional, identifiable individualities, that as community life in the villages

5 *Carpets: From the Tents, Cottages and Workshops of Asia*, Barrie & Jenkins, London, 1983.

breaks down or evolves, the making of something precious and beautiful for the honouring of family or guests is being lost.

Of course, in a market where there is over-production of fine wine, and exceptional competition from new producer countries, growers must make wines which will please their customers, but not, let us hope, at the price of sacrificing their traditional individualities.

There is one enormous difference between oriental rugs and modern red Burgundies: the wines are so much more easy and straightforward to buy. And the cost per bottle is very modest, when one considers how much love and care has often gone into it.

At least one active trader who is an enthusiast for strongly oaked red wines has close contacts with a Côte d'Or cooperage, and sells serious quantities of barrels on its behalf, for all I know earning a commission on every barrel sold, which would be a clever way to a few extra bucks.

Altering the product to fit the market (which is what is happening here) can falsify the taste of consumers, particularly new ones, so they end up being disappointed by, or disliking wines which do not conform. Something very similar happened in the United Kingdom up to 1973 (Britain's entry into the Common Market) when the palate of most consumers was completely falsified by clever, but spurious blends despatched in bulk from Burgundy for baptizing with well-known Burgundian place-names, once the Channel had been crossed. It was perfectly legal at the time, but resulted in many British consumers being totally unfamiliar with the taste of pure Pinot Noir.

Over-reliance on new oak is dangerous for the Burgundians, as many New World areas will soon come close to regional and village red Burgundy qualities – as soon as they have access to decent Pinot Noir vine plants, have identified their prime sites, and can get their hands on sufficient well-weathered oak staves of good origins for their barrels.

Burgundy is a gigantic jigsaw puzzle, and of course one can only do a jigsaw if one likes that sort of game. This book is not the photo on the lid, but, armed with it, anyone who wants to get to work can do the puzzle.

In Part One, the most wide-ranging revision has been to the Tasting chapter. Over the last twenty years I have completely had to rethink my wine-buying and wine-tasting, as the raw materials are now so different. Faulty wines are now really rare, and so are grossly unauthentic bottles. There is so much good wine around, the problems are completely different. A lot relate to value, rather than authenticity or quality.

What are Burgundy's prospects looking like for the millennium? Extremely bright, I think, for it is claiming back the undisputed position it once held for hundreds of years: that of the region making the most exciting red wines in the world. Throughout the Middle Ages, Bordeaux was nowhere near to challenging it.

Its best sites have been identified, its soils are being studied and naturally enriched and the health of its plant material has been improved, while its variety has been retained. Wine-making skills to handle most weather conditions are widely available. Great swathes of its best vineyards are now mature, their roots pushing downwards as much as 70 metres into the mineral-rich rocks.

Nowhere else on the globe is such a varied, brilliant wine culture in place, thriving already, yet poised to realize its full potential.

2

Tasting

———

We need a new approach to tasting red Burgundies. Why? Because Burgundy is still seen as a minefield by many consumers, traders and writers. Yet of all the classic areas, these wines, both red and white, are the most straightforward and immediate in their impact, and we do not have to buy and age them for years to see what it is all about.

In the recent past, it is true that there have been some unpleasant, expensive surprises, for instance 1983 red Burgundies, which were often overrated. But now, there are rapidly increasing quantities, each vintage, which give no disappointments at all.

People often only think of red Burgundy in terms of the peak of the pyramid, which is a big mistake. That peak is often a sharp and painful spike. A specialist US wine retailer, such as Rick Ostrand of State Line Liquors, Elkton, Maryland, in a store full of top bottles (none being sold simply on the strength of a score out of 100, which is the route many US retailers now take) when asked if he had plenty of Burgundy enthusiasts might say: 'No, maybe five collectors, and they shop in every store in the country to get what they want. One in Hawaii, two in Washington DC, one in California. And me being drawn into the trap of buying thirty cases of Bourgogne *rouge* and twenty cases of village wine to be allocated three cases of the *Grand Cru* everyone wants – it's infernal.' If consumers only pursue the rarest, exquisite bottles, they are often frustrated.

Robert Parker added to the confusion over how and when to drink Burgundy when he wrote, 'The window of opportunity for drinking red and white Burgundy is ... one of the smallest of any great wine in the world ... The optimum drinking window for most red and white Burgundies is small, and closes quickly.'[1] This can only have been written by someone who does not really understand the region's wines, which five pages later he frankly admits: 'It would appear that no matter how much time, effort and money is spent trying to understand the wines of Burgundy, to a large extent they remain an unfathomable mystery.'

His concept of a narrow drinkability window is totally inappropriate. Only the briefest acquaintance with white Burgundy can demonstrate that these wines – from Bourgogne *blanc* up to *Grands Crus* – are perfectly able to taste delicious when youthful in barrel, when recently bottled, as they age, and once fully mature. Like most fine wines, they may suffer after bottling, but brief bottle-sickness is no different from that which affects Cabernet Sauvignons, Merlots, Syrahs, Sémillons, Chenins, Sauvignons or other fine wines. (It is due to the actual bottling operation, which may include pumping, filtering, some aeration etc.) He appears completely to misunderstand the way in which most red Burgundies, and Pinots Noirs, develop.

For three or four years from the time their fermentations are completed these wines can taste perfectly delicious, from the barrel (so cellar-door callers may have wonderful treats) and for a couple of years after they are bottled, while the wines are still purple-red and vibrantly youthful. Very often, there is no bottle-sickness period, or the wine will have gone through it before being despatched.

Then, almost inevitably, there comes a period when the lively young fruitiness diminishes and disappears. One might call this a window of undrinkability. It is a period of adolescence, through which almost all red Burgundies and Pinots Noirs have to pass. When a red Burgundy's youthful fruitiness is being lost, and it is achieving maturity, it is at its least attractive. It is important to understand that this phase exists, and to watch out for it, otherwise one may open, and waste, fine-potential bottles by trying them, and agonizing over them, at a time when they should not be touched.

It does not take much tasting experience with Pinots to recognize that a given aroma is neither one thing nor the other, neither young Pinot, nor aged and spicy. When trying a bottle reveals that the

---

1 *Burgundy: a Comprehensive Guide to the Producers, Appellations and Wines,* Simon & Schuster, New York, 1990, p. 54.

remembered fruity youthfulness is diminishing, one should compare notes with friends or one's supplier before uncorking any more. The best Burgundies are made by growers who talk to each other, and share discoveries; ditto, the drinking of the best bottles.

Tasters can be divided into two groups. Group 1 are those who are uncertain of their skills, and anxious that lack of knowledge bars them from deciding for themselves. In wine matters, they remain dependent on others. Group 1 people often have an eye on names and labels and tasting scores, and they often miss out on wine's pleasures.

Group 2 people are those who have made the jump, who look forward to putting their nose into a strange glass of wine as soon as it is poured. They know that finding words to describe or talk about a wine is difficult, but they will have a go. If you are not yet part of Group 2, I hope this book will help you, particularly this chapter.

You can quickly learn to assess Burgundy if you concentrate on what is in the glass. Do not worry about what someone else thinks the wine should taste like. Modern red and white Burgundies are the easiest wines in the world to enjoy (not the cheapest, true, but that is about their biggest drawback).

During the 1980s it became fashionable to depend on buying wine by numbers (particularly on American 100-point scales). But if you follow numbers you can miss the point completely. If you let other people do the tasting, you cannot catch wine's pleasures. So how does one move from Group 1 to Group 2, from being a miss-the-pointer to being a pleasure-catcher?

Wine-tasting, if you approach it as a pleasure-catcher, is not difficult at all. A contrary message, however, is being put out by wine-writing (whether on back-labels, in price-lists, articles, journals or books) which relies on wine-making technicalities, strings of adjectives and 100-point scales, which imply a precision which does not exist. The 100-point scales may be fine for professionals trained to use them accurately, tasting in laboratory-type conditions. The Union Internationale des Oenologues, for instance, has developed a sophisticated 100-point assessment scheme, and the Institute of Masters of Wine an English adaptation, but you cannot use them at speed, in the field, when assessing dozens of wines in a short time. From the consumer's point of view, 100-point scales are a long-term, counter-productive menace.

It is only possible to enjoy red Burgundy to the full if you talk about it. 'Words spoken off the cuff, even if they are clumsy, are the most meaningful', says Emile Peynaud, after a lifetime teaching people to express their thoughts, when they taste wine, immediately they are conceived. He may not be Burgundian, but he certainly inspired himself from drinking red Burgundies. If you talk about red Burgundy, you will soon learn to judge it and to love it. If you don't, you won't.

In fact, it is best to start tasting white Burgundy. As Peynaud has pointed out,[2] white wines have little or no tannin, and have a simple balance of flavours, by comparison with reds. Their basic taste structure is sweetness–acidity, the sweetness coming from the fact that alcohol has a sweet taste, and gives a softness to the first impressions of a wine on the palate. 'We normally sweeten straw-berries, fruit salads or lemon juice to make their acidity tolerable', says Peynaud. The sweet and sour tastes do not cancel each other out, they just need to be in balance.

This is the first point to look for, tasting white Burgundy, after one has plunged one's nose in the glass looking for pleasant or unpleasant aromas. The unpleasant ones might be chemical (for instance, sulphurous), or mouldy (caused by a faulty cork). The positive thing to look for is something fresh not stale – it does not matter what. Then – is it flowery or fruity ? It should not be vegetal or leafy. You might look out for coconut or vanilla, which are very common (from ageing in new oak). If you notice those aromas, take a pause. Do you really want them ? Are they overwhelming the wine's own fruitiness?

That'll do for starters, on whites, except for a visual check of course. Clear, not hazy (but no need to insist on transparency). As to the hue, the colour, check it against something white, otherwise you may get a false impression.

Go through these simple steps a few times, voicing impressions as you go. You are leaving miss-the-pointers behind.

Moving to red Burgundies, there is an extra dimension to their structure, for red wine is fermented with its skins, pips and some-times stalks. It picks up a different texture from these, and different sorts of flavours.

If we think of Bordeaux wines, or Cabernet Sauvignons, these

2 *The Taste of Wine*, translated (brilliantly) by Michael Schuster, Macdonald Orbis, London and Sydney, 1987.

wines are agreeable to the extent that the acidity and bitterness in them are balanced by their alcohol content. Red Burgundy is completely different – often low in acidity (for various reasons) and naturally lower in tannins than wines from the Bordeaux grapes, red Burgundies are often just mildly fruity, soft, and flabby. Adding sugar to boost alcohol (known as chaptalization) is now endemic to Burgundy; most growers do it like breaking bread at mealtimes. Although there is a tendency towards a more intelligent use of sugar in wine-making, this is still Burgundy's Achilles heel.

So, if you want to enjoy good red Burgundy, from every level of its pyramid, from Bourgogne *rouge* up to *Grand Cru*, you must start by first considering its alcohol content. High alcohol makes wine sell fast when young. High alcohol wines win tasting competitions. But the fruitiness of high alcohol wines dries out with bottle-age. Beware of them if you are buying wine for drinking over several months, or for some years' maturing.

An appropriate alcoholic degree is a quality element, don't get me wrong, 11.5° or 12° being a level below which it is circumspect for red Burgundy not to drop.[3] Too high a degree of alcohol can diminish the intensity of a wine's odour, as Peynaud so rightly says. Look out for high levels of alcohol, for they easily confuse one's judgement of a wine's true quality.

Red Burgundy has often been criticized for its light red colour, and indeed Pinot Noir naturally gives wines which are paler than those of Cabernet Sauvignon, which has recently become the world's most fashionably planted red grape variety. During the 1980s the colour of many red Burgundies has been deepened by changed methods of wine-making: cold-soaking the grapes before fermentation begins, or lengthening the vatting. One cannot tell much, these days, from looking at a Burgundy's colour. Deepness does not equal quality; on the contrary, it can indicate over-extraction of solid matters from the skins. Nor does paleness equal inferiority. I look for brightness, for purple signs of youthful life, in young red Burgundy.

In aroma red Burgundy (forget Gamay for the moment, we are considering Pinot Noir) must be split, as we have seen, into youthful wines with their aromas, and aged wines which are quite

3 'This level of alcohol is required before the mucous surfaces, bathed in saliva, can feel the softening, penetrating, solvent effect of alcohol' (Emile Peynaud, *The Taste of Wine*).

different. The two are separated by the window of undrinkability, mentioned above, when one should close the shutters on one's stocks. If the wine was good in the first place, it will come good again, if it is coolly, damply stored – but patience is needed.

Youthful wines will either have the mouth-wateringly appealing, lively, spicy fruitiness of good red Burgundy, or a heavier, richer more complex aroma because a different wine-making method – longer vatting – has aimed for a more tannic construction, and the wine is destined to be aged. Tannin is simply masking its fruit, temporarily.

The word aroma is usually used of what we perceive with the nose in young wines, the word bouquet being used when wines have aged.

Concerning the bouquet of aged red Burgundy (which is really a completely different wine) a complex spiciness appears which seems both fresh and ancient. There may be roasted, or smoky elements, suggestions of baked red fruits, gamey smells, a leathery character, sometimes smells of certain fungi. There are over 250 chemical substances present in wine, and as many adjectives to describe aromas and bouquets. The good host and the good guest both try to be precise.

Red Burgundy should have a palpable, succulent, attractive texture, and this is what I look for to replace the bland, soft alcoholic cover which is still too common. Red Burgundy is absolutely yummy, with the most sensuous mouth-feel – silky, never cloying – of any liquid in the world. Red Burgundy should have a focused intensity of flavour which persists after spitting or swallowing. This length of after-taste, allied to complex bouquet and seductive texture, is what constitutes great red Burgundy.

It is essential to talk about the Burgundy one is tasting, to discuss and argue over aroma and flavour. Only then may one tolerate or dismiss, as appropriate.

Consider a cheese board, instead, with some Pecorino from Sardinia. You nibble a crumbly, tasty piece; it is flavourful, with a sharp but agreeable bite to it. Suddenly you realize it tastes a bit mouldy, you've chewed on some rind, it is a bit acrid. But you don't send the cheese back to the monger. You can enjoy the character and quality of the cheese, while also seeing the mouldy, acrid component.

Wine of course is quite different when it tastes *really* mouldy –

from corkiness or bunch-rot at harvest-time, for instance – and a whole bottle sometimes has to be rejected, and sent back for refund. However, imperfections can be worth discussing and analysing. They may have the same charm and originality as a flawed pattern in a nomad rug, where you see what the weaver intended. You may see where a skein of wool ran out, the next being of slightly different colour, or where a geometric pattern was modified to accommodate a corner. Wine faults may be minor, forgivable faults, which it is preferable to accept, rather than insisting on something impeccable.

TASTING BURGUNDY ON THE SPOT

The best way of getting to know the wines of Burgundy is by tasting them on the spot. Of course, it is not the only way, but I think it is probably the quickest.

The constant passage of tourists, buyers, writers – and no doubt free-loaders – in the famous villages is such that Burgundian hospitality is sometimes stretched beyond its limits, particularly if family privacy is intruded upon at mealtimes, or on Sundays. I strongly advise having an introduction, and one must always telephone in advance, not just drop in.

As soon as you leave the beaten track the story can be totally different. I remember making a first visit, in the rain and fog, to an isolated red Mâcon property, to be met by a smiling, chewing Burgundian. It was 12.15 p.m., an unpardonable hour to turn up, given French lunch customs. Without a moment's hesitation came: 'We didn't wait, would you like to eat with us?' There was blanquette de veau, sautéed cauliflower, home-made goat's cheese, with white and red, both delicious. Smiles and stories (and a television set going strong throughout). I had arrived cold, late and downhearted, and was sent on my way completely revived.

It might seem that Burgundy is a perfect hunting ground for the private wine enthusiast, for the great wines of any vintage are produced in such small quantities that little is available for importers. Dealing direct with growers can be expensive and risky, and there is a temptation for a grower to dispose of his second-rate wines to inexperienced or unsuspecting travellers; however, buying a case or two of wine on one's way through Burgundy is an experience which is not to be missed. You will be welcomed right through the year, but the first problem is to find your proprietor.

Rainy days in January and February are good, for it is a slack time of year in the vines and there is a fifteen-month-old wine for tasting, soon to be bottled. The great horizontal presses are ranged silently against the walls of the vat-rooms, surrounded by geraniums in pots and tubs of orange trees (the oranges still on them), both brought in from the frosts. April is perhaps best, before growers get really busy in the vines; and Burgundy's weather in April can be wonderful.

Cleanness of cellar floor, pipette and glasses do not necessarily mean a thing. One may note whether all the casks are fully topped up, for this is perhaps the most important part of *élevage*; one will welcome the sight of new oak barrels. Personally I do not like to see a cellar-full, for the taste of oak, if overdone, can dominate a wine's aromas for years. But these expensive items are rarely indulged in by half-hearted wine-makers. If one is lucky, and gets to taste every wine in the cellar which is still in barrel (there may be ten or more *cuvées*, from two different vintages) one will have a very good idea of the wine-maker. Anybody can pull off one or two good *cuvées*, but making good wine from Bourgogne up to *Grand Cru* is something else.

Be cagey about telling the grower that the wine you are tasting is *très grand vin, magnifique, formidable*. Remember the Burgundy Buyer's Law, the only one worth memorizing: The Price of Burgundy is Set by Demand. Production costs are relevant for mediocre Burgundies, and lousy ones, but they are virtually irrelevant for good Burgundy.

It is worth practising phrases like *Ce sont mes premiers jours en Côte d'Or*, and *Je suis ici pour apprendre*. Indeed this last may be spoken at least three times in a 60-minute tasting session, and you may be amazed by its wonderful effects. As a wine is poured one may ask *Parlez-moi un peu de ce vin, je vous prie*, and later say, *Qu'en pensez-vous?*, putting the stress on *vous*. Burgundians love talking about their wines, and most are astonishingly open about them if they sense an appreciative listener.

But how does one taste? Given normally functioning senses, does it really only require enthusiasm and a croissant- rather than a bread-line income? I maintain so, and after a few years of attentive tasting one becomes so familiar with certain basic colours, smells and tastes (as long as one is training oneself on authentic examples) that one tastes with confidence.

For the first two or three years I was in the wine trade, I was secretly beset with dread lest I had a defective palate. The difference between wines seemed so small. I came from a family which drank wine only rarely, and it is regular tasting which allows one to build up one's knowledge. There is no substitute for experience; so if you lack confidence about your tasting, do not despair, just start working on it.

'It seems to me sometimes,' writes Pierre Poupon, 'when I taste with extra attention, that antennae are growing at the base of my nose.'[4] Tasting requires concentration, and quiet and space and light. It is much easier to assess a wine if one is tasting it blind than if one has read the label or been told what it is. It is also easier if there is a range of six to ten wines, all anonymous. The object is not to attempt to identify them, but to arrive at an honest assessment without being influenced by what one *thinks* the wine should taste like. One makes notes about each wine's looks, aroma, taste, and comes to a conclusion. And then, having seen the key, goes back to re-examine whether one's assessment is wildly out of line with what a given wine *should* taste like. If one is prepared to taste wines blind, one can call oneself a wine-taster.

Do not expect a Burgundian grower or shipper to put his wines up blind to you, though he may do if you get to know him. After all, he is trying to sell them, and telling you that you are about to taste Vosne-Romanée Les Suchots will predispose you to like it. Or will it?

You must decide what importance you attach to authenticity, for the wine trade is still not completely of one mind on the subject, nor are those who write on Burgundy. Parker, for instance, seems to avoid addressing the subject, while Johnson states that Burgundy is either pure or it is nothing.[5] Growers, brokers, *négociants*, importers and merchants all know that what keeps them in business is providing the customer with wines she or he will enjoy. Nowhere is the reconciliation of attractiveness with authenticity more difficult than in Burgundy.

How does one recognize a pure Burgundy from one diluted with

4 *Nouvelles Pensées d'un dégustateur*, Confrérie des Chevaliers du Tastevin, Nuits-Saint-Georges, 1975.
5 *The Story of Wine*, Mitchell Beazley, London, 1989.

10 or 15 per cent of fortifying wine from the south? This is a minor issue today, but old bottles surface, and we should not forget yesterday's problems. It is very difficult. Familiarity with the unblemished article is the first requirement, and one of this book's main objectives is to indicate how to find it. Authentic red Burgundy is essentially clean-tasting, and leaves the mouth fresh. With practice you will recognize the distinctive Pinot Noir flavour and know when it is masked by bone-setter Mediterranean red. Remember that it is a characteristic of the Pinot Noir grape, when grown in Burgundy, to produce wines which are light in colour and alcohol. Is the wine you are tasting heady and alcoholic?

It is also essential to familiarize yourself with the taste of old Grenache (for instance, bottle-aged Châteauneuf du Pape and Gigondas), to be aware of Roussillons, and Italian reds, and even old *cru* Beaujolais. A memory-flash which takes you forth in these directions, when you thought you were in for a noseful of pure Pinot Côte d'Or, can be a sure giveaway.

Fortifying from the south is on the wane (getting subtler every vintage) so more relevant today is the question: how does one recognize an over-chaptalized Burgundy? This is tricky, for alcoholic richness makes wines which win blind tastings, and immediately impress a neophyte. Take a good look at the way the wine slides back down the inside of your glass, after you twirl it. Those oily-looking droplets falling slowly back like tears: are they appropriate in the vintage you are tasting? They are part alcohol, part glycerol, but in a light year their origin will be sugar-bags, not the sun. I dread the sight of large alcohol droplets on the inside of my red burgundy glass; it usually means a heavy-handed wine-maker.

It is difficult to detect over-chaptalization from just smelling a wine, but taste it, and you can soon work it out. It will be mouth-filling, and round, and at first impression perhaps satisfying. But is there intense Pinot fruit, is there concentrated, textured flavour? Good red Burgundy is tactile yet subtle. It should never pack a noticeable, alcoholic punch.

How can one define the difference between a fine bottle and a great bottle of wine? Not by their classifications, nor their origins or ages. It is the effect on the drinker which matters. A fine wine will have a lovely colour, attractive bouquet, and the balance, flavour and smoothness to be expected of it. A great wine will have all these things, but in addition something to make the pulse race, to make one exclaim, 'How *can* it smell and taste like that? That is amazing!' A fine wine may remind one of flowers or spices or fruits, but there is something animal, often something erotic about great Burgundy. *Un verre de Nuits prépare la votre* goes the old saying about Nuits-Saint-Georges. Perhaps I should translate the play on words: 'A glass of "Night" paves the way for yours.'

Of course, a great bottle of Burgundy is one whose cork is out, with a friend opposite you, holding an empty glass.

BURGUNDY TASTING: HOW LONG TO CRACK IT?

You must keep going until you find a wine that tastes as if it had come seeping up from under the ground. You must keep tasting red Burgundy until you get the 'aha!' response. Burgundy is not for assessing, collecting or classifying, it is for grazing. Don't buy on other people's tasting notes, talk to a stock-holder, buy and try, then – if you are not satisfied – change suppliers. It is only by talking about wines that they can be fully appreciated, but most people never learn to talk at all. Don't set your sights on the expensive and rare bottles, they are not what it is about, at all. Trust yourself: you know more than you think you do.

Some people are very modest, say they know nothing, and are casting about for an expert in whom to trust. But this route no more leads to enlightened happiness than casting about for a drug-dealer, declaring one feels depressed, and buying the product. It is two quick steps to being hooked up to the dealer.

It is necessary for all of us – consumers, traders and writers – to become more acute, and more demanding, in our tasting of Burgundy. It is not the growers or merchants themselves, nor the French regulatory authorities, who can blast out of existence those mediocrities which continue to bedevil the place, and render it confusing, sometimes still a minefield. Some French gloss over the problems, some do not recognize them, some profit from them. An increasing number, of course, recognize them very well, and it is they from whom we shall hope to be buying.

3

The History of Burgundy Wines

—

'Beginning this work, I would like to have written on the opening page the name of the man who first tried to cultivate the vine in the Côte d'Or; he who, divining the perfume beneath the rock of our hillsides which the plant knows how to extract, installed the first vine and ran off the first wine.' Thus Dr Lavalle, writing in 1855, opened his *Histoire et statistique de la vigne et des grands vins de la Côte d'Or*. Since then there has been much research, but we are no closer to knowing for certain who began it all.

FROM EARLY TIMES TO THE BARBARIANS

Popular tradition in Dr Lavalle's time had it that the Gaulish conqueror Brennus was responsible for importing the first vine into Burgundy. The story went that he brought it back with him after his invading exploits against the Romans. In recent times the theory has been picked up by the late Pierre Forgeot in his *Origines du vignoble bourguignon*, published in 1972.

The Iron-Age Celtic tribes living in the region we now know as Burgundy may have got their first taste of wine from the Phoenicians. Legend has it that around 1300 BC the latter travelled to England after tin. Their route lay up the Rhône valley and then down the Seine and they would have carried gifts with them, for instance wine, for the tribes likely to bar their passage.

The discovery in January 1953 of a burial-ground dating from about 500 BC at Vix near Châtillon-sur-Seine in northern Burgundy has supplied some evidence. Vix is situated on the Mont Lassois, commanding the Seine Valley (near where it becomes navigable) and the tin route from Italy to the Cornish mines. Here the Celts had an encampment in the sixth, fifth and fourth centuries BC and they may have exacted payment from travellers along the route.

Although the magnificent shoulder-high Vix vase, capable of holding 1,250 litres, could equally have been used for carrying olive oil or wine, an Etruscan wine jar and a complete Greek wine service were also discovered at the same time. It seems reasonable to assume from these objects that first the Phoenicians, and then the Phocaeans[1] around 500 BC, were paying for their passage with money, presents and wine. Imported wine was therefore known in Burgundy by this time.

The next important fact is the invasion of Italy by the Celts. There were minor invasions between 590 and 550 BC, but the main movement took place around 400 BC. Authors such as Plutarch and Pliny, the naturalist, attribute the motive for the invasion to the Celts' passion for Italian wine. Titus Livius wrote in the first century BC, 'The Gauls penetrated the rich plains of Lombardy, installed themselves, then summoned their brothers who came in compact masses to invade the wine country.' As many as 300,000 are thought to have made the march. The Celtic tribes settled in different parts of Italy, the Aedui between Milan and Lake Como. The Aedui are the ancestors of today's Burgundians. Courtépée describes how the Aedui (*Eduens* in French), based on their capital Bibracte, were first amongst the independent peoples. They were to earn the description of brothers, friends and allies of the Roman people, and to be the first Gauls to be admitted to the Senate.

Diodorus, a Greek historian of the first century BC, relates that, once arrived in Italy, the Celts started cultivating the land and lost their nomadic instincts. There was plenty to learn on the subject of viticulture, as the Italians practised propagation by cuttings, layering (known as *provignage* in French, and indeed in use until the nineteenth century) and grafting, even on to vines already in production. If young vine plants were to be transported, roots and soil were established in a basket buried in a shallow pit. At a given moment, the young vine was severed from its parent, and the basket lifted without the roots being disturbed. Around 280 BC the Gauls attempted to invade Greece and Macedonia but were driven back,

1 From Phocaea, an Ionian city of Asia Minor.

and from 238 the Aedui began to lose ground in Lombardy to the Romans. This lasted for a century and during this period it seems likely that certain tribes began their way back over the Alps to their old homelands.

P. Forgeot concludes from this story as follows:

> It seems unthinkable and illogical that a people liking wine, who to a large extent invaded Italy because of it, who were reputed for their intelligence and manual skill, who lived for several generations in a land of famous vineyards, who became farmers and vignerons, who were able to learn everything on the subject of vines and wine, should not have started producing it in Gaul, immediately they returned home there from Italy.

The plantation of vineyards from 200 BC onwards is therefore possible. Sadly, Monsieur Forgeot could provide no evidence. And what happened, one wonders, to his wine-making Aedui for the five centuries from 200 BC onwards? Initially there was relative peace in the region, but soon they were invaded by the *Sequanes*, then the *Helvètes*, then enemies from Germany. They then allied themselves with the Romans to fight the Bretons and, finally, there was the revolt of the Gauls under Vercingetorix, which resulted in Caesar's victory at Alésia in 52 BC and the Roman subjugation of Gaul. The development of a wine-growing area at this time seems unlikely, and in the absence of evidence can only be considered hypothetical.

As Professor R. Dion has shown, the origins of French viticulture go back to the establishment of a Greek colony at Marseilles around 600 BC. The wine trade was one of the principal means used by Mediterranean societies to acquire slaves before the times when their armies were large enough to carry off whole nations into bondage. The Gauls would exchange a slave for a measure of wine, indeed sell themselves as a last resort. If the wine could be provided on the doorstep of the people who were prepared to pay so high a price for it, all the better. Much Greek colonization was done with this aim, he says. Tradition has it that the hostility of the Celts prevented the extension of the vineyard area by the Greek colony. But, as the centuries passed, there was a gradual extension along the trade routes.

There is a first-century BC mention in Cicero of the vines of central Gaul, and Columella at the beginning of the first century AD was writing that the vine was tended in almost every climate and

area of Gaul. Caesar's *Commentaries* have been variously inter-
preted. On the one hand they do not specifically mention viticulture
in Burgundy, on the other they seem to imply that it was present in
most areas.

Towards the end of the first century (AD 92) the Emperor Domitian issued an edict which prohibited the extension of vineyards in
Italy, and ordered the uprooting of half the vineyards in the prov-
inces. Many texts show that the reason for Domitian's edict was
economic. There was overproduction of cheap wine in the Roman
Empire, indeed in Ravenna it was cheaper than water. One motive
was probably to favour Italian wine-growers by cutting competition, and another to encourage the growing of corn. It would seem
that Domitian did not put his edict into effect. It was rescinded by
the Emperor Probus in AD 281, and there is no evidence that it
had the slightest effect in Burgundy.

From the second century AD we at last begin to get the archaeo-
logical finds which have previously been lacking pointing to the
existence of a commercial vineyard area. A gravestone found at
Corgoloin shows a Celtic god whose right hand holds what may be
a vine; other gravestones have reliefs featuring grapes and the god
of wine. More important, as E. Thevenot has shown, from around
AD 150 wine amphoras disappear from Burgundy. True, the distinction between amphoras used for wine and those used for oil or fish
sauce is a delicate one; true also that it is possible that the amphoras
were replaced by wooden casks;[2] nevertheless the disappearance of
wine amphoras may indicate that local production was now
enough to satisfy demand.

Between AD 253 and 277 however, barbarians (Franks, Alamans
and the Vandals under Crocus) returned to the area. Many Roman
villas were destroyed, and fortified camps were built to shelter the

---

2 The earliest mention of barrels in France is at the 51 BC siege of Uxellodunum
(now Vayrac in the Lot), when barrels were used for defence, filled with
inflammable matter. Jean Taransaud (*Le Livre de la tonnellerie*) claims that this is
when barrels were invented; however it is pre-dated by their appearance in
Herodotus, as Edward Hyams has shown. In *Dionysus, a Social History of the
Wine Vine* (Sidgwick & Jackson, London, 1987) he tells how the Babylonians
obtained their wine from the country of the Armenians above Assyria. It was
floated down the Euphrates in boats made of skins stretched over willow-hulls,
the casks being made of the wood of the palm-tree. He concludes, 'The Armenians
were the first coopers, or they may have bought their wine-casks in Assyria.'

local population, like the one whose remains can be found on the Mont Saint-Désiré, above the vineyards of Beaune.

There is also at last some written evidence: a document of AD 312 known as the Panegyric to Constantine, which was spoken by the orator Eumenius. R. Dion explains that the Emperor had recently reduced the taxes of the Autun citizens, and that the object of the Panegyric was to thank Constantine while showing that the tax exemptions were well deserved by the impoverished citizens.

Mention is made of the *Pagus Arebrignus*, the area around Beaune and Nuits, where the vine was cultivated. A convincing picture is painted of abandoned vineyards and age-old vine-stocks whose roots have become confusingly interlaced. But it appears that these vineyards were once an object of admiration, surely evidence of an established wine-growing area. Burgundy's renown dates from this moment: AD 312.

The fall of the Roman Empire and the invasions of the barbarians had seemingly little effect on viticulture. The area under vines stayed much the same, and Gregory of Tours was announcing in the sixth century that the land round Dijon produced a considerable amount of quality wine.

Les Burgondes, the people who have given their name to this region, originated in Scandinavia. Their traces can be found in Norwegian, Swedish and Danish place names.[3] They made their way south through Germany at the beginning of the Christian era, and founded a kingdom along the Rhône valley in AD 456, taking advantage of the decline of the Roman Empire to establish themselves in Lyon and then Dijon. They reigned until 534, when their kingdom was split up and shared by the Franks after a defeat in battle.

THE MONASTERIES

Soon afterwards the first large gift of land including vines was made to a Burgundian abbey – by Gontran, King of Burgundy, to the Abbey of Saint-Bénigne in Dijon in 587. At the beginning of

3 Perhaps I may be forgiven for not going any deeper into this, for, as the Abbé Courtépée warned, '*L'étymologie du mot de Bourguignons est une de ces vaines recherches qu'il faut abandonner à l'oisiveté et à la fiction de ceux qui s'en occupent.*'

the sixth century, Amalgaire, Duke of Lower Burgundy, founded the Abbey of Bèze, which was to give its name to one to the region's greatest wines. Dr Lavalle tells us that he endowed it with vines situated at Chenôve, Marsannay, Couchey, Gevrey, Vosne and around Beaune, along with the vignerons needed to cultivate them. Charlemagne gave a large area of vines between Aloxe and Pernand (it still bears his name) to the Abbey of Saulieu in 775. Church records of donations from now on serve to announce that, one after another, celebrated growths were producing wine. Aloxe had appeared in 696, then Fixey (733), Santenay (858), Chassagne (886), Savigny (930), and Pommard (1005). The oldest mention of the fame of Beaune's wine is in a book by Guillaume le Breton at the beginning of the thirteenth century.[4]

Two religious orders played large parts in the plantation and development of vineyards. The first was Cluny, founded in 910 in the Mâconnais, which at its height controlled 1,450 monasteries and 10,000 monks; and then Cîteaux, founded in 1098 in the plain opposite the Côte de Nuits by Robert, Abbot of Molesme. Both received donations of land and vineyard at the time of the crusades. The Cistercians created the Clos de Vougeot, planting vines for the first time on a hillside dotted with scrub, and building the famous wall, the château and its presses; they also owned vines on the Côte de Beaune.

One of Burgundy's most brilliant public-relations coups was the gift of thirty barrels of Beaune and Chambertin by Jean de Bussière, Abbot of Cîteaux, to Pope Gregory XI in Avignon. Some years later Jean de Bussière was made a cardinal, but better still the Papal Court got a taste for the wines. Petrarch was to write that the Cardinals did not want to quit France and return to Rome because Beaune wine would no longer be available to them.

The Cistercians and then the Valois dukes (to whom we shall come in a moment) made Burgundy the first wine of Europe; the coronations of both Charles VI in 1321 and Philippe VI in 1328 were celebrated at Reims with Beaune wine. It was made to spout from a stag's nostrils.

---

4 Two Beaune wine-growers, both established in 1270 (Clerget-Buffet et Fils and Raoul Clerget et Fils), are the sixth and seventh oldest businesses in the world according to the *Guinness Book of the Business World*, 1976.

THE VALOIS DUKES

Although the fame of the wines was spreading, Burgundians had problems at home. In 1349 plague struck the region. It caused many deaths including that of all Beaune's *curés*. Because of the decreased work-force, the vineyards suffered neglect, and for fourteen years there were virtually no harvests. Then it was noted that a vine in the hamlet of Gamay not only withstood disease but was also producing sizeable crops. It was propagated and, under its village's name, planted along the Côte. But it failed to give quality wines as the Pinot had done, and soon was attacked. The first of many instructions to uproot the *'très mauvaiz et très-desloyaul plant, nommez Gaamez, du quel mauvaiz plant vient tres-grant habondance de vins'* was issued by Duke Philip the Bold in 1395. His vineyards had the reputation of producing the best, most precious and proper wines of the Kingdom of France for the nourishment and sustaining of human creatures. So that they should recover their lost renown, the use in the vineyards of manure from cows, goats, horses and other beasts, animal's horns, or bone-scrapings was forbidden.

In France at this time the king was confronted by great fiefs which were nominally subject to the French crown but in fact independent: Normandy, Guienne, Gascony, Toulouse, Burgundy. The French kings had the habit of allotting great territorial domains to princes of the blood, and Burgundy was granted to his fourth son Philip by John II 'the Bountiful' in 1363. Under the reign of Duke Philip and his successors John the Fearless (1404–19), Philip the Good (1419–67), and Charles the Bold (1467–77), Burgundy enjoyed its period of greatest glory and pre-eminence. The four Valois dukes were ambitious, able, flamboyant rulers, whose lands (covering an area the size of England and Wales) straddled the border between France and the Holy Roman Empire. In a century they came close to hiving off an independent kingdom for themselves.

The first Duke Philip had earned himself the title of 'the Bold' by his courage on the battlefield of Poitiers at the age of fourteen. He was to marry the heiress of Flanders, and through his wife also became ruler of Franche-Comté, Artois, Nevers and Rethel. He laid the foundations of the Burgundian state to which would later be added Tonnerre and the Mâconnais, Hainault, Brabant, Holland,

Limbourg, Luxembourg, Picardy and, briefly, Lorraine. By 1392 he also had his hand on the French Treasury. An unfortunate king was on the throne, Charles VI, who 'during his protracted fits of madness, capered about the corridors of the royal palace howling like a wolf; or else, believing he was made of glass, proceeded with the utmost caution, for fear of breaking himself'.[5] Thanks to economic upsurge in the Low Countries (Brussels and Antwerp were expanding, Bruges was the busiest port in Europe), Philip the Bold had the finances to maintain his position as regent over Brittany, Savoy and Luxembourg; he was the undisputed master of France, and even laid plans in 1386 to invade England. But he never crossed the Channel.

His son John the Fearless helped Henry V of England to victory by his absence from the French army at the battle of Agincourt. He led the Burgundians in bloody civil war against the Armagnacs, and spent most of his reign trying to keep control of the French government. He resorted to the assassination of his rival Louis of Orléans in a Paris street in 1407, openly admitting it, but was himself murdered by his political opponents twelve years later, having been lured to a 'diplomatic parley' with the Dauphin.

The next Great Duke of the Occident, Philip the Good, allied himself with the English in 1420, and handed over Joan of Arc (in exchange for 10,000 gold crowns), who had fallen into his hands beneath the ramparts of Compiègne. Under his rule Burgundy remained hostile to France and there was a more or less permanent Anglo-Burgundian alliance. Philip had simple tastes in food, according to Bishop Guillaume Fillastre, who wrote that frequently he left partridges on one side for a Mainz ham or a piece of salt beef. This did not prevent him entertaining visitors, as in 1450 when some Scottish knights and squires travelling with William Earl of Douglas partook of this banquet: 2 hares, 10 pheasants, a heron, 4 bitterns, 156 rabbits, 72 partridges, 10 geese, 12 water-birds, 34 dozen larks, 231 chickens and 56 brace of pigeons. Philip the Good founded the Chivalric Order of the Golden Fleece, including among its members noblemen from throughout his territories as well as foreign rulers, such as the Kings of Aragon and Naples, and Prince John of Portugal. A resident agent was maintained at the

5 From Richard Vaughan's *Valois Burgundy*, Allen Lane, Penguin Books, London, 1975, to which this account owes much.

Papal Court, and gifts of wine or tapestries despatched to Rome from time to time. Thus he hoped to widen his influence and strengthen his alliances.

He was in no doubt about the duchy's wines, declaring that the Dukes of Burgundy were immediate lords of the best wines of Christendom. In 1441 he forbade the planting of vines in unsuitable land around Dijon, which noble town was described by its mayor and corporation in 1452 as being based on the culture of vines, with wine its chief merchandise. R. Vaughan has shown that the main commercial and agricultural activity of the Duchy was the export of fine wines, mainly to Paris and the Low Countries.

Duke Philip the Good appointed an Autun burgess, Nicolas Rolin, to be his chancellor, the most important, influential and best-paid Burgundian official. Rolin amassed a fortune while serving the duke, and in 1443 endowed a poor-house and hospital, the Hôtel-Dieu in Beaune. He donated no vines to it, but one of its finest red Beaune wines always bears his name.

The next duke, Charles the Bold, saw himself as a new Alexander – had not his father carried the same name as Philip of Macedon? A German cleric, Conrad Stolle, reported 'that the Duke of Burgundy claimed there were only three lords in the world, one in Heaven, that is God; one in Hell, the devil Lucifer; and one on earth, who will be he himself'. He had a passion for military campaigning, and fought to consolidate and unify the Burgundian state. He temporarily acquired Upper Alsace, and for a year Lorraine, thus almost joining his northern and southern possessions. He dressed even more ostentatiously than his predecessors, in jewelled hats – were they ducal, archducal or regal? – his robes, and even armour, glittering with rubies, pearls and sapphires. When he visited the emperor he wore a floor-length ermine-lined open-fronted cloth-of-gold mantle, with underneath a pearl-bordered coat, studded with diamonds. One of his plumed and jewelled hats cost nearly £500, so the ducal accounts record.

Burgundian power reached its zenith under Charles, whose allies were listed by one of his officials as the pope, the emperor, the kings of England, Aragon, Scotland, Denmark, Portugal, the dukes of Brittany and Austria, the house of Savoy, the doge and signory of Venice, the elector-palatine of the Rhine, the dukes of Bavaria, Cleves and Guelders and my lords the archbishop-electors of Mainz, Trier and Cologne. But it was not to last.

The kings of France and the emperors resented and feared the upstart state on their borders. The dukes had failed to impose centralized administration, or centralized justice, on their scattered territories. The energetic, violent Charles alarmed his neighbours, not without reason, and they proved formidable, determined enemies.

He was brought down by an alliance between Austria, Lorraine, the confederate cantons of Switzerland, and the towns of Strasbourg, Basel, Selestat and Colmar. Twice he allowed his army to be taken by surprise and defeated while campaigning against the Swiss. He then shifted the theatre of war northwards, in an attempt to reconquer Lorraine which was slipping from his grasp. Against the advice of his captains he laid siege to Nancy during the bitter winter of 1476–7. Four hundred of his soldiers froze to death on Christmas Eve, and on 5 January his army was routed by the enemy. Valois Burgundy collapsed with the death of Charles the Bold before the walls of Nancy. He had only one child, a girl promised in marriage to Maximilian of Austria, son of the emperor. There was no one to carry on the fight, and Louis XI, King of France, rapidly annexed the duchy.

Charles's body lay undiscovered in a frozen stream for two days. He had been felled by a battle-axe; when found his corpse was half-devoured by wolves, so legend has it. Many believed that he had survived and would return after seven years, and bills of exchange in Burgundy were held until that time had elapsed.

Valois Burgundy was broadly contemporary with the Italian Renaissance, but unheedful of it. The dukes looked to the north for their artists and craftsmen. Philip the Good employed Jan van Eyck, sending him to Portugal to paint Henry the Navigator's sister, the Infanta Elizabeth, before he married her. He appointed van Eyck official court painter, and stood godfather to his son, believing that he would never find his equal in artistic skill. Roger van der Weyden (whose *Last Judgement* can be seen at the Hôtel-Dieu in Beaune) may also have been employed by the dukes. The outstanding name in sculpture is that of the Dutchman Claus Sluter, employed by Philip the Bold at the Charterhouse of Champmol just outside Dijon. R. Vaughan describes him as the greatest sculptor then living outside Italy; at the very moment when Donatello and Ghiberti were competing to produce the bronze doors of the Baptistry in Florence, Sluter was at work on the statues of a monumental

Crucifixion for the Valois duke, parts of which can still be seen in Dijon.

The dukes commissioned illuminated manuscripts, and built up one of the best princely libraries of their day, over two hundred of these books being now preserved in the Royal Library of Belgium in Brussels. Their court was of great splendour, and a cause of admiration throughout Europe, as was its feasting. 'We went to see my lord of Burgundy at dinner, and saw all the majesty and all the triumph which occurred when he dined', declared some deputies from the city of Metz, obviously impressed, at the court of Charles the Bold.

The Valois dukes were not great builders, and little of their architecture survives except part of the ducal palace in Dijon, and the Tower of Duke John in the Rue Etienne-Marcel in Paris. (Here the 'Fearless' Duke locked himself up, under bodyguard, in a sort of fortified bedroom with a bathroom beneath it.) In music however R. Vaughan considers that the Burgundian impact was important and long term. The court chapel employed some of the foremost musicians of the day, and a Netherlandish tradition was built up which under Maximilian was to influence German music-making significantly.

The vineyard enactments of the two Valois Philips were well-meaning but ineffective. A multiplicity of complaints against vines planted in land more suitable for crops caused an investigation under King Charles VIII in 1486, and further regulations in 1567. In 1590 there were calls for vineyards to be uprooted, in 1628 and 1731 new plantations were forbidden. Just before the French Revolution the Abbé Courtépée was writing that a new order like that of Philip the Bold was much needed, for the *gamet* (Gamay) had been planted in land more suitable for wheat. In 1855 Dr Lavalle exclaimed, 'God knows with what terrifying activity the vulgar plant has driven out the noble one, and what progress it makes each day. Our ancestors would have been appalled!'

Nevertheless the popularity of the wines had continued to grow, and under Louis XIV they received two useful puffs. The first occurred when, after 1693, Guy-Crescent Fagon, the king's doctor, prescribed *vieux Bourgogne* (in place of Champagne) to bring relief to the king, who was periodically subject to attacks of gout.[6] The

6 I am indebted to Richard Olney's *Romanée-Conti*, Flammarion, Paris, 1991, which clearly separates fact from myth here (as with several other Burgundian legends).

second was thanks to a Mâcon vigneron named Charles Brosse who drove a cart laden with barrels from Chasselas near Juliénas to Versailles. During Mass the Sun King noticed Brosse, who seemed to remain standing while everyone else knelt. But Brosse was a giant, and he seized the opportunity of speaking to Louis to ask him to taste his wine. The king approved of it, and the court followed suit.

THE EXPORT OF BURGUNDY WINES

The earliest shipments of Burgundy across the Channel, according to A. L. Simon's *The History of the Wine Trade in England*,[7] took place during the reign of Henry II (1154–89). Rouen had an important trade in the wines of Normandy and the Seine Valley, though A. L. Simon describes them as very inferior compared to the produce of the Burgundy vineyards. Burgundy merchants used to bring their wines to Rouen, where they sold them to the local traders, who had a monopoly on navigation from their city to the Channel. In 1212 King John purchased 348 casks of wine for £507.11s., of which 26 came from Auxerre (3 came from Germany, 8 from Anjou, 54 from the Orléanais and Île-de-France, 267 from Gascony). During the same reign the Abbot of Fécamp paid two barrels of Auxerre wine for letters patent enabling him to bring a shipload of wine to England before the feast of Saint Peter in Chains. King John stocked his cellar in part by imposing fines on his subjects, the Bishop of Winchester being relieved of a cask of good wine for not reminding the King to give a girdle to the Countess of Albemarle.

A. L. Simon declared that the fame of the wines of Auxerre in England is more ancient than that of Bordeaux wines, even if their consumption during the Middle Ages was always less; this of course because Gascony was English for the three hundred years after Henry II had married Eleanor of Aquitaine.

Those Burgundies that reached Britain came sometimes via Rouen, sometimes via Flanders. In 1512 Louis XII sent thirty-six puncheons of *Vin de Beaune cleret* to James IV of Scotland; in 1537 Auxerre wine was sent from Rouen direct to Thomas Cromwell

---

7 Reprinted by the Holland Press, London, 1964.

in London; in 1538 an advice from Brussels referred to wines of Burgundy (*Borgoyn*) sent to Henry VIII.

A. L. Simon goes on to describe that Burgundy was greatly appreciated in England during the seventeenth century, but never common, its scarcity and consequent high price being due to the difficulties of bringing it over, usually down the Yonne and the Seine, via Paris and Rouen. Louis XIV made a present of 200 *muids* of very good Champagne, Burgundy and Hermitage wines to the King of England in 1666.

Julian Jeffs in *The Wines of Europe*[8] writes that only wealthy connoisseurs could afford to import Burgundy. He instances John Harvey, first Earl of Bristol, who imported red and white Burgundies between 1700 and 1739, though in very small quantities as compared with claret. A century later English cellar-books still feature it rarely.

The Burgundy wine trade began to organize itself during the eighteenth century, and a number of the companies established at that time are still in business. Champy was founded in 1720, Bouchard Père in 1731, Poulet in 1747, Chanson in 1750. Until then most exports of Burgundy went to Belgium, indeed the Belgians came regularly after the harvest to visit growers' cellars with a Beaune commission-agent. The wines travelled north on vast carts; risk of robbery was high, as was the chance that wine would be tapped on the way.

AFTER THE FRENCH REVOLUTION

The multiple ownership of most of Burgundy's vineyards dates from the French Revolution. After the suppression of religious orders and the flight or guillotining of the nobility, their lands were declared national assets and sold. The Clos de Vougeot was to be reunited under one owner in the nineteenth century, but the majority of famous sites were irrevocably split.

The second important repercussion of 1789 was increased demand and consumption of wine. The Gamay was again widely planted.

In common with France's other vineyard areas, Burgundy had to

8 Faber and Faber, London, 1971.

fight two deadly threats in the nineteenth century. The first was a disease called Oidium, or powdery mildew, which attacks the green organs of the vine. It was first discovered in Margate, Kent in 1845 and may have come to Britain on an ornamental plant, perhaps from America. By 1852 it was endemic in all France's vineyards, reducing the crop substantially. Fortunately a remedy was at hand, for it was discovered that dusting with finely-ground sulphur was effective in combating the disease. Tens of thousands of tons of sulphur are used in vineyards to this day in the fight against Oidium.

The second threat was to appear in a Hammersmith greenhouse in 1863 and soon after in the south of France. A burrowing vine louse had been imported into Europe on vines sent from the United States. Small yellow insects were to be seen on the roots of dying vines, sometimes so numerous that the roots appeared to be varnished yellow. In 1868 the insect was identified as 'phylloxera', and named *vastatrix*, the devastator. 'Gentlemen, it is disastrous: it goes forward like an army, laying waste all before it', declared a vineyard manager to a scientific commission. Over the next fifteen years it was to invade every vineyard area in France, costing the country more than twice the indemnity (5,000 million francs) paid to the Germans after the Franco-Prussian War.

The cure was not so rapidly discovered as had been that for Oidium. The Government offered a 300,000-franc prize, and was deluged by crazy suggestions: burying a live toad under each vine; watering the vineyards with white wine, or sea-water; applying hot sealing wax to the pruning cuts. Five years of experiments failed to provide the answer, but two processes seemed promising. The first was flooding, which killed the insects but was impractical on hillside sites; the second, injection of the soil with carbon bisulphide (CS_2), a heavy liquid with an unpleasant smell. It is an effective fumigant but dangerous, since its vapour is toxic, and it is liable to catch fire or explode when being manipulated. Although it killed the phylloxera, the vineyard was immediately open to infection again. The first process was used in the flat plains of the Midi, indeed flooded vineyards can still today be seen from the Marseille–Toulouse *autoroute*; the second had its adherents in Burgundy until 1945, the last vineyard to be so treated being Romanée-Conti.

The solution to the problem proved to be grafting on to resistant American root-stocks. According to G. Ordish, to whose book *The*

Great Wine Blight[9] I am much indebted, the suggestion was first made in 1869 by Gaston Bazille at a congress in Beaune, but neither he nor Léo Laliman (who claimed to have been the first to indicate that certain American vines were resistant to phylloxera) ever saw the prize-money.

It was many years before the solution was universally adopted, the interval seeing fierce disputes between proponents of carbon bisulphide and grafting. The pest reached the Côte d'Or officially in July 1878, though Burgundians believed their vineyards would be immune from harm. They claimed that it only attacked poorly-tended vines, or those pushed to give enormous yields. A year later thirty-four infected centres were to be found in Beaune, and local government was forced to take action.

Searches and treatments with carbon bisulphide became compulsory. They were unpopular, as the first treatments had killed the vines as well as the phylloxera. G. Ordish describes how 160 growers in Chenôve chased the treatment team out of the area, saying they were more to be feared than the aphid itself. A decree of 1874 had prohibited the introduction of American vines into Burgundy, for it was feared that growers would replant and produce directly from them, causing deterioration of quality and increased yields. The realization that resistant vines were invaluable as root-stocks, on to which the traditional varieties could be grafted, was not widespread until the mid–1880s.

The Société Vigneronne de Beaune brought in three skilled craftsmen-grafters in 1886, though a decree permitting the introduction of foreign vines into the Côte d'Or was not passed until June 1887. That year free grafting courses were set up in thirteen communes. It was evident that if complete reconstitution of the vineyards was necessary, a vast quantity of plants would be needed. Skill at the grafting table was to become a necessary accomplishment for the wine-grower.

By 1890 the chemists, advocating treatment with carbon bisulphide, were in retreat before the Americanists; it was estimated that 1,000 hectares had been replanted with transatlantic vines. 1893 was the critical harvest, when wines from grafted vines could be tasted and compared. A Meursault Goutte d'Or was awarded a Paris Gold Medal the following spring, and its owner decorated

9 Sidgwick & Jackson, London, 1987.

with the medal and cross of the Mérite Agricole. After so many years of wondering whether the vineyards were doomed, the relief must have been tremendous.

From now on the search began for the most suitable stocks to use in the alkaline soils of the Côte. Equally the door was open to experimentation with high-yielding types of Pinot, with sometimes disastrous effects on quality, as will be seen. The worst consequence of the destruction of Burgundy's vineyards by the phylloxera was not the modification of the style of wine, but the opportunity it gave to vineyard owners to replant with Pinots known for their high yields.

A subsidy was paid to growers for reconstitution, as it had been for treatment; however, it represented only 18 per cent of the cost in the case of a grower doing his own grafting, 8 per cent for those who bought the plants. Many small growers had chosen emigration to Algeria or the United States, to become Burgundian farmers as well as wine-growers, or had gone to work for large estates who needed labour for chemical treatments, or to organize flooding. The vineyards lost about 6,000 people through emigration, and the area under vines was never remotely the same again.

It is the cheap table wine areas in the plain which have never been replanted – no great surprise, and no great loss, for *vin ordinaire* can be produced more economically in southern France. The completion of the Marseilles–Lyon–Paris railway line in 1856 had brought Midi wines easily and cheaply to the Burgundian and Paris markets. Of 31,000 ha. of *vin ordinaire* vineyard in the Côte d'Or in 1882 a mere 929 ha. were left by 1988. The area planted with fine varieties in 1882 had been just over 3,000 ha. In 1988 there were 8,076 ha. producing *appellation contrôlée* (AC) wines. In the adjoining *départements* – Yonne to the north, and Saône-et-Loire to the south – plantations also stood at record levels, total AC vineyards in the three *départements* standing at 21,689 ha. by 1988. So great an area under fine vines has never before been seen in Burgundy.

TWENTIETH-CENTURY BURGUNDY

Methods of vineyard cultivation and wine-making have been completely revolutionized over the last hundred years, as we shall see in the coming chapters.

4

Climate, Rock and Soil
(what the French call terroir)

French is more concise here than English, for this complex subject is covered in one word, where we need three. In Burgundy, they love the word *terroir*, and have virtually turned it into a religion. Indeed, if one accepts Erich Fromm's definition of religion as 'any group-shared system of thought and action that offers the individual a frame of orientation and an object of devotion'[1] then *terroir* in Burgundy is definitely a religion, a sort of harking back to the pagan veneration of trees, plants, hills and springs.

CLIMATE

Unless the weather is favourable to the vegetative cycle of the vine and the maturing of its fruit, good wine cannot be made. So before looking at soil, type of vine or working methods, we must examine the climate: rainfall, wind, temperature, hours of sun and relative humidity. I am greatly indebted to S. Taboulot and his colleagues of Météo-France at Dijon-Longvic, to R. Gadille's *Le Vignoble de la Côte bourguignonne*,[2] and particularly to the table, 'Climate: a comparison of regions in Australasia and France' (the material in which was collated by Dr Richard Smart) which appears in James Halliday's *Wine Atlas of Australia and New Zealand*.[3] This table, and the text accompanying it, make riveting reading for anyone interested in how global warming and climate change may come to affect French vineyards.

1 *To Have or to Be?*, Erich Fromm, Jonathan Cape, London, 1978.
2 Les Belles Lettres, Publications de l'Université de Dijon, Paris, 1967.
3 Published by Angus & Robertson-HarperCollins, London, 1991.

Rainfall

Over 1 mm of rain falls in Burgundy on about 115 days of the year, averaging 732 mm per annum over the period 1961–92. The months of April, February, July and March tend – in that order – to be the driest (April being often a perfect month for visiting Burgundy). May can be very wet. It is difficult to generalize about rainfall during July, August and September, but the first two months are normally dry, with the third beginning a phase of diminishing rainfall which is accentuated in October. Regular light rains are more characteristic than heavy storms, but the latter do occur, particularly in June, the record being 52 mm in less than an hour on 16 July 1947.

Vineyard development is favoured by dryness at the end of the winter, which allows the soil to warm up, but often compromised by rain during June, when the vine is in flower. If the rains are heavy and persistent, either the flowers can be destroyed, or their fertilization can be hampered by low temperatures, both causing *coulure* or a reduction in the size of the harvest. A dry July is favourable since it brings the growth period to a halt and advances the date of the *véraison* when the grapes turn colour. This process is helped by rain in early August, but if the month is persistently wet, an attack of grey rot can be unleashed.

Many vintages have been saved by the diminishing rainfall of September and particularly early October, for this dryness is sometimes enough to halt the development of grey rot, and bring the grapes to maturity.

There are considerable local differences in rainfall in Burgundy; Saint-Romain for instance in the Hautes Côtes regularly receives more rain than Dijon. The plateaux of the Hautes Côtes are wetter than the Côte d'Or throughout the year, as is the plain during the summer. As one progresses south, through Chagny and Mâcon to Lyon, the rainfall increases, particularly in July and August. In spite of the disadvantages of a wet May–June and an uncertain summer, the vineyards of the Côte d'Or benefit from two favourable factors as regards rain. Protection is afforded by their sheltered position halfway up hillsides, and also by their very northerliness, for rain-bearing clouds from the south have often shed their moisture by the time they reach the Côte d'Or.

The prevailing winds of Burgundy are those from the west (which often bring rain), south-west, north-east and north. The last, known as *la bise*, is the coldest, but has the merit of often drying out the vegetation after the rain.

Temperature

Below are the monthly centigrade temperatures, averaged over the thirty-year period 1961–90:

January	1.6°
February	3.6°
March	6.5°
April	9.8°
May	13.7°
June	17.2°
July	19.7°
August	19.1°
September	16.1°
October	11.3°
November	5.6°
December	2.3°

As may be seen, the lowest monthly averages are met in January, December, and February. April's 10° encourages budding and May's 13° some rapid growth. In June, a temperature of 16° is desirable for a successful flowering period, this factor being more influential than the rainfall. July usually sees the highest average temperatures (around 20°), coming at the moment of lightest rain, and this should ensure an early *véraison*. Days of intense heat (30° or over) are occasionally met with in June and September, but most often in July and August. When they occur in June, often in three- to five-day periods, they can be most beneficial to the flowering. Intense heat combined with lack of rain can delay the *véraison*, but scorching of the grapes has scarcely been met with since 1727 and 1819.

There are about sixty-six days of frost in Dijon, of which four-teen or fifteen go down to −5°. Frosts of −8° are regularly met with in December and January. So long as the weather is dry the Pinot vine has nothing to fear, since it can support −17° without harm, but spring frosts are another matter. A late budding is therefore desirable so that damage can be limited.

As far as local differences are concerned, comparison between Saint-Romain in the Hautes Côtes and Auxonne in the plain reveals that the former is cooler from March to June but warmer from July to October. From July to September the temperatures on the Côte Châlonnaise are notably lower than those at Dijon. The Côte de Nuits regularly harvests its grapes a week later than the Côte de Beaune, and while some growers on the former Côte might attribute this to undue haste on the part of the Beaunois, it certainly reflects the cooler climate just a few kilometres farther north.

If we look elsewhere in France, the vineyards of Champagne, being somewhat closer to the ocean, are cooler than those of Burgundy, those of Alsace warmer, though in both cases the differences lessen in the autumn. Bordeaux's monthly average temperatures are always higher than Burgundy's, and it has a decidedly warmer August and September.

Sunshine

There is a heliograph at Dijon which records the hours, though not the intensity, of the sunlight. During the thirty years 1961–90 Dijon received an average of 1,831 hours of sun per annum during a theoretical total of 4,476 hours of daylight. Since 1949 the twelve sunniest years have been:

1959	2,530 hours
1949	2,296 hours
1955	2,285 hours
1953	2,166 hours
1976	2,152 hours
1952	2,139 hours
1989	2,126 hours
1962	2,068 hours
1957	2,051 hours
1967	2,042 hours
1971	2,024 hours
1985	2,010 hours

1990 comes in thirteenth position, with 1,978 hours. 1965 holds the record for the most sunless summer since 1949: 1,583 hours, just 35 per cent of the hours of light.

July stands out as the sunniest month, followed by June, then

August, May and September. The long hours of sunshine in Burgundy are tied to two factors: the latitude, giving more daylight, and the area's continental position, which causes it to be affected during the summer by anti-cyclones. Sunshine goes a long way to compensate for less happy rainfall and temperature averages.

Relative humidity

A study of rainfall alone is not enough to give an idea of the dampness or dryness of Burgundy.

The annual average relative humidity of the air at 13.00 hours showed the following figures for the period 1926–35:

Marseille	58 per cent
Bordeaux and Dijon	65 per cent
Reims	66 per cent
Strasbourg	68 per cent

There is a remarkable similarity in humidity between Bordeaux and Dijon throughout the vine's vegetative cycle. The Bordelais starts the day damper (and often foggier) because of the closeness of the ocean, but the air dries out to Dijon's level by 13.00 hours, then further by the evening. Reims and Strasbourg are damper than Dijon throughout the day.

During April and May Marseille is more often than not damper than Dijon, and on six occasions between 1945 and 1963 the Côte d'Or enjoyed a relative humidity during July, August and September, comparable to that of the Mediterranean region.

If all four factors are considered together it is to be noted that Burgundy's climate is remarkably like that of Bordeaux, although its average temperature is lower and its rainfall less favourably spread over the months. Until the decade of the 1980s, Burgundy's weather tended to be most irregular from year to year, this being one of its fundamental characteristics. The region owed its fame to the wines produced after good summers.

Global warming and climatic change

If we compare the recent average daily temperatures, and the hours of sun, for those summer months in Burgundy which ripen the grapes, the results (see Tables 1 and 2) are a little startling.

Table 1   Monthly averages of daily temperatures in °C (8 observations per day, averaged)[4]

	July	August	September
1963–72	19.7	18.5	15.8
1973–82	19.6	19.4	16.2
1983—92	21.2	19.8	16.2

Table 2   Average total hours of sun per month

	July	August	September
1953–62	245	242	209
1963–72	266	207	191
1973–82	252	231	194
1983–92	289	253	191

If average summer temperatures have risen by 0.4°–1.5°C, when we compare the decades 1963–72 and 1983–92, does this mean that global warming is already affecting our Burgundies? One cannot jump to that conclusion on such slim evidence, and indeed if one adds in the figures for June (1963–72: 17°, 1973–82: 17.7°, 1983–92: 16.6°) we find a decrease. I wonder what the next decade will bring?

There have been major climatic swings in the past, of course. Halliday[5] refers to the exceptionally warm period from the late 1400s to the mid-1500s, when vineyards flourished in England, and at one point the Rhine stopped flowing and could be crossed by foot. He describes how this was followed, in the 1690s, by a run of catastrophic vintages and a great freeze in 1709 which caused near total destuction of French vineyards. He feels that global warming is 'far from an unmitigated disaster for vignerons, and in particular for those in New Zealand.' The latter are making wine, as are Burgundians, at the cool limits of where the grape will ripen; indeed Auckland, Marlborough, Nelson, Canterbury and Tasmania (in Australia) all appear *cooler* than the French classic regions of Bordeaux, Burgundy and Champagne.

Halliday appears to believe that downunder he will see tempera-

4 Source for Tables 1 and 2: France-Météo, Météorologie Nationale, Service Interrégionale Centre-Est, Station de Dijon-Longvic.
5 *Wine Atlas of Australia and New Zealand.*

ture increases of between 1.5° and 4.5°C by the year 2030, this year having been selected because it is 'well within the commercial life expectancy of a vineyard planted in 1990'. He concludes that if these temperature increases are seen in Europe 'the axis for premium wine production would shift to the north, creating great wealth and opportunity for some, but causing immense problems for areas such as Bordeaux, Burgundy and Champagne . . . Bordeaux may cope to a degree (Cabernet Sauvignon is a flexible variety), but Pinot Noir is very intolerant and exacting, so what is the future of red Burgundy? And what of Champagne? Only time will tell.'

I have not succeeded in unearthing any research into climate change in the Côte d'Or, and its influence on the wines, but I am sure something is under way. The BIVB's Service Expérimentation is in full fermentation throughout the year, and no doubt they will publish when they are ready.

On a smaller scale, it would be possible to take the study of microclimate much further. Statistics collected at Mercurey, Saint-Maurice-les-Couches, Santenay, Meloisey, Chorey-lès-Beaune, Comblanchien, Meuilley, Morey and Marsannay would show many subtle, local differences, and go some way to explaining the varied successes of the villages. It might call into question, for instance, the enthusiasm shown by the authorities for planting Pinot Noir, not Chardonnay, all over the Hautes Côtes, so not everyone would welcome a radical approach to climatic research.

These local climates are influenced not just by altitude, but by depressions in the hillsides, by the orientation of the slopes, by the opening up of combes leading back through the Côte, by the closeness of the woods. If Burgundians were as interested in the detail of microclimate as they are in the detail of subsoil they could discover all sorts of things.

Microclimate cannot, of course, be divorced from the differences in soil and subsoil. It would be fruitless to search for the origin of the diversity of Burgundy's villages and *crus* solely in the distribution of microclimates. The answer lies largely in the rocks and soils.

FISH-ROES, SEA-LILIES AND BABY OYSTERS: BURGUNDY'S ROCK FORMATIONS

Some knowledge of how Burgundy's rocks and soil were formed is necessary, I think, if one is to understand the wines. So prepare yourself, please, for a rapid 400-million-year survey of the Burgundian scene.

Europe's geological history is long and complicated. The heart of the continent is known as the Baltic shield (which roughly approximates to present-day Sweden and Finland), continuing eastwards as the Russian platform. Around this shield various mountain ranges have been formed at different times.

There were three main periods of mountain-building. The first affected Northern Scandinavia, Scotland, Wales and much of Ireland. It was first studied in Scotland and because of this christened Caledonian. It took place during the Silurian period, about 400 million years ago (see the geological time-scale, Table 3).

The seas were inhabited by trilobites, sea-lilies and brachiopods; the first animals, such as millipedes, were gaining a foothold on land, as were the first seedless plants.

About a hundred million years later a second folding of mountains took place, called Hercynian, from the Latin name for Harz Mountains. The Harz form only a small part of this fragmented range, which stretches from the west coast of Europe (Cornwall, Brittany and Portugal) to Poland. The Massif Central and Morvan, on whose eastern edge the vineyards of Burgundy are to be found, was formed at this period. Sharks dominated the seas, while on land amphibians (evolved from fish) became an important group, and giant tree ferns grew.

Millions of years passed, while the jagged outlines of the Massif Central mountains were ground down by the erosive action of water, wind and sun. Near Autun a great lake existed, the home of fish, microscopic algae and giant frogs. During the Jurassic period (135–95 million years ago) the whole of Burgundy sank beneath shallow seas. Archaeopteryx, or some other ancestral bird, took wing, great dinosaurs roamed the land, while on the sea-bed marine sediments were slowly laid down. The shells of myriads of baby oysters piled one on another, while the skeletons of countless crinoids or sea-lilies were compacted together; from such petrified remains limestone rock is formed. Jurassic limestone rocks,

Table 3   The geological time-scale (in millions of years)

0	
	Pliocene
7	
	Miocene
26	
	Oligocene
38	
	Eocene
54	
	Palaeocene
65	

TERTIARY

CRETACEOUS (70)

135 —

JURASSIC (60)

195 —

TRIASSIC (30)

225 —

PERMIAN (55)

280 —

CARBONIFEROUS (65)

345 —

DEVONIAN (50)

395 —

SILURIAN (40)

435 —

ORDOVICIAN (65)

500 —

CAMBRIAN (100)

600 —

PRECAMBRIAN

4500

interspersed with marlstones, are fundamental keys to the excellence and variety of Burgundy's wines. We will come across their outcrops on hillsides from Chablis down to Mâcon.

The sedimentary rocks formed at this period have three origins. That just described is biological and, as well as baby oysters and sea-lilies, there were molluscs and sea-urchins, brachiopods and corals, foraminifera (protozoa with a calcite skeleton) and calcareous seaweeds. Such rocks consist almost entirely of fossils. A second type results from the erosion of nearby land-masses above sea-level, in this case not the Morvan, Massif Central or Jura, as these were also submerged, but the Ardennes and the schistous mountain-mass of the Rhineland. These rocks are composed of fine particles of clay and sand, gravel and marl (itself a calcareous mudstone). They form the marlstones which outcrop on both Côte de Beaune and Côte de Nuits. The third type of rock is caused by the precipitation of carbonate of lime from sea water and its subsequent accretion around a nucleus, for instance skeletal debris. Millions of such tiny grains packed together form oolitic limestone (so named from its distant resemblance to fish-roes), the same rock which forms the Cotswolds, and stretches in a great swathe of wonderful building material from Dorset up to Yorkshire.

The Jurassic period was followed by the Cretaceous, then the Tertiary. The seas finally withdrew from Burgundy about 70 million years ago, when dinosaurs and pterodactyls were dying out. During the Tertiary period, flowering plants like magnolia were appearing alongside ferns, conifers and ginkgoes, and mammals were evolving rapidly; many fish and reptiles resembled those of today.

At this time the third great phase of European mountain-building took place, a mere 35 million years ago. The Pyrenees, the Apennines, the Atlas and the Alps all date from then. A depression began to form south of Dijon, which was to sink further during the Miocene period, to become the rift-valley of Bresse. Palms and Judas-trees flourished at its edges. The great Alpine upheaval caused faults to form on the Côte in a north–south direction, and many of the old Hercynian rifts moved again. This is the moment when Burgundy acquired the geological structure we can see when we visit it today, its Jurassic bedding planes dipping towards the Saône.

Figure 2 shows the Côte between Dijon and Meursault, viewed from the plain. The outcrop of Liassic marls north of Gevrey is the same rock which is responsible for the rich pastures of the Auxois, the finest grazing ground for white Charolais cattle. Above it is Bajocian (so-called because first studied at Bayeux) crinoidal limestone. This is most characteristically formed from the accumulation of the broken stalks of crinoids or sea-lilies; it is a powerful rock, resistant to erosion, from which were cut the dark stones of the Vézelay basilica. Next comes a layer just 8 to 10 metres thick, of softer marly limestone. It is characterized by the presence of innumerable tiny oysters, steely-blue on extraction, turning yellow after contact with the air. They outcrop in the lower third of the Côte between Gevrey and Nuits and have an undoubted influence on the wines. The oyster is, of course, a coastal animal; these lived and died at the edge of a shallow Jurassic sea.

Above these marls comes Bathonian limestone, again compact and resistant, laid down by deeper seas. First 10 metres of pink Prémeaux stone with flints, then 20 metres of white oolite, easily broken down by frost. Above this comes Comblanchien 'marble', one of the hardest limestones, frost-resistant and taking a good polish. It forms the precipitous, picturesque walls of many of the combes or dales which lead back from the Côte, and old Dijon is largely built of it. The next Callovian layer was formed when the seas became shallower again, 155 million years ago. Large oysters in banks of oolitic limestone alternate with marl. Above it is a thin layer of ferruginous oolitic marls (exploited in the Châtillonnais during the Iron Age). Then comes a 100-metre layer of marly limestone, known as the Argovian, of great importance on the Côte de Beaune; finally compact coralline limestone containing fossilized sea-urchins, the Rauracian. This is resistant to erosion and caps many of the hills of the Côte de Beaune and both Hautes Côtes.

Figure 2 shows that the layers of rock form a shallow ridge, known as an anticline, at Gevrey, and a basin, or syncline, at Volnay, so different sediments outcrop at different levels all along the two Côtes.

To complicate matters further, the Alpine upheavals caused faults in the bedding planes so that not all of the Côte de Nuits hillsides have a regular succession of rocks. Chenôve, Nuits-south, Prémeaux and Comblanchien are straightforward Bathonian; but Gevrey-south has a double outcrop of Callovian. The maximum of complexity is to be found, according to R. Gadille, on the

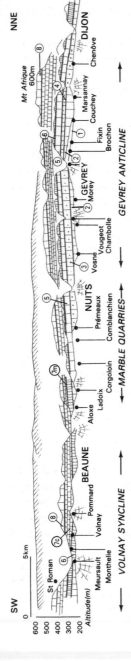

FIGURE 2. The rock strata of the Côte de Beaune and the Côte de Nuits (Adapted from Pierre Rat, *Bourgogne-Morvan*, Masson & Cie, Paris, 1972.)

In the foreground: the front has the form of an 'S' due to two transversal movements. Where the combes open out, old sedimentary cones can be seen, which the Dijon–Beaune road climbs or cuts through.

In the middle ground: hillocks and slabs of Rauracian limestone in the Arrière-Côte, which also follow the 'S' design.

On the horizon: line of the Montagne, eroded to 600 m. Comblanchien limestone, which is quarried on the Côte at around 260 m, can be found at a height of 640 m in the Montagne section.

Types of Rock Outcrop

1. Summit of Liassic marls, outcropping in the vineyards in the heart of the Gevrey anticline.
2. Crinoidal limestone (Bajocian).
3. Upper Bajocian (marls with *acuminata* oysters).
4. White oolite (Middle Bathonian).
5. Comblanchien limestone (Middle and Upper Bathonian).
6. Callovian limestone (pearly slabs).
7. (m) Argovian marly-limestone (slopes of Mont Afrique, hill and vineyard of Corton).
   (c) Argovian limestone (south of Beaune).
8. Compact Rauracian limestones, forming the caps of the hills.

Echézeaux hillside, where lower Bathonian and upper Bajocian interplay the length of the slope.

On the Côte de Beaune there are fewer faults, but more variations in the characteristics of the rocks. Between Ladoix and Savigny, and between Pommard and Saint-Aubin, the Argovian sediments are mainly gritty marl; yet between Savigny and Pommard they contain thick layers of oolitic and crinoidal limestone. By contrast the normally limestone Rauracian includes marly layers . . . it is very confusing!

Geologists would divide the southern section of the Côte de Beaune into a separate Côte de Santenay, as here the rock formations of the Côtes of both Nuits and Beaune are found, from Liassic up to Rauracian. There are many dislocations due to tectonic faults, caused at the time when the Alps were thrown up.

The vineyards of Mercurey are established on Liassic slopes of marl and limestone debris, with the higher sections on middle-Jurassic Bathonian. Buxy-Montagny's bedrock dates from the period between these two, the Bajocian. The limestone strata end in the southern Mâconnais, giving way to the granite of the Beaujolais. We shall look more closely at these in the chapters on each region.

Far to the north in the Yonne *département*, we shall find Chardonnay grapes growing on Jurassic strata, though they are younger deposits than we have so far met. Bitter quarrels raged in the 1970s over whether Chablis vines might rightfully be planted on Portlandian as well as Kimmeridgian limestone. They were resolved by permitting certain extensions, forcing Burgundians to accept that other factors than bedrock contribute to their wines' quality and character.

The role of the underlying rock is at least four-fold. Its disintegration partly forms the topsoil, as we shall see in a moment; it permits the penetration of vine roots to varying degrees, being a crucial source of minerals and nutrients; it helps or hinders the draining of rain-water, and may or may not prove a reserve of moisture during dry spells.

Upper Bathonian or Comblanchien stone is hard, with few fissures, slowing root penetration. Callovian and Bajocian marly limestones on the other hand are often split, containing pockets of red silt which permit the roots to descend easily. Excessive water retention after rain is not normally a problem on the slopes of the Côte. Trouble comes however from the fact that many of the Jurassic strata are relatively impermeable – Liassic marls, Bajocian, Argovian, Comblanchien, sometimes Rauracian – and this may contribute to soil erosion in heavy rain. Land where the slope is shallow, such as the Gevrey vineyards between the road and the railway, or the lower part of the Clos de Vougeot, depend on their subsoil for drainage. In Gevrey this is satisfactory, for the vines are on accumulated banks of Tertiary or Quaternary pebbles. Lower Clos de Vougeot is planted on Pliocene and alluvial deposits, and heavy rains are harmful to quality.

During dry periods most of the Côte's limestones and marlstones provide some reserves of water, the vine's ability to benefit depending on the depth of its roots. Vineyards on banks of pebbles (situated opposite the openings in the Côte where streams have washed sediments down into cone-shaped deposits in the valley) inevitably suffer from their excellent drainage.

The Côte de Nuits and Côte de Beaune are orientated differently, the former facing almost due east,[6] the latter south-east. Certain vineyards are exceptions to this rule however, for instance Les Varoilles in Gevrey which faces south.

Vines generally grow on the Côte at altitudes between 200 and 300 metres, but most of the best growths are located between 250 and 300 metres, in the hillside's navel. The width of the band of vines is variable, with extremes on the Côte de Nuits at Prémeaux (750 metres) and Gevrey-Chambertin (2,000 metres). Meursault presents the broadest swathe on the Côte de Beaune (2,500 metres).

The angle of the slope, with its influence over drainage and the amount of sun available to the vine is a vital factor in determining quality wine production. R. Gadille goes so far as to say that quality is more bound up with the angle of slope than with the bedrock. She classifies slopes of less than 3 per cent as plateau or plain, and it is only exceptionally that quality vineyards are to be found on them.

---

6 There is advantage in an eastern orientation, as P. Pacottet noted in *Viticulture* (Paris, 1905), for the sun dries the dew or the humidity of the soil from the first hour of the day: 'It touches the skin of the grape, still damp from the night, and colours it without scorching it.'

THE SOIL

'This obscure, little-loved world'

You can grow a vine virtually anywhere, so long as it is not in standing water. Good drainage is the first essential, so the fact that Burgundy's best vineyards are on slopes is not surprising. Pebbles and small broken stones also help the rapid evacuation of water.

Broadly speaking, the soil of the Côte is a complex and extremely varied mixture of particles from the different rocks and sediments which have outcropped and decomposed on the upper parts of the slope, intermixed with decaying vegetal matter.

Certain slopes suffer more than others from erosion. R. Gadille[7] mentions those of Aloxe, Beaune, Pommard and Volnay where the factors of steep slopes, relatively impermeable soil and subsoil, and the whole hillside being under mono-culture, can sometimes have catastrophic effects. Before and after planting a minimum level of topsoil must be maintained – now, thanks to tractors, a lighter job than when soil was carried up painfully by the backload, as it was in Burgundy for centuries. The composition of this replacement topsoil is of fundamental importance, and it is no longer permitted to cart it from plain or plateau, as it used to be.[8] For instance, it is recorded that in 1749 the Croonembourg family spread 150 cart-loads of 'new turfed soil', brought from the mountain, on to their Romanée vineyard, and at the end of the nineteenth century one could see numerous holes up in the hills, dug for the same purpose, so contemporary writers affirm. This centuries-old practice must have contributed to diversifying the naturally evolved soils. Today, soil may be enriched with compost, and more and more estates are turning to this, as an alternative to mineral fertilizing.

Vine has been planted on vine in the best sites of Burgundy, for ten – in some cases fifteen – centuries. This intensive cultivation has slowly changed the properties of the vineyards. Organic material (humus) in the soil has diminished; reserves of mineral elements have been exhausted, top soils have been eroded, and in some

---

7 *Le Vignoble de la Côte bourguignonne.*
8 In 1829 a report by the Prefecture in Dijon on the state of viticulture in France since the Revolution gave three causes of the success of new vineyard plantings: the transport of earth, the choice of vine, and persistent work. There was no mention of the natural virtues of the site.

cases toxic metal residues (copper, from anti-mildew spraying, for instance) have built up.

For centuries the spreading of manure in a vineyard was strictly prohibited. In 1395 Philippe le Hardi's Edict declared that it gave a bad taste to the wine. In 1732 the preamble to a decree of the Parlement de Bourgogne ran as follows: 'Burgundy is renowned for the excellence of the wines it produces and this reputation is beginning to decline; it is not that our precious vineyards have lost anything of their quality, but people are corrupting them by making them too fertile.' Those who had taken manure into their vines would have to remove it or pay a fine of twenty *livres*. In 1845 the congress of French vignerons in Dijon continued to forbid the use of manure.

In his study of France's vineyards in 1867 Guyot noted, on the vineyards of the Côte d'Or, 'One only manures Pinot vines at the moment of layering, but one earths them up occasionally – above all one carries the soil back up from the foot to the top of the vines every six to eight years.'

When the vineyards were reconstituted after phylloxera organic farm manure was used, with vegetable waste, grape skins, pips and stalks. Bit by bit animal livestock disappeared from the villages of the Côte, and obtaining manure from farms became expensive and difficult. By the mid–1950s salesmen were active, recommending mineral fertilization, the four main elements being nitrogen, phosphorus, magnesium and potassium. It is worth briefly considering their roles, one by one, for their present imbalance in many of Burgundy's best vineyards is one of the main reasons for our disappointments with the wines. It may take decades to rectify some of the fertilization errors of the last quarter century.

Nitrogen

Nitrogen is an essential constituent of living matter, but it must be used with prudence in viticulture, for its effects on growth and yield are great. 'Any excess of nitrogenous fertilizer favours the vine's vigour to the detriment of the quality of its harvest', states Jacques Delas, of INRA (Institut National de la Recherche Agronomique) Bordeaux.[9]

9 'Action des principaux eléments de la nutrition de la vigne', BIVB, Beaune, 1991.

Too much nitrogen may damage our health, as recent tests have shown, causing increased levels of histamine and ethyl carbamate. The first plays a role in human allergic reactions, the second may be carcinogenic at high levels.[10] Canada has, since October 1985, fixed a maximum level for ethyl carbamate in imported wines.

Excessive use of nitrogen is easily spotted by professionals: deep green leaves, shoots of thick diameter. In spite of its negative aspects, intelligent, appropriate use of nitrogen is entirely beneficial in vineyard care, enabling the vigneron to guide skilfully the length of the vegetative cycle, for instance. But the amounts need to be calculated exactly and prudently, according to the vine's vigour and needs.

Phosphorus

Vines only need moderate quantities of phosphorus, and this is usually achieved by a normally developed association between the root system and fungi in the soil, to draw in naturally occurring phosphates. Phophorus deficiency is very rarely noted. However, research shows that the fertilizer salesmen may have been hyperactive in the Yonne, where 'phosphate levels are, more often than not, abundantly excessive around Chablis.'[11] This is not damaging to quality, but it seems to have been a glaring waste of money.

Magnesium

Magnesium is a constituent of chlorophyll, the pigment which permits plants to fix the energy in light and to synthesize sugars. It plays a crucial role in the maturation of grapes and in neutralizing organic acids. Magnesium deficiency occurs if it is insufficiently present in the soil, if a particular root-stock absorbs it poorly, or if there has been excessive potassium fertilization (more on this, below).

These problems can be lessened, long term, by appropriate choice of root-stock and lowering potassium levels. Short term, they are being treated by the spreading of magnesium salts on soil or grapes.

10 Results obtained in 1990 on tests started in 1969 on Merlot vines at Domaine INRA de la Grande Ferrande.
11 Jean-Paul Voilliot, 'Bilan physico-chimique de l'Yonne', Station Agronomique de l'Yonne, BIVB, 1992.

R. Bernard comments, 'Correction of this accident . . . is obtained fairly quickly. Prevention would, however, have been more economical.'

Potassium

This is the element which is causing the gravest problems. Jacques Delas (cited above), when speaking in Vosne-Romanée in January 1992, described potassium's good points. It is a very mobile element within the plant, neutralizing certain acid products, and being necessary for photosynthesis, so favouring sugar production. It plays a part in the movement and accumulation of sugars, and in helping the plant to survive dry periods. Potassium deficiency causes reduced yield, and a fall-off in quality. However, if used to excess, it damages quality in several areas. Firstly, there is an antagonism between potassium and magnesium, which can induce a deficiency of the latter, and a drying out of the stalk of the grape-bunch, impeding maturation. Secondly, potassium blocks the entry of calcium, which is naturally abundant in Burgundy's soils, into the vine's system. Calcium is needed to make the pectins used for the pecto-cellulose membrane of the plant, without which the plant, and particularly the grapes, are susceptible to attacks of grey rot. Thirdly, potassium neutralizes the natural tartaric and malic acids found in grapes. This brings about a diminution in the acidity of grape-juice and wine, giving wines which can lack flavour balance, and the ability to age harmoniously.

Root-stocks play a part in this process, for certain absorb more potassium (SO4 for instance) than others (Riparia), with corresponding effects on wine acidity. Chemical weed-killing in the vineyard will also exacerbate absorption of potassium, for it favours root development by the vine in the highest soil levels. These surface levels hold recent, and possibly ancient, fertilizer reserves. (Both potassium and phosphorus leach very slowly downward through the soil.) When weeds are destroyed by ploughing, rather than chemically, at the same time the shallow levels of vine root development are disturbed and partly cut through, forcing the vine to send its roots more deeply downwards.

When rain falls just before the harvest the vine sucks up a potassium-rich solution, if its roots are highly developed near the surface. This causes a major fall in acidity in the grapes, just before they are picked. Many domaines on the Côte de Nuits suffered in this way during the 1992 vintage, for instance.

The Saône-et-Loire and the Yonne have both published statistics showing the extent of potassium excesses in vineyard soils. Analyses of 600 samples of vineyard soils taken between north Beaujolais and southern Côte d'Or show that, 'Concerning potassium oxide (K_2O), the levels are high in all soil types.'[12] The story is the same in Chablis and the Auxerrois, where Jean-Paul Couillaut[13] reports that 'potassium is the element where exaggerated use has been the most flagrant'. Analysis of 300 Yonne soil samples between 1989 and 1991 showed that 67.5 per cent had excessive potassium levels, 20.7 per cent insufficient levels, and only 11.7 per cent had 'normal' levels. Quite obviously, there has been no scientific, managed approach to fertilizing.

And what of the Côte de Beaune and the Côte de Nuits? I have found no published figures, but suspect that the situation is worse than in the Yonne, for the Côte d'Or has been more prosperous.

Raymond Bernard has remarked (mildly) that 'there is a certain divergence in points of view between respect for quality . . . and the lure of profit'. He went on to say that fertilizer purchase had often been irrational, influenced solely by salesman's prompting. Its cost was very low, compared to the value of the wines being produced and in most cases the vigneron 'thought he was acting for the best'. While wines were selling well, it seemed sensible to restore regularly to the vineyard some of those minerals and elements which were annually harvested or cut away. The cost of fertilizers was easily recouped, with interest, by increased yields.

Analysing the soils

So far as I know, the most detailed, published soil analyses and classifications in Burgundy are those of R. Gadille, in *Le Vignoble de la Côte bourguignonne*.[14] Madame Gadille took ninety soil

---

12 Claude Defranoux and Jean-Paul Goursaud, *Laboratoire de Mâcon 1988–91*, BIVB, Beaune, 1992.

13 Jean-Paul Couillaut, *La Fertilisation du vignoble de l'Yonne*, BIVB, Beaune, 1992.

14 Her soil samples were mostly taken at a depth of 30–40 cm, the principal nutrition level of vines. On the skeletal plateau soils, samples were taken at 5–10 cm, in the plain a second sample at 60 cm.

samples from plateau, hillside and plain from Chenôve down to Dezize-lès-Maranges. She covered Chambertin, Clos de Vougeot and the Montrachets; Marsannay, Corgoloin, Saint-Romain and Meloisey; Beaune Les Grèves, Pommard Les Rugiens, Meursault Les Perrières; Corton, Musigny, Magny-lès-Villers, and many others. The angles of slope were recorded, and the soils analysed for alkalinity, texture, presence of stones and pebbles larger than 2 mm in diameter, active lime, organic nitrogen, phosphoric acid, presence of magnesium, potassium, sodium and trace elements.

On the hillsides one finds moderately alkaline soils:[15] rendzinas, brown chalky soils and brown chalky clays. The first are usually high up the slope, stony and particularly suitable for white wines. The second are by far the most common, medium-textured with a higher proportion of silts and clays. They often occupy the whole of the vineyard area, almost always the lower third of the slope, and produce most of Burgundy's finest wines. The third group is normally found at the foot of the hillside, and is composed of over 70 per cent fine silt and clay.

The varying quantities of active lime, organic nitrogen, phosphoric acid and magnesium in the soil do not appear to have a determining influence on the quality or diversity of the wines produced. Nor are sodium levels particularly significant, though it is curious to note the relatively high levels in the great white vineyards Meursault Les Perrières and Montrachet. The role of potassium as a factor for growth and fruit development was little understood for many years, its effects being thought to be highly beneficial. Potash fertilizers were widely used, resulting in soil imbalances which it will take many years to rectify, as we have seen.

Many trace elements are found in the soil, including manganese, chromium and cobalt. These are held, when sprayed in pulverized form on to the vines, to be beneficial by encouraging the accumulation of sugar (manganese), favouring fertilization (chrome), and speeding the maturity (cobalt). The relationship between their presence in the soil and viticultural success is, however, difficult to evaluate. Other trace elements present are lead, gallium, beryllium, molybdenum, tin, vanadium, copper, nickel, strontium, barium, lithium and rubidium. The slopes of Marsannay and Dezize have higher than average levels of strontium, barium and lithium; those

15 pH 7.9–8.3.

of Puligny and Meursault a little more beryllium; Fixin and Beaune seem relatively poor in manganese; Gevrey, Vosne, Flagey, Vougeot, Beaune, Pommard have lower than average traces of tin. It is tempting to conjecture that the presence of some of these elements is a negative influence on quality, but one must be cautious, for the vine does not always assimilate the elements available to it. No pattern emerges to link particular types or qualities of wine with specific trace elements.

Madame Gadille drew more interesting conclusions from looking at the soil's texture and structure. The proportion of pebbles and small broken stones influences the drainage; that of fine clay particles the fertility, she found.

Pebbles of over 1 cm diameter are often a major part of vineyard soils, particularly at the middle and top of the slopes. They absorb heat during the day, liberating it at night, but their presence in a vineyard is irregular and difficult to chart. Small broken stones (2 mm to 1 cm in diameter) are more widespread. R. Gadille records their incidence (as a percentage of the total weight of the sample), feeling that they play an undoubted role in obtaining quality wines.

In a rendzina soil such as Morey-Saint-Denis Les Monts Luisants, they represent 30–35 per cent, in normal brown chalky soils between 10 and 30 per cent, in chalky clays as little as 5 per cent. On a famous vineyard slope the proportions can vary considerably. The top section of Chambertin has about 30 per cent, the middle and bottom 8–12 per cent. Over the road in Charmes-Chambertin the figures are 15–20 per cent, further downhill 5 per cent, then 10 per cent. The superiority of clay-rich Bâtard-Montrachet over vineyards below it may be partially explained by the 10 per cent of small stones, compared to less than 5 per cent downhill.

Soil particles are graded by size into sand, fine sand, silt, fine silt and clay. The proportion of clay particles is capital, for they retain water and form the soil solution in which the roots of the vine develop and draw nourishment. R. Gadille shows that fine wines are made on soils with contrasting proportions of clay particles. She feels that a high proportion of clay particles contributes to a wine's staying power, but if this is not counterbalanced by adequate small stones to ensure good drainage (the case in Chenôve, Clos du Roi (bottom), Fixin and Corgoloin) then the necessary texture is not achieved, with consequently less successful wines.

Table 4   Percentage of clay particles in soil samples

	%
Bâtard-Montrachet	approx. 50
Musigny	44–9
Chenôve, Clos du Roi (bottom)	approx. 45
Fixin	approx. 45
Corgoloin	approx. 45
Pommard Les Rugiens	37–40.5
Clos de la Roche	36–40
Clos Saint-Denis	36–40
Chambertin	30–40
Corton	approx. 30
Blagny-Meursault	28–40
Montrachet	32–6
Chevalier-Montrachet (top)	approx. 20

Enter Claude Bourguignon

Clay particles may indeed hold a major key to explaining Burgundy's diversity and quality, as Claude Bourguignon is presently discovering. He is an agronomic engineer, and one of the leading Burgundian soil researchers. He runs the Laboratoire Analyse Microbiologique des Sols at Marey-sur-Tille, an hour's drive north of Côte de Nuits, his speciality being research into the life of the soil. Initially a researcher at INRA (Institut National de la Recherche Agronomique, Paris), he quit the national institute when he found his research into the life of the soil discouraged or blocked.

He is currently engaged in some of the most exciting vineyard soil research to be found anywhere in France. In Bordeaux he has numbered, or numbers, among his clients Châteaux Latour, Pavie-Macquin and Haut-Marbuzet, in the Loire Domaines Huet and Coulée de Serrant, in the Languedoc the Mas de Daumas Gassac. In Burgundy he works with the Domaines de la Romanée-Conti, Leflaive, Lafarge, Lafon, Leroy, Rateau, Jean Trapet and others.

His research is not restricted to vine soils. He is also unravelling why essence of geraniums, grown on the island of Réunion in the Indian Ocean for use in the perfume business, has lost its concentration, and why black truffles no longer grow in their old profusion on the oak-tree roots of the Périgord. (The answer to both problems appears to lie with the microbial life of their soils.)

Over the last twenty years there has been such enormous progress in oenology, the science of wine-making, that there is no longer cause for poor wines to be made (so long as the decisions are in well-qualified hands). Oenologists constantly find, however, that they are faced with grape-juice which is out of balance. You cannot make top wine with bad juice, so why are the vineyards producing grapes with acidity levels which are insufficient, juices which need large doses of sulphur dioxide to protect them, juices with insufficient sugars?

Bourguignon points the finger at the soils, and firstly to a physical problem, their compaction. Only thirty years ago vineyards were cultivated by horses and people, treading lightly and irregularly along the rows. Today, tractors weighing up to 8 tonnes repeatedly make identical tracks between the vines, compacting it as never before. There is twice, or three times, as much microbial activity between individual vines along each row (where the soil escapes compaction) as between the rows. Ploughing has often been abandoned in favour of herbicides, so nothing aerates the ground between the rows.

To reverse this process, vine-straddling tractors may have to be designed with wide, floppy, low-pressure tyres which do not crush the soil. Tyre pressure controlled from the cab already exists for wheat farmers, who travel on roads at 3 kg/cm^2, then may deflate to 300 g/cm^2 on their fields. Behind the wheels, claws can scratch air back into the soil after the passage of the machine.

The other aspect of soil aeration is the work of the fauna – earthworms, spiders, and the thousands of little insects – *acariens*, *colemboles* – which make galleries and holes. (In a forest, 60 per cent of the soil is made up of emptyness, of air holes.) For the fauna to live, you need organic matter, and in many Burgundy vineyards there is none left. More important, they cannot survive the massive, toxic doses of pesticide which have been regularly applied over recent decades. Many vineyards in the Côte d'Or are more devoid of microbial life than the Sahara desert, so Bourguignon's researches show. The soil is completely blocked.

When he analyses the Côte d'Or's vineyard soils he examines where the rootlets are attacking and breaking down the pebbles, thanks to bacteria. Pressure of the root attacking the rock has been calculated as 200 kg/cm^2, and it is well acknowledged that roots can go down rock fissures, at times creating their own cracks, to formidable depths. The record for a vine root in France is in Burgundy, measured in a Comblanchien quarry on the Côte de Nuits: 70 metres below the surface. (This is beaten by a pot-holer's discovery of wild cherry roots, in a cave in the Jura, at 140 metres).

There is enormous diversity in the clays of the Côte d'Or's vineyards, so Claude Bourguignon is finding. This is not altogether surprising, for during the aeons of the Jurassic period different rivers would be bringing their sediments from different bedrocks or combinations of bedrock : slates, granites, shales, schists. Clays are apparently like the leaves of a book, and there are many different qualities. Their greatest significance in wine-making may relate to measurement of their specific internal surfaces (which contain the negative charges which, thanks to positively-charged calcium, magnesium, iron and aluminium, will fuse with humus to give fertile soil). Normally, measuring the internal surfaces is time-consuming and costly, but he has developed and patented a method which is speedy and inexpensive.

Analysing the internal surfaces of the clays of the *Grands Crus* of the Côte de Nuits, Claude Bourguignon never finds the same results. This is a new discovery, and a totally new slant on *terroir*. Clos Vougeot, as expected, has wide differences, and there is even a small difference between the top and bottom of La Tâche. Soils growing red wines consistently have higher internal surface levels in their clays than those producing whites. Moving to the Côte de Beaune, he finds similarities between the soils of Pommard and those of the Côte de Nuits; interestingly, we are in a village with a reputation for wines of structure and ageing capacity. And he finds that the best white wines are coming from sites with lower internal surface levels. For instance, Chevalier or Bâtard-Montrachet might have 30–100 square metres of internal surface for each gram of clay, where village Puligny-Montrachet may have as much as 400 square metres per gram.

Will the INAO find these soil analyses of interest, or value, I wonder, as they periodically assess where to draw *appellation* lines? Will Bourguignon's advice be sought, for instance, before deciding on the merits of raising Meursault's Clos des Perrières to *Grand Cru* status, or extending that status to all, or part, of what is currently called Meursault Perrières *Premier Cru*? There is often antagonism between self-employed wine researchers and those within the state's centrally- and regionally-funded bureaucracies, but it is not too much to hope that the benefits of Bourguignon's researches may be drawn on by the Dijon and Beaune establishments over the coming years.

'The only planet in the solar system...'

Consumers, their watchdogs and law-makers are increasingly concerned over noxious residues in wine. This provides impetus to those growers who themselves welcome the search for other ways than pesticides, herbicides, fungicides and mineral fertilizers with which to tend the vines. There is rapidly increasing interest in organic viticulture, and to a better thought out, more reasoned approach, throughout Burgundy, as we shall see in the chapter on vines and viticulture. In addition, some influential domaines have gone further, embracing or experimenting with bio-dynamic methods.

Bio-dynamic agriculture has a fundamentally different approach to soil and plant life from that traditionally held in Burgundy, as François Bouchet would have it.[16] The earth should not be considered as a support-system, whose prime role is to hold reserves of the minerals dumped on it by humans. On the contrary, in its broad sense (mother rock, tillable soil, airy environment) it is an organization apart. The earth is often disrupted, he tells us, owing to ill-considered additions of minerals, and a poison soup of pesticides and herbicides in the cultivable layers, so that it can no longer produce harmonious, balanced vegetation:

> As with an ill person who has become dependant on this or that medicine, it is only slowly that health and balance may be re-established – but this balance is everything ... Having 25 years of bio-dynamic practices, I believe that re-conversion of a vine-yard succeeds so long as the grower advances with wisdom and tranquillity – not a brutal re-conversion, but modulated. Habitual treatments are progressively replaced by the application of techniques which will bring the domaine bit by bit to the bal-

16 He is an adviser on bio-dynamic agriculture, and a wine-grower at Château Gaillard, 49260 Montreuil-Bellay in the Loire. He was here speaking at a Rencontre technique interprofessionnelle organized in April 1991 by the BIVB in Mâcon.

anced state being sought. At present one may say that a period of three years seems necessary ...

Claude Bourguignon does not preach bio-dynamic methods, but many of them, although appearing cranky (as we shall see) give results which entirely fit his purposes. He laid out his philosophy to 500 Burgundians in Mâcon, in April 1991, on the theme 'A New Approach to the Fertilization of Agricultural Soils':[17] 'The only planet in the solar system to possess a soil is Earth. Indeed, it gave its name to our planet. In order for soil to exist we need two sources of matter: mineral matter from the mother rock, and organic matter from vegetal litter.' He went on to describe the birth of soil, from the fusion of clay with humus (both charged negatively) thanks to positively charged cations – calcium, magnesium, iron and aluminium. 'Every person working in agriculture should know these basics of soil fertility, which depends directly on the quality of these primordial elements.' A few growers must have crouched lower in their seats at this moment, no doubt avoiding his passionate, challenging gaze. Certainly I feel like ducking down – how could I have written so many pages, in 1982, on Burgundy's soils with so slim an understanding of their real dynamics?

Luckily, it is not too late. Claude Bourguignon tells us that it takes 3,000 years for a soil to be constituted, and 10 to 100,000 years for it to mature in our climates. So, thirty years of twentieth-century misuse does not sound completely terminal. He adds,

> Recent progress in meteorology and oceanography has highlighted how complex, and how fragile are the two environments: atmosphere, and sea. By contrast, it is rare to meet people who understand how soils function, and who are moved by their pollution, or erosion. And yet – most of our foodstuffs come out of the soil. Into this obscure, little-loved world I propose to lead you, describing its dynamics, the reactions which occur there, and the micro-organisms which lodge within it.

The objective is to understand the fundamental and complex relationships which bind soil, microbes and plants.

This is not the place to attempt to lay out in full Claude Bourguignon's analysis of soil dynamics, but, having glanced at how

17 Rencontre technique, *Qualité hygiénique des vins et environnement*, BIVB, Beaune, 25 April 1991.

soils are born (from the fusion of clay with humus, thanks in Burgundy principally to calcium, from its native limestone), let us now turn to how they mature, and die.

In our climates, he explains, rocks may yield one tonne of clay per hectare per year, and natural forest litter give 2 tonnes of humus per hectare per year, of which one tonne will be mineralized in the year. Soils can therefore grow deeper at the rate of two tonnes per hectare per year. Earthworms play a major part in maturing these layers, being capable of eating 200–300 tonnes of soil per hectare per year, in other words, a total mashing of the soil every ten years.

When man cultivates the topsoil he suppresses the humus layer. If he does not counter this by making humus through composting he will block the maturing of his soil, for the bedrock will continue to produce clay particles, but these will be washed away by rain-water. Claude Bourguignon states that the spreading of compost and humus at a rate of 1 to 2 tons per hectare per year is indispensable for the maturing of an agricultural soil.

In the wild, the soil dies or is destroyed when the mixture of organic and mineral matter becomes so thick that erosion by wind and water carries it away, to form sediments on the floors of oceans. The bedrock is again revealed, and the cycle of soil creation restarts. When farming land is cultivated, the soil is eroded if levels of humus fall away and compost is not supplied. Bourguignon calculates that erosion in OECD countries currently averages 10 tons per hectare per year. If this continues, they could be deserts, like North Africa, within a hundred years. Farmers must be encouraged to recapitalize their soils by adding organic matter in the form of composting, by adding good clays to young soils, and by bringing the necessary limestone links, in the form of calcium carbonate.

Returning to the Côte d'Or's vineyard slopes, he shows that an understanding of how, when and why plants absorb elements from the soil will explain why intensively cultivated plants need chemical treatments to protect them from ill health. They are in fact being overdosed with nitrogen, potassium and phosphorus, and starved of those elements which are naturally mobilized by microbes. 'When you treat such ill plants you finish off the destruction of the microbes, and increase the deficiencies of trace elements. This is the infernal cycle of fertilizers and pesticides. To break it, one must restore soil to the place it merits at the heart of agriculture.'

When I first visited Claude Bourguignon north of Dijon, after reading his book *Le Sol, la terre et les champs*[18] he ended the meeting with an invitation:'Would you like to see the life of the soil? When I show this to cereal farmers they cannot believe it.' He walked to a flower-bed ('These soils are alive', he said; 'I don't treat them') and collected a small bottle of earth. He shook it with water, added a colouring agent, then put it on a slide on his microscope. I shall never forget the sight, abundant with activity: tiny specks of solid particles (clays and other inanimate matter) were bathed in liquid which teemed with swimming, turning, thrashing, pulsing little organisms – bacteria, yeasts, microbes of all sorts, he said. 'You get to recognize them, with practice.' How did this compare – I could see thousands of living organisms in this speck of muddy ooze – with soils from chemically-treated vineyards? 'You will see one or two movements there. Many of the Côte d'Or's vineyards are more devoid of microbial life than the Sahara desert.'

So, what is to be done? 'It is no good pouring the same fertilizers on to different soils, one must get to know one's soils and approach them along three routes: fertilizing the soil, fertilizing the microbes within it, and fertilizing the plants that grow on it. This is the geology of the future, and it will transform the farmer's role, turning it into the most exciting calling of the year 2000.'

Claude Bourguignon is one of Burgundy's most precious assets, it seems to me, guiding those Burgundians who have not yet homed in on these problems (dozens already have) firmly back to specialist fine wine-making. He speaks a language – which is also a religion – that every single Burgundian, from Châtillon down to Chânes, can understand, and in which many have total faith (even though they may not fully understand it): the language of *terroir*.

Terroir analysis – a new direction?

A future line of soil research is to quantify the proportion of soil of vegetal, rather than mother-rock, origins in Burgundy's vineyards. Old root cells from buried, decayed vines may make up 70 per cent of some soils, so recent scannings by Claude Bourguignon suggest. So six centuries of monoculture – or more – could prove to be the real creators of these soils.

If these observations can be verified Burgundians could relax. It

18 Editions Sang de la Terre, Paris, 1991.

will be centuries before the best New World *terroirs* catch up, and by then Burgundian *terroirs* will be somewhere else.

5
Vines and Viticulture

ORIGINS OF THE VINES

One cannot help wondering at the diversity and number of France's vine-types, and at the affinity that some seem to have with certain geographical areas, soils or climates. It would be too long a story to go into the origins and history of all Burgundy's vines, but of one, the Pinot Noir, something of interest may be said.

Deciding the ancestry of French vines is a difficult problem, complicated by the fact that the phylloxera wiped out much of the evidence a hundred years ago. Did the vine spring from the land of France itself, or was it imported, there to be acclimatized? A great stir was caused in 1879 by the discovery near Sézanne in Champagne of the fossil remains in tertiary deposits of the leaves and branches of a vine. This was immediately named *Vitis sezannensis*, and proclaimed the ancestor of the Pinots of Epernay and Rheims. Unfortunately, a glance at the other fossilized flora on the site revealed that *Vitis sezannensis* was growing in a humid subtropical climate which has long since moved on from western Europe. Professor Dion[1] dismisses it, saying that its fruit would have been quite unsuitable for making into wine.

Fossil remains of *Vitis vinifera*, the wine-maker's vine, have been found in northern Italy, in Tuscany, and near Montpellier in quaternary deposits. During the Ice Age it would seem that the wild vine was driven back to two warm areas, one around the Mediterranean, the other south of the Caspian between the Black Sea and the Indus. As the last glaciers retreated the vine advanced north-

---

1 Professeur Dion, *Histoire de la vigne et du vin en France des origines au XIXème Siècle*, Paris, 1959.

wards, and fossils of the neolithic period have been found in several parts of the Neckar valley, near Heilbronn. The climate has since cooled, and now the northern limit of the wild vine in France is just south of this. Before the phylloxera destroyed them, wild vines were common along the banks of streams in the Languedoc, on the hills of the Vivarais and in the alluvial soils of the Rhine in Alsace.

The wild vine in France appears to thrive in moist soils, and gives fruit which is too small and acid to produce wine. In addition it rebels against pruning, and many botanists have sought to show that the cultivated vine could not have descended from such a stock. However, between the Black Sea and the Caspian in one of the two areas to which the vines retreated in the Ice Ages, Russian botanists have identified over sixty forms of wild vine, certain of them able to produce wine. Armenia and Azerbaijan, south of the Caucasus mountains, are the regions whence might originally have come the plants which have developed into Pinot, Cabernet, Riesling and so many others. But there is no evidence to prove this actually happened. Indeed the difference in the climate forces Professor Dion to the conclusion that such a transplantation is most unlikely.

Studies of vine genetics indicate that certain of the vines producing today's famous French wines are not far removed from wild vines. Professor Dion writes, 'The original savour of the great wines made from . . . the Pinot of the Côte d'Or is, to a large extent, an effect of the still close relationship which this vine has with the wild species. The botanist Louis Levadoux classes the Burgundian Pinot . . . in a group of archaic vine-types which, he says, one could also call wild-vine vines. "They are characterized by a high vinous value and often by a savour of the grapes which resembles that of the wild vine." ' The thought, I must admit, delights me, for there is something untamed and ferocious about the smell and taste of top Pinot wines, particularly when they are young or still maturing.

The French appear to have satisfied themselves that the Pinot was not imported from the eastern Mediterranean. They do not deny, however, that the know-how to cultivate it was originally brought by the Greeks. It happened in the sixth century BC with the founding of the Greek colony at Marseille, as we have seen in the chapter on Burgundy's history. Mention was also made in that chapter of the phylloxera (first discovered in Burgundy in July 1878) and it will be remembered that the most effective method of combating the root-sucking louse was to graft French *Vitis vinifera* on to louse-resistant root-stocks.

PREPARING THE LAND

For its root system to develop well, a vine demands that the land be well prepared before plantation takes place. The land must be well broken up (to a depth of about 60 cm), and the soil finely divided for the vine to establish itself. Reclaiming land for cultivation and initial heavy ploughing are often done by an outside contractor who will disinfect the soil at the same time, rendering it at least temporarily free from virus diseases. Before the phylloxera Burgundian vines were planted higgledy-piggledy, and since it was impossible to get a plough into the vineyard, all cultivation was done by hand. As many as 25,000 vines were found per hectare, the vegetation in each case being attached in a bundle to a wooden vine-prop, made from oak, chestnut or acacia. These were not always easy to acquire, and in the centre and east of France one can still see acacia copses which were planted to furnish vine-props. Plantation density is believed in Burgundy to be a crucially important quality factor; the closer the vines are one to another the more their individual vigour is limited, and their root systems forced to develop. Rejuvenation of the vineyard took place by layering (*provignage* or *marcottage*), a shoot from an old vine being led beneath the surface of the soil so that it rooted independently. Today, vines are no longer planted 'in a crowd' as it was known, but in lines, where the distance between the rows and between each vine is approximately equal (varying from 1 m to 1.25 m) and giving densities per hectare of 8,000 to 10,000 vines.

VINE GRAFTING

The first root-stocks were pure American: *Vitis riparia*, *Vitis rupestris* and *Vitis berlandieri*. The first two do not thrive in lime-rich soil, and the third (originating in the hot and dry southern states of the USA) does not adapt well to the Burgundian climate. The affinity between root-stock and graft is also of major importance. One root-stock will prove too vigorous, causing the flowers to abort; another will fail to bring the grapes to maturity on time; a third will be responsible for low production of sugar; a fourth will encourage foliage rather then fruit. For a hundred years crossings have been made between the different American vines and between French and American vines to produce the ideal root-stocks for various combinations of soil, climate and graft.[2]

These are generally known by numbers; 3309, for instance, a productive *Riparia* × *rupestris* crossing realized in 1880 by G. Couderc which was for long the most widely used Côte d'Or root-stock, both for Pinot and Chardonnay. In lime-rich soil, however – such as most hillside vineyards of the Côte – it developed a physio-logical ailment known as chlorosis (which results in a yellowing of the green parts of the plant), and in the 1930s its popularity waned in favour of another Couderc hybrid, this time *Riparia* × *berlandi-eri*, No. 161–49C. I find it difficult to take an interest in root-stock crossings. How much pleasanter would it not be to evoke the lost vines of the Côte, with their intriguing names: Tinevache and Amandelle, Machuzé, Enfariné. But to hurry past 3309 and 161–49C, not to mention SO4, 5BB and 41B, would be to neglect vital pieces of the Burgundian jigsaw.

Hybrid No. 161–49C is of medium vigour and can withstand up to 25 per cent of active lime in the soil. It is popular with wine-growers, as it favours production and advances maturity. But it is sensitive to disease, and because of this was often replaced by SO4. This is also a *Riparia* × *berlandieri* crossing, but a very vigorous one. It was developed in Germany and seemed to have many of the qualities sought: good resistance to chlorosis and other diseases; good fruit production at an early date, and the ability to withstand

2 George Ordish's *The Great Wine Blight* was republished by Sidgwick & Jackson in 1987 with a new chapter. In it he told us that the scientific name of the phylloxera has been changed – we ought now to be calling it *Daktulosphaira vitifoliae*; informed us of work by Russian chemists which has produced hexachlorobutadiene (HCBTD), which keeps root infestation by the louse below damage levels (he alleges a conspiracy of silence in the West on this chemical); and warned of a new form of phylloxera, called Type B, which appeared able to attack the 'resistant' roots of American vines. How right he was about the last point (this is what is destroying many Californian vineyards, some of which were injudiciously planted on Franco-American hybrid root-stocks, not resistant, all-American ones).

periods of drought as well as to tolerate humid subsoils. It also took well at the moment of grafting. A third *Riparia × berlandieri*, called 5BB, can be used in the thin soils high up on a hillside; planted anywhere else its great vigour produces abundant foliage at the expense of the crop. All of these have been crossings of two American vines. There is one Franco-American hybrid, a *Vinifera × berlandieri*, No. 41B, with the highest known tolerance of active lime. We will come across it in the chapter on wines of the Yonne *département*. Its major fault is its heavy cost, the union of stock and graft being difficult to achieve.

Since September 1988 it has been illegal in Burgundy to plant on other than certified clonal root-stocks. The elimination of viruses through clonal selection has meant the rehabilitation of some valuable root-stocks which had been abandoned (*Riparia Gloire* for instance).

Now that virus-free clonal selections of dependably productive Pinot Noir and Chardonnay are widely available, it is vital to marry these with less vigorous root-stocks (if disastrous over-production is to be avoided). For the new clones, SO4, 5BB and 41B are no longer appropriate, so it is recommended,[3] instead, that a choice be made between 161–49C or Fercal (for Pinot), and these two with Riparia, 3309C, and 101–14MG for Chardonnay.

'It is agreed that wines from grafted vines must be as good as those from ungrafted. Whoever would affirm the contrary would unleash the self-interested thunderbolts of trade and producers', declared a director of Burgundy's Oenological Institute in 1907. At that time, when pre- and post-phylloxera Burgundies were available for direct comparison, judgements were contradictory and inconclusive. Whether or not the quality has suffered can never be established, but it is certain that the wines have been modified, if only because the density of vine plantation has been dramatically changed, that is, cut from around 25,000 vines per hectare to half that number, or less. The root systems of the old French vines probably explored different soil horizons from those now used by louse-resistant stocks. Today, if weedkillers have broadly replaced ploughing, the superficial root-systems cause vineyards to be quickly influenced by sudden rains or periods of drought. A. Ger-

3 by GRAPVI, the Groupement Régional d'Amélioration et de Prémultiplication de la Vigne du Centre-Est.

beaut, G. Constant and L.-N. Latour report with regret that the risks inherent in late harvesting, which generates quality, have somewhat increased.

The other side of the coin is very positive, however, for several root-stocks advance the maturity of the grapes, and also increase natural sugar production. R. Bernard concludes that there has been an improvement rather than a drop in quality since grafting was introduced. Raymond Bernard, now retired, was for many years a Professor at the Lycée Viticole et Agricole de Beaune, and one of the most respected experts in Burgundy. He headed the Dijon Regional Delegation of the Office National Interprofessionnel des Vins, having been posted to Dijon in 1956 after four years under Professor Branas at Montpellier researching into vine virus diseases and the selection of vine-types. His brief covered viticulture throughout Burgundy and the research he initiated, with H. Biol of the Institut Technique du Vin in Beaune, has had profound effects on replanting since the early 1970s. His successor at ONIVINS since 1992 is Pierre Labruyère.

CLONAL SELECTION OF VINES

Since cultivation of the vine began one can imagine that there have been attempts to improve the plant, with the objects of increasing productivity, enhancing quality or selecting strains which will be resistant to a certain disease. This can be done in two ways: selection in the mass, or selection by clones.

The first consists of marking individual vines within a vineyard just before the harvest so that wood for grafting (or in the old days for layering) is taken only from healthy, vigorous specimens. The method is insufficient however to combat certain virus diseases, and here clonal selection is the answer. A clone is the whole family of direct descendants of a single mother-vine. There are different stages in the process, the first being the selection of the mother-vine or head of the clone, based on its healthy looks and the abundance, regularity and quality of its production. It will take some years for this vine to yield enough shoots for grafting and planting to take place to establish a sizeable collection of identical plants, whose performance can be watched, and whose grapes vinified and wine tasted.

Clonal selection began around 1960 in Burgundy, because of the spread of infectious degeneration or fan-leaf (known in French as *court-noué*) amongst Chardonnay vines. This disease had become a major problem, from 1947 onwards, on the Côte de Meursault, and by 1970 it was thought that 20 per cent of the production of Montrachet was being lost to it. Once affected, vines took on a stunted appearance, their leaves becoming deformed and nettle-like, their yields falling away – until death overtook them ten or fifteen years after planting.

The microscopic carrier of the fan-leaf virus can be destroyed by chemical disinfection of vineyards at replanting time, but there is a danger of recontamination taking place from mud-laden boots, tractors or implements. Clonal selection of virus-resistant families of vines has proved to be the long-term solution.

Let us now turn to the Pinot Noir, looking first at the past. Before the phylloxera, the system of rejuvenating the vine by layering guaranteed that the same types of Pinot Noir were perpetuated in any one vineyard. The complete reconstitution with grafted vines which became necessary gave growers the opportunity to choose higher-yielding varieties, and it is hardly surprising, given the losses they had recently suffered, that many chose this path. R. Gadille describes the conditions of the reconstitution as being pretty anarchic, and the consequences are still with us.

There are many different types of Pinot Noir in Burgundy, some famous, some infamous, as we shall see in a moment. In parallel with the work to find virus-free Chardonnays in the 1960s, clonal research took place on Pinot Noir. To start it off, nearly 160 different types of Pinot were collected and planted for observation. There were *Pinots fins*, *moyens* and *gros* and many *Pinots droits*; Pinots from the Jura, the Côte Chalonnaise, Champagne and Switzerland; Pinots with cylindrical bunches, pine-cone bunches, bunches with ears and bunches with shoulders. They were planted on the same root-stock, in identical ground, and all trained, pruned and treated similarly. Their growth and development were charted, particularly with regard to their resistance to grey rot and virus diseases,[4] as were the yields per hectare, the natural alcoholic degrees and other important characteristics of the grapes.

4 *Court-noué*, described above, is the principal virus disease, but *enroulement* is also serious. In the latter case, the leaves of the Pinot Noir become thick, and roll up underneath. Sugar production is impeded with the loss of 1–1.5° in the wine.

By the late 1970s, healthy, virus-free clones of Pinot and Chardonnay had been isolated and could be propagated, so they were let loose into the hands of growers. Healthy Pinots and Chardonnays must be preferable to sick ones, went the theory. Some of them, however, simply produced dependable crops of inferior wine, damaging the reputation of clonal selection along the way.

THE SECOND CLONAL WAVE

Burgundians do not like publicly admitting a mistake, but in May 1992 the Chambre d'Agriculture de Saône-et-Loire stated, 'The urgency of the problem compelled us to act fast, and different types of clone were authorized. Certain of these are perhaps not compatible with the production of great red wines, nor of white wines with complex aromatic character. This is why a second wave of clonal selection has begun.'[5]

Somewhat late in the day, quality criteria are to be rated as highly as those of vine health and yield. And the importance of preserving the best of the immensely-varied genetic stock is to be recognized. A second wave of collections has been undertaken, with 300 different types of Chardonnay being assembled, nearly 100 Pinot Noir and about 20 Aligoté.

One experimental centre is a vineyard high on the Montagne de Beaune called Les Chilènes, containing ten Pinot Noir clones (planted on root-stock SO4) which was installed on the domaine of the Lycée Viticole de Beaune in 1980, giving its first harvest in 1983. Amongst the ten were the three Pinot Noir clones Nos. 115, 114 and 113 which were being most actively promoted by nurseries at the time, on the strength of the earliest trials. Many factors were analysed to assess the performance of each clone, for instance: yield, natural sugar, total acidity and pH levels, number of bunches per vine, average bunch weight, weight of the branches after pruning, the vigorousness of growth, the susceptibility to grey rot, the tendency for flowers to abort (*coulure*) or grapes to grow small and hard (*millerandage*). Small-scale vinifications of the grapes of course took place each year, and after five years it was possible to

5 *La Sélection clonale en Saône-et-Loire: synthèse de résultats,* Service Viticole, Mâcon.

start drawing conclusions – albeit cautiously, for the vines were still very young, and micro-vinifications are not the same as the real thing.

Clones 115 and 114 gave wines which were rated highly in the tastings. Both are very vigorous vines, and highish yielders, but also very sensitive to grey rot. Both tend to give wines with good sugar levels, but low acidity. Clone 113 did consistently badly in tasting trials (lack of colour and aroma), though it yielded less than the other two, and was a good natural sugar producer.

After five years it was realized that most of the clones needed pruning differently, to harness their energies and reduce yields. So, many were converted from *Guyot simple* (which allows 6 fruiting buds on the main shoot, and two on the reserve branch) over to *Cordon de Royat* (four fruiting buds on each of two branches). It was also decided to add less fertilizer each year.

Clonal stock is multiplied in three ways in the Côte d'Or. The 10 hectare experimental Mont-Battois domaine overlooking Beaune produces 1 million graftable buds per annum; certain growers (Jacob in Echevronne, the Lycée Viticole in Beaune, for instance) give back prunings from their mother-vine plantations, each spring; thirdly, vine nurserymen use grafts from their own plantations.

For Pinot Noir, there is now over-production of clones 115, 114 and 113, and much of the wood is left unharvested. Clones 667 and 777 have so far been little multiplied; what is available is presently not enough to satisfy demand. For Chardonnay, clones 76 and 95 are widely available, followed by the rarer clones 124, 131 and 548. There is good availability of Gamay and Aligoté (except clone 651, for the latter).

The research continues to find clones giving not just health but higher quality. Also, it is felt advisable that at least 10–15 recommendable clones of each vine type should be identified, to provide diversity, and limit the risks of future weaknesses or proneness to disease.

There is understandable anxiety that wine flavours could become standardized, if just one or two clones were universally planted. This is a valid fear, though it may be remembered that when the old-fashioned selection from the mass was practised, it was perfectly possible for a grower to perpetuate down the generations his reliance on a very limited number of vine-types – those already present in his particular vineyards.

Over 10 million grafts were produced in 1988 (all vine-types added together) in Bourgogne Franche-Comté, 54.3 per cent being certified clones.[6] This sounds a lot, but it was calculated that by this time only 4 per cent of the region's vines were of certified clonal stock (rather more Chardonnay – 6 per cent – than Pinot Noir – 2.5 per cent). If one believed that wine quality in Burgundy had been degraded, or its character standardized, one could hardly lay the blame at the door of clonal selection, at that time.

There is one enormous *caveat* about clones: clonal plant material is much more vigorous and fertile than unscreened stock. Pruning needs to be adapted, use of fertilizers cut back, and crop-thinning possibly practised in summer, if excess production is to be avoided.

Writing in 1988, Raymond Bernard pinned the responsibility for the quality of Burgundies firmly on the grower:

The producer now has at his disposal a limited number of clones, both the Pinot Noir and the Chardonnay, which have been subjected to elaborate experiments, with the sole object of improving quality. The new plant material is in excellent health, and consequently more fruitful, so the vigneron should reconsider certain practices and do everything possible to diminish the plant's vigour. Having chosen a clone of low productivity and good quality, it is incumbent on him to choose the weakest root-stock he can, while making sure that it is compatible with the soil to be planted. He may also wish to reconsider the pruning method, while keeping the same number of fruit-bearing eyes. By abandoning the *Guyot simple* ... in favour of the *Cordon de Royat* ... he can diminish the yield, the reason being that the eyes at the base of the shoot, near where it grows from the previous year's wood, are less fruitful than those further along it.

He must also carefully consider the use of fertilizers, and not make over-generous applications, for this not only causes high yields, but also often results in imbalances in the wine's structure ... Fertilization should be diminished, and in some cases abandoned. In recent years, excessive use of fertilizers, par-

6 'Viticulture et sélection, organisation de la selection et travaux sur les variétés régionales', Service Viticole Chambre de'Agriculture, Mâcon, May 1992.

ticularly potassium, has taken place, well beyond the needs of the plant.[7]

Elsewhere, writing with Michel Leguay, Bernard states, 'Nitrogen is generally not to be recommended.'

The objectives of these steps are yields for Pinot Noir of 40–45 hl/ha. and for Chardonnay of 50–60 hl/ha. Leguay and Bernard continue, 'Concerning Pinot Noir, yields of 40–50 hl/ha. may appear at first sight high. However, the level at which quality deteriorates differs from Pinot to Pinot and from clone to clone, and it is only logical to think that this critical level is higher if plant material of proven health, better fertility and demonstrable quality is being used.'

From the above it can be seen that identifying the best clones is just the first step. Persuading the conservative, traditional Burgundian grower to plant them, and to abandon the root-stocks he knows for new ones, while learning a whole new pruning method (which demands considerable skill to establish) are some of the next steps. He must also decline the blandishments of the agro-chemical industry. Monsieur Bernard has been calling for a revolution in vineyard practices.

THE PINOT NOIR

The most illustrious vine of Burgundy is the Pinot Noir, the same variety of vine that is grown in Champagne on the Montagne de Rheims, in Alsace, Sancerre, Germany, Switzerland and, with increasing distinction, in many vineyard areas of the New World: California, Oregon, Victoria and Western Australia, and Martinborough, New Zealand, for instance. Its wine is first mentioned in the accounts of Philippe le Hardi, Duc de Bourgogne, in 1375, for he sent before him to Bruges a consignment of *vin de pinot vermeil* for his entertaining. The records show that various notables drank it with him, including the '*conte de Sallebrucke, Elion de Granson, Othes de Granson et autres Anglois... le duc de Lancastre, le*

---

7 Raymond Bernard, *La Selection clonale, facteur d'évolution qualitative de la production viticole en Bourgogne*, Cahiers du Centre d'Etudes Régionales de Bourgogne, No. 4, La Vigne et le vin de Bourgogne: Science et Réglementation, pp. 73–8, Dijon, 1988.

conte de Salabery'. The English were tasting Pinot wine from the very first year of its recorded existence.

The Pinot Noir has thick, dark green leaves of medium size and small compact bunches (7–10 cm), shaped, so it is said, like a pine-cone, whence its name. The grapes are egg-shaped, blue-black and thick-skinned. Some Pinots *teinturiers* (with black skin and red juice) exist, but in Burgundy all the Pinot's red colouring matter is contained in the skins, the juice and the pulp being colourless. It buds and ripens early, and can withstand winter frosts down to –17°C. According to P. Galet[8] its wines reach their highest qualities in dry calcareous soils in a temperate climate, such as the Côte d'Or. In hot dry areas the wines have no style. He lists many synonyms: Pineau, Franc Pineau, Noirien, Savagnin noir, Salvagnin (Jura), Morillon, Auvergnat, Plant doré, Vert doré (Champagne), Burgun-der (Germany), Plant de Cumières, Cortaillod (Switzerland), Blauer Klevner, Schwartz Klevner (Alsace), Chiavenese (Tyrol), and others.

The Pinot Noir is a very large family, with over 1,000 individual types or clones, their productivity varying from almost total ster-ility to yields of over 100 hectolitres per hectare. Some are named after villages – Pinot de Pernand, de Pommard, de Santenay, others after growers – Pinot d'Angerville, Pansiot, Gouges, Crépet, Lié-bault. The most infamous of the various types are probably the *Pinots droits* or straight-growing Pinots. Legend has it that the first *Pinot droit* was discovered in Richebourg around the turn of the century by a vigneron named Thomas. Where surrounding Pinots trailed along the ground, easy preys to mildew, this one grew straight and healthy up its post. Cuttings were therefore taken and propagated.

The traditional Pinot whose shoots grow sideways (known as *Pinot fin*, *Pinot classique*, or *Pinot tordu* (twisted) when compared to *Pinot droit*) makes extra work for vignerons. For if a clear way for tractors is to be maintained through the vines, three passages on foot are required during the summer to lift its young shoots up between the wires. The shoots of the *Pinot droit* grow vertically, but what endeared it most to the vigneron's heart was that its yield was larger and more regular than that of the classic Pinot.

In the hands of a man who pruned short, or who was prepared, immediately after the flowering, to thin out the young bunches of

---

8 *Cépages et vignobles de France, Tome II*, Paul Dehan, Montpellier, 1958.

grapes if the crop looked excessive, this reliable, time-saving vine could produce good quality. Such a man was hardly the rule, however, and many people believe that, even in careful hands, *Pinots droits* give inferior quality, and that the generally big grapes produce wines lacking in character and short in life span. The issue is confused by there being different types, some bigger yielders than others. Today, virtually no one admits to still having some in their vineyards. The spread of *Pinots droits* over the last fifty years, particularly on the Côte de Nuits in Vosne-Romanée and Vougeot, illuminates an amazing fact: that there was precious little legislation, and no effective control over the type of Pinot Noir which could be planted in Burgundy.

Few people plant *Pinots droits* now, for clonal selections give the guranteed, higher yields, with guaranteed built-in health. From 1971 a number of Pinot Noir clones were identified as virus-free, and recommended for planting. The most successful of these has been Clone 115. This is one of the less productive, and a good sugar-producer, with grape bunches averaging 70 to 95 g in weight. For a decade it regularly topped the clone tasting-panel results. It is the most widely planted, and still recommended. Clone 114 is still distributed, but it yields smaller crops than No. 115, and is usually less liked by tasting panels. Of the other Pinots recommended in 1971, Clone 111 was little planted, and rated no more than average on tasting. Clone 113 was widely championed for its 'aromatic finesse' for planting with 115, but is now no longer recommended, for quality reasons. Of the second generation of clones, the best may be No. 777, which originated in Morey-Saint-Denis, and produces small to medium-sized bunches. It buds late and matures early, giving deep-coloured wine of good length and ageing potential. Clone 667 gives bigger yields. It also originated in Morey, and has characteristics similar to 115, alongside which it is often planted. Clone 828 has only been authorized since 1985, but appears promising. It is reported to be one of the lower yielders, giving many small bunches and wines of good structure. Clone 943, selected by the Lycée de Beaune, has been authorized since 1989; as yet it is too early to draw conclusions.

CHARDONNAY

There is a village called Chardonnay in the Mâconnais, but whether it gave its name to the vine or vice versa is not known for certain. The Chardonnay is responsible for all the great white Burgundies. It is a handsome vine with large thin leaves and bunches of grapes which are less tightly packed together than the Pinot Noir, beautifully golden at vintage time. Quality differences between vintages are less marked with Chardonnay. It is a smaller family than the Pinot Noir, but P. Galet lists even more synonyms: Chardennet, Chardenai, Chardonnet, Chaudenay, Pinot Blanc (Cramant), Pinot Blanc Chardonnay (Marne), Arnaison Blanc, Arnoison (Touraine), Aubaine, Auvernat Blanc; Auxois Blanc, Auxerrois Blanc (Lorraine), Beaunois (Chablis), Epinette Blanche (Champagne), Morillon Blanc (Yonne), Arboisier (Aube), Blanc de Cramant (Marne), Rousseau or Roussot (Val de Saône), Gamay Blanc (Lons-le-Saunier), Moulon (Poligny), Melon Blanc (Arbois), Luisant (Besançon), Noirien Blanc and Chaudenet (Côte Chalonnaise), Plant de Tonnerre (Yonne), Mâconnais (Isère), Petite Sainte-Marie (Savoie), Petit Chatey (Jura), Weisser Clevner or Klawner (Germany, Alsace). This vine buds a little after the Pinot Noir and also ripens later. Its yield can vary from 15 to 100 – or more – hectolitres per hectare depending on the richness of the soil.

There are plantations in the Mâconnais of a white Chardonnay *musqué*, which gives wine with a Muscat-like flavour (considered beneficial by some, in small doses, as part of a blend); and in the most northerly of the Côte d'Or's vineyards there are traces, so Raymond Bernard states[9] – I have never seen such a vine – of a Chardonnay *rosé*.

Chardonnay clones have a more uniform appearance than is the case with Pinot Noir; however there are big quality differences. The levels of natural sugar production, the strength of aromatic expression, the finesse and ageing potential all vary considerably. Three clones currently stand out for their quality and relatively moderate yield levels. Clone 76 originated at Azé in the Mâconnais; it is valued for its regular yields and fine, floral character. It is often planted with Clone 95 (originating in Meursault) which gives wine of greater structure, and good ageing potential. Both have been

---

9 *Le Vin de Bourgogne*, Editions Montalba, Lausanne, 1976.

approved since 1971. Clone 548 (which dates from 1978) produces small bunches and lower yields than the first two. If allowed to overripen it gives heavy wines, but picked at the right time it is balanced, with complex aromas and good potential. In the second division one finds the aromatic Nos. 96 and 124, and more full-bodied No. 131 (but all are over-productive if their vigour is not carefully controlled). There is one recommended Chardonnay with Muscat character: No. 809, which originated in Bissy-la-Mâconnaise. Its yield is reasonable, the bunches below average in size, the Muscat character delicious as a table grape, or as 5–10 per cent of a Chardonnay blend. Several clones were widely planted after approval in 1971 (Nos. 75 and 78, for instance), but are now recognized as giving commonplace, insipid or neutral wine which needs to be drowned in better-quality *cuvées* – or the vineyards grubbed up. As in the case of Clone 113 for Pinot Noir, many people believe they should never have been approved in the first place.

GAMAY

The Gamay grape may have originated in the Côte d'Or, for there is a hamlet of that name just behind Chassagne-Montrachet. It produces its best wines further south on the light soils of the Beaujolais, and we shall return to it in the Beaujolais chapter in Part Two. In northern Burgundy it forms, with the Pinot Noir, a part of the blend of Bourgogne Passe-Tout-Grains, and can feature in Crémant de Bourgogne. On its own it is sold as Bourgogne Grand Ordinaire, and some very respectable wines are appearing under this surprising label. In the nineteenth century it invaded many fine vineyards on the Côte Dijonnaise, its yield being greater than that of the Pinot Noir. No mention of this grape would be complete without another passing reference to Philippe le Hardi's Edict of 1395 ordaining the rooting up of this *mauvaiz plant* from Burgundy's vineyards. The Gamay managed to hang on, and now, no longer *desloyaul*, has gained respect south of Mâcon.

Gamays have been split into two groups – high yielders and quality Gamays – since the nineteenth-century work of Viala and Vermorel, so the Sicarex Beaujolais affirms.[10] In the first group are found Gamay Picard and Gamay Tachon, in the second Petit Gamay rond, Gamay Geoffray and Gamay de Vaux.

Beaujolais and Burgundy growers may presently choose from six Gamay clones, several having originated from the earliest sweep for suitable material, which was in the Loire. Two clones give moderate yields and wines of fine quality: Clone 509, approved since 1976, gives naturally sweeter-than-average juice, and wines which age well. Clone 358 is more productive, but produces reasonably structured, balanced wines. Higher yielders are Nos. 222 and 282, whose wines are fruity and balanced, if the crop sizes are limited. The two most recent recommendations, both originating in the Beaujolais, are the vigorous Clone No. 656, whose production can be excellent if the grapes are not overabundant, and No. 787, available from spring 1994, for which great things are being claimed.

ALIGOTÉ

The fourth vine of importance in Burgundy is the Aligoté. Its wine is white, higher in acidity than that of the Chardonnay, refreshing and clean when young and at its best. Its yield is regular, higher than the Chardonnay's, and it is planted on less favoured slopes. One of the minor delights of the Burgundian wine business is finding an excellent Aligoté. Certain villages have a reputation for this wine, P. Bréjoux mentioning: Pernand-Vergelesses, Villers-la-Faye, Saint-Aubin, Bouzeron, Chagny and Rully.[11] That from Bouzeron now has the right to its own *appellation contrôlée*; those from Pernand and Saint-Aubin have almost disappeared, for their best slopes have increasingly been replanted to Chardonnay, which sells more readily, and at a higher price. This is a major problem for Aligoté; it tends to be relegated to the less favoured sites, where it may have difficulty ripening.

The productivity and health of Aligoté was much more satisfactory than with the other varieties, so clonal research has been on a smaller scale. Two clones originating from Marey-lès-Fussey in the Hautes Côtes appear superior: Clone 264 gives good natural

10 Jean-Michel Desperrier, *Historique de la sélection du Gamay et comment choisir ses plants certifiés*, 210 en Beaujolais, UIVB, Villefranche, December 1990.
11 *Les Vins de Bourgogne*, Société Française d'Editions Vinicoles, Paris, 1967.

sugars, and yields below average; Clone 651 performs well in tricky vintages, and also shows well in comparative tastings.

PINOT BLANC AND PINOT GRIS

The Pinot Blanc was for long confused with the Chardonnay; it is a permitted vine variety for white Burgundies. It is said to be a mutation of the Pinot Noir, and not widely planted, its wine being, according to R. Bernard 'common and bereft of seductiveness'.[12] The white Pinot Beurot on the other hand is much praised, yet even more rarely planted. This is the Pinot Gris, known as Ruländer in Germany, and Tokay in Alsace. Its wine is richer in natural alcohol than that of the Pinot Noir. It used to be found interplanted with Pinot Noir on the Côte, as was the Chardonnay, and together they represented 5–7 per cent of red vineyards, adding perfume and finesse to the wine. The practice has been abandoned and the vines grubbed up, for the consumer has not been looking for these qualities in red Burgundy. There are small plantings of Beurot on the Côte and Hautes Côtes de Beaune: old ones at Senard, new ones at Simon Bize, Joseph Drouhin and Thévenot-le-Brun, amongst others.

In the chapter on wines of the Auxerrois, mention will be made of four vines special to that region, the red César and Tressot, and the white Sacy and Sauvignon.

The survey of Burgundian grapes is completed by reference to the white Melon de Bourgogne, still permitted in the legislation for the lowest AC of the area, Bourgogne Grand Ordinaire. It is extremely important in the Loire, where it produces Muscadet, and has indeed been renamed the Muscadet vine. In Burgundy it was very rare to meet it. However good white wine is now again being made from Melon in the new vineyards of Vézelay, so perhaps it will spread out from there.

---

12 There have been other mutations: P. Galet records that a certain Camuzet of Vosne-Romanée discovered a Pinot Noir in 1899 bearing black, grey and white grapes, and that some years previously the three colours had been seen on the same grape, like segments of melon.

HOW VINEYARD UPKEEP HAS EVOLVED OVER THIRTY YEARS

It is often said, but hard to prove, that red Burgundy has changed in character. It is certain, however, that tending the vineyards has been *twice* transformed within a century.

Until the late nineteenth century, as we have seen, vines were planted higgledy-piggledy (*en foule*, in a crowd), and all cultivation was done by hand. Digging was bound to be shallow, and weed-killing was simply scratching the surface.

The first transformation happened after the phylloxera, when replanting took place in rows, the vines being trained up posts and wires, at half the previous density per hectare. Horse-drawn implements did the ploughing, much of the weeding, and the anti-disease treatments. The second took place from the 1950s, when vine-straddling tractors rapidly took over, and chemical weed-killers began to replace ploughing.

From the phylloxera until the 1960s it was common for the vineyards to be ploughed four times a year. Most Burgundians see this as the 'traditional' way of cultivating, when of course it is but a tiny span in the region's 1,600-year wine-making history. At the end of winter the soil would be tumbled down from around the vine-stocks (where it had been piled up the previous autumn, to protect the graft-joints from frost), and the row ploughed 10–15 cm deep, with a smoothing-down of the earth around the vines. In May, a second ploughing would leave the soil flat, then a third, before the grapes began to mature, destroyed weeds and aerated the ground. The fourth ploughing took place after the vintage, piling up soil protectively around the vine.

Robert Boidron has shown that there were many beneficial effects to this ploughing.[13] Casual weeds were destroyed, and the soil was made more porous, so encouraging water absorption and diminishing surface water streaming. The mineralization of nitrogen was favoured, manure and fertilizers buried and incorporated, and vine-stock graft joints covered. With the cutting through of surface rootlets the vine was forced to develop deeper root systems. On the other hand, there could be damaging effects. The arrival of

13 'Des Labours à la non-culture – quelle évolution dans les techniques d'entretien du sol', Colloque à Nolay, BIVB, Beaune, 1990. Boidron is head of the Service Viticole de Saône-et-Loire.

powerful tractors and mechanized ploughing resulted in some root systems being mutilated, the ground became compacted, and soil erosion became more common.

The use of weed-killers, which were cheap and simple to employ, became widespread in the 1960s. Sometimes they were used across the whole soil surface, sometimes just along the row, with between-rows being controlled by ploughing, or the sowing of selected grasses. Simazine was the weed-killer most widely used, but resistant strains of weeds soon appeared – to be combatted by a host of chemicals, in the familiar spiral. Concern over residues grew during the 1980s, and permitted levels have now been reduced. Simazine doses were halved, for instance, by a notice in the *Journal Officiel* of 13 July 1990.

Chemical weed-killing sometimes ushered in permanent non-cultivation, and experience showed that vines could survive, and thrive, without disturbance of their soil. Indeed, a bonus proved to be that old vines found new vigour, and escaped uprooting, when their useful lives had seemed to be at an end. In spite of the financial and manpower savings, non-cultivation did not become dominant in Burgundy, however. Growers feared that vines would suffer if the soil was not turned, even if they could not say why. And they were concerned by the side-effects of herbicides in the soil, plant and grapes – and how right they were. In any case, by the mid-1970s resistant weeds were appearing, and generally more of them.

It was also becoming evident that non-cultivation was having certain side-effects on both soil and plant. The repeated passage of tractor wheels along the same tracks compressed the soil, rendering it less permeable. So, rain-water tended to stream away, and there was a need to evacuate larger quantities of water from the vineyard. Obviously, this resulted in lower reserves of water deep down, which was beneficial in wet, but harmful in dry, years. The soil became a better conductor of heat, warming up more quickly by day, and cooling more slowly at night. If a stony, pebbly layer formed on the surface, this effect was reinforced.[14]

Non-cultivation allowed root systems near the surface to develop, with various effects. Summer rains were more immediately absorbed by the vine, prolonging the period of growth to the detri-

14 François Champagnol, 'La non-culture et ses effets', Progrès Agricole et Viticole, 15 November 1989.

ment of maturity, and encouraging rot. Absorption of summer rains brought with it greater quantities of nitrogen and potassium fertilizers, causing a drop in wine acidity.

Obviously the use of fertilizers needs to diminish in non-cultivated vineyards. Perhaps more crucially, however, it is felt that minerals are drawn from the surface area, and the role of deep root systems is lessened. 'Now, it is from those minerals which are drawn up from the mother-rock, and from a regular water source provided by deep roots, that the effect of *terroir* is best expressed' wrote Robert Boidron on a critical factor which touches Burgundian hearts, and their most profoundly-held beliefs.

Grass-sowing

The sowing of grass in one row for every two rows between vines, or one in three, is commonly practised, and is the subject of research at the Mont-Battois Experimental Domaine on the Montagne de Beaune. The reasons for doing it are to limit erosion, for the live green carpet of grass keeps the soil in place, and to limit yields from vigorous vines, for which, read clones. If you produce competition for water and nitrogen in the surface layers, the vine's roots must be sent down deeper, though you might say this is shutting the stable door after the horse has bolted – for why are the vines too vigorous in the first place?

In 1986 a survey[15] estimated that vineyards in Burgundy were being tended as follows: localized weed-killing 10 per cent, traditional ploughing 11–25 per cent, non-cultivation 51–75 per cent. But since then there seems to have been a partial return towards traditional cultivations. (Traditional, however, in this case means the methods of the eighty years from phylloxera to the 1960s.)

It is common to find that weed-killer will be applied at the end of winter, and be followed by shallow scratchings of the soil. It has proved impossible to control the evolving weed stocks by poisoning them, and growers are happy to break up the soil surface, thus reducing water-streaming. Manure and fertilizers can be buried, and soils decompacted. Not least, aesthetically, a cultivated vineyard has the edge over one where grass and weeds are growing,

15 Yves Heinzle, '2ème symposium sur la non-culture de la vigne,' Montpellier, November 1986.

which seems neglected. We are not seeing a return to the old methods, but a balance between old and new.

Crop-thinning

Done at the right time, ideally as the grapes are turning colour (*véraison*), crop-thinning can substantially improve Pinot Noir quality, as Didier Sauvage has shown.[16]

For the three years 1989, 1990 and 1991 there were important gains in sugar production (nearly two degrees for 1989, one degree each for 1990 and 1991) when the crop was reduced from 14–17 bunches to 10 bunches per vine. Total acidity was slightly better, as was colour intensity in the finished wine. In both 1989 and 1990 the crop-thinned samples showed better in tasting tests, giving more complete, more structured wines. However, I cannot believe that most Burgundians will countenance clipping off 30 to 40 per cent of their harvest to gain a degree or two extra of alcohol. Such things come more cheaply from sugar bags; no doubt the respected Monsieur Sauvage is being asked to think again.

Leaf and vine canopy management

A more open-minded and scientific approach to growing vines is spreading along the Côte, altering in small ways some traditional habits. For instance, the key role of the leaf as sun-catcher – the crucial factory producing starch and sugars for plant and fruit – is becoming better understood. A radioactive tracer (carbon dioxide, marked with carbon 14), if photographed in the leaves and branches, allows a researcher to see how carbohydrates produced within it may migrate within the plant.

Carbohydrates are synthesized from light energy and the carbon dioxide found in water and air. This, of course, is photosynthesis, and the sugars and starches produced may then migrate in different directions, depending on the time of year. Initially they take over from the reserves stored in trunk, roots and branches, to help build the new vegetation. Later, towards the end of the growing cycle,

16 Chambre d'Agriculture de Saône-et-Loire, Service Viticole (Pinot Noir Clone 292, Rully), Compte rendu des travaux, May 1992.

sugars migrate to the grapes, and starch is stored within the vine-stock for the following year's spring start-up.

Maximum leaf productivity is achieved when the leaf is exposed directly to sunlight.[17] It is only one tenth, or one hundredth, as effective if the leaf is hidden respectively by one, or two, leaf layers, though agitation by wind can allow otherwise hidden layers to play a useful role. There is therefore every reason to discourage thick, dense blocks of foliage, which may also create an unfavourable, humid atmosphere. The leaves should be spread out widely, without overlapping.

Just before the vintage, old leaves at the bases of the fruit-bearing canes turn yellowish and thicken, playing little or no further role in photosynthesis from the end of September. They may advantageously be plucked off, bringing light and air to the bunches (so discouraging grey rot) while also speeding the grape-pickers in their search for bunches.

Generally in the Côte d'Or rows of vines are planted on an east–west axis, facing up and down the slopes, so that each row may receive along its southern side the full heat of the midday sun. Pruning, attaching of branches, and clipping of straggling shoots and non-fruit-bearing branchlets should all focus on filling the maximum sun-catching space, while not shading the next row.

Tests on clipping Pinot Noir, pruned by the widely used *Guyot simple* method in Rully,[18] show a significant gain in natural alcohol, as well as yield, if additional leaves are left at the top of the row. Raymond Bernard and Michel Leguay state, 'Let us remember that one or two extra adult leaves per branch are capable of increasing by 1° the alcoholic richness of the harvest. Natural enriching of the harvest, as you know, is the best, since every increase in sugar levels is accompanied by a greater concentration of the juice and its other constituents, notably tannins, colour and aromas.'[19]

The Côte d'Or's vineyard layout and vine-training system evolved with the post-phylloxera replanting, from the previous crowding into a disciplined scheme of parallel rows. This is easy to farm mechanically, initially by horse, now by vine-straddling tractor.

17 Raymond Bernard and Michel Leguay, *Rôle déterminant du feuillage de la vigne dans la qualité de ses vins*, ONIVINS, Dijon, BIVB, Nolay, 1990.
18 Chambre d'Agriculture de Saône-et-Loire, Compte rendu des travaux, 1989.
19 *Cahiers du centre d'études regionales de Bourgogne*, no. 4.

When vines are planted densely (in Burgundy, about a metre apart) there is competition between the vines, mainly for water and minerals. Leaf growth is limited, and the yield per vine is low. Overall yield per hectare is maximized by a large number of plants per hectare. The low yields per vine give enhanced concentration of character, it is thought, the object being to produce top quality fruit. The grower will aim to spread out the foliage so this may produce the required sugar and acid levels, discourage disease and rot, and reduce shading the fruit. Having established the chosen training system, he or she will aim to maximize production, without diminishing quality, and of course the vineyard must be reasonably efficient and practical to farm.

In Burgundy, the trellis system almost universally used is a vertical, single hedge, the shoots and foliage being gathered up between two wires (which lie on the ground in spring) once they have grown. Vertical trellises have many advantages. They are the cheapest to install, and, once the trailing shoots have been gathered in or clipped away, tending or treating foliage and grapes is easy, as is mechanical harvesting, though this is rare in the best vineyards. The leaves can be spread out effectively, not bunched. Mildew and mould are discouraged, and preventive sprays and powders penetrate well.

Leaf-plucking by hand or machine, to allow sun-rays to reach the fruit, is perfectly feasible, though as yet not greatly practised in Burgundy. Vertical trellising lends itself to mechanical pre-pruning, and mechanical shoot-positioning, in parts of the New World. One suspects these may find their way into Burgundy's vineyards, if plantings of regional *appellations* resume; however traditional habits take a long time dying. Trimming the tops of the canopies is necessary to prevent shading of the adjoining row, and this is commonly carried out by tractor in the Côte d'Or.

Fighting grey rot

Science has provided the means to fight most of the diseases and pests which threaten the vine, with the principal exception of grey rot, which is one of the vine's most damaging disorders. When more than 10–15 per cent of the grape bunches are affected by the fungus, there is loss of yield, and drop in quality. Grey rot is a cryptogamic disease,[20] the fungus responsible for it being the famous *botrytis cinerea*. In many vineyard areas, given the right weather conditions, this fungus causes noble rotting of the grapes and makes possible the production of unctuous dessert wines, such as Sauternes. But in Burgundy it is feared and fought, particularly by makers of red wines, for it destroys the colour cells. Wet weather and high yields are the determining factors. Fifteen hours of rain, with a temperature of 15–20°C, are enough to allow contamination by the fungus. If cochylis caterpillars have attacked the grapes, scarring and splitting the skins, the rot can establish itself even more easily. Once it has a hold, the size of the harvest becomes seriously reduced. It might be hoped that there could be a corresponding gain in sugar content, as with Trockenbeerenauslesen or Bordeaux's dessert wines, but this is rarely the case. Instead there is destruction of the red colour cells once the grapes are affected. The fungus attacks the natural sugars in the grape, forming secondary products which can make later clarification of the wine difficult. Volatile acidity will be raised, and enzymes produced which will provoke a brown turbidity (*casse oxydasique*).

Grey rot has been a major problem since the mid-1960s, and of course it is better to prevent than cure it. Attacks are worst on heavy, clay-rich, water-retaining soils. Here drainage systems may be installed when the vineyard is planted, and can bring relief. Certain vigorous root-stocks (SO4 and 5BB, to a lesser extent 41B) are those most often associated with grey rot attacks. Certain vine-clones are susceptible: those where the grapes are tightly packed in the bunch, those where maturity of individual berries comes early, and those where grape skins are on the thin side. Jean-Paul Couillault[21] adds that vigorousness and high productivity are also key factors which encourage grey rot.

The vigneron can encourage or minimize grey rot attacks according to his work in the vines. Fertilizing with nitrogen and adding organic material will increase the vine's vigour; these must be reduced, or stopped, when rot-favouring weather conditions might coincide with forceful growth. Failure to prevent damage by caterpillars (*tordeuses de la grappe*) feeding on the grape bunches has been shown to be very harmful: once they have munched their way

20 A cryptogam is a plant with no stamens or pistils, and therefore no proper flowers.
21 *Méthodes de lutte prophylactique contre le botrytis*, BIVB, Beaune, 1990.

in, rot follows fast. Spraying to prevent, or wipe out, caterpillar attacks is therefore crucial, and choice of anti-mildew products can also have beneficial secondary effects against grey rot; copper salts, for instance, may help reduce its spread.

When pruning and training the vines the aim should be to allow grape bunches to hang airily, and for water to clear from leaves and shoots as fast as possible. So vegetation must be spread out, not tightly bunched. Unproductive shoots and excessive leaf-growth may be cut away. Just before harvest, leaves may be plucked from around the bunches, to diminish the likelihood of late rot attack. Ploughing after fruit-setting, particularly if followed by rain, will invariably cause an outbreak. Most growers are familiar with these steps, but they also need to use preventive chemical sprays. The fungicides of the late 1970s are no longer effective, for botrytis families soon built up resistance. The struggle evolves afresh each season, as new resistant strains appear.

In 1990, three specific anti-rot treatments were being recommended, using two products: Sumico L, after the flowering (to prevent rot taking hold on the floral heads), with two applications of Silbos DF, the first just before the grapes swell to form a tight bunch (so that fungicide may be sprayed within the bunch), and again 15 days later, before the grapes turn colour. Success with treatments seems to depend in equal measure on four factors: the fungicide, the date, the dose and the effectiveness of the sprayer-pulverizer at reaching the grapes.

Grey rot is a European, not just a Burgundian, problem, and a research programme, instigated by Moët-Hennessy, is under way. 'We are ill-protected against the fungus', says Professor Roger Bessis,[22] going on to admit that the genetic character of the parasite is unknown, and that the way it attacks the tissues of the vine and grape, as well as how the cells respond, are very little understood. At Professor Bessis's Dijon University laboratory studies are under way into how the vine itself resists the parasite. It seems that compounds from the chemical group called phytoalexines appear in cells once they are under attack. Botrytis can be stopped if these molecules appear fast and in high concentrations. One such molecule, called resveratrol, has been synthesized and the laboratory is seeking to understand how it succeeds in blocking the fungus. Such

22 'Comment attaquer la pourriture grise?' Colloque, Nolay, BIVB, 1990.

research might end in the discovery of a means to stimulate the vine's own immune systems, so that rot may effectively be resisted from within.

On the grey rot problem there is perhaps one insufficiently tapped resource: all the practical experience on the hillsides and in the villages. If you taste from cellar to cellar you regularly hear growers say: 'This *cuvée* didn't have a whiff of rot, but that one – same treatments, same aspect, but badly affected.' Each grower has his or her own theory in explanation, yet these experiences and observations are neither collated, nor analysed. Perhaps they would contribute to prevention, if conclusions could only be drawn.

Harvesting machines

Grape harvesting machines work by thrashing and beating the sides of the vine-row with narrow, plastic poles like giant's chopsticks. The grapes fall off the stalks and are caught, with their juice, and collected in tanks. The method is forbidden in the Beaujolais, where the bunches must arrive whole and intact at the vat-house. In northern Burgundy, it is very little practised on Pinot Noir, for its grapes are difficult to detach from their stalks, and, from a quality point of view, the results have often been unimpressive.

Chardonnay and Aligoté, however, are another matter, particularly in Chablis, the Auxerrois and the Mâconnais. Harvesting costs are reduced by 30–40 per cent, and another considerable gain from machine-harvesting is that you can pick grapes at speed, exactly when they are ripe. Hand-picking can mean that, for reasons of cost, and owing to organizational difficulties, you start picking unripe grapes, and end, three weeks later, with grapes which are rotting. A machine allows you to pick at optimum grape maturity.

The choice between hand- and machine-picking largely depends on the size of the estate. It is not difficult to organize family and friends to pick 5–10 hectares of vineyard (different parts of which may ripen perfectly, one after the other, over ten days or so, given Burgundy's differing microclimates). Twenty hectares or more is something else, and the big Chablis and Mâconnais estates solve this problem by machine-picking. In the Yonne there were over five times as many machines per hectare of vineyard as in the Côte d'Or, in 1989.[23] As the Revue des Oenologues has asked, is this not preferable to depending on the Algarve olive harvest, or the starting date of semesters at French universities, for the pickers to arrive?

Machine-harvesting Chardonnay means that a skin-contact exchange with the juice inevitably takes place before pressing. Rot on the grapes will tend to be dissolved in the juice. Leaves, stems, bits of bark, clips from the vine-trellising, who knows? Maybe also snails browsing under the leaves, all are harvested, along with the second-crop, usually unripe grapes, which hand-workers would not dream of picking.

If Chardonnay yields are excessive and the grapes unripe, machine-harvesting exacerbates the leafy, grassy aromas which so easily mar Mâcon-Villages and Chablis. However, if the fruit is ripe, and the machines are operated, not too fast, by growers intent on fine quality, and if wine-making is then adapted to machine-harvested grapes, superb results can be achieved, particularly if the wines are to be drunk when young.

On the Côtes de Beaune and Chalonnaise, by contrast, there are many white-wine-growers who believe that noble grapes are brutalized by these machines, indeed some think that any remaining harvesting machines should be retired to Beaune's Musée du Vin.

Organic approaches

Talking to some of those involved in plant protection in Beaune, or some of the viticulture specialists in Dijon, is like discussing the problems of the United Kingdom's National Health Service with a British doctor. You scratch beneath the surface and find that it is not a National Health Service, but a Sickness Service. These unbelievably hard-working doctors are treating the sick and picking up the pieces after disasters, with virtually no one being involved in either educating us into healthy living, or teaching us about preventing ill health. It does, however, seem that reliance on killer chemicals is being increasingly questioned in Beaune and Dijon, and that the reasoned approach is gaining ground.

Not so long ago, the vigneron sprayed regularly, to a rhythm dictated by the local Plant Protection Service. Increasingly,

23 'La Récolte mécanique en Bourgogne', in *Vinification: l'expérience bourguignonne, résultats d'essais*, Vol. 2, BIVB, Beaune, July 1993.

treatments must be soundly reasoned out (this is *la lutte raisonnée*) before they are made, firstly, to choose products which are least harmful to man, plants and soil, secondly to treat only when it is necessary. Traps will be set for insects, for instance, to establish the dangers, before any spraying. Products will be chosen if they are not harmful to the natural predators. Of course, there are risks, but an extra benefit is that it reduces costs.

La lutte intégrée (integrated prevention) takes matters a step further, adopting natural products as insecticides, for instance (which are not necessarily more expensive).

La lutte biologique (organic viticulture) means the elimination of all synthesized products, and the use only of natural products, such as sulphur, or copper sulphate, whose constituents occur in nature. Weed-killers are not used on the soil; it is ploughed.

Of course, great commercial risks are taken, as leaves and fruit may be badly damaged if pests get out of control or weather conditions are really difficult, allowing rot to spread. But in theory the vine's natural immune systems will be strengthened as the soil is cleansed of chemicals, and revivified with compost and humus.

Fighting spiders and caterpillars biologically

The red and yellow spiders which today often damage vines have their own natural predators; the destruction of these predators by the mindless use of chemicals is almost certainly the main cause of recent spider population growth in vineyards.

Since 1988, Burgundians have been researching whether natural enemies of the spiders, already present in vineyards, may be bred and reintroduced to control them. The best predator appears to be *typhlodromus pyri Scheuten*. This is tiny, blind, pear-shaped insect, half a millimetre long, which has three pairs of legs when larval, four when adult. It has feelers and pincers with which to grab its prey, which it then empties by suction, taking on the colour of whatever it has eaten.

When *typhlodromus* was bred and released in vineyards in Jully-lès-Buxy and Nuits-Saint-Georges it was found that no pesticide was needed to control spider populations in the two years which followed. Typhlodromes happily fly down the rows from vine to vine – no doubt pursuing spiders – but rarely from one row to another. So release sites must be planned accordingly. 'The control of ravaging spiders by using their own natural enemies has become a reality if one only takes sufficient trouble to reconsider the normal treatment programmes' concludes Gilles Sentenac of ITV.[24]

In Alsace, a keen-eyed vine technician, M. Montavon, noticed that the normally translucid eggs laid by grape caterpillars were sometimes black. In 1986 it was discovered that this was because the eggs of these caterpillars had been invaded by a parasite: minuscule wasps, called *Trichogramma daumala* and *T. cacoeciae*. In 1987 the Organization Professionnelle de l'Agriculture Biologique en Alsace put 4 hectares of vines at the disposal of INRA Colmar,[25] so that the little wasps might be released to lay their eggs. There was a 60–90 per cent success rate.

Trichograms had already been used for the biological control of maize pyrale-moths, indeed in 1990, 10,000 hectares of maize were protected, thanks to wasps bred by INRA Antibes. In Alsace, they are mindful of the arguments for reducing insecticide treatments, which may be as high as ten to twelve per year. They wish to avoid being confronted by problems of pesticide residues in wine, not to mention increased resistance by the pests. The concept of preserving the environment is entirely at one with the image of wine quality – and as well as endearing oneself to foreigners and greenies one also earns the thanks of bee-keepers, who have been known to blame vine-treatment products for damage to their livelihoods.

You need to release 400,000 to 600,000 little wasps per hectare for the desired effect, six times a year, to coincide with two generations of caterpillar. A grower must observe each vineyard carefully, bearing in mind microclimate and weather patterns. He may lay food traps or sexual traps for the pests, in order to estimate their egg-laying dates. Of course, pesticide treatments which would wipe out the wasps must be avoided. These lay their eggs inside the eggs of the moth, which then do not turn into caterpillars, but instead become food for the little wasps. Inoffensively, these then protect the vineyards.

In 1991, in Alsace, just ten to twelve hectares were being thus experimentally treated. The system is expensive, but a factory for

24 *Lutte biologique contre les acariens phytophages*, ITV, Beaune, April 1991.
25 To the Director of whose Zoological Laboratory I am greatly indebted for this account: Marc Stengel, whose findings were published by BIVB-Technovin Qualité Hygiénique des Vins et Environnement, Mâcon, 25 April 1991.

breeding trichograms year-round is under study. Marc Stengel summarizes (and this surely applies equally to Burgundians as to Alsace vine-growers): 'The success of the method will be tied to the will of the vine-growers to choose this biological method in preference, adapting the whole protection programme (fungicides etc.) to the use of trichograms in the vineyards . . . it ought to be possible, soon, to reduce populations of grape caterpillars to below the level at which they are damaging.'

The cosmic approach

No discussion of organic viticulture and wine-making in Burgundy would be complete without also covering bio-dynamic methods, though at present barely two dozen estates have significant experience in this field. (See Appendix D for a list of certain organic wine-growers in the Côte d'Or, several of whom work bio-dynamically.)

Those working their vines bio-dynamically are operating in three areas: the mineral, the vegetable and the animal kingdoms. They time their work to relate to the movements of the planets, and with the greatest consideration for the air and the soil which surround their plants. They never forget that over 90 per cent of the dry matter needed by a plant is drawn from the air: carbon, oxygen and hydrogen (the sugars $C_6H_{12}O_6$).

Having tasted blind, in June 1993, two samples each of Domaine Leflaive's Puligny-Montrachet Clavoillon and Bâtard-Montrachet 1991, one made traditionally and one bio-dynamically, in both cases finding the bio-dynamically made wine the better, I had no alternative but to try to open my mind to how the rhythms of the cosmos may be impinging on Burgundy. There is quite a lot to take on board.

We must consider the zodiac, for instance – the band of constellations in front of which the moon and all the planets travel their predestined paths. Many believe that this passage in front of the constellations stimulates forces which exercise influences over matters on earth.

It is not hard to accept the gravitational influence of the moon over liquids on earth – witness the tides. If the seas can be moved, so surely can the sap, or the fluids in the bodies of insects, animals or humans.

Certain periods each month are seen as favourable for sowing, for weeding or hoeing, and for harvesting, depending on the plant being cultivated.

During the course of its revolution around the earth in 27 days, the Moon passes in front of the twelve constellations of the Zodiac, and transmits to earth forces which express themselves by way of the four elements. These forces activate a 'fructification' in the plant, in four different organ areas (root, leaf, flower, fruit). By choosing the right moment to sow, to tend or to pick we can stimulate the plant's growth and good health... Each impulse lasts 2–4 days. This fundamental framework can be disrupted by a waxing or waning moon, and by certain planets being in opposition to each other. Such periods are unfavourable for sowing or harvesting.[26]

Plants are broadly divided into four groups: root plants (radish, carrot, beetroot, celeriac, etc.), leaf plants (spinach, salads, cabbage, parsley, etc.), flower plants (including sunflowers, flax, rape, and those cultivated for cutting), and fruit plants (pulses, peas, maize, courgettes, and of course vines). Approximately every nine days the moon passes in front of the same equilateral triangle of forces, each relating to Earth–Root (the constellations Taurus, Virgo and Capricorn), Water–Leaf (Cancer, Scorpio, Pisces), Air–Flower (Gemini, Libra, Aquarius) and Fire–Fruit and Grain (Aries, Leo, Sagittarius). Sowing, weeding or picking will best take place according to the calendar showing the activity's favourable dates. Sometimes it may be necessary to rise before dawn to treat at 5 a.m.

For instance, if treating grapes to protect them against grey rot, one would arrange to do this when the moon passes in front of a fire constellation: Aries, Leo or Sagittarius.

Preparations based on silica (crystals of quartz) are often deemed appropriate in the mineral kingdom. Sulphur mixed with a resin extract is often used against oidium (nothing revolutionary about this, and it is now recommended by the Service de la Protection des Végétaux), and traditional copper sulphate Bordeaux mixture against mildew. The disadvantage of the latter is that it does not penetrate into the plant, so is easily washed away by rain. Against other pests, such as spiders, caterpillars and fungal attack, infusions

26 Translated from *The Sowing Calendar of Maria Thunn* (a German disciple of Rudolf Steiner).

of nettle, valerian, camomile, thuja, yarrow, oak-bark, dandelion, bracken and *prêle* will be prepared. Bracken, nettle and *prêle* are apparently rich in silica, and one never sees these plants themselves affected by grey rot or fungal attack. Silica may play an important role in reinforcing the pecto-cellulose membrane of the grape skin.

The infusions are extremely diluted, in homoeopathic doses, and then 'energized', being mixed and stirred up in a small, open-top, motorized chestnut barrel. To ensure a good result they must be applied speedily.

From the animal kingdom, cattle manure is applied, as part of a compost supplied by the Syndicat d'Agriculture Bio-dynamique in Paris (in the case of Domaine Leflaive, for instance), or made on the estate (as at the Domaine de la Romanée-Conti). The compost strengthens root activity, encouraging the creation of a rich and complex clay–humus soil structure, favourable to microbial life.

Another preparation comes from cattle excrement inside a hollow heifer's horn, buried in the soil on a certain date and dug up on another. This might sound close to witchcraft, but if the microbes inside it are then identified and counted the concentration is found to be enormous, way above what may be produced in the laboratory, with many different types of bacteria, yeast, and fungus. Once diluted for use according to the doses prescribed, the microbial count is reduced to that appropriate to fertilizing a field of alfalfa or lucerne, cultivated by traditional methods.[27]

It is easy to smile incredulously, but what surely matters is whether these methods work. These are new departures for most Burgundians, but one domaine on the Côte with over ten years bio-dynamic experience is Jean-Claude Rateau in Beaune. I found his wines excellent and individual.[28]

Studying the air is not such a stupid idea, given the extent to which the vine relies on it for its carbon, oxygen and hydrogen. But there is very little research into it, or into matters atmospheric, and how they impinge on wine-making. You cannot make money out of the air; no doubt that is the problem.

Chemical fertilizers are another matter, of course. Let us just

27 Laboratoire Analyses Microbiologique des Sols, Marey-sur-Tille, 21120, Is-sur-Tille.
28 I warmly recommend Fiona Beeston's chapter on Nicolas Joly in *The Wine Men* (Sinclair-Stevenson, London, 1991). His dry white Loire, Clos de la Coulée de Serrant, has been cultivated bio-dynamically since the early 1980s.

consider the profits made by companies producing fertilizers, which throw plants off-balance, creating the need for pesticides to protect them (from parasites which were previously unthreatening). These disordered plants, or the fruit from them, go to nourish humans, who in turn find their health thrown out of balance. They will be treated with medicines and drugs manufactured by the companies which produce the fertilizers and the pesticides. That sort of profitable cycle attracts massive investment funds, just as surely as tobacco companies pour money into research, attempting to show that smoking is not as dangerous to health as one or two people think.

Calling for research into the insubstantial air or cosmic forces is unlikely to cause a queue of cheque-carriers. But the soil is something else. It is surely most regrettable that properly funded scientific research into soil life is so bare, and indeed so little encouraged, in a wine region whose constant obsession is the uniqueness, the richness and the diversity of its *terroirs*.

Cultivating vineyards according to the rhythms of the cosmos might seem on first acquaintance completely cranky, but an open mind, and a determination to judge by results, not preconceptions, is surely called for. There appears to be something in it. Time and experiment will eventually, no doubt, demonstrate how much.

Yields remain the greatest problem

The principal cause for concern in the vineyards of Burgundy is over-yields, however. Healthier vines, advances in cultivation methods, over-permissive legislation and lax controls jointly explain the increases. Have things now gone too far?

Between 1974 and 1990 the yields in France's *appellation contrôlée* vineyards increased by one hectolitre per hectare, every year, according to the INAO.

The problem is not restricted to Burgundy, of course. In the *Revue du Vin de France*[29] Michel Bettane, one of France's most knowledgeable wine writers, pointed his finger at the classed growths of the Médoc at the same time as he singled out Puligny-Montrachet, Corton and Chambertin Clos de Bèze for what he termed scandalous increases in yields. He contrasted them with

29 October 1993.

appellations which have stayed reasonable in their production levels: Volnay, Nuits-Saint-Georges, Romanée-Conti, Pomerol, Sauternes and Bandol, for instance. We shall return to the problem when we look at the laws and controls in Chapter 8: Naming, Controlling and Letting Go.

Over the centuries there have been many examples of wine reputations being destroyed by excess yields. For instance, here is Pliny on Falernian, the most famous wine of the Roman world: 'The reputation of this district . . . is passing out of vogue through the fault of paying more attention to quantity than to quality.'[30] And here is a letter of 3 May 1786 from Margue, steward of the Prince de Conti, to the latter's *régisseur* in Beaune: 'Besides, his Serene Highness in no way wishes that one should lean towards producing a large quantity of wine, but towards quality: you know that a vine too loaded with fruit produces only mediocre wine without quality. I beg you, Sir, to tell the vigneron to prune the vineyard accordingly. Such are the last wishes of the Monseigneur.' Finally, here is R. Bernard: 'One must therefore find the balance between a vine's possibilities and the pursuit of the best product, bearing in mind the rule which proclaims the incompatibility of quantity and quality, time and again confirmed.'[31]

The Institute for vine and wine at Dijon University (Institut Universitaire de la Vigne et du Vin)

Dijon University's achievements in the wine field have blazed less spectacularly than those of Bordeaux or Montpellier, but this may be due to change.

From 1994 the three *départements* concerned with wine at Dijon University are being brought together under one new roof. Previously, oenology was attached to chemistry, and viticulture to biology, and there was an independent experimental centre based at Marsannay. The aim is to make Dijon University's newly-named Institute for Vine and Wine the leading research and teaching centre for cool-climate wine studies. How could Burgundy be properly catered for by Bordeaux or Montpellier, with their different grapes and climates? How, indeed?

30 Quoted in William Younger, *Gods, Men and Wine*, The Wine and Food Society and Michael Joseph, 1966.
31 *Le Vin de Bourgogne.*

Four years of study, after the *baccalauréat*, are envisaged, partly oenology, partly viticulture. Links have been made with Champagne, Alsace, the Jura and Beaujolais, and are planned, I understand, with Germany and Switzerland. No news, as yet, of overtures in the direction of Russian River Valley, Carneros, Yamhill, Pemberton, Lilydale, Martinborough, or the Cape – to mention just seven – but French siege mentality will perhaps evolve, and arms one day be stretched beyond Europe.

Jacques Marquis d'Angerville of Volnay is the first president, and Roger Bessis (Dijon's Biology Professor, with considerable experience in wine-related research) the first director.

On the vine front, for ten years Dijon has been developing *in vitro* cultures, regenerating vines from plant cell cultures. These vine embryos are referred to as somaclones. It is thought that this work can be used in at least two ways: to produce vines identical to those in the vineyard, but more rapidly, and to produce clones with specific attributes, for instance, a greater resistance to grey rot. Here, we meet resveratrol again, the antimicrobial compound produced by plants in response to infection, or various stresses. Resveratrol can help the vine withstand an attack of grey rot, but, sensationally, it is also thought to be of value to humans in protecting them from heart disease. Certain authors have suggested that 'the reduced serum lipid levels observed in humans as a result of drinking wine might be attributed to the presence of this compound in wine. Therefore, this provides a possible explanation for the cardioprotective action of wine and now constitutes an active field of research.'[32] Analysis of resveratrol in Burgundy wines (Pinot Noir, Chardonnay and Aligoté) has indicated that 'resveratrol could reach high concentrations in red table wines, while those produced from white grapes contained low levels of resveratrol'.

Professor Bessis and his colleagues at Dijon have succeeded in synthesizing resveratrol, and his further research findings are awaited with enthusiasm.

Funds may not be sufficient for soil studies to feature high on the

32 P. Jeandet, R. Bessis, B. Maume and M. Sbaghi, 'Analysis of resveratrol in Burgundy wines', *Journal of Wine Research*, vol. 4, no. 2, Institute of Masters of Wine, London, 1993; and P. Jeandet, M. Sbaghi and R. Bessis, 'The production of resveratrol by grapevine *in vitro* cultures, and its application to screening for grey mould resistance', *Journal of Wine Research*, vol. 3, no. 1, Institute of Masters of Wine, London, 1992.

institute's priorities, initially, which seems a pity, given Burgundian obsession with *terroir*. Will Claude Bourguignon's findings relative to the causes of vine disease, and soil imbalance, be treated during the courses, I wonder?

The Marquis d'Angerville has said that he sees one of the institute's functions as being the 'recycling of professionals . . . in the sense of permanent retraining, to stay abreast of evolving techniques'. So maybe some technicians who have set their faces against organic solutions will be encouraged to incorporate them into the university's syllabus. It is intended that business management and living languages may be obligatory parts of the courses. Change is undoubtedly in the university air.

THE EXTENDED PINOT NOIR FAMILY

Many famous villages of the Côte have twinned themselves abroad (Puligny with Johannisberg, Beaune with Katsunuma, Gevrey with Nierstein). They could do worse than to consider closer links with just one honourable, yet struggling, village each in a lesser sector of Burgundy – the Auxerrois, the Mâconnais, the Couchois, the Hautes Côtes, the Chalonnais. Here growers can barely afford sufficient vat capacity, and techniques, education, even cleanliness can still be rudimentary. These villages carry abroad the names of Burgundy, yet many will cease to make wine at all, owing to competition from better organized foreigners, unless something is done.

In the famous villages, growers have inherited mega-valuable land, by the luck of the birth lottery. This has now permitted them to invest, and study, and master many of the problems of two decades ago. Some such growers could perhaps now look to their wider interests.

If more Burgundians (not just the established globe-trotters) only travelled more frequently to other Pinot Noir vineyard areas they would realize how close are the Pinot Noir family interests. Perhaps trips would sometimes need to be accompanied by a bilingual Burgundy enthusiast who could try to defuse any whiff of chauvinism, if ever it threatened – perish the thought. If they tasted at Ata Rangi or Wignalls, at Ponzi or Williams Sellyem, at Saintsbury, Calera or Acacia, at Coldstream Hills, Diamond Valley and all around Halliday's Melbourne 'dress circle' they would see that every vineyard has its own *terroir*. The battle between red Burgundy and other Pinot Noir areas is meaningless. If a Pinot Noir battle needs to be waged it is that between between mediocrity and excitement.

Another struggle, one day, could be between the succulently delicious, user-friendly Pinot Noirs (whether red Burgundy or other), and the impressive, but often austere Cabernet Sauvignons and Cabernet blends. But that is another campaign, and one that can only start to be fought once decent quantities of delicious red Burgundy, and Pinot Noir, become available at approachable prices.

Which country, region, district, village or site is yielding the exciting quality is pretty irrelevant. It will always be difficult and expensive to achieve, wherever it is grown. But as the Dessendre family, who almost single-handedly kept Burgundy's best red grape going in the Couchois district might say, Pinot-cchio people should try to work together.

6

Wine-making and Tending

WHAT IS THE TRADITIONAL APPROACH?

Burgundian red-wine-making is obsessed by tradition, the word being almost universally trotted out, whatever wine-making methods are being used. But which tradition?

Dr Lavalle[1] states that the principal points of wine-making in Burgundy have been the same in every epoch from the sixth to the nineteenth century: bring together the grapes in vats, let them ferment there a certain time, squash them, then press them. Removing the stalks was never suggested, and juice was never left in contact with the skins and stalks for more than a few days. He admitted, however, that personal taste and the fashion of his time had varied the details. At the expense of finesse and bouquet all the white *Pinots blancs* and *Pinots beurots* were being pulled up from the vineyards, where for centuries they had been planted amongst *Pinots noirs*, to obtain wines of deeper colour and more firmness.

Louis Latour[2] would disagree with Lavalle. He has argued that until the revolutionary construction of the Clos Vougeot vat-house by the monks of Cîteaux in the twelfth century, no one would have risked open vat fermentation, because of the danger of vinegariness. Red grapes might have been squashed by foot, but they would assuredly have been pressed, the juice being separated from the skins, before fermentation *in barrel*. Red Burgundy prior to Cîteaux would have been pale in colour, for it would have been made rather like white Burgundy is today.

1 *Histoire et statistique de la vigne et des grands vins de la Côte d'Or* 1855 reprinted by Fondation Geisweiler, Nuits-Saint-Georges, November 1972.
2 Vinification d'autrefois en Bourgogne, the opening essay of the BIVB's *Vinification: l'expérience bourguignonne, résultats d'essais*, Beaune, July 1993.

The motives for Cîteaux wishing to produce deeper coloured red Burgundy may be understood by studying history, so Latour affirms. It was the time of the Cathar heretics, who questioned the realities of the Bible and the Christian story. If Cîteaux could produce red wine closer to the colour of Christ's blood, which wine represented at the Mass, the message of the Gospel would be strengthened. This was the mission, so Latour would have us believe, of the theologian-oenologists who revolutionized Burgundian wine-making when Cîteaux was at the the height of its power.

Those are just two attempts to define traditional red Burgundy wine-making, but there are probably as many different 'traditional' approaches as there are wine-makers stating that they use them. What seems certain is that Burgundy's great reputation was made by fast maturing, light red wines. Only in the nineteenth century did deeper coloured wines, with greater body, make their appearance. The fashion has lasted 150 years (with some ups and downs) but, in the context of a reputation which goes back 1,500 years, has by no means become entrenched. If only our expectations of red Burgundy were less hidebound we would more often be delighted with it.

When A. Jullien wrote *Topographie de tous les vignobles connus* (Paris, 1816) red Burgundy from the Côte d'Or of a good year united, for him, in just proportions all the qualities which constituted perfect wines ... a beautiful colour, much perfume and a delicious taste. At the same time, they were full-bodied, fine, delicate and racy, without being too heady. Here is James Halliday on the same subject, in January 1992: 'intense yet delicate, powerful yet elegant, piercing yet silky; above all else, the wine should be long on the palate, with a lingering finish and after-taste.'[3] The descriptions are almost interchangeable.

Wine-making on the Côte de Beaune was first described in detail by the Abbé Tainturier in 1763. On the first day the vigneron would fill his vat with grapes, on the second he would climb naked into it, piercing with difficulty to the bottom of the vat, and going back and forth. 'Soon the broken grape gives out its juice, he can move more freely, the squashing is less impeded – an hour or two of this exercise is needed for a vat of 20–25 hogsheads. After three or four hours, if the juice is of fine red colour, with a lively and penetrating

3 Lecture at Institute of Masters of Wine Seminar, 1992.

aroma, it is time to draw off the vat.' One could say that was traditional wine-making on the Côte de Beaune.

A different technique was used on the Côte de Nuits, where the juice and grapes were not drawn off for pressing until after the fermentation had been completed. Vatting times on both Côtes depended to a large extent on the ambient temperature, varying, according to Dr Morelot in 1819, from thirty hours to eight or ten days, if it took that long for fermentation to begin. The longer vatting did not relate to the wine-maker's desire to extract colour through maceration. As Dr Lavalle describes, vat-houses often had no roof, and the doors were ill-fitting. It was a matter of luck if the temperature inside the vat-house rose above the outside, so it might take a week or more for fermentation to begin. So cold-soaking red Burgundy prior to fermentation may certainly be described as traditional, if somewhat *faute de mieux*.

The main innovations in the wine-making technique, which resulted in deeper coloured Burgundies being produced in the nineteenth century than at any time previously, can be found in the instructions issued by Chaptal (who was Napoleon's Minister of Agriculture), published in 1801. The harvest could be improved by the addition of sugar; squashing the grapes could be done by means of a 'long-handled plane'; one or two cauldrons of boiling must could be added to the vat, and the floating hat of grape skins could be kept beneath the surface by means of a close-fitting cover. This produced a style of wine which foreigners particularly appreciated, and wines which were sturdy enough to travel well. The arrival of the railways must have made easier the transport of Rhône or Midi wines used for 'improving'; and brandy was beginning to be added to wines destined for export markets.[4]

Writing on Côte d'Or vinification in 1864 A. de Vergnette-Lamotte declared that 'We have had to conform to the taste of the drinkers ... by using large wine tuns we can obtain up to twenty days' vatting, and deliver for consumption wines which are rich in extracted matter and above all heavily charged with tannins.' There was at the time very little legislation or control to protect the consumer from substitution or fraud. Dr Lavalle encountered a *négociant* based outside Burgundy and asked him how he had managed

---

4 This practice, known as *vinage*, was still common for wines despatched in bulk from Beaune to the United Kingdom until the mid-1960s.

to amass enormous profits in so few years, to be told: 'It is by always selling Burgundy without either harvesting or buying any.'

No doubt the style of wine he was blending was the deep coloured, full flavoured wine which the nineteenth century liked, a far cry from the partridge-eye tinted wine from the vermilion *pinot* which was transported to Reims to celebrate the coronation of Charles IV in 1321 or that of Philip VI in 1328.

CHOOSING THE HARVEST DATE

Wine is only made once a year, the raw materials and the ambient temperature being different each time. How tremendous it must be thus to bring twelve months' work to completion!

The choice of the best date for picking is a vital one. In the eighteenth century, so the Abbé Tainturier tells us, even the behaviour of the wasps around the bunches had to be taken into account when arriving at the decision. He felt that one needed cooked, roasted and green grapes ('*de cuyt, du roty, du verd*'), to produce fine, balanced wine. In the nineteenth century, when demand for deeper coloured, fuller wines made itself felt, there was a tendency to harvest late, and in 1822, for instance, the result was wines which failed to last in bottle.

Today, ripeness of the grapes is mainly thought of in terms of sugar content. Indeed one of the cornerstones of AC legislation (though Burgundians constantly ride rough-shod across it) is the minimum natural sugar level, laid down by law, for each *appellation*. But other constituents of the grapes mature at different speeds and times, their optima not necessarily coinciding with peak sugar production: the aromatic compounds, the colour and tannins, the tartaric and malic acids, for instance. When to pick the grapes is not a simple matter in Burgundy, for they mature at widely different moments, depending on soil types, slope and orientation, vine age, pruning, clonal variety, yield, etc.

Publicly proclaiming the start of the vintage (the *ban des vendanges*) is a very old tradition, dating back to early feudalism; indeed Dr Lavalle writes that it may be traced through barbarian laws to Roman legislation. The idea is to ensure that no grapes are picked before they are ripe, but it also allows itinerant pickers to be forewarned of the start-day, for the harvesters to work more effectively in a group. And in feudal times, it allowed for the lord of the manor to precede, by a day, his vassal's vintaging, thus gaining an advantage. The vintage date is one of the hardest fought discussions in Burgundy today, and quite rightly too. Until 1979 the *ban des vendanges* was fixed by order of the *Préfet*. Since 1985 the BIVB has been following the fortunes of eighteen vineyards from Santenay up to Marsannay, aided by the Beaune Lycée Viticole. Since 1988 it has collaborated with Professor Bessis at Dijon University to keep tracks on a network of selected, cloned vineyards 'to define maturity references', though this is still at experimental stage.

A system has existed since the 1950s for growers' unions, the INAO and the Station Oenologique de Bourgogne to arrive at a date for the start of the Côte d'Or's harvest, and similar arrangements exist in the other districts. In 1992, for instance, six different start-dates were agreed, from Mâcon up to Chablis: 10 September for the villages of the Mâconnais, 12th for Givry, Rully, Montagny and the Côte de Beaune, 15th for Mercurey, 18th for the Côte de Nuits, 19th for the Yonne's regional *appellations,* 21st for Chablis. But the system is sometimes unsatisfactory; for instance in 1991 it is generally agreed that on the Côte de Beaune the starting pistol was fired too late.

Surely it is time for the legislation to catch up with the fact that hundreds of Burgundy domaines now have owners, or managers, who are qualified oenologists, or have top qualifications from the Lycée Viticole de Beaune, or a comparable establishment. It is ludicrous for a committee to impose picking dates on such people. They should be allowed to register as 'domaines of high technical capacity' for instance, and granted the freedom to act independently, to pick their grapes, for instance, exactly when they think best. This would not stop them being liable to flash visits, if the fraud squad inspectors felt so inclined. After all, these wines will be subject to the INAO's strictest scrutiny, anyway, with Draconian blind tasting by highly critical assessors (during the *labellisation* process – for which reference may be made to the section on *appellation contrôlée* in Chapter 8). So there is a police force, and a safety net, both securely in place. And there is the market. Such wines are non-essential, luxury products, which will be subject to public commentary, with the trade and media sieving which now regularly accompanies high profile domaines. Centralized French bureaucracy has too much of a stranglehold on fine wine-making. Its Jacobin grip could perhaps be loosened from those qualified to run their own affairs.

SUGAR LEVELS IN THE GRAPES

The practice of adding sugar to grape-must when sunless summers have failed to ripen the fruit completely is very old. The monks of Cîteaux, for instance, were adding small pieces of white sugar to light wines in the late eighteenth century. Unfortunately chaptalization (as it is called, after Chaptal, Napoleon's Minister of Agriculture) is often overdone, for growers, brokers and merchants know that alcoholic strength goes a long way towards making up for a lack of real flavour. It is also a highly effective money-spinner, for it swells the volume of wine. A kilo of beet-sugar resold as a litre of *Grand Cru* represents a very tidy profit.

During the 1960s, 1970s and early 1980s, many red harvests in the Côte d'Or had not reached maturity when they were picked, if one took as maturity the official natural grape-sugar level laid down by the AC laws. This was because yields were too high, and to some extent because the sugar minima had been set too high, at unrealistic levels. Growers made up the deficit by additions of sugar, breaching the law when the crop was finally declared under the chosen AC, while the fraud squad turned a blind eye. One may think of 1967, 1968, 1970, 1972, 1973, 1974, 1975, 1977, 1980, 1982, 1984 and 1987.

In these years it was basically the overladen vines which failed to reach the minimum degrees. A 35–40 hectolitres per hectare yield could reach the minimum, even in 1982 or 1984. The Chardonnay produces sweeter grapes than the Pinot or Gamay, and it is fair to say that the minimum is practically always reached with white wines. The problem was the reds.

From 1988 to 1993 Burgundy enjoyed an unparalleled succession of warm or hot summers. Thanks to this run of weather, attaining the legal minimum sugar levels has became less of a headache. Also, vineyards which have been replanted with clonal stock yield better sugar levels, though this still represents a tiny percentage of the total.

The law in France states that a declaration of intent to chaptalize must be made. Careful vinifiers often do not add the sugar all at once, for a tempestuous fermentation might be unleashed, taking the temperature above the 35°C danger level. They add it little by little during the vatting time, and this has the immeasurable advantage of extending the fermentation, achieving a long-drawn-out extraction of colouring matter, flavours, aromas and fine tannins. Australian Pinot Noir wine-makers seeking to emulate the velvety texture of red Burgundy, who operate in a country where the addition of sugar is illegal, envy the French their freedom to add sugar in this way, for it greatly adds to the seductive feel of a wine. Californians can have similar feelings of envy, all the while musing that some Burgundians do not realize how lucky they are.

Since 1987 it has been tolerated (though not legalized) in France to fractionalize the addition of sugar. You make a declaration at the beginning of the amount you plan to use, then add it in two or three goes, or more, keeping a record in the vat-house notebook (*carnet de cuverie*) of when, and how much. In the French manner, the law will one day catch up with what has been happening for ages, no doubt, and properly legalize fractionalized chaptalization, which is entirely beneficial.

Seen from Australia, where chaptalization is illegal and consequently some Pinot Noir wine-makers must feel (if they stay within the law) that they are being asked to make Pinot with one arm tied behind their backs, Burgundy's freedom to chaptalize can appear highly desirable. 'Undoubtedly', write Halliday and Johnson,[5] 'chaptalisation adds roundness and fatness to the texture of the wine.' They also state, 'Chaptalisation is a religion in Burgundy', and later,

Chaptalisation is considered quite essential to the making of burgundy regardless of the naturally available sugar in the grapes. This view is challenged by a few iconoclasts such as Hubert de Montille ... but his is a voice in the wilderness. Its many proponents say quite simply that '*it is for the feel in the mouth*', an oblique reference to the fact that (particularly if it is added progressively in small amounts towards the end of the primary fermentation) it 'stresses' the fermentation and leads to an increase in glycerol.

5 *The Art and Science of Wine.*

These passages give a false impression of its benefits, for they do not refer to over-chaptalization, which has been, and remains, one of Burgundy's greatest banes. It is now the single greatest cause, I believe, of consumer dissatisfaction, though this is not yet widely recognized. Sugar disguises so many faults, and it disguises so well the absence of true concentration. It gums up origins, it renders wines pleasing to neophytes, it makes them easily saleable when young, and it turns people's heads while all unaware. Excess alcoholic strength kicks Burgundies off-balance time and time again. Of course, that is not the root of the problem, which is that yields have been a bit too high for ages, and that the consumer's palate has now got acclimatized to what is getting, mostly, delivered.

De Montille is certainly not a voice in the wilderness. He is greatly admired in Burgundy, now as twenty years ago, and increasingly, I think, emulated. But it all depends on the consumers. If most buyers persist in imagining that red Burgundy must be 13° and new-oaky (hedonistic gob-stopping wines, every one) his bottles will continue to escape the media limelight. They will go, like those of like-minded growers, into the cellars of those who can age them properly, and will like or love them.

In 1992 James Halliday[6] (who has a passion for red Burgundy and its grape, a personal experience of wrestling with it, and a global overview of all its manifestations which are second to none) wrote of Pinot Noir, 'No other variety is so sensitive to yield, and in particular to the adverse effects of excessive yield.' He went on: 'It is my conviction first quality pinot noir cannot be made from grapes yielding in excess of 3 tonnes per acre (48 hl/ha.), and a counsel of perfection (assuming a vine in good health and balance) would suggest no more than 2 tonnes per acre (32 hl/ha.).' And yet he praises Burgundian chaptalization practices! Without realizing it, perhaps he draws strength from the countless bottles of unbalanced red Burgundy he sees. For indeed, the more those Burgundians persist, the faster will come the day when his Melbourne dress circle may aspire truly to rub shoulders with one of those admired Burgundian Côtes . . .

6 ibid.

DE-STEMMING, ACIDIFYING AND CRUSHING

There is immense variety in growers' practices concerning de-stem-ming. The advantages may be summarized as follows: more wine can be put into a vat, and there is less *marc*[7] to press at the end of fermentation, for the stems may represent 30 per cent of the volume of the harvest; the alcoholic degree is slightly increased; tannin content in the wine is minimized as are vegetal aromas, for the stalks may contribute not a little, in both cases, if given the chance. Acidity may be beneficially higher, for reasons which will be explained below. In years of imperfect maturity, mellowness, finesse and quality are often improved.

However certain wine-makers continue to add a proportion, or all, of the stalks. Some do it simply because they always have, and they like the results. Others believe that well-ripened, woody stems allow a wine's tannic and structural potential to be fully realized. The stalks favour aeration, and absorb heat, allowing the fermen-tation to proceed more smoothly. Because they act as drains, stalks are helpful during pumping over and punching-down, discouraging a jam-like consistency in the must. The ratio of solids (skins, pips and stalks) to liquid (the juice) has been unbalanced by modern treatments which produce healthier, bigger grapes. Many growers feel that at least some stalks are necessary to redress the balance. Another advantage in placing some of the grapes uncrushed in the vat is that their cool juice is only liberated during punching-down later on, resulting in a slowly progressive fermentation, and helping to keep down the temperature in the vat.

One of the most serious problems in Burgundy at present is that the red wines often lack sufficient acidity. The prime cause, as we have seen, is that too much potassium fertilizer has been well-meaningly, but mindlessly, spread on the vineyards. But it is exacer-bated by other factors, for instance, over-use of a vigorous root-stock, SO_4 (which sucks up potassium), and the use of weed-killers instead of ploughing, causing the vine's root systems to develop on the surface, exactly where the potassium residues are to be found.

This state of affairs causes more growers to de-stalk their bun-ches than used to, in order to eliminate potassium-rich stalks from

---

7 This is the mass of skins, pips and stalks left behind after the wine has been run off. It is later distilled to produce a spirit, itself called *marc*.

the fermentations. Wines of low acidity not only tend to taste flat and heavy, they are more open to bacterial and microbial spoilage, particularly since red Burgundies tend to be low in tannin (which itself plays a beneficial, antiseptic, role).

In the long term, the acidity problem is being resolved by reducing potassium fertilization, by the use of less vigorous root-stocks, and by a return to ploughing, or a combination of all these. In the short term, Burgundian technocrats are calling for permission from the Common Market to add tartaric acid, even in years when they have chaptalized. Many leading growers would support this, for if added in the proper amounts at the start of fermentation the result can be good. Others, however, find that acidifying red Burgundy brings an angularity to the finished wine. Acidifying is often found in California, where the climate, and cultural practices, have made it common. But such acidities rarely blend harmoniously with a wine's natural richness and fruit. You find that you taste the elements separately.

If Brussels gives permission for acidification of Burgundies, in years when they are also sugared, perhaps this will be for a limited period – say five years – so holding a threat over growers, encouraging them to bring their soils back into balance.

Crushing of course often takes place as the bunches are being de-stemmed. Many growers favour partial, rather than total, crushing of the grapes, which helps the fermentation to start promptly, yet also prolongs it, for sugar is released slowly during its course. Some crushing of Pinot Noir grapes is essential to set in motion the process of colour and flavour transfer from skins to juice. Cultured yeasts, sulphur and chaptalization sugar can all be mixed in efficiently if the fruit has been crushed. A good mechanical crusher needs to explode the grape, but not to grind it; if the latter has occurred, astringent or stemmy flavours may be found in the wine.

FERMENTATION AND THE BASICS OF WINE-MAKING

Fermentation is the process by which sugar is decomposed into ethyl alcohol and carbon dioxide, by the action of enzymes in yeasts. Thus grape-juice becomes wine. There are various side-products and the process is extremely complex – fortunately beyond the scope of this book, since it is beyond my comprehension. There are various types of yeast, the most important in winemaking being *saccharomyces ellipsoideus* and *saccharomyces oviformis*, the latter working well in the later stages of fermentation. In order for yeasts to develop and perform their work, various phosphates and nitrogenous compounds must be present, and the temperature needs to reach around 20°C. At over 35°C they suffer, and stop multiplying, which will bring about a halt in fermentation. Lack of oxygen also prevents multiplication of the yeasts, and for this reason aeration of the must is strongly recommended early on in the fermentation. The antiseptic sulphur dioxide (SO_2) is vital to modern wine-making. It eliminates non-productive yeasts, destroys harmful bacteria, and protects the must from oxidation in the early stages.

There are differences in the making of red, rosé and white wines, the most obvious being that the red wines are completely fermented with their skins, and rosés partly fermented with their skins, while white must is first removed from the skins by pressing. I will deal briefly with the different methods (leaving Beaujolais wine-making to its own chapter).

RED WINES

Old vats and new

Red Pinot Noir grapes are brought whole and uncrushed to the vat-house, whose vats, pipes, presses, pumps and implements have previously been carefully cleaned. Much water needs to flow for cleaning and rinsing before the vintage starts.

Vats in Burgundy are traditionally of cylindrical shape, made of iron-hooped oak staves, open at the top. Open-topped enamel-coated metal vats, stainless steel, and cement vats are also seen, stainless steel and metal being the most convenient to cool and warm, for water can either be run down their sides, or pipes for cooling or warming can be snaked around them, top and bottom. The vats need to be open at the top to allow for punching-down (*pigeage*) of the floating mass of grape skins which rises to the surface, buoyed up by carbon dioxide, once juice is liberated from the grapes and fermentation has got under way. We shall return to punching-down, which is vitally important with red Burgundies, below.

Open-top oak vats have some disadvantages: temperature control during fermentation is not easy, they are difficult to disinfect, and there can be alcohol loss through evaporation.

Over the last decade an increasing number of Burgundians have installed slowly moving conveyor-belts, on which the grape bunches are placed, so they may be picked over for unripe or rotted fruit, and mouldy stems. At the same time, leaves or other extraneous matter can be removed prior to vatting. Domaine de la Romanée-Conti was the pioneer, I believe. This practice is best done under cover in the vat-house, and appears entirely beneficial. At some domaines, warm air may be blown over the bunches as they leave the conveyor-belt, driving off moisture without heating the grapes, if these had to picked under, or immediately after, rain.

Two new methods for enriching rain-affected harvests are now under trials in Burgundy. That of the Durafroid company evaporates water from heated Pinot Noir must before fermentation, by running air through it. Some growers are anxious at the idea of their musts being oxidized, but the first results I saw were good. The Entropie method originated, I gather, in the Arabian Gulf, at factories making sea water drinkable by concentration in a vacuum. The must enters a pressurized tunnel, where the vacuum is sufficient for it to boil at between 20°C and 30°C, the evaporated water being discarded. With both methods the sugars are concentrated, and also, to different extents, the acidity, colouring matter and tannins, as the water is driven off. The Entropie method appears to be twice as costly as the Durafroid, but wine-makers may be able to group together to share an investment, if either or both systems receive official approval.

Sulphur dioxide

Sulphur dioxide (SO_2) is the most indispensable product used in wine-making, its use going back to the Romans. Because of its anti-oxidant and anti-microbial roles, it is universal in wine-making, even for organic wine-makers. Individual's tolerances vary, of course. It can cause headaches, and it destroys Vitamin B1. If the sulphur level in a wine is high, you may feel the blood pounding behind your forehead within moments of swallowing. (This is not uncommon.)

Good wine-makers everywhere are trying to reduce the amounts being used. The problem is that it has many beneficial effects; were it to be eliminated, the taste of wines would be irrevocably changed, indeed altered beyond recognition, and for the worse.

Sulphur is an antiseptic, acting against moulds and undesirable microbes which impair quality (lactic and acetic bacteria). Amongst other properties, it blocks wild yeasts, allowing cultivated yeasts to develop, and protects wine from oxygen.

Sulphur dioxide is normally added at the beginning of fermentation, in doses of between 3 and 5 grams per hectolitre in respect of a healthy harvest (up to double these doses if there is rot).

On average 85 per cent of a French person's sulphite consumption originates with wine.[8] The authorities (Office Mondiale de la Santé) have fixed a 'daily admissible dose', which corresponds to half a litre of wine per day for wines containing 100 milligrams per litre of SO_2. Most red wines are well below this; however whites are often above it, particularly dessert wines.[9] For those wishing to reduce sulphite consumption, the obvious route is to go for dry red wines whenever possible.

Temperature and duration of fermentation and vatting

It used to be thought important that fermentation should begin within twenty-four hours or at most two days of vatting, to avoid the risk of oxidation of the must. The Côte d'Or being northerly, it was not unusual to have to heat the must.

There are various methods of doing this, the most common being the plunging of *drapeaux* (which look like portable wall-radiators) into the juice. Hot water or steam is run through them until 20°–22°C is achieved, at least in a section of the vat. Pod-shaped electrical plungers are also effective. Alternatively, part of the must can be heated in a cauldron, then returned to the mass; and fires can be lit to increase the temperature of the vat-room. The first vats

8 Philippe Trollat, *Bourgogne, la revue du vin*, no. 13, BIVB, June 1992.
9 *Vinification: l'expérience bourguignonne, résultats d'essais*, pp. 39–40. The legal maximum levels of SO_2 in wine since 1987 have been 160 mg/l for red wines, 210 mg/l for dry whites and *rosés*, and 260 mg/l for wines with more than 5 g/l residual sugar.

filled are always the tricky ones, and some growers prepare a starter of actively fermenting must (*pied de cuve*). A few rows of vines are picked some days before the main harvest, and the must warmed until fermentation begins, and a great quantity of yeasts have developed. The addition of this fermenting must to the first vats is usually enough to get them going.

Since the mid–1980s, however, many growers have returned to the practice of letting their vats macerate at cool temperature for two, five, seven or sometimes more days, before fermentation begins. Some let this happen naturally, and if it starts after two, or four, days *that* becomes one of the characteristics of the vintage. Others use their cooling equipment to bring down the vat temperature and hold it at a given level, with or without the addition of sulphur dioxide. The respected Vosne-Romanée grower Henri Jayer, for instance, has favoured four or five days of pre-fermentation maceration. Several growers have been influenced by Jayer's approach to reintroduce the cold soak, pre-fermentation maceration which used to be common in Burgundy, when vat-houses were open sheds, temperature control did not exist, and if the weather at vintage time was cool.

Enter Guy Accad, a catalyst of change

Accad has been an important catalyst of change and self-questioning in Burgundy, though many would prefer to cast him in the role of scapegoat. His setting up as an independent Nuits-Saint-Georges-based oenologist in the mid–1970s coincided with the arrival, at prices growers could afford, of cold-making machines which revolutionized what wine-makers could do with their fermenting vats. He initially made his name as a super-doctor for ill wines, then succeeded in persuading those growers who had had cause to be grateful to him (particularly after the tricky 1983 and 1984 vintages) to buy cooling equipment. The summer of 1985 was very hot; 'Equip yourselves with refrigeration', he said, and they did. Suddenly, in a Vosne-Romanée world where such names as Engel or Mongeard-Mugneret had held sway, Confuron-Cotetidot and Pernin-Rossin sprang up from obscurity.

Accad was one of the first to highlight the imbalances in Burgundy's soils, due to excess potassium fertilizing. Some of this fertilizing had been encouraged by government laboratories, so his criticism was not always welcome in university or official circles. He is a determined individualist, often challenging the Establishment view, and Burgundy is certainly large enough, I would imagine, to leave space for such questioning.

Accad admires the fruity, floral aromas of red Burgundy, and seeks to slow down their degradation towards aromas recalling leather, game, mushrooms, humus, or decaying animal matter. He believes that wines will be more elegant if these evolutions happen slowly. By macerating the grape skins, prior to fermentation, in a watery solution (their own juice), rather than in an alcoholic solution (prolonging the maceration after fermentation) he believes greater finesse, more aromas and fewer rustic tannins will be extracted. Certainly, very deep colours are extracted, which helps the wines to sell well. Sulphur (he admits to 8 g/l) and low temperatures are necessary to prevent fermentation starting.

Of course, the wines taste different, in exactly the same way as strawberry jam tastes different if you leave the berries in the fridge to soak overnight, rather than boiling them up to make the jam straight away. With Accad's methods you may get wines with blackcurrant and other piercing red fruit aromas, and personally I prefer the aromas I already know and love in red Burgundies. Accad replies that his methods produce wines closer in taste to those of pre-phylloxera Burgundy, when the vineyards were planted 25,000 vines per hectare, though how this belief can be justified I could not discover.

Some of his finest achievements have perhaps been at estates where matters were sometimes less than brilliant before his arrival (Confuron-Cotetidot, Pernin-Rossin, Batacchi, Lalarme), and particularly in vintages of imperfect maturity, such as 1987. At Grivot's the highly qualified and equally passionate Etienne Grivot no doubt took what he chose of Accad's instructions, rather than following them blindly. The jury is still out over certain Grivot results as at Château de la Tour, Senard and the Clos de Tart. Given Guy Accad's declared objectives it will be only fair to assess the wines, alongside their peers, when they are aged and mature. As growers in the most famous sites increasingly learn to fly with their own wings, perhaps Accad and others will be able to give greater time to Bourgogne *rouges*, Hautes Côtes and other regional wines, where the needs are certainly still being felt.

Punching-down

Punching-down is traditionally, and still in the 1990s commonly, done with the legs and feet, the treaders clinging to the sides of the vat, or to planks stretched across it. If not done by feet, legs and bodies, individuals may stand beside the vat and use a plunger, a long pole with a wide, inverted plastic soup-bowl shape on its end, to achieve a similar effect. Pneumatically- or hydraulically-driven systems can be installed above open vats, mechanizing the process almost completely, without changing the method.

There are several ways of trying to replicate the results achieved by punching-down. Stainless steel vats, either fixed or rotating, containing paddles, or plungers, or spiral coils or ledges exist in several designs, in regular use.

Three or four systems have been developed, which may be seen at Moillard in Nuits, at Bouchard Père, Louis Jadot and the Cave des Hautes Côtes in Beaune, and at Jean-Marc Joblot in Givry. They are described in these sections, in Part Two, where they are installed. J. Faiveley in Nuits-Saint-Georges was one of the first to install pneumatic punching-down, and a new hydraulic system may be seen at the Cave Cooperative of Buxy-Montagny, on the Côte Chalonnaise. These are amongst the best wine-makers to have sought mechanization of the Pinot Noir wine-making process.

Few small estates have taken that route, and many proprietors, even those with oenological degrees and modern installations, remain convinced that humans are the most effective means of achieving the mingling of fermenting must with skins, and the gentle, long-extended extraction of the grape's most precious properties. Only a swimming body can discover overheated pockets in a large vat, and mix them back into the mass. Such beliefs are perfectly tenable in small-scale domaines, of which Burgundy, of course, is full.

If the picking takes place in hot weather it is often necessary to cool the must, and here again the *drapeaux* can be used. The object of macerating the grape skins in the juice is to extract the colouring matter, aromas and tannins. Twice (or more often) a day it is common to push the floating *chapeau* of skins and stalks beneath the surface of the wine, and to break it up so that dissolution of the skins be encouraged. Particularly early on, the must can be pumped over from the bottom of the vat, to encourage the multiplication of the yeasts, which is essential if total transformation of sugar into alcohol is to take place.

Many growers find it desirable or essential to let the fermentation temperature rise to 30–33°C (at some stage, for in this way particularly complex, rich aromas may be achieved.

Drawing off juice

The 1982 red Burgundy harvest was very large. Although healthy, it often proved disappointing, for many wines tasted diluted, owing to high yields. Conscientious growers in subsequent years began to consider drawing off juice, at the start of vatting, so as to increase the proportion of solid matter (grape skins) in the vat. In the process, several made delicious *rosés de Pinot Noir*, which, although they could not be sold at First Growth prices, made their friends very happy. Drawing off juice is a method to be used if pruning has been too generous, if bunch-thinning was insufficient in the summer, or if late rains cause the juice in the grapes to increase in volume. As more high-producing clones come into full production it is likely to be more widely necessary.[10]

Local or cultured yeasts

Until the 1970s the vast majority of Burgundy wine-makers relied on the native wild yeasts present in vineyards and vat-houses for their fermentations. This had two main shortcomings: fermentation could be slow to start, and the final transformation of sugars (when high alcohol levels start to inhibit yeast activity) could be very difficult. Also, if not controlled by sufficient sulphur, wild yeasts such as *s. brettanomyces* or *s. dekkera* could bring undesirable aromas.

In 1988 it was estimated that a mere 30 per cent of French wines were vinified in the presence of selected, dried active yeasts. The practice began to spread in Burgundy during the 1980s, strains being chosen for their ability to transform sugar efficiently, to multiply rapidly, and to survive in alcohol. There are many occasions when adding yeasts is beneficial, for instance in cold or rainy years,

10 The BIVB's *Vinification: l'experience bourguignonne*, pp. 47–9, sets out the interesting results of recent research into drawing off juice.

when yeast populations may be insufficient. If grapes have been attacked by grey rot, toxins may be present which are inimical to yeasts. Certain yeast strains produce more deeply-coloured wines, or certain aromas. Special yeasts are appropriate for making Crémant de Bourgogne, and others suit certain grape-types. For instance different ones would be appropriate for Sauvignon de Saint-Bris and Bourgogne Irancy.

Some yeast strains were retained because they provided a specific aromatic compound. For instance, strain 71B synthesizes amyl acetate (a substance which recalls the aroma of bananas) in great quantity. This can be of interest for Beaujolais Nouveau, which will be drunk young. Some consumers, understandably, object to this character, so a vat so treated may need to be blended with others where, for instance, yeast L 2056 (which originated in the Côtes du Rhône) is used. This yeast helps colour extraction, giving complex, tannic wines which reflect the character of the grape. By 1993, the BIVB was able to itemize thirty different yeast strains, some appropriate for getting the fermentation going, some for restarting a stopped vat, or for other specific objects. Most go by numbers, but there is a Cocktail Bouchard, and U. C. Davis has selected another, called Killer Montrachet.

Fearing that the individual character of their wines might be prejudiced by commercial yeast cultures from outside the area, Burgundians had begun a research project in 1985 to identify the best local yeasts. The laboratories of Dijon, Beaune and Mâcon were all involved, and over 1,000 different strains isolated and multiplied, from sites all over Burgundy.

By May 1988, it could be reported that four yeasts had been identified for further research, with one seeming exceptional.[11] The researchers noted that most of the indigenous flora had given very irregular results, and also that wines produced with commercial yeast strains performed well in tasting tests.

In 1992 one white yeast and two reds were released for use. The white, called Bourgoblanc, originated in the Mâconnais, the two reds (Bourgorouge 1 and 2) both originated in Aloxe-Corton. Bourgoblanc is described as an efficient producer of alcohol, which carries on working well at high levels, and gives wines which taste fat,

11 M. Feuillat and M. Obisanya, 'Rapport d'activities de recherche et d'expérimentation, commission 'Recherche, Progrès et Qualité', FIVB

round, powerful, balanced and long. Bourgorouge 1 is apt for deep coloured wines with tannic structures. It regularly gave better-coloured wines than the control samples, in its tests. Bourgorouge 2 is more suitable for supple, early-maturing red wines, and seems destined for regional Pinots and Gamays.

The new yeasts will certainly be very useful in rotten harvests, when doses of SO_2 necessary for antiseptic purposes tend to knock out indigenous yeasts, giving rise to the need for cultured yeasts. And certainly for regional and village wines one imagines they will be of very great benefit.

But there are big question marks. Will cultured yeasts wipe out the natives? And to what extent may the use of one white, and one red yeast for the Côte d'Or's First Growths and Great Growths gum up their site-specific originalities?

Many of the finest growers believe cultures are pollution, and are sticking to their indigenous yeasts. They do not mind sacrificing a bit of alcoholic strength in order to sleep soundly, without worries of having diluted or diverted their wines' time-honoured specificity.

By the turn of the century, however, when more conclusions can be drawn, and perhaps more yeasts have been released, one can imagine two or three cultured yeasts for red wines on the Côte de Nuits, and two or three more for different villages of the Côte de Beaune and for Mercurey, and that as the choices expand, so top growers may use them more often.

Length of vatting time

During the 1960s and 1970s red Burgundy was often criticized for being light in colour, and for having lost its ability to improve with age. Trade was not always buoyant, and growers and merchants probably saw fast turnover red Burgundies as one way out of the problems of high interest rates, expensive stock-holding, and sluggish trade.

At the Station Oenologique in Beaune, Director Max Léglise stated, on the subject of short vatting periods of five to six days, 'This question, which in the past caused great discussions, is a false problem . . . one has recently been able to prove by simple experiment that an excessive length of vatting time for a harvest where the stalks have been removed brings no extra enrichment to the wine in the way of body or colour.'

All oenologists and growers do not agree with this, however. For instance, if one turns to Dr Emile Peynaud (admittedly a Bordeaux man, but one respected far beyond the borders of the Gironde) one learns something very different. In his book on wine-making for the layman, *Connaissance et travail du vin*,[12] he explains that the colour of red wines, and a large part of their savour, comes from the class of aromatic organic substances known as phenolic compounds, which are found in the skins, pips and stalks of the grape. There are two main types: the anthocyanins (or red colouring matter) and the tannins. The former pass from the skins into the must rapidly during the first three or four days of vatting if the grapes are squashed and the must is agitated. Thereafter the intensity of colour of the wine can actually diminish as the anthocyanins fix themselves to the pips or stalks. The tannins are dissolved into the liquid at a regular rate throughout the maceration, and it is they which constitute the colouring matter in a fine wine when the anthocyanins have virtually disappeared after two or three years' ageing.

M. Peynaud concludes,

The maturation, good conservation and colour intensity of *vins de garde* require sufficient concentrations of tannins. For, after several months or years, the colour of a wine no longer corresponds to the presence of anthocyanins found in the grape – they have for the most part disappeared – but to that of tannins. In addition, the anthocyanins have little savour. The quantity of tannins decides the sapidity and the longevity. For all wines which get their qualities from a certain degree of ageing, the success of a vinification is based on a compromise between the necessity of guaranteeing them a good richness in tannins and the contrary necessity of assuring them a certain suppleness when they are young at the moment when habitually they are judged.

There is a case for some red Burgundy to be vinified to be drunk young: some regional and village *appellations*, sometimes the wines of immature or rot-affected, light vintages; but longer vinifications have come back into fashion for those wines selling for the highest

12 Dunod, Paris, 1971.

prices, where a certain depth of colour, with richness, complexity and length of flavour are, quite reasonably, expected.

The final stages of red-wine-making are the running-off of the wine and the pressing of the skins and pips. The most unpleasant and tiresome activity of the harvest – the forking out of grape skins from a vat laden with CO_2 and alcohol fumes – is now being done on the larger estates by modern pumps which can handle solids and liquids together. The first pressing is almost always included with the free-run juice (*vin de goutte*). Subsequent pressings should be kept apart if they have unpleasant characteristics – often the case when grey rot is common.

The malolactic fermentation

The malolactic fermentation (transformation, by the action of bacteria, of malic acid into lactic acid) is now encouraged by maintaining the temperature of the new-wine cellar near to 18°C, not racking the wine off its lees, and sometimes by inoculating with lactic bacteria. This means that it is left on the deposit of dead yeast cells, bacteria and particles of grape skin which form the sediment at the bottom of barrel or vat. The transformation of malic acid into lactic acid is positively sought for red wines, as it brings about a softening of the wine; also, if not encouraged when the wine is young, there is a danger it will take place after bottling, making the wine gassy and out of condition. However, it is capricious, and some wines take a year or more to complete it.

WHITE WINES

White Burgundies are dry wines, the sugars fermented right out of them, down to the last unfermentable (and from a tasting point of view imperceptible) one or two grams per litre. In the Burgundian wine culture it is considered sloppy wine-making to market white wines with residual sugar. The challenge is to achieve elegantly rich fruit, aroma, flavour and texture, with a dry finish, and for each wine to sing out its geographical origin. The makers of New World Chardonnays who rely on residual sugars for their final effects – and there are many – are playing with an oddly shaped ball, in a different game.

In white-wine-making, complete cleanliness is even more important than with red wines. The whites generally have a higher acidity and are more corrosive, particularly after the addition of SO_2.

The grapes are brought whole to the vat-house, and there pressed rapidly, great care being taken to minimize oxidation of grapes and juice. Screw presses and pneumatic presses have now almost entirely replaced basket presses in which pressure was applied by a hydraulically powered ram. Modern presses have various programmes, so pressure, duration of pressing, and number of times the cake is split up and re-pressed can all be varied by the operator.

In years when grey rot has attacked, the different pressings should be kept separate, as the second and third are likely to contaminate otherwise clean-tasting must. Sulphur dioxide is added. As we have seen, this is an antiseptic which kills bacteria, eliminates unwanted wild yeasts, and protects the juice from oxygen, so preventing browning.

Fine aromas may be encouraged if solid matter in the must is allowed to settle in vat prior to fermentation. Particularly in years of rot, or when the vintage takes place in muddy conditions, it is wise to allow a twelve-hour settling or *débourbage* in vat, before the must begins to ferment. This permits mineral impurities and particles of grape skin or dirt to sink to the bottom of the vat, whence the must is racked off. The addition of selected yeast will then be advisable.

In Chablis, the Mâconnais, and in respect of Aligotés and minor Chardonnays from regional *appellations* of central Burgundy, fermentation often takes place in tank or vat (which may be wooden tuns, glass-lined cement, stainless steel, or enamel-lined metal). Such wines may see no small-barrel-ageing at all. Temperature control is vital, or the contents of a vat may heat up beyond the desirable 15–20°C levels, with loss of fruity and floral aromas.

The greatest richness, complexity of fruit and length of flavour in white Burgundies is achieved when fermentation takes place in oak barrels, the standard capacity in Burgundy being 228 litres. The temperature will be that of the cellar itself – 15°C and upwards.

The wines can go on fermenting throughout the winter, and often take a year to finish their malolactic fermentations; they will be left unracked until the process is complete.

A happy medium must be found for filling the barrel: too full, and the yeast will not develop; too empty, and the must may oxidize. Most of the best growers rouse their casks periodically with stainless steel stirrers, to mix up the yeast solids (known as lees) which have fallen to the bottom, for three to six months after the harvest.

It is widely recognized on the Côte de Meursault, and in most wine regions round the world specializing in Chardonnays, that more softened, and better integrated, oak flavours are obtained when wine is fermented from the start in oak barrels, than if it is fermented in vat and then aged in barrel. Nevertheless in Burgundy much Pouilly-Fuissé from the best sites, many top Chablis, many decent Chalonnais whites, and even certain Côte de Beaune whites (Bonneau du Martray's Corton-Charlemagne, Latour-Giraud's Meursault Genevrières and several Bouchard Père *appellations* spring to mind) are either partly, or totally, fermented in tank before being barrelled for storing. This Burgundian part-vat, part-barrel habit is traditional (whatever that means) but I wonder if it is always appropriate in today's markets, given the prices Burgundians prefer to charge?

A number of substances in the oak are directly absorbed into the wine and have fundamental influence on its taste and aromas. Indeed, as Larry Brooks and Mel Knox have pointed out,[13] of the ten odour categories into which Emile Peynaud divides wine aromas, half can be directly or indirectly linked to barrels. Without going deeply into the flavour chemistry of oak, a coconut-like aroma can be obtained from barrels, dependent on how much they were toasted over the flames used to bend its staves when it was made; vanillin aromas are also dependent on toasting, as also on how long the wood was open-air seasoned prior to the barrel being manufactured. Other wood compounds impart a spice-like character, sometimes described as clove or carnation; this too is dependent on seasoning the wood. Essential oils, and 'furfurals' (produced from toasting wood sugars) bring other flavours, perhaps reminiscent of bitter almond or caramel, or subtly contributing to, or acting on, existing tastes. Tannins in the wood bring colour and astringency, and vitally protect the wine from oxidation. Some of the yeasts which are transforming sugar into alcohol also act on the wood-derived compounds to transform their flavours. Knox gives

13 *Flavors and Chemistry of Wine Barrels*, Knox-Fax Industrial Publications, San Francisco, 1992.

as an example bitter-flavoured furfurals, which 'are transformed by the yeasts into compounds which have a range of flavour from smoked meat to leather'. Bacteria can be similarly influential; 'in the case of white wines the barrel contributes compounds that the bacteria can transform from relatively flavourless preceptors to highly aromatic ones in the smoke, clove and coffee groups.'

While some Burgundian wine-makers have gone into the influence of oak on the character of their wines in detail, and some habitually age staves in their back gardens, or at their chosen coopers, to ensure they have the requisite open-air seasoning, it seems to me that too little care is given in Burgundy to oak grain width, oak stave ageing under the rain and wind, oak origin, and oak toasting. Burgundians like to think that *terroir* gives their wines their flavour – when often it is *quercus sessiflora*, or *quercus robur* – the sessile or the pedunculate European oaks which flourish in central France, in the Vosges, the Cher and in Burgundy itself. And not always the good characters we love, either, for improperly weathered staves, inappropriately matched to the wine they contain, split from broad-grained, fast-grown trunks, can have devastating effects on the Chardonnay's subtleties. Too many Burgundians have never ventured into an oak forest, never watched a stave-splitter at work, never pored over grain widths, and never chosen their toasts. At great cost, they put blind faith in their cooper, or buy from a local man without questioning.

The temperature and humidity of the cellar or store where the white wine lies in barrel are of crucial importance, but it is only since the mid-1980s that air-conditioning and humidification have slowly started to spread to the best domaines. Puligny (where there are no cellars, because of the high water table) was the first to realize what had been happening in hot summers. Next door, in Meursault, growers still sometimes speak admiringly of the deep, cool, damp cellars at Comte Lafon, without realizing that a not-very-great-investment would permit them to get quite close to recreating those conditions.

As Halliday and Johnson have written,[14] in France 'The emphasis has always been placed on *terroir*, which has justified a basically fatalistic approach to grape-growing and wine-making.'

14 *The Art and Science of Wine.*

Skin contact

Some research has been undertaken into the benefits, or not, of juice and skin contact for white Burgundies. Chardonnay is a grape variety which is only slenderly aromatic, its grapey character being weakly expressed, compared for instance to Sauvignon *blanc* or Gewürztraminer. If the skins are left in contact with the pressed juice, so the theory grows, a greater quantity of flavours will be extracted and a more robust, fuller wine produced.

The traditional approach, which still holds good for the best villages like Chassagne or Meursault, is to separate juice from skins as fast as possible. These wines need vinification in barrel, and contact with the lees over many months to achieve their flavours and mouth-feel.

For regional Chardonnays (Mâcon-Villages or Bourgogne *blanc*, for instance) skin contact lasting 12–16 hours can be beneficial.[15] It can personalize them and add value. Such wines are made for youthful drinking, so the downside of macerating juice with skins – that such wines can age disappointingly with bitter tannins, developing undesirable aromas, having shown appealingly while young – is not the major factor.

Mâcon-Villages, Chablis and Bourgogne *blanc* are often machine-harvested today, which means that grapes that have been plucked off their stems soak in their juice from fields to vat-house. Skin contact here comes automatically.

It can be counter-productive if you macerate underripe grapes (it will give aromas of green vegetation) or rotten grapes (something rather worse!). You often get leafy, vegetal aromas in wines from famous, hot-summer vintages for the simple reason that yields were too high; so the fruit was unripe when picked.

A beneficial side-effect of macerating on the skins is that the malolactic fermentations start and finish more speedily than for traditionally made wines. There is little point oak-ageing such a wine; the new oak character would subdue the beneficial skin-contact character.

The French have come to skin contact a decade or so behind some of the best New World white-wine-makers. Denis Dubour-

15 Laboratoire de Biochimie Alimentaire (Ecole Nationale d'Ingénieurs des Travaux Agricoles de Dijon), FIVB, June 1989, and BIVB's *Vinification: l'expérience bourguignonne*.

dieu in Bordeaux, for instance, was still recommending it at a time when David Ramey in Sonoma was moving on, abandoning the idea. But there is still plenty of room for research and discussion, and of course for a method to work in Cadillac, Gironde, which bombs in California . . .

ROSÉ WINES

There are two types of *rosé* wine, the less common being *vin gris*. This is made from red grapes which are pressed immediately and give a pale grey-pink wine, when vinified away from the skins. True *rosés* are also made from red grapes, the skins being allowed to macerate a day or two in the must before this is drawn and they are pressed. Choosing the moment to draw off the vat to give the aromas and exact *rosé* tint required is a delicate decision. Pale *rosés* may stay as little as 3–6 hours on the skins, deeper coloured wines up to 24 hours. Vinification then proceeds as for a white wine.

Rosés represent only a tiny proportion of Burgundian production, the most famous being Marsannay *Rosé*. There is also Mâcon, Beaujolais, Bourgogne, Bourgogne Passe-Tout-Grains and Bourgogne Grand Ordinaire.

SPARKLING WINES

Although there were some good ones, Sparkling Burgundy (Bourgogne Mousseux) used often to be made from the produce of underripe grapes and low quality fruit, the sparkling process serving to disguise wine-making faults and excessive acidity. Base wines used to be the regional *appellations*, Bourgogne Aligoté and Bourgogne Grand Ordinaire, the latter being mainly made from Côte d'Or Gamays and Sacy grapes from the Yonne. Thirty per cent of noble grapes (Chardonnay, Pinot) had to be used in the *cuvées*, which in the old days could be white, *rosé* or red. Today, Bourgogne Mousseux may only be red, and it must have a minimum of 30 per cent Pinot, or Gamay from the *crus* of the Beaujolais (César and Tressot are permitted from the Yonne), the balance being other Gamays. But its production is minimal.

A new *appellation*, Crémant de Bourgogne, was created in 1975, imposing higher standards than previously. Discipline begins in the vines, where the grapes must be hand-picked before complete maturity, when their potential alcohol has reached 8°. They must be taken, uncrushed, to the press-house in perforated containers; any free-running juice (which could oxidize) slips through the holes and is lost. In order to obtain one hectolitre of juice, 150 kg of grapes must be used, in contrast to Bourgogne Mousseux, where 130 kg may be pressed to yield a hectolitre. For Crémant de Bourgogne at least 30 per cent of the blend must come from one, or a combination, of these 'first category' grapes: Pinot Noir, Pinot Gris, Pinot Blanc and Chardonnay, the balance coming from 'second category' grapes: Gamay, Sacy and Melon. In the Yonne the Sacy, which used to be widely planted, is admitted as a 'first category' grape, so long as it does not constitute more than 50 per cent of the final blend. The base wine must be tasted by a commission, and not bottled for its second fermentation until after the 1 January following the harvest. Crémant de Bourgogne must then age at least nine months on its lees, at the end of which the same commission must taste and pass the finished product. These controls have undoubtedly raised Crémant de Bourgogne to quality levels which allow it to challenge, and indeed defeat, inferior Champagnes.

The sparkle is obtained by adding a dose of sugar and yeast to the wine when it is bottled. A secondary fermentation takes place in bottle, and since the carbon dioxide cannot escape, it dissolves into the wine. The Champagne process of *remuage* and *dégorgement* is then needed to eliminate the sediment of dead yeast cells which have formed during the fermentation. Over a period of two to three months, the bottles are tipped upside down into a vertical position, being shaken every other day, so that the sediment slips down on to the cork. The necks of the bottles are then passed through a bath of brine at lower than freezing temperature, so a bullet of frozen wine forms in the bottle-neck. When the cork is removed, the pressure inside the bottle expels bullet and sediment. The bottles are then topped up, their sweetness is adjusted, and they are re-corked. After a period they are ready to be drunk.

Burgundians know very well what has sometimes been going on over the border in the Aube, the southernmost section of the Champagne wine-field, only a few kilometres away from Châtillon in northern Burgundy: yields of over 100 hl/ha. – sometimes 120 hl/ha. – with lorries moving grapes, under cover of night, from the

Aube to the Marne, or vice versa, depending on where the yields are short. A car goes in front, and one behind, to watch out for Customs patrols. There are some very wealthy farmers in the Aube, sellers of grapes, not wine-makers, living a life of relative ease: pruning, treatments, harvest; it doesn't add up to much more than two or three months' work, if you are highly mechanized, the philosophy being *Je ne cultive pas de la vigne pour faire des feuilles* (I'm not tending vineyards in order to produce leaves). This sort of exaggeration has contributed to bringing Champagne's reputation downwards, and Crémant de Bourgogne is one of the wines to be benefiting.

Nearly five million bottles of Crémant de Bourgogne were sold during 1991, France accounting for nearly three-quarters of this total, the United Kingdom being the leading export market. On both sides of the Channel Crémant is mainly drunk in people's homes (rather than in bars, hotels or restaurants). There are many excellent value, well-made, correctly aged, celebratory bottles to choose from.

DEALING WITH A POOR HARVEST

The ability to vinify off-years is one of the aspects of Burgundy that has most changed since the late 1970s. And the attitude to off-vintages. It is a pity growers so rarely reflect the light years by lightening their prices, but very few people just give up now, certainly not if they are bottling themselves.

There used to be three main schools of thought about how to deal with red grapes when a poor summer had failed to develop their colour cells fully, or when grey rot had attacked them.

A large proportion of vignerons used to believe that producing acceptable wine from rotten or unripe grapes was impossible, saying, 'On ne peut pas faire du vin vivant avec des raisins morts'. All one could do was chaptalize strongly and vat for a brief period, so that the taste of rot did not get into the wine. If the result lacked colour, at least one's neighbour's was no better. And what was a *négociant* for, anyway?

In the early 1970s Monsieur Léglise at the Station Oenologique recommended a more positive approach. He suggested that the rotten bunches be dipped for three minutes into grape-must pre-

heated to 80°C, so that colour extraction from the skins be acceler-
ated. Taken to extremes, this could involve the installation of costly
heating and cooling apparatus as at Domaine Drouhin-Laroze
(q.v.); however, many estates and merchants economized by using
double-wall, steam-heated copper basins to heat part or all of the
must.

In the late 1970s, it seemed likely that the use of copper basins
would spread. Many wine-makers with high ideals believed that
they could be used with moderation on, say, one-third of the harvest in an off-year; and that colour was gained without undue loss
of character.

However, there was another successful approach to off-vintage
wine-making which did not involve must-heating. It worked on the
principle that rotten grapes should be removed by careful sorting,
either to be left in the vineyard or vinified apart. The Pousse d'Or
estate in Volnay, for instance, was one of the first to extract mouldy
red grapes, press them, sulphur and fine the resultant must, and
then add back small portions (if free of any taint of rot) later.
It made many successful off-vintage *cuvées* from the mid–1960s
onwards, which sold happily under *Premier Cru* labels.

This method has carried the day, allied with improved techniques
of grey rot prevention and protection in the vineyards. But from
1985 to 1993 Burgundy has been spared a disastrous year such as
1963 or 1968. Growers hold their breaths for a really wet summer
or autumn.

Technical research was coming to similar conclusions, in Burgundy and elsewhere. 'Eliminating rotten grapes at the moment of
picking is still the only method which allows one to maintain the
potential quality, for wine-making purposes, of the healthy part of
the harvest', said Denis Dubourdieu (a leading Bordeaux research
scientist and wine-maker),[16] speaking to Burgundians in Nolay in
1990.

His audience, in the main, agreed, but it is far more easily said
than done. Partly rotten grapes will almost inevitably slip through
the controls. When there is rot in the harvest, particular care needs
to be taken not to bruise or damage grapes during transport or
mechanical pressing of the bunches. If this is neglected, the wine

16 Denis Dubourdieu, *Modification de la composition des mouts par botrytis
cinerea*, Institut d'Oenologie, Université de Bordeaux II, BIVB, Nolay, 1990.

may prove difficult to filter. De-stalking may be reduced, so that a higher concentration of tannins may help protect wines from oxidasic casse.

Tastes of rot or mould may be minimized by a speedy start to fermentation (with yeast cultures) and possibly a bentonite or casein fining during fermentation (for white wines) or just after it (for reds). Both fining agents can absorb certain undesirable odours.

Letting white wine musts settle and fall bright is desirable, but difficult, so a gelatine and silica-gel fining may be advisable, to help sedimentation. Products such as thiamine, glucanase and ascorbic acid may be added, to reduce the need for sulphur dioxide, to help filtrability, and to prevent oxidation. During red wine fermentation one may try to avoid grape maceration at highish temperatures.

Where these steps are not taken, or are ineffective, odours and tastes which reduce the wine quality and typicity are common. Fruity and floral aromas will be absent, as will freshness and finesse. A plummy smell may develop, or fungal or iodine aromas; also vinegariness, oxidation, dry mushroom, mouldiness. When such wines age, they take on heavy notes, honeyed, camphorous, earthy.

Such wines are rarely found under the labels of those domaines or *négociants* we all associate with the *crème de la crème* of Burgundy. The wines are handled by second division *négociants*, blended, assembled, fined, filtered and maybe refrigerated or pasteurized in attempts to remove the offending characteristics. They end up tasting bland and neutral, vaguely Pinot-perfumed but without quality, without the rush of flavour, freshness and individuality one expects (given the price). These are *sous-seuil* wines, of course, which should really be withdrawn from commerce. At the very least, they should be declassified from *Grand* or *Premier Cru* status. But it would need the Burgundians themselves to wish for this.

TERROIR OBSESSION

Burgundians are often so obsessed by their *terroirs* that they sometimes forget to make their wines delicious. Where are the growers who pursue, in little-known villages, on less-favoured sites, or in areas making regional *appellations*, that seductive, silky texture which only Pinot Noir – of all the vine-types in the world – can give, when skilfully vinified? We shall meet some in Part Two, but there are not enough. Many are caught by outmoded snobbisms in an earth-bound trap which has them groping for flavours which relate to their second-division soils. Or they are emphasizing tannins and structure, so they can pretend that their wines will develop into respectably fine old bottles, once sufficiently aged.

In Beaujolais, it is the opposite. They have been pursuing deliciousness and supple drinking so determinedly for twenty years that many have lost track of their *terroirs* completely. Chiroubles can be taken for Beaujolais-Villages, Moulin à Vent can be made for early drinking, and Morgon has often completely lost that individuality which used to make tasters declare *'Ça morgonne!'*

TENDING

Wine-making is a round-the-clock job. The well-equipped vat-room which is run by someone who combines understanding of the processes involved with adaptability to the differing conditions of each vintage will regularly produce acceptable, maybe even excellent, young wine. But the story does not end there. For a further six to twenty-four months the wine must be watched and tended before it can be bottled. This *élevage* requires common sense and meticulous attention to detail, more than technical know-how and flair.

Wine deteriorates from contact with the air and from microbe attacks. The first is prevented by regular topping-up of containers, the second by decanting or racking clean wine away from the lees which fall to the bottom of barrel or vat, by the use of an antiseptic such as sulphur dioxide, and by control of cellar temperatures.

The ideal temperature for the storage of wine is 12°C, a variation of 2°C in either direction being tolerable. Underground cellars supply such conditions, and when wines are stored above ground (as for instance at Puligny where the water-table is high) great care must be taken to avoid temperature fluctuations. Where wines are kept in wood, the humidity of the air should be near to saturation point if evaporation is to be minimized. The humidity of Burgundy's cellars, cut into the limestone, is usually satisfactory.

The most elementary danger to wine is *piqûre*, vinegariness. A whiff of vinegar as one enters is a sure sign of a badly run cellar, that somewhere will be found a leaking stave or barrel-head, an unrinsed pipe, or a small stagnant pool of wine left over from a racking-operation. *Pour faire du bon vin, il faut utiliser beaucoup d'eau* (to make good wine, you must use a lot of water) goes the old saying, and every cellar should have a tap. Evaporation of wine stored in cask varies (depending on the temperature, humidity, quality and thickness of the wood, and alcoholic degree) from half a glass to a bottle per week. It is 1 per cent per year in a humid cellar, 4–5 per cent above ground. E. Peynaud[17] affirms that out of a hundred litres of new wine, only ninety litres are left at the moment of bottling.

The law states that topping-up should be done with the same wine, or one of a superior *appellation*. It is a law which is neither respected nor enforced, and indeed, in the cellars of the Côte d'Or (whether grower or *négociant*) there is such a multitude of *appellations* it is a practical impossibility. If I were a Côte d'Or grower with a dozen *appellations* I guess I would top up my reds with a decent, clean-flavoured Pinot of similar age. If I had three or four *Premiers Crus* or *Grands Crus* I would hope to top them up with a wine of similar stature. But identical geographical origin into each would I think be unachievable, and to expect it as hopeless a quest as asking a much-*toqued* chef whether he had someone verify if the bees indeed restricted themselves to firtree buds when gathering the honey which went into his dish of *Canette de Bresse laquée au miel de bourgeons de sapin au serpolet et navets confits*.

In the bad old days, some merchants used to top up with the cheapest wine in the cellar, and sometimes this was not even an *appellation contrôlée* wine. It was a powerful, deep-coloured *vin de consommation courante*, whose influence on the *cuvée* was perceptible after the wine was bottled. Imagine – 10 per cent of topping-up wine was *bound* to leave a mark, if it was deep-coloured, or from a strong-tasting grape-type other than Pinot.

This topping-up factor remains a crux today, with *négociants* who buy heavily cropped, light-coloured Pinots in vintages of imperfect maturity. When, today, I put my nose into a red wine with a Burgundian label and am whisked straight southwards towards the Mediterranean (it still happens, though certainly less often than it used to) my thoughts immediately go to the contents of the

17 *Connaissance et travail du vin.*

négociant's stainless steel topping-up can. It looks like a garden watering-can with a long spout, and the topping-up wine inside it is still sometimes responsible for a *négociant*'s identifiable house style.

One of the best places to train one's nose to pick up this character is pre-sale tastings of old Burgundies coming up for auction, where there can be a rich harvest from ancient *négociant* bottlings.

Barrel ageing

We first considered new oak barrels in the section relating to white-wine-making. With red wine ageing, the use of new oak is equally influential, and the spread of the use of new oak barrels one of the most marked developments in Burgundy since the early 1980s. Too much new oak, or the wrong sort, makes wine banal and standard-izes it, Burgundians are concluding,[18] but its appropriate use is here to stay.

Traditionally in Burgundy a proportion of new barrels would be acquired as old ones wore out, started to weep or could no longer be repaired. This barely perceptible 'new oak' character (coming from perhaps 15 per cent new barrels) provided a subtle, discreet, additional aroma dimension. If we were lucky, that is, and the wine was not damaged by the 85 per cent ancient, sometimes damaged, vinegary or mouldy barrels which tradition revered . . .

Tests in Burgundy organized by René Naudin of ITV Beaune in the late 1970s showed that tight-grained oaks from Tronçais, Vosges and Burgundy (Mercurey and Cîteaux) rated more highly than loose-grained Limousin (whose aromas could be one-dimen-sional, with a bitter finish). Oaks from Tronçais and Vosges left their mark on wines quite quickly (6–8 months), whereas oaks of Burgundian or Limousin origins took longer to have effect. After three years bottle age, however, the differences due to varying oak origins were much reduced. In cases where wines had been aged in metal casks, in old oak, or in old oak repaired with some new staves, the results were always inferior to the wines aged in new wood.

Within a given forest, oak of tight, medium and wide grain (corresponding to the annual growth rings in the trunk) may be produced. The width of the grain depends on the soil and altitude,

18 *Bourgogne, la revue du vin*, No. 18, December 1992.

on the species of tree itself, and on whether it is growing in the middle, or at the edges of the wood. R. Naudin conducted further tests in the late 1980s, to investigate whether grain-type or forest origin was the more important factor in barrel-ageing wine.[19] He concluded that forests have their own specific taste characteristics, and that each grain-type has a different effect during barrel-ageing.

Broadly speaking, fine-grained oak is greatly to be preferred to coarse-grained for the finesse of the aromas it gives. The thicker the annual rings, the less it will be liked as a barrel stave. This fact greatly simplifies the barrel-buying task, for it does not take much practice to be able to pick out fine-grained from coarse-grained barrel staves. A barrel can be assessed in seconds by examining the stave-ends carefully. A proportion of coarse-grained staves are acceptable; they bring vanilla aromas, complementing the tight-grained's spicy backbone.

Just as important as the geographical origin and the width of the oak grain is the method of drying the staves, and the way they are made up into barrels, being heated and toasted in the process.

The drying of the oak is crucial, for the 70 per cent residual humidity of the wood at the moment the tree is felled needs to fall to around 15 per cent when the barrel is made. A month in a drying room at a temperature of 40–60°C will de-humidify the wood, but wines then aged in such wood may have a strong, tannic aftertaste. Eighteen to thirty-six months of natural drying in the open air produces a quite different result, and improves the taste of wines which subsequently come into contact with it. The French researcher N. Vivas has shown that chemical constituents such as tannin, cellulose and lignin are transformed by the action of the enzymes in the wood, and those secreted by mould, this being dependant on the ultra-violet sun-rays, rainfall, and seasonal temperature changes.[20] Ideally, French oak should be weathered for one year for every 10 mm of stave thickness. Burgundy barrel staves are nearly 30 mm thick, compared to 20 mm for Bordeaux *barriques*. One may speculate that the reason for this difference is that Pinot

19 Vincent Bouchard, 'Burgundy study with new oak', International Oak Symposium, San Francisco State University, June 1993.
20 Nicolas Vivas, Research-Oenologist Tonnellerie Demptos, 'The phenomena of oxidoreduction related to wood ageing', Libourne-Montagne Agricultural and Viticultural College seminar, June 1992.

Noir, which lacks the tannic structure of the Bordeaux red grapes, benefits from less oxygen absorption during its ageing.

Research continues in the open air, in the rain and the wind, to establish the importance of weathering. If you look at the ground under the tall stacks of staves in a barrel-maker's wood-park, you see deep, dark brown stains on the gravel. These appear to be the wood tannins washed out of the oak by months, sometimes years, of seasoning under the elements. However, an Australian researcher, Mark Sefton,[21] suggests that the reactions are much more complicated than has been thought, and that seasoning concentrates some of the oak-wood components, subsequently influencing wine flavour. One French cooper, Boutes, sometimes weathers his oak staves by submerging them under water, so I am told.

The dense structure of oak wood, with its minute pores, allows the diffusion of tiny doses of oxygen into wine, bringing about its slow maturation in barrel. At the same time, tannins and other products are ceded from the wood. These may be aggressive and hard-tasting if the wood is immature or half-dried, but if the tannins are mature they are like a herb or spice in the hands of a good cook – entirely beneficial to flavour. And as we saw with white wines, various extractable components of the wood are dissolved into the wine, giving some recognizable aromas: clove, carnation, coconut, undergrowth, vanilla, caramel, smokyness.

Whether the staves are sawn or split in the traditional way is also a major factor. Sawing is thought to expose more grains, so yielding more raw tannins to the wine, and tasters prefer wine from split-wood barrels. The vast majority of French oak is split, so that the shaped staves follow the grain of the wood, thus also minimizing leaks. However, sawing is less labour-intensive, and yields about twice as many staves from each trunk. A corner-cutting cooper might include sawn staves in what purports to be a barrel made from split ones.

When the barrels are put together, the method used to curve the staves is important, the use of steam having a neutral influence, that of flames bringing a more aromatic, vanilla note – indeed

21 M. A. Sefton, I. L. Francis, K. F. Pocock, P. J. Williams, 'Influence of seasoning on the sensory characteristics and composition of oak extracts', Australian Wine Research Institute, International Oak Symposium, San Francisco State University, June 1993.

caramelized, if the barrel is held over the fire for too long, or smoky, if a lid is left on during heating. The Beaujolais cooper Dargaud & Jaegle offers shaping in cauldrons of boiling water, I understand, and Seguin-Moreau of Cognac are developing an automatically-controlled process for barrel-toasting which should bring greater consistency.[22] 'The level of toast . . . has profound flavour effects', writes Mel Knox,[23] 'the more slowly this is done the better it is for both flavour and structure. A deep medium toast produces the most desirable character for most woods, but there is variation in effect depending on their geographic origin.' The other crucial point about toasting is that the darkened, sometimes charred and blistered wood provides a buffer between the alcohol in the wine and the wood tannins. Red Burgundies aged in lightly toasted barrels may be pleasingly fruity, but quite tannic in the after-taste; the same wine in medium toasted barrels will be less tannic, but may have aromas of vanilla and coffee; in a heavy toast barrel there may be aromas of (Knox again) roasted coffee beans, toasted bread, ginger, nutmeg, and smoked meats.

It is possible to reproduce some of these aromas by submerging a plastic tray, holding freshly toasted, smoothly-planed oak staves, within a vat – so taking the 'barrel' to the wine, rather than vice versa. Or indeed by suspending a sack of toasted oak chips in a volume of wine. 'Chips are one of the cleanest ways to get a decent oak flavour into bulk wine,' stated Phil Burton of Barrel Builders, St Helena, Napa, at a San Francisco Oak Symposium in June 1993.[24] 'There are hundreds of tons of chips used annually, although very few wineries will admit usage . . . Costs for chips range from $1.50/lb to $4.00/lb . . . A wine-maker can add a reasonably complex oak character to a thousand gallons of wine for about $25.00.' I believe it is rare in Burgundy at grower level.

There seems to be little organized pooling of the results of barrel-ageing research in Burgundy at grower and *négociant* level. Many are familiar with R. Naudin's work, but individuals experiment independently, in parallel with each other. The same, inconclusive

22 Pascal Chatonnet, 'Effects of heat on the composition of oak wood: importance and control of heating operations in cooperage', International Oak Sympsium, San Francisco State University, June 1993.
23 *Flavors and Chemistry of Wine Barrels.*
24 'Oak chip use in wine', International Oak Symposium, San Francisco State University, June 1993.

experiments are run by dozens of growers at the same time. Run haphazardly and unscientifically, with the results unrecorded (though impressions will be spread by word of mouth) it seems a great waste of resources. Controlled experiments could be co-ordinated by the growers' unions (encouraged by the INAO), but it would need a dynamic Union President or two to get such co-operation off the ground.

Nor do we find in Burgundy an open-minded *négociant* house with the foresight of a Robert Mondavi, running oak experiments in carefully structured, relevant tests over many years alongside what is done (in a limited way) by the authorities. Of course, they would need to be as generous-minded as Robert Mondavi in making available the results of their research to the rest of the wine trade, which rather goes against the grain; indeed the whole idea could be anathema to some Beaunois.

A dismayed Jean-François Bazin writes of the threats to French wine from an Anglo-Saxon world of competing, unregulated wine regions, and from foreign wine commentators, where English, the language of the Tower of Babel he seems to think, is taken as gospel. He believes that 'From now on, the old Burgundy–Bordeaux debate has been completely overtaken by events. Today, the game is being played out between the French team, and that of the Rest of World.'[25] He is succumbing to siege mentality, like many Burgundians who have not travelled enough in non-French Pinot Noir and Chardonnay regions. He appears unaware of the enor-mous global affection for, and fascination with, red Burgundy, when it delivers the expected pleasures and excitements. The chal-lenge can be met, and without great difficulty, but there would have to be a changing of gear on the technical front by many Burgundi-ans, and it might be helpful if a five-year moratorium was put on their use of the word *terroir*.

Racking from barrel

Racking, the moving of wine from one barrel to another, is a less frequent operation in Burgundy, where it may be done two or three times, than in Bordeaux, where half a dozen rackings are not

25 *Chambertin: La Côte de Nuits de Dijon à Chambolle-Musigny*, Jacques Legrand, Paris, 1991.

uncommon. The purpose is to draw the wine off from the dead yeast cells, microbes, organic acid crystals, and any other solid particles which collect at the bottom of the barrel or storage tank. Some growers still rack their wines too often, avoiding boredom on rainy days, when they cannot go working in the vines. Excessive rackings cause a wine to dry up and loose fruit. In a light year, there is good reason to leave well alone, perhaps storing wine in a tank rather than a barrel, touching it as little as possible. If a grower has sufficient cellar space, and enough tanks, a decision may be taken to remove white wines from barrels to store them in bulk for some months prior to bottling, as at Domaine Leflaive, for instance. Oak influence on the wine will be limited, and the *cuvée* be completely homogenous. Some red Burgundies appear to be nourished by their lees, just like the great whites, if they are left on them after the malolactic fermentation has finished.

Two particular wine-making faults can be met with in Burgundies, both red and white: smells of sulphides and mercaptans, and of a wild yeast, *brettanomyces*, known as brett. Halliday and Johnson cover both problems in depth in the wine faults chapter of their book,[26] which is an essential reference book for every wine enthusiast who lacks a technical training. Hydrogen sulphide (the smell of rotten-egg gas) is produced during fermentation, but also originates with the elemental sulphur used to control oidium in the vineyard, and to disinfect barrels and vats. It can react with other chemicals in wine to form sulphur compounds called mercaptans, whose smells can be varied and unwelcome. Halliday and Johnson list burnt rubber, tar, rotten game, fowl manure, rancid garlic, leather and gravel as some of the aromas. Brett is a wild yeast which 'reacts with lysine (an amino acid) to create a taste which is exceedingly difficult to describe, but which in American technical literature is described as producing odours suggesting ammonia, mouse droppings, burnt beans and the pungent scent of barnyard animals'. Proper levels of sulphur dioxide should prevent *brettanomyces*, but those growers seeking to reduce sulphur levels can easily find their wines tainted by this microbial spoilage.

But what is a taint, and what an acceptable, constituent part of the wine's complexity? The answer will be different for different

26 *The Art and Science of Wine.*

tasters, of course. Halliday has described the bouquet of Pinot Noir like this:

> Pinot Noir, whether from Burgundy or elsewhere is a fruit-driven wine, and this should be reflected in an intense, fragrant bouquet. It should also be complex: the simple, mono-dimensional strawberry confection bouquet can signal a perfectly enjoyable glass of Pinot, but never a great one. The fruit aromas are typically described as falling within the strawberry, red cherry, plum spectrum, with secondary characters like violets (seen or believed to be seen in Europe more than in Australia), truffles (likewise), tobacco (particularly immature Pinot), stemmy/leafy/sappy notes, and oak spices. All of these are to be found in greater or lesser degree in a top Pinot Noir ... [He goes on] Particularly where some whole berry or bunch fermentation has been used, a certain gaminess akin to the character of (very) well-hung meat will be found. Additionally, sulphide and lees residues clearly leave their mark.

I certainly oversimplified the case when I wrote in 1982 'Great Burgundy smells of shit', and now find that, just as noticing volatile acidity may cause me to reject a wine as vinegary (but some volatility is present in all wines, to some degree) so if I perceive decaying vegetable and animal smells, or farmyard aromas, I now mostly find them unacceptable. In Burgundy it used to be quite common to celebrate the earthy, gamey, elemental aromas which were present, and they were often thought to be linked to the wine's geographical origin. We did not realize the extent to which a smell recalling chicken's innards, for instance, might be more due to microbial activity in the lees of the barrel than the subtle mixture of marls, clays, pebbles and limestone on the vineyard slope.

Infrequent racking, the by-products of fermentations, and microbial activity may all account for aromas which are either desirable, or anathema, to consumers. 'Sweaty saddle' aromas, depending on the levels found, can be acceptable or not. But when Californian wine-makers studiously eliminated them they found that something was missing in their Pinot Noir bouquets, rendering them dull. If you clean up Pinot completely, you can find that you have lost the point.

We have seen that the malolactic is to be encouraged after vinification. To achieve this, the grower will ensure that his white wines are left on their original fermentation lees, for this encourages the development of the bacteria which will transform the malic into lactic acid, and he may raise the temperature of the cellar to between 15°C and 18°C. He will avoid using the inhibiting antiseptic sulphur dioxide. In certain years the transformation takes place rapidly and easily, in others it is troublesome, and wines may be inoculated with lactic bacteria to encourage it.

Some red Burgundies used to be bottled with the malolactic fermentation uncompleted, when oenologists had not yet mastered this period of a wine's development, and growers were unaware of its importance. Sometimes no harm came of it, but occasionally an increase in temperature would provoke a fermentation in the bottle. There would be a noticeable prickle on the tongue, due to the carbon dioxide gas being produced, and a loss of bouquet.[27]

Today, white Burgundies (Pouilly-Fuissé, for instance) are sometimes bottled when the malolactic fermentation has been completely, or partially, blocked, so that a certain fresh acidity may be retained in the wine. These wines may need sterile filtration, however, to keep them stable, so there may be a diminution of taste qualities due to this tight filtration, noticeable particularly when the wine is young. Jacques Lardière, the wine-maker of Louis Jadot, wrote in 1993 that for twenty years his company had been retaining part, or all, of the malic acidity in some of their white Burgundies.[28] The New World saw the Chardonnay of Burgundy as a wine with new barrel and lactic aromas, but was it not a Pavlov-like reaction to limit wine-making to this technique? Buttery or milky aromas can erode the aromatic spectrum, particularly if new wood has been used. Malic acidity can be an open-sesame for a wine's bouquets. Lardière believes that a malolactic fermentation policy for each wine should be considered on its merits. If barrel-aged and carefully tended such wines offer few risks of refermentation. They require

---

27 Gas in a bottled wine may also be caused by two other factors. If the wine was bottled at cold cellar temperature there may have been some carbon dioxide still dissolved in it, which will become perceptible on warming up. Alternatively, it may have had some unfermented sugar upon which yeasts or microbes have got to work, with consequent production of alcohol and carbon dioxide. Such wines should be decanted before serving and left to stand in a warm place. After several hours they may taste in good condition. If they do not, they should be returned to the supplier.

28 *La Malolactique*, in BIVB's *Vinification: l'expérience bourguignonne*, vol. 2.

fining and 'normal' (in other words, not sterile) filtration prior to bottling.

An occasional complaint about white Burgundy is that it contains a deposit of crystals. These are identified by the customer as particles of broken glass, undissolved sugar, or, correctly, as a precipitation of tartaric acid. This organic acid is found naturally in the grape, a proportion of it crystallizing out during the ageing process before bottling. To encourage it, the cellar doors can be left open to allow freezing winter air to penetrate, or the wine can be refrigerated if the right equipment is available. If tartrate crystals are found in a bottled wine they should never cause dismay, for their appearance will have brought about a natural softening of the wine. If the bottle is handled carefully, the wine can be poured out perfectly clear, and not a drop need be lost.

Before a wine is bottled it should be brought to a stage where it is biologically and chemically stable. One might assume that this has been achieved when the fermentation of sugars has been completed, and all the malic acid transformed into lactic acid; however, the last 2 grams of sugar are unfermentable. Microbes in the wine may attack these, if warmth stirs them into action. Other bacteria may attack and transform the lactic acids. A wine may have picked up unwanted traces of copper or iron during vintage or cellar manipulations, or may rapidly deteriorate on contact with air owing to the presence of *oxydase*, a secretion common in years of grey rot. The protein found in white wines can make them susceptible to hazing.

Analyses by a professional laboratory reveal such likelihoods, and will be accompanied by instructions for treatment, preventive or curative. Many products may be used: citric acid, gum arabic, potassium ferrocyanide, calcium phytate, bentonite and others.

A fining is often recommended for fine wines, both red and white, before bottling. Whites of egg, gelatine, isinglass, caseine and bentonite are the most common agents, bringing about a coagulation of solid particles in suspension within the wine, which fall to the bottom of barrel or tank, there to be left after racking. Wines are stabilized by fining, and then often receive a light filtration to clarify them before bottling. Some estates refuse to use filters, feeling that every manipulation removes something of the natural qualities of the wine, and that the customer's insistence on clarity has gone too far. It is natural for fine wines to throw a deposit. A slight haze is indeed as harmless in one's Bâtard as in one's Bavarian, Belgian or Burton draught beer.

One of the main reasons why estate-bottling growers have so often achieved equal, or greater, quality status to *négociants* in Burgundy is that they are willing to take more risks than big companies with their wines. Big firms like to be secure, so they centrifuge, and refrigerate, to remove tartaric acid crystals, they filter – by various methods – they add finings, then filter again to remove any traces of treatments, and to polish the wines to crystal clarity. There have been many improvements in vinification during the 1980s, but fine products are often spoiled by over-zealous tending, pumping and bottling. Tightly run, quality-conscious *négociants* with no conflicting obligations to go cultivating the fields can, however, do immaculate jobs of tending. And at grower level, some mobile bottling plants can also be too safety-conscious, wishing to protect themselves against complaints.

Filtration for Burgundies

'Filtration properly carried out does not strip or attenuate a wine; it clears it of internal impurities and improves it. To deny this is to say that a wine's quality is due above all to foreign substances in suspension' – so Emile Peynaud in *The Taste of Wine*. This may be true with Bordeaux, Cabernet Sauvignons and many wines, but it is questionable with Pinots Noirs and red Burgundies; witness the many top growers, and merchants such as Louis Jadot or Faiveley, who find it worthwhile to risk problems after bottling in order to bottle wine unfiltered. If pad-filtration has taken place, what was delicious in cask can taste, in the months after bottling, diminished and stripped of life, its texture altered. Whether the quality fully returns is a moot point, on which there is plenty of disagreement. It very much depends on how lightly, and how carefully, the filtration was done.

Murky wine does not exactly look appetizing, clarification treatments being designed to remove the tiny bits of grape skin, yeast remnant and possibly also those potentially damaging bacteria remaining after the natural processes of wine-making.

This is best left to the wine-makers to decide. Most Burgundians prefer to filter or fine their wines as little as possible, or not at all. Every vintage, *cuvées* need to be handled individually.

Robert Parker has (with the Californian importer Kermit Lynch) been waging a vociferous campaign on behalf of non-filtration for red Burgundies, which is attractive in principle, but not entirely practical. 'No filtration' would be a simple slogan, to which we could all relate, but the campaign is proving counter-productive, some French growers now blithely offering as unfiltered wines which have been 'sensitively' tended, in the way they best see fit. Filters are quite small, and not difficult to hide when visitors are due. Given the changing temperatures into which their bottles travel once out of their cellars, beyond the control of their trade customers (who may well have arranged air-conditioned transit and storage) suppliers often prefer to play safe. When wine goes out of condition the bottler usually has to pick up the tab.

This will come as no surprise to Robert Parker, who, after fourteen years of tasting young Burgundies was by 1992 'convinced . . . that there is little correlation between what many growers present from cask and what ultimately is put in the bottle. This lamentable situation exists nowhere else in France . . . In Burgundy, growers have a tendency to show only their best lots to visiting wine writers.'[29] I have not found this to be true at all, and believe Parker is unwise to generalize about Burgundian growers and wine writers simply because his own experiences have not been good. Clearly he is anguished by the problem, but the causes may not lie solely with the growers. Burgundy growers are in my view exceptionally open about what they show from barrel, if writers take the time, show genuine interest and listen carefully. Of course, they do not always respond well when writers lecture them.

If Parker does not trust Burgundians to deliver according to sample (which is what he appears to be alleging) presumably he is also becoming dubious about non-filtration claims. Unless infrared surveillance videos have covered their entire establishments, or independent observers have slept round the clock between the barrel ranks to vouch for the accuracy of non-filtration claims, not everyone will choose to swallow them all. The French Fraud Repression Squad is not greatly bothered by non-filtration claims at present, I believe, as this would be a minor infraction.

It is indisputable that pad-filtration takes away colouring matter, with which are associated flavours and aromas. It does not remove

29 *The Wine Advocate*, 1990 Burgundy review, published 1992.

bacteria from the wine, but there are sterile pads, and other filtration methods, which can do this. When red Burgundies are being aged in barrel (not necessarily new barrels) the clarification process can take place in the barrel, and the wine be bottled clear, without filtration, perhaps after an appropriate fining. The tannins in the wood contribute to the clarification process, and a grower may use enzymes to help. It is virtually unthinkable to attempt to bottle unfiltered, if ageing large volumes in vat. Nor may it be feasible in years when the grapes were imperfectly healthy, or if the pressing of the grape skins was other than gentle.

So, a specialist grower or shipper, working carefully with small quantities, can deliver clear, unfiltered wines if operating a barrel-ageing policy. A label mention, front or back, seems highly desirable, even mandatory, so clients may be warned of greater than normal deposits, and the need to rest the bottle, and pour carefully or decant.

In *Connaissance et travail du vin* published in 1970, Emile Peynaud wrote, 'The generalization of the filtration of wines dates from the last twenty or thirty years. It spread bit by bit in all wine regions as technical progress was made, and in response to commercial demands. The use of younger wines, and the development of wine bottling, make filtration almost obligatory. The resistance to the use of filtration in certain regions came from the reproaches made against it that it thinned wines down, and emaciated them . . .' He went on to conclude that pumping, aeration, the use of less-than-perfect filtration materials or equipment, and improper methods can all contribute to it sometimes being harmful.

Robert Parker's campaign (even if he sometimes takes it quite over the top) is timely and welcome, and we should also be grateful to Kermit Lynch for having wakened many of us up to the ease with which more Burgundians can re-embrace a perfectly sound old practice.

But consumers must store these bottles in cool conditions, or microbes may attack the unfermentable, imperceptible gram or two of sugar left in most wines. As Halliday and Johnson write, 'Heat can trigger unwelcome bacterial activity, leading to 'off' odours, cloudiness and occasionally worse'.[30]

30 *The Art and Science of Wine.*

Wine contaminants

A feature of the last decade in the wine world has been the sudden eruptions of scandals about residues and contaminants in wines. The worst of these have happily been irrelevant to Burgundy: the addition of di-ethylene glycol to Austrian wines, as a flavour-enhancer, or the deadly methanol – wood alcohol, to boost strength – to certain Italian wines, for instance. But the presence of hista-mine in wine (to some extent influenced by excess nitrogen fertilizing) has caused concern for public health in Holland, and after the Chernobyl catastrophe I believe there were repercussions relating to the release for sale of Beaujolais Nouveau.

Research is currently being undertaken into histamine and ethyl carbamate levels, lead and cadmium residues, and procymidone (the latter can be found in wine after certain anti-grey rot treatments).

In the late 1980s the USA forbade wine imports if procymidone levels were above a certain level. Bordeaux, Beaujolais and Bur-gundy alone estimate that this and other actions relating to residues may have caused a drop in turnover in excess of 300m francs up to the end of August 1991. As a result, they have been taking the problem very seriously.

Concerning ethyl carbamate, Canada imposed maximum levels in 1985, without proper discussion or research (as the French would see it). This product is found naturally in all wines, and at higher levels in those grapes which reach maturity with difficulty: Pinot Noir, Chardonnay, Riesling, Gewürztraminer. Levels increase as wines age.

Certain wines appear to cause headaches, or in other ways make consumers unwell, in respect of which the presence of histamine, or other possibly toxic by-products of wine-making, like putrescine, may well be relevant. In Holland a Bordeaux wine containing 10 mg/l of histamine and 20 mg/l of putrescine was recently declared unfit for consumption, after a complaint from a consumer.

World over-production of wine currently runs at many millions of hectolitres per annum, at a time of falling consumption. New wine-producing and wine-exporting countries regularly appear, and recently established ones increase their productions. Tariff barriers within the GATT countries may be coming down, but the French feel that these are being replaced by finicky application of technical obligations. Sophisticated new methods of analysis now make it possible to detect infinitely tiny residues. So new barriers are thrown up, on the surface to protect consumers and the environment, but also, insidiously, as disguised trade barriers protecting domestic productions, reducing consumer choice and restricting the spread of French culture through an already too English-speaking world.

'Wine contaminants can be innumerable, it all depends on the level fixed for these products to be considered as such.' Thus wrote Professor Alain Bertrand, a leading figure in the research at the Institut d'Oenologie de Bordeaux.

Problems with corks

It is not just with Burgundies that we notice more faulty corks, but the reasons are hard to unravel. Is it because of intenser cultivation of the self-sown cork forests in southern Portugal, where trees are now pruned more severely to allow cattle to graze beneath them and other crops to grow? Is it that disease is on the increase, and early death of the trees more common? Traditionally cork-oak bark was stocked in the forest for two years before being made into corks. This period has often been reduced to 2–3 months or less, which can make your hair stand on end, if you think what it would do to wine if you lodged it in a barrel made of two-month-felled oak staves, as opposed to two-year weathered. Many manufacturers use archaic methods and rudimentary techniques, although there are also some technically well-equipped companies.

Corks have three functions: to be water-tight, to be chemically neutral, to be easy to extract. Often quality controls (except visual ones) are lacking, and standards too low. Bark origins can be unknown.

Burgundians individually source the best corks they can, but this sometimes results in identical research being done by several domaines, without the benefits being pooled. Why should one give a neighbour the benefit of one's researches?, it may be asked.

Recently at a leading Côte de Nuits estate I was asked to help extract a swollen, sticking cork, the comment being made that it was perhaps Sardinian ('We test Portuguese, Sardinian, Spanish'). Possibly we were tasting from a limited batch of experimental bottles, but I found myself thinking that there ought to be industry-wide research into cork origins, or at least more pooling of findings between domaines of top-quality standing, to save me (or some other hapless consumer) spending money on a bottle of *Grand Cru* only to find I had been let down by an over-active Portuguese cattle-grazing mixed farmer.

7

Growers, Traders, Media and Consumers

―――――

THE GROWERS

Traditionally in Burgundy the grower had two functions: he cultivated the vineyard and he made the wine, as we have seen in Chapters 5 and 6. Increasingly now he also bottles it, and sells it under
his own name.

Pierre Poupon compared the first two activities in 1975: 'There
are many good vignerons, but few skilful wine-makers. The work is
not the same. One takes place the whole length of the year, the
other in a few days. A person can reflect while tilling, can think
while pruning, but when wine-making there is no time left. One
must act, and act fast.'[1] A man or woman only makes wine thirty or
forty times in his or her life, the conditions and raw materials being
different each time, so it is not surprising that many mistakes used
to be made, before technical education became valued. Burgundian
grapes would get thrown into a vat or press with very little fore-
thought, indeed, vintage after vintage, the fruits of eleven and a half
months of patient labour were sometimes spoiled through lack of
training, lack of application – and the knowledge that mistakes
could be painlessly corrected by blending.

Things have improved immensely during the 1980s, as we have
seen in the chapters on viticulture and wine-making. It is now
estimated that half the Côte d'Or's annual harvest,[2] in a good year,
is bottled at the estate, the figure for *Premiers* and *Grands Crus*
being certainly higher. This is quite a contrast with 1969, when a

1 *Nouvelles Pensées d'un dégustateur,* Confrérie es Chevaliers du Tastevin, Nuits-
Saint-Georges, 1975.
2 Sylvain Pitiot and Jean-Charles Servant, *Les Vins de Bourgogne,* Presses
Universitaires de France, Paris, 1992.

leading Côte d'Or broker estimated that a mere quarter of the *Premiers* and *Grands Crus* production, in a good year, was being bottled at the estate. Today, approximately a third of the Yonne's harvest is domaine-bottled. The Côte Chalonnaise and Mâconnais bottle about 30 per cent, the Beaujolais 10–15 per cent.

It is difficult for a vigneron to adapt to successful tending and bottling. Many come to it first because wine is selling badly in barrel and prices are on the floor, but they have enough cash reserves not to have to sell their stock at the bottom of the market. At this stage many rely on mobile bottling plants, installed on the back of a lorry, which move from courtyard to courtyard throughout Burgundy. Since the bottler usually has no idea how the wines have been tended before his arrival he often plays safe when it comes to sulphur levels, stabilizing treatment and filtration.

Mobile bottling plants are highly active throughout Burgundy, and in some cases damaging to quality. You do not need to pasteurize, today, to ensure a sterile, stable product – which is what most mobile bottlers want, to protect themselves from responsibility for problems. Sterile filtration will remove not just bacteria and yeasts, but much of the wine's stuffing, fruit and life. Recent improvements in vinification can be laid to waste in a moment by over-zealous final treatment and bottling.

Many estates are now equipped to do their own bottling; however the correct procedures are not always followed, for instance the unifying of hogsheads in a vat, or the bottling of that vat in one uninterrupted operation. As a result, irregularities in quality are sometimes found from bottle to bottle when growers' wines are served.

Great wine is not made by chance, and almost never by growers under financial pressure. Not only must yield be restricted, but new casks may need to be bought and a fine wine used for topping up. Money must be purposely tied up, by making wines of such a style that they need considerable ageing. Many families have other priorities.

During the 1970s an increasing number of private customers and foreign buyers discovered that they could go directly, or via a broker, to the growers. In some cases stocks dropped, old vines were pulled up so that yields might reach levels to meet the new demands, and off-vintages were bottled when they barely had the stuffing to proclaim their origins with pride. Technical mastery was undervalued. Wines from the greatest, historic sites were made to give rapid pleasure. It is still happening, and the quality of many domaine-bottled wines is low. The evocative words are by no means a guarantee of perfection.

Domaine-bottling has seen an enormous expansion since the late 1960s. The vigneron discovered that his empty winters could usefully be filled, and that much satisfaction, as well as excellent profits, were to be had.

Initially, very few ever sent out a price-list, took a stand at a country fair, or rang a doorbell to sell their wines. Demand from American importers and the home market created the supply, and then the Belgians, the Swiss, and the British joined in. The Americans began to realize back in the 1930s that they could obtain top quality wines and eliminate a middleman by buying direct from growers. Initially unpopular because they only bought in famous years, they nevertheless sometimes paid in advance. Such clients now are rare.

Ask such a proprietor how he got his clientele and he may reply 'la boule de neige' (the snowball). He had a friend, who told his relations, who brought their friends. Over the years countless snowballs have been dislodged from the Golden Slope, to begin their rollings up, down and around Europe, North America, Japan, South-east Asia and Australasia. Each year they get bigger and each year fresh ones get dislodged.

A high proportion of estate-bottled wines are sold to passing Frenchmen, on the road to and from Italy, the Alps and the Côte d'Azur. Not only is the Frenchman convinced that he gets a finer wine (just as chickens collected from the farm are automatically superior to the town-sold article), he also gets it cheaper while having the satisfaction of doing the government out of several francs in Value Added Tax, for transactions between private client and vigneron are sometimes in cash.

Young growers starting bottling today find the competition much tougher, and need serious selling skills – often from their partner in life – to build a clientele.

A glance at Part Two will show that a high proportion of the best estates now practise it extensively. The global recession and slump in wine prices in Burgundy from 1991 have meant that many new families have started bottling. In the main these newcomers will not be touched on in Part Two, where I seek to highlight experienced bottlers.

There has been a startling transformation in the balance of power in the Burgundian wine trade since the early 1960s. Already by 1976 P.-M. Doutrelant was writing: 'In the Burgundian economy, the vigneron wears the trousers. The merchant follows.'[3] Unlike their Bordeaux equivalents (who commercialize the vast majority of château-bottlings), the Burgundian merchants have largely let the estate-bottling business pass them by. For a time merchants who felt uneasy about domaine-bottling growers put a brave face on it, saying that it was a good thing for the grower to learn the difficulties of selling wine in bottle. Many, like Louis Latour, thought the growers would fall flat on their faces – which they largely did not. Now the best and most successful merchants have either established, or extended their estates, or linked themselves irrevocably with top growers in partnership, for instance Faiveley, Louis Jadot, Joseph Drouhin, and the relative newcomer Antonin Rodet.

Why is more wine not estate-bottled? It is mainly a question of finance. If one examines the difference between selling the 1992 in bulk and bottle, one finds that it incurred its first costs in November 1991, when the winter pruning took place. If one took as example a vineyard that needed replanting, there would be four additional years before the first crop could be sold. The vineyard was tended and treated throughout the spring and summer of 1992, and the proprietor's family fed, so it is not surprising that many wines were put on sale after the harvest, that is to say in November 1992. Many owners waited until the spring for a better price. So the seller in bulk financed his operations for between twelve and eighteen months, and the terms of payment which the buyer negotiated may have extended this by a further six months. The grower wishing to sell wine in bottle must age it a further twelve to eighteen months in wood, continue to cultivate his vineyard and feed his family, finance the bottling expenses, and then let the wine rest a little in bottle. He will not start getting paid for November 1991's work until spring or autumn 1994. It is not surprising that most proprietors start domaine-bottling in a small way. Also, it is undoubtedly a lot of trouble. *Il faut aller moins souvent à la pêche si on fait de la bouteille* (there's less time for fishing if one goes in for bottling).

3 *Les Bons Vins et les autres*, Editions du Seuil, Paris, 1976.

The good proprietor in less famous villages like Savigny, Saint-Romain or Givry must bottle to make a decent living, for his wine gets a relatively poor price from a merchant. Often growers sell any famous names they own in bulk, because of the high prices they command. They will bottle for themselves the cream of their lesser-known *cuvées*, the value-for-money wines.

Maurice Vollot, a Savigny wine-broker, used to see two extreme types of grower on the Côte, the *Bourguignon de terre* and *Bourguignon de table*. The first is in service to his vines, rising at dawn, in bed by early evening: a professional who spends vintage-time in the vat-house rather than supervising the pickers, and whose barrels are always topped up. The second, round and purple like a ripe grape, may own and cultivate vines, but he also goes *à la chasse*. Above all he eats well, and when he says of a wine: *Ça irait bien avec une bécasse* (That would go well with a woodcock) you know he speaks from experience. Of his stomach he will say, as he pats it fondly, *Monsieur, ça, c'est du Pinot*. When strangers are around he sees himself as a one-man repository of all Burgundy's folklore. They both hold the same opinion about one thing, however. Their own wine is the best. Maybe there are just a few wine-makers who do not think this. When the future Pope John XXIII visited the Hospices de Beaune as Papal Nuncio, he admitted to M. Louis-Noël Latour that he too was a wine-grower. He said that he knew there must be better wines than his in Italy, everyone said so and he agreed. But his own was the one for him.

Today, there is a third Burgundian, whom one might call the *Bourguignon à tout-faire*. He must be a master of plant husbandry (including the organic approach), of wine-making, tending and bottling, a business manager, and a travelling salesman. Some are also tasting and gastronomic gurus, some tourist guides, and all, of course, need to find time for families and friends, while not refusing a warm welcome to curious visitors, who may be hangers-on or valuable customers (it is hard to know) but who sometimes drop by without any warning.

BROKERS

Wine-brokers are at the hub of Burgundian trading. Buying and selling wine can be a delicate, emotional business, for two or three transactions may decide a family's annual income and form a judgement on twelve months' work. The *courtier*, or broker, is the intermediary who smooths the way for the deal. I declare an interest since I work as consultant to a French wine brokerage company, and could easily over-praise good broking.

He neither buys nor sells any wine himself, being paid by commission. Once a deal has been struck, he produces a written confirmation and, one hopes, keeps an eye on the wine, for he guarantees that the delivery, perhaps three or six months later, corresponds to the wine originally sampled.

Dr Lavalle has recorded that in Burgundy until the sixteenth century it was almost always the *jurés-tonneliers*, the corporation of coopers, who were charged with tasting the wines offered for sale, to value them or establish if they had been spoiled or adulterated. Thereafter, gentlemen known as *gourmets* took over the responsibility for fixing prices, verifying if the wine indeed came from the vineyard indicated by the seller, whether it was pure Pinot or a mixture of Pinot and Gamay, and whether white wines had been mixed in, or various vintages. More often than not these *gourmets* were also brokers, their responsibility being to conduct the foreign merchant to the cellars, and not allow any wine to be sold if not of good quality. In those days it was a buyer's market, the broker being rewarded only by the grower, at the rate of *dix sols par queue*. The *queue* represented 456 litres or two of today's *pièces*, there being twenty sols in the *livre tournois* or franc.

Although today some foreign merchants are very successful in dealing directly with Burgundy growers, many use brokers, perhaps one who is a qualified oenologist, and it is easy to see why. In an hour or two the importer can be given an idea of the availability of wine and the tendency of prices. His person-on-the-spot will know that one grower has sold most of the cellar; that another had trouble with overheating during the vinifications; that a third has a stack of old vintages on offer; that a fourth's head has been swollen out of recognition by media attention. The broker may help growers to allocate stocks between markets (when demand is buoyant) and to weed out slow or unreliable payers.

Many growers have but a rudimentary grasp of the nuts and bolts of exporting, and the broker provides a follow-up service after the importer has flown home, ensuring that treatments are carried out, special labels affixed, collections co-ordinated, invoices established, and payments distributed on time.

It is less easy to appreciate the value of the broker's contribution to the local trade. When I was living in Burgundy in the late 1960s I was often surprised at the arm's-length treatment of the vignerons by Burgundian merchants, many of whom would not then be seen within miles of the growers – not to taste, not to talk, certainly not to socialize. Their buying was done without contact with the vineyard owners, after assembly of samples by their brokers. While the best brokers certainly fulfil a useful role, it seems to me that some must have been a block to communication between grower and local shipper. It has been estimated that brokers are involved in 60 per cent of today's trade in Burgundy.

THE MERCHANTS

Vous faîtes notre travail a traditional *négociant* has been heard to say to a domaine-bottling grower: 'You are doing our job, taking the bread out of our mouth.' Of course, it is true, they are. And why? Because many *negociants* did their jobs badly, for ages. They were wealthier, and thought they inhabited a superior planet. Some became contemptuous and arrogant. When a crisis arrived, some went under, if they did not change. Nepotism often played its part in that.

The role of the merchant was defined in Poupon and Forgeot's *Les Vins de Bourgogne* (eighth edition, 1977) as buying fine wines, usually young, at the property, assuring them the care, treatment and maturation necessary to develop their natural qualities, correcting any possible faults, and thus satisfying the tastes and requirements of the customers.

That formula has proved to be only patchily successful in respect of Burgundy's greatest wines. Buying wines with faults, which the *négociant* hoped his skills would correct, is the key to the problem, and at the root, I believe, of the loss of independence of many famous old names (Thomas-Bassot, Lionel Bruck, Charles Viénot, Pierre Ponnelle, Chauvenet, Bouchard Aîné, for instance) who now shelter under Jean-Claude Boisset's giant trading umbrella in Nuits-Saint-Georges. Buying wines with faults reduced a firm's costs, but whatever you blended with them the final result never hit the heights. And it did nothing for one's image or brand. Cheap wines with faults need distilling, or declassing to a lower level of *appellation*.

A dynamic young *négociant* starting out today (there are a few) might define his or her (I do not know any of these) role quite differently, highlighting the ability to select and decline. Having no obligations relating to viticulture, he can tend and bottle wines so as to maximize their qualities. In theory, a *négociant*'s cellar should be able to express the multiple subtleties of Burgundy's sites with more diversity than a group of growers' wines. But in practice, this has been hard to achieve, and most *négociants*' ranges have a sameness to them, and an overriding family resemblance, which may come honestly from the personal vision and tastes of the buyer, but must sometimes be ascribed to a lack of imagination by the cellar-master – handling everything, from Pouilly-Fuissé through to Chablis, in the same way, for instance – or of course to carelessness with topping-up. Few *négociants* allow themselves to surprise us with the unexpected, the untypical, the daring; they tend to play for safety.

By holding large stocks, *négociants* can guarantee a regular supply of wine from year to year, and to some extent smooth out dramatic price fluctuations at the property, and this can be very precious, particularly to restaurants. Many merchants specialize in export, and their efforts have undoubtedly brought wealth and prestige to the region, dating back to the mid-eighteenth century, when the first firms were founded, often combining wine-dealing with trade in cloth with the Low Countries.

Pitiot and Servant record that there are 140 firms in the four *départements* of vinous Burgundy,[4] employing 3,600 people, and that they despatched 3.75 million hectolitres (500 million bottles) in 1990, 60 per cent of the trade going to export markets. A lot of that will have been Beaujolais, and about 45 per cent of the trade is in *vins de marque* – branded table wines and *vins de pays* – so has little to do with Burgundy, except that the address on the label, or the brand association, may help the sale.

First as regards turnover in 1991 was the Patriarche group (including Kriter), its sales being around 540m fr. Then followed Georges Duboeuf 472m fr., Jean-Claude Boisset 248m fr., Picard

4 *Les Vins de Bourgogne.*

242m fr., Loron 198m fr., De Villamont 187m fr., Mommessin 159m fr., Louis Jadot 153m fr., Joseph Drouhin 140m fr., Louis Latour 139m fr., Bichot 122m fr., Moillard 121m fr., Chauvenet 120m fr., Reine Pédauque 117m fr.

The largest vineyard-owners amongst the *négociants'* families are: Patriarche (123 ha.), J. Faiveley (112 ha.), Bouchard Père (93 ha.), Joseph Drouhin (62 ha.), Protheau (59 ha.), Bichot (56 ha.), Louis Jadot (45 ha.), Louis Latour (45 ha.), Chanson (42 ha.) and Reine Pédauque (38 ha.). Rodet owns or controls over 150 ha., Picard over 90 ha. Out of a total of 5,000 ha., 800 ha. of AC vineyard were owned by merchants by 1962, according to Françoise Grivot.[5] I would estimate that the merchants' share had stayed about the same, around one-sixth.

Only fifteen years ago one would find fine merchants with large vineyard estates selling their poor wines, after a light vintage, to the second division where they would be lost in the blending vats. With today's improved techniques in vineyard and vat-house (particularly the appearance of conveyor belts, where unripe and rotten grapes may be removed prior to vatting) this practice is diminishing. Many merchants now buy grapes, rather than wine, so as to ensure wine-making to their specifications, Bouchard Père having made some of the most significant investments to permit expansion of grape-buying.

OLD RIVALS COMING TOGETHER

The lack of co-operation between growers and merchants worried leading members of each side for years. Attempts were made to get together before the First World War, and later in 1942 and 1957, but success was not finally achieved until 6 July 1966 when the Comité Interprofessionnel de la Côte d'Or et de l'Yonne pour les Vins d'Appellation Contrôlée de Bourgogne was founded. In 1989, this became the BIVB, the Bureau Interprofessionnel des Vins de Bourgogne. It covers Yonne, Côte d'Or and Saône-et-Loire, but not the Beaujolais, which went its own way, judging its Gamay needs to be completely different from those of the Pinot and Chardonnay. The Rhône *département*, where Beaujolais is grown, is part of the

5 *Le Commerce des vins de Bourgogne*, SABRI, Paris, 1962.

next regional administration southwards, and no doubt draws on separate regional funds.

The BIVB has technical, business and communication roles to play on behalf of Burgundian growers and merchants, and gives me every impression of efficiency and dynamism. There are regular symposia on technical matters (which never used to occur), and controversial problems are attacked with relish. It is also involved with marketing and promotion.

MEDIA AND MERCHANTS

'The newsletter writers have become agents of change in how Burgundies get sold', wrote Matt Kramer, in *Making Sense of Burgundy*,[6] and 'The difficulty is that these advance reports whip up a buying frenzy among Burgundy lovers, who, knowing the small quantities available, are afraid they are going to miss out. The only reasonable advice is: Resist it. Talk to your merchant.'

No one can stop writers wishing to spread good news, but if wines are praised to the skies before their prices have been struck the consumer is a loser. The wine writer enriches the grower, and undermines the role of the buyer, if he or she blurts good news too soon.

The wine media – particularly Robert Parker and the *Wine Spectator* – have immensely contributed to opening new consumers' eyes to fine wine and to discovering new sources. Wine traders cannot turn back the clock to times when the media was not omnipresent, any more than a professional diplomat can prevent a television crew interviewing enemy generals or politicians during a war, and thereby maybe altering its course. But there is constructive comment, and its opposite.

Merchants in the 1980s depended too much on wine writers to sell their Burgundies. They did not do enough original buying prospection themselves, and were not close enough to their consuming customers to pass on the good news, around an open bottle. Merchants have only themselves to blame if they find the prices of their favourite wines have climbed out of reasonable reach because of media hype.

6 William Morrow, New York, 1990.

8

Naming, Controlling and Letting Go

ARTIFICIAL WINE

When the phylloxera destroyed France's vineyards towards the end of the nineteenth century, an artificial wine industry soon appeared to take their place so that the demand might continue to be satisfied. Concentrated must (grape-juice) was imported from abroad, water, sugar and colouring matter were added, and the result sold as wine.

But then other ingredients such as animal blood, chemicals and industrial alcohol appeared. According to J. Capus, who was to become Minister of Agriculture, by 1905 fraud was more and more frequent and dangerous because of the advances of science. As the vineyards were replanted, natural wine (which, being from young vines, was not of exactly marvellous quality) found itself in competition with the artificial product. M. Charles Quittanson has written that it was after pressure from producers with their backs against the wall, and consumers whose well-founded interests were wronged, that the law of 1 August 1905 was born.[1]

The French claim that this was the first major legislation in the world to govern the naming of wine by its geographical origin. It was certainly pre-dated by an enactment of Charles VI in February 1416, confirmed by François I in August 1527, which stated that 'all sorts of wines harvested above the bridge at Sens, as much those of the Auxerrois as those of the Beaunois . . . which travel on the Yonne river shall be called Vins de Bourgogne'. Philippe-le-Hardi, Duke of Burgundy, was much ahead of his time when he ordered

1 He was for many years Inspecteur Divisionnaire du Service de la Répression des Fraudes et du Contrôle de la Qualité as well as Chef de la Brigade Nationale de Surveillance des Vins et Eaux-de-Vie à Appellations d'Origine.

the uprooting of the Gamay vine from the vineyards of Dijon, Beaune and Chalon on 31 July 1395, as were the consular deliberations of Saint-Georges d'Orques in the Midi on 31 May 1744. These ordained that the wines of the nearby communes of Laverune and Saint-Jean de Vedas should neither be blended with Saint-Georges d'Orques, nor allowed to use its name. None of these, however, can be called major legislation.

The 1905 Act was mainly concerned with protecting the consumer from fraudulent *vins ordinaires* and in this was extremely successful. The law made it necessary for a vineyard owner to make a declaration of the amount of wine produced each year, and at the same time the Service de la Répression des Fraudes was set up. It stated that a wine might only bear an *appellation d'origine* if it came from the usual zone where such wines were produced. In addition, it limited chaptalization (the addition of sugar at the vintage), for there had been abuses. *Appellation d'origine contrôlée* came later, as will be seen.

In 1906 the Société des Viticulteurs de France organized a sort of Congress of Names of Origin. Representatives from the great fine-wine regions were asked to describe their local wines, for the 1905 law had declared its intention of mapping out the regions. J. Capus reported from the Gironde, and issued a warning: 'Now that names of origin are protected, it would be possible for certain proprietors, one must admit it, to plant in unsuitable soils of a famous region vine-types which produce large quantities of mediocre wine; in this way they would have wines of absolute authenticity, but of an inferior quality, capable of disqualifying the region.'[2] Sad to relate, this is exactly what happened, and it took thirty years to put it right.

The law-makers of the time had failed to understand that the soil and the vine are both vital influences on a wine's character, and many proprietors compounded this misunderstanding. They claimed that, just as a son carries his father's name simply because he is the son, so any wine produced in, say, the Gironde, might call itself Bordeaux. They missed the point that a consumer does not order a Bordeaux solely in order to drink a wine from this region;

---

2 Where Capus is quoted his words are taken from his *L'Évolution de la législation sur les appellations d'origine*, Louis Larmat, Paris, 1947.

he wants a wine with the smell and taste he is used to, or which made the region famous.

The decree of 1905 established that the wine-producing regions should be delimited by administrative order. This soon led to trouble, for a Paris-based body can have little understanding of the delicate questions of soil-types, climatic conditions, vine species, or vinification methods, and the parts they all play in a region's wine-making. The new powers were first put to the test in the Champagne district, where there was much dissatisfaction. Large quantities of grapes were being brought into the district from outside, there to be vinified and christened Champagne. There were two rival factions in the Champagne province: the vignerons from the Marne and the vignerons from the Aube *départements*. Both *départements* form part of the historic province of Champagne and both claimed the right to the name Champagne for their sparkling wine. However, the soil and grapes, as well as the climate, were different. It was hoped that a government order would settle the dispute. By the decree of 17 December 1908 the Aubois were denied the right to the *appellation d'origine Champagne*. One might imagine that the vignerons of the Marne would have been satisfied but they were not, for part of the Aisne *département* was included, and the latter's wines, according to the Marnais, resembled *la purée des haricots*.

The vintages of 1907, 1908, 1909 and 1910 had been appalling; many vineyards were mortgaged and the vignerons faced with bankruptcy. Again the government acted, by legislating that the production of Champagne and that of sparkling wine made from grapes grown outside the Champagne area must take place in two different buildings. The new decree did nothing to help the Aube *département*, however, and its vignerons turned militant.

Patrick Forbes describes the scene:

> In Troyes there were processions, huge demonstrations and disorders of a grave nature including the burning of tax papers; Bar-sur-Aube, in the heart of the vineyard district, hung out red flags and chanted the Internationale. Thoroughly alarmed, the Government prepared to give in; on 11 April, the Senate was persuaded to pass a resolution recommending that the law of 17 December 1908, which had delimited the Champagne district, should be annulled forthwith.[3]

3 *Champagne, the Wine, the Land and the People*, Gollancz, London, 1967.

When the Marne vignerons heard of this intention, *they* rioted. Merchants' houses were sacked and wine ran in the streets.

DRAWING BOUNDARIES

By June 1911, although certain regions such as Cognac, Armagnac and Banyuls had been successfully delimited, the government had come to realize the foolishness of imposing solutions from Paris. It was agreed that the local courts should be given the power to map out an *appellation d'origine*. However, legislation was slow to come, and the war then provided an interruption. It was not until 6 May 1919 that power was finally given to the local courts to decide in the event of conflicts, upon intervention of the persons concerned. In addition, it was declared that every vintager who intended to give a name of origin to his product must indicate this in his harvest declaration. The declarations were made public for anyone's inspection. *Appellation d'origine* wines were to be made in accordance with the established, honest, local customs (*les usages locaux, loyaux et constants*). Wine merchants were to keep a record of all *appellation d'origine* wines entering and leaving their premises.

The law of 1905 had made it clear that, for instance, wine produced in Languedoc could not be called Bourgogne; that of 1919 enabled court cases to be brought to establish just how far down the hillside and into the plain one might produce wine and call it Bourgogne. Between 1920 and 1934, many legal delimitations of villages and vineyards took place.

These were heroic times when men such as the Marquis d'Angerville and Henri Gouges (the latter succeeded the former as President of l'Union Générale des Syndicats pour la Défence des Producteurs de Grands Vins de Bourgogne) led the fight against malpractices. Because local merchants were among the first to be taken to court, d'Angerville of Volnay and Gouges of Nuits-Saint-Georges found that their traditional market closed its ranks against them. They were forced to tend and bottle their wines themselves, and sell them direct to the public. It is from this moment that the domaine-bottling movement begins to gather strength.

Although the Service for the Repression of Frauds had been created in 1905, merchants were not effectively controlled until after 1919, and even in 1925 one could buy a good wine in Beaune called Beaune – but it might have come from anywhere. Things are better nowadays.

THE RIGHT VINES, SOILS AND YIELDS

The 1919 Act was bad law because of its omissions. It gave no lead on permitted grape varieties and failed to state the maximum amounts of wine which any vineyard might produce. The result was that many proprietors bought *ordinaire* from merchants, declared a large production of *appellation d'origine* wine, and received certificates for what they had declared. In the 1920s it was as simple as that.

As Capus had predicted, unsuitable soils of a famous region were soon being planted with vines. One such was the palus-land of Barsac, in the Bordeaux area, which is close to the river and made up of alluvial soils which had hitherto produced cheap red *ordinaires*. They were now turned over to producing white wines simply because these would have the right to the famous commune name.

All sorts of grape-types came to be planted in famous villages, often giving vast productions of strange-tasting wines. Some of the greatest abuses were due to hybrid Franco-American vines. The American vines had of course originally been introduced to combat phylloxera, for their roots were resistant to the louse and the French vines could be grafted on to the transatlantic stocks. The hybrids were crossings between the two nationalities; they were sometimes known as *producteurs directs* because they produced wine directly, without grafting. They yielded an inferior-quality wine, but nothing prevented their being planted in France's most famous vineyards. 'The new legislation, far from protecting buyers, thus exposed them to a fraud which it authorized', wrote Capus.

During the 1920s, the importance of listing permitted grape varieties thus came to be realized. So on 22 July 1927 a new Act was passed to allow local tribunals to decide which vines might produce *appellation d'origine* wines, and hybrid, direct vines were denied this right. It was in 1930 that the Pinot Noir was legally defined as Burgundy's noble grape, with the Gamay and others being permitted in certain circumstances.

The new law of 1927 had two main disadvantages. Firstly, it was optional, which meant that in many famous regions where the tribunals had not regulated the names of origin, large-yielding vines were still being planted in totally unsuitable soils. Secondly, it did not enable tribunals to fix a minimum alcoholic degree for an *appellation*. (A few, however, went beyond the strict text of the law to do so.) The result of the second omission was that *appellation d'origine* wines of a mere 7° were produced at a rate of 120 to 200 hectolitres per hectare, or four times the normal yield.

At this time, the words *appellation d'origine* on a label offered one of four different types of guarantee:

1. In a few rare cases, judgements by tribunals had laid down area, vines and minimum degree. Châteauneuf du Pape was one of these, thanks to the leadership of the Baron Le Roy.
2. A few rare regions had applied the law of 1927 strictly. Minimum degree was left to the conscience of the producer.
3. In two famous Bordeaux districts, the law of 1927 was misunderstood and ill-applied. The palus-land of Saint-Emilion, often under water, was confirmed in 1934 as part of the Saint-Emilion *appellation* and in 1932 the tribunal of Bordeaux judged that the palus-land of Barsac and Sauternes had a right to these famous names. The Bordeaux Court of Appeal scandalously confirmed this in 1934.
4. In most regions, however, the law had not come into operation and all sorts of wines and soils were producing *appellation d'origine* wines.

SEPARATING GREAT FROM GOOD (OR ORDINARY)

Names of origin thus offered some or no guarantees to the consumer, and the whole system risked falling into discredit, to say the least. The confusion was then further aggravated by the producers of *vins ordinaires*. These wines were obliged by law to display their alcoholic degree on the label, where *appellation d'origine* wines were not. Unfortunately, however, the latter had no legal definition, so quantities of wines which had never been anything but ordinary were declared with a name of origin.

A multiplicity of names resulted for other reasons as well. The law which forbade merchants to launch fictitious *Crus* or *Châteaux* applied only to *vins ordinaires*. So the *Châteaux* were launched with an *appellation d'origine*, and if there were no traditions for using one, this did not prevent a court case being brought so that a new region could be legally mapped out. Local court decisions tended to favour local interests.

From 1927, there was a mounting crisis owing to over-production of *ordinaire* in France and Algeria, which resulted in the Statut Viticole of 1931. This statute forbade the plantation of vineyards for a ten-year period by properties larger than 10 hectares; taxed high yields and big harvests; blocked a percentage of a large estate's wines at the property, and obliged proprietors to have their wines distilled if total production exceeded a fixed maximum. The producers of *appellation d'origine* wines were exempt from these measures; so again many improvised names of origin were created in areas which had traditionally produced *vins ordinaires*. The importance of the *scandale des appellations d'origine*, as it came to be called, can be seen from the following figures:

Quantity of wine declared with an *appellation d'origine*
1923   less than 5 million hectolitres
1931   over 9.75 million hectolitres
1934   over 15.5 million hectolitres

The law of 1927 had been known as the Loi Capus, and it was again Capus who prepared the new law, which was passed on 20 July 1935. He was aided by, amongst others, the Marquis de Lur Saluces of Château d'Yquem; Baron Le Roy de Boiseaumarié of Château Fortia, Châteauneuf du Pape; and from Burgundy, the Marquis d'Angerville and Henri Gouges. The memory of the last two is preserved not at the foot of statues but more appropriately (and with great distinction) by their heirs on wine labels, every good vintage. Further details can be found in the Volnay and Nuits-Saint-Georges chapters of Part Two.

The new law had two objects: firstly, to enable the consumer to tell the difference between the name of origin given to a *vin ordinaire* and that given to a fine wine, and secondly, to discipline the production, and control and guarantee the quality of fine wines. This was to be achieved by eliminating ignoble vines and unsuitable soils, establishing a minimum degree and a maximum yield and laying down procedures for viticulture and vinification. On the subject of differentiating between fine wine and other, Capus wrote, 'We cannot forbid wine-growers to give their wines, whatever they are, a name of origin. But we can let the consumer know that certain names correspond to prime-quality wines. These *appellations d'origine* will be known as *contrôlées* (AOC, or AC for short). This qualification will be applied to them in price-lists and will be shown on labels. By this fact alone, a selection will be established amongst *appellations*.' Ordinary wines carrying a name of origin were to be described as having an *appellation d'origine simple* (AOS).

After the failure of the administration's efforts to delimit the Champagne area, there was no question of it controlling the factors of production. The state and the wine-growers had to combine and work together, and the Comité National des Appellations d'Origine des Vins et Eaux-de-Vie[4] was founded to co-ordinate them, financed by a tax of two francs per hectolitre of AC wine. The decisions of the *Comité*, issued in the form of decrees in its official bulletin, were to become law. The members of the *Comité* were chosen by the state: two-thirds from the presidents of those viticultural associations in AC areas, which had been at least ten years in existence; the other third from representatives of the Ministries of Agriculture, Finance and Justice.

The INAO was reorganized in 1967. It is responsible to the Ministry of Agriculture, which nominates its director. It is composed of a National Committee of 64 members: a president, 25 producers, 16 *négociants*, 9 'qualified people' (oenologists etc.), 8 people representing the various ministries, and 5 commercially qualified people, including *négociants*. There was no one to represent foreign customers' interests (in spite of the fact that they are the principal market for many of the greatest AC names), and above all no one to represent consumers' interests.

The National Committee has a subsidiary executive board and a permanent commission of ten people to deal with current affairs. There is a total administrative staff of about 140, in twenty centres throughout France as well as Paris. Part of the INAO's job is to make technical, practical and legal studies of all the problems

4 Later the name was changed to Institut National des Appellations d'Origine des Vins et Eaux-de-Vie (INAO).

related to AC (which extends to cheese, pottery, etc.), including production and composition, and the ways in which products are presented and sold. Its activity is thus not simply limited to the definition of *appellations contrôlées*. It is charged with studying and proposing any measure which may favour the improvement of quality or regulate the market and must contribute to the defence of the *appellation* system. This is enforced by two bodies, the Service de la Répression des Fraudes et du Contrôle de la Qualité (the Fraud Squad) and the Direction Générale des Impôts – the latter being involved because of the fiscal element covered by the transport documentation.

Capus commented that the 1935 legislation provoked sharp hostility among a large number of merchants. A Bordeaux daily paper wrote that the new law would bring ruin to merchants and growers alike. Fearing that this opposition might reach the Chambre des Deputés and the law perhaps be repealed, a transitional period was allowed when both AOS and AOC existed in the same region, the latter being applicable only after a request from a grower that his wine should be submitted to the controls. This transitional period ended on 3 April 1942. In the next four years the average production of AC wine was 4.75 million hectolitres, whereas in 1934 we have seen that it was 15.5 million hectolitres. The new law thus removed over a thousand million litres per annum of spurious *appellation* wine from the market.

This was a major achievement, but abuses still existed. Although the grower was now controlled, and the wholesaler obliged to keep records of the amount of AC wine bought and sold, the retailer and bar-keeper fell outside the law. *Vin ordinaire* was sold as AC wine in cafés and restaurants simply by refilling empty bottles bearing AC labels. This fraud attained prodigious proportions, said Capus. It was the basis for the oft-heard claim that Lyon and Paris each consumed the whole annual Beaujolais production.

A law of 18 December 1949, completed by a decree of 30 November 1960, established a group of *appellations* known as Vins Délimités de Qualité Supérieur (VDQS). These wines are often described as being halfway in quality between *vins ordinaires* and AC wines. In fact this is unfairly derogatory, for many of them are of greater quality then AC wines. From the beginning all VDQS wines have had to be approved by a tasting panel before reaching the market. (Only from the 1979 vintage have most AC wines had to submit to this stringent control, and not even then in Burgundy, because of the success of Burgundian pressure groups – as we shall soon see.) There is only one VDQS in Burgundy, Sauvignon de Saint-Bris, discussed in the chapter on wines of the Yonne (Chapter 10).

This is not the place to go into the reasons why France has saddled herself with three separate, complex, but almost identical categories for describing wines by their geographical origin. Not only are there AC and VDQS, but also *vins de pays*. The latter appeared with the abolition of *appellations d'origine simples* (which, as we have seen, were names of origin given to ordinary wines) by the law of 12 December 1973. They are mainly from the Midi: attempts to produce individual wines of quality, in contrast to the mass of Midi plonk which is good only for assembly in vast vats, where the grossest defects are merged together to form the Frenchman's palatable though mediocre staff of life.

The main reason for the three categories is the self-protective stance of France's old-established wine regions. Several, particularly in the Midi, were slow to adopt a policy of quality. Since the National Committee of the INAO had strong representation from the original AC areas, there was a policy of excluding new areas from joining the club, particularly if they were likely to bring large productions of reasonably priced fine wine in with them. At the same time the lucky members of the club have extended where possible their production areas, and selected special strains of noble vines with the object of increasing yields. By 1973, these initiatives were bearing great fruit: 13.6 million hectolitres of AC wine were produced, the VDQS contribution taking the total to over 17 million hectolitres. Over 20 per cent of the French harvest masquerading as quality wine! We were back to 1934.

The cascade system – not abolished but truncated

It was time for new legislation, and the problems to be tackled were those of excessive yields and poor quality. There had already been straws in the wind, for instance the AC Châteauneuf du Pape took a most interesting initiative by its decree of 2 November 1966. A basic figure for the yield was fixed, which could be lowered but not raised. The total yield for a vineyard could not be more than 20 per cent above the basic figure, otherwise the whole quantity produced lost its right to the AC. The same system applied to the Rhône AC Tavel and the Corsican Patrimonio.

The trouble with the AC system until 1974 was that it set a limit on the amount of wine which could be bought and sold under each famous *appellation*. But there was *no limit* on the amount of wine that a vineyard could produce. A 'cascade' system of naming was in force which allowed a grower in Pommard, for instance, to produce 80 hectolitres per hectare of wine from a vineyard. Of this one identical wine, 35 hectolitres were called Pommard, 15 hectolitres Bourgogne, and the rest was *vin rouge*. And there were several markets (Holland, Germany and particularly the UK) which were delighted to purchase these over-productions, baptizing them Pommard as soon as they had crossed the frontier. 'Where's the harm in that?' I hear you cry. Were these wines not harvested on Pommard soil, had not the advent of fertilizers, the advances in grafting techniques, the better use of sprays caused a genuine increase in the yield of good wine beyond the out-of-date legal maxima? Well, yes and no. First of all, there were many years when poor weather at the flowering in June was responsible for containing a vineyard's yield naturally within the legal limits. It was the case in 1969 and 1971, and in those years over-production scarcely existed. Secondly, years of plenty such as 1970 and 1973 produced thin wines which often lacked colour and substance.

There are still a few people who mourn the passing of the days before 1 September 1973 when AC legislation came into force in the UK. The British wine trade was delighted to purchase, and the Burgundians to supply, what they called over-productions of Côte d'Or communes. This is what Michael Broadbent was referring to when, as Chairman of the Institute of Masters of Wine in 1969, he wrote of 'the cynical devaluation of well-known Burgundy commune and vineyard names over a long period by the trade on both sides of the Channel'. These wines were not genuine Burgundies at all, or only very, very rarely. They were weak-bodied Pinots, strengthened from the south to produce drinkable blends which were easy to sell under famous names. This style of wine completely falsified the consumer's ideas about the taste of Burgundy.

New legislation to control vineyard yields (Decree 74/872) was introduced on 19 October 1974, and made immediately applicable to the 1974 vintage. One cannot help wishing that a simpler solution had been found; the one adopted is extremely complicated.

The old law had established a maximum-yield figure for each AC. This figure was retained in Burgundy, and named as the 'basic yield' (*rendement de base*) of the *appellation*. The old law had also permitted the maximum-yield figure to be reviewed annually to take account of bounteous or niggardly years, and this concept too was retained. Each wine-growers' syndicate might propose its idea of a suitable annual yield (*rendement annuel*) to the regional committee of the INAO, who would pass it up to the National Committee for a decision. New ground was broken with the introduction of an absolute maximum for each vineyard, known as the 'classification ceiling' (tautology has crept into the French *plafond limite de classement*, which is abbreviated to PLC). This absolute-maximum figure is arrived at by adding a percentage (typically in Burgundy 20 per cent) to the annual-yield figure. The cascade system which allowed a given AC vineyard to produce an unlimited quantity of wine, perhaps 90 hectolitres per hectare, with imaginary lines being drawn through the vat specifying that 35 hectolitres of this one identical wine could be called Vosne-Romanée, 15 hectolitres Bourgogne and 40 hectolitres *vin rouge*, was finally abolished. Henceforth the produce of a vineyard could only be sold under one name.

So far so good. In 1975, a year of grey rot on the Côte d'Or, growers' syndicates suggested annual yields in line with the damage suffered in the vineyards. In Gevrey-Chambertin, Fixin, Morey-Saint-Denis and Vosne-Romanée the basic yields held good at 35 hl/ha. Nuits-Saint-Georges and Chambolle-Musigny (apparently worse hit by rot than Vosne-Romanée, or else setting their sights higher) dropped their annual yield to 28 hl/ha. Aloxe-Corton went to 20 hl/ha., being particularly affected by rot.

What is not so splendid, however, is the action taken when the annual yield plus the agreed percentage is exceeded. In this case a grower has only to send the excess over the limit to the distillery or vinegar factory to be allowed his certificate for the rest – so once again an imaginary line is being drawn through a vat of wine, with the two sections being given a different name. Above the line it's vinegar, below it's Puligny-Montrachet – but Puligny-Montrachet from a vineyard which has grossly overcropped. To do the lawmaker justice, he was at the same time intending that wine produced in excess of the annual yield should be subjected to blind tasting control. In Burgundy, however, his intention has been almost totally frustrated by the local, vested interests.

All AC wines must be tasted (but Burgundy is an exception)

A decree was published in 1974 (No. 74/871), which laid down that all wines to be offered with an AC must be subject to analysis and tasting. There are possibilities for reassessment of wines which are not approved at the first examination. A five-year introductory period was allowed in Burgundy, which meant that the legislation would come into force for wines of the 1979 vintage.

An attempt was being made to move from quantitative to qualitative control. The INAO knew how much Burgundy was made each year, and had for some time been effective in ensuring that no more should be sold than had been harvested. That is what the Marquis d'Angerville cried out for in the 1920s and that had pretty successfully been achieved. But the AC system did *not* guarantee the authenticity nor the quality of the wines bearing AC names. Decree 74/871 was an attempt to draw the net tighter, and it was opposed by Burgundian growers because they knew certain wines would lose their right to famous names in the off-vintages, as indeed they should.

Burgundian growers resisted this control and, with an unbelievable smoke-screen, had it so watered down that it ended up with no bite left whatsoever.

They claimed that there were too many small *cuvées* of wine on the Côte d'Or for them all to be tasted, and that the inspectors would surely be hoodwinked by the growers. The growers would manage to submit samples of a good wine twice, and then attribute the second certificate to a poor *cuvée* which would thus escape analysis. In any case, should not the tasting take place further down the line in the merchants' cellars? Why should growers be controlled if merchants could go on blending as before? They questioned whether there were enough qualified people to form tasting panels, and whether these were capable of judging the wines when young, which would appear necessary given that much wine changed hands in the three months after the vintage.

They successfully bullied the authorities into accepting that a grower's whole cellar could be released for sale on the strength of one (sometimes two) samples having been collected and approved. The grower himself or herself is often openly involved in the choice of which wine will be taken for tasting ('don't take that, it is not tasting well today'). The sample is collected by a local person, and tasted by a team composed mainly, sometimes entirely, of locals.

After a time it was noticed that tasting panels hesitated to refuse wines (surprise, surprise). In order to paper over the cracks in the system, the idea of a 'yellow card' (as on the football pitch, when a player has his name taken) was introduced. When there is doubt over a wine, it gets its certificate, but the grower receives a yellow card, which obliges him to receive at least one visit from an oenologist (paid for by the Chamber of Agriculture) to explain where he has gone wrong. He is not penalized, he is educated. The next year, in theory, the commission will be stricter.

In the meantime, you might notice, the consumer lost out again. Matters might change if consumer interests were represented on the tasting panels, but that is highly unlikely. Interest in fine Burgundy by consumers, traders and reporters (of many nationalities) is now extremely keen, but it is insufficiently harnessed.

The main problem is that the lobbies of the local *Syndicats* (growers' unions) are extremely strong, and the INAO lamentably pusillanimous. Many well-qualified, young growers would like to see matters changed, but are outnumbered by reactionaries in the *Syndicats*. Young oenologists may hang back from serving on the tasting panels, knowing them to be sometimes farcical, sometimes frightening.

Given that the private, internal controls do not work (any more than internal regulation of financial or insurance markets in London's Square Mile succeeded in preventing inefficiency and fraud on massive scales) consumers and traders should become more publicly voluble. Writers can have some influence, but their position is not as strong as that of traders and consumers working together. Those growers selling *Grands Crus* at high prices when they taste no better than village wines need publicly deriding, from outside the region. The French cannot do it, they get accused of being unpatriotic. Foreigners, however, need not be so inhibited. Wine is meant to be fun after all, not a painful rip-off. Laughter may yet prove stronger than the legislation.

CURRENT ISSUES

Analysis by magnetic nuclear resonance can now permit very accurate readings by the Répression des Fraudes of how much sugar has been added – if they choose to go that route (though it is not certain the analysis would stand up in court). But the authorities have been unwilling to use it, in exactly the same way that they have been unwilling to move against growers whose grapes were being harvested below the legal sugar levels at vintage time. The fraud squad inspectors do have teeth, but they are often unwilling to use them. As Pierre Boisset has pointed out,[5] they play the role of sheepdogs.

Today in the vineyard areas, the INAO is responsible for deciding what yield is compatible with correct levels of quality. In theory, the local interprofessional organizations have to decide what should be released on to the market.

With the 1992 harvest (a large one, which arrived at a time of slumped fine wine sales) the INAO used its quality control powers as an economic lever. It blocked at the property those volumes produced between the base yield and the PLC, the aim being to get trade moving again. The BIVB delegated to individual growers' unions the decision to apply for these volumes to be deblocked. By December 1992, virtually everyone had applied for the blocked stocks to be released, the honourable exceptions having been Musigny and Bonnes Mares, Corton and Corton-Charlemagne (amongst the *Grands Crus*), Chambolle-Musigny, Vougeot, Aloxe-Corton, Pernand-Vergelesses and Côte de Nuits-Villages (amongst the villages), and one lone regional *appellation* – Mâcon-Villages (the Mâconnais at the time was awash with white wine stock).

It would be possible to increase alcoholic content by adding concentrated must (*moût concentré rectifié*). But apparently there is no means of analysing how much has been added, so the authorities are unwilling to permit its use. Added to which, there is not enough Pinot Noir planted in France to supply reasonable volumes of concentrated Pinot must. It would have to be concentrated Aramon, or Carignan, or Grenache, which could have the same damaging

5 *Millésimes et campagnes: les carnets d'un acheteur de vins*, Robert Laffont, Paris, 1989.

influence on Burgundies as must-concentrates from southern Italy have had on Chianti. If alcoholic levels need increasing, sugar is undoubtedly preferable to concentrated musts.

Two amendments to the legislation were being sought in May 1993, through official channels up to Brussels. The first was that Burgundy should move from being a zone where chaptalization to give 2° additional alcohol is permitted, to one allowing 2.5 additional degrees. There is a danger, however, that if that were permitted, Burgundy might lose the facility to add acidity when the wines need it. Given that excessive potash fertilizing over decades is a root cause of low acid levels in the grapes, Burgundy sometimes really *does* need the facility to acidify.

The second was that adding the chaptalization sugar should be permitted in small doses, rather than in one dollop. This fractioned chaptalization is now 'tolerated' by the authorities – for it makes excellent wine-making sense – but the legislation currently bans it.

Some of the most interesting current discussions revolve around whether Burgundy should *reduce its minimum degrees*. Each *appellation* has a minimum degree set for it, but in practice – as is widely acknowledged – the authorities turn a blind eye in unripe years. It would be too unpopular to declassify thousands of growers' wines, so illegal doses of sugar are let through while the authorities wink, blink, or go on holiday.

But why were the levels set where they were? It dates back to the 1930s, when *appellation contrôlée* wines were of very minor importance in the French wine world. France was primarily a *vin de table* drinking country, and fine wine exports were insignificant, compared to today. In the minds of a *vin de table* grower, and the legislators of the time, alcoholic strength was the keynote to quality. Even though Burgundy was a northerly area, if it had pretensions to quality its natural alcohol levels had to be set high – higher than those of *vins de table* (which in the Midi fluctuated around 8.5° to 10°). So, for a Volnay to be called Volnay, or a Mercurey Mercurey it was stated it must attain a minimum of 10.5° naturally – it was purporting to be a quality wine, was it not? That meant a high natural sugar level. This level was good for all the village wines of the Côte, with *Premiers Crus* half a degree more, and *Grands Crus* another half degree. Of course, at the time, the yields were lower, so perhaps naturally these levels were achieved more easily than they are today.

Setting minimum degrees a bit high would help to keep the yields down, so the theory went. But in practice, yields crept up, and fraudulent quantities of sugar got chucked in, to bring alcoholic levels up to what the market expected. Now, of course, the consumer's palate has become accustomed to highly chaptalized Burgundy. Yields have continued to climb, as will be seen from a glance at Figure 3.

Today, do we judge and buy fine wine by its alcoholic content? Fine wine should be harmonious, be aromatic, be delicate, be characterful, be smooth. Probably over 12° alcohol – or at least over 11.5° – is needed for our palates to be satisfied with a fine wine's body and weight, but if drink-driving legislation is drawn tighter, and if concern over the effects of total alcohol absorption on our brains, and our general bodily health, is sustained, perhaps in future we should consider demanding lower total alcohol levels in our finest wines. Red Burgundy of 13° may become the exception, not the rule.

Instead of seeking to move Burgundy into the 2.5° chaptalization zone, the authorities might do well to knock half a degree off all the minimum levels. Let us admit it, these levels are not respected, anyway, nor have they been, for decades. They could realign with reality and common sense.

At least decisions could be taken at local levels, which is what the Marquis d'Angerville was considering, I believe, when he suggested to me, regarding chaptalization, 'It should be variable from year to year, to be decided locally. [That meant by the President of the local growers' Union]. The whole of France is not the same. Nature often makes a laughing-stock out of people.'

As vineyards are replanted with healthy clonal vines, and efficient yeast strains are increasingly available, obtaining higher alcoholic degree becomes easier. And conceivably, global warming will bring extra warmth to the Côte (see Climate, in the chapter on *terroir*). More immediately, Brussels has stepped in, with the aim of reducing production, as will be seen later in this chapter.

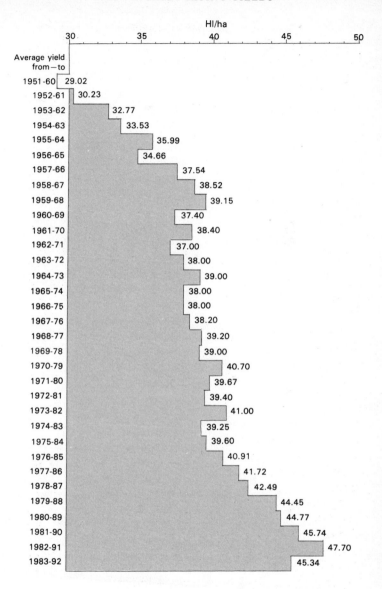

HI/ha

Average yield from—to	
1951-60	29.02
1952-61	30.23
1953-62	32.77
1954-63	33.53
1955-64	35.99
1956-65	34.66
1957-66	37.54
1958-67	38.52
1959-68	39.15
1960-69	37.40
1961-70	38.40
1962-71	37.00
1963-72	38.00
1964-73	39.00
1965-74	38.00
1966-75	38.00
1967-76	38.20
1968-77	39.20
1969-78	39.00
1970-79	40.70
1971-80	39.67
1972-81	39.40
1973-82	41.00
1974-83	39.25
1975-84	39.60
1976-85	40.91
1977-86	41.72
1978-87	42.49
1979-88	44.45
1980-89	44.77
1981-90	45.74
1982-91	47.70
1983-92	45.34

FIGURE 3. Evolution of the ten-year average yield of AC wines in the Côte D'or, 1951–92
(Source: INAO, Dijon)

Defending *appellation contrôlée* internationally

The INAO spends a lot of time and money trying to prevent, or reduce, the use of French wine names for non-French wines. According to Jérome Agostini,[6] two of the most abused names are Chablis and Burgundy (Sauternes and Champagne being the others). Sporadic problems like Sri-Lanka Chablis, Zimbabwe Burgundy or India Champagne are relatively easy to eradicate, but Canadian wine production (Ontario and British Columbia have 40 brands of 'Chablis' and 12 of 'Burgundy' between them) is thornier. The INAO estimates that a quarter of Australia's white-wine-makers use the word 'Chablis', and 12 per cent cling to the word 'Burgundy'. The USA is the biggest headache: counterfeiters (as the French see it) produce half a million hectolitres of 'Burgundy', and up to 3 million hectolitres of 'Chablis' a year – in three colours, and not forgetting 'Chablis with a twist'. These ancient abusive practices are deeply entrenched, and digging them out a costly job.

In March 1994, however, a Bi-lateral Wine Agreement between Australia and the European Community came into force which will result in the phasing out, at dates to be agreed, of the use by Australian wine-makers of names such as Chablis, Burgundy and Champagne for their wines. In exchange, Australian wines were assured of freer access into European markets. Here, the INAO appears to have pulled off a fine achievement.

INAO in the 1990s: which way forward?

Most of the wine legislation in force was designed to regulate and control production by a hidebound bunch of ill-educated peasants some of whom could barely read (and if they could, only did so when forced). It was set up when French wine exports were completely on the floor. Not only are the children and grandchildren of those peasants today in many cases highly educated, with top qualifications, many have trained internationally. They are certainly as well qualified as some Paris-influenced committee to decide whether a touch of natural tartaric acid should be added, or not, to their wines, and whether picking should start on Wednesday, Friday or next Monday. How can committees possibly come up with the

6 Jérome Agostini, Division Juridique et Etranger INAO, 'La Défense des AOC au plan international', Puligny-Montrachet, January 1991.

right day to start fruit-picking, in Burgundy's multitude of microclimates? Burgundy growers are forced to work within a legal straitjacket designed to address the problems of fifty years ago.

Many INAO bureaucrats seem to have become marginalized, and the thinly-spread fraud inspectors seem often irrelevant. Paris should consider further decentralizing, and, particularly, letting more decisions be taken by the individual producers.

Safeguards, of course, would be necessary. If domaines wished to have a freer hand in responsible decision-making they would have to apply, and be registered. But it would seem reasonable to trust those with qualifications and experience – for instance, oenologists. A BTSA qualification, and maybe also a BTAO, along with three years' wine-making experience, must also, surely, be worth something.[7]

At times the INAO seems completely out of touch with the real world of wine-drinking outside France. This has been seen, for instance, in its regular attempts to insist that names of grapes should not be permitted on regional *appellations*, with the outcome that Bourgogne Pinot Noir and Mâcon-Villages Chardonnay might become illegal. Why do they not urge (on the grounds that it is a loyal, local and constant tradition – which, I hasten to add, it is not) that all those selling wine should breakfast on raw garlic before visiting a customer, and speak only in the language of Racine, so that potential buyers may have the fullest possible benefits of France's ancient culture?

I realize that they are trying to add value to French wines, and that insistence on *geographical* origin (with names which cannot be used by other countries) is the only way they know to ensure that promotional work paid for with French funds will not be applied to the same grapes used elsewhere. But those horses bolted decades ago, and they would do well to recognize it.

Instead of which they breathe heavily over impoverished, hardpressed farmers up and down France, urging them to Sisyphean struggles with their local grape varieties, often obscure, often unloved by consumers (one thinks of the broad slopes of the Midi, where Grenache, Cinsault and Carignan – to name just the famous ones – have been encouraged while Cabernet Sauvignon, Sauvignon

7 These qualifications are to be had from the Lycée Agricole et Viticole in Beaune:
BTSA, Brevet de Technicien Supérieur Agricole ,option 'viticulture-oenologie';
BTAO, Brevet de Technicien Agricole, option 'viticulture-oenologie'.

Blanc and Chardonnay may be forbidden). Some of the best hill-sides and soils of France can not be planted with France's best grapes. The vineyards of the New World (some of them completely non-existent ten years ago) have been given, with this decision, years and years' worth of head starts.

Or they deny them the right to attempt to improve quality by adapting pruning and trellising methods in line with modern techniques (one thinks of the rigid approach to vine training for the regional *appellations* of the Côte d'Or).

Additional, solid value could be added to French wines not by interfering with the salesmen, who have enough problems, or the marketing – there are experts in each country to handle that – but by wading into the mediocrities at production level, to downgrade them, to declass them, fast, irrevocably, and now. If that were to happen (instead of fraud inspectors wasting time and money catching out well-meaning firms in minor illegalities) Burgundy's reputation could move upwards as steeply as a Mirage jet taking off from Longvic.

Perhaps they need to start dismantling certain sections of the AC edifice. It is historic, magnificent, solid – but now dated. Power and freedom could be released downwards.

Competition for Burgundy has got stiffer from outside France, but also from within it – for instance from the Midi, where fine wines are increasingly being produced, inexpensively, too, if often with unheard-of *vin de pays* names. New distribution methods and patterns, which touch young clients, are often used more effectively by new products than old ones. Certain overseas markets are saturated with fine wine, and certain are turning to protectionism, favouring their local productions. Anti-alcohol groups have been voluble, economies in recession, and wealth-growth has been non-existent. Events in the early 1990s have forced a new realism on Burgundy's wine traders.

Given these threats and challenges, Burgundy needs to eliminate whatever is not characteristic, whatever is mediocre, and whatever leaves consumers in doubt as to its value and uniqueness.

Brussels targets chaptalisation, and much else

There has been enormous global overproduction of wine since the mid-1980s. The European Commission has estimated that, if current trends continue, there will still be a surplus of 39 million hectolitres per annum by the year 2000, this being more than a fifth of Europe's wine production.[8] The excess each year is distilled, at great cost to taxpayers.

In summer 1994 the Commission issued new proposals to address the problem, treating table wine and quality wine regions alike. Burgundian authorities were outraged, seeing it as an unjust, and potentially mortal, thunderbolt. A 17 per cent decrease in production was being sought, to be achieved by reducing alcoholic degree, reducing chaptalisation, reducing yields and ripping out vineyards. 'The heart of the Burgundian system is affected' wrote the BIVB, grouping together the views of both growers and *négoçiants*.

Burgundians may come to recognize that from economic, quality and image standpoints they made a grave tactical error seeking to increase chaptalisation levels in the early 1990s, from 2° to 2.5°. Chaptalisation is Burgundy's Achilles heel, but a part of the body they do not enjoy seeing fingered. Brussels appears now to have placed it, along with yields, firmly in the public eye.

Jancis Robinson has written:[9]

The observer may wonder ... why in an age in which many consumers wish to curb their consumption of alcohol, and there is a global wine surplus, the wine industry systematically and deliberately increases the alcohol content of so many of its products, in many cases to compensate for overcropped vines.

Why, indeed?

No doubt partly in response to the Brussels initiative, during the first few days of the 1994 vintage the INAO agreed, following requests from Burgundian wine-growers, that all the minimum, natural alcoholic degrees of Burgundy's *appellations*, throughout the Yonne and Côte d'Or – regional wines, village wines, *Premiers Crus* and *Grands Crus* – should be cut by a half degree. The Mâconnais and Côte Chalonnaise were split: Rully and the Pouillys staying put, but Mercurey, Bouzeron, Bourgogne (*rouge*) and northern Mâconnais dropping the half degree, for instance.

The first straws in the wind had appeared in the Beaujolais the

8 *The Oxford Companion to Wine*, ed. Jancis Robinson, Oxford University Press, Oxford, 1994
9 *ibid.*

previous year, when a half degree was knocked off the minimum natural alcoholic levels of all Beaujolais, Beaujolais-Villages and *crus*, and this was repeated in respect of the 1994 Beaujolais vintage, for all *appellations*.

These moves call into question laws which date back fifty years. It is an admirable, historic about-turn, which may have highly beneficial consequences.

PART TWO

9

Introduction to Part Two

Part Two describes the people, places and wines of Burgundy, village by village, from the Yonne and Chablis in the north down to the Mâconnais and Beaujolais at Burgundy's southern edge.

For each region, village and *Grand Cru* I give figures showing the average production over the five vintages 1988–92. I think this will be of more interest than, for instance, the ten-year average 1983–92 (for during that decade there was much vineyard expansion and replanting), or simply showing the production figures for the most recent vintage.

In 1991, plantation rights in Burgundy were blocked, the French authorities recognizing that they were faced with fine wine over-production and an economic recession. This meant, and will mean until the law is changed, that no additional vineyard land could be brought into production. (Growers are not prevented from renewing existing vineyards, nor from switching production rights from, for instance, some old Aligoté vines they are happy to pull up in order to plant some *appellation* Santenay land which was lying fallow. But they cannot plant up the Santenay unless they pull up the Aligoté.)

If a consumer, wine writer, wine buyer, retail shop manager or tasting group organizer wishes to obtain up-to-date production figures, I recommend a faxed enquiry directly to the BIVB in Beaune, or the UIVB in Villefranche for matters relating to the Beaujolais (both of whom I have found very efficient; details are in Appendix E). Such annual production figures, set against these five-year averages from the years leading up to the blocking of plantation rights, should make interesting comparisons, and help one to set claims about future vintages (their small size, for instance) in proportion.

Production figures are shown as cases of 12 bottles of 75 cl., calculated on the basis that 1 hectolitre yields 11 cases, from figures supplied by BIVB and the UIVB (their sources being the Direction Générale des Impôts). I have rounded the figures down to the nearest hundred cases, for village and regional ACs, and to the nearest ten cases for *Grands Crus*.

Where vineyard surfaces are shown, these relate to the position in 1991 or 1992, however indicated (sources being BIVB and UIVB).

Over seven hundred Burgundy producers are described or listed: the leading domaine-bottling growers, cooperatives and merchants.

The sizes of *Grand Cru* (Great Growth), *Premier Cru* (First Growth) and commune vineyards are given in hectares, as accurately as possible. After every grower's name is shown the total size of his or her vineyards in hectares. There may be a difference between the total figure and the sum of the individual vineyards, to be explained either by regional *appellations* (such as Bourgognes, Passe-Tout-Grains, Aligotés and Bourgogne Grand Ordinaires), or by young vineyards not yet in production. A percentage figure follows, which shows the approximate proportion of the total harvest which, in a good year, is bottled at the estate. When a grower owns more than one First Growth in the same village, the name of the village is not repeated. The word 'Monopole' appears whenever a grower is sole proprietor of the listed vineyard; there are 150 of these, summarized in Appendix A. Often a grower or merchant owns vineyards in several communes. Details of the grower's estate appear wherever the vat-house and cellars are located; in the case of merchants, where his business is based. The same vineyard may be spelt differently by two growers. Where there is no accepted, correct form, I have tried to follow the spelling which appears on individual grower's labels. First Growths are named and listed individually, except where two or more small-holdings are commonly vinified together, when a simple *Premier Cru* total is given.

The figure in brackets after a merchant's name indicates the year the company was founded. No percentage figure is given after merchants' vineyard possessions for they practically always bottle all their wines themselves.

Metric measures have not been converted into their British or American equivalents, for these details will chiefly be of interest to the visitor to Burgundy. When discussing wine with a proprietor, it is essential to feel at home with hectolitres and hectares. Here is a simple conversion table:

1 hectare (ha.): approximately 2½ acres
1 hectolitre (hl): 100 litres: 22 gallons or 11 dozen bottles
1 barrel (*une pièce*): 228 litres: 25 dozen bottles
(In Chablis the standard barrel is the *feuillette*, holding 132 litres; Mâconnais-Beaujolais barrels hold 212–16 litres.)

Be warned, however, that vineyard owners will often confuse matters by talking not of hectolitres and hectares, but of quarter-casks and *ouvrées*, the game being played with the persistence of estate agents calculating property values in a mixture of old centimes and new francs. The *ouvrée* is an old measure equivalent to 0.0428 ha. It is most often met with in the following sort of conversation: 'In the old days yields were far smaller; my father used to make a quarter-barrel (*quartaut*) per *ouvrée*. If he made half a barrel it was miraculous. But these days people make a whole barrel, even two barrels.' Here are the modern equivalents:

quartaut à l'ouvrée: 13.5 hl/ha.
½ *pièce à l'ouvrée*: 27 hl/ha.
1 *pièce à l'ouvrée*: 54 hl/ha.
2 *pièces à l'ouvrée*: 108 hl/ha.

There is scarcely an estate which does not bottle off the odd barrel of wine for family consumption; overnight it can begin to commercialize such wine as domaine-bottled. However, it takes practice to succeed in this, so I have tried to make a choice of those estates equipped and experienced in wine-making, tending and bottling, to whom I would go, or have gone, first when buying wine in bottle. Selection was made after consultation with merchants, brokers, growers, traders and consumers, and regular reference to recent Burgundy books (details of which will be found in the Bibliography). Most of these growers own more than 5 hectares, and bottle over 50 per cent of their produce in a good year.

I have also often described estates and merchants I avoid buying from, for various reasons. Burgundy is a confusing place, and the reader needs help forming his or her own judgement. One must try mediocre and poor bottles to appreciate fully the brilliance of the best wine-makers. Neither readers nor the Burgundians should take my strictures too seriously, however; they are only one person's impressions, included because I think it is constructive to do so. Given the speed with which Burgundy is currently changing, evolving and improving, the bottle which disappointed me (if it was not an accidental aberration) has possibly by now been followed by a younger vintage which would delight me. As will be seen, I have not attempted quality assessments of every establishment described, but give leads or hints where I believe these may be of value.

The accuracy of my figures cannot be guaranteed. A proprietor who in fact bottles all his wine in a fine year may only have admitted to bottling 60 per cent for fear merchants would black him the next bad year. Also there may be some duplication of vineyards. An ageing proprietor who has leased out his vines on the half-fruit system may have declared himself the owner of all the land even though he only sells half of the wine; the lessee may have done the same.

I have tried to keep abreast of marriages and deaths, of changes within businesses, of land acquisitions and sales, but am aware that errors will have crept in. I should be most thankful for any corrections from readers (however angry). Please fax details directly to me in London (0) 171 226 4575; all contributions will be gratefully acknowledged, and mistakes rectified when the book is reprinted.

To spend half a page describing a merchant's own vineyards may be said to be missing the point if they represent a mere 5 per cent of his turnover. But often they are his prestige products, and ownership of vineyards is of increasing importance as more growers refuse to part with their wines to the trade. Many merchants only differ from their colleagues by their vine possessions.

The *appellation* laws stipulate different minimum, and now maximum, levels of sugar in the grapes for each wine of Burgundy, but I have not listed them. They are often ignored by growers, brokers, merchants and enforcement authorities when it suits them, and we might as well ignore them too. As discussed in Part One, there has probably been too much concern with natural sugar levels, and this can often divert attention away from more crucial matters, such as intensity of fruit, length of flavour and texture.

10

The Yonne: Chablis, Auxerre and New Yonne Vineyards

The vineyards of the Yonne *département* are mainly situated in two valleys, the Yonne and its tributary, the Serein. The latter is the narrower, and consequently more subject to spring frosts. In twenty communes in the low hills and combes which border the Serein are to be found the vineyards of Chablis. We shall come to them in a moment, but first let us look at the wine history of the area.

Vines ran up to the walls of Auxerre as long ago as AD 680, so the account of Bishop Vigile tells us. And from the beginning, the small craft of the Yonne river, which runs past the town, were responsible for distributing the wines. Nearby Chablis and its territory belonged to the monks of Saint-Martin de Tours, who had arrived in the area, at the Abbey of Auxerre, around 530. They had fled before the Vikings, who were sailing up the Loire, carrying with them the relics of Saint Martin. In 867 Charles the Bold made a gift to these monks of the small monastery of Saint-Loup, which had been founded in Chablis by Sigismond (first Christian king of the *Burgondes*) in 510. Another monastery was to play a part in establishing the renown of Chablis, that of Pontigny, 20 kilometres away, which was founded by Cîteaux in 1114. It is a magnificent white church, almost the size of Notre Dame, where three Archbishops of Canterbury, including Thomas à Becket, gained sanctuary in the Middle Ages. Although the monks had a small vineyard called *la Vieille Plante* nearby, they lost no time in seeking agreement with those of Saint-Martin de Tours to exploit land at Chablis. A house was obtained in 1118, with enclosable land and thirty-six *arpents*[1] of vineyard.

At this time it was said of the Comte de Gatinois that his Auxerre

1 An old French measure roughly equal to an acre.

vines gave 'delicious wine beyond all expression'. Two kings, François I and Henry IV, looked favourably on the region, the one allowing its wines to be sold throughout the kingdom, the other removing taxation on them.

'Few wine reputations in France are so anciently attested as that of Auxerre', writes Professor Dion. 'From the twelfth century, at a time when texts concerning the export trade of wines are still silent about Beaune and Bordeaux, clerks are using emphatic adjectives: *superlativum, pretiosissimum,* to describe Auxerre's wines. One sees King John being given a *tonneau,* in 1203, in gratitude for affixing the royal seal on an act confirming an agreement between the Earl of Leicester and the Bishop of Lincoln.'

Through the centuries, Paris was the outlet for the wine of the region, as for its wood, its charcoal, its cattle and its building stone, which went down to the capital via the Yonne and its tributaries. Often the barrels did not stop in Paris, but went on to Rouen, Normandy and overseas. The correspondence of the Chevalier d'Eon, who lived in London in the eighteenth century, shows that wine from nearby Tonnerre was much appreciated in England at that time.

Professor Dion describes how, by the seventeenth century, 150 itinerant merchants habitually brought Yonne wines for sale in Paris. It was fashionable for nobles, churchmen and bourgeois (described in 1607 as *ces gros-milours, ces ventres-gras*) to own their own vines in the region. But disaster was to overtake the Auxerrois.

Because of its proximity to Paris, the north and the east of France, it became a most important table-wine production area in the eighteenth and nineteenth centuries, indeed the most important in Burgundy. In 1788 there were 32,000 hectares planted, in 1888 over 40,000 hectares. Three-quarters of the production was red wine, one quarter white, but Pinot Noir and Chardonnay had given way before large-yielding varieties, particularly Gamay and Sacy. Only in the small enclave of Chablis and its nearest communes had the Chardonnay retained its hold.

The vineyards of the Auxerrois received three body-blows during the second half of the nineteenth century, from which they are only now coming round. Mildew ravaged them, the phylloxera devastated them, and then they lost their traditional market to wines from the Midi, which could reach Paris cheaply thanks to the

Table 5   AOC and VDQS vineyards and wines of the Yonne *département*

| | Vines in production (ha.) | | |
	1981 vintage	1991 vintage	vines
LE CHABLISIEN			
Chablis *Grand Cru*	91	98	Chardonnay
Chablis *Premier Cru*	474	692	Chardonnay
Chablis	924	2,140	Chardonnay
Petit Chablis	113	305	Chardonnay
Chablisien subtotal:	1,602	3,235	
L'AUXERROIS			
Bourgogne *blanc* (Côtes d'Auxerre)	29	142	Chardonnay
Bourgogne *rouge* (Côtes d'Auxerre)	189	366²	Pinot Noir and César
Crémant de Bourgogne (*blanc* and *rosé*)	191	157	Chardonnay, Pinot Noir, Sacy, Aligoté, Melon de Bourgogne
Bourgogne Aligoté	152	200	Aligoté
Sauvignon de Saint Bris	63	69	Sauvignon
Bourgogne Passe-Tout-Grains	71	75	Gamay (66%)
Bourgogne Grand Ordinaire			Pinot Noir (33%)
blanc	56	31	Sacy and Melon
rouge	19	18	Gamay and Pinot Noir
Auxerrois subtotal:	770	1,058	
Yonne grand total	2,372 (ha.)	4,293 (ha.)	

Notes

(In 1975, the comparable Yonne grand total was a mere 1,743 ha.)

2 This total includes that for Bourgogne Irancy, amounting to 119 ha. The figure for 1981 is not available.

newly opened railways. Of the 40,000 hectares planted in the 1880s there remained by 1968 a mere 3,617 hectares, over half of which was table wine for home consumption. But there has been a quality wine renaissance (the total area under *appellation contrôlée* vines more than tripling since 1968). By 1991 there were fewer than 800 hectares left of *vin ordinaire*. The details of the quality wines are shown in the Table, comparing 1981 with 1991, so that recent trends may be seen.

There is little change in Chablis *Grand Cru*, for the total area had already been pretty much planted up. New *Premiers Crus* have been established by deforesting appropriate hillsides, and by protecting, thanks to new anti-frost technology, slopes which were previously not worth planting. But the biggest jump is for basic Chablis, where the surface has more than doubled in ten years.

In the Auxerrois, Aligoté has expanded gently, Chardonnay and Pinot Noir more spectacularly, both being now destined to be sold as Bourgogne Côtes d'Auxerre.

CHABLIS

Chablis is to wine what Corot is to paintings: three out of four are false – or so the saying used to go. Perhaps it is still true if one takes into account all the Californian, Australian, Canadian and other wines whose makers cannot be bothered, or are unable, to build a reputation in their own right; fortunately it is no longer the case with Chablis AC.

As we have seen, the grape is the Chardonnay, locally known as Beaunois. It is grown on clayey-limestone hillside and plateau soils, which are sometimes stonier, and often deeper, than those of the Côte d'Or. The bedrock is 20 million years younger, being upper Jurassic.

Yonne vines must be grafted on to specially lime-resistant root-stocks, and, before the arrival of virus-free clonal root-stocks, similar errors occurred in the Yonne (with 41B, for instance) as we saw in the Côte d'Or.

The Yonne experimented with clonal selection of Chardonnays in liaison with the Côte d'Or, establishing fourteen families in 1974. Almost all Chablis replanting is now with clonal Chardonnay. Because of the greater richness of the soil the pruning is different

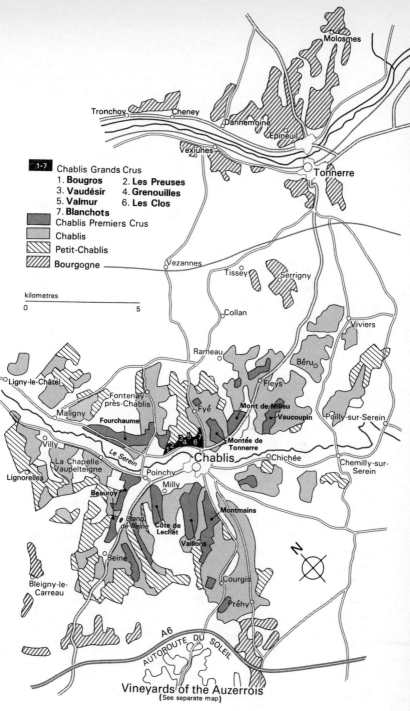

Molosmes

Tronchoy Cheney Dannemoine

Vexilles Épineuil

Tonnerre

1-7 Chablis Grands Crus
1. **Bougros** 2. **Les Preuses**
3. **Vaudésir** 4. **Grenouilles**
5. **Valmur** 6. **Les Clos**
7. **Blanchots**
Chablis Premiers Crus
Chablis
Petit-Chablis
Bourgogne

kilometres
0 ———————————— 5

Vezannes
Tissey Serrigny
Collan
Viviers
Rameau Béru
Fleys
Ligny-le-Châtel
Fontenay- Fyé Mont de Milieu
près-Chablis Vaucoupin
Maligny Poilly-sur-Serein
Fourchaume
3 5 7
2 4
1 6 **Montée de
Tonnerre**
Villy **Chablis**
Le Serein Chichée
La Chapelle- Poinchy Chemilly-sur-
Vaupelteigne Serein
Lignorelles **Milly**
Beauroy **Montmains**
Étang
de Beine **Côte de
Lechet**
Beine **Vaillons**
N
Bleigny-le- Courgis
Carreau Préhy

A6
AUTOROUTE DU SOLEIL
Vineyards of the Auzerrois
(See separate map)

Vineyards of Chablis and the Tonnerrois

from the rest of Burgundy, being a double Guyot with two long fruit-bearing canes. They are often bent downhill, to diminish vegetation and encourage the production of fruit.

Frost protection

Frost has always been a far greater problem in Chablis than elsewhere in Burgundy. In the years 1945, 1951, 1953 and 1957 the crop was totally wiped out; from 1955 to 1961 parts of the vineyard were touched every year except 1958. The *Grands Crus* were always the worst hit, for the narrow Serein valley tends to trap cool air masses, to the extent that growers gave up replanting. The great vineyards of Clos and Grenouilles were stubble-fields on which children tobogganed in the winter only forty years ago. The most dangerous period has always been 15–31 May, for if young buds are caught then it is too late for them to shoot again.

Anti-frost systems are normally installed in the vineyards around 25 April, when the pruning and one ploughing have taken place. Various methods have been tried: paraffin candles (which tend to burn the nearby vines); various heaters using fuel-oil; and thermostatically-controlled gas burners, though these sometimes fail to raise the temperature sufficiently. The most imaginative and effective (but it is expensive) installation is a network of underground pipes and over-vine sprinklers connected to pumps on the river Serein, or a man-made lake. The sprinklers come into operation when the temperature drops to freezing, covering the young shoots with a thin layer of ice; they are then as snug and safe as snowdrops under the snow. It needs a lot of water, and the likelihood of frost on subsequent days is increased once you start to sprinkle, because of the increased humidity in the vineyard. But it is an economical system, if requiring delicate handling. One of the first installations protected Fourchaume, taking its water from a specially dug horseshoe bend of the Serein; another was the artificial lake on the road between Chablis and Auxerre, which sprays vineyards in the communes of Beine, Poinchy and Milly.

In the thirty years after Louis Bro published, in 1959, *Chablis, porte d'or de la Bourgogne* the area under vines increased six-fold. This was partly due to the possibility of protection against spring frosts, and the ease with which land could be chemically disinfected (thus eliminating the need for ten or fifteen years between grubbing up and replanting a vineyard). Progressively more estates moved over to cultivating the vine exclusively, thereby requiring a larger area under cultivation. It corresponded also with the world's thirst for Chardonnay becoming established.

There are Chablisiens who still remember well the years after the Second World War, when there were many old vignerons, for much labour had been lost to the towns. A vigneron would have cows and cornfields, and in order to make ends meet the wives would keep rabbits, hens and a pig. The local *négociant* was really someone in those days. As Michel Rémon (previously owner of Regnard/Pic, now retired) used to recall, when he went a few kilometres down the road from Chablis, to La Chapelle perhaps, the word would go round the hamlet, 'He's here, he may drop in'. There was an additional link in the distribution chain, for Regnard would use a *courtier de campagne* to aid the transaction. One such broker was Simon of Fleys, a bachelor. The broker had title to a free lunch whenever a deal had been done and the wine taken away, and Monsieur Simon would artfully insist on his right even if he had arranged three deliveries in a morning, storing up free lunches for days ahead.

The vigneron-raconteur Robert Fèvre used to recall pressing in the old days, when the whole Chablis harvest went through twenty-six presses owned by twenty-two families. Five men were needed to turn the press, and even then they only managed one day-time and one night-time *marc*. The small vigneron would bring his grapes to a bourgeois house; they would be pressed, and the must carried back to his cellar slung between the shoulders of two men walking in step. A crown of rye straw would be put in the container to prevent the must from slopping over. The owner of the press would obtain payment according to the number of *feuillettes* produced.

And those *cabanes*, shaped like igloos, of which just one remains to be seen, at the Domaine de Vauroux . . . When earth was brought by donkeys from hill-top or valley to replace the winter's erosions, the large stones would be set on one side. Communal effort would then build them into domed shelters, with a hole in the top, which let the smoke out, or the sun in, and could be blocked in times of rain. Since there was no cement, something had to be done to fill the crevices between the stones. So a trench would be dug round the outside of the *cabane* and earth piled against it, at least high enough to keep the draughts above the heads of those sitting inside, their backs against the stones.

It was a harder life in those days, of course. Père Collet, for instance, used to recall the spring frosts of 1926, 1927 and 1928 when as a newly married man he had no wine to sell for three consecutive years.

In addition to Chablis itself, nineteen communes have the right to the *appellation*. Progressing down the Serein valley they are: Poilly, Chemilly, Préhy, Chichée, Béru, Viviers, Courgis, Fleys, Milly, Fyé, Rameau (a hamlet of Collan), Beine, Poinchy, Fontenay, La Chapelle, Lignorelles, Villy, Maligny and Ligny-le-Châtel. It is a pretty valley, the roadsides dotted with cowslips in April. Only twenty years ago, if you went for a walk in the mixed evergreen and deciduous woods you could still see traces of old rows of vines, for many of these woods had been vineyards. Now many are again, thanks to land reclassification and bulldozers, for the look of the hillsides around the town has been greatly transformed over the last two decades.

This was not achieved without controversy, the two main rivals in the disputes having been Jean Durup of Maligny, and William Fèvre of the Domaine de la Maladière in Chablis, each heading up rival growers' unions in the district. Bitter argument revolved around what should constitute the specified area where First Growth Chablis, Chablis and Petit Chablis should be grown.

Chablis was recognized by the tribunals in 1923, and the INAO in 1938, as being grown on a subsoil of Kimmeridgian limestone (the name comes from the Dorset village of Kimmeridge). Petit Chablis could be grown anywhere else within the twenty communes, theoretically on as many as 17,000 hectares. It was Jean Durup's contention that this was a major error – for was not orientation and altitude of the vineyard frequently of greater importance? Had not some Chablis always anyway been grown on Portlandian limestone?

He succeeded in persuading the INAO to appoint a highly qualified commission of experts to reopen the investigation, and in November 1976 decrees were published which more or less vindicated his views, removing the reference to Kimmeridgian and taking into account all factors, such as aspect and microclimate, when arriving at the classification. Much of the land around Monsieur Durup's home village of Maligny was upgraded from Petit Chablis to Chablis, to the fury of Monsieur Fèvre and his supporters, whose battle-cry remained Kimmeridge. They lodged an appeal against the 1976 decrees before the Council of State, the highest court in the land for disputes between individual and the state, but it was doomed to fail. As a consequence, many south-, and south-east facing hillsides in the little valleys which stretch sideways from the Serein have been de-forested, and are now planted up to Chardonnay vines, are frost-protected, and yield wines called Chablis or Chablis *Premier Cru*. This latter *appellation* came a bit fast, it may be argued, for unproved vineyards planted entirely with young vines; but no doubt the political pressures to go the whole hog – all the way to First Growth status from Day One – were extremely heavy.

There are forty named Chablis First Growths (*Premiers Crus*), but some are completely obscure. As one finds in Chassagne-Montrachet, where the name Morgeot may be applied, for the sake of simplicity, to many little-known First Growth names, certain First Growth names are umbrellas for lesser-known sites. There are seventeen such flagship names, as follows:

MONT DE MILIEU

MONTÉE DE TONNERRE, Chapelot, Pied d'Aloup, Côte de Bréchain

FOURCHAUME, Vaupulent, Côte de Fontenay, L'Homme Mort, Vaulorent

VAILLONS, Châtains, Sécher, Beugnons, Les Lys, Mélinots, Ron-cières, Les Epinottes

MONTMAINS, Forêt, Butteaux

CÔTE DE LÉCHET

BEAUROY, Troesmes, Côte de Savant

VAU LIGNEAU

VAU DE VEY, Vaux Ragons

VAUCOUPIN

VOSGROS, Vaugiraut

LES FOURNEAUX, Morein, Côte des Prés Girots

CÔTE DE VAUBAROUSSE

BERDIOT

CHAUME DE TALVAT

CÔTE DE JOUAN

LES BEAUREGARDS, Côte de Cuissy

It is hard for an outsider to understand why two names from the hamlet of Fyé (Côte de Vaubarousse and Berdiot) should have been imposed on us as flagship First Growths. Equally with Chaume de Talvat, Côte de Jouan and Les Beauregards, all apparently flagships from the commune of Courgis. It is, however, comprehensible if one considers the occasional pusillanimity of the INAO, which can have the greatest difficulty in saying no to vineyard owners and a comparable problem dragging into consciousness some semblance of a thought-process on the needs of overseas consumers (which in the case of Chablis represented, in 1989, 90 per cent of the market).

The seven *Grands Crus* in Chablis are long established, and uncontroversial, just over 100 hectares being now in production. In descending order of size they are: Les Clos (26.05 ha.), a good example of which is the most perfectly balanced Chablis for bottle-ageing, being harmonious, rich yet steely; Vaudésir (14.71 ha.) ripe, spicy and complete; Valmur (13.2 ha.), which rarely has the elegance of Vaudésir, but can be full and soft while ageing well. The last two *Crus*, however, have sections which are less well-orientated than others, so there are wide differences in ripeness. Blanchot (12.72 ha.) can have a touch of hardness when young, but is perfumed and harmonious; Bougros (12.63 ha.) is the burliest of the seven, sometimes short on perfume and elegance in this fine company; Preuses (11.44 ha.) often achieves succulent ripeness, and can be enjoyed when youthful (Moutonne is an enclave which straddles Preuses and Vaudésir – see Domaine de la Moutonne); Grenouilles (9.38 ha.) combines piercing fruitiness with racy elegance and aptitude for ageing.

Visiting Chablis

The obvious drive around the district is to aim towards the hill of *Grands Crus*, out of Chablis, across the Serein river. It is worth going up to the Panorama des Clos, a look-out from the woods above the *Grand Cru* Les Clos, reached after driving uphill past the vineyards. When you come back down, from Chablis, take the road towards Ligny-le-Châtel, alongside First Growth Fourchaume all the way to Maligny, where you turn left, through Villy, towards Lignorelles. You climb over a plateau towards Beines, then drive past its lake, past Préhy and Milly to regain Chablis.

More unusual is the road towards Auxerre via Courgis. This gives superb views of the church of Sainte Claire, surrounded by vines on a hilltop, beside Préhy – one of Chablis's most beautiful and enduring images. Leaving Chablis for Courgis, wooded, south-facing hillsides may still be seen, where one may fantasize about hiring a bulldozer, reclaiming scrubland, and creating a great Chablis domaine from scratch. But one would have to contend with the locals, who are very adept at keeping outsiders at bay . . . Chablis vineyards peter out as you climb upwards towards Auxerre, then suddenly you drive under the *autoroute*, and down into another valley. This is quite different countryside, with cherry trees and old man's beard and patchy plots of vines. This is Chitry, no longer Chablis, and struggles to survive. The fortified church, a great dungeon tower in place of a choir, is magnificent.

Present tendencies, current concerns

Petit Chablis and Chablis are almost entirely machine-harvested today, and so are many First Growths. A number of domaines are implacable hand-harvesters: Vincent Dauvissat, Joseph Drouhin, Jean-Marie Raveneau, Laurent Tribut, and many others hand-harvest their First and Great Growths, Jean-Paul Droin, William Fèvre, Domaine de la Meulière, Jean Collet amongst them.

So long as harvesting machines are really well looked after between harvests they can do excellent work, but not every estate has presses of the right size to handle speedily the quantities of grapes being machine-picked. If grapes and juice have to wait, oxidation can occur. Pneumatic presses have often replaced Vaslin chain-and-compressing-plate presses, but the latter still do excellent work if slow, long programmes are chosen, and the cake of skins and pulp split up three times rather than five or six.

Most planting, and replanting, has been with cloned Chardonnays, which are efficient alcohol producers, and this has resulted in an increase in the amount of juice that is naturally rich in sugar. As elsewhere in Burgundy, excess use of potassium fertilizer causes musts to be low in acidity, but since consumers generally prefer white wines which are low in acid, and since most Chablis is not made for maturing, the drop in acidity levels cannot be considered serious. Indeed it probably contributes, along with the higher alcohol levels, to the wines' popularity.

Dried yeast cultures are widely used, and inoculation with lactic bacteria, to speed the malolactic fermentation, is becoming more common. Many large estates find that yeast cultures bring about more regular fermentations, giving clean, dependable wines, with less risk of hydrogen sulphide smells, and with natural alcohol production maximized.

The use of new oak has spread, and it is now quite common to find strong aromas of vanilla and new wood in a glass of First Growth and Great Growth Chablis. It makes them often very delicious indeed, or turns them into caricatures, depending on one's point of view. They can be difficult to tell apart from other good white Burgundies, but this is a problem which growers could rapidly, and economically, resolve, should consumers manifest genuine boredom with oak. The best growers are using new wood with subtlety.

The Chablisiens are almost pathologically incapable of discussing their wines openly, in company, except in the blandest possible terms. Perhaps it is not surprising, the district having been so riven by the schism over vineyard extension that emotions and rivalries still run high.

Around a table of Chablis wine-growing enthusiasts there is a taboo about saying something critical – even if the spirit is constructive or enquiring – about another grower's wine. I remember at a spectacular tasting of Chablis from 1988 back to 1959, being served a Chablis Fourchaume from Roger Seguinot (a senior figure, and grower's doyen). It should have been exquisite, but the colour had been bleached by over-sulphuring at bottling, and the nose was unbelievable, like leaning over the crater (while breathing in) of Mount Etna. If this had been Sonoma or Adelaide – or even Ruoms or Limoux – a red-faced grower would, I think, have been on his feet apologizing to tasters for his slip of the wrist with the sulphur-dose. But this was Burgundy (to be fair, the problem is certainly not restricted to Chablis). Monsieur Seguinot stayed firmly in his seat while we spluttered and whispered.

When William Fèvre was fighting to restrict vineyard expansion in the 1970s he wrote in *Les Vrais Chablis et les autres*, 'If Chablis were to produce 200,000 hl through expansion on to the plateaux opened to its development by the decrees and survey of 1976, it would cease to occupy a place "in the first ranks of the wines of France", as Guyot described it in 1868. It would fall to a level alongside many foreign dry white wines which call themselves Chablis.' That production level has now been reached (207,000 hl in 1992), without, however, the reputation of Chablis disintegrating. But with prices running (in 1993) at levels where growers barely recover their costs, in a world market for Chardonnay which looks decidedly crowded, I believe growers and *négociants* would do well to attempt more open discussion, and more public tasting, of wines within the district, before they are exported. They may have satisfied themselves that their best *terroirs* have now been identified, they may have invested in planting them up, but some have still to master certain technical turns-of-the-wrist which ensure that consumers and traders regularly consider their wines to be of dependable, top quality.

Chablis growers

CHRISTIAN ADINE   17 ha. (55 per cent)
DOMAINE LES BONNES VIGNES
DOMAINE DE LA CONCIERGERIE

Chablis Montmains 3.35 ha., Butteaux (BIO) 1.1 ha., Côte de Cuissy 0.76 ha., Chablis (BIO) 3.7 ha., Chablis 8 ha.

Christian Adine was one of the first to adopt an organic approach to viticulture, forming a group of fourteen growers in 1991, on the arrival of Jean-François Crochet at the GETEVAY research station in Auxerre. Two years later interest in the reasoned-out approach had exploded, and the number had swollen to 150 members.

Since 1992, a third of Adine's domaine has been tended biologically. After three years the wines will qualify for the mention BIO (according to the rules of the Bio-Bourgogne group). This is an excellent source.

Christian Adine, rue Restif de la Bretonne, Courgis, 89800 Chablis

DOMAINE BAILLARD   15 ha. (15 per cent)

Chablis Fourchaume 0.26 ha., Vaillons 0.75 ha., Montmains 1 ha., Montée de Tonnerre 0.15 ha., Chablis 12.6 ha., Petit Chablis 0.3 ha.

The eldest Servin son, Jean, has created this estate independently of the family domaine (see Domaine Servin, below), from a combination of his wife's, purchased, and rented vines. Each business has a harvesting machine, so they take turns to work speedily together in each other's vineyards, the aim being to fill a trailor as fast as possible, cutting down oxidation time between vines and press-house. His temperature-controlled vat-house was completed in 1989.

I have the impression that chaptalizations here are kept to a minimum. Some barrel-fermentation takes place, but this is primarily a good source of interesting straight Chablis.

Jean Servin, route d'Auxerre, 89800 Chablis

MICHEL BARAT   15 ha. (65 per cent)

Chablis Vaillons 3 ha., Côte de Léchet 3 ha., Mont de Milieu 1 ha., Fourneaux 2 ha.

Supple, cleanly-made wines, for drinking youthful.

Joëlle et Michel Barat, 6 rue de Léchet, Milly, 89800 Chablis

J. BILLAUD-SIMON   20 ha. (60 per cent)
DOMAINE DE MAISON BLANCHE

Chablis Les Clos 0.5 ha., Vaudésirs 0.75 ha., Les Preuses 0.5 ha., Blanchots 0.25 ha., Montée de Tonnerre 2.5 ha., Fourchaume 0.3 ha., Mont de Milieu 4 ha., Vaillons 4 ha., Chablis 7 ha., Petit Chablis 0.5 ha.

Technically sophisticated, this domaine has very high-perform-ance equipment. Eighty per cent of its vineyards are superbly placed on the Serein's right bank, but so far for me the wines have lacked personality and length. Nothing has been spared however, so it could only be a matter of time before really fine wines become available here.

Bernard et Samuel Billaud, 1 quai de Reugny, BP 46, 89800 Chablis

DOMAINE PASCAL BOUCHARD   22 ha. (100 per cent)

Chablis Les Clos, Blanchot, Fourchaume, Mont-de-Milieu, Mont-mains, Beauroy, Chablis, Petit Chablis.

Pascal et Joelle Bouchard, 17 blvd Lamarque, 89800 Chablis

JEAN-MARC BROCARD, SARL   67 ha. (100 per cent)
DOMAINE SAINTE-CLAIRE

Chablis Beauregard 2 ha., Chablis 45 ha., Bourgogne Chardonnay 7 ha., Pinot Noir 4 ha., Bourgogne Irancy 1.3 ha., Sauvignon de Saint-Bris 4 ha., Aligoté de Saint-Bris 3 ha.

This estate has appeared since 1974, from the tiny seed of 2.5 ha. of old vines from Brocard's wife's family. Their vines now completely surround the compact, beautiful fifteenth-century church of Sainte Claire, which stands isolated on a ridge, beside the village of Préhy. It is thought that after the burning of their homes during the religious wars the villagers chose to reconstruct the houses some distance away, where they would be better sheltered from the sweeping winds.

This is such a large estate that consistent quality escapes them (it cannot be easy to ripen grapes on some of their windswept slopes). But I have had excellent Brocard bottles (stony-dry, full of vivacity – there are few oak trials here), including those from grapes bought in for the merchant's business, run in tandem.

Jean-Marc Brocard, Préhy, 89800 Chablis

LA CHABLISIENNE   1,000 ha.

Every third bottle of Chablis sold world-wide comes from here. This co-operative dates back to 1923, and speaks for 250 Chablis wine producers. Its influence has been steadily growing, thanks to high standards, its investments in wine-making and storage capacity (so vital to successful dry white-wine-making), and the calibre of the people, such as Nathalie Fèvre on the technical side, who work here. In terms of turnover (maybe quality too) this is now Burgundy's leading co-operative.

Less entirely admirable, perhaps, is its habit of returning co-operative-made bottles to the growers who adhere to it, for labelling with the grower's name. This is a common practice by French wine co-operatives – particularly widespread in Champagne – and results in consumers innocently believing that the wine was made by such and such grower, when all that person did was stick a label on wine made co-operatively in monster vats. The position could be made quite clear by a law-change obliging the label to state 'Vinifié et mis en bouteilles par la coopérative de Chablis – Jacques Fèvre, Adhérant et Membre', for instance. The word 'co-operative' is not always a sales aid, but other French co-operatives resolve this problem by calling themselves Groupement de Producteurs, Confrérie des Vignerons, etc.

La Chablisienne aims, by the mid-1990s, to have brought the working practices of all its members up to European standards. It is engaged in an official national Certification Process (ISO No. 9002), set by the Association Française d'Assurance Qualité (AFAQ), recognized by the Common Market, which, if it meets the parametres over three years (1992–4) will greatly strengthen its position as a supplier to volume buyers.

It is a terrific source for straight Chablis, and *Premiers Crus*, at a good price. *Grands Crus* may not often reach the level of the best specialist growers, but the old vines *cuvée* is dependably well made. Hervé Tucki et Alain Cornelissens, 8 blvd Pasteur, BP 14, 89800 Chablis

DOMAINE DU CHARDONNAY 30 ha. (20 per cent)
ETIENNE BOILEAU

Chablis Montée de Tonnerre 2.15 ha., Montmains 3.8 ha., Mont de Milieu 0.4 ha., Vaillons 0.75 ha., Vaugiraut 1.2 ha., Chablis 12.8 ha., Petit Chablis 8.9 ha.

Here the grander First Growths (Mont de Milieu, Montée de Tonnerre) may be barrel-fermented. There is a connection with William Fèvre's Domaine de la Maladière, in that Boileau pays Fèvre for use of his equipment, space and services during wine-making and ageing – the wines, however, being quite separate. Etienne Boileau, Moulin du Pâtis, 89800 Chablis

CLAUDE ET JEAN-LOUIS CHEVALLIER 10 ha. (15 per cent)

Chablis Vau-Ligneau 0.1 ha., Chablis 9.8 ha., Petit Chablis 0.17 ha.

Barley, wheat, rape-seed, sunflowers and peas for cattle-feed were the traditional Chevallier preoccupations, until, finding they had classified land in Courgis and Beine, they planted vineyards in 1987. The wines are made in spotlessly tiled, temperature-controlled new premises, in a converted old barn, between Beine and Saint-Bris. It will be most surprising if award-winning Chablis does not issue from this address. Claude Chevallier, 89290 Montallery

DOMAINE JEAN COLLET ET FILS   30 ha. (80 per cent)
DOMAINE TUPINIER

Chablis Valmur 0.53 ha., Vaillons 4 ha., Montmains 6 ha., Epinotte 3 ha., Mont de Milieu 0.5 ha., Montée de Tonnerre 1.6 ha., Chablis 13 ha., Petit Chablis 1.3 ha.

A grand old Chablis name, but bottles during the 1980s could be unreliable. A new *chai* opened in 1991, matters have improved, and I have recently had full-bodied, powerful wines from this address, if sometimes over-wooded.

Gilles Collet, 15 av. de la Liberté, 89800 Chablis

DOMAINE DU COLOMBIER   20 ha. (90 per cent)
GUY MOTHE ET SES FILS

Chablis Bougros 1.3 ha., Fourchaume 2.2 ha., Vaucoupin 0.5 ha., Chablis 14.8 ha., Petit Chablis 1.2 ha.

Guy, Jean-Louis et Thierry Mothe, Fontenay, 89800 Chablis

DANIEL DAMPT   17 ha. (60 per cent)

Chablis Vaillons 4 ha., Côte de Léchet 2 ha., Fourchaume 0.6 ha., Beauroy 0.4 ha., Chablis 10 ha.

Dampt married Jean Defaix's daughter. There are fine wines here.

Daniel Dampt, 89800 Milly

BERNARD DEFAIX ET FILS   23 ha. (40 per cent)

Chablis Côte de Léchet 7.8 ha., Vaillons 2 ha., Les Lys 1 ha., Chablis 10.3 ha., Petit Chablis 1.9 ha.

This is obviously the place to come for Côte de Léchet, where they aim for clean expressions of origin, without artifice (for which read wood). The 'x' in Defaix, incidentally, is silent.

Bernard, Sylvain et Didier Defaix, 17 rue du Château, 89800 Milly

DOMAINES DANIEL ET ETIENNE DEFAIX   26 ha. (96 per cent)

Chablis Blanchot 0.15 ha., Vaillon 4.5 ha., Côte de Léchet 3.5 ha., Les Lys 4 ha., Chablis 12.8 ha., Petit Chablis 0.3 ha., Bourgogne (*rouge*) 0.47 ha.

This estate is highly interesting and unusual, for the yeasts and lees are roused monthly, being kept in suspension in the vats for up to eighteen months. This gives thicker-tasting wines than is current in Chablis, the aromas not so much floral and fruity as candle-waxy, buttery or yeasty. By keeping the yeasts in suspension, Daniel Defaix lessens the need for sulphur and feeds his wines throughout the year. The results can seem bizarre, or original, innovative and delicious, according to one's tastes and moods.

Daniel et Etienne Defaix, 14 rue Auxerroise, 89800 Chablis

JEAN DEFAIX   8 ha. (60 per cent)

Chablis Côte de Léchet 2.5 ha., Vaillons 2.5 ha., Chablis 3 ha.

Splendid bottles, from a grower in his early sixties who has the wine-making touch, and a real feeling for what he is doing.

Jean Defaix, 89800 Milly

CAVES JEAN DAUVISSAT   6 ha. (80 per cent)

Chablis Preuses, Vaillons, Montmains

A well-known Chablis surname, and a confident, smiling grower, but I am not at all convinced of this Dauvissat's wine-making skills.

Jean Dauvissat, 3 rue de Chichée, 89800 Chablis

DOMAINE JEAN-CLAUDE DAUVISSAT   35.9 ha. (80 per cent)

Chablis Vaulignot 12 ha., Mont de Milieu 1.3 ha., Chablis 20 ha., Petit Chablis 0.3 ha., Aligoté 0.3 ha.

One of the places to come to taste the produce of the newly planted First Growths – in this case Vaulignot – which caused so much controversy when the woods were cleared. The vines are still a little young, and Beines-based Chablis is not always the easiest to ripen, but these wines can look good.

Jean-Claude Dauvissat, 10 Grande Rue, Beines, 89800 Chablis

VINCENT DAUVISSAT   10 ha. (100 per cent)
RENÉ DAUVISSAT

Chablis Les Clos 1.5 ha., Les Preuses 1 ha., La Forest (Montmains) 4.5 ha., Vaillons 1.4 ha., Séchet 0.8 ha., Chablis 0.96 ha.

This is a famous, traditional estate, with fine sites and skilfully made wines. René Dauvissat's sister married François Raveneau, and the two domaines have similar aims.

They have been bottling since 1931, for grandfather Dauvissat loved his wines, and loved tasting them. Vincent has worked with his father René since 1979, the wines being made in a neat, attractively tiled fermenting-room, then aged below ground, partly in *feuillettes*, the local small barrels. One wonders how these small Chablis barrels (132 litres, whereas Bordeaux and Burgundy barrels are 70 per cent bigger) originated. Is it really that the entrances to Chablis cellars are tiny, the cellars themselves narrow and low? Does it relate to the devastating spring frosts, which often cut yields down to the smallest quantities? Certainly they have advantages, for instance being easy to handle, when full. Much Chablis used to go in *feuillettes* to the cramped cellars of Paris restaurants. Chablis in *feuillette* will settle, and fall bright, more rapidly than in a larger barrel, given the proportionally greater mass of wood and air to wine. In a vineyard area where holdings were often tiny, it was an advantage to be able to ferment in small containers.

The First Growth La Forest (part of Montmains) is a wine to look out for here (the 's' is not sounded). It is often unflattering when young, but develops complex undergrowth aromas, with beautifully balanced ripeness and length. Les Clos and Les Preuses can be as wonderful as any bottle in the region.

Vincent Dauvissat, 8 rue Emile Zola, 89800 Chablis

DOMAINE JEAN-PAUL DROIN   13 ha. (60 per cent)

Chablis Vaudésir 1.2 ha., Les Clos 1 ha., Valmur 1 ha., Grenouilles 0.5 ha., Vaillons 2.5 ha., Montée de Tonnerre 1.75 ha., Montmains 1 ha., Vosgros 0.6 ha., Fourchaume 0.4 ha., Côte de Léchet 0.15 ha., Chablis, Petit Chablis

We are in highly competent hands here, tasting *Grands Crus* out of new oak, and *Premiers Crus* from one-year-old, or older, barrels, under vaults as ancient as the Droin family's vigneron origins:

1752. The grapes may be machine-harvested, but the wines none the worse, it seems, for that.

Jean-Paul et Catherine Droin, 8 blvd de Ferrières, 89800 Chablis

DUPLESSIS PÈRE ET FILS   5.28 ha. (40 per cent)

Chablis Les Clos 0.36 ha., *Premiers Crus* 4.4 ha. (Montmains, Montée de Tonnerre, Fourchaume, Vaillon), Chablis

Memories of old barrel stocks, late bottlings and errors with sulphur levels (too high) in the early 1980s have caused me to hesitate before ordering a Duplessis bottle, but matters may be improving. When good, these wines certainly have personality.

Marcel et Gérard Duplessis, 5 quai de Reugny, 89800 Chablis

DOMAINE JEAN DURUP   115 ha. (80 per cent)
DOMAINE DE L'EGLANTIÈRE
DOMAINE DU CHÂTEAU DE MALIGNY
DOMAINE DE LA PAULIÈRE
DOMAINE DES VALÉRY

Chablis Fourchaume 17.5 ha., Vau de Vey 15 ha., Montée de Tonnerre 1.5 ha., Montmains 1.1 ha., Chablis 78.9 ha., Petit Chablis 1 ha.

A dynamic, enormous estate, where the quality can vary from excellent (I declare an interest, having often been a customer) to merely passable. Barrel-ageing does not feature. It is essential to taste and select, for they do not have only top *cuvées* for sale. Michel Poitout and Jean Durup probably know this very well, but have perhaps been preoccupied with restoring the Château de Maligny, its moat, cellars and park, while expanding their hillside winery sideways into newly-acquired neighbouring buildings.

Michel Poitout et Jean Durup, 4 Grande Rue à Maligny, 89800 Chablis

DOMAINE DU CHÂTEAU DE FLEYS   6 ha. (60 per cent)

Chablis Mont de Milieu 4 ha., Chablis Clos du Château de Fleys (Monopole) 0.86 ha., Chablis 1.5 ha.

Vineyards under sole ownership, with château names, are rare in

Chablis. Its aspect is not ideally sun-facing, however this estate has the potential to deliver fine wine.
André Philippon, Fleys, 89800 Chablis

DOMAINE FROMONT-MOINDROT   9 ha. (100 per cent)

Chablis Beauroy 4.25 ha., Chablis 4.75 ha.

These vines are tended by M. Bitouzet of Savigny-lès-Beaune, and the grapes divided up at harvest time, one third being vinified by Fromont.
Jean-Claude Fromont, 8 rue Guy Dupas, 89144 Ligny-le-Chatel

VINCENT GALLOIS   12 ha. (65 per cent)
LA VALLÉE AUX SAGES

Chablis 7 ha., Petit Chablis 5 ha.

Lignorelles is the place to come for Petit Chablis, and this cellar has one of the best.
Vincent Gallois, Lignorelles, 89800 Chablis

GAUTHERIN RAOUL ET FILS   12 ha. (80 per cent)

Chablis Vaudésirs 0.81 ha., Grenouilles 0.22 ha., Clos 0.17 ha., Vaillons 3.68 ha., Montmains 0.68 ha., Mont de Milieu 0.26 ha., Chablis 6.25 ha.

Alain Gautherin, 6 blvd Lamarque, 89800 Chablis

DOMAINE DES GENÈVES   10 ha. (50 per cent)
DOMINIQUE AUFRÈRE

Chablis Mont de Milieu 1.5 ha., Vaucoupin 1 ha., Chablis 5 ha., Petit Chablis 1 ha.

In an ideal world, this above-ground storage space would no doubt be temperature-controlled. This is an unpretentious source.
Dominique Aufrère, route de Collan, Fleys, 89800 Chablis

DOMAINE ALAIN GEOFFROY   30 ha. (100 per cent)
DOMAINE LE VERGER

Chablis Fourchaume 1.5 ha., Beauroy 7 ha., Vau Ligneau 3 ha., Chablis Domaine Le Verger 17 ha.

'For tradition and quality, we use new wood of course!' states this big estate. Fruit and oak do not always marry equably, but when they do, the wines can be balanced and lively.

Alain Geoffroy, 4 rue de l'Equerre, Beines, 89800 Chablis

CORINNE ET JEAN-PIERRE GROSSOT   12 ha. (75 per cent)

Chablis Vaucoupin 0.9 ha., Mont de Milieu 0.65 ha., Fourchaume 0.25 ha., Côte de Troëmes 0.18 ha., Chablis 7.93 ha., Petit Chablis 0.28 ha.

An ambitious young couple whose wines, for me, have not yet lived up to hopes and expectations. But this is a domaine to watch, as their vineyards age and their wine-making experience increases.

Corinne et Jean-Pierre Grossot, Fleys, 89800 Chablis

LAMBLIN FILS, SA   7 ha. (1920)

Chablis Valmur 0.6 ha., Chablis Mont de Milieu, Beauroy, Fourchaume, Chablis

Eleven Lamblin generations have tended vines or wines, dating back to 1712, and this firm now claims to be the largest Chablis merchant to have entirely retained family control. Once in the picturesque rue Chante-Pinot in Maligny, they now have impressive modern installations with membrane filters, sterile bottling and full temperature control, just north of the village. Some of the *vin de table blanc* despatched under their labels can have done little to add lustre to the Lamblin name.

Michel et Didier Lamblin, Maligny, 89800 Chablis

DOMAINE LAROCHE   95 ha. (100 per cent)

Chablis Clos 0.8 ha., Blanchot 4.27 ha., Bouguerots 0.31 ha., Four-chaume 7 ha., Vaillons 5.8 ha., Montmains 0.48 ha., Beauroy 1.3 ha., Vaudevey 11.5 ha., Montée de Tonnerre 0.04 ha., Chablis 47 ha., Petit Chablis 1.27 ha.

One of the greatest success stories of the district over the last two decades, this estate and company have expanded enormously, while holding on to top quality as they grow. Michel Laroche is a dynamic trader; the bottles may not come cheaply but they are dependable, and often highly delicious.

Michel Laroche, L'Obédiencerie, 22 rue Louis Bro, 89800 Chablis

ROLAND LAVANTUREUX   18 ha. (75 per cent)

Chablis 10 ha., Petit Chablis 3 ha.

A name worth seeking out for straight Chablis and Petit Chablis.

Roland Lavanturex, 4 rue Saint Martin, Lignorelles, 89800 Chablis

DOMAINE LONG DEPAQUIT   35 ha. (100 per cent)

Chablis Moutonne (Monopole) 2.35 ha., Les Clos 1.54 ha., Vaudé-sirs 2.6 ha., Preuses 0.25 ha., Blanchots 1.65 ha, Les Lys 1.7 ha., Vaillons 3.91 ha., Beugnons 2.21., Vaucoupins 3.45 ha., Chablis 15 ha.

A famous old estate which has doubled in size since the Bichots of Beaune reached agreement with six out of seven of the Long Depaquit heirs. This estate accounts for over 8 per cent of Chablis *Grands Crus*.

I have had excellent bottles, but believe the wines could be more regularly exciting if the tending and bottling in Chablis took place with greater care.

Gérard Vullien, 45 rue Auxerroise, 89800 Chablis

DOMAINE DE LA MALADIÈRE   50.2 ha. (100 per cent)
WILLIAM FÈVRE
JEANNE PAULE FILIPPI
ANCIEN DOMAINE AUFFRAY
VIGNOBLE JEAN MARIE BONNET

Chablis Les Clos 3.41 ha., Valmur 1.82 ha., Les Preuses 2.54 ha., Bougros 6.23 ha., Vaudésir 1.2 ha., Grenouilles 0.57 ha., Vaulorent (dit Fourchaume) 3.64 ha., Vaillons 2.86 ha., Lys 0.98 ha., Montée de Tonnerre 1.57 ha., Montmains 1.43 ha., Forêts 0.77 ha., Beauroy 1.12 ha., Chablis 14.47 ha., Chardonnay (Vin de Pays) 1.94 ha.

A high-profile domaine, and the leading exponent of Chablis fermented and aged in wood. Fèvre is the largest owner of *Grands Crus* (with 15 per cent of the total) having vines in every one except Blanchots, but from this vineyard he buys in grapes, as also from those First Growths where he is not a proprietor, in order to be able to offer examples of the 'totality of the *crus* of Chablis'. Wood ageing is 'to give the wines depth and bouquet', and applies to all First and Great Growths. The best vineyards of Chablis are the equal, he would have us know, of the finest Meursault and Puligny-Montrachet, and all his highly active commercial life has been bent towards having his customers accept this judgement. Although France is his largest single market, 80 per cent of his production is exported.

The creation of this estate during the last thirty years by the determined William Fèvre undoubtedly stimulated others to expand and replant. He was one of the first to fight frosts in the 1950s. On the one hand, this is a traditional domaine, hand-harvesting its best fruit, feeding and lodging 80 people throughout the harvest. On the other, Fèvre is the most global wine-maker of the district. For instance, his straight Chablis musts may be held in storage tanks for several months, so that wine-making could theoretically take place *throughout the year.* His barrel stocks are thus most efficiently in constant use, and he has available freshly made young wines, full of youthful fruitiness. I first saw such an approach to white-wine-making at Brian Croser's winery at Piccadilly, in the hills above Adelaide. No kookaburras perch on the end of Fèvre's vineyard-posts, but a New World spirit walks between his vats. He keeps an eye on Chile, too, making Chardonnay in partnership with a winery in the Maipo Valley.

Fèvre was identified, like no other Chablisien, with the 1970s–80s fight against 'abusive extension' of Chablis's production area, which he would have restricted to vines on Kimmeridgian strata. That battle was lost, but his fight continues against the 'abusive use' of the word Chablis for wines made outside France.

What of the wines? They are highly dependable, often beautifully balanced and delicious. Just occasionally I have wished the oak-ageing element was more integrated, but that is probably related to my usually tasting these wines when young. New oak puts up the price of the finished bottle, too, and can play straight into the hands of New World Chardonnay growers who do not benefit from the exceptional, unique situations of Chablis's stony hillsides, each with its *terroir*, but Monsieur Fèvre and his family are certainly aware of this.

William Fèvre, 14 rue Jules-Rathier, 89800 Chablis

DOMAINE DES MALANDES   25 ha. (90 per cent)

Chablis Vaudésir 0.9 ha., Les Clos 0.53 ha., Vau de Vey 3.52 ha., Fourchaume 1.25 ha., Montmains 1.18 ha., Côte de Léchet 1.4 ha., Chablis 15 ha., Petit Chablis 1 ha.

Fermentation and ageing are in tank – no oaking – giving rich, harmonious wines of much elegance.

The only *Grand Cru* Chablis I know of in British hands is made and bottled here: one-third of a hectare of Vaudésir, belonging to wine trader Mark Reynier. It was bought by his grandfather in the 1930s, when much of the vineyard was still abandoned to the weeds.

Lyne et Jean-Bernard Marchive, 63 rue Auxerroise, 89800 Chablis

DOMAINE DES MARRONNIERS   15 ha. (60 per cent)
BERNARD LEGLAND

Chablis Montmains 2.5 ha., Chablis 9.8 ha., Bourgogne (blanc) 0.7 ha.

This is recently established, the first vines having been planted in 1977. Most wine-making and storing is in vat, but trials with one- to four-year-old Limousin oak barrels have proved cost-effective and in demand.

Bernard Legland, Préhy, 89800 Chablis.

DOMAINE DE LA MEULIÈRE   12.5 ha. (100 per cent)
CHANTAL ET CLAUDE LAROCHE

Chablis Mont de Milieu 3 ha., Vaucoupin 0.55 ha., Les Fourneaux 0.5 ha., Chablis 6.2 ha., Petit Chablis 2.25 ha.

These wines have sometimes gone under the name of Claude Laroche, but confusion occurred with the mega-Laroche of Maligny, so a new domaine name was adopted. Here is a family who until 1972 used to sell everything to the local Chablis trade. They have been bottling their total production since 1982, and deliver dependably (with minimal sulphur levels), after hand-picking and vat-ageing. (I declare an interest, having bought and sold bottles from here.)
Chantal et Claude Laroche, 89800 Fleys

J. MOREAU ET FILS, SA   70 ha.

This company makes and distributes the wines of the 70 ha. Domaine Moreau, consisting of: Chablis Les Clos 7 ha. (of which 2.14 ha. constitute the Monopole Clos des Hospices, which before the Revolution belonged to the Hôpital de Chablis), Valmur 2 ha., Vaudésir 1 ha., Vaillons 10 ha., Chablis Domaine de Biéville 50 ha.

The firm is owned, like Calvet (whose activities are centralized here), by Hiram Walker, itself a subsidiary of Allied Domecq. Ninety-five per cent of its sales are in export markets. As with Lamblin, this firm's reputation has perhaps been diluted by strong associations with a dry white table wine brand, but it is certainly capable of making top Chablis too.
D. A. Oud, Christian Moreau et Julie Campos, route d'Auxerre, 89800 Chablis

LOUIS MICHEL ET FILS   21 ha. (100 per cent)

Chablis *Grands Crus* 2.2 ha. (Grenouilles, Vaudésir, Les Clos), *Premiers Crus* 13.8 ha. (the most reputable being Montmains, Montée de Tonnerre, Séchets), Chablis 5 ha.

Louis Michel would recall his father pulling up their Les Clos vines in 1959. After eighteen harvests they had produced wine precisely twice, so often had the frosts struck. But in the thirty years which followed, the estate quintupled in size.

This has been a highly dependable source of unwooded, vibrantly fresh Chablis which ages beautifully if well stored.

Louis et Jean-Loup Michel, 11 blvd de Ferrières, 89800 Chablis

DOMAINE DE LA MOUTONNE   2.35 ha. (100 per cent)

Chablis Moutonne (Vaudésir and Les Preuses) 2.35 ha.

For years the whereabouts of one of Chablis' best-known wines, Chablis Moutonne, was obscured by disputes. There were wrangles over alleged abuses of the name and squabbles between the heirs to the estate. Was it a brand or a vineyard? No two Chablisiens seemed to agree.

Thanks to an article by Pierre Bréjoux, published in 1978 in *La Revue du vin de France*, all became clear. I am indebted to it for much of what follows.

Pissatif et leger, faict saulter le buveur comme un petit mouton: so wrote the monks of the Abbey of Pontigny about their Chablis in the eighteenth century. They owned a vineyard of 1.11 ha. in the *climat* of Vaudésir, known as La Moutonne, which was sold to Simon Depaquit at the Revolution. His descendants, the Long-Depaquit family, extended the Moutonne name to cover wine from nearby plots in the *Grand Cru* Les Preuses, then further adjoining Vaudésir rows. Louis Long-Depaquit also owned vines in Les Clos, Valmur and *Premiers Crus*. Moutonne became for a time a commercial brand covering wines from several origins.

In 1950 an agreement was reached that the *appellation* should only be used on wines from a plot of 2.35 ha., situated in the *Grands Crus* Vaudésir and Les Preuses.

There are really, therefore, eight *Grands Crus* in Chablis (Moutonne being the eighth), even if the decree formalizing this state of affairs never saw the light of day. The little lamb is allowed to jump, but its competitors no doubt take pleasure in noting that this Monopole is denied total *Grand Cru* recognition.

After Louis Long-Depaquit's death in 1967, the seven heirs took time dividing their valuable inheritance. The vineyard now belongs to the Société Civile de la Moutonne, the shares being owned by Bichot (82.5 per cent) and Drouhin (17.5 per cent) of Beaune, the wine being made and handled by Bichot. Half of the vineyard is so steep that cultivation is done by winch.

Gérard Vullien, 45 rue Auxerroise, 89800 Chablis

GEORGES PICO   18.5 ha. (75 per cent)
DOMAINE DE BOIS D'YVER

Chablis Montmains 4 ha., Beauregard 1 ha., Chablis

On brief acquaintance I have found a certain hardness of finish to the basic Chablis here. Pico has been bottling since the mid-1980s; the Montmains can be a big step up.

Georges Pico, Grande Rue Nicolas Droin, Courgis, 89800 Chablis

GILBERT PICQ ET SES FILS   12 ha. (65 per cent)

Chablis Vosgros 1.5 ha., Chablis 10 ha.

A good source of basic Chablis, and Chichée's little-known First Growth, Vosgros.

Didier Picq, 3 route de Chablis, 89800 Chichée

DOMAINE PINSON   11 ha. (90 per cent)

Chablis Les Clos 2.6 ha., Mont de Milieu 4.75 ha., Montmains 1.1 ha., Forêt 0.68 ha., Chablis 1.25 ha.

This is a long-established domaine bottler, and a hand-harvester, but my recent experiences with their bottles have been disappointing.

Laurent et Christophe Pinson, 5 quai Voltaire, 89800 Chablis

JEAN-MARIE RAVENEAU   6.88 ha. (100 per cent)
FRANÇOIS RAVENEAU

Chablis Clos 0.5 ha., Blanchot 0.65 ha., Valmur 0.75 ha., Montée de Tonnerre 2.15 ha., Chapelot 0.34 ha., Butteaux 1.73 ha., Vaillons 0.4 ha., Monts Mains 0.36 ha.

Impossible to write objectively about this family's wines, for I have been buying them for home consumption and trading for nearly thirty years. I stumbled on a bottle of Chapelot 1961 in a local hotel in the mid-1960s, and promptly walked round in the hope of meeting the person who made it. This was François Raveneau *père*, at the time also a broker (he still is, in a small way).

His son Jean-Marie began making the wine around 1984, after studies at the Lycée Viticole in Beaune. He is a lean, fiercely involved individualist, working in tight conditions, making long-flavoured Chablis which demands at least six to eight years' bottle-age in most vintages. They can be quite off-puttingly closed or ungainly after bottling, but with cellarage can develop considerable complexity.

In spite of media-interest – Italian, French, English-speaking – he has kept his cellar-door prices reasonable and rock steady, which is quite a feat.

Jean-Marie Raveneau, 9 rue de Chichée, 89800 Chablis

A. REGNARD ET FILS (1870)

One of the most respected Chablis merchants, this now belongs, with its subsidiary Albert Pic, to Ladoucette, of Pouilly-Fumé fame. A speciality is First Growths assembled together, branded for simplicity as Pic Premier, in a de luxe bottle.

de Ladoucette, 89800 Chablis

GUY ROBIN   14 ha. (60 per cent)

Chablis Valmur 2.7 ha., Vaudésir 0.28 ha., Blanchot 0.2 ha., Les Clos 0.16 ha., Bougros 0.14 ha., Montée de Tonnerre 3.2 ha., Vaillons 2 ha., Montmains 1.4 ha., Mont de Milieu 1 ha., Chablis 2.5 ha.

A famous cellar, the source of bottles which may be fabulous or disastrous, but are unlikely to be boring.

Guy et Denise Robin, 13 rue Marcelin-Berthelot, 89800 Chablis

DOMAINE SERVIN   29 ha. (95 per cent)

Chablis *Grand Cru* Blanchot 0.92 ha., Les Clos 0.88 ha., Preuses 0.86 ha., Bougros 0.7 ha., Montée de Tonnerre 3.7 ha., Vaillon 3.65 ha., Chablis 18 ha.

One of the oldest-established Chablis bottlers, championed by Alexis Lichine back in the 1950s. These wines are now harvested and pressed in tandem with Domaine Baillard (run by François

Servin's elder brother Jean) after which the vinifications go their separate ways. Some good 1990 and 1991 wines were made; this domaine could be back on an upward path.

François Servin et Mme Servin, Domaine Servin, 89800 Chablis

SIMONNET FEBVRE ET FILS (1840) 3.57 ha.

Chablis Preuses 0.30 ha., Mont de Milieu 1.36 ha., Chablis 1.91 ha.

For many years, half of this company's turnover was in sparkling Chablis, which has an interesting origin. After the Napoleonic wars a certain Tisserand began putting a bubble into his local wines (Chablis is in fact closer to the Champagne than the Côte d'Or wine-field). Bearing the noble name of Moët the wines sold successfully in England for several years until one day his customer omitted to pay for a large consignment. Since a court action could hardly be brought, Tisserand went out of business. His equipment was bought by the first M. Febvre, who wisely began production under his own name. The company owns a couple of hectares in Chablis Preuses and Mont de Milieu and is broker for several Beaune merchants. It also handles a little red and *rosé* Irancy.

Jean-Pierre Simonnet, 9 av. d'Oberwesel, 89800 Chablis

BERNARD TREMBLAY ET FILS 11 ha. (50 per cent)
DOMAINE DES CHENEVIÈRES

Chablis Fourchaume 1.5 ha., Côte de Léchet 0.5 ha., Chablis 7.5 ha., Petit Chablis 1.5 ha.

Bernard Tremblay, 1 rue des Vignes, La Chapelle Vaupelteigne, 89800 Chablis

GÉRARD TREMBLAY 34 ha. (100 per cent)
DOMAINE DES ISLES

Chablis Valmur 2 ha., Fourchaume 6 ha., Montmains 1.5 ha., Côte de Léchet 3 ha., Beauroy 0.5 ha., Chablis 15.5 ha., Petit Chablis 5.5 ha.

I have had some dreadful bottles from this man, smelling of green stalks, leaves – unripe fruit, in short, from high yields, I imagine, unless it was from tattered vegetation left in the wake of a harvest-

ing machine. To put another view, Parker has found these model, fruity, non-oaked Chablis, although in point of fact, Tremblay told me that he has experimented quite a lot with new oak.
Gérard Tremblay, 12 rue de Poinchy, 89800 Chablis

DOMAINE LAURENT TRIBUT   4.05 ha. (100 per cent)

Chablis Beauroy 0.65 ha., Montmains 0.2 ha., Chablis 3.2 ha.

Until the 1992 vintage these hand-harvested wines were made and aged alongside the excellent wines of Vincent Dauvissat (Monsieur Tribut married his sister) in Chablis ('same style, same objectives'). A vat-house is under construction in Poinchy for subsequent years.
Laurent Tribut, 15 rue de Poinchy, 89800 Poinchy

OLIVIER TRICON   24 ha. (100 per cent)
DOMAINE DE VAUROUX

Chablis Bougros 0.63 ha., Montmains 1.27 ha., Montée de Tonnerre 1.07 ha., Chablis 20.75 ha.

Olivier Tricon has merchant as well as grower status, allowing him to buy in First Growth grapes (the domaine being overly weighted towards straight Chablis). It is an isolated farm 3 km outside Chablis towards Avallon, and has been the scene of experimental low-temperature tank fermentation, and limited cask experiments (on sometimes imperfectly ripe fruit, in my experience).
Jean-Pierre et Claude Tricon, route d'Avallon, 89800 Chablis

CHÂTEAU DE VIVIERS   25 ha.

Chablis Vaillons 0.5 ha., Vaucoupin 2.5 ha., Chablis 22 ha.

Like Long-Depaquit and Moutonne, this is part of the Bichot stable, though in this case the wines are distributed by their *sous-marque* Lupé-Cholet. The wines have been made in Viviers, but Beaune-bottled.
Gérard Vullien, 45 rue Auxerroise, 89800 Chablis

DOMAINE VOCORET ET FILS   34 ha. (100 per cent)

Chablis *Grands Crus* (Blanchot and Les Clos) 3.55 ha. (Valmur being replanted), Forêts or Montmains 5.1 ha., Vaillon 3.39 ha., Montée de Tonnerre 1.4 ha., Mont de Milieu 0.17 ha., Chablis 20.72 ha.

This was one of the original Chablis domaines to export to the USA, as early as the mid–1950s. The quality can be patchy.

Patrice et Jérome Vocoret, 40 route d'Auxerre, 89800 Chablis

YONNE WINES OTHER THAN CHABLIS

Wines of the Auxerrois

As we saw on p. 201 the Auxerrois produces all manner of wines. They come from four principal communes: Saint-Bris-le-Vineux (the most important), Chitry, Irancy, and Coulanges-la-Vineuse. The first two produce mainly white wines, the last two mainly reds. For much of this century the area lived in the shadow of Chablis; indeed at one time it hoped for an extension of that *appellation*. Was not Chitry part of the canton of Chablis, with its vineyards on similar Kimmeridgian subsoil? But it is in a different watershed, on the wrong side of the *autoroute*; an AC such as 'Bourgogne des environs de Chablis' was not to be. For long the communes sought to offer a range of wines which were complementary to their famous neighbour, but now they are developing their own identity, focused on the French market, and Paris in parti-cular. This of course was always where the wines of Auxerre used to be shipped when river transport was the vital key to vineyard prosperity.

A relic from those times is a white grape, the Sacy, found here and nowhere else in Burgundy. It is a high yielder, giving rather acid wine, which went to make sparkling Sekt in Germany in the years up to the flotation of the Deutsche Mark in 1970. When this market had collapsed, the growers decided to do the job of making it sparkling themselves, forming a company of collective interest, the Société d'Intérêt Collectif Agricole du Vignoble Auxerrois. They leased underground cellars in a disused limestone quarry at Bailly, a hamlet of Saint-Bris. Its stone once went to build the Panthéon. Champagne methods are used on *assemblages* of the local grapes to make good value Crémant de Bourgogne. The Sacy is fast disappearing, little-mourned : 400 productive hectares in 1958 were down to 82 hectares by 1988. Crémant in future will be made from Pinot Noir, Aligoté, Chardonnay, remnants of Sacy and Melon de Bourgogne, and some Gamay for the *rosé* (see Cave de Bailly, below).

The still wines of the Auxerrois start with a surprise: Burgundian Sauvignon *blanc*. There are also light and perfumed Pinots, steely-fruity Chardonnays and inexpensive Aligotés. This is the place to come for affordable Burgundy, though of course one must not expect it to taste like Côte de Nuits or Beaune.

Here too are wines which are not over-alcoholic. A Pinot Noir above 12.5° would taste spirity, burning the mouth, quickly showing its imbalance. Most growers understand this, and are careful not to tip in too many sugar bags.

The Sauvignon grape has been found at Saint-Bris since the mid-nineteenth century, at that time being mixed in with other wines. Now grown and vinified apart, Sauvignon de Saint-Bris has enjoyed VDQS status (but may imminently move up to AC, changing its name to Saint-Bris). It has served to lure Parisians and foreign buyers in search of value for money away from Sancerre and Pouilly-Fumé. The wine of the Aligoté grape is not very pronounced, indeed there is nothing in its character to hook the private customer – that is the role of the Sauvignon, and within a year or two that customer will happily be buying both. Not to mention the red! There has been much replanting with Pinot Noir, as well as Chardonnay, and Bourgogne *rouge* and *blanc* (made respectively from these grapes) may now be called Bourgogne Côtes d'Auxerre.

The best spot for red wines is Irancy, and 1976 saw the arrival of a strange sort of village-regional *appellation* – Bourgogne Irancy – for wines from that commune and neighbouring Cravant and Vincelottes. Palotte is the best-known Irancy hillside, but other vineyard names are also beginning to appear.

The village of Irancy entirely fills the flat space in the centre of its amphitheatre of vines, its church tower rising elegantly off-centre from the houses which tightly surround it. Almost all the roofs are right-angled and red wine-lees coloured, spotted with grey lichens. Something should be done to prevent any more hangars going up to jar the roof lines, and perhaps an orientation table and some benches could be built in one of the many old cherry orchards

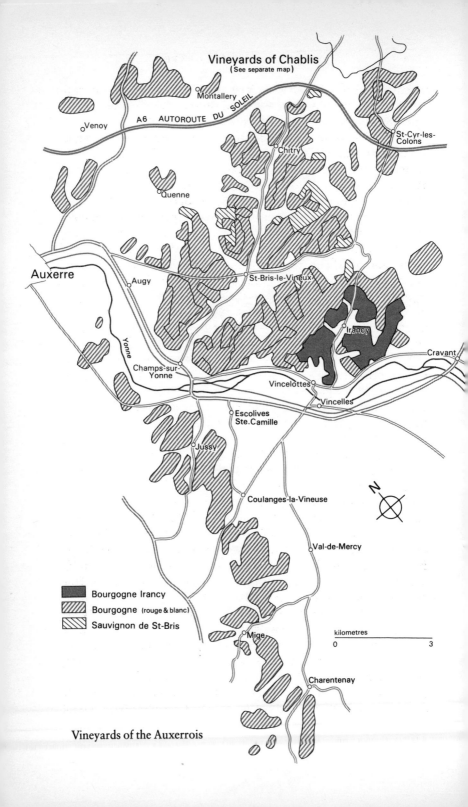

Vineyards of Chablis
(See separate map)

Montallery

Venoy

A6 AUTOROUTE DU SOLEIL

St-Cyr-les-Colons

Chitry

Quenne

Auxerre

Augy

St-Bris-le-Vineux

Irancy

Cravant

Yonne

Champs-sur-Yonne

Vincelottes

Vincelles

Escolives
Ste.Camille

Jussy

Coulanges-la-Vineuse

N

Val-de-Mercy

Bourgogne Irancy

Bourgogne (rouge & blanc)

Sauvignon de St-Bris

kilometres

0   3

Mige

Charentenay

Vineyards of the Auxerrois

commanding this lovely view. The amphitheatre cannot vie with Vergisson for grandeur, but it is one of Burgundy's most exquisitely beautiful vineyards.

In addition to the Pinot Noir, some César (otherwise known as Romain) is planted. This is a singular vine, with jagged leaves, big long bunches and an irregular production, whose introduction to the area is attributed to one of Caesar's legionaries. A bas-relief dating from the second or third century discovered at Escolives, between Coulanges and Auxerre, shows a small, naked vintager picking a bunch of grapes whose leaf, much indented, has been recognized as the local César. Its wine is very deep in colour, full of tannin and backbone. Normally it is planted in among the Pinots, in the proportion of 5–10 per cent, giving body to the light wines. It has a reputation for being *ingueulable* (undrinkable) if ever vinified on its own. Michel Esclavy and Luc Sorin both made César *cuvées*, but the first has now retired, and the second sold up and moved away.

César has not really staged a come-back to coincide with the renaissance of estate-bottling in the Auxerrois over the last decade, and many Irancy growers do not bother with it. It adds a *je ne sais quoi* of interest to Bourgogne Irancy, helping to lift the *appellation* from the mass of indistinguishable regional Bourgognes, but it has perhaps appealed more to writers looking for novelties than to consumers, it appears. Unless the growers put their hearts into incorporating it smoothly into their blends César looks destined to disappear.

Michel Esclavy has not given up championing it, however, believing it to be a superb vine, which must not be lost. In the days when Raymond Bernard of ONIVIT in Dijon could turn a blind, but encouraging, eye in their direction one grower each on the Côte de Beaune and Côte de Nuits planted César, for some trial vinifications. The bunch hangs long and loose, so very rarely rots, the alcohol yield is high, the crop is low. However, in the Côte d'Or the grapes may split when ripe if not harvested promptly. The wine is deep-coloured and somewhat astringent. No doubt today's Côte d'Or authorities are unwilling to allow experimental plantings to spread, for fear that growers would use César as a medicine wine, giving deeper colour to the Pinots. The fact that consumers often complain about the pale colour of Pinots would no doubt be thought completely irrelevant. César in the Côte d'Or has no legal existence within the *appellation contrôlée* system, for the vine is only permitted in the Yonne. 'It is a pity that a vine like that should not be better known', said one of the Côte d'Or growers who incorporates it into his Bourgogne *rouge*. I would heartily agree, given its history, possibly extending back 2,000 years, and the need to add interest and specificity to so many regional red Burgundies. If it can ripen in the Auxerrois, what about the Hautes Côtes, or the Mâconnais?

Returning to the Yonne, the legislation still permits Bourgogne *rouge* to be made from the Tressot grape, but this really has disappeared. It was a low-yielder, and its wine without merit, according to Michel Esclavy. It is surprising it should have lasted to the twentieth century, for in a letter from Charles VI of 1394 mention is made of a fifteen-year-old grape-picker at Saint-Bris being struck down and killed by the owner of a vineyard because he *mettait des treceaux et autres raisins avec des pynoz*. This is one of the earliest mentions of the Pinot grape known to Professor Dion.

In Saint-Bris are some wonderful old ashlar stone houses, proof of the area's richness – presumably thanks to its wines – in the days before road and rail. Parisians then would barely have heard of the wines of the Côte d'Or, and Chablis was also less highly rated than Auxerre.

At times of plagues and epidemics during the Middle Ages, the nobility and wealthy merchants of Auxerre would move out to take advantage of Saint-Bris's healthier air. Their presence perhaps partly accounts for the magnificence of the church, and also some of the fortifications, for an influx of wealthy families would certainly have attracted brigands and pillagers from their hide-outs in the surrounding forests, and steps would have been taken to ensure protection, and give thanks for safe delivery.

Chitry is best known for its whites – Bourgogne Côtes d'Auxerre *blanc* and Bourgogne Aligoté Côte de Chitry, but suffers from being on the edge of two vineyard areas, Chablis and Auxerrois. This has always been its role, for in the past its principal street represented the dividing line between the province of Champagne and that of Bourgogne. Many of Chitry's whites go to make Crémant, at the Cave de Bailly.

Irancy and Saint-Bris, on the other hand, are on the move, showing signs of prosperity; they are even planting rose-bushes at the end of the vine rows. Coulanges-la-Vineuse (dedicated to red wine-making, where Pinots Noirs are slowly reclaiming the hillsides) is much more isolated, and has further to climb back.

The restaurant Le Saint-Bris is a well-maintained cog at the hub of Saint-Bris village life, and a fine place for lunch when visiting growers in these four villages. Food is copious, hot and fast (and absolutely nothing to do with *le fast-food*). One may start with a salad of sliced, waxy potatoes, flecked with garlic and shallot, round a pyramid of light slices of *boudin noir*, and end with a home-made tart of plums and walnuts. If, with the main course, one would like a Pinot Noir at cellar temperature, not the warmth of the room, one has only to ask, and up it comes, well chilled from one of Saint-Bris's deep, historic cellars. Mother is in the kitchen, daughter rushes the hot plates out front – and chooses the wine-list, all of it growers' bottles.

Other wines of the Yonne: Tonnerre, Epineuil, Joigny and Vézelay

The reputation of the wines of Tonnerre goes back to the tenth century, and thanks to water-transport on the Armançon, a tributary of the Yonne, they were often served at court in Paris and exported on down the Seine. Their eclipse after the phylloxera and the arrival of the railways bringing Midi wines cheaply to Paris was almost total, but a revival is in progress. Rosemary George has described[1] how André Durand, an Epineuil teacher and subsequently its mayor, awakened interest in the abandoned Epineuil hillsides above Tonnerre, and succeeded in attracting growers from afar (a Parisian, two Champenois, a Chablisien and a grower from Châteauneuf du Pape) to replant with Pinot Noir. Jean-Claude Michaut (q.v.) is a leading grower.

In the mid-1980s France's Minister of Agriculture was for a time Henri Nallet, the mayor of Tonnerre. From this moment dates the revival of white-wine-growing round Tonnerre, spurred on by the success of the red Epineuil (see Caveau des Fontenilles and Emmanuel Dampt). *Appellation contrôlée* status came quickly – in 1988 – and over 70 hectares will be in production by the mid-1990s.[2]

---

1 *The Wines of Chablis*, Sotheby Publications, London, 1984.
2 According to Jacques Dupont of *Gault & Milau*, September 1993.

One principal grower – Jacques Vignot – undertook the replanting of the Côte Saint-Jacques above Joigny, whose vines had disappeared just like the others of the Yonne, but the vineyard area is now being extended, thanks to Michel Lorain and his associates (see Joigny, Les Petits Propriétaires du Vignoble, below). Another three star chef (Marc Meneau) is also a leading light behind the renaissance of the vineyards of Vézelay (see La Vézelienne). These are not the only pockets of Yonne viticulture; the Brigand family, outside Châtillon, has the most northerly outpost of Burgundian vines I know, and there are villages such as Vaux, near Auxerre, where planting is spreading.

The fascination with Pinot Noir and Chardonnay, the ease with which travellers may visit these unexpected cellars, and the closeness of Paris and other centres of population seem to be enough to bring these abandoned hillsides back into cultivation. The livings are as yet tenuous, so visitors can usually be sure of very warm welcomes.

Growers of the Yonne (other than Chablis)

CAVEAU DES FONTENILLES   32 ha. (50 per cent)

Bourgogne Chardonnay 22 ha., Bourgogne Pinot Noir 10 ha.
For the renaissance of the vineyards around Tonnerre, twenty-eight growers have grouped together to vinify and market their wines in common. Planting started in the late 1980s; by the 1995 harvest the vineyard area in production will have risen to 80 hectares, they say.
Place Marguerite de Bourgogne, 89700 Tonnerre

CAVES DE BAILLY   350 ha. (100 per cent)

Sparkling Crémant de Bourgogne (*blanc* and *rosé*) accounts for 85 per cent of the production here, the balance being split equally between Saint-Bris Sauvignon and Bourgogne Aligoté.

The co-operative was founded in 1971, after the collapse of the German market for the rather acid produce of the local Sacy grape. For years, much of this had been sold to Henkell, as a base-wine for making Sekt. (The Sacy is now disappearing, for it gives too low a degree to be of interest.)

The growers determined to sparkle their wines themselves, and leased 4 hectares of old limestone quarry, with origins allegedly going back to the twelfth century, in the cliffs overlooking the Yonne at Bailly. Initially it was dripping wet, but they succeeded in canalizing the water down into the Yonne.

You drive your car straight into the rocks, if you want an *apéritif*, or some bottles. Eighty per cent of their Crémant production is Blanc de Noir (the proportions of the blend being 60 per cent Pinot Noir, 20 per cent Aligoté, 5 per cent Sacy, the balance Chardonnay) – very fresh and finely-balanced, too.

José Martinez, SICA du Vignoble Auxerrois, Bailly, 89530 Saint-Bris-le-Vineux

DOMAINE BERSAN ET FILS 35 ha. (100 per cent)
DOMAINE SAINT-PRIX
DOMAINE BELLE-CROIX
BERSAN ET FILS, SARL

Chablis 4 ha., Bourgogne Côtes d'Auxerre (Pinot Noir) 8 ha., (Chardonnay) 3.5 ha., Saint-Bris (Sauvignon) 7 ha., Bourgogne Aligoté 7.5 ha., Bourgogne Irancy 1 ha., Bourgogne Passe-Tout-Grains 3 ha.

The Auxerrois often has frost problems, which is the reason, so they say, this family has a *négociant* identity as well as vineyards, enabling it to buy in grapes or must, to maintain availabilities, if disaster has struck the vines.

Until 1986 everything was done in cramped cellars next to the church, but now there is a spacious winery uphill from Saint-Bris's Auxerre gate. The Pinot Noir ferments in closed, stainless steel vats, the stalk-hat turned by hydraulic piston punchers carrying horizontal grids, with flaps which open as the piston cuts down through the hat, to close beneath it. As the grid rises, the floating mass of skins is broken, turned and dampened.

The cellars by the church are one of the show-places of the Auxerrois. Parts date from the eleventh century, with vaulted ceilings and side-arches, like the nave of a chapel, the builders surely being those who put up Saint-Bris's spacious church next door. One may see where the grapes were tipped straight in from the street, into what may be an eleventh-century vat. The horse-operated press is nearby, and down a tunnel is the cellar's bread oven, for this is an underground home, where families would hide during feudal raids and religious wars, from the invading English or the Vikings. Human bones were found, when the Bersan family dug out these twisting passages, and we may be sure that throats were cut down here, by men-at-arms in the dark.

Have no fear about today's welcome, however, from the Bersan brothers: tall Jean-Louis, or the red-bearded, rugby-playing, Jean-François. The wines are dependable and varied, made for youthful drinking.

Jean-Louis, Jean-François et Annick Bersan, 20 rue de l'Eglise, 89530 Saint-Bris-le-Vineux

LÉON BIENVENU   12 ha. (100 per cent)

Bourgogne Irancy Palotte 0.4 ha., Bourgogne Irancy (*rouge* and *rosé*) 10 ha., Passe-Tout-Grains 1.5 ha.

One will find wines of a reasonable standard here, if without originality. Bienvenu is President of the Irancy Syndicat de l'Appellation and is lobbying the authorities for the name to stand on its own – Irancy – where at present only Bourgogne Irancy is permitted. With his cap on the back of his hair, leaning on a well-wiped wooden counter (worn smooth by daily use, like a stone step) he may uncork a ten-year-old bottle. It seems just as good as much Givry or Marsannay, so why not?

Léon Bienvenu, 89290 Irancy

GILBERT ET RÉGINE BRIGAND   8.5 ha. (70 per cent)

Pinot Noir 5 ha., Chardonnay 2 ha., Pinot *blanc* 1.5 ha., and Gamay 0.2 ha. produce red, white and *rosé* Bourgogne, Crémant and Passe-Tout-Grains

Vines were probably first planted around Châtillon after the foundation of the Benedictine Abbey of Molesmes, by Saint Robert, in 1075. There were 2,400 ha. of vineyard here, up to the phylloxera, much of the wine going down the Seine to Paris on barges.

The Brigand family uses the old Abbey buildings, with an elegant curling oak stair, and a broad, flat-vaulted cellar. They own the 2.3 hectare Clos which was originally worked by the monks. This has a sloping, southern exposure among orchards, on a pine-capped hillside, with long views over the Seine's flat plain. Word has it that this look-out spot was settled, in the Dark Ages, by Mongolian foot-soldiers, out of the steppes. With a name like Brigand, who knows what the origins of this family might have been? Today, as well as wine-makers they are vine nurserymen, supplying cuttings to Burgundians, but particularly the Champenois – for the Champagne vineyards of the Aube begin just 10 km away.

They plant *pinots blancs*, for if they are caught by frosts in the spring – often the case – they will shoot again, which Chardonnay will not. The red wines here are light-coloured, of course – tender when ripe, spicy and lively.

In Châtillon's museum, the bronze Greek or Etruscan *Vase de Vix* – possibly used for storing wine – should not be missed. It is enormous, the size of a man, with a frieze of charioteers round its rim, and serpents, lions and Gorgon's heads on the handles: a wonderfully preserved treasure from the grave of a Celtic priestess or princess, probably buried about 500 BC.

And only 30 kilometres away, in a narrow, wooded valley, is the Abbey of Fontenay, the best-preserved Cistercian monastery to have survived, anywhere. It is far more evocative of mediaeval monastic life, in the days when the Clos Vougeot's cellar was being built, than Cîteaux itself.

Gilbert et Régine (his sister) Brigand, Massingy, 21400 Châtillon-sur-Seine

BERNARD CANTIN   7.5 ha. (70 per cent)

Bourgogne Irancy 5.4 ha., Bourgogne Passe-Tout-Grains 0.8 ha.
Bernard Cantin, Le Moutier, Irancy 89290 Champs-sur-Yonne

CLOS DE LA CHAINETTE, DOMAINE DU   4.5 ha. (100 per cent)

Clos de la Chainette (Monopole), Bourgogne *rouge, blanc* and *rosé* 4.5 ha.

This vineyard is in the middle of town, and claims origins going back to A.D. 650. It has 1,500 customers, acquired more because of the wine's picturesque renown than the quality of recent vintages; M. Millière is working to improve matters.

Thierry Millière, Centre Hospitalier Specialisé en Psychiatrie, 4 av. des Clairions, 89011 Auxerre, Cedex

RENÉ ET WILLIAM CHARRIAT   9.5 ha. (95 per cent)

Bourgogne Irancy *rouge* and *rosé* 9 ha.
One of the half-dozen best addresses for Irancy.
René Charriat, 69 rue Soufflot, 89290 Irancy

ANITA ET JEAN-PIERRE COLINOT

Bourgogne Irancy Palotte 0.3 ha., Les Mazelots 2 ha., Côte de Moutier 0.3 ha., Les Bessys, Vauchassys, Les Cailles

Jean-Pierre is an effusive fast-talker, who will insist you study the well-thumbed Gault & Millau pages from the time when he was grower of the year, and those showing his blonde Anita as a *Guide Hachette* heart-throb. But these wines are made with passion and individuality, the different hillsides fermented and vat-aged (no barrels here) separately. His Pinot Noirs are often little more than 12°; bottled when youthful, they give a lovely balance of richness and fruit.

If you are lucky (and his mother hasn't double-bolted the doors separating her home from his) you may be shown the old below-ground vats, lined with stone slabs, dating back at least two centuries and still in use, which inspired the design of his new ones. There are many attentions to detail: he may even show you the *new sponge* he uses to clean his vats. His mother was a Polish refugee; she is an elegant, well-preserved, determined lady, and for many years he made the wine for her. Now strong demand from French customers has enabled him to set up independently.

Anita et Jean-Pierre Colinot, rue Chariats, 89290 Irancy

ROBERT COLINOT PÈRE ET FILS   4 ha. (100 per cent)

Bourgogne Irancy 3.5 ha., Bourgogne Palotte 0.25 ha., Bourgogne Cailles 0.25 ha.
Mme Rosa Colinot, rue Soufflot, Irancy 89290

ROBERT DEFRANCE   6 ha. (80 per cent)

Bourgogne Saint-Bris (Pinot Noir) 1.5 ha., Chardonnay 1 ha., Sauvignon de Saint-Bris 0.5 ha., Bourgogne Aligoté 3 ha.
Robert Defrance, 5 rue du Four, 89530 Saint-Bris-le-Vineux

ROGER DELALOGE   6 ha. (60 per cent)

Bourgogne Irancy *rouge*, *rosé*, Bourgogne Aligoté, Crémant de Bourgogne
Roger et Annie Delaloge, ruelle du Milieu, 89290 Irancy

ANTOINE DONAT   10 ha. (100 per cent)
VIGNOBLE DESSUS BON BOIRE

Bourgogne Chardonnay and Pinot Noir
   The whites here are likely to be more dependable than the reds, many Pinots in this area having originated in Champagne, so being not the most suitable stocks for still red-wine-making. But there can be pleasant surprises.
Antoine Donat, Vaux, 89290 Champs-sur-Yonne

RAYMOND DUPUIS   6 ha. (100 per cent)

Bourgogne Coulanges la Vineuse 5 ha.
Raymond Dupuis, 17 rue des Dames, 89580 Coulanges-la-Vineuse

DOMAINE FÉLIX ET FILS   31 ha. (50 per cent)

Saint-Bris (Sauvignon) 6.13 ha., Bourgogne Côtes d'Auxerre (Chardonnay) 4.08 ha., (Pinot Noir) 5.24 ha., (César) 0.1 ha., Bourgogne Irancy 2.1 ha., Chablis 0.99 ha., Petit Chablis 1.31 ha., Aligoté 9.37 ha.
   This place may look a little chaotic, but the whites go into bottle young and fresh, and the reds can have a chewy, characterful appeal which is worth experiencing. Harvesting has been mechanized since 1980, bottling being done by a roving plant from the Mâconnais, SOBEMAB (which is very active in the Auxerrois). This is one of Saint-Bris's oldest families, Nicolas Félix having been second alderman in the revolutionary year 1789.
Hervé Félix, 17 rue de Paris, 89530 Saint-Bris-le-Vineux

MICHEL ESCLAVY

Bourgogne *rouge*, Sauvignon de Saint-Bris

Most of Monsieur Esclavy's grapes go to the Cave de Bailly, but he still makes a little pure César and some Sauvignon *blanc*.

Michel Esclavy, 89530 Saint-Bris-le-Vineux

PATRICE FORT   17 ha. (90 per cent)

Bourgogne Irancy 3 ha., Saint-Bris (Sauvignon) 2 ha., Bourgogne Côtes d'Auxerre (*blanc*) 2 ha., (*rouge*) 4 ha., (*rosé*) 2 ha., Aligoté 2 ha.

The young Patrice Fort had responsibilities at Château de Puligny-Montrachet, in the Laroche era, before returning to make wine in the Auxerrois. The story goes that his grandmother planted 12 hectares of vineyard, just before her death, although unsure if a family member would take them on. Patrice picked up the gauntlet, and now makes some of the best value, most lively (no barrels here, at present) wines of the district.

Patrice Fort, 13 route des Champs, 89530 Saint-Bris

DOMAINE FOURNILLON-CHAMPEIX   12 ha. (10 per cent)

Chablis Fournaux 0.3 ha., Chablis 5 ha., Bourgogne Epineuil 3.25 ha., Bourgogne Chardonnay 1.1 ha., Bourgogne Grand Ordinaire Pinot Noir 0.25 ha.

Here, 12 km from Tonnerre, may be seen pre-phylloxera vines growing healthily, producing Bourgogne *blanc*. They are Chardonnay *franc de pied*: ungrafted Chardonnays, in clay soil, planted originally in a crowd, as the saying went, but now pushed into rows. Madame Champeix believes they owe their survival to a thin, surface layer of sand which prevented the hatching of the phylloxera's eggs. Cuttings from these old vines went to vine research stations at Montpellier and Mulhouse, and have been used to replant many fine white Burgundy plots.

Mme Champeix (née Forgeot) et Gérard Fournillon, Bernouil, 89360 Flogny-la-Chapelle

DOMAINE MICHEL GARLAN   7 ha. (50 per cent)

Bourgogne Irancy 7 ha.

The biological, or, as they say reasoned-out, approach to vine-tending is made here; I have not yet come across the wines.

Michel Garlan, 6 Les Promenades, 89290 Irancy

GHISLAINE ET JEAN-HUGHES GOISOT   23 ha. (80 per cent)
HUGHES GOISOT
DOMAINE DU CORPS DE GARDE

Sauvignon de Saint-Bris 5 ha., Bourgogne Côtes d'Auxerre (*blanc*) 6 ha., (*rouge*) 5 ha., Bourgogne Aligoté 7 ha.

Sauvignon grapes are generally harvested at the beginning of the vintage, to highlight their herbaceous fruit intensity, but not here, where they seek citrus fruit, not vegetal, aromas, and pick them at the end. The result is spicy and complex: New World Sauvignon *blanc* rather than Sancerre in character.

The wines are made in twelfth- and thirteenth-century cellars, some being stored in an eleventh-century guardroom with a fine ribbed vault intersection. Into this underground world a passage once lead from the town's south gate, which was so narrow that if its guardian died defending it his body entirely blocked the access. The passage is now closed off, but one can climb up five or six steps in the total dark until stopped by a damp earth wall, reflecting on the bodies of men-at-arms who might have fallen beneath one's feet.

The Goisots briefly considered moving their wine-making to larger, easier premises, but cannot conceive of these old cellars without wines being made within them. 'An atmosphere is released from these walls which forces us to vinify in a certain way, thinking of the generations who have passed under these vaults. A cellar is dead when it is only used for bottle storage', says Jean-Hughes Goisot.

These are some of the finest wines of the Auxerrois, the Aligoté uncomplicated but richly fruity, the Chardonnay complex and ripe, the Pinot lively and suave, well worth ageing. The cellar is barely five hours' drive from the Channel tunnel.

Ghislaine et Jean-Hughes Goisot, 89530 Saint-Bris-le-Vineux

JOEL GRIFFE   8 ha. (20 per cent)

Sauvignon de Saint-Bris 1 ha., Bourgogne (*rouge*) Côtes d'Auxerre 1.2 ha., Bourgogne Aligoté Côtes de Chitry 3.3 ha., Crémant de Bourgogne 3 ha.
Joël Griffe, 15 rue du Beugnon, Chitry le Fort, 89530 Saint-Bris-le-Vineux

PETITS PROPRIÉTAIRES DU VIGNOBLE DE JOIGNY

Bourgogne (*blanc*) 7 ha.

Seven hundred hectares of vines existed around Joigny at the the time of the Revolution, supplying Paris, thanks to transport down the Yonne, and local needs. The railways and phylloxera almost killed this production off completely, but now there is a small revival (see also, below, Alain Vignot).

Twelve small proprietors have grouped together, around Michel Lorain of the Restaurant Côte Saint Jacques in Joigny, to replant up to 15 of the 90 hectares which were classified in March 1989, as Bourgogne. Their first harvest is scheduled for 1995, from an initial plantation of 5 hectares of Chardonnay. Given the likely difficulties of ripening Pinot Noir so far north, and following soil analysis and advice from Claude Bourguignon of LAMS, they decided to concentrate on white wine. At some future stage they may try to produce a *vin gris* (traditional in Joigny) from Pinot Noir.
Michel Lorain, 43 faubourg de Paris, 89300 Joigny

JEAN-PIERRE MALTOFF   10 ha. (100 per cent)

Bourgogne (*rouge* and *rosé*) Coulanges-la-Vineuse 9 ha., Bourgogne Grand Ordinaire Gamay 1 ha.

Maltoff is President of the Coulanges growers' union, and like many of the fifteen estate-bottling growers here, sells his wine primarily to passing consumers. Gamay is planted as a thirst-quencher; his first vinification was 1987.
Jean-Pierre Maltoff, 89580 Coulanges-la-Vineuse

MICHEL MARTIN   13 ha. (70 per cent)
ANDRÉ MARTIN

Bourgogne Coulanges-la-Vineuse 10 ha., Bourgogne Chardonnay 1 ha.

Nothing heavy about these red wines (indeed I think this is the lightest, softest young Pinot I know), which are mainly destined for sale in France.

Martin has been replanting these stony hillsides (with the regular yielder Clone 115) and sometimes makes a refreshingly delicious *rosé*.

Michel Martin et Mme André Martin, 40 rue des Dames et 61 rue Andre Vildieu, 89580 Coulanges-la-Vineuse

JEAN-CLAUDE-MICHAUT   15.5 ha. (97 per cent)

Bourgogne Epineuil (*rouge* and *rosé*) 11 ha., Chablis Vaucoupin 0.5 ha., Chablis 3 ha., Bourgogne (*blanc*) 1 ha.

Michaut was a pioneer replanter (from 1978) of the hillsides above Tonnerre, where Bourgogne Epineuil is grown. Now that his vines have aged the wine (which undergoes longish storage in large wooden vats) has more stuffing; it is still light, but has an appealing, soft, attractive fruitiness.

Jean-Claude Michaut, Epineuil, 89700 Tonnerre

JEAN PODOR   5.2 ha. (70 per cent)

Bourgogne Irancy 2 ha., Les Mazelots 1.1 ha., Palotte 0.5 ha., Bourgogne Passe-Tout-Grains 1.4 ha.

Can Monsieur Podor, standing beside his ancient, blackened barrels in dark blue, peaked cap, smoke a whole own-rolled cigarette without removing it from his beard? I haven't seen it, but am sure he can. He is a delightful, modest wine-maker, the contents of his bottles being just occasionally disastrous, but also sometimes excellent. Irancy may sometimes be a little rustic, but if you have a rich, old one, it's a great treat which slows you down, which makes you reflective.

Jean et Antoinette Podor, chemin des Marteaux, 89290 Irancy

DOMAINE G. VERRET ET FILS   42 ha. (75 per cent)
DOMAINE DU PARC

Chablis Beauroy 6 ha., Bourgogne Irancy 10 ha., Sauvignon de
Saint-Bris 6 ha., Chablis 2.5 ha., Bourgogne Côtes d'Auxerre 3 ha.,
Aligoté 9 ha., Crémant de Bourgogne 5 ha.

A sizeable estate for Burgundy, providing a living to three house-
holds, this has been a valued supplier to the British Embassy on the
rue du Faubourg Saint-Honoré (which surely shows discrimination
on the part of our diplomats, good Auxerrois wines being highly
rated in Paris, while remaining remarkably good value).

M. et Mme Georges, Claude et Jacky Verret, 7 route de Champs,
89530 Saint-Bris-le-Vineux

SICA LA VÉZELIENNE   50 ha.

This co-operative of ten growers vinifies half the production of the
fledgling Vézelay vine district. Seventy per cent is Chardonnay,
giving Bourgogne *blanc*, 15 per cent Pinot Noir (Bourgogne *rouge*)
and 10 per cent the unusual Melon de Bourgogne (which is damned
before birth by its derogatory *appellation* Bourgogne Grand
Ordinaire).

Marc Meneau, the brilliant restaurateur of L'Espérance in Saint-
Père-sous-Vézelay, has been one of the main movers in the replanting of Vézelay's vineyards. There are 300 hectares of suitable land
(currently 100 hectares are planted) dotted amongst fir-tree woods,
on the south and south-east facing slopes of several narrow valleys
around the basilica. Only the top of the slopes is classified, for fear
of frosts. Cultivation is largely manual, for these steep slopes would
need four-wheel-drive vine-straddlers, and at present such an
investment is not cost-effective.

Marc Meneau's first vintage was 1989, and the grapes went
to Nuits-Saint-Georges and Chablis for vinification (the reds to
Faiveley, the whites to Michel Rémon). Now he delivers them to this
co-operative. Since 1990 Bernard Raveneau, elder brother of Jean-
Marie in Chablis, has been helping with wine-making, and from
January 1993 has been full-time with La Vézelienne. He is making
soft, supple Bourgogne Chardonnay of high quality (at an unpretentious price), and sometimes pulls off a fresh and spicy Pinot
Noir. The Melon de Bourgogne (the same grape which gives Musca-

det de Sèvre et Maine, when planted at the mouth of the Loire) can be full of round fruitiness, for youthful drinking.

Very little help comes from the INAO in Paris over use of the perfectly valid name of origin Vézelay to launch these unknown, excellent wines. Perhaps the growers will register a brand – Henri de Vézelay, or some such – to circumvent the stuffy bureaucrats.

Bernard Raveneau, SICA La Vézelienne, Saint-Père, 89450 Vézelay

CAVES ALAIN VIGNOT   9 ha. (100 per cent)

Bourgogne Côte Saint-Jacques Pinot Noir 5 ha., Pinot Gris (producing *vin gris*) 4 ha.

Jacques Vignot was the frontiersman who reclaimed the fine slopes above Joigny for Pinot Noir (and Pinot Gris), the first authorization for use of the word Bourgogne being 1975. He lacked, however, the wine-making skills to make high-flying wines. His son Alain has doubled the vineyard area, while remaining a mixed farmer – wheat, barley, sunflowers, depending on the year.

Alain et Annie Vignot, 16 rue des Près, Paroy sur Tholon, 89300 Joigny

11

The Côte de Nuits: Dijon, Marsannay and Fixin

DIJON, LARREY AND CHENÔVE

Larrey is the most northerly village of the Côte de Dijon, but it has virtually disappeared beneath the suburbs of the town. Already in 1892 Danguy and Aubertin described how country houses had been built halfway up the slopes, thus gaining a magnificent view. Vineyards were probably planted there contemporaneously with those at Chenôve; they certainly existed in AD 587, and in the seventh century Duke Amalgaire gave vines from this commune to the Abbey of Bèze; we will meet the duke again later, in Gevrey-Chambertin.

Neither of the villages has right to a commune *appellation*, but both produce some good Bourgognes. Larrey's best-known vineyard is Les Marcs d'Or, whose wines did not lack finesse, according to the early nineteenth-century writer Dr Morelot. It used to belong to the cellist Maurice Maréchal, and faces north-east, which is rare on the Côte. I understand that his son has so far won the battle to prevent a school being built on the vineyard. The only Larrey wine I have come across is the Bourgogne Montre-Cul of Charles Quillardet, now part of Patriarche.

Chenôve may have got its name from the fact that chanvre, or cannabis, was cultivated there. In the old days, the territory was divided between three owners: the chapter of Autun, the Benedictines of Saint-Bénigne and the Dukes of Burgundy, who owned the famous Clos du Roi with its vat-house and magnificent presses. The Clos du Roi now belongs to M. Michel Pont of Volnay and Savigny (see p. 391), the presses to Messrs Pascal of Dijon. They were constructed by Alix de Vergy in 1238.

It is recounted that in 1648 the wines of Chenôve sold at higher prices than those of Gevrey. Perhaps the presence of the Duke of Burgundy's Clos had an influence on demand.

There are three or four attractive interior courtyards in Chenôve and on the main square a fifteenth-century façade which has been turned into four separate houses. Around the sanatorium grows the most northerly forest of cedars in Europe, so the locals claim.

I know of one estate-bottling grower based in Plombières-lès-Dijon:

JEAN DUBOIS   6.5 ha. (100 per cent)
DOMAINE DE LA CRAS

Bourgogne (*rouge*) 4 ha., (*blanc*) 2.25 ha.

These vines are planted on a dry, thistle-infested plateau above Dijon, between Plombières and Corcelles-lès-Monts (near where the *autoroute* starts for Paris). Gamay and Aligoté used to grow here, for Dijon's cafés, until the 1914–18 war killed many vignerons, and the land was abandoned. Monsieur Dubois has set aside his unprofitable arable lands, and now makes unsophisticated, prize-winning red and white Burgundies, from Pinot Noir and Chardonnay.

Jean Dubois, Domaine de la Cras, 21370 Plombières-lès-Dijon

MARSANNAY

This has been the first village *appellation* of the Côte de Nuits coming south from Dijon, since it received the right, in 1987, to label its wines with its own name, rather than send them primarily for blending as Côte de Nuits-Villages.

Marsannay is no little village of the Côte, but virtually a suburb of Dijon, home to 6,000 people. Vines cover a fifth of the area of the commune, however, and were mentioned as far back as the seventh century.

The villages of Marsannay and Couchey used to be best known for their *rosé*, which could be called Bourgogne Rosé or Bourgogne Clairet with the addition of either Marsannay or Marsannay-la-Côte. The wine is made by vinifying Pinot Noir grapes as if they were white. The last pressings give a rose-tinted must which should be enough to give the wine its grey-pink colour. If not, three bottles

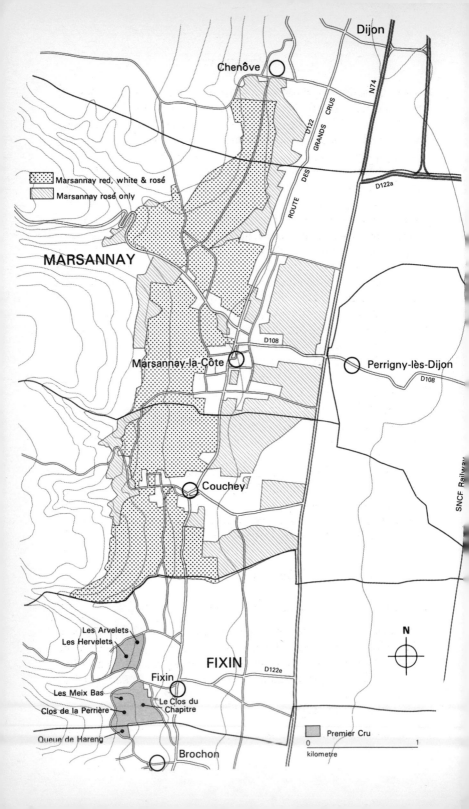

per hogshead of red Pinot from Marsannay have been known to do the trick. It is a full-bodied dry *rosé* with a clean Pinot flavour.

Marsannay has been producing wine since at least AD 658. It has had periods of great poverty, for instance after the Battle of Rocroy in 1643, when the population was reduced to thirty, of which two handled half the pruning, as the remainder were so miserable. But during the eighteenth century Dijon doubled in size, and the nearby villages were planted with Gamay to quench its thirst. Couchey and Marsannay-la-Côte made fortunes and they showed it by building enormous town halls and churches which can still be seen (Marsannay pulling down a Romanesque church to do so). In 1855 Dr Lavalle wrote that there was not enough Pinot in the communes to make a single *cuvée spéciale*, and in 1918 the situation had scarcely changed.

Even though the village has its own *appellation*, as yet it is hard to see a recognizable character in the wines of Marsannay, white or red. At best they are clean and fresh and fruity, but they lack an identifiable, original character. Perhaps more concentrating and less enriching are needed, and maybe the 10/10 route might be considered: drop production by 10 per cent, and increase price by 10 per cent. Of course, growers would have to go travelling, with their samples, to sell at the higher price, but concentration and length of fruit rarely fail to hook consumers. At present people try the new name, but are not smitten.

There are no First Growths in Marsannay. The 1991 vineyard land planted was 97.42 ha. Pinot Noir, and 7.47 ha. Chardonnay. Since the *appellation* is a recent one, there is no average five-year figure, but 1991 and 1992 averaged shows production running at 62,000 cases of red and *rosé*, with 3,900 cases of white.

Main Marsannay and Couchey growers

DOMAINE BART   19 ha. (50 per cent)

Chambertin Clos de Bèze 0.42 ha., Bonnes Mares 1.12 ha., Chambolle-Musigny 0.11 ha., Fixin Les Hervelets 1.43 ha., Côte de Nuits-Villages 0.4 ha., Marsannay (*rosé* and *rouge*) 8.5 ha., Marsannay (*blanc*) 0.5 ha., Santenay (*rouge*) 1.6 ha., (*blanc*) 0.4 ha., Aligoté 2.3 ha.

Bart is a cousin of Bruno Clair, and many of the best vines here –

◁ Chenôve, Marsannay, Couchey and Fixin

Clos de Bèze, Bonnes Mares, Santenay – were once part of Domaine Clair-Daü. I have heard good things of this range.
Martin Bart, 24 rue de Mazy, 21160 Marsannay-la-Côte

DOMAINE BRUNO CLAIR   20 ha. (100 per cent)

Chambertin Clos de Bèze 1 ha., Gevrey-Chambertin Clos Saint-Jacques 1 ha., Les Cazetiers 0.87 ha., Clos du Fonteny (Monopole) 0.67 ha., *Premier Cru* 0.22 ha., Morey-Saint-Denis en la Rue de Vergy (*rouge*) 0.64 ha., (*blanc*) 0.51 ha., Savigny-lès-Beaune La Dominode 1.1 ha., *Premier Cru* 0.6 ha., Vosne-Romanée Champs Perdrix 0.92 ha., Chambolle-Musigny Les Véroilles 0.72 ha., Marsannay (*rouge*) Les Vaudenelles 1.95 ha., Grasses Têtes 1.35 ha., Les Longeroies 1.25 ha., (*blanc* – Chardonnay and Pinot Blanc) 2.03 ha., (*rosé*) 2.8 ha.

Superb wines are made here, in spacious underground stone cellars, from simple Marsannay *rosé* (which needs a year or more in bottle to develop its character), through white wines from Chardonnay, Beurot and Pinot Blanc, to the grandest Côte de Nuits bottles for long ageing.

A family domaine has been reborn around the questing, anxious Bruno Clair, when, in the early 1980s, many feared the worst for Domaine Clair-Daü's fortunes, which during the period 1980–5 passed from the control of Bruno's father Bernard to his sister Noëlle Vernet. The latter finally, and mercifully, sold her vines and interests into American control (Louis Jadot and Kobrand) in 1986. The original Domaine Clair-Daü was dismembered (Bernard Clair-Daü taking his share to the Fougeray domaine), but the benefits have been considerable.

Domaine Clair-Daü had invented the Bourgogne *rosé* of Marsannay on 22 September 1919, at a time of faltering wine sales. Bruno's grandfather Joseph Clair had just married Miss Daü, having been billetted opposite her, and fallen quite in love, when resting from the Verdun trenches.

I suspect that interest in Marsannay *rosé* will continue to dwindle in favour of white and red, but if the latter's particular character is to be discovered it may well be here, where three different *cuvées*, from specific sites, are made each year, as well as a simple village version. The old vines Dominode, and the Cazetiers, are famous wines, but wherever one sees bottles from this estate one should buy and try them, from the bottom of the range to the top.

Bruno Clair makes wine with a light touch, and seems to welcome input from his friends: co-worker and oenologist Philippe Brun, or André Geoffroy, for instance, who vinifies here – notably a fine Fixin – sharing Clair's facilities. Clair is an unusual Burgundian, who, as Fiona Beeston described in *Mes Hommes du vin*,[1] was a shepherd on the barren plateaux of the Lozère, in the Massif Central, for four years before returning to establish his vine domaine.

Bruno Clair et Philippe Brun, 5 rue du Vieux Collège, 21160 Marsannay-la-Côte

CLÉMANCEY FRÈRES   6.5 ha. (20 per cent)

Fixin Hervelets 1.8 ha., Marsannay Champs Perdrix 1 ha., Côte de Nuits-Villages 0.3 ha., Bourgogne

The Clémanceys are mixed farmers. With vineyards, they grow wheat, oil-seed rape, winter barley and have land set aside, lying fallow.

Hubert et Pierre Clémancey, 31 et 33 rue Jean Jaurès, 21160 Couchey

COLLOTTE PÈRE ET FILS   8.5 ha. (70 per cent)

Marsannay (*rouge*) 3 ha., (*rosé*) 2.5 ha., (*blanc*) 0.5 ha., Bourgogne (*blanc*) 0.5 ha., Aligoté and Passe-Tout-Grains

Good Marsannay, both white and red, is to be had here.

Philippe Collotte, 44 rue de Mazy, 21160 Marsannay-la-Côte

DEREY FRÈRES   18 ha. (60 per cent)

Gevrey-Chambertin 0.8 ha., Fixin Hervelets 0.7 ha., Fixin 3.8 ha., Marsannay and Marsannay *rosé* 9.2 ha., Bourgogne (côteau de Couchey) 0.7 ha.

The Derey brothers cultivate Montre-Cul, along with Patriarche, who bought the Quillardet domaine. The family bought its

---

1 The title was feebly rendered into English as *The Wine Men* (by Fiona Beeston, and published by Sinclair-Stevenson, London, 1991).

Hervelets from Noisot, the Napoleonic grenadier who set up the well-known monument to the emperor above Fixin.

Albert and Pierre Derey, 1 rue Jules Ferry, 21160 Couchey

DOMAINE FOUGERAY DE BEAUCLAIR   20 ha. (95 per cent)
DOMAINE FOUGERAY

Bonnes Mares 1.6 ha., Fixin 1.02 ha., Gevrey-Chambertin 0.27 ha., Vosne-Romanée Damodes 0.2 ha., Marsannay (*rouge*) Clos du Roy 0.27 ha., Les Longeroies 0.45 ha., Grasses Têtes 0.81 ha., Les Saint-Jacques 0.45 ha., Les Favières 0.53 ha., Marsannay (*blanc*) 1.42 ha., (*rosé*) 3.87 ha., (*rouge*) 0.87 ha., Côte de Nuits-Villages 1.38 ha., Savigny-lès-Beaune Les Gollardes (*rouge*) 1.5 ha., (*blanc*) 0.26 ha., Bourgogne (*blanc*) 0.5 ha., Aligoté 1.68 ha.

This estate dates from 1986, when Bernard Clair-Daü leased his Bonnes Mares (representing the totality of that *appellation* to be found in Morey), along with other vines, to the Fougerays, who since 1972 had owned vines on the Côte de Nuits and in Savigny. Clair has a 10 per cent sleeping interest in the business.

Fougeray tries hard. The wines can be good, but also sometimes below expectations, over-crafted, with oak showing through, and maybe not the finest oak. With so many *appellations*, and all the single vineyard red Marsannays, it cannot be easy to harvest everything at optimum ripeness, nor to make a success of each *cuvée*. But this couple is extremely, some might say fanatically, determined, and it is likely the wines will continue to improve.

Jean-Louis et Evelyne Fougeray, 44 rue de Mazy, 21160 Marsannay-la-Côte

JEAN FOURNIER   12 ha.

Gevrey-Chambertin 0.55 ha., Marsannay Clos du Roy 1.25 ha., Marsannay 6 ha., Marsannay (*blanc*) 0.33 ha.

Jean Fournier has been running this estate single-handed since the age of seventeen. The reds are perfectly correct, but don't fly very high in my experience.

M. et Mme Jean Fournier, 34–39 rue du Château, 21160 Marsannay-la-Côte

JEAN-PIERRE GUYARD   14 ha. (60 per cent)

Fixin Hervelets 0.25 ha., Gevrey-Chambertin 0.25 ha., Fixin 1.5 ha., Marsannay (*rouge, rosé* and *blanc*) 9 ha., Bourgogne and Aligoté
M. and Mme J.-P. Guyard, 4 rue du Vieux Collège, 21160 Marsannay-la-Côte.

DOMAINE HUGUENOT PÈRE ET FILS   17 ha. (70 per cent)

Charmes-Chambertin 0.25 ha., Gevrey-Chambertin *Premier Cru* 0.5 ha., Marsannay Clos du Roy 1 ha., Marsannay La Montagne 0.7 ha., Marsannay 5 ha., Fixin 3.5 ha.
Huguenot was instrumental in obtaining the *appellation* Marsannay for the wines of this village. I have found the wines perfectly correct.
Jean-Louis Huguenot, 7 ruelle du Carron, 21160 Marsannay-la-Côte

CHÂTEAU DE MARSANNAY

(See Patriarche Père et Fils, in Beaune)

PHILIPPE NADDEF   4 ha. (75 per cent)

Mazis-Chambertin 0.4 ha., Gevrey-Chambertin Cazetiers 0.3 ha., Champeaux 0.4 ha., Gevrey-Chambertin 1.3 ha., Marsannay 1.5 ha.
Philippe Naddef, 30 rue Jean Jaurès, 21160 Couchey

SIRUGUE PÈRE ET FILS   10 ha. (30 per cent)

Gevrey-Chambertin 0.6 ha., Fixin and Côte de Nuits-Village 2.5 ha., Marsannay (*rouge* and *blanc*) 5 ha.
Jean-Marie et Maurice Sirugue, 2 rue Pasteur, 21160 Couchey

FIXIN

Until Marsannay gained the right to its own *appellation*, Fixin was the first village AC south of Dijon; with its First Growths and its historic Clos it is still the beginning of the Côte de Nuits proper.

It was named Fiscinus in 830, Fiscentiae in 995. Its best-known vineyard has always been Clos de la Perrière, and the Marquis Loppin de Montmort used to sell this at the same price as Chambertin. The vineyard is named after a once-famous quarry, and is attached to a manor house which was originally a hunting lodge for Duke Odo II; then it belonged to the Abbey of Cîteaux. Jean-François Bazin tells us that the monks established a Hospice in the *manoir*[2], a nursing home for unwell monks, up on the slope where the air is good.

Next door is the Clos du Chapitre, which lies at the heart of the hill, giving in theory the best wine of the village. Also well known is the Clos Napoléon, previously Aux Cheusots or Les Echézeaux, which borders Fixin's melancholy curiosity, the Parc Noisot. Claude-Charles Noisot was a *commandant aux grenadiers* in Napoleon's Guard who commissioned the Dijon sculptor Rude to erect a memorial to the Emperor. Bonaparte is cast in bronze, at the moment when he 'awakens to immortality' on a rock in Saint Helena. Noisot's last wish was to be buried in the park, upright, with his sabre raised, mounting a deathly guard on his emperor; however the rock was too hard, so J.-F. Bazin recounts, so he was cheated of his wish.

The following vineyards are classified *Premiers Crus*:

Arvelets, Les
Clos de la Perrière
Clos du Chapitre
Clos Napoléon (Aux Cheusots and Le Village)
Hervelets, Les
Meix Bas, Le
Queue de Hareng
Suchot, En

First Growth and commune Fixin covered in 1991 an area of 93.7

---

2 *Les Grands Vins de Fixin*, Editions de Saint-Seine-l'Abbaye, 1994.

ha. The five-year average production (1988–92) for red Fixin was 43,600 cases, for white (averaged over 1991 and 1992) 440 cases.

Main Fixin growers

DOMAINE BERTHAUT 13 ha. (70 per cent)

Fixin Les Arvelets 1 ha., Les Crais 1.5 ha., Les Clos 1 ha., Fixin 7 ha., Gevrey-Chambertin *Premier Cru* 0.3 ha., Gevrey-Chambertin
  Savigny is not the only village of the Côte with wall inscriptions. Over M. Berthaut's garden gate is written *Prend garde a toy maro 1693 (maro* is *maraudeur)*. Elsewhere can be seen: *Bien faire vax mieu que dire* and *Tout par amour et rien par forse.*
  One may expect balanced, lively wines here.
Vincent et Denis Berthaut, 9 rue Noisot, 21220 Fixin

CAMILLE CRUSSEREY 4 ha. (10 per cent)

Fixin Hervelets 0.8 ha., Clos du Meix Trouhans (Monopole) 1.8 ha., Les Herbues 0.8 ha.
Camille Crusserey, Clos du Meix-Trouhans, 21220 Fixin

RENÉ DEFRANCE ET FILS 4 ha. (50 per cent)

Fixin, Côte de Nuits-Villages, Bourgogne *rouge*
René Defrance, 38 route des Grands Crus, 21220 Fixin

DOMAINE PIERRE GELIN 16.5 ha. (100 per cent)
GELIN-ET-MOLIN

Chambertin Clos de Bèze 0.6 ha., Mazis-Chambertin 0.38 ha., Gevrey-Chambertin 1.8 ha., Fixin Clos du Chapitre (Monopole) 4.78 ha., Clos Napoléon (Monopole) 1.8 ha., Fixin Les Hervelets 0.6 ha., Fixin 2.55 ha., Passe-Tout-Grains and Aligoté
  Gelin is the largest proprietor in Fixin. He and his brother-in-law André Molin exploit a very fine ensemble, both Monopoles Clos having their own *cuveries* within their walls. The village church stands below them, the twelfth-century manor of La Perrière above, and in between their rolling hillside of vines. When I first visited it, the youngest vines in the Clos du Chapitre dated from 1948, but

approximately 40 per cent of the old vines have now been replanted.

These wines are substantial and rich, with country, rather than sophisticated, charms, but very good.

Stephen Gelin et André Molin, 2 rue de Chapitre, 21220 Fixin

DOMAINE DE LA PERRIÈRE   5.18 ha. (50 per cent)

Fixin Clos de la Perrière (Monopole) 5.18 ha.

These are historic buildings, as we have seen, and the vineyard has one of the oldest reputations in Burgundy, on a wonderful mid-slope site. I have found the wine chewy and rather rustic, lacking middle-palate, and think it is sometimes left too long in barrel. They can make rich wine in a year like 1990, but seem to lack the *savoir-faire* to make something excellent in lesser vintages. There is an old crusher and Vaslin press which are becoming museum pieces like the mediaeval wine-press, which they believe dates from the twelfth century. This vat-house-cellar is in a time-warp, virtually unchanged over the twenty years since I first saw it.

Joliet *père* is to be joined by his son, who has studied at Beaune's Lycée Viticole, but I cannot see attitudes or wine-making approaches being about to change. The wine has been distributed by a variety of shippers, particularly Moillard and Dufouleur Père et Fils.

Philippe et Bénigne Joliet, Manoir de la Perrière, 21220 Fixin

12

Gevrey-Chambertin and Brochon

Danguy and Aubertin believe that it was probably a Roman colony which first reclaimed the Brochon hillsides from brambles to plant vines. Traces of their occupation in the form of coins, sculpted monuments and tombs have been found, as have remains of a Merovingian settlement in the form of large numbers of graves. The place was known as Bruciacus in the sixth century, Briscona villa in 878. Eleven of the southern *lieux-dits* of the commune of Brochon have right to the AC Gevrey-Chambertin, the remainder being Côte de Nuits-Villages or Bourgogne.

Gevrey-Chambertin, situated 13 km south of Dijon, is the largest village *appellation* of the Côte de Nuits. First Growth (73.85 ha.) and commune Gevrey-Chambertin (331.85 ha.) cover a total of 405.7 hectares. Together, the five-year average production (1988–92) was 191,100 cases.

Some of the longest-living village wines come from the hillside between Gevrey and Brochon, the reason being that *Grands Crus* and *Premiers Crus* are so thick on the ground to the south of Gevrey that much of the commune wine comes from over the *Route Nationale* 74 down towards the railway.

The most important vineyard owner in the history of Gevrey-Chambertin is the Abbey of Cluny. Its first acquisition was land which had been given to the Abbey of Sainte-Bénigne by Richard le Justicier, Duke of Burgundy, in 895; it purchased much more in 1275 from another Burgundian duke, Robert II. One of its abbots, Yves de Poissey, had begun the construction of the château on the rue Haute in 1257, and this, with its four strong towers, served as a refuge for the local population in times of invasion. Part of the château still stands and can be visited.

Gevrey-Chambertin is the birthplace of Gaston Roupnel, a pro-

fessor at the Lycée de Dijon and historian of the French countryside. Between the two World Wars he wrote many purple passages
on wine; here he is on Chambertin:

> On its own, it is all that is possible in great Burgundy. Tough
> and powerful like the greatest of Cortons, it has the delicacy of
> Musigny, the velvet of Romanée, the perfume of a high Clos
> Vougeot. Its colour is that sombre scarlet which seems to
> imprison in its garnet reflections all the glory of a setting sun.
> Taste it: feel in the mouth that full and firm roundness, that
> substantial flame enveloped by the mat softness of velvet and the
> aroma of reseda! Chambertin, king of wines!

No village in Burgundy has more *Grands Crus* than Gevrey,
which added Chambertin to its name by *ordonnance* of Louis
Philippe in 1847. Chambertin Clos de Bèze vineyards cover 14.91
hectares and Chambertin 12.64 hectares, making a total of 27.55
hectares for the top two *Grands Crus*. Both wines are red, the five-
year average production (1988–92) totalling respectively 5,290 and
5,360 cases. Chambertin Clos de Bèze may be called Chambertin
on its own, but the opposite is not permitted. The Clos de Bèze was
first planted after Duke Amalgaire had given a parcel of land to the
Abbey of Bèze in 630. Tradition has it that a peasant named Bertin
who owned the adjoining plot to the south decided to plant it with
the same vines as the monks; its wine was perfect and soon the field
(known in 1219 as Campus Bertini) became called the Champ de
Bertin, then simply Chambertin.

The two vineyards (whose wines are said to taste the same) are
divided between twenty-five owners. They have not always been as
famous as they are today. Danguy and Aubertin record that their
reputation was made in the eighteenth century, when the owner of
the Clos supplied the Palatine court and Napoleon Bonaparte, the
queue of Bèze-Chambertin being worth only 30 *livres* in 1651, but
700 or 800 *livres* by 1761.

The Burgundian politician and Dijon journalist Jean-François
Bazin has shed light on Napoleon's liking for Chambertin, quoting
from Frédéric Masson (*Napoléon chez lui, la Journée de l'Empér-
eur aux Tuileries*). It would seem that the emperor drank scarcely
any wine except five- to six-year-old Chambertin, much diluted
with water (*très trempé d'eau*). There was no cellar at the Tuileries
nor any of the palaces. The wine cost six francs a bottle, and was

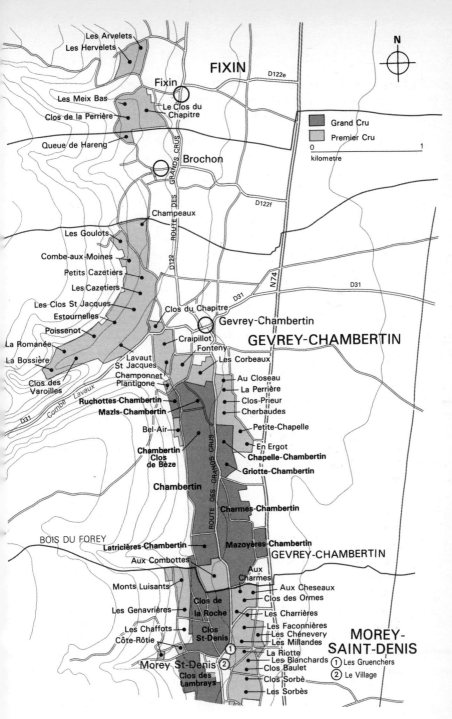

Gevrey-Chambertin

supplied on a sale-or-return basis by the firm of Soupé et Pierrugues, 338 rue Saint-Honoré, in uniform bottles marked with a crowned N, manufactured at Sèvres. Either Soupé or Pierrugues accompanied the imperial headquarters on campaign, Bonaparte declaring that he had never been deprived of his wine 'even in the middle of the sands of Egypt'.

A second division of *Grands Crus* in the village are: Charmes-Chambertin (30.39 ha., average harvest 12,166 dozen bottles); Chapelle-Chambertin (5.04 ha., 2,250 dozen bottles); Griotte-Chambertin (2.34 ha., average harvest 1,450 dozen bottles); Latricières-Chambertin (7.43 ha., average harvest 2,970 dozen bottles); Mazis-Chambertin (8.55 ha., average harvest 3,660 dozen bottles) and Ruchottes-Chambertin (3.13 ha., average harvest 1,350 dozen bottles). Mazoyères-Chambertin used occasionally to be found, but the vineyard has been merged with the more easily pronounceable Charmes-Chambertin, which it touches.

Charmes-Chambertin covers the biggest area of the satellite *Grands Crus*. In parts adjoining Morey-Saint-Denis, in parts stretching right down to the *route nationale*, it has the least personality of these second division *Grands Crus*. A good one is densely, richly fruity, but good ones are hard to find. Chapelle-Chambertin is leaner, and matures relatively soon. Griotte-Chambertin sometimes has an aroma of roasted cherries, as the name suggests; it can be wonderful. Latricières is often closed and tannic when young, Mazis can flash with individuality, and a lingering, powerful fruit. These three are the most interesting, Ruchottes, placed high on the slope, having, for me, not yet yielded up its striking message.

The following are currently classified as *Premiers Crus*:

Bel-Air
Bossière, La
Cazetiers, Petits
Cazetiers, Les
Champeaux
Champonnet
Chapelle, Petite
Cherbaudes
Clos des Varoilles (Les Varoilles)
Clos du Chapitre
Clos Prieur-Haut (Clos Prieur)

Clos Saint-Jacques, Le
Closeau, Au
Combe aux Moines
Combottes, Aux
Corbeaux, Les
Craipillot
Ergot, En
Estournelles
Fonteny
Goulots, Les
Lavaut Saint-Jacques
Perrière, La
Plantigone ou Issart
Poissenot
Romanée, La

The origins of some of these names are intriguing. For instance, there is a spring near the Le Poissenot, where Marie-Hélène Land-rieu-Lussigny believes the monks of Cluny built a fish-pond (when they lived in the old château in Gevrey),[1] excavations having revealed the remains of a likely construction. They left other memories: Combe aux Moines, where the monks perhaps worked or walked, and Clos Prieur, the land no doubt belonging to a Cluniac prior. Not a First Growth, but adjoining the main road is Clos de la Justice, probably the site of the gibbet, where criminals used to be executed and left in view of passers-by.

Main Gevrey-Chambertin growers and merchants

DOMAINE DENIS BACHELET   2.6 ha. (100 per cent)

Charmes-Chambertin 0.43 ha., Gevrey-Chambertin *Premier Cru* 0.27 ha., Gevrey-Chambertin 0.93 ha., Côte de Nuits-Villages 0.16 ha., Bourgogne (*rouge*)

Quantities are minuscule but I have found these Gevrey-Chambertins immaculate, even in a tricky vintage like 1986.

Denis Bachelet, 54 route de Beaune, 21220 Gevrey-Chambertin.

1 *Les Lieux-dits dans le vignoble bourguignon*, Editions Jeanne Laffitte, Marseilles, 1983.

LUCIEN BOILLOT ET FILS   13.75 ha. (65 per cent)
BOILLOT PERE ET FILS

Fixin 0.11 ha., Gevrey-Chambertin Les Corbeaux 0.29 ha., Les Cherbaudes 0.34 ha., Gevrey-Chambertin 5.5 ha., Nuits-Saint-Georges Les Pruliers 0.53 ha., Côte de Nuits-Villages 0.2 ha., Beaune Les Epenottes 0.2 ha., Volnay Les Angles 1.14 ha., Les Caillerets 0.35 ha., Volnay 2.55 ha., Pommard Les Fremiers 0.57 ha., Les Croix Noires 0.37 ha., Pommard 0.25 ha., Bourgogne (*rouge*) 1.3 ha.

This estate was established over one decade, from the small beginnings of a hectare of vines in Gevrey-Chambertin in 1978, to the renting of chunks (Pommard Fremiers, Beaune, Volnay Caillerets, Bourgogne) of the original Domaine Henry Boillot in Volnay, ten years later. Its origins lie in the decision of the two sons of Henry Boillot – Jean and Lucien – to go their separate ways.

Louis et Pierre Boillot, 1 rue docteur Magnon-Pujo, 21220 Gevrey-Chambertin.

PIERRE BOURÉE FILS   (1864) 4 ha.

Charmes-Chambertin 0.7 ha., Gevrey-Chambertin Champeaux 0.13 ha., Clos de la Justice (Monopole) 2 ha., Beaune Epenottes 1.20 ha., Gevrey-Chambertin 0.3 ha., Bourgogne.

A family-controlled, specialist merchant well placed to select and tend small lots of top Côte de Nuits reds. Theirs has seemed to me a sturdy, burly style, corresponding well to old-fashioned British perceptions of what Burgundy should taste like, which I do not share – but perhaps I underrate these wines, many of which are evidently built to last.

Bernard Vallet, route de Beaune, 21220 Gevrey-Chambertin

ALAIN BURGUET   5.18 ha. (80 per cent)

Gevrey-Chambertin Champeaux 0.18 ha., Gevrey-Chambertin 4 ha., Bourgogne (*rouge*) 1 ha.

Alain Burguet is a conscientious wine-maker, and also a Mr Fixit: not much escapes him in Gevrey, and on the northern Côte de Nuits. His wife Dominique is an export broker, working for Becky Wasserman. His Vieilles Vignes Gevrey-Chambertin *cuvée* is his most dependable, long-living bottle, but all his wines have bounce, and powerful fruit, without over-extraction or aggressive tannins.

There are many carefully tended barrels of different ages in this cellar, and you do not pick up new-oak flavours in the finished wines. He works with the lowest possible levels of sulphur, and retains some dissolved carbon dioxide at bottling times, which he likes for the freshness it brings, but the presence of this gas means he cannot use finings (they would not settle). He prefers low-pressure infusorial earth filtration, the earth being an inert siliceous material which is a filter aid. 'Filtration frightens people,' says Burguet, 'but if you know how to filter . . .' Jean-Marc Boillot in Pommard has a similar philosophy, I believe.

Alain Burguet, 19 rue de L'Église, 21220 Gevrey-Chambertin.

DOMAINE CAMUS PÈRE ET FILS   16.8 ha. (70 per cent)

Chambertin 1.75 ha., Latricières-Chambertin 1.5 ha., Charmes-Chambertin 3 ha., Mazis-Chambertin 0.33 ha., Mazoyères-Chambertin 4 ha.

Why are these wines not top drawer? I suspect they are handled too much, and sometimes bottled too late. I have had *Grands Crus* from here which could pass for village wines, if you had not seen the label, and think there should be a more rigorous policy of downgrading, if necessary after bottling. Camus has wonderful vineyard sites, but the wine-making has been insufficiently quality-driven, or perhaps quite simply the yields have been too high, or maybe both.

I think Monsieur Camus's wine-making starts from the point of view that what he produces from these great sites is *inevitably* good, and that the market will adapt to it. He is a High Priest of *terroirism*. Foreign commentators can only spend a limited number of hours tasting his wines; how can they possibly know something he doesn't already know himself?

His old-fashioned philosophy is disconcerting in someone who, having been the INAO's Burgundian regional delegate for many years became, in 1993, President of the BIVB, in succession to Didier Mommessin. He gives much time to bureaucratic duties, speaking to the world – in particular no doubt to law-drafters of Brussels – on behalf of Burgundy, and indeed often has to tell the

Burgundians themselves, in the subtlest possible way, what he thinks is best for them.

Hubert Camus, 21 rue Maréchal de Lattre-de-Tassigny, 21220 Gevrey-Chambertin

DOMAINE PHILIPPE CHARLOPIN-PARIZOT   11 ha. (100 per cent)

Charmes-Chambertin 0.33 ha., Clos Saint-Denis 0.33 ha., Gevrey-Chambertin 3 ha., Morey-Saint-Denis 1 ha., Chambolle-Musigny 0.6 ha., Vosne-Romanée 0.33 ha., Marsannay (*rouge*) 3 ha., (*blanc*) 1 ha., Fixin 0.3 ha. As manager: Chambertin 0.21 ha., which is owned by Mme Jocelyne Barron.

Charlopin *père* was a foundling orphan, brought up by the state, who handed on just 1.5 ha. to his straight-talking son Philippe, who has been bottling since 1984. He has a conveyor-belt on which to spread out the grapes, so as to eliminate anything unripe or mouldy, prior to a week's low temperature maceration, then a further two weeks' fermentation. His wines are often bottled early, and can have splendid fruit. Charlopin used to be based in Marsannay, but moved to the old Quillardet cellar on Gevrey's main road in 1993.

Philippe et Sonia Charlopin-Parisot, route nationale, 21220 Gevrey-Chambertin

MICHEL CLUNY ET FILS   6 ha. (50 per cent)

Chambolle Musigny Les Noirots 0.4 ha., Gevrey-Chambertin Champeaux 0.1 ha., Gevrey-Chambertin 4 ha., Côte de Nuits-Villages 0.77 ha.

Michel Cluny, 5 rue du Tilleul, Brochon, 21220 Gevrey-Chambertin

DOMAINE PIERRE DAMOY   9 ha. (70 per cent)

Chambertin Clos de Bèze 5 ha., Chambertin 0.5 ha., Chapelle-Chambertin 2.25 ha., Gevrey-Chambertin Clos Tamisot (Monopole) 1.5 ha.

Damoy has the largest area of Clos de Bèze; I have often found the wines disappointing, and suspect that the yields were too high. I understand that there have been dreadful tragedies in Jacques

Damoy's family: the death of his wife, and of a son. From 1992 his nephew Pierre Damoy (who has a general agricultural qualification) took over. That summer, he green-harvested in July, to reduce the crop. The resulting 1992s were deeply-coloured and mouth-filling, and I see that his Chapelle-Chambertin scored highly in the 'Ambassadeurs' tasting in Gevrey-Chambertin in September 1994. There may still be a long row to hoe to take the estate into the top league.

Jacques et Pierre Damoy, Le Tamisot, 21220 Gevrey-Chambertin

DOMAINE DROUHIN-LAROZE   15 ha. (100 per cent)

Chambertin Clos de Bèze 1.5 ha., Clos de Vougeot 1.5 ha., Bonnes Mares 2 ha., Latricières-Chambertin 0.75 ha., Chapelle-Chambertin 0.5 ha., Mazis-Chambertin 0.25 ha., Gevrey-Chambertin *Premier Cru* 2 ha., Chambolle-Musigny, Morey-Saint-Denis

A high concentration of wonderful vineyard sites here, and a starry clientèle. The approach to this immaculate property has more the feel of a *Grand Cru* bourgeois estate in Bordeaux than a Burgundy domaine.

I expect these wines to give enjoyment relatively early, and not to show outstanding depth of flavour, nor structures appropriate for the long haul. However, a generation change is subtly taking place, so matters may evolve.

Bernard Drouhin, 20 rue du Gaizot, 21220 Gevrey-Chambertin

DOMAINE BERNARD DUGAT-PY   4 ha. (40 per cent)

Charmes-Chambertin 0.24 ha., Gevrey-Chambertin Petite Chapelle 0.05 ha., Lavaut Saint-Jacques 0.17 ha., Gevrey-Chambertin 2.9 ha., Bourgogne (*rouge*) 0.6 ha.

These wines are cellared in Gevrey's old leper-house, construction of which started uphill, away from the village, in AD 1075. It is a high, cool, airy, early Gothic vault.

Dugat bought his first vineyard when fifteen years old, and although still in his thirties has made nineteen harvests. He stopped putting potassium on his vineyards in the 1970s. Before that, fertilizer had been spread by hand, but with the arrival of machines it became easy to increase the doses, leading to masses of green leaves and over-vigorous vines. He has only been bottling since 1989, and the availabilities are tiny, as may be seen. The family used to be vine nurserymen, and I suspect may have been able to choose their own small grape Pinots, which might partly account for the succulent, mouth-filling flavours in these wines, the absence of excess fertilizer in the soil perhaps contributing to their welcome freshness of fruit. Bernard Dugat-Py, rue de Planteligone, cour de l'Aumônerie, 21220 Gevrey-Chambertin

DOMAINE CLAUDE DUGAT   3 ha. (90 per cent)

Charmes-Chambertin 0.31 ha., Griotte-Chambertin 0.15 ha., Gevrey-Chambertin Lavaut Saint-Jacques 0.3 ha., *Premier Cru* 0.29 ha., Gevrey-Chambertin 1.65 ha., Bourgogne (*rouge*) 0.3 ha.

The Dugats were stonemasons from the Creuse, who came to Burgundy to build the locks of the Canal de Bourgogne in the early nineteenth century. Settled in Gevrey, they first built a house and dug a well. Their descendants have rebuilt and restored the thirteenth-century Gevrey tithe-barn beside the church at the top of the village, themselves carving the great oak beams needed to recreate the ceilings. Here used to be stored one sheaf of corn for every twelve, and one pint of wine for every twenty-six, to which the canons of Langres Cathedral had rights. Once the *Grange*, now the *Cellier des Dîmes*, this beautiful building can accommodate 96 people to sit at tables and taste (two hours cost 1,400 fr. in 1993).

Claude Dugat and his father Maurice (now retired – his last wine being Lavaut Saint-Jacques 1991) also dug a deep, damp cellar where their wines age (in François Frères barrels). They do not hurry the start of their fermentations, nor do they vat for extra tannins at the end. These are wines which age well, but are rich and harmonious when young.
Claude Dugat, Cellier des Dîmes, 1 place de l'Eglise, 21220 Gevrey-Chambertin

DOMAINE DUROCHÉ   8.24 ha. (80 per cent)

Chambertin Clos de Bèze 0.25 ha., Charmes-Chambertin 0.41 ha., Gevrey-Chambertin Lavaut Saint-Jacques 1.2 ha., *Premier Cru* 0.4 ha., Gevrey-Chambertin 4.2 ha.

One may have an opportunity to check the efficacy of machine harvesting here. Trials began in 1981, and a machine was bought in

1991. It is not used in the *Grands Crus*, where the vines are old, but picks the Lavaut Saint-Jacques, as well as the basic *appellation*. I have never seen these wines alongside their peers; given that machine-picked Pinots tend to receive a poor press, a blind comparison would be revealing.

Gilles Duroché, 48 rue de l'Eglise, 21220 Gevrey-Chambertin

FRÉDÉRIC ESMONIN   7 ha. (100 per cent)

Ruchottes-Chambertin 0.5 ha., Griotte-Chambertin 0.5 ha., Mazis-Chambertin 0.3 ha., Gevrey-Chambertin Estournelles Saint-Jacques 1 ha., Lavaut Saint-Jacques 0.25 ha., Corbeaux 1.5 ha., Gevrey-Chambertin 2.5 ha.

A domaine which has been bottling only since 1987. Frédéric's father André Esmonin is a respected Gevrey grower who cultivates Mazis-Chambertin for the Hospices de Beaune. His wines traditionally went for tending and bottling to top stock-holders like Jadot or Leroy; however from the 1991 vintage all has been bottled here. Frédéric formed a company, Société Les Etournelles, enabling him to buy additional wine (mainly from Gevrey-Chambertin). However this remains a small-sized affair. The wines can be irregular, but I have had excellent examples from both barrel and bottle.

Frédéric Esmonin, 1 rue de Curley, 21220 Gevrey-Chambertin

DOMAINE MICHAEL ESMONIN ET FILLE   6 ha. (80 per cent)

Gevrey-Chambertin Clos Saint-Jacques 1.6 ha., Gevrey-Chambertin 3.9 ha., Côte de Nuits-Villages 0.29 ha., Bourgogne (*rouge*) 0.42 ha.

Sylvie Esmonin is an Ingénieur-Agronome who qualified from ENSA Montpellier specializing in viticulture and oenology. She works with her father (who took over from *his* father) who says of himself, 'I am a vigneron, from the head to the feet, and the feet to the head.' Their wines used to go mainly to the best *négociants-éleveurs* of both Côtes. Only from the 1987 vintage did the domaine start bottling in significant quantity. Mlle Esmonin takes up the story: 'Ninety per cent of the 1987 and 1988 vintages were sold abroad, thanks to the comments of Mr Parker in *The Wine Advocate*. With the 1989 vintage the domaine opened itself to France . . .'

It may be significant that many of this domaine's Pinots are planted on root-stock 161–49, which used to be disease-prone, and was consequently unpopular with growers, but is now recognized as one of the best available. But of course an immense number of tiny attentions to detail throughout the year in vine and cellar combine to account for the complexity and balance of these wines. There is 100 per cent de-stemming, but that alone would not account for their silky elegance. As significant is perhaps the leaving of the wines on their original lees, without racking, longer than is common. Many red-wine-makers rack immediately the malolactic fermentations are finished, but not here, so the healthy lees presumably 'nourish' the wines, just as happens in Meursault, Puligny and Chassagne.

Michel et Sylvie Esmonin, 1 rue Neuve, Clos Saint-Jacques, 21220 Gevrey-Chambertin

JEAN-CLAUDE FOURRIER   8.5 ha. (80 per cent)

Griotte-Chambertin 0.26 ha., Gevrey-Chambertin Clos Saint-Jacques 0.89 ha., Gevrey-Chambertin Combes aux Moines 0.35 ha., Gevrey-Chambertin *Premier Cru* 1.22 ha., Vougeot *Premier Cru* 0.34 ha., Gevrey-Chambertin 2.7 ha., Chambolle-Musigny 0.68 ha., Morey-Saint-Denis 0.64 ha.

Jean Claude et Anne-Marie Fourrier, 7 route de Dijon, 21220 Gevrey-Chambertin

GEANTET-PANSIOT   12 ha. (100 per cent)

Charmes-Chambertin 0.5 ha., Gevrey-Chambertin Poissenot 0.6 ha., Gevrey-Chambertin Vieilles Vignes 4 ha., Gevrey-Chambertin 4 ha., Marsannay Champs Perdrix 0.5 ha., Bourgogne (*rouge*)

This little-known estate has been bottling since the late 1950s, and has tripled in size since I first visited. Very stylish wines which can mature relatively early for Gevreys, but will surely also age magnificently.

Vincent Geantet, 3 & 5 route de Beaune, 21220 Gevrey-Chambertin

GOILLOT-BERNOLLIN 5.5 ha. (40 per cent)

Gevrey-Chambertin 3.9 ha., Bourgogne (*rouge*) 0.4 ha., Aligoté 0.37 ha.

On brief acquaintance these wines seem fine, harmonious and characterful. The estate has only recently begun to bottle.

Laurent Goillot-Bernollin, 29 route de Dijon, 21220 Gevrey-Chambertin

DOMAINE HARMAND-GEOFFROY 6 ha. (100 per cent)

Mazis-Chambertin 0.17 ha., Gevrey-Chambertin Clos Prieur 0.42 ha., *Premier Cru* La Bossière (Monopole) 0.45 ha., Gevrey-Chambertin *Premier Cru* 0.42 ha., Gevrey-Chambertin 4.22 ha., Bourgogne (*rouge*) 0.25 ha.

This estate owns the Monopoly of the First Growth part of the La Bossière vineyard, which lies uphill and west of Clos des Varoilles, in the combe above Gevrey. It was planted up in 1987–8. Grape bunches are de-stalked, and the vattings shortish. These wines can be charming, and come round quite rapidly for Gevrey.

Gérard Harmand, 1 place des Lois, 21220 Gevrey-Chambertin

DOMAINE HERESZTYN 10.3 ha. (60 per cent)

Clos Saint-Denis 0.33 ha., Morey-Saint-Denis Les Millandes 0.43 ha., Gevrey-Chambertin Les Goulots 0.6 ha., La Perrière 0.45 ha., Les Champonnets 0.4 ha., Les Corbeaux 0.3 ha., Gevrey-Chambertin 4 ha., Bourgogne

Chantal Heresztyn, 27 rue Richebourg, 21220 Gevrey-Chambertin

PHILIPPE LECLERC 8 ha. (100 per cent)

Gevrey-Chambertin Les Cazetiers 0.65 ha., Les Champeaux 0.65 ha., La Combe aux Moines 0.65 ha., Gevrey-Chambertin Les Platières 2 ha., Bourgogne (*rouge*) 3.5 ha.

And now for something completely different, a simple, rigid, established wine-making formula (very successful too) from a grower who disguises himself around Gevrey as a latter-day, sword-flashing musketeer. These wines are often aged two and a half years in oak, entirely new ('total burn, including the ends', says Monsieur

Leclerc) for the First Growths, after long, extractive vattings. 'I have never filtered a wine in my life', says Leclerc, which must endear him to someone we know, and sure enough, this is one of only eleven producers in Burgundy to merit a top rating of five stars in Robert Parker's book. 'Wine remains unfathomable', Leclerc *père* used to tell his son; 'just as one might have known a thousand women in one's life, but on dying still not understand them.' Leclerc gets a kick from exporting small quantities in all global directions – where I am sure their hedonistic gobs of fruit make them flashy ambassadors for Gevrey, and sure-fire winners in some tasting competitions.

In musical terms, these wines are the lower side of grunge. The man is achieving volume and distortion (but that, of course, is not difficult). Where is the melody?

To be a little fairer, the full rich fruit of his Combe aux Moines 1991 was marrying superbly with the oakiness when I tried it. It should make a spectacular bottle.

Philippe Leclerc, 9 rue des Halles, 21220 Gevrey-Chambertin

RENÉ LECLERC   10 ha. (80 per cent)

Gevrey-Chambertin Combe aux Moines 0.82 ha., Lavaut Saint-Jacques 0.52 ha., Clos Prieur 0.36 ha., *Premier Cru* 1 ha., Gevrey-Chambertin 5 ha., Bourgogne (*rouge*) 1.5 ha.

René Leclerc is Philippe's brother, but the approach is more pragmatic and flexible here. I much prefer these wines.

From this estate may also be bought wines from the Domaine des Chézeaux, which owns over half of Griotte-Chambertin, with some Chambertin, Clos Saint-Denis and Chambolle-Musigny Charmes. The vines are tended, and the wines made and sometimes bottled by Ponsot of Morey, who keeps two-thirds of the production for his pains and costs.

René et François Leclerc, 28 route de Dijon, 21220 Gevrey-Chambertin

HENRI MAGNIEN ET FILS   3 ha. (100 per cent)

Ruchottes-Chambertin 0.16 ha., Gevrey-Chambertin Les Cazetiers 0.6 ha., Gevrey-Chambertin *Premier Cru* (Estournelles Saint-

Jacques, Lavaut Saint-Jacques and Champeaux) 0.86 ha., Gevrey-Chambertin 0.6 ha.
Henri et François Magnien, 17 rue Haute, 21220 Gevrey-Chambertin

JEAN-PHILIPPE MARCHAND (1984)

This company, and its associate Alfred Salbreux, distributes the wines of the domaine of the same name, and the Domaine Claude Marchand (based in Morey-Saint-Denis), consisting of 8 ha. in total:
Clos de la Roche 0.15 ha., Griottes-Chambertin 0.2 ha., Charmes-Chambertin 0.45 ha., Chambolle-Musigny Les Sentiers 0.25 ha., Morey-Saint-Denis Les Millandes 0.8 ha., Gevrey-Chambertin Les Combottes 0.3 ha., Cherbaudes 0.25 ha., Gevrey-Chambertin 3 ha., Morey-Saint-Denis 0.8 ha., Chambolle-Musigny 0.5 ha., Bourgogne (*rouge*) 0.4 ha., Aligoté 0.4 ha.

Clive Coates has sniffed out that father and son (Claude and Jean-Philippe) make their wines diametrically differently:[1] the father de-stemming, then macerating ten to twelve days, the son cold-soaking whole bunches, then vatting for fourteen. Both could do better, says Coates, so perhaps we should watch this space for developments.
Claude et Jean-Philippe Marchand, 1 place du Monument, 21220 Gevrey-Chambertin

DOMAINE MARCHAND-GRILLOT ET FILS   8 ha. (50 per cent)

Ruchottes-Chambertin 0.07 ha., Gevrey-Chambertin Petite Chapelle 1 ha., Perrières 0.3 ha., Gevrey-Chambertin 5 ha., Morey-Saint-Denis 0.4 ha., Chambolle-Musigny 0.3 ha.

Most of these bottles – of good, steady quality – go to passing European consumers, who are warmly welcomed, I am sure, by Michel Marchand (who started bottling in 1973) or his son Jacques.
Jacques Marchand-Grillot, 13 rue de Gaizot, 21220 Gevrey-Chambertin

---

1 *The Vine*, no. 97, February 1993.

DOMAINE MAUME   3.76 ha. (90 per cent)

Mazis-Chambertin 0.67 ha., Charmes-Chambertin 0.17 ha., Gevrey-Chambertin Lavaut Saint-Jacques 0.28 ha., Champeaux 0.27 ha., Gevrey-Chambertin 2 ha.

A tiny estate whose wines are worth seeking out.

Bernard F. Maume, 56 route de Beaune, 21220 Gevrey-Chambertin

DENIS MORTET   12.7 ha. (100 per cent)

Clos de Vougeot 0.31 ha., Chambertin 0.14 ha., Gevrey-Chambertin Lavaut Saint-Jacques 1.17 ha., Champeaux 0.28 ha., Gevrey-Chambertin Vieilles Vignes 0.86 ha., Gevrey-Chambertin En Motrot (Monopole) 0.5 ha., Gevrey-Chambertin 5.78 ha., Chambolle-Musigny Beaux-Bruns 0.22 ha., Bourgogne (*rouge*) 0.94 ha., (*blanc*) 0.6 ha., Marsannay Les Longeroies 0.48 ha., Passe-Tout-Grains 0.21 ha., Aligoté 0.3 ha.

The first vintage that the Mortet brothers vinified separately was 1992 (previously, prior to their father's retirement, their wines had appeared as Charles Mortet et Fils). This is the new-oak brother, it seems, on the first year's showing, but the estate looks set to produce fine and balanced wines.

Denis Mortet, 22 rue de l'Eglise, 21220 Gevrey-Chambertin

THIERRY MORTET   4 ha. (75 per cent)

Gevrey-Chambertin Clos Prieur 0.3 ha., Chambolle-Musigny Beaux Bruns 0.25 ha., Gevrey-Chambertin 3 ha., Bourgogne (*rouge*) 0.5 ha., (*blanc*) 0.3 ha., Aligoté

Thierry Mortet, 21220 Gevrey-Chambertin

NAIGEON-CHAUVEAU ET FILS   (1890)

This firm distributes the wines of Domaine des Varoilles (12.75 ha.), Domaine Pierre Naigeon, and Domaine Paul Misset as well as owning vines in its own right – in total, no less than five Gevrey-Chambertin Monopoles and three *Grands Crus*:

Clos de Vougeot 2 ha., Charmes-Chambertin 0.75 ha., Bonnes Mares 0.5 ha., Gevrey-Chambertin Clos des Varoilles (Monopole) 5.97 ha., La Romanée (Monopole) 1.06 ha., Champonnets 0.66

ha., Clos du Meix des Ouches (Monopole) 1.05 ha., Clos du Couvent (Monopole) 0.5 ha., Clos Saint-Pierre (Monopole) 0.4 ha., Clos Prieur 0.33 ha.

There has been an admirable, and exceptionally rare, policy, here, for light vintages: 'If for climatic or other reasons quality does not live up to expectations the Domaine des Varoilles will . . . *draw back from using its grand* appellations, *and use simple village names* [my italics]. This occurred in 1981 and 1984, and – for vines less than 20 years old – in 1982 and 1985.'

This 'draw-back' policy is the Burgundian equivalent of the *bordelais* practice of offering the wine from younger vines under a second label. If it were to become more widespread on the Côte d'Or (relating to *Grands Crus*, where it is most needed) it would result in an enormous improvement to Burgundy's reputation.

In 1989, the Rolaz family bought Naigeon-Chauveau, and half the Domaine des Varoilles. There is a high proportion of old vines in these estates, and the wines require bottle age to show their best; they can appear to lack life when young. I gather that Jean-Pierre Naigeon continues as the wine-maker, helped by Roger Guillemaud, who has assisted here for thirty years. Jean-Pierre Naigeon makes four-square wines for the long haul, but I wonder if they ever really supple up. (Serena Sutcliffe has written of a special punching down technique, involving cables, but I have never been shown that.)

Jean-Pierre Naigeon, BP 7, 21220 Gevrey-Chambertin

DOMAINE LES PERRIÈRES   12.5 ha. (75 per cent)
DOMAINE DE LA TASSÉE

Gevrey-Chambertin Petite Chapelle 1 ha., Champerrier 1 ha., Chambolle-Musigny Les Charmes 0.75 ha., Les Baudes 0.5 ha., Gevrey-Chambertin 3.5 ha., Chambolle-Musigny 2.5 ha., Savigny-lès-Beaune, 1.5 ha., Marsannay (*rouge*) 0.33 ha., Bourgogne (*rouge*) 0.5 ha.

François et Christine Perrot, 3 av. de la Gare, 21220 Gevrey-Chambertin

DOMAINE HENRI REBOURSEAU   13.69 ha. (50 per cent)

Clos de Vougeot 2.21 ha., Chambertin Clos de Bèze 0.33 ha., Chambertin 0.46 ha., Mazy-Chambertin 0.96 ha., Charmes-Chambertin 1.31 ha., Gevrey-Chambertin Fonteny 0.88 ha., Perrière 0.13 ha., Gevrey-Chambertin 7.13 ha.

Pierre Rebourseau chose one of his grandsons, Jean de Surrel de Saint-Julien, to take over management of the family property, established by General Henri Rebourseau in Gevrey-Chambertin in 1915. His first solo harvest was 1981, when he was aged twenty-three and without formal wine-making training. This is not necessarily a problem; many excellent growers pick up wine-making from a father, relation or friend.

This is a spacious, walled property in a park with lawns and cedar trees, overlooking a six-hectare block of Gevrey vines, extending to the main road. The cellars are equipped with stainless steel vats, heat and humidity control. He handles grapes from wonderful origins, though during the 1980s with uneven success. The light-styled wines appeared to suit the French and Swiss markets, but was the vineyard potential being fully realized? 'After ten years, one vinifies better', says de Surrel, and I think these wines will be worth following closely in the 1990s.

Jean de Surrel, 10 place du Monument, 21220 Gevrey-Chambertin

PHILIPPE ROSSIGNOL   3.13 ha. (100 per cent)

Gevrey-Chambertin 1.38 ha., Côte de Nuits-Villages 0.96 ha., Bourgogne *rouge* 0.78 ha.

Rossignol is an adviser to eastern France's largest mutual bank, the Crédit Mutuel, which gives him an interesting overview of the great domaines of the Côte de Nuits, brimful, some of them, with *Grands Crus*, but also lines of credit, and heavy stocks.

His wines, when young, are often charmless, oak-marked and tannic, but this worries him not a jot. 'I think this has a future', he may say, and like as not it does. I wonder if he nevertheless does not sometimes misjudge his yields a bit. He refuses to envisage green-harvesting, preferring to be in the vines with his pickers at vintage-time, selecting best bunches. Here is yet another Burgundian individualist's approach.

Philippe Rossignol, 61 av. de la Gare, 21220 Gevrey-Chambertin

DOMAINE ROSSIGNOL-TRAPET   13.2 ha. (100 per cent)

Chambertin 1.6 ha., Latricières-Chambertin 0.74 ha., Chapelle-Chambertin 0.54 ha., Gevrey-Chambertin Petite Chapelle 0.52 ha., Clos Prieur 0.28 ha., *Premier Cru* 0.4 ha., Gevrey-Chambertin 5.5 ha., Morey-Saint-Denis Rue de Vergy 0.3 ha., Beaune Teurons 1.43 ha., Les Mariages 0.32 ha., Savigny-lès-Beaune Bas-Liards 0.26 ha., Bourgogne (*rouge*) 0.2 ha., (*blanc*) 0.68 ha.

This estate came into being on the splitting up of the old Domaine Louis Trapet between Jean Trapet and his sister, who married Jacques Rossigol of Volnay. It is a family affair, with broad smiles in view, whichever son, or sister Sophie, is wielding the *pipette*, mother and father being rarely far away.

When the domaine was setting itself up independently in the early 1990s I remember wondering how four or five equally involved family members could end up agreeing on who made the wine, or how – but the results seem to get better each year (I declare a trading interest, however). Is Nicolas Rossignol (the helmsman), inspired by such brilliantly intense wines as Louis Trapet's 1969 Chambertin, reducing imperceptibly the alcoholic strengths while increasing the fruit intensity, and concentration? I hope so, but note that R. Parker has thrown a ton of bricks 'at the 1991 Chambertin. The two Rossignol sons were tasting wines in Yarra Valley, and other fine Pinot places, in early 1994, so will be lobbing the bricks back soon, I suspect.

Jacques, Nicolas et David Rossignol-Trapet, rue de la Petite Issue, 21220 Gevrey-Chambertin

DOMAINE JOSEPH ROTY   8.5 ha. (100 per cent)

Charmes-Chambertin 1 ha., Mazis-Chambertin 0.25 ha., Griotte-Chambertin 0.2 ha., Gevrey-Chambertin Clos Prieur 0.34 ha., Les Fontenys 1 ha., Clos de la Brunelle (Monopole) 0.26 ha., Champs Chenys 1.15 ha., Marsannay (*rouge, rosé* and *blanc*) 2.5 ha., Gevrey-Chambertin, Bourgogne (*rouge*), Bourgogne Grand Ordinaire

The Roty family has been making wine here since Louis XIV, we may be told – eleven generations since 1710. No clones here, no cultured yeasts, and no more than a third new oak barrels for ageing. The wines have long, cool macerations: perhaps a pre-fermentation week at 15°, then two weeks when the temperature will be systematically lowered, when they reach 25°, back down to 22°. He draws the vat off when the floating hat of grapeskins sinks, the whole process often lasting a month. In the vat-house Joseph Roty is now interchangeable with his son, he says.

I once made the mistake of writing that this estate was the new star in the Gevrey firmament. Monsieur Roty thanked me for bringing him new customers from abroad, then proceeded to make a 1982 vintage which left one or two people quite seriously alarmed. I think his yields got out of control, so he stirred and stewed, no doubt wishing to extract what good he could.

The quality see-sawed during the 1980s, though I gather recent vintages have been less irregular, and very successful. If Al Hotchkin (Burgundy Wine Company, New York, 1993) can ask $225 per bottle for Roty's Mazis-Chambertin 1985 (the most expensive Gevrey *Grand Cru* from a total listing of 57) Monsieur Roty seems to be doing fine. But I often wonder about the people who bought the 1982, and some of the other vintages since.

Joseph et Philippe Roty, 21220 Gevrey-Chambertin

DOMAINE ARMAND ROUSSEAU 14 ha. (100 per cent)

Chambertin Clos de Bèze 1.41 ha., Chambertin 2.15 ha., Clos des Ruchottes-Chambertin (Monopole) 1.06 ha., Gevrey-Chambertin Clos Saint-Jacques 2.21 ha., Clos de la Roche 1.48 ha., Charmes-Chambertin and Mazoyères 1.36 ha., Mazy-Chambertin 0.53 ha., Gevrey-Chambertin Cazetiers 0.75 ha., Lavaut Saint-Jacques 0.50 ha., Gevrey-Chambertin 2.26 ha.

This is one of Burgundy's great, traditional domaines, of course, and Charles Rousseau one of the Côte's best-loved, most courteous growers (now ably seconded by his son Eric, though the latter sometimes has difficulty getting a word in edgeways). The estate recently bought additional rows in both Clos de Bèze and Chambertin.

Whatever country it may be, I expect to be in the hands of a knowledgeable, conscientious Burgundy-lover if I track down Armand Rousseau's importer or distributor. Of course, not all his bottles will be great (no one's are) but they will normally be harmonious, elegant, rich and individual. There are no pumps in this cellar; bottling takes place by gravity, after a light filtration to ensure the wine is clean, and contains no solid impurities.

At times the wines evolve more quickly into spiciness than I expect from *Grands Crus* in this village (which of course has a reputation for longevity), but that can be the delicious, Rousseau way. At other times they look decidedly below their peers, but it can be a mistake to judge them harshly when young.

Charles et Eric Rousseau, Domaine Armand Rousseau, 21220 Gevrey-Chambertin

SÉRAFIN PÈRE ET FILS   4.35 ha. (100 per cent)

Charmes-Chambertin 0.12 ha., Gevrey-Chambertin Les Cazetiers 0.23 ha., Le Fonteny 0.23 ha., Gevrey-Chambertin Vieilles Vignes 1.67 ha., Gevrey-Chambertin 1.39 ha.

These are fresh rich wines, though sometimes rather strongly new-wooded.

Christian Sérafin, 7 place du Château, 21220 Gevrey-Chambertin

DOMAINE TORTOCHOT   9.40 ha. (50 per cent)

Chambertin 0.39 ha., Charmes-Chambertin 0.57 ha., Mazis-Chambertin 0.41 ha., Clos de Vougeot 0.21 ha., Gevrey-Chambertin Lavaut Saint-Jacques 0.62 ha., Les Champeaux 0.4 ha., Gevrey-Chambertin, Morey-Saint-Denis

Monsieur Tortochot must be past his seventieth birthday, but the quality seems to get better by the year. I do not think there is great regularity here, but have tasted some exceptionally rich and balanced wines.

Gabriel Tortochot, 12 rue de l'Eglise, 21220 Gevrey-Chambertin

DOMAINE LOUIS TRAPET   11.50 ha. (75 per cent)

Chambertin 1.9 ha., Latricières-Chambertin 0.75 ha., Chapelle-Chambertin 0.6 ha., Gevrey-Chambertin Petite Chapelle 0.7 ha., Clos Prieur 0.5 ha., Gevrey-Chambertin 5 ha., Marsannay 0.85 ha., Bourgogne (*blanc*) 0.4 ha., Passe-Tout-Grains

Domaine Louis Trapet has had the reputation of a great domaine (bend the knees on entering) but routine and ruts also became established, with not enough questioning, not enough comparing.

The domaine is on the main road, and I imagine there are always passers-by dropping in to say the wines are rare and wonderful. But it seems only reasonable that, if it stays aware of the prices charged by other domaines (which it quite understandably does) it should also keep track of the alternative quality levels.

In the late 1980s, the *Grands Crus*, when I tasted them carefully, sometimes seemed no better than decent village, or *Premier Cru*, wines. Jean Trapet (now aided by son Jean-Louis) *père* is a charmingly tolerant, respected Gevrey figure, and a generous host. His wines have generally been better than Camus or Damoy, but is that enough?

The late Louis Trapet's 1969 Chambertin is one of the best Chambertins I ever met.

Jean et Jean-Louis Trapet, 53 route de Beaune, 21220 Gevrey-Chambertin

G. VACHET-ROUSSEAU PÈRE ET FILS   7 ha. (100 per cent)

Mazis-Chambertin 0.53 ha., Gevrey-Chambertin Lavaut Saint-Jacques 0.68 ha., Gevrey-Chambertin 5.58 ha.

Ploughing and organic fertilizers are in use here, I gather.

Gérard Vachet, 15 rue de Paris, 21220 Gevrey-Chambertin.

13

Morey-Saint-Denis

The first mention of Morey is in 1120, when the place was known as Mirriacum Villa. The Abbey of Cîteaux was given a part of the village by Savaric de Vergy that year, and in 1171 another religious foundation, the Abbey of Bussières, received a donation of Morey land from the High Constable of Burgundy, Guillaume de Marigny. There have been many proprietors, including the Abbey of Saint-Germain-des-Prés in Paris.

The name never used to be well known. To some extent this was because the wines were sold as Gevrey-Chambertin or Chambolle-Musigny until the AC laws were introduced; also the village is a small one, with less than a quarter as much land under vineyard as at Gevrey, and there is no single outstanding vineyard like Chambertin or Corton to make its reputation. But a generation of wine merchants and writers saying that this was the best-value village of the Côte de Nuits has had its effect, and by the 1976 vintage, Morey-Saint-Denis was fetching the same price as Vosne-Romanée. Saint-Denis was tacked on to Morey as recently as 1927, but it is by no means agreed that this is the finest vineyard of the commune. Of the wines in general, Pierre Bréjoux said that they have 'a more tender firmness than those of Gevrey'.[1]

There are five *Grands Crus* on the commune:

1. Bonnes Mares (1.51 ha.; for production, please see Chambolle-Musigny) The majority of this vineyard is in Chambolle-Musigny, indeed the Morey section is entirely in the hands of Fougeray de Beauclair.

2. Clos Saint-Denis (5.89 ha. The five-year average production

1 *Les Vins de Bourgogne*, Société Française d'Editions Vinicoles, Paris, 1967.

(1988–92) for Clos Saint-Denis was 2,530 cases.) These vines originally belonged to the Collégiale of Saint-Denis de Vergy, founded in 1203.

3. Clos de Tart (7.53 ha. The five-year average production (1988–92) for Clos de Tart was 2,510 cases.) A parcel of land known as 'Climat de la Forge' was sold to the nuns of Notre Dame de Tart near Genlis in 1141. The vendor was the Maison-Dieu in Brochon, the acquisition being confirmed by Pope Lucius III in a bull of 1184. The property was sold at the time of the Revolution to a M. Charles Dumagner of Nuits for 68,200 *livres* (charges in addition). Today, it is under the sole ownership of Mommessin.

4. Clos de la Roche (14.5 ha. The five-year average production (1988–92) for Clos de la Roche was 6,220 cases.) This vineyard has expanded over the years, for in Dr Lavalle's time (1855) it was less than a third its present size.

5. Clos des Lambrays (7.71 ha. The five-year average production (1988–92) for Clos des Lambrays was 3,245 cases.) This vineyard was upgraded from First to Great Growth status in 1981.

The following are currently classified *Premiers Crus*:

Blanchards, Les	Côte Rotie
Chaffots, Les	Faconnières, Les
Charmes, Aux	Genavrières, Les
Charrières, Les	Gruenchers, Les
Chenevery, Les	Millandes, Les
Chéseaux, Aux	Monts Luisants
Clos Baulet	Riotte, La
Clos de la Bussière	Ruchots, Les
Clos des Ormes	Sorbès, Les
Clos Sorbè	Village, Le

First Growth 36.45 ha. (red) and 1.51 ha. (white), plus 50.6 ha. (red) and 1.28 ha. (white) commune Morey-Saint-Denis cover a total of 89.84 ha. The five-year average productions (1988–92) for Morey-Saint-Denis for reds and whites were respectively 39,600 and 1,240 cases.

Main Morey-Saint-Denis growers

PIERRE AMIOT ET FILS   10 ha. (100 per cent)

Clos Saint-Denis 0.25 ha., Clos de la Roche 1.5 ha., Charmes-Chambertin 0.3 ha., Morey-Saint-Denis Les Millandes 0.42 ha., Les Ruchots 0.6 ha., Aux Charmes 0.46 ha., Les Chenevery 1 ha., Gevrey-Chambertin Combottes 0.7 ha., Chambolle-Musigny Les Baudes 0.35 ha., Morey-Saint-Denis 2.5 ha., Gevrey-Chambertin 0.5 ha.

Wonderful vineyard sites, but I think the yields have been too high for a solid reputation to be built.

Pierre, Jean-Louis et Didier Amiot, 27 Grande Rue, 21220 Morey-Saint-Denis

GUY CASTAGNIER   4 ha. (50 per cent)
CASTAGNIER-VADEY

Clos de Vougeot 0.5 ha., Clos de la Roche 0.53 ha., Charmes-Chambertin 0.39 ha., Clos Saint-Denis 0.35 ha., Chambolle-Musigny 0.33 ha., Gevrey-Chambertin 0.25 ha., Morey-Saint-Denis 0.19 ha.

Castagnier tends the wines of Domaine Christopher Newman (q.v.)

CHRISTOPHER NEWMAN   1.25 ha. (100 per cent)

Latricières-Chambertin 0.53 ha., Bonnes Mares 0.33 ha., Mazis-Chambertin 0.19 ha.

No *Premiers Crus* here, but well-made, supple village wines, and some intense, ripe *Grands Crus* for mid-term ageing. Newman who is the only American owner of *Grands Crus* on the Côte de Nuits, so far as I know (Matt Kramer's book has the story).[2]

Guy et Sylvie Castagnier-Vadey, 20 rue des Jardins, 21220 Morey-Saint-Denis

DOMAINE DUJAC   11.35 ha. (100 per cent)

Clos de la Roche 1.95 ha., Clos Saint-Denis 1.47 ha., Charmes-Chambertin 0.8 ha., Echézeaux 0.69 ha., Bonnes Mares 0.43 ha.,

2 *Making Sense of Burgundy*, William Morrow, New York, 1990.

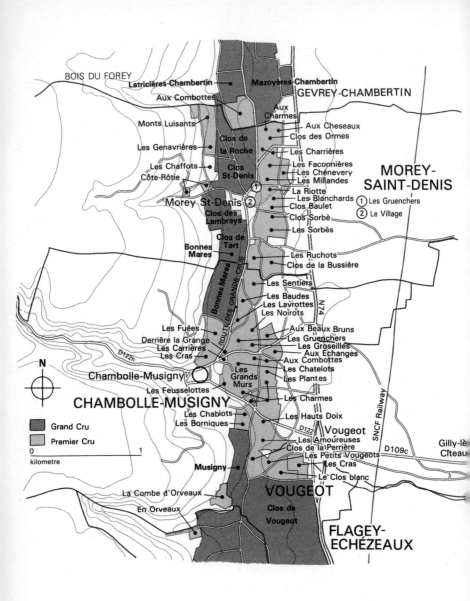

Morey-Saint-Denis and Chambolle-Musigny

Gevrey-Chambertin aux Combottes 1.15 ha., Chambolle-Musigny Les Gruenchers 0.33 ha., Morey-Saint-Denis *Premier Cru* 0.54 ha., Chambolle-Musigny 0.53 ha., Vosne-Romanée Les Beaumonts 0.25 ha., Morey-Saint-Denis (red) 2.63 ha., (white) 0.58 ha.

Jacques Seysses has been one of the main catalysts of information exchange on the subjects of red Burgundy and Pinot Noir. A regular supporter of Oregon's Pinot Noir Festival, he tastes and travels widely outside Burgundy and within it.

His wines are perfumed, silky, spicy, and elegant, the style consistent and recognizable. Lovers of four-square, deep-coloured, so called old-fashioned Burgundy should stay away. The prices have been known to rise and fall, which adds uncommon interest for traders. Ted Lemon made wine here before moving to Meursault, then California. Jean-Pierre de Smet, now at Domaine de l'Arlot, worked and trained with Dujac before going to Prémeaux.

There is no de-stemming, yet the wines never seem to have harsh tannins, perhaps thanks to gentle handling, and pneumatic pressing. His delicious Morey *blanc* might receive three or four hours of skin contact, which is rare in Burgundy. Indigenous yeasts are used. Enzymes may help clarification, for Seysses does not like to filter (and states 'unfiltered', when applicable, on his front labels).

He has been responsible for vinifying, on behalf of a Californian firm who rented a cellar in Morey and bought white grapes, a number of Meursaults in the name of Druid Wine. Some of Burgundy's best grower-vinifiers thus turn their hands to grapes from other estates.

It is beyond the scope of this book to attempt to go into the clonal and pruning research work done in Dujac fields by Christophe Morin, the vineyard manager, to whom Jacques Seysses pays high tribute. There are a dozen different clones in these vines: six alone in Clos de la Roche, on three different root-stocks. At least one, Clone 123, is virtually unique to Dujac, having been eliminated from the official recommendations since it tended to suffer from the virus disease *enroulement*. Seysses kept it, taking the risk, for he liked its small berries. Echézeaux and Bonnes Mares were entirely replanted to clones in the early 1980s, and as their yields settle down and pruning is adapted – a fan system, with two canes each bearing three buds being installed, in preference to Cordon de Royat – the qualities of both look set to rise.

If general conclusions can be drawn from these researches, and experiences shared, they could one day be of immense value to other Burgundians.

Jacques et Rosalind Seysses et Christophe Morin, 7 rue de la Bussière, Morey-Saint-Denis, 21220 Gevrey-Chambertin

ROBERT GROFFIER PÈRE ET FILS   7 ha. (65 per cent)

Chambertin Clos de Bèze 0.45 ha., Bonnes Mares 1.5 ha., Chambolle-Musigny Les Amoureuses 1.60 ha., Les Sentiers 1.07 ha., Hauts-Doix 1 ha., Gevrey-Chambertin 0.9 ha., Bourgogne (*rouge*)

This is the largest owner of Amoureuses, and a beautiful *cuvée* it often is. The wines are rich, but also charming and supple.

Robert Groffier, 35 route des Grands Crus, Morey-Saint-Denis, 21220 Gevrey-Chambertin

DOMAINE DES LAMBRAYS   13.2 ha. (100 per cent)

Clos des Lambrays 8.66 ha., Morey-Saint-Denis *Premier Cru* 0.35 ha., Morey-Saint-Denis 1 ha., Corton Clos des Maréchaudes 0.52 ha., Aloxe-Corton Les Maréchaudes 1.44 ha., Aloxe-Corton 0.5 ha., Puligny-Montrachet Cailleret 0.38 ha., Folatières 0.3 ha.

When top Burgundy is made by a manager – as is the case here – rather than an owner, the most exciting quality can elude their joint grasps. To pull it off, you *have* to take risks, it is no good playing for safety – which a conscientious, highly-qualified person (which Thierry Brouin certainly is) might find himself doing.

The Clos des Lambrays is often silky, perfumed, fine – and gives much pleasure. Surely, from this stony hillside, it should flash with brilliance and mystery. But standards are high; for instance, after August hail in 1991, the entire Lambrays crop was declared as Morey-Saint-Denis *Premier Cru*, and a beautiful, chewy wine it made, keenly priced too.

During the early 1990s it was widely believed that chunks of Saier Mercurey (for details of which, please see that village, where the wine is made) or other vineyards were for sale. But in 1993, on the contrary, they were buying, not selling: part of Chartron's precious Puligny-Montrachet Cailleret, for instance. The Saiers apparently often surprise us.

Fabien et Louis Saier (owners), Thierry Brouin (manager), 31 rue Basse, Morey-Saint-Denis, 21220 Gevrey-Chambertin

DOMAINE GEORGES LIGNIER ET FILS   14 ha. (50 per cent)

Clos Saint-Denis 1.6 ha., Clos de la Roche 1 ha., Bonnes Mares 0.3 ha., Charmes-Chambertin 0.1 ha., Gevrey-Chambertin Combottes 0.45 ha., Morey-Saint-Denis Clos des Ormes 1.8 ha., Gevrey-Chambertin 1.5 ha., Chambolle-Musigny 1 ha., Morey-Saint-Denis 2 ha., Bourgogne (*rouge*) 0.3 ha., Passe-Tout-Grains 1.5 ha., Aligoté 1.5 ha.

Little has changed in this courtyard in thirty years, and below ground, space being tight, every metre of passage is neatly put to good use. Lignier is a slim, reflective figure, his views carefully wrought. Traditional family, village and regional values are held in high regard, and this includes supplying top *négociants* of both Côtes with his wines in barrel. Generally these wines are very pleasing, and mature fairly early.

Georges Lignier, 41 Grande Rue, 21220 Morey-Saint-Denis

HUBERT LIGNIER   7.5 ha. (50 per cent)

Clos de la Roche 0.8 ha., Charmes-Chambertin 0.1 ha., Morey-Saint-Denis and *Premier Cru* 3 ha., Gevrey-Chambertin and *Premier Cru* 1.2 ha., Chambolle-Musigny and *Premier Cru* 0.7 ha., Bourgogne (*rouge*) 0.65 ha., Aligoté 0.65 ha.

Not so sure a touch here, I feel, as at Georges Lignier. There are good wines, but also those overly tannic, or lacking concentration. Other observers find them classic and beautiful, rating the estate very highly. Remington Norman records two individual First Growth plots: Gevrey Les Combottes 0.14 ha., and Chambolle Les Baudes 0.17 ha., (which must be fiendishly difficult to vinify individually) but Lignier combined them with his village holdings when he gave me his details.

Hubert et Romain Lignier, 45 Grande Rue, 21220 Morey-Saint-Denis

JEAN-PAUL MAGNIEN   4.5 ha. (80 per cent)

Charmes-Chambertin 0.2 ha., Clos Saint-Denis 0.32 ha., Morey-Saint-Denis Faconnières 0.57 ha., Gruenchers 0.25 ha., Clos Baulet 0.12 ha., Monts Luisants 0.14 ha., Morey-Saint-Denis 0.92 ha.,

Chambolle-Musigny Sentiers 0.41 ha., Chambolle-Musigny 0.26 ha.

Some of these may seem a little rustic, some a bit high in alcohol for my taste, but this is a source worth exploring.

Jean-Paul et Marie-Odile Magnien, 5 ruelle de l'Eglise, 21220 Morey-Saint-Denis

HENRI PERROT-MINOT 10 ha. (90 per cent)

Charmes-Chambertin 1.6 ha., Morey-Saint-Denis La Riotte 0.55 ha., Rue de Vergy 1.7 ha., Chambolle-Musigny Combe d'Orveau 0.5 ha., Gevrey-Chambertin 1.8 ha., Bourgogne (*rouge*), Passe-Tout-Grains, Aligoté

I have had varied experiences with these wines.

Henri Perrot-Minot, 54 route des Grands Crus, 21220 Morey-Saint-Denis

DOMAINE PONSOT 10 ha. (100 per cent)

Clos de la Roche 3 ha., Clos Saint-Denis 0.5 ha., Latricières-Chambertin 0.5 ha., Chambertin 0.15 ha., Griotte-Chambertin 1 ha., Chapelle-Chambertin 0.5 ha., Chambolle-Musigny Les Charmes 0.6 ha., Gevrey-Chambertin 0.5 ha., Morey-Saint-Denis *Premier Cru* Monts Luisants (*blanc*) 1.5 ha., Morey-Saint-Denis 1.5 ha.

One of the most distinguished domaines of the Côte de Nuits. Ponsot, like Gouges and Rousseau, was estate-bottling from the early 1930s. As Andrew Barr revealed in 1992,[3] from these vineyards have been selected five of the first Pinot Noir clones to be approved and distributed: 113, 114, 115, 667, 777. Others are following, for instance 778, which may prove just as fine as the rot-resistant, high-quality 777. The mother vines, selected by Jean-Marie Ponsot for planting in 1954, may still be seen in the Clos de la Roche.

Since 1990 only one *cuvée* of Clos de la Roche issues from here, labelled 'Vieilles Vignes', the wine from the younger vines in their Clos de la Roche plots going into Morey-Saint-Denis *Premier Cru* or village wines. Latricières-Chambertin is due to disappear from the estate's list of properties, but the area of Clos de la Roche to be

---

3 *Pinot Noir*, Viking Penguin, London, 1992.

increased by 0.5 ha. This wine has been increasingly dependable and wonderful, where in the early 1980s it could be patchy. Robert Parker is often a great enthusiast for Ponsot wines, and we may note how the prices uncannily track his tasting numbers.
Jean-Marie et Laurent Ponsot, Morey-Saint-Denis, 21220 Gevrey-Chambertin

JEAN RAPHET ET FILS   12 ha. (40 per cent)

Chambertin Clos de Bèze 0.21 ha., Clos de Vougeot 1.5 ha., Charmes- Chambertin 1.5 ha., Clos de la Roche 0.38 ha., Gevrey-Chambertin Lavaut Saint-Jacques 0.22 ha., Gevrey-Chambertin Les Combottes 0.17 ha., Morey-Saint-Denis Les Millandes 0.13 ha., Gevrey-Chambertin 3.9 ha., Chambolle-Musigny 0.86 ha., Morey-Saint-Denis 0.53 ha., Bourgogne (*rouge*) 1.3 ha.

Uneven results here, with bottles sometimes just rich and supple, sometimes really brilliant.
Jean Raphet, 45 route des Grands Crus, 21220 Morey-Saint-Denis

DOMAINE LOUIS REMY   2.65 ha. (100 per cent)

Chambertin 0.35 ha., Latricières-Chambertin 0.58 ha., Clos de la Roche 0.66 ha., Chambolle-Musigny *Premier Cru* 0.75 ha., Morey-Saint-Denis 0.24 ha.

A tiny estate with well-placed vines and an uneven track record, which under new owner-management may be firmly on the way up.
Mme Chantal (née Remy), place du Monument, 21220 Morey-Saint- Denis

DOMAINE BERNARD SERVEAU ET FILS   7 ha. (80 per cent)

Morey-Saint-Denis Les Sorbets 1.63 ha., Chambolle-Musigny Les Amoureuses 0.28 ha., *Premier Cru* 1.08 ha., Chambolle-Musigny 0.37 ha., Nuits-Saint-Georges 0.26 ha., Bourgogne (*rouge*) 2.2 ha.

Since the 1991 vintage I suspect an improvement in quality here, but am far from convinced by Matt Kramer that Serveau is Morey's 'supreme producer', his wines 'Cistercian austere', and Les Sorbets 'seemingly light, but as focused as a laser beam'.
Jean-Louis (fils) et Bernard Serveau, 37 Grande Rue, Morey-Saint-Denis, 21220 Gevrey-Chambertin

DOMAINE DU CLOS DE TART   7.5 ha. (100 per cent)
MOMMESSIN, SA

Clos de Tart (Monopole) 7.5 ha.

This is one of the rare places in Burgundy where press-house (with original press dating from 1570), *cuverie* and cellar are all to be found within the Clos.

My feeling is that the owners have recently used too much new oak on this wine, and that vanilla flavours may continue to dominate the fruit of many of their vintages of the 1980s.

If only a member of the Mâcon-based Mommessin family, or a senior person from the firm, lived in or really near Morey, tasting up and down the Côte, taking day and night responsibility for this great wine, Clos de Tart could surely become one of the most scintillating bottles of the Côte de Nuits. As it is, Accad was appointed to make the wines from the 1991 vintage onwards. Tasting the 1992 in March of the following spring, I found it bright red purple, briary, spicy, intensely fruity. The words sound good, but it seemed, at that stage anyway, outlandish.

An article in *Vinum* magazine sheds light on Accad's methods for this 1992.[4] The unwilling observer was Henri Perraut, manager of Clos de Tart for 25 years, soon due to retire. It appears that half the harvest was de-stemmed, which then macerated at around 8° for up to ten days, while sufficient tannins and colouring matter were extracted. Accad then stopped the refrigeration, allowed the must to warm up, and added cultured yeasts. For the next two to three weeks the temperature was regularly controlled, never allowed over 30°, but being brought down to 12° if things seemed to be going too fast.

Didier Mommessin, Morey-Saint-Denis, 21220 Gevrey-Chambertin

DOMAINE TAUPENOT-MERME   9 ha. (100 per cent)

Charmes-Chambertin 1.5 ha., Gevrey-Chambertin 2.5 ha., Chambolle-Musigny 1 ha., Morey-Saint-Denis 1 ha., Clos des Lambrays (a few rows)

To venture here is to risk being gently bullied by a vivacious Madame Taupenot. You ask for the Gevrey 1990, and she will give you the 1988; you ask for Morey and she replies, 'No, taste the

4 *Vinum*, no. IV, 1993.

Chambolle.' I find the wines can be agreeable, but lack concentration and potential.

Jean et Denise Taupenot, 33 route des Grands Crus, Morey-Saint-Denis, 21220 Gevrey-Chambertin.

J. TRUCHOT-MARTIN   7 ha. (50 to 75 per cent)

Charmes-Chambertin 0.66 ha., Clos de la Roche 0.43 ha., Gevrey-Chambertin Les Combottes 0.16 ha., Gevrey-Chambertin 0.6 ha., Morey-Saint-Denis Clos Sorbès 0.95 ha., Morey-Saint-Denis 1.43 ha., Chambolle-Musigny Les Sentiers 0.66 ha., Chambolle-Musigny 0.33 ha., Bourgogne 0.68 ha.

M. et Mme Jacky Truchot, 43 Grande Rue, Morey-Saint-Denis, 21220 Gevrey-Chambertin

14
Chambolle-Musigny

Known as Cambolla in 1110, also Campus Ebulliens (*Champ Bouillant* or boiling field), Chambolle seems to have taken its name from the turbulent flood-waters of the Grone stream which used to cause severe damage. Musigny was added in 1878.

'In the opinion of many persons,' writes Dr Lavalle, 'this commune produces the most delicate wines of the Côte de Nuits.' This is echoed by many writers. Chambolle wines also have a seductive vinosity and exceptionally elegant aromas.

Only 30 per cent of Chambolle's vineyards are owned by Chambolle residents, so Julie Morrison discovered, while working and living in the village,[1] which was one of the first in the Côte d'Or to protect its vineyards from encroaching development. She recorded how the roles of Chambolle vintners had changed dramatically since 1970, domaine bottlings having risen from a mere 8 per cent to around 50 per cent twenty-five years later.

There are two *Grands Crus* in the village:

1. Musigny (9.1 ha. (red), 0.55 ha. (white). The five-year average production (1988–92) for red Musigny was 3,670 cases, for white 150 cases.

The Musigny vineyard (without doubt one of Burgundy's greatest sites) is situated to the south of the village, near the Clos de Vougeot. The earliest record of it dates from 1110, when the Canon of Saint-Denis de Vergy, Pierre Cros, gave his field of Musigné to the monks of Cîteaux. Good Musigny is very finely balanced, with aromas of the sweetest complexity and a lingering, dreamy aftertaste.

---

1 'Chambolle: life in a small wine town', American Magazine, 1980s.

2. Bonnes Mares (13.65 ha.) The five-year average production (1988–92) for Bonnes Mares (including the wine produced in the commune of Morey-Saint-Denis) was 5,310 cases.

Bonnes Mares would seem to take its name from the verb *marer*, to work the vines, thus meaning well-tended vines. This is a four-square, densely textured wine, which is often richly spicy.

The following are classified *Premiers Crus*:

Amoureuses, Les	Doix, Les Hauts
Baudes, Les	Echanges, Aux
Beaux Bruns, Aux	Feusselottes, Les
Borniques, Les	Fuées, Les
Carrières, Les	Grands Murs, Les
Chabiots, Les	Grange, Derrière la
Charmes, Les	Groseilles, Les
Châtelots, Les	Gruenchers, Les
Combe d'Orveau, La	Lavrottes, Les
Combottes, Aux	Noirots, Les
Combottes, Les	Plantes, Les
Cras, Les	Sentiers, Les

First Growth (44.09 ha.) and commune Chambolle-Musigny (99.3 ha.) cover 143.4 hectares. Together, the five-year average production (1988–92) was 65,200 cases.

Main Chambolle-Musigny growers and merchants

DOMAINE BERNARD AMIOT   6 ha. (60 per cent)

Chambolle-Musigny Les Charmes 0.33 ha., Les Chatelots 0.33 ha., *Premier Cru* 0.66 ha., Chambolle-Musigny 3 ha.
Bernard Amiot, 21220 Chambolle-Musigny

DOMAINE AMIOT-SERVELLE   6.5 ha. (80 per cent)

Clos de Vougeot 0.4 ha., Chambolle-Musigny Charmes 1.44 ha., Amoureuses 0.44 ha., Derrière la Grange 0.36 ha., Chambolle-Musigny 2 ha., Bourgogne (*rouge*)

This domaine is the successor to Domaine Servelle-Tachot, which last bottled in 1989.

Christian et Elizabeth Amiot, rue des Tilleuls, 21220 Chambolle-Musigny

DOMAINE GHISLAINE BARTHOD   6.64 ha. (75 per cent)

Chambolle-Musigny Charmes 0.25 ha., Les Cras 0.87 ha., Beaux-Bruns 0.73 ha., Véroilles 0.37 ha., Châtelots 0.23 ha., Les Baudes 0.19 ha., Les Fuées 0.24 ha., Chambolle-Musigny 1.87 ha., Bourgogne (*rouge*) 1.38 ha., Passe-Tout-Grains and Aligoté
   Deep-coloured wines here, which, on brief acquaintance, I have found delicious. There must be some cold macerating pre-fermentation, I would imagine.
Ghislaine Barthod-Noellat, rue du Lavoir, 21220 Chambolle-Musigny

DOMAINE BERTHEAU ET FILS   7 ha. (60 per cent)

Bonnes Mares 0.34 ha., Chambolle-Musigny Amoureuses 0.32 ha., Charmes 0.66 ha., *Premier Cru* 0.88 ha., Chambolle-Musigny 3 ha., Bourgogne
   I have found these wines likeable but not irresistible. But they can be keenly priced, which is particularly welcome on the Côte de Nuits.
Pierre et François Bertheau, 21220 Chambolle-Musigny

DOMAINE MICHEL MODOT   7 ha. (50 per cent)

Chambolle-Musigny Charmes 0.5 ha., *Premier Cru* 0.5 ha., Chambolle-Musigny 4 ha., Hautes Côtes de Nuits 1.2 ha., Bourgogne and Aligoté
Michel Modot, rue Basse, 21220 Chambolle-Musigny

DOMAINE MOINE-HUDELOT   6.8 ha. (100 per cent)

Musigny 0.12 ha., Bonnes Mares 0.32 ha., Clos de Vougeot 0.15 ha., Chambolle-Musigny Amoureuses 0.19 ha., Charmes 0.19 ha., *Premier Cru* 2 ha., Chambolle-Musigny 3 ha., Bourgogne
Daniel Moine, Les Feusselottes, 21220 Chambolle-Musigny

JACQUES FRÉDÉRIC MUGNIER   4 ha. (80 per cent)
CHÂTEAU DE CHAMBOLLE-MUSIGNY

Musigny 1.13 ha., Bonnes Mares 0.35 ha., Chambolle-Musigny Les Amoureuses 0.52 ha., Chambolle-Musigny Les Fuées 0.71 ha., Chambolle-Musigny Les Plantes 0.47 ha., Chambolle-Musigny 0.8 ha.

Most Burgundy books cite Chambolle as the place to come for delicacy, and finesse, on the Côte de Nuits, but in the 1960s and 1970s it was hard to single out a domaine in Chambolle which was making wine to fit that particular expectation. But here, surely, is one, since Frédéric Mugnier's taking up the reins in the early 1980s. Frédéric Mugnier, Château de Chambolle-Musigny, 21220 Chambolle- Musigny

DOMAINE GEORGES ROUMIER ET FILS   14.5 ha. (100 per cent)
and DOMAINE CHRISTOPHE ROUMIER   0.8 ha. (100 per cent)

Bonnes Mares 1.8 ha., Musigny 0.1 ha., Clos de Vougeot 0.3 ha., Ruchottes-Chambertin 0.5 ha., Charmes-Chambertin 0.3 ha., Corton-Charlemagne 0.3 ha., Chambolle-Musigny Les Amoureuses 0.5 ha., Les Cras 1.6 ha., Chambolle-Musigny 5.4 ha., Morey-Saint-Denis Clos de la Bussière (Monopole) 2.5 ha., Bourgogne 2 ha.

Christophe Roumier is a marvellous ambassador for the Côte de Nuits. His English is excellent, and his technical mastery much admired. The domaine has sometimes sugared its wines a half degree, maybe a degree, beyond the ideal, for my taste. I do not notice it when tasting in the cellar, but at home, with a bottle of Bourgogne *rouge*, Chambolle or Charmes-Chambertin with friends, I find myself wishing the wines were more airy. What this domaine delivers (very reasonably priced), corresponds exactly to a wide-spread perception of how top Côte de Nuits should taste, but I believe that not a customer would abandon him if he moved towards a slightly lighter style.
Jean-Marie et Christophe Roumier, Chambolle-Musigny, 21220 Gevrey-Chambertin

HERVÉ ROUMIER   9 ha. (70 per cent)

Bonnes Mares 0.7 ha., Clos de Vougeot 0.55 ha., Echézeaux 0.36 ha., Chambolle-Musigny Les Amoureuses 0.21 ha., Chambolle-Musigny 3 ha., Bourgogne 4 ha.

Hervé Roumier learned wine-making with his father Alain – for long, manager at Comte de Vogüé – I gather, and worked in Napa at Carneros Creek in the early 1980s.

Hervé Roumier, Chambolle-Musigny, 21220 Gevrey-Chambertin

HERVÉ SIGAUT   3.5 ha. (80 per cent)

Chambolle-Musigny Les Charmes, Les Fuées, *Premier Cru*, Chambolle-Musigny, Pommard.

Hervé Sigaut, 21220 Chambolle-Musigny

DOMAINE DU COMTE GEORGES DE VOGUE   12 ha. (100 per cent)
DOMAINE DES MUSIGNY

Musigny (*rouge*) 6.5 ha., (*blanc*) 0.4 ha., Bonnes Mares 2.5 ha., Chambolle-Musigny Les Amoureuses 0.5 ha., Chambolle-Musigny 2 ha.

This famous estate owns 70 per cent of the *Grand Cru* Musigny and nearly a fifth of Bonnes Mares. Its wines are made under and around the same fifteenth-century house in Chambolle which was inhabited – perhaps even built – by an ancestor of the present owners. Few estates in Burgundy have held their vineyard lands so long.

From the 1960s to the mid-1980s these wines were often smooth and velvety, but could lack flesh and savour. I have drunk some wonderful bottles, but also those I felt were over-chaptalized. It is hard to forget this, for of course they were always expensive. Given the exceptional nature of de Vogüé's holdings on the village's best hillsides, these wines were sometimes below expectations. Family-owned French estates can be rigid in their unquestioning acceptance of the methods-in-place; one finds it in Bordeaux, on the Loire, in Provence, just as in Burgundy.

A new wine-maker, François Millet, arrived to tend the 1985. It must have taken him some time to get into his stride, for his previous experience had not been on the Côte de Nuits. By the early 1990s, however, the domaine had been brought up to the highest quality level, and Millet now speaks of his wines like a native. Musigny comes from an astonishing and fabulous *terroir*; the 1992 vintage is the embodiment of tranquil force. Millet is assisted by a new vineyard manager, and a new commercial manager with experience at Joseph Drouhin.

In future, not much will be left to chance, I think. For instance, after the estate suffered 60 per cent hail damage in 1991, a team of 60 people was reportedly equipped with eyebrow tweezers to pick out split grapes. Millet had done a small, pre-harvest vinification, which revealed that there was a *goût de sec* (a dry taste of rot) in the offing, and it was necessary to react. The resulting wines seem immaculate.

The owner of the domaine is the late Comte Georges de Vogüé's only daughter Elizabeth (who was married, until his death in 1989, to Baron Bertrand de Ladoucette – the uncle, incidentally, of Patrick de Ladoucette, who owns Chablis Regnard and makes Pouilly-Fumé at Château du Nozet). Madame la Baronne appears to have put together a fine team to revitalize this great estate.

Baronne Bertrand de Ladoucette et Jean-Luc Pépin, rue Sainte-Barbe, 21220 Chambolle-Musigny

CHÂTEAU ANDRÉ ZILTENER

'You are in an old Priory, where the monks of Cîteaux used to live, in the days they had the Clos de Vougeot. Walk through, visit the cellars – we have arranged them in our own way.' They have indeed, including a white-cassocked, ghostly monk descending a staircase, with a lamp, also plaster-cast monks at an eternal meal (inspiration for this must have come to Bâle businessman Ziltener at a Chevaliers du Tastevin banquet). It is a cellar-visit with a difference, open all year round including Sundays, and more amusing than Reine Pédauque or Patriarche on the Beaune boulevards. One pays to go in (40 fr. in 1991), but can hone one's palate on eight to ten wines (all bought in by the *négoce*; Ziltener's production from his Gevrey-Chambertin La Justice vineyard goes to Bâle) and keep a tastevin.

Famille Ziltener, rue de la Fontaine, 21220 Chambolle-Musigny

15

Vougeot

———

As I was walking away from the Château du Clos de Vougeot, a gust of wind blew a sheet of paper into my hands. It was obviously a speech, here translated:

Chers Confrères [it began] the time has come to admit that the reputation of the Tastevinage label is not as high as it could be. While it is true that many *tasteviné'd* wines are excellent, it is also true that an enormous quantity of those bottles wearing Tastevinage labels go straight on to supermarket and shop shelves, to be bought by neophytes who don't know any better. This helps to sell large quantities of wine that otherwise might stick around. The Confrérie makes decent money from selling the labels, but let us think back to what we were trying to do in 1950, when we launched it: to create a range of wines which was above average.

Burgundy's problems during the 1960s and 1970s were such that I believe we somewhat lost our way. The Confrérie exists to promote the wines of Burgundy, so that business will go well. But perhaps we have allowed ourselves to be influenced too much by powerful, wealthy local interests – you all know who I mean: those *négociants* who submit quantities of samples, some of them skilfully arranged blends, in the hope that one here, one there, will slip past our guards.

Is it not time to put an end to that? If not, we could admit that we are irremediably compromised, and leave the field free to other tasting panels, more careful with their choice of judges, more rigorous in their assessments, to carry on the banner. Several of us have tasted at the Ambassadeurs Tasting in Gevrey on the day of the Roi Chambertin – yes, conditions were indeed a bit cramped. Some of us have *even* ventured as far as Mercurey, coming away from both impressed at the professionalism.

Personally, I do not accept that we should leave the field. There is work to be done, and we should act. For instance, by making a charge for each wine submitted to our panels: 200 fr. for regional ACs, 300 fr. for village wines, 400 fr. for *Premiers Crus* and *Grands Crus*. If we hit the right figures, this should make those proprietors and merchants hesitate, who in the past have repeatedly sent us doubtful bottles. And we should state, even more clearly than in the past, that only wines which seem to correspond 100 per cent to the *appellation* whose name they bear will be allowed through.

In future, I suspect we may have fewer bottles to judge here, at least initially. I am really desolated that the numbers invited to make up juries and stay to lunch may drop. But this will give us an opportunity to weed out undesirable elements – perfidious Anglo-Saxon skunks, for instance, who are always talking of the value and excitement they claim to find in those copy-cat wines produced beyond the shores of our beloved hexagon. My Ladies and My Sires, such wines have no history, I assure you. Nor do they speak to us of the nobility of *terroir*. And they will *never* – believe me – be served at the tables of the Popes in Avignon. *Never* . . . [Here the writer had halted.]

Had this speech been given, or was it a first draft? Whose was the hand? It must have been written, with all its imperfections, by a younger generation *négociant*, I suspect, who loved the place, and its wines when they were good, but who believed that the time had come for the Confrérie to cut the bull, and stand up more proudly. Perhaps he also believed that tasters should be allowed to see the labels, after they had handed in their marks. In this way, those brilliant growers and *négociants* with demonstrably outstanding wines would be thanked, congratulated and fêted, without delay. And judges would cease to allow mediocrity and fraud to hide behind the brown paper of anonymity. No need to be ashamed to face the fact, it would just be part of progress. Perhaps he also hoped that wines might be served at the banquets carrying the names of the properties from which they sprang, thereby surely increasing the interest and quality of the wines being served, for it was well known that many of the best wine-makers were unwilling to sacrifice quantities of their best bottles to the anonymity of the Confrérie's banquets. For once, Burgundians might admit to learning something from the Bordelais, who were proud to serve their best wines, loud and clear with the châteaux named, at their festivities.

Suddenly, the wind tore the paper from my hand, high up into the air over the vines. Would it go uphill, towards Le Musigny – that most subtle, elegant, delicious expression of life's fleeting pleasures? Or would it go downhill towards the road, the mud and the lorries, over the monks' much-breached mediaeval, limestone wall, with its tasteless gateways? Another gust took it higher – it was impossible to see which way the wind would take it.

The Confrérie des Chevaliers du Tastevin has been spectacularly successful in publicizing the wines of Burgundy. It was founded in 1934, when cellars were full and buyers scarce, and one of the proprietors of Richebourg was sending his wine to a Lyon café for sale by the carafe. Since no one wants our wines, let us invite our friends and drink together, ran the idea, and soon it became apparent that people would pay a great deal to have dinner at the Clos de Vougeot.

The Confrérie is now a brilliantly successful, male-dominated club, mainly for the wealthy, which draws in distinguished outsiders: top footballers, astronauts, politicians, businessmen, musicians, diplomats, and people from all walks of life, if they are Burgundy-enthusiasts. Many people only attend one *chapitre* per lifetime, and a marvellous experience it can be (as it was for me).

But at its banquets, you cannot really discuss the wines in a true Burgundian fashion, as they do not tell you who made them. This is an old *négociant* attitude (above all, don't give credit to a grower) and one I find out-moded. When, as a guest Tastevinage judge I found myself jumping with excitement over an outstanding Nuits-Saint-Georges *Premier Cru* (on 28 March 1992) I would have been really grateful to know who had made it. I could learn a lot from talking to whoever was responsible, and might write about the methods, to the benefit of others. And I could certainly make many customers and friends extremely happy if I knew where to buy the bottles.

At a Tastevinage, the wines are often judged when very young (some might add: at their best, before their alcohol has dried them out). To give examples: giving Tastevinage honours to a Hautes

Côtes de Beaune 1990 in March 1992 may be acceptable, but to do the same for a Chambolle-Musigny *Premier Cru* 1990 (which can only have had a few weeks ageing, after early bottling) seems like asking for trouble. The system as it stands gives shelter to the mediocre, gives scant encouragement to the brave and brilliant, and serves the consumer pretty poorly.

The Confrérie is very international, and I wonder if it might consider filling what I think is a gap in Burgundy's cultural coverage: the sponsoring of the translation into French, and publication, of the best of the overseas research into cool-climate Chardonnay and Pinot Noir, their pruning and training, their vinification, and their ageing. Some of the Roseworthy, Davis or Oregon research gets an airing in existing Burgundian publications, but the coverage is spotty, and one feels that Burgundians would really prefer not to have to read what these foreigners are up to. These foreigners have the most inadequate understanding of, and respect for, *terroir* – in any case, all their *terroirs* are ignoble. Sponsoring could even extend to commissioning studies, who knows?

Sixty years after the Confrérie's foundation, selling Burgundy is a completely different problem, so the organization needs some new objectives. Millions of people are happy to pay good money for fine Burgundy, but consumers are often still disappointed, when the wines do not live up to the hype. Come on, Confrérie, don't be content with looking at the *status quo*, do something different! At least, please consider updating the dreadful label.

Let us return to the wine. The *Grand Cru* Clos de Vougeot occupies 50.59 ha (of which 46.27 ha. was in production in 1991). This accounts for over four-fifths of the land under vines in the commune. The five-year average production (1988–92) for Clos de Vougeot was 19,400 cases.

This is the part of the Côte nearest to the monastery of Cîteaux, which is 10 kilometres into the plain. From 1110 onwards the monks started to receive gifts of land, so Dr Lavalle tells us, their poverty, saintliness and the austerity of their rule contrasting keenly with the opulence of other abbeys. The vineyard was too far from the monastery to be cultivated by the monks themselves, so a *maître du cellier* was appointed. The young wine spent its first year next to the vat-house in the vines, then being moved to greater safety at a château in the village of Vougeot. By the fifteenth century the

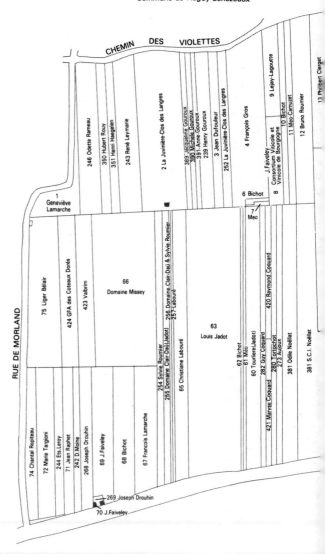

Commune de Flagey-Echézeaux

CHEMIN DES VIOLETTES

RUE DE MORLAND

1 Geneviève Lamarche

246 Odette Rameau
350 Hubert Rouy
351 Henri Haegelen
243 René Leymarie

2 La Juvinière-Clos des Langres

389 Jacqueline Gouroux
390 Michèle Gouroux
391 Anne Gouroux
239 Henry Gouroux

3 Jean Dufouleur

252 La Juvinière-Clos des Langres

4 François Gros

9 Lejay-Lagoutte

13 Philibert Clerget

6 Bichot
8 Consortium Viticole et Vinicole de Bourgogne
J.Faiveley
7 Meo
10 Bichot
11 Meo-Camuzet
12 Bruno Roumier

74 Chantal Ropiteau
72 Marie Targioni
244 Ets Leroy
71 Jean Raphet
242 D.Moine
268 Joseph Drouhin
69 J.Faiveley
68 Bichot
67 Francois Lamarche

75 Liger Bélair

424 GFA des Coteaux Dorés

423 Valbrim

66
Domaine Missey

254 Sylvie Roumier
255 Domaine Clair-Dau/Jadot
256 Domaine Clair-Dau & Sylvie Roumier
257 Labouré
65 Christiane Labouré

63
Louis Jadot

62 Bichot
61 Méo
60 Tourliere(Jadot)
421 Maryse Coquard
282 Guy Coquard
280 Tortochot
273 Aujoux
381 Odile Noëllat
420 Raymond Coquard

381 S.C.I. Noëllat

269 Joseph Drouhin
70 J.Faiveley

Commune de Chambolle-Musigny

272
Jean-Charles Nourissat

379 S.C.I.Noëllat

402 Marie Rabut

403 Colette Gros

Les Amis du
Clos Vougeot

26

320 Colette Gros

329
Drouhin-Laroze

330 Labet-Dechelette

378 Odile Noëllat

25

23
Alfred Haegelen

24
Méo-Camuzet

Ch. du Clos de Vougeot

264 Ch.de Marsannay

17 Renée Jayer

18
Paulette Engel

19 Drouhin-Laroze

265 Christian Confuron
392 Christian Confuron 393 Andrée Noëllat

21 Mongeard Mugneret
410 Madeleine Hudelot
409 Georges Hudelot
408 Alain Hudelot

35
Méo-Camuzet

34 Marie Mugneret
33 Domaine Lamarche
32 Bernard Chezeaux
31 Geneviève Lamarche
30 Geneviève Lamarche

29
L'Héritier Guyot

36 Gunter Rey
262 Chantal Lescure
37 Scea les Beaux Monts
275 Clos de Thorey
274 Clos de Thorey
39 Champerdry (Henri Roch)
38 Clos de Thorey

40 Jousset-Drouhin

41 Jousset-Drouhin

42 Ch.de la Tour

51
Labet-Dechelette

43
Labet-Dechelette

384
Domaine Jacques Prieur

372 Daniel Chopin

CHEMIN DU CLOS DE VOUGEOT

401 Bernard Clerc
54 Domaine Missey
53 Henri Rebourseau
50 Labet-Dechelette

49
Jean Grivot

48 Labet-Dechelette
47 Consortium Viticole et Vinicole de Bourgogne
J.Faiveley
46 Joseph Confuron
266 Michel Noëllat

383 Bernard Raphet
413 Bernadette Raphet
412 Gerard Raphet
411 Jean Raphet
376 Jean Raphet
375 Jean Raphet
374 Jeanne Charvet
373 Jeanne Charvet

45 J.Prieur

N74

Vougeot →

303

monks' vineyard had been enclosed within the great wall which can still be seen.

The Clos de Vougeot was confiscated for the nation in 1789, but was not split up for another hundred years. In 1860 the English tried to acquire it, offering 2.5 million francs, but their offer was disdainfully thrust aside, so Camille Rodier tells us.[1] It was sold in 1889 for 600,000 francs to six Burgundians, five of them wine-shippers, and two years later the six had become fifteen. By 1977 the Clos had been divided into 107 plots, shared between 75 owners. By 1993 this had risen to 82, but it is estimated that there are approximately 50 actual vinifiers, for several owners share facilities.

The Clos de Vougeot has the most varied subsoil of any *Grand Cru* in Burgundy. There are six types according to R. Gadille:[2] Bathonian and Bajocian limestone, Bajocian, Aquitanian and Pliocene marls, and alluvial deposits. In 1832 A. Jullien wrote: 'The vines placed in the upper section give a very fine and delicate wine; the low sections, above all those which border the main road, give something much inferior.'[3] Today, more than one Burgundian has been heard to say that the low land, being somewhat imperfectly drained, would be more aptly used for beetroot cultivation. Indeed, when filming in the alluvial south-east corner of the Clos with an American video crew in 1987 I was astonished to find one grower cultivating a healthy crop of asparagus between each Pinot. After a heavy storm, such as occurred in summer 1993, the lower vines may be temporarily submerged under water, so I understand.

If soil analysis, and well-organized comparative blind tastings (such as those put on by the Clos de Vougeot growers themselves in the context of the biennial Grands Jours de Bourgogne) become more common perhaps we shall one day see the Clos being classified more appropriately than today. There are enormous differences – pebbly land at the top, heavy soil at the bottom – and no grower in his or her right mind would choose to buy at the bottom, with its lower potential for finesse. If there *are* three, or more, *terroirs* in the Clos (and analysis of the internal surfaces of the clays, and other elements, may soon confirm if the myth is based on reality) they

1 *Le Clos de Vougeot*, Librairie L. Venot, Dijon, 1949.
2 *Le Vignoble de la Côte bourguignonne*, Les Belles Lettres, Publications de l'Université de Dijon, Paris.
3 *Topographie de tous les vignobles connus*, de Lacroix et Baudry, Paris, 1832.

could fit neatly into the well-known Burgundian AC pyramid: a village wine – Vougeot du Clos; a First Growth – Vougeot *Premier Cru* du Clos; and the wine of classic *Grand Cru* status – Clos de Vougeot. But Burgundy's *Grands Crus* were not solely mapped out by reference to *terroir*, as a reading of J.-F. Bazin's account of the creation of the satellite-Chambertins quickly demonstrates.[4] Commercial interests and precedent weighed, and still weigh, heavily. A Clos de Vougeot review is extremely unlikely.

The map of the Clos de Vougeot to be found on pp. 302–3 shows the position of the various owners' plots. I am particularly indebted to Les Amis du Clos for their help in updating it.

The following are classified *Premiers Crus*:

Clos Blanc, Le (La Vigne Blanche)
Clos de la Perrière
Cras, Les
Vougeots, Les Petits

First Growth and commune Vougeot covers 14.15 ha., producing on average 5,290 cases of red and 1,190 cases of white wine per vintage.

Main growers and merchants in Vougeot

DOMAINE BERTAGNA   28 ha. (100 per cent)

Chambertin 0.2 ha., Clos Saint-Denis 0.5 ha., Clos de Vougeot 0.3 ha., Vougeot Clos de la Perrière (Monopole) 2 ha., Les Petits Vougeots 2.5 ha., Les Cras 1.2 ha., Clos Bertagna (Monopole) 0.3 ha., Chambolle-Musigny Les Plantes 0.2 ha., Vosne-Romanée Les Beaux Monts Bas 1 ha., Nuits-Saint-Georges Les Murgers 1 ha., Hautes Côtes de Nuits 16 ha., Bourgogne (*rouge*) 2 ha.

The Reh family has owned this estate since 1982 and much renovation has taken place, including the creation of a country house hotel with twelve guest rooms, bicycles being provided for wanderers. From the 1988 vintage a white Vougeot *Premier Cru* has been available.

There is a sizeable production from Hautes Côtes de Nuits vines

---

4 *Chambertin: La Côte de Nuits de Dijon à Chambolle-Musigny,* Jacques Legrand, Paris, 1991.

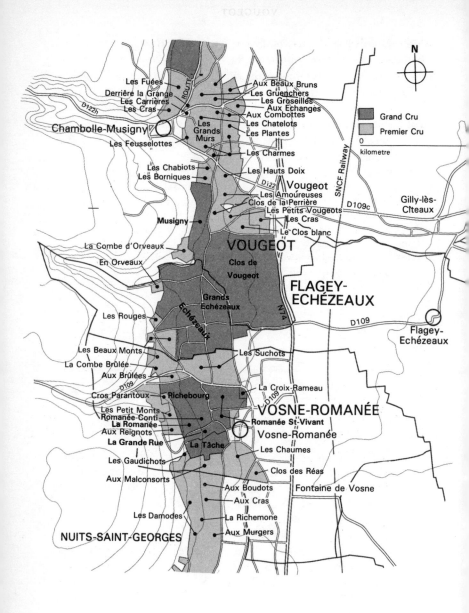

Vougeot, Flagey-Echézeaux and Vosne-Romanée

(declared either with that name, or as Bourgogne *rouge*) located uphill from the pine woods above Nuits-Saint-Georges. Because of its altitude this ripens six to eight days later than the village wines of the Côte.

The labels may be understated, but these wines are mouth-fillers, strong on spice and character.

Eva Reh, Mark Siddle et Roland Masse (manager), rue du Vieux Château, 21640 Vougeot

GEORGES CLERGET   4 ha. (100 per cent)
MICHEL CLERGET
CHRISTIAN CLERGET

Echézeaux 0.8 ha., Chambolle-Musigny Les Charmes 0.5 ha., Chambolle-Musigny 0.6 ha., Vougeot *Premier Cru* 0.46 ha., Vosne-Romanée Les Violettes 0.38 ha., Morey-Saint-Denis 0.4 ha.

Master of Wine, Doctor of Philosophy, Remington Norman condescendingly twits Monsieur Clerget for not spending more money on new oak, which he seems to think would give the wines 'firmer backbone and naturally greater power'. Naturally greater power? The point about this cellar, to my mind (as one who has sometimes bought here), is the conscientious, unpretentious production of reliable, fine wine, offered at fair prices. Burgundy would be immensely poorer if those growers who bring Monsieur Clerget's skills, and modesty, to their work all started heavily new-oaking their best *cuvées*.

Georges et Christian Clerget, route nationale 74, Gilly-lès-Cîteaux, 21640 Vougeot

L'HÉRITIER-GUYOT   11.5 ha.

Clos de Vougeot 1.36 ha., Vougeot *Premier Cru* Clos Blanc de Vougeot (Monopole) 2.28 ha., Vougeot *Premier Cru* Les Cras 1.42 ha.

Three-quarters of the activity of this company has been in cassis and liqueurs, and the wine-making sometimes less than imaginative (masses of new wood being thrown at the Clos Blanc). Since 1990 changes are under way, I understand, studies into wood origins being pursued with the cooper François Frères, for instance. They buy in as many grapes as they harvest, so should be worth watching.

Mme Marie-José Mermod, Gilly-lès-Cîteaux, 21640 Vougeot

ALAIN HUDELOT-NOELLAT   10 ha. (100 per cent)

Romanée-Saint-Vivant 0.46 ha., Richebourg 0.28 ha., Clos de Vougeot 1.09 ha., Vosne-Romanée Suchots 0.43 ha., Beaumonts 0.32 ha., Malconsorts 0.13 ha., Nuits-Saint-Georges Murgers 0.67 ha., Vougeot Les Petits Vougeots 0.54 ha., Chambolle-Musigny 2.5 ha., Vosne-Romanée 0.68 ha., Nuits-Saint-Georges 0.2 ha., Bourgogne (*rouge*) and Passe-Tout-Grains

I have had some magnificent wines from here, yet for some reason no consistent image of a high quality domaine is yet established.

Alain Hudelot-Noëllat, 21640 Vougeot

CHÂTEAU DE LA TOUR   5.39 ha. (100 per cent)

Clos de Vougeot Château de la Tour 5.39 ha.

Guy Accad was consultant wine-maker to this estate, which is the largest owner of Clos de Vougeot, having its *cuverie* within the Clos, for the six vintages 1987–92. This resulted in deeper-coloured, more richly fruity, broadly flavoured wines than I normally expect in Clos de Vougeot. How will they develop? Certainly as young wines, I prefer the old-fashioned approach to Pinot Noir wine-making (because I adore those aromas). But I had to admire what was achieved here with the by-no-means-simple 1987 vintage, and gave it a pass-mark when I found myself judging it blind, at a Fleurons de Bourgogne tasting in Mercurey in March 1992, while writing 'lacks the finesse/delicacy of the year'. Probably I should have been grateful.

M. Labet parted company with Accad in time to make the 1993 vintage independently. He says that, although still inspired by his techniques, he will aim for greater roundness, and something more fanciful (*un peu de fantaisie*). Perhaps he came to find Accad-style wines monotonous. Also at this address are to be found the wines of the:

DOMAINE PIERRE LABET   5 ha. (100 per cent)

Beaune Couchérias 0.75 ha., Beaune Clos des Monsnières (*rouge*) 0.8 ha., (*blanc*) 1 ha., Savigny-lès-Beaune Vergelesses (*blanc*) 0.3 ha., Bourgogne (*rouge*) 1 ha.

François Labet, Château de la Tour au Clos de Vougeot, 21640 Vougeot

16

Vosne-Romanée and Flagey-Echézeaux

If word came down that the Côte de Nuits was to sink beneath the seas, its vineyards returning to submarine ooze as in Jurassic times when the rocks first formed, but that one village might be saved, I would have to cry out, 'Vosne!' Of course there are times when these wines disappoint, and moments when the prices asked for them seem outrageous, but, although Chambolle-Musigny runs it close, this is Burgundy's most fascinating spot, these wines its most perfectly balanced, flashingly brilliant, magically textured, thought-provoking and exciting.

There are six *Grands Crus* in the village, some of the most famous and expensive wines in the world. In alphabetical order, with their vineyard areas in production in 1991, and their five-year average productions (1988–92) they are: La Romanée (0.85 ha. – 330 cases); La Tâche (5.83 ha. – 1,880 cases); Richebourg (8.03 ha. – 2,690 cases); Romanée-Conti (1.8 ha. – 550 cases); Romanée-Saint-Vivant (9.06 ha. – 3,250 cases); and a new arrival: La Grande Rue (1.65 ha.). This has just been promoted from First Growth; its production in 1991 was 570 cases.

For centuries Romanée-Conti has been judged the finest. At the Revolution a document declared that its wine was the most excellent of all the vineyards of the Côte d'Or, indeed of all the vineyards of the French Republic, and could give life back to the dying. La Tâche is rarely other than spectacular and fascinating; Richebourg (obtainable from several sources, where the previous two are owned by one estate) often a powerful, complex wine of lingering allure. These three are the most valued, sought-after wines of the village. La Romanée I have hardly ever tasted; like La Grande Rue it is in the hands of one owner. Romanée-Saint-Vivant covers a larger area, and has several owners; if often outclassed by the first three, in any other company it would be outstanding.

Flagey-Echézeaux is a small village in the plain which belonged to the Abbey of Saint-Vivant in 1188. A thin wedge of this commune divides the wines of Vougeot from those of Vosne-Romanée, Flagey enjoying the latter *appellation*.

There are two *Grands Crus* on Flagey's territory: Grands Echézeaux (8.63 ha.) and Echézeaux (34.03 ha.), their five-year average productions (1988–92) having been respectively 2,940 and 13,530 cases. The first makes rare, beautifully balanced, spicily complex wine, the second larger volumes which are, at their best, magnificent.

The following are classified as *Premiers Crus*:

Beaux Monts Bas, Les
Beaux Monts Hauts, Les
Beaux Monts, Les
Brulées, Aux
Chaumes, Les
Clos des Reas
Combe Brulée, La
Croix Rameau, La
Cros Parantoux
Gaudichots, Les
Malconsorts, Aux
Monts, Les Petits
Orveaux, En
Reignots, Aux
Rouges du Dessus, Les
Suchots, Les

First growth and commune Vosne-Romanée represented in 1991: 152.26 ha., the five-year average production (1988–92), both together, being 69,800 cases.

Main Vosne-Romanée growers

DOMAINE ROBERT ARNOUX   12 ha. (95 per cent)

Romanée-Saint-Vivant 0.35 ha., Clos de Vougeot 0.45 ha., Echézeaux 0.95 ha., Vosne-Romanée Suchots 0.5 ha., Chaumes 0.75

ha., Hautes Maizières o.6 ha., Nuits-Saint-Georges Corvées Pagets o.65 ha., Procès o.6 ha., Vosne-Romanée 1.5 ha., Nuits-Saint-Georges 1.95 ha., Bourgogne (*rouge*) Passe-Tout-Grains and Aligoté

Principal clients here are French, Swiss and German. In the past these wines have been too powerful for me. Monsieur Arnoux has been recently joined by a son-in-law.

Robert Arnoux et Pascal Lachaux, 3 route nationale, 21700 Vosne-Romanée

JACQUES CACHEUX ET FILS   4.57 ha. (90 per cent)

Echézeaux o.66 ha., Vosne-Romanée Croix Rameau o.16 ha., Suchots o.43 ha., Vosne-Romanée 1.7 ha., Nuits-Saint-Georges o.77 ha., Bourgogne (*rouge*) o.45 ha., Passe-Tout-Grains

I expect these wines to be precise examples of their origins, carefully made.

Jacques et Patrice Cacheux, 58 route nationale, 21700 Vosne-Romanée

RENÉ CACHEUX-BLÉE   2.5 ha. (30 per cent)

Vosne-Romanée Suchots o.95 ha., Beaumonts o.18 ha., Vosne-Romanée o.78 ha., Bourgogne (*rouge*) o.55 ha.

René Cacheux-Blée, 21700 Vosne-Romanée

SYLVAIN CATHIARD   3.84 ha. (50 per cent)

Romanée-Saint-Vivant o.17 ha., Vosne-Romanée Malconsorts o.74 ha., Suchots o.16 ha., Reignots o.24 ha., En Orveaux o.29 ha., Chambolle-Musigny Clos de l'Orme o.43 ha., Nuits-Saint-Georges Murgers o.48 ha., Vosne-Romanée o.85 ha., Nuits-Saint-Georges o.13 ha., Bourgogne (*rouge*) o.34 ha.

Some of these *appellations* still appear under the label Domaine Cathiard-Molinier, being separately vinified by Sylvain's father.

Sylvain Cathiard, 20 rue de la Goillotte, 21700 Vosne-Romanée

J. CONFURON-COTETIDOT   9.5 ha. (100 per cent)

Clos de Vougeot 0.25 ha., Echézeaux 0.25 ha., Vosne-Romanée Suchots 1.94 ha., Vosne-Romanée 1.45 ha., Nuits-Saint-Georges *Premier Cru* 1 ha., Nuits-Saint-Georges 0.55 ha., Chambolle-Musigny 0.9 ha., Gevrey-Chambertin 0.4 ha., Bourgogne (*rouge*) 0.5 ha.

The vines are said to average 60 years, some going on 80; about 15 per cent new wood is regularly used. Lots of stalks are left in, and vatting is long, giving tannic, deep-coloured wines which leave question marks over their final balance. Guy Accad has been influential here. As Fiona Beeston has described, Jacky Confuron is a fanatic for *pigeage* (punching down),[1] immersing himself up to the neck in the dangerous, carbon-dioxide laden atmosphere of an open vat to extract colour, fruit and body. 'It is at this moment', she wrote, 'that the true relationship between Confuron and his wine is established. A product for which one risks losing one's life takes on a different dimension.'

Jacques et Jean-Pierre Confuron-Cotetidot, 10 rue de la Fontaine, 21700 Vosne-Romanée

COQUARD-LOISON-FLEUROT   8.36 ha. (75 per cent)

Grands Echézeaux 0.18 ha., Echézeaux 1.29 ha., Clos de la Roche 1.17 ha., Clos Saint-Denis 0.17 ha., Charmes-Chambertin 0.32 ha., Clos de Vougeot 0.64 ha., Gevrey-Chambertin 0.21 ha., Chambolle-Musigny 0.8 ha., Vosne-Romanée 1.68 ha., Morey-Saint-Denis 0.78 ha., Bourgogne 1.11 ha.

Of the two Morey *Grands Crus*, Clos de la Roche is the finer, Clos Saint-Denis much stronger tasting in the mouth, they find.

Two small, smiling ladies present these fine wines, as yet little-assessed by English speaking commentators (but Gault & Millau rate them well; most of the bottles stay in France).

Mme Sylviane Fleurot, 5 rue Haute, 21700 Flagey-Echézeaux

---

1 *La Revue du Vin de France*, September, 1989.

DOMAINE RENÉ ENGEL   6 ha. (65 per cent)

Clos de Vougeot 1.5 ha., Grands Echézeaux 0.5 ha., Echézeaux 0.55 ha., Vosne-Romanée Les Brûlées 1 ha., Vosne-Romanée 2.50 ha.

Here is an open-hearted wine-maker, with some of the most perfectly situated vineyards on the Côte de Nuits. He is attached to tradition, yet engaged in modest experiments with different barrels and vatting methods. Sometimes spicy, sometimes with old-fashioned smells of decaying leaves, these wines are not overstated; they have balance, richness and potential.

Philippe et Mme Pierre Engel, place de la Mairie, Vosne-Romanée, 21700 Nuits-Saint-Georges

JEAN FAUROIS   1.5 ha. (100 per cent)

Vosne-Romanée Chaumes 0.24 ha., Vosne-Romanée 1 ha., Nuits-Saint-Georges 0.09 ha., Passe-Tout-Grains

The 1990 vintage was the last for this estate's Clos de Vougeot, for those vines have now reverted to their owner Méo-Camuzet, as will the Chaumes one day. Jean Faurois having retired, and his son Christian being Jean-Nicolas Méo's right-hand man, the family vines are now tended by his mother. This is a dependable, if tiny, source, the wines being bottled unfiltered, with a sensible explanatory back-label.

Mme Jean Faurois, 21700 Vosne-Romanée

DOMAINE FOREY PÈRE ET FILS   3.73 ha. (40 per cent)

Echézeaux 0.3 ha., Vosne-Romanée Les Gaudichots 0.1 ha., Nuits-Saint-Georges Les Perrières 0.42 ha., Vosne-Romanée 1.33 ha.

Jean et Régis Forey, Vosne-Romanée, 21700 Nuits-Saint-Georges

DOMAINE FRANÇOIS GERBET   15 ha. (80 per cent)

Clos de Vougeot 0.3 ha., Echézeaux 0.2 ha., Vosne-Romanée Aux Réas 2 ha., Vosne-Romanée *Premier Cru* Les Petits Monts 0.5 ha., Vosne-Romanée 1 ha., Hautes Côtes de Nuits 10.5 ha.

Marie-Andrée et Chantal Gerbet, Vosne-Romanée, 21700 Nuits-Saint-Georges

DOMAINE JEAN GRIVOT 13.2 ha. (100 per cent)

Richebourg 0.32 ha., Clos de Vougeot 1.88 ha., Echézeaux 0.59 ha., Vosne Romanée Beaux Monts 0.94 ha., Les Rouges 0.34 ha., Suchots 0.22 ha., Brûlées 0.15 ha., Chaumes 0.15 ha., Reignots 0.09 ha, Nuits-Saint-Georges Boudots 0.86 ha., Pruliers 0.76 ha., Roncières 0.5 ha., Chambolle-Musigny Combe d'Orveau 0.62 ha., Vosne-Romanée 3.12 ha., Nuits-Saint-Georges 2.12 ha.

Impossible for me to write objectively of these wines, which I have often bought, sold and drunk with pleasure. Etienne Grivot was for five years Guy Accad's highest-profile client (they parted company just before the 1992 vintage). He first involved Accad in his domaine for soil analyses, wishing to bring his vineyards back into balance, then used low temperature pre-fermentation maceration to varying extents for the five vintages 1987–91 inclusive. His aim throughout has been to make well-structured wines for long-term ageing, not easy-pleasing bottles for early consumption.

The controversial element of Accad-influenced wine-making is whether the site-specific character of each wine is highlighted and brought to its finest expression (which is what most Burgundians seek) or whether, alternatively, technology gets in the way of the *terroir*. Much ink and argument has flowed without answers being found. We need to wait until the mid- to late 1990s for wines from top sites from a number of vintages to mature, and then be tasted alongside their peers, and also served in the contexts for which they were made.

The estate now incorporates the vineyards of Domaine Jacqueline Jayer, Etienne Grivot's aunt, and I think the wine-making will go from strength to strength.

Jean et Etienne Grivot, 21700 Vosne-Romanée

GROS FRÈRE ET SOEUR 15.4 ha. (100 per cent)

Richebourg 0.69 ha., Clos de Vougeot (Musigni) 0.75 (Garenne) 0.8 ha., Grands Echézeaux 0.37 ha., Vosne-Romanée 3.27 ha., Bourgogne Hautes Côtes de Nuits (*rouge*) 3.27 ha., (*blanc*) 0.94 ha., Bourgogne (*rouge*) 3.32 ha., Passe-Tout-Grains 1.9 ha.

Bernard Gros et Mlle Colette Gros, 21700 Vosne-Romanée

DOMAINE ANNE ET FRANÇOIS GROS   4.53 ha. (100 per cent)

Richebourg 0.6 ha., Clos de Vougeot Grand Maupertuis 0.93 ha., Chambolle-Musigny 1.1 ha., Vosne-Romanée 0.4 ha., Bourgogne (*rouge*) 1.5 ha.

After health problems, François Gros has associated himself with his daughter Anne to work his estate. From 40 per cent in bottle for the 1988 vintage, the domaine had progressed to bottling all its production by the 1990. They have increased the proportion of new oak being used for the *Grands Crus*. The wines of these first years seem relatively soft, though not without richness, intensity and promise.

Anne Gros et François Gros, rue de la Fontaine, 21700 Vosne-Romanée

DOMAINE JEAN GROS   18.8 ha. (100 per cent)
DOMAINE MICHEL GROS

Richebourg 0.4 ha., Clos de Vougeot 0.21 ha., Vosne-Romanée Clos de Réas (Monopole) 2.12 ha., Vosne-Romanée 2.55 ha., Nuits-Saint-Georges 0.38 ha., Chambolle-Musigny 0.48 ha., Bourgogne Hautes Côtes de Nuits (*rouge*) 9.32 ha., (*blanc*) 1.54 ha., Bourgogne (*rouge*) 1.27 ha., Passe-Tout-Grains 0.52 ha.

Mother and son work closely here, and a lot of thought goes into retaining the best of traditional practices, while incorporating modern advances. They aim to reach at least 30°C at some point in the red fermentations, which begin with pumping over and addition of yeast, and possibly tartaric acid adjustment. Once half the sugars have been transformed, the vats are covered over, except for twice-daily punching down periods, with a pneumatic jack puncher. The *Grands Crus* are aged entirely, the *Premiers Crus*, half, in new oak – of varied origins, but strongly burned over the flames. The object of this policy is to protect the wines from green wood tannins, and to gum together flavours associated with different oak origins. While it may oak-mark the wines when they are first in barrel, a balance of flavours will have been achieved by bottling time. The Monopole Clos des Réas can be particularly succulent.

This is potentially a top source for red Hautes Côtes de Nuits, of which they make enough vats to be able to eliminate (if this policy were to be embraced) any which fall below the highest standards.

Mme Jean Gros et Michel Gros, 3 rue des Communes, 21700 Vosne-Romanée

DOMAINE HAEGELEN-JAYER   4.5 ha. (65 per cent)

Clos de Vougeot 0.86 ha., Echézeaux 0.16 ha., Nuits-Saint-Georges Damodes 0.32 ha., Vosne-Romanée 1 ha., Chambolle-Musigny 0.18 ha., Nuits-Saint-Georges 1.5 ha., Bourgogne (*rouge*) 0.4 ha.

In the late 1980s I found the tannins of these wines too intrusive for my taste, but M. Haegelen has increased his bottlings and now exports to several countries.

Alfred Haegelen, 4 rue Croix Rameau, 21700 Vosne-Romanée

DOMAINE HENRI JAYER   5 ha. (100 per cent)
DOMAINE GEORGES JAYER

Details of the Jayer landholdings may be found elsewhere (see Emmanuel Rouget, Jayer's nephew, below). Rouget cultivates the vineyards, and the wines are split up after the harvest.

Echézeaux, Vosne-Romanée Cros Parantoux, Vosne-Romanée Beaumonts, Vosne-Romanée, Nuits-Saint-Georges, Bourgogne (*rouge*) and Passe-Tout-Grains are those one may find tended here. There are complicated arrangements between Henri Jayer and his brothers Georges (whose wines he tends) and Lucien (who tends his wines independently). All three Jayer names may be found on labels.

Henri Jayer says he has not been putting potassium in his vineyards for thirty years; you could not get fertilizer during the war, and after it, he was happy with his small bunches and high proportion of solid matter to juice. François Faiveley (who introduced me to a bottle of Cros Parantoux) has said that Jayer's secret is firstly yields, secondly yields, and thirdly yields (he meant low).

Jayer adds other details: as few rackings as possible, and always when there is high pressure (to keep the lees pinned to the bottom of the barrel). Complete de-stalking, for tannins from the stalks bring nothing but astringency. Tronçais barrels from François Frères, medium burn. Picking grapes into 25–30 kg containers, so they are not squashed and can be sorted for unripeness and mould ('Burgundy needs to revise its picking methods', he says, but it is in fact now quite common to do as he suggests). Reduce vat tempera-

ture to 15° for 4–5 days at the start, to obtain stable colour; after, to let it climb to 34°. Never use cultured yeasts, it standardizes. (I suspect he has never tried them.) 'It is not the vocation of Pinot Noir to have a violet colour. It must not be like Syrah. It must be beautiful to look at.' A glass of Vosne-Romanée 1992 is perched on a barrel at eye-height. He goes on: 'Look at the glints of brilliance – step back. Like silk fabric flashing in the sun.'
Henri Jayer, 21700 Vosne-Romanée

DOMAINE FRANÇOIS LAMARCHE   8 ha. (90 per cent)

La Grande Rue (Monopole) 1.6 ha., Grands-Echézeaux 0.5 ha., Clos de Vougeot 1 ha., Echézeaux 1 ha., Vosne-Romanée Malconsorts 0.5 ha., Suchots 0.75 ha., Vosne-Romanée 1 ha.

For many vintages these wines (previously Henry Lamarche) were wan and wispy, left too long in wood. I thought the family very lucky to have *Grand Cru* status finally accorded to La Grande Rue. Apparently the quality is climbing back up.
M. et Mme François Lamarche, 21700 Vosne-Romanée

DOMAINE LEROY   22.42 ha. (100 per cent)

Grands Crus: Chambertin 0.5 ha., Latricières-Chambertin 0.57 ha., Clos de la Roche 0.67 ha., Musigny 0.27 ha., Clos de Vougeot 1.91 ha., Richebourg 0.78 ha., Romanée-Saint-Vivant 0.99 ha., Corton-Renardes 0.5 ha., Corton-Charlemagne 0.43 ha..
Premiers Crus: Gevrey-Chambertin Combottes 0.46 ha., Chambolle-Musigny Les Charmes 0.22 ha., Vosne-Romanée Beaux Monts 2.61 ha., Aux Brûlées 0.27 ha., Nuits-Saint-Georges Les Boudots 1.19 ha., Vignerondes 0.38 ha., Savigny-lès-Beaune Narbantons 0.81 ha., Volnay-Santenots 0.35 ha.
Village and regional: Nuits-Saint-Georges Lavières 0.68 ha., Aux Allots 0.51 ha., Bas de Combe 0.15 ha., Vosne-Romanée Genevrières 1.23 ha., Chambolle-Musigny Fremières 0.35 ha., Gevrey-Chambertin 0.11 ha., Pommard Vignots 1.26 ha., Trois Follots 0.07 ha., Auxey-Duresses (*blanc*) 0.23 ha., Bourgogne (*rouge*) 0.76 ha., (*blanc*) 0.61 ha., Aligoté and Passe-Tout-Grains

This estate has been built up rapidly, no expense spared, from the purchase of the vines and buildings of Domaine Charles Noëllat of

Vosne-Romanée in April 1988, from Domaine Remy in Gevrey-Chambertin, and from other vineyards.

At the time, Mme Bize-Leroy was a co-director of the Domaine de la Romanée-Conti. The Noëllat holdings clashed directly with vineyards owned by that estate (Richebourg, Romanée-Saint-Vivant). After her departure as a DRC director in 1991 the two domaines had completely separate managements. In less than a year, to the astonishment of many, cultivation at Domaine Leroy went over to bio-dynamic methods.

When I visited the estate in August 1993, I was struck by Mme Bize-Leroy's openness. In the DRC days she often used to play cards from close to her chest, when fielding questions or critical comment, so this was a welcome change. For instance, one of her initial 'golden rules' for Domaine Leroy was that vineyard regeneration would be by selection from the mass (rather than with clonal stock). In fact cuttings from her own vines proved to be virus-ridden, so had to be burnt. That set-back (and the consequent replanting with clones) could be openly discussed. In her attempts to return to healthier methods of vineyard care a helicopter was used to spray against bunch mildew in 1993 on the Côte de Nuits (there had been 42 tractor-treatments the previous year, resulting in soil compaction). But this proved a very expensive error, for helicopter spray nozzles cannot aim accurately at the bunches. There was almost total crop destruction in some vineyards. Had less green methods been adopted, there would have been fruit to harvest.

Wine-making objectives here are no de-stemming, two pneumatic punchings-down per day, and long vattings. The traditional, open-topped wooden vats are all, I believe, equipped with stainless steel temperature-controlling coils installed near their bases, a brilliant concept, which I know of nowhere else. It requires regular pumpings-over to equalize the temperatures within each vat, but eliminates the need for cooling systems (radiator-like heat exchangers) being humped from vat to vat. No doubt the system runs on auto-pilot throughout the night. This makes it easier to achieve extended vatting times, helped by whole, uncrushed grapes yielding their sugars only gradually from day to day.

Initially André Porcheret, Mme Bize-Leroy's wine-maker, had experimented with horizontal heat-exchangers in alimentary plastic positioned under the hat of grape-skins, in each vat's warmest area, but these proved impractical to install and use.

Yields at Domaine Leroy vineyards appear to be extremely low, partly due, perhaps, to imperfect, or missing, vines in old vineyards, but more likely to a policy of severe pruning. The wines I tasted have been balanced, varied, wonderful, and most exciting. And not just the *Grands Crus*; the Vosne-Romanée Beaumonts, for instance, were the most beautiful I have ever seen. Of the prices, some observers calculate that they are unsustainable. Are yields of 25 hl/ha. conceivable, indeed, on a wider basis, in Burgundy?

If a grower does the calculation, it is illuminating. In 1993, a First Growth Vosne from a vineyard which had yielded 45 hl/ha. had the prospect of selling at 70 fr. to 140 fr. per bottle, in a highly recessed, stock-charged market. The same name, at half the yield, if perceived to be one of the best and most exciting wines in the world could fetch more than double – so long as there were enthusiasts to spread the news. 'Thank goodness for Mr Parker, and for the *Wine Spectator*', acknowledged Mme Bize-Leroy, with disarming frankness.

Her policy demonstrates that there is a market for outstanding wines at high prices, which is an example to the whole of Burgundy. Bio-dynamic methods permitting, this Domaine looks set fair to deliver some truly superlative bottles of Burgundy.
Mme Bize-Leroy, Domaine Leroy, 21700 Vosne-Romanée

DOMAINE MANIÈRE-NOIROT   10 ha. (50 per cent)

Echézeaux 0.25 ha., Vosne-Romanée Suchots 1.5 ha., Nuits-Saint-Georges Damodes 1.4 ha., Boudots 0.6 ha., Vosne-Romanée 1.5 ha., Bourgogne (*rouge*)
Marc Manière, rue de la Grand' Velle, 21700 Vosne-Romanée

DOMAINE MEO-CAMUZET   15 ha. (100 per cent)

Clos de Vougeot 3 ha. (top), Richebourg 0.35 ha., Corton 0.45 ha., Vosne-Romanée aux Brûlées 0.7 ha., Cros Parantoux 0.3 ha., Les Chaumes 2 ha., Nuits-Saint-Georges aux Boudots 1.05 ha., Aux Murgers 0.75 ha., Vosne-Romanée 1.3 ha., Nuits-Saint-Georges 0.55 ha., Bourgogne (*rouge*) 0.45 ha., Hautes Côtes de Nuits Clos Saint-Philibert (Monopole) (*blanc*) 3.6 ha., Passe-Tout-Grains 0.5 ha.

This estate has moved only recently from obscurity to prominence. It used to sell a mere 10 per cent of its wine in bottle, the vineyards being looked after by share-cropper vignerons, whose remuneration each year was half the fruit. The most famous of these was Henri Jayer, who, although retired, has an advising role at the domaine, for wine-making and tending. Bit by bit, as the vignerons reach retirement age, the estate is taking back its vineyards to exploit them directly.

The domaine was built up by Etienne Camuzet, who was the Côte d'Or's *deputé* to the Assemblée Nationale 1902–32. He bought the Château du Clos de Vougeot at this time, passing it on to the Confrérie des Chevaliers du Tastevin in 1945. On the death of his childless daughter Maria Noirot, the vineyards came to Camuzet's great-nephew, Jean Méo, a distinguished *Polytechnicien*, President Director-General of Elf petrol, and a technical adviser to General de Gaulle. Indeed, the General consoled himself with a bottle of Méo's Clos de Vougeot the day after his last referendum. *On ne va pas se laisser abattre*, he said, *va donc me chercher un vin Méo* (This must not get us down – go and bring me one of Méo's wines). The date was 17 April 1969, the wine Clos de Vougeot 1964 (so being drunk before its fifth birthday).

These are splendidly rich wines, of elegance and length (but I am not objective, having sometimes bought and sold them) surely owing much of their concentration to yield-limitation. They are flattering in youth, though I can be shocked by the high new-oakiness (100 per cent new wood being used).

The wines are egg-white fined (though some *cuvées* may not need fining), but not filtered, and gravity-bottled directly from each barrel. *Cuvées* will have been unified at the second racking, three or four months before bottling, leaving the possibility of bottle variations and deposits, which seems a reasonable risk to ask consumers to run.

Jean-Nicolas Méo, 11 rue des Grands Crus, 21700 Vosne-Romanée

DOMAINE GÉRARD MUGNERET   8 ha. (100 per cent)

Echézeaux 0.64 ha., Chambolle-Musigny Les Charmes 0.25 ha., Vosne-Romanée Les Suchots 0.38 ha., Nuits-Saint-Georges Les Chaignots 1.27 ha., Les Boudots 0.42 ha., Vosne-Romanée 2.5 ha., Gevrey-Chambertin 0.25 ha.

Gérard Mugneret maintains his father René's tradition of egg-

white fining, no filtration, and sealing his bottles with wax. These wines are worth tasting, but there is no point dropping by without a rendezvous; if there is outdoor work, the family is in the vines.
Gérard Mugneret, Vosne-Romanée, 21700 Nuits-Saint-Georges

DOMAINE MONGEARD-MUGNERET   20 ha. (100 per cent)

Clos de Vougeot 1 ha., Grands Echézeaux 1.8 ha., Echézeaux 3.2 ha., Richebourg 0.32 ha., Vosne-Romanée Les Orveaux 1.2 ha., Suchot 0.5 ha., Les Petits Monts 0.33 ha., Vougeot 0.6 ha., Vosne-Romanée 2 ha., Nuits-Saint-Georges 0.59 ha., Fixin 1.3 ha., Savigny-lès-Beaune Narbantons 1.5 ha., Savigny-lès-Beaune 0.6 ha., Puligny-Montrachet 0.33 ha., Bourgogne (*rouge*), Passe-Tout-Grains

Mongeard is an intriguing grower, still close to the earth yet very active in Burgundian wine trade life (President of the Association des Viticulteurs de la Côte d'Or, Vice-President of the Commission Technique of the BIVB). I have had excellent, mature bottles from here, but his wines have generally tasted better for me from barrel than bottle. He has wonderful sites, and recently exchanged some Echézeaux (of which he has quantities) for Puligny-Montrachet with Bernard Clerc, which is imaginative and unexpected.
Jean et Vincent Mongeard, 21700 Vosne-Romanée

DOMAINE MUGNERET-GIBOURG   8.5 ha. (100 per cent)
DOMAINE GEORGES MUGNERET

Clos de Vougeot 0.34 ha. (top), Echézeaux 1.2 ha., Ruchottes-Chambertin 0.64 ha., Nuits-Saint-Georges Chaignots 1.27 ha., Vignes Rondes 0.26 ha., Chambolle-Musigny Les Feusselottes 0.46 ha., Vosne-Romanée 3.5 ha., Bourgogne (*rouge*) 0.8 ha.

Almost all of this estate is cultivated on the half-fruit system by local vignerons, so regrettably there is only half as much wine available under these labels as at first sight would appear.

Dr Georges Mugneret, a much respected Côte de Nuits wine-maker, died in 1988, since when his widow, now aided by two daughters (Mme Nauleau being a fully-fledged oenologist) has ably maintained the traditions. One may expect elegant yet characterful wines from this source, expressing their origins precisely.

Mme Georges Mugneret, Mme Teillaud et Mme Nauleau, 5 rue des Communes, 21700 Vosne-Romanée

DENIS MUGNERET ET FILS   7.2 ha. (50 per cent)

Richebourg 0.52 ha., Clos de Vougeot 0.72 ha., Nuits-Saint-Georges Les Saint-Georges 1.14 ha., Boudots 0.61 ha., Vosne-Romanée *Premier Cru* 0.16 ha., Vosne-Romanée 1.4 ha., Nuits-Saint-Georges 0.68 ha., Gevrey-Chambertin 1.16 ha., Hautes Côtes de Nuits 0.58 ha., Bourgogne (*rouge*), Aligoté and Passe-Tout-Grains

There are four barrels of Richebourg in this cellar (half the production from the Liger-Bélair *métayage* they cultivate) – an intense and chewy wine. Dominique Mugneret seems a talented young man, with a bright enquiring eye, and, with experience, may well deliver good bottles.

Denis et Dominique Mugneret, 14 route nationale, 21700 Vosne-Romanée

MICHEL NOËLLAT ET FILS   19 ha. (50 per cent)

Clos de Vougeot 0.47 ha., Echézeaux 0.47 ha., Chapelle-Chambertin 0.36 ha., Vosne-Romanée Suchots 1.77 ha., Beaumonts 1.92 ha., Chambolle-Musigny Les Feuselottes 0.92 ha., Nuits-Saint-Georges Boudots 0.46 ha., Morey-Saint-Denis 1.6 ha., Vosne-Romanée 1.72 ha., Nuits-Saint-Georges 1.6 ha., Chambolle-Musigny 1.33 ha., Fixin 1.77 ha., Bourgogne (*rouge*), Aligoté and Passe-Tout-Grains

With its extensive, fine vineyard sites, this has been an interesting source since the days when the late Michel Noëllat's late father Henri was between the vines. I suspect that local *négociant* scouts often succeed in extracting the domaine's best *cuvées*, for the estate-bottled offerings can show signs of dilution and over-sugaring. Early-maturing, many go to passing French consumers.

Cousins of Ghislaine Barthod-Noëllat in Chambolle, Alain and Jean-Marc Noëllat are slowly bottling more over the years.

Alain et Jean-Marc Noëllat, 5 rue de la Fontaine, 21700 Vosne-Romanée

ANDRÉ PERNIN-ROSSIN   6.9 ha. (100 per cent)

Clos de la Roche 0.04 ha., Morey-Saint-Denis Monts Luisants (*rouge*) 2.33 ha., Nuits-Saint-Georges Richemone 1.32 ha., Vosne-Romanée Beaux Monts 0.45 ha., Reignots 0.1 ha., Vosne-Romanée 0.82 ha., Chambolle-Musigny *Premier Cru* 0.13 ha., Morey-Saint-Denis 1.06 ha.

Guy Accad was involved here from 1982 to the 1988 vintage inclusive, however with mixed results for the 1987 vintage, which caused a change of adviser.

These wines nevertheless show the characteristics – deep red purples, intensely briary, raspberry aromas, rich fruitiness – one associates with Accad-influenced wine-making. You like them or you do not, it is truly a matter of taste.

André Pernin-Rossin, 21700 Vosne-Romanée

RION PÈRE ET FILS   7 ha. (100 per cent)

Clos de Vougeot 0.75 ha., Nuits-Saint-Georges Les Murgers 0.77 ha., Les Damodes 0.5 ha., Vosne-Romanée Les Chaumes 0.5 ha., Chambolle-Musigny Les Lavrottes 0.4 ha., Nuits-Saint-Georges 1.6 ha., Vosne-Romanée 0.5 ha., Chambolle-Musigny 0.4 ha.

Bernard Rion, Vosne-Romanée, 21700 Nuits-Saint-Georges

DOMAINE DE LA ROMANÉE-CONTI   27 ha. (100 per cent)

Romanée-Conti (Monopole) 1.8 ha., La Tâche (Monopole) 6.06 ha., Richebourg 3.51 ha., Romanée-Saint-Vivant 5.29 ha., Grands Echézeaux 3.53 ha., Echézeaux 4.67 ha., Montrachet 0.67 ha., Bâtard-Montrachet 0.17 ha., Vosne-Romanée Suchots 1.02 ha. Petits Monts 0.4 ha.

The owner of the most famous *Grands Crus* on the Côte, a maker of richly complex, long-lasting wines, one of the first and most consistent advocates of estate-bottling – for many people the Domaine de la Romanée-Conti is *the* domaine in Burgundy. In addition to its two famous Monopoles Romanée-Conti and La Tâche, the DRC owns nearly half of Richebourg, over half of Romanée-Saint-Vivant, and over a third of Grands Echézeaux. With the Richebourg and Grands Echézeaux *appellations*, DRC has for decades set the standard by which all others are measured.

Since the early 1990s the estate has been taking advice from
Claude Bourguignon on the health of its soils. It has stopped using
fertilizers, and now makes its own fermented compost (ground-up
pruning shoots, with pips and stalks from the pressings and cattle
manure), which is spread on the land, according to need, to revitalize the soil's microbiological activity, and improve its texture,
with the object of allowing the vine to defend itself as naturally as
possible against its enemies. Magnesium is provided to help absorb
old excess potassium dressings. Although the domaine does not use
the word biological, those are its methods. Pesticides, herbicides
and synthetic chemical products have been set aside.[2]

The average age of the vines is now most impressive. In 1993
they were: Romanée-Conti 47, La Tâche 45, Richebourg 30,
Romanée-Saint-Vivant 28, Grands Echézeaux 45, Echézeaux 35,
Montrachet 60.

The estate was, I believe, the first to install a conveyor-belt table
for hand-sorting unripe or rotten grapes in the vat-house, after
grape-picking. This was in 1977, after the experience of 1976,
when, as often, they had delayed harvesting to achieve extra
maturity, but then been caught by a rapid development of botrytis
mould. The conveyor-belt is now perforated, to allow drips of
water to escape (if grapes are picked under rain) while the sorting
process goes on.

Fermentation takes place in nine traditional, open-topped round
or oval wooden vats, in respect of the four top wines. The Grands
Echézeaux and Echézeaux have since 1989 fermented in eight rectangular, open-topped, stainless steel box-vats equipped with automatic punching-down. It seems to me that the quality of the
Echézeaux, in particular, has taken a serious leap forward since it
has been made in vats with automatic punching-down; the 1990
and 1993 seemed marvellous, for instance, when tasted young. In
the days when *pigeage* of the whole cellar was with the legs and
feet, one can imagine that thigh, calf and arm muscles (needed for
hanging on to the edges of the vats) would have been really aching,
and bodily exhaustion be setting in, by the time vintage workers
had attended to the Romanée-Conti, La Tâche, Richebourg,

---

2 Dr Sylvain Bihaut, *Le Vin authentique: ecologie et oenologie*, Editions Sang de la
Terre, Paris, 1993.

Romanée-Saint-Vivant and Grands Echézeaux. Echézeaux must sometimes have been the last *Grand Cru* in line.

Since the 1991 harvest there are different cellars for each vintage maturing in barrel, the second one being that under the old Marey-Monge buildings at the foot of Romanée-Saint-Vivant by Vosne-Romanée's church, where the natural temperature and humidity are excellent.

In common with several other of Vosne's best estates (Henri Jayer, Méo-Camuzet, Leroy), the DRC buys its barrels from the Saint Romain cooper François Frères. However, it invests in staves for three years' natural drying and leaching in the rain, sun and open air, to ensure that its barrel wood is appropriately matured. The whole harvest has been put into new wood for the last fifteen to twenty years. This policy can result in markedly oaky wines in light vintages, if they are tasted when young; however the flavours of long-aged oak staves of the best possible origins subsequently seem to marry exceptionally beautifully with the vinosity of the individual wines.

The estate sometimes bottles a small quantity of wine not aged in new oak, for instance La Tâche 1991, to be able to compare the two types of storage. My personal preference (at a tasting in July 1993) was not for the new-oaked Tâche. The wines, however, were made for maturing, not for enjoyment when two years old.

At different stages since the war the two families (de Villaine and Leroy) who own this domaine must have considered employing a full-time oenologist as wine-maker, yet set their faces against the idea. No doubt they have access to Burgundy's finest (but who, I wonder, might that be?) in the same way that they can call on the services of Claude Bourguignon or Raymond Bernard whenever they need them.

Input from an exceptional oenologist might allow the domaine to make greater successes of the really tricky years, when there is immaturity, rot or rain – perhaps avoiding embarrassments such as the loss of the 1992 Montrachet, due to a halt in fermentation. However, that has not been the chosen route, and perhaps today the need for it is less.

Overall responsibility at the domaine was for many years shared, as is well-known, by Mme Bize-Leroy and Aubert de Villaine, and their joint actions often produced wonderful results. Whilst I believe that in the 1960s and 1970s the yields, and consequent chaptalizations, were sometimes on the high side, nevertheless, the DRC has generally set extremely high standards. Its wines have been not only the most expensive, but very often the most exciting, in all Burgundy.

In 1991 Mme Bize-Leroy was ousted by the shareholders from her position as co-director, after disagreements over how the DRC wines were then being distributed. As we have seen (above), she now competes from Domaine Leroy.

In the past, the Domaine de la Romanée-Conti's position has been an isolated one, somewhat cut off from developments at other top estates. I wonder if the departure of Madame Bize-Leroy may usher in a decade of greater exchange of ideas with other like-minded wine-makers elsewhere on the Côte de Nuits and the Côte de Beaune? Research now moves so fast, and there are so many observant, highly qualified, expert producers at work, that greater exchanges may prove beneficial.

This would come naturally to Aubert de Villaine, who, with his wife Pamela, rapidly took their domaine in Bouzeron to prominence – and held it there, making simple, regional *appellations* of top quality and individuality. His greater personal involvement in decision-making at the DRC is surely very welcome.

On the retirement of André Noblet in 1984 responsibility for the vineyards fell to Gérard Marlot, splitting the DRC's viticultural and wine-making activities into two, Noblet's son Bernard in due course becoming manager of vat-house and cellars. But the overall wine-making responsibility lies, I believe, with Aubert de Villaine. Now in his fifties, he is conscious that a mere dozen vintages may be left to him, health and good luck permitting, before retirement looms. Given the low yields that the domaine is now achieving, given his involvement with its great sites, and given the experience of thirty years of DRC vintages under his belt, we can surely look forward to many spectacular and wonderful bottles from the coming vintages.

Aubert de Villaine et H-F Roch, Domaine de la Romanée-Conti, Vosne-Romanée

EMMANUEL ROUGET   4.9 ha. (100 per cent)

Echézeaux 1.5 ha., Vosne-Romanée Cros Parantoux 0.72 ha., Beaumonts 0.25 ha., Vosne-Romanée 1.2 ha., Nuits-Saint-Georges 0.45 ha., Bourgogne (*rouge*) 0.3 ha., Passe-Tout-Grains 0.45 ha.

Rouget is Henri Jayer's nephew, and tends his vines on the half-fruit system, the uncle helping with vinification and *élevage*. Between them they misjudged the sugar level of the 1989 Nuits-Saints-Georges, I felt, but that was early days in the collaboration. The same wine in 1990 was a model of delicious, restrained harmony, when three and a half years old.

I have not yet met Monsieur Rouget, feeling that he must have had more than enough media-beating on his door. These visits can be counter-productive, it often being in consumers' interests to let the trade do the news-gathering, while prices are being discussed.
Emmanuel Rouget, Flagey-Echézeaux, 21700 Vosne-Romanée

ROBERT SIRUGUE   10 ha. (60 per cent)

Grands Echézeaux 0.15 ha. Vosne-Romanée Petits Monts 0.5 ha., Vosne-Romanée 4.5 ha., Bourgogne (*rouge*) 3.5 ha., Passe-Tout-Grains

I expect fine wines here, particularly the village Vosne-Romanée.
Robert, Jean-Louis et Marie-France Sirugue, 3 av. du Monument, 21700 Vosne-Romanée

JEAN TARDY   5 ha. (100 per cent)

Clos de Vougeot (top) 0.25 ha., Nuits-Saint-Georges Boudots 1.05 ha., Vosne-Romanée Chaumes 1.54 ha., Chambolle-Musigny Les Athets 0.32 ha., Nuits-Saint-Georges 0.42 ha.

This Clos de Vougeot is in the sloping Grand Maupertuis section, adjoining Grands Echézeaux; the Boudots is currently planted with seventy-year-old vines. All wines go into new oak, states Olivier Tardy – America is the main market.
Jean et Olivier Tardy, 21700 Vosne-Romanée

DOMAINE DU CHÂTEAU DE VOSNE-ROMANÉE   4 ha.

La Romanée (Monopole) 0.85 ha., Vosne-Romanée aux Reignots 1.68 ha., Vosne-Romanée du Château (Monopole) 1.46 ha.

La Romanée has been in the Liger-Belair family for three and a half centuries, the wines being bottled and distributed by Bouchard Père et Fils (q.v.).

17

Nuits-Saint-Georges and Prémeaux

This is an important commercial centre for the area, grouping ship-pers, brokers, liqueur-makers, fruit-juice factories, label-printers and sparkling-wine manufacturers. It used to have strategic import-ance as a frontier town on the French border with Franche-Comté, but today there are few traces of its mediaeval battlements, indeed few attractions for the tourist.

Nuits stands on a stream, the Meuzin, which flows down from two villages in the Hautes Côtes, Arcenant and L'Etang-Vergy. In 1747 its flood-waters caused the death of five adults and seven children. Over the years it has carried down alluvial deposits to the detriment of the commune's low-lying vineyards, and those along its banks.

Look for the rock, if you want to find texture in the wine. Some of the best vineyards are in the adjoining commune of Prémeaux (whose wines have right to the Nuits-Saint-Georges *appellation*) in a narrow strip between hill-top and plain.

One can enjoy Nuits-Saint-Georges from an early maturing vin-tage when it is five years old, but wines from rich years may not reach their peak until they are twenty. There is a big difference in the character of wines from the Vosne side of the commune (Boudots, Damodes, some Murgers) which have a silky richness approaching the perfections of Vosne. Wines from the south side of the commune (Vaucrains, Les Saint-Georges, Cailles, and the First Growths of Prémeaux) can be rough and ungainly when young, with sometimes animal, sometimes furry aromas, verging on veg-etable decay – which can be off-putting to the unwary. I do not think this character relates solely to the wine-making and tending. They need deep, dark, long cellarage.

It is often worth decanting Nuits-Saint-Georges, at the moment of serving. There can be specks of deposit to leave behind, and a little prior aeration will speed its development in the glass, as may be found if the nose is kept close to the wine as it swirls.

The following are classified as *Premiers Crus*:

Commune of Nuits-Saint-Georges:
Argillats, Aux
Boudots, Aux
Bousselots, Aux
Cailles, Les
Chaboeufs, Les
Chaignots, Aux
Chaines Carteaux
Champs Perdrix, Aux
Château Gris (Les Crots)
Clos des Porrets Saint-Georges (Poirets)
Cras, Aux
Crots, Les
Damodes, Les
Murgers, Aux
Perrière Noblot, En La
Perrières, Les
Poirets, Les (Porrets Saint-Georges)
Poulettes, Les
Procès, Les
Pruliers, Les
Pruliers, Les Hauts
Richemone, La
Roncière
Rue de Chaux
Saint-Georges, Les
Terres Blanches, Les
Thorey, Aux
Vallerots, Les
Vaucrains, Les
Vignerondes, Aux

Commune of Prémeaux-Prissey:
Argillières, Les
Clos Arlot
Clos de la Maréchale
Clos des Argillières
Clos des Corvées
Clos des Corvées Pagets
Clos des Forêts Saint-Georges (Forêts)
Clos des Grandes Vignes
Clos Saint-Marc (Aux Corvées)
Didiers, Les
Perdrix, Aux

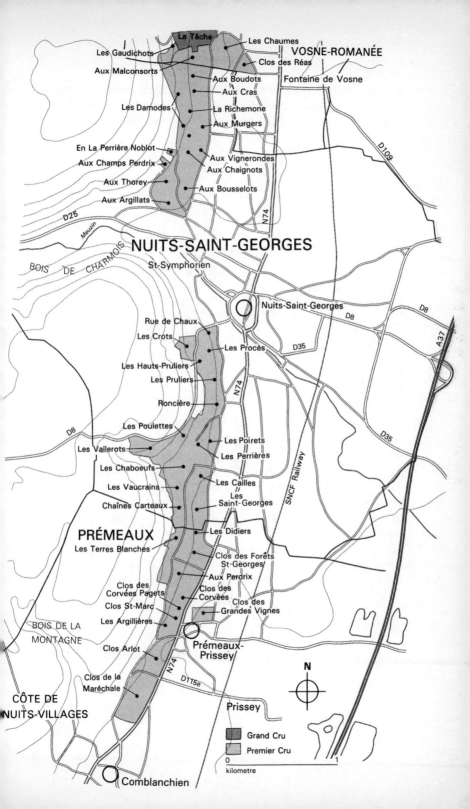

The First Growth and commune vineyard area covers a total of 297.33 ha. The five-year average production (1988–92) was 139,200 cases of red Nuits, and 750 cases of white.

Main merchants and growers

JEAN CLAUDE BOISSET, SA (1961)

This publicly-quoted company, now the largest wine-trader on the Côte de Nuits, distributes exclusively the following:
Domaine Pierre Ponnelle (12.9 ha.): Charmes-Chambertin 0.73 ha., Bonnes Mares 0.7 ha., Musigny 0.21 ha., Clos Vougeot 0.36 ha., Corton Clos du Roi 0.49 ha., Vougeot Le Prieuré (*rouge*) 1 ha., (*blanc*) 0.82 ha., Nuits-Saint-Georges Les Damodes 0.93 ha., Clos des Corvées Paget 0.3 ha., Beaune Grèves 0.33 ha., Clos du Roi 0.11 ha., Chambolle-Musigny 0.53 ha., Marsannay 0.27 ha., Côte de Beaune Pierres Blanches (*blanc*) 3.72 ha., (*rouge*) 1.86 ha., Bourgogne (*blanc*) 0.52 ha.
Domaine Claudine Deschamps (total 6.73 ha.): Gevrey-Chambertin Bel Air 1.02 ha., Les Goulots 0.16 ha., Gevrey-Chambertin 5.55 ha.

There are also 10 ha. of Hautes Côtes de Nuits, five ha. of white being under the Domaine de Charmont label, the balance of red under the name of Edouard Delaunay et ses Fils.

An enormous and influential firm, but a top reputation for quality in the Côte d'Or presently escapes it. Their wines seem often designed to be reliably inoffensive. The firm certainly has many technical skills, and the ability to clean out, or blend away, both faults and imbalances. One might be very grateful to be spared unpleasant surprises, and to have a low-cost bottle, but if one considers how many thousands of cases (maybe hundreds of thousands) of such wines are despatched from the street of the Brothers Montgolfier one may conclude that little is being done to add lustre to Burgundy's reputation, or its long-term prosperity, by the thrust of Boisset's buying.

This dynamic business provides employment for over 200 people, and has absorbed many loss-making, old-established Burgundy *négociant* names: Charles Viénot (possibly founded 1735), Bouchard Aîné & Fils (1750), Jaffelin (1816), Morin Père & Fils (1822), P. de Marcilly Frères (1849), Thomas-Bassot (1850), F.

Chauvenet (1853), Pierre Ponnelle (1875), Edouard Delaunay et ses Fils (1893), Roland Thévenin and Lionel Bruck. As well, there have been numerous names on brass plates outside his Nuits offices: Raoul Henri, Francis Borelli, Blaise de Chantdieu, Desonvelle, Mayet & Fils, Antoine Demelo, Julien de Moissac, Lionel de Pontbriand (who really exists – I shared a judging table with him at the Tastevinage in March 1992), Tollinche Frères. There are surely many more.

When Boisset purchased these companies he also sometimes acquired stocks of *négociant* Burgundies going back decades which now make intriguing, time-warp tasting. And young vintages are still being laid away in the old-fashioned styles: Nuits-Saint-Georges Clos des Corvées Paget 1990 Charles Viénot, for instance, or P. de Marcilly Réserve Bourgogne (*rouge*) 1988, or Double Blason 1985, remind me of *méthode ancienne* Doudet-Naudin bottlings, with a leathery, thick-textured, old-style *négoce* character which is not to my taste.

Patriarche group may have the largest wine cellars in Burgundy but Boisset claims the biggest barrel-hall (temperature- and humidity-controlled, with a capacity of 3,500 barrels) under one roof. These barrels are often building blocks for Boisset blends, I believe, a proportion of strongly-oaked Chardonnay or Pinot being useful for adding character to bought-in wines which lack it. Some of their fastest-selling brands, Charles de France Chardonnay de Bourgogne for instance, ape ill-balanced New World Chardonnays – or so it seemed to me, in respect of the 1992 vintage, which sold a quarter of a million bottles – in their reliance on wood-flavour input.

With the 1993 vintage Boisset became one of the largest grape buyers in Burgundy. He has constructed an impressive stainless steel vat-hall with pneumatic press and robotized punching-down machinery whose first results, whether Bourgogne Pinot Noir or Chambertin Clos de Bèze Domaine Dr Marion, looked encouraging. Bought-in grapes represent only a tiny fraction of Boisset's needs, however, and anyone trading internationally in Burgundy will probably be familiar with this group's ability to quote prices which awaken curiosity, while defying competition (and sometimes belief). This can be achieved, no doubt, by buying when prices are on the floor.

Wines from the Pierre Ponnelle and Claudine Deschamps

domaines are vinified in Prémeaux, partly in old, open-topped wooden vats, partly in auto-punching rotaters or in an Amos horizontal-axis vat with a 'hedgehog' cap-disperser. Impressively, they go to the trouble of racking into half-barrels and quarter-casks, so that, when topping up, like may be topped up with like – which is rarer than one might expect in Burgundy, given local obsession with the subtleties of exact territorial origin. The wines are not bottled at the domaine, however, but 'for hygienic and stability reasons' go down the bottling lines at the Nuits-Saint-Georges *négoce*.

The Pierre Ponnelle and Claudine Deschamps domaine wines that I have tasted (only a limited number, mainly from barrel) certainly seemed harmonious and fine, but I doubt they are yet at the level of their *appellation* peers from Jadot or Drouhin, for instance, or top growers in the individual villages. When a big volume *négociant* controls major domaines (as here, or at Bichot, for instance) there must be frictions between the wine-making styles. If a really top wine-maker had total, independent responsibility for the Pierre Ponnelle domaine (including bottling) the results might put some of Maison Boisset's wines to shame, causing consternation. It is perhaps better that the domaine wines should not be too exceptional, or at least that, if they start out great in barrel, they should be tamed by their education and upbringing (for which, read treatment and filtering) to join the family harmoniously.

One of the most interesting wines I tasted at Boisset's in April 1994 was a Pinot Noir de Bourgogne 'Charles de France' 1992. The character was Pinot plus wood, with a fresh, fruity finish, the alcohol level being around 12.5°. Boisset may well have perceived the enormous potential in Burgundy to buy genuine Pinot grapes from fine, established, limestone-rooted plants, to vinify well, tend carefully and sell profitably. Such grapes have lowly *appellations*, like Bourgogne *rouge*, so are often despised and neglected by those obsessed with selling famous names, but modern vinification controls and working closely with growers to keep yields within reasonable levels can achieve excellent results. Boisset is not the first name to come to mind when thinking of close working collaborations between *négociant* and grower, however, so perhaps there is room for other leading vinifiers to supply this market, if it exists : reasonably-priced, youthful, softly fruity, aromatic yummy young Pinot. It does not sound very Burgundian, but consumers appear to love it when the Pinots come from Carneros, Sebastopol, Willamette, Yarra, Albany, Canterbury or Wanaka – to mention just a few *terroirs* from outside the French hexagon. It must be worth paying a bit more attention to lowly Bourgogne *rouge*, one would think.

Cheap, mid-priced, expensive – there is plenty of price-choice here at Boisset, but these wines do not have the incisive individuality of the greatest Pinots Noirs from Burgundy's best *terroirs*, in my, admittedly limited, experience. The company delivers vast volumes of wine which novice – and some less-than-novice – consumers find delicious, but I do not advise Burgundy enthusiasts to shop here yet, for I have sometimes had the greatest difficulty tasting the differences between the individual village names.
Jean-Claude Boisset, rue des Frères Montgolfier, 21700 Nuits-Saint-Georges

JEAN CHAUVENET   6.7 ha. (35 per cent)

Nuits-Saint-Georges Les Vaucrains 0.4 ha., Les Bousselots 0.55 ha., Les Perrières 0.22 ha., Nuits-Saint-Georges 4.8 ha., Vosne-Romanée 0.35 ha., Bourgogne (*rouge*) 0.5 ha.
Jean Chauvenet, chemin de Gilly, 21700 Nuits-Saint-Georges

CHAUVENET-CHOPIN   9.5 ha. (50 per cent)

Nuits-Saint-Georges Murgers 0.43 ha., Aux Argillats 0.35 ha., Aux Thorey 0.11 ha., Chambolle-Musigny 0.45 ha., Nuits-Saint-Georges 5 ha., Côte de Nuits-Villages 2 ha., Bourgogne
Hubert Chauvenet-Chopin, 97 rue Félix Tissérand, 21700 Nuits-Saint-Georges

DOMAINE GEORGES ET MICHEL CHEVILLON   8 ha. (70 per cent)

Nuits-Saint-Georges Les Saint-Georges 0.45 ha., Les Porêts 0.63 ha., Champs Perdrix 0.35 ha., *Premier Cru* 0.64 ha., Nuits-Saint-Georges 3.2 ha., Vosne-Romanée 0.35 ha., Bourgogne Hautes Côtes de Nuits (*blanc*) Les Chaumes 0.7 ha., Bourgogne (*rouge*)

These wines can be perfectly acceptable, but I do not expect them to be as dependably elegant as at Robert Chevillon. Stocks of old vintages run back eight years.

Michel Chevillon, 41 rue Henri de Bahèzre, 21700 Nuits-Saint-Georges

ROBERT CHEVILLON   13 ha. (80 per cent)

Nuits-Saint-Georges Les Saint-Georges 0.62 ha., Les Vaucrains 1.6 ha., Pruliers 0.61 ha., Chaignots 1.52 ha., Perrières 0.58 ha., Roncières 1 ha., Cailles 1.18 ha., Bousselots 0.55 ha., Nuits-Saint-Georges 3.26 ha., Bourgogne (*rouge*) 0.76 ha., Aligoté, Passe-Tout-Grains

Bottles from this highly-rated domaine can be magnificent: chewy, spicy and smooth, with lots of character.

Robert, Bertrand et Denis Chevillon, 68 rue Félix Tisserand, 21700 Nuits-Saint-Georges

GEORGES CHICOTOT   5.5 ha. (50 per cent)

Nuits-Saint-Georges Les Saint-Georges 1.14 ha., Vaucrains 0.3 ha., Pruliers 0.25 ha., Rue de Chaux 0.3 ha., Nuits-Saint-Georges 3 ha.

Georges Chicotot, 12 rue Paul Cabet, 21700 Nuits-Saint-Georges

DUFOULEUR FRÈRES   7 ha.

Clos de Vougeot, Musigny, Mercurey Clos l'Evêque, Mercurey, Côte de Nuits-Villages

For reasons which Jean-Louis Dufouleur would not divulge, this company prefers to keep the details of its vineyard holdings secret. J.-F. Bazin states,[1] however, that the holding is 0.2085 in Clos de Vougeot, and 0.098 in Musigny, with 2 ha. in Mercurey. (It must be quite tricky to vinify the Musigny.)

The family properties may also include vines in Nuits-Saint-Georges Les Saint-Georges, Chambolle-Musigny Argillières, Gevrey-Chambertin, Nuits-Saint-Georges and Côte de Nuits-Villages, being offered under various names: Domaine des Dames Ursulines, Domaine des Saint-Georges and Domaine Jean Dufouleur, all made in the so-called Château de Nuits-Saint-Georges. This

---

1 *Chambertin, la Côte du Nuits de Dijon à Chambolle-Musigny,* Jacques Legrand, Paris, 1991.

is a nineteenth-century construction on the corner by the traffic lights as you drive north, leaving town.

Jean, Hubert, Philippe, Jean-Louis Dufouleur, BP 5, route de Dijon, 21700 Nuits-Saint-Georges

DUFOULEUR PÈRE ET FILS, SA (1848)
DOMAINE GUY DUFOULEUR 14.38 ha.

Nuits-Saint-Georges Les Perrières 0.93 ha., Poulettes 0.57 ha., Les Crots 0.5 ha., Chaîne Carteau 0.2 ha., Nuits Saint Georges 1.78 ha. Santenay 1.69 ha., Hautes Côtes de Nuits (*rouge*) 7.21 ha., (*blanc*) 1.4 ha.

Offered wines from both Dufouleur companies, and asked to choose between them, I would definitely plump for these, hoping to taste interesting wines.

M. et Mme Xavier Dufouleur, 17 rue Thurot, BP 27, 21700 Nuits-Saint-Georges

MAISON JOSEPH FAIVELEY 112 ha. (1825)

Chambertin Clos de Bèze 1.29 ha., Latricières-Chambertin 1.2 ha., Mazis-Chambertin 1.2 ha., Gevrey-Chambertin Les Cazetiers 2.04 ha., Gevrey-Chambertin La Combe aux Moines 1.08 ha., Gevrey-Chambertin *Premier Cru* 0.48 ha., Gevrey-Chambertin 1.08 ha., Musigny 0.03 ha., Chambolle-Musigny *Premier Cru* 0.44 ha., Clos de Vougeot 1.28 ha., Echézeaux 0.86 ha., Nuits-Saint-Georges Les Saint-Georges 0.29 ha., Les Porêts 1.69 ha., Les Damodes 0.81 ha., Clos de la Maréchale (Monopole) 9.55 ha., *Premier Cru* 1.18 ha., Nuits-Saint-Georges 4.02 ha., Corton Clos des Cortons Faiveley (Monopole) 2.97 ha., Corton-Charlemagne 0.53 ha., Mercurey Clos du Roy 2.54 ha., Clos des Myglands (Monopole) 5.48 ha., La Framboisière (Monopole) 2.81 ha., Clos Rond (Monopole) 5.06 ha., Les Mauvarennes (Monopole) 11.28 ha., Mercurey (*blanc*) Clos Rochette (Monopole) 1.6 ha., Mercurey (*rouge* and *blanc*) 13 ha., Rully (*rouge* and *blanc*) 6.25 ha., Montagny 4 ha.

François Faiveley moves discreetly between the worlds of grower and *négociant* – at the highest quality level – with curiosity and enthusiasm. No shipper is more welcome in the cellars of the best domaine-bottlers on the two Côtes.

He makes outstanding red wines, with great capacities for ageing and developing. This has been consistently true, and his Mercureys (previously perhaps a little neglected) have significantly improved over the last ten years. All his Côte Chalonnaise wines are vinified in Mercurey at his Domaine de la Croix Jacquelet, those from the Côtes de Beaune and Nuits in Nuits-Saint-Georges.

Vintage-time in the Faiveley vat-houses (equipped with automatic punching-down) must be frantic. Given the size of the estate, it is astonishing that his wine-making, both red and white, is so dependably successful.

Certain *cuvées* are hand-bottled, barrel by barrel, without filtration, and then carry a matt gold, lozenge-shaped medallion above their main front label stating clearly how they were handled – an admirable way to proceed.

François Faiveley, 8 rue du Tribourg, 21700 Nuits-Saint-Georges

MICHEL GAVIGNET   9 ha. (100 per cent)

Nuits-Saint-Georges Les Chaboeufs, Nuits-Saint-Georges Les Bousselots, Côte de Nuits-Villages, Bourgogne Hautes Cotes de Nuits
Philippe et Michel Gavignet, 22 rue Thurot, 21700 Nuits-Saint-Georges

S. GESSEAUME   4 ha. (80 per cent)
D. CHOPIN-GESSEAUME

Nuits-Saint-Georges Pruliers 0.5 ha., Cailles 0.25 ha., Chaignots 0.2 ha., Nuits-Saint-Georges 2 ha.
S. Gesseaume et G. Chopin-Gesseaume, 32 rue du Tribourg, 21700 Nuits-Saint-Georges

DOMAINE HENRI GOUGES   14 ha. (90 per cent)

Nuits-Saint-Georges Clos des Porrets Saint-Georges (Monopole) 3.5 ha., Les Pruliers 1.7 ha., Les Saint-Georges 0.95 ha., Les Vaucrains 0.98 ha., Les Chaignots 0.5 ha., La Perrière 0.39 ha., Nuits-Saint-Georges 4 ha., Bourgogne (*rouge*) 1 ha., (*blanc*) 1 ha.

With the Marquis d'Angerville from Volnay, Henri Gouges was at the forefront of the battles against fraud in Burgundy in the 1920s. He died in 1967, leaving an estate of low-yielding Pinots, and one of the most ancient names for domaine-bottling.

Wine-making takes place in closed vats (unusual for Burgundy). The aromas and flavours of Nuits-Saint-Georges can be quite shocking (gamey, earthy, astringent) in certain wine-making hands. During the early years of the 1980s the domaine appeared to be subduing these violent characteristics, and perhaps allowed the pendulum to swing too far away from the structured fruitiness expected of this village's wines.

In 1988 a piston-driven punching-down system was installed, with automatic pumping over, without aeration, of the fermenting must. Since then, the wines have been more richly fruity and complex, but as Christian Gouges points out, the weather has been regularly helpful. Burgundians often downgrade the importance of their own input, attributing successes to the weather and the *terroir*.

Two white wines are made, originating from 1934, when Henri Gouges noticed a partly mutated Pinot Noir in his vineyards, bearing white as well as red grapes. He took cuttings of the white shoot, and planted up 0.33 ha. of La Perrière. This produces an unusually full-bodied white Nuits-Saint-Georges; the domaine now also has 1 ha. Bourgogne *blanc* planted with the same white Pinot.

Christian et Pierre Gouges (grandsons of Henri Gouges), 7 rue du Moulin, 21700 Nuits-Saint-Georges

HOSPICES DE NUITS-SAINT-GEORGES   8.1 ha.

Nuits-Saint-Georges *Premier Crus*: Les Saint-Georges 0.95 ha., Les Didiers (Monopole) 2.45 ha., Les Porêts 0.18 ha., Les Rues de Chaux 0.3 ha., Les Boudots 0.2 ha., Les Murgers 0.17 ha., Les Corvées-Pagets 0.35 ha., Les Vignerondes 1 ha., Nuits-Saint-Georges 2.5 ha.

A much smaller estate than the Hospices de Beaune, but there has been dependably high-quality wine-making here for several years. The wines are sold by auction at the end of March, following the harvest.

Hospices de Nuits-Saint-Georges, rue Henri Challand, 21700 Nuits-Saint-Georges

LABOURÉ ROI (1832)
COTTIN FRÈRES

This firm has exclusive distribution of four Burgundian estates which are bottled by Labouré-Roi, Négociant-Eleveur in Nuits-Saint-Georges:

Domaine Chantal Lescure (16.2 ha.): Clos de Vougeot 0.31 ha., Vosne-Romanée Suchots 0.42 ha., Pommard Les Bertins 1.67 ha., Beaune Les Chouacheux 1.51 ha., Chambolle-Musigny 0.25 ha., Nuits-Saint-Georges Les Damodes 1.01 ha., Pommard 4.12 ha., Volnay 0.26 ha., Côte de Beaune Grande Châtelaine (*rouge*) 3.06 ha., (*blanc*) 1.5 ha., Bourgogne (*rouge*) 1.61 ha.

Domaine René Manuel (5 ha.): Meursault Clos des Bouches Chères (Monopole) 1.51 ha., Poruzot 0.6 ha., Clos de la Baronne (Monopole) (*rouge*) 1.53 ha., (*blanc*) 0.72 ha., Bourgogne (*blanc*) 0.61 ha.

Domaine Daniel Seguinot (8 ha.): Chablis Fourchaume 4 ha., Chablis 4 ha.

Domaine Litaud Frères (3.9 ha.): Pouilly-Fuissé 3.5 ha., Saint-Véran 0.39 ha.

This, however, is only a tiny part of the story, for annual sales have grown from 10,000 to 1 million cases in the twenty years to 1994, the firm being now one of Burgundy's ten largest wine businesses. Labouré-Roi belongs to the brothers Armand and Louis Cottin, the former having trained as an engineer in the oil and construction industry, the second in the Lyon silk trade. There are five in-house oenologists, I was told, but they do not buy grapes to vinify. They source a quarter of their needs thanks to a partnership policy with growers: 'We de-isolate them, and supply them with new barrels. We like the contact with growers, we are peasants ourselves' said Armand, tongue in cheek, no doubt. He is an indefatigable traveller, and his wines are to be found on many airlines. The business has grown, I suspect, because its sales people are so close to its customers, and its buyers quick on their toes to secure fine stock if they see a market.

The wines taste straight, by which I mean they appear to speak clearly of their territorial origins – my if-not-forget-it first essential for red Burgundy. Top quality and volume sales stick together like olive oil and vinegar in this region, however, so the firm is sometimes a victim of its own success.

Two recent grower partnerships are with the 30 hectare Domaine Ropiteau-Mignon in Meursault and the 44 hectare Domaine Michel Pont in Volnay and Savigny-lès-Beaune, both major owners of fine sites. The latter might benefit enormously from Labouré-Roi wine-making input, I believe. I look forward to following this dynamic firm's wines in coming years.

Armand et Louis Cottin, BP 14, rue Lavoisier, 21700 Nuits-Saint- Georges

DOMINIQUE LAURENT

'Why is it in Burgundy', asks recently-established *négociant* Dominique Laurent, 'that one finds the greatest number of bad bottles?' and answers it, in part, by pointing the finger at over-intrusive wine-tending. On a very small scale, he practises tailor-made tending, with minimal use of sulphur, and his bottles are certainly worth watching out for (though with circumspection, if found in the tropics).

Dominique Laurent, 2 rue Jacques Duret, 21701 Nuits-Saint-Georges

DOMAINE XAVIER LIGER-BELAIR   3.5 ha.

Richebourg 0.5 ha., Clos-Vougeot 0.75 ha., Nuits-Saint-Georges Les Saint-Georges 2.25 ha.

The Liger-Belair company (whose origins date back to 1720) is owned by Dufouleur Père & Fils, which also bottles and distributes the lion's share of this Domaine, one of the largest owners in Nuits Les Saint-Georges.

Xavier Dufouleur, rue Thurot, 21700 Nuits-Saint-Georges

DOMAINE COMTESSE MICHEL DE LOISY   3 ha. (70 per cent)

Clos de Vougeot 0.64 ha., Vougeot *Premier Cru* Les Cras 0.15 ha., Nuits-Saint-Georges 1.03 ha., Hautes Côtes de Beaune 0.15 ha., Crémant de Bourgogne 1 ha.

These Clos de Vougeot vines have been in the family (whose connections included Maison Labouré-Gontard, founded 1823) since the end of the nineteenth century. Vougeot Les Cras is a recent purchase, the first harvest being 1993. An interesting estate, making a bit of everything – regional and village reds, sparkling, and an inky-black Clos de Vougeot, all edges and corners when young, not for the faint-hearted. These wines need laying away.

Françoise de Loisy Loquin, 30 rue Général de Gaulle, 21700 Nuits-Saint-Georges

LUPE CHOLET, SA (1903)

This firm was bought in 1978 by the three Bichot brothers, Albert, Bernard and Bénigne, who run the Beaune-based *négociant* Albert Bichot. There are many subsidiary wine labels under the Bichot umbrella in Beaune, but Lupé-Cholet has a more separate identity. It owns and vinifies two wines from the commune of Nuits: Nuits-Saint-Georges *Premier Cru* Château Gris (Monopole) 2.8 ha., and Bourgogne (*rouge*) Clos de Lupé (Monopole) AC 2.2 ha., as well as a 22 ha. Chablis estate. The Domaine du Château de Viviers consists of 3 ha. each of Vaillons and Vaucoupins, with 16 ha. Chablis, these wines being made in Chablis. All the wines have been Beaune-bottled.

Investment in Nuits is under way, I understand, to enable Lupé-Cholet to buy in grapes, vinify and tend more of its own wines. Until 1993 the wine-making has been mainly Château Gris and Clos de Lupé. Perhaps most *élevage* will one day take place independently of the Beaune firm; bottling looks set to stay in Beaune, however, down one of the Bichot bottling lines after pre-bottling treatments and filtration.

Benoît de Truchis, av. du Général de Gaulle, 21700 Nuits-Saint-Georges

DOMAINE MACHARD DE GRAMONT 23 ha. (80 per cent)

Vosne-Romanée Les Gaudichots 0.25 ha., Nuits-Saint-Georges Les Damodes 1.1 ha., La Perrière Noblot 2 ha., Les Argillats 1.2 ha., Les Hauts Poirets 0.6 ha., Les Poulettes 0.25 ha., Les Vallerots 0.75 ha., *Premier Cru* 0.8 ha., Chambolle-Musigny, Aloxe-Corton, Savigny-lès-Beaune Guettes 1 ha., Vergelesses (*blanc*) 0.2 ha., Beaune Les Chouacheux 1 ha., Couchérias 0.38 ha., Pommard Clos Blanc 1.6 ha., Puligny-Montrachet Les Houillères 1.4 ha., Chorey-lès-Beaune, Bourgogne Hautes Côtes de Beaune

Remington Norman describes exhaustively the recent background of the two Machard de Gramont estates in his *Great Domaines* book, where may be found the story of the pressure cooker heiress, the Bouchard sulphur manufacturer, the Bichot wife, and *pigeage à la main*.

In the early 1990s the estate acquired land in the rare First Growth Vosne Les Gaudichots, abutting La Tâche; it needed to clear a henhouse, fruit trees, brambles and brushwood before replanting. On my limited acquaintance, these wines have perhaps not always had the personalities or sparks they might have had, but they appear carefully-made and rich.

Arnaud Machard de Gramont, 6 rue Gassendi, 21700 Nuits-Saint-Georges

BERTRAND MACHARD DE GRAMONT 4 ha. (60 per cent)

Nuits-Saint-Georges Hauts Pruliers 0.58 ha., Les Allots 1 ha., Vosne-Romanée Les Réas 0.53 ha., Nuits-Saint-Georges 1.4 ha., Bourgogne (*rouge*) 0.5 ha.

Bertrand Machard de Gramont is a Dufouleur grandson, who did a year's *stage* with de Vogüé in Chambolle, then stayed there a further three.

A small domaine like this has all the time in the world for those tiny details of tending which so often take growers' wines into a fascination league way beyond what most large *négociants* aspire to. For instance, if the acidity strength permits, he will fine carefully, then bottle without filtration. Five or six barrels will be left to settle in vat for a week, then a morning allowed to draw the clear wine off by gravity, into bottle, leaving the finings behind. But you cannot proceed like this all the time. If the pH levels were 3.60 to 3.65, for instance, it would open doors to bacterial growth, bringing bitterness, and the spoilage smells of the poultry-yard. (The implication, if one listens carefully to this grower and his broker, is that lecturing growers to bottle without filtration can be counter-productive.)

Bertrand Machard de Gramont, 13 rue de Vergy, 21700 Nuits-Saint-Georges

DOMAINE TIM MARSHALL   1.9 ha. (100 per cent)

Nuits-Saint-Georges Les Perrières 0.26 ha., Aux Argillats 0.18 ha., Chambolle-Musigny Les Cras 0.34 ha., Les Feusselottes 0.5 ha., Chambolle-Musigny 0.16 ha., Bourgogne (*rouge*) 0.25 ha., (*blanc*) 0.18 ha.

Tim Marshall is a Yorkshireman turned Burgundian, who, until scuttling his wine-broking business in 1993, pointed more than one confused Anglo-Saxon buyer in the direction of authentic, high-quality Burgundy. The wine from his own vineyards is mainly sold in France. He believes in slow fermentations, total de-stemming, and less new oak than in the past. He is a partner in the Meursault *négociant* ECVF Jean Germain.

Tim Marshall, 47c rue Henri Challand, 21701 Nuits-Saint-Georges

ALAIN MICHELOT   7.9 ha. (80 per cent)

Nuits-Saint-Georges Les Saint-Georges 0.2 ha., Vaucrains 0.68 ha., Cailles 0.88 ha., Porrets Saint-Georges 0.55 ha., Chaignots 0.4 ha., Richemones 0.55 ha., Champs Perdrix 0.52 ha., Nuits-Saint-Georges 2.75 ha., Morey-Saint-Denis Les Charrières 0.23 ha., Morey-Saint-Denis 0.27 ha., Bourgogne (*rouge*) 0.8 ha.

Here is a confident, reflective wine-maker, who adapts his methods to the year, and often succeeds well in vintages where others falter. He might remove 95 per cent of the stalks, then keep the fermentation going for eighteen or twenty days if possible, creating 'hot spots' in the vats, using ambient yeasts and progressively added sugar. Rackings will be minimal, the object (regularly achieved) being age-worthy wines, with character, balance and smoothness.

The estate was built up between the wars by Alain's father Emile Michelot, who began bottling for private customers and top restaurants – the latter being where to look, for these rich wines.

Alain Michelot, 8 rue Camille Rodier, 21700 Nuits-Saint-Georges.

P. MISSEREY, SA   6 ha. (1904)

Nuits-Saint-Georges Les Vaucrains 2 ha., Les Cailles 1 ha., Les Saint-Georges 1 ha., Aux Vignes Rondes 1 ha., Aux Murgers 1 ha.

The Misserey family has owned vines for four generations. It sells its grapes for vinification, tending and bottling by the company.
Olivier Lanvin, BP 10, 3 rue des Seuillets, 21702 Nuits-Saint-Georges

MOILLARD-GRIVOT (1850) 40 ha.

Chambertin Clos de Bèze 0.23 ha., Chambertin 0.06 ha., Bonnes Mares 0.15 ha., Clos de Vougeot 0.6 ha., Romanée-Saint-Vivant 0.17 ha., Vosne-Romanée Les Malconsorts 3.42 ha., Les Beaux Monts 0.93 ha., Nuits-Saint-Georges Clos de Thorey (Monopole) 4.11 ha., Clos des Grandes Vignes (Monopole) 2.12 ha., Les Richemones 0.89 ha., Les Porrets Saint-Georges 0.54 ha., Nuits-Saint-Georges 2.05 ha., Corton Clos du Roi 0.83 ha., Corton-Charlemagne 0.23 ha., Beaune Grèves 2.19 ha., Hautes Côtes de Nuits (*rouge* and *blanc*). The firm also distributes Corton Clos de Vergennes (Monopole) 2 ha.

The origins of this company go back as far as 1848, to the marriage of Marguerite Grivot and her vineyards with Symphorien Moillard and his.

Although owning 40 hectares of vines, the company is essentially a specialist merchant, now second in turnover on the Côte de Nuits to J.-C. Boisset. The Thomas family entirely owns the company. Moillard has three functions, according to its managing director, Denis Thomas: it owns the well-situated vineyards listed above; it was one of the first companies in Burgundy to buy grapes from the growers and assume responsibility for the vinification; and it fills the traditional role of buying, tending and bottling. There is a fourth: it acts as a stockholder and, to some extent, a banker for the Burgundy trade, as many firms draw wines from it, then put their own labels on.

It has experimented with must heating and new methods of vinification with the object of producing wines which are more 'supple and complete'. Yves Thomas was one of the first to design a vat (back in 1982) which would automatically do the job of punching down, which has been manufactured or adapted by at least three companies, so his son claims. Stainless steel rotating paddles and screws within the vat extract colour, tannin and glycerine more efficiently and rapidly than the traditional *pigeage*. One experimental vat increased to eight, and now to twenty-four or more.

Traditional, open vats may be used for small quantities of *Grands Crus*.

The firm sometimes uses pasteurization to solve a wine's stability problems, best results being achieved when the process is applied to young wines. Moillard exports extensively to around forty different countries.

I have found these wines a bit irregular, at times dense and well-balanced, showing lively fruit and potential, at others merely respectable, but unexciting. Sometimes they are excellent.

Denis Thomas, 2 rue François Mignotte, 21700 Nuits-Saint-Georges

DOMAINE BARBIER   14 ha. (65 per cent)

Gevrey-Chambertin 0.3 ha., Nuits-Saint-Georges 0.3 ha., Santenay 0.55 ha., Chassagne-Montrachet (*rouge*) 0.2 ha., Savigny- lès-Beaune 0.4 ha., Hautes Côtes de Beaune 2.1 ha., Hautes Côtes de Nuits (*rouge*) 4.5 ha., (*blanc*) 1.8 ha.

The Barbiers also run Moingeon-Gueneau Frères, whose sole activity is the making of Bourgogne Mousseux and Crémant de Bourgogne.

Vincent et Rémi Barbier, 2B rue des Seuillets, 21700 Nuits-Saint-Georges

DOMAINÉ-PRIEURE ROCH   3.8 ha. (100 per cent)

Clos de Vougeot 0.58 ha., Vosne-Romanée Clos Goillotte (Monopole) 0.55 ha., Hautes Maizières 0.6 ha., Vosne-Romanée 0.7 ha., Bourgogne Grand Ordinaire (*rouge*) 0.7 ha., (*blanc*) 0.62 ha.

Domaine-bottled BGO (Bourgogne Grand Ordinaire) is extremely unusual, BGO being usually despised, since it normally grows beyond the pale, over the railroad tracks, off-bounds from the magic-touched lands with pukka *appellations*. The white is made from stirred-up, barrel-fermented Chardonnay, the red from Gamay, with a proportion of Pinot, all grown in the plain below Vosne, at Boncourt-le-Bois. Both wines are excellent, and go to show that *terroir* counts for little if the wine-maker is a well-funded fanatic; in this case, he has the grandest connections with Vosne-Romanée, and is married to Jean-Louis Fougeray's daughter.

His wine-maker is Philippe Pacalet, who works with minimum sulphur levels (like Pacalet's uncle in the Beaujolais, Marcel Lapierre).

The wines of finer origins age in barrels from the Domaine de la Romanée-Conti, of which Henry-Frédéric Roch is now co-director, alongside Aubert de Villaine. His mother, Mme Pauline Roch is Mme Bize-Leroy's older sister. His own estate, once a Nuits Priory, is easy to find: the old Peugeot garage on the main road into Nuits going north, on the left before the lights, the pumps replaced by outsize, varnished oak quarter-vats. These bottles are very interesting, but one may need ample funds, for Leroy incantations were being chanted, it seemed to me, when they prepared the price-list.
Henry-Frédéric Roch, rue Général de Gaulle, 21700 Nuits-Saint-Georges

DOMAINE HENRI ET GILLES REMORIQUET   7.8 ha. (75 per cent)

Nuits-Saint-Georges Les Saint-Georges 0.2 ha., Rue de Chaux 0.4 ha., Les Damodes 0.5 ha., Les Bousselots 0.4 ha., Nuits-Saint-Georges 3.3 ha.

Gilles Remoriquet has been active in young growers' associations, and, on paper, seems to be doing many of the right things in vineyard and cellar. The bottle to stop me in my tracks from this address has not yet come my way.
Henri et Gilles Remoriquet, 25 rue de Charmois, 21700 Nuits-Saint-Georges

Main Prémeaux growers and merchants

BERTRAND AMBROISE   14 ha. (40 per cent)

Corton Le Rognet 0.7 ha., Nuits-Saint-Georges Rue de Chaux 0.4 ha., Vaucrains 0.12 ha., Nuits-Saint-Georges 3 ha., Côte de Nuits-Villages 2 ha., Bourgogne (*rouge*) 6 ha., (*blanc*) 0.5 ha.
Bertrand Ambroise, rue de l'Eglise, 21700 Prémeaux-Prissey

DOMAINE DE L'ARLOT   14 ha. (100 per cent)

Romanée-Saint-Vivant 0.25 ha., Vosne-Romanée Les Suchots 0.85 ha., Nuits-Saint-Georges Clos des Forêts Saint-Georges

(Monopole) 7 ha., Clos de l'Arlot (Monopole) (*rouge*) 2 ha., (*blanc*) 1 ha., Côte de Nuits-Villages Clos du Chapeau (Monopole) 1.5 ha.

Cellars and buildings here date back to the seventeenth century, surrounded by a nineteenth-century park: quite a contrast to most Côte de Nuits domaines. The property was bought by the French insurance company AXA in 1987 (which also owns Quinta do Noval, Château Pichon-Longueville-Baron and other Bordeaux châteaux), and has been much improved.

Jean-Pierre de Smet took his wine-making inspiration from Jacques Seysses, and these spacious old cellars are not the place to come for rustic, tannic expressions of the stony slopes of Nuits. These are amiable wines (particularly the Clos de l'Arlot), but there are also rich, elegant *cuvées* of the highest quality which are destined for ageing. This is also a rare source of white Nuits.

Jean-Pierre de Smet, Prémeaux, 21700 Nuits-Saint-Georges

DOMAINE JEAN-JACQUES CONFURON 7 ha. (90 per cent)

Romanée-Saint-Vivant 0.5 ha., Clos de Vougeot 0.52 ha. (top), Vosne-Romanée Beaux-Monts 0.3 ha., Chambolle-Musigny *Premier Cru* 0.35 ha., Nuits-Saint-Georges Chaboeufs 0.48 ha., Boudots 0.3 ha. (Les Fleurières) 1.23 ha., Chambolle-Musigny 1.15 ha., Côte de Nuits-Villages Les Vignottes 1.3 ha., Bourgogne (*rouge*), Aligoté

Working conditions used to be very simple here, but a fine new cellar and vat-house have been built. Having sometimes bought here, I look forward to tasting again.

Sophie et Alain Meunier, Prémeaux-Prissey, 21700 Nuits-Saint-Georges

R. DUBOIS ET FILS 17 ha. (100 per cent)

Nuits-Saint-Georges Clos des Argillières 0.43 ha., Les Porêts Saint-Georges 0.57 ha., Chambolle-Musigny 0.25 ha., Vosne-Romanée 0.2 ha., Nuits-Saint-Georges 3 ha., Beaune 0.3 ha., Savigny-lès-Beaune 0.8 ha., Côte de Nuits-Villages 3.75 ha., Hautes Côtes de Beaune (*blanc*), Bourgogne (*rouge*) 4.5 ha.

Highly mechanized, this estate can be a good source for bottles at low-end or mid-price, but I would not personally choose its First Growths.

Régis Dubois, Prémeaux-Prissey, 21700 Nuits-Saint-Georges

DOMAINE DES PERDRIX 12 ha. (50 per cent)

Echézeaux 1.5 ha., Nuits-Saint-Georges Les Perdrix (Monopole) 3.5 ha., Nuits-Saint-Georges *Premier Cru* 1 ha., Vosne-Romanée 1.5 ha., Nuits-Saint-Georges 1.5 ha.

Most of these wines go to French regulars.

Bernard et Thierry Mugneret-Gouachon, Prémeaux-Prissey, 21700 Nuits-Saint-Georges

DOMAINE DU CHÂTEAU DE PRÉMEAUX 10 ha.

Nuits-Saint-Georges *Premier Cru* 0.9 ha., Nuits-Saint-Georges 2 ha., Côte de Nuits-Villages 1.5 ha., Bourgogne *rouge* 4 ha., Passe-Tout-Grains 0.5 ha., Bourgogne Aligoté 0.8 ha.

Alain Pelletier, Prémeaux-Prissey, 21700 Nuits-Saint-Georges

DOMAINE DANIEL RION ET FILS 19.08 ha. (100 per cent)
DOMAINE MICHÈLE ET PATRICE RION

Clos de Vougeot 0.73 ha., Vosne-Romanée Les Beaumonts 1.07 ha., Les Chaumes 0.42 ha., Vosne-Romanée 1.87 ha., Chambolle-Musigny Les Charmes 0.41 ha., Les Beaux Bruns 0.32 ha., Les Cras 0.46 ha., Nuits-Saint-Georges Les Hauts Pruliers 0.42 ha., Aux Vignes Rondes 0.46 ha., Clos des Argillières 0.72 ha., Les Terres Blanches (*Pinot blanc*) 0.55 ha., Nuits-Saint-Georges 2.45 ha., Côte de Nuits-Villages 1.55 ha., Bourgogne Pinot Noir 2.22 ha., Passe-Tout-Grains 0.66 ha., Hautes Côtes de Nuits (*blanc*) 2.3 ha., Chardonnay 0.22 ha., Aligoté 1.26 ha.

Patrice Rion is one of Burgundy's leading and most accomplished wine-makers, operating from a purpose-built (1980) winery and cellar, always pushing out frontiers, whether it be towards organic vine-growing, comparison of barrel sources, or getting the most out of his Passe-Tout-Grains.

There is a similarity about the wines in this cellar which can detract from the pleasure of tasting up the range; however, that is a small price to pay for luscious, ripe fruitiness, which is what we, most dependably, will get. These wines, after all, are made to be drunk bottle by bottle, on all sorts of occasions, not to make barrel-tastings for cellar-rats tasting them all over half an hour.

I have sometimes found myself wondering why he applies similar wine-making methods to First Growths and to Bourgogne from the *bas de côteaux* (the flat-lands). Low temperature maceration gives rich purple colours, certainly, with a lot of fruit. We need these things in Bourgogne *rouge*, or Côte de Nuits-Villages. In Chambolle Charmes, or Vosne Les Chaumes, on the other hand, I wonder. However, Rion's wines get finer each time I taste them. Marked by his personality, they have a family resemblance.

Here there is no recital of *terroir* clichés, as often voiced by technically unsound traditionalists. Instead, you learn that he is bottling his best wines into special bottles with high protection in the glass against ultra-violet rays, so the wines will suffer minimum damage in the distribution channels. Patrice Rion's consumers are being considered right down the line. And of course there are trials with wood origins, ages and coopers. Irrespective of this subtle experimentation, we may count on the highest level of grower dependability.

Patrice Rion, Prémeaux, 21700 Nuits-Saint-Georges

Côte de Nuits and Hautes Côtes de Nuits ▷

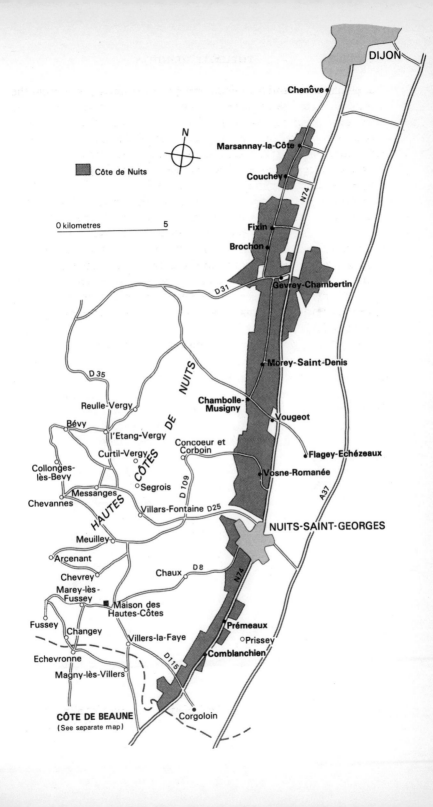

Côte de Nuits

N

0 kilometres   5

DIJON

Chenôve

Marsannay-la-Côte

Couchey

N74

Fixin

Brochon

Gevrey-Chambertin

D 31

Morey-Saint-Denis

D 35

Reulle-Vergy

Chambolle-Musigny

Bévy

l'Etang-Vergy

Vougeot

Curtil-Vergy

Concoeur et Corboin

Flagey-Echézeaux

Collonges-lès-Bevy

CÔTES DE NUITS

Vosne-Romanée

Segrois

D 109

Messanges

A 37

Chevannes

HAUTES

Villars-Fontaine   D25

NUITS-SAINT-GEORGES

Meuilley

Arcenant

Chevrey

Chaux   D 8

Marey-lès-Fussey

N74

Maison des Hautes-Côtes

Fussey

Changey

Villers-la-Faye

Prémeaux

Prissey

Echevronne

Comblanchien

Magny-lès-Villers

D 115

CÔTE DE BEAUNE
(See separate map)

Corgoloin

18

Côtes Frontier Land: Côte de Nuits-Villages, Côte de Beaune-Villages, Hautes Côtes de Nuits and Hautes Côtes de Beaune

COTE DE NUITS-VILLAGES

Between Prémeaux and Ladoix, the first village of the Côte de Beaune, the scenery changes abruptly, for the Côte is dominated by large tips, the refuse of marble quarrying. Quarrying on a large scale dates from the Second Empire, when mechanical saws made it possible to obtain thin slabs, two to four centimetres thick, and the new railway carried the marble to the capital. The first quarry is above the Poirets vineyard of Nuits-Saint-Georges. It produces Rose de Prémeaux, not a wine but a compact light-pink limestone, in which can be seen the fossilized holes of tiny organisms which burrowed in the ooze before it solidified. It takes an excellent polish. Comblanchien marble proper is the stratum above the Prémeaux. It is a clear beige colour, and was used to build the Paris Opéra and Orly airport. It is also widely seen in the Côte d'Or, as flooring in the houses of successful growers and shippers.

Leaving Nuits on the road towards Beaune one crosses three communes, Prémeaux-Prissey, Comblanchien and Corgoloin, some of whose wines may be sold under the *appellation* Côte de Nuits-Villages. Fixin and Brochon at the northern extremity of the Côte de Nuits also have that right.

Côte de Nuits-Villages is an *appellation* which may be applied to wines from Fixin (if they are not well-placed enough to be called Fixin, but better situated than to rate as Bourgogne) and from good sites in the four other villages: Corgoloin, Comblanchien, Brochon and Prémeaux. In 1991 there were 154.15 ha. in production for red wines, with a tiny amount for white: 1.13 ha., the five-year average production (1988–92) for Côte de Nuits-Villages being 74,800 cases of red wine, and 750 cases of white.

Côte de Nuits-Villages growers (based in Comblanchien and Corgoloin)

DOMAINE CHOPIN ET FILS   11.5 ha. (60 per cent)

Nuits-Saint-Georges Murgers 0.34 ha., Nuits-Saint-Georges 1.72 ha., Chambolle-Musigny 0.39 ha., Côte de Nuits-Villages 6.09 ha., Bourgogne (*rouge*) 1.23 ha.

It is tempting to transfer allegiance to this grower, given that Chopin-Groffier rarely has enough wine, but the latter is in a different league.

Yves et André (père) Chopin, Comblanchien, 21700 Nuits-Saint-Georges

DANIEL CHOPIN-GROFFIER   7 ha. (90 per cent)

Clos de Vougeot 0.35 ha., Nuits-Saint-Georges Chaignots 0.4 ha., Vougeot 0.4 ha., Nuits-Saint-Georges 0.5 ha., Côte de Nuits-Villages 3.3 ha., Bourgogne (*rouge*) 1.7 ha., (*blanc*) 0.3 ha.

A terrible old-parchment label, but it takes more than that to discourage a serious Burgundy lover, and here one does not have to seek out *Grands* or *Premiers Crus*; the Bourgogne *rouge* can also be wonderful.

Daniel Chopin, rue Claude Henry, 21700 Comblanchien

RENÉ DURAND   15 ha. (90 per cent)

Corton-Rognet 0.36 ha., Aloxe-Corton 0.83 ha., Nuits-Saint-Georges 0.3 ha., Ladoix 0.75 ha., Côte de Nuits-Villages 10 ha., Bourgogne and Aligoté

These red wines may age one-third in new oak, the balance in slightly older barrels and, unusually, large casks or tuns, so the fruitiness may be preserved.

René Durand, Grand'Rue, Comblanchien, 21700 Nuits-Saint-Georges

GERARD JULIEN   12 ha. (90 per cent)

Echézeaux 0.23 ha., Nuits-Saint-Georges 2 ha., Côte de Nuits-Villages 1 ha., Corton-Renardes 0.16 ha., Aloxe-Corton 0.6 ha.

I have found this a useful source of dependable values, particularly the Côte de Nuits-Villages.

Gérard Julien, Comblanchien, 21700 Nuits-Saint-Georges

DOMAINE DE LA POULETTE   14 ha. (80 per cent)

Nuits-Saint-Georges Vaucrains 2 ha., Les Poulettes 1 ha., Chaboeufs 0.5 ha., Vosne-Romanée Suchots 0.25 ha., Nuits-Saint-Georges Les Brûlées 1 ha., Côte de Nuits-Villages 4 ha.

Mme Michaut-Audidier, Corgoloin, 21700 Nuits-Saint-Georges

CÔTE DE BEAUNE-VILLAGES

Côte de Beaune-Villages is an *appellation* which may be applied to red wines from good sites in sixteen communes of the Côte d'Or and Saône-et-Loire. The wine is made from land classified good enough to carry the individual *appellations* of those villages, if the growers so wish, the relevant *appellations* being: Auxey-Duresses, Blagny, Chassagne-Montrachet, Chorey-lès-Beaune, Ladoix, Maranges, Meursault, Monthelie, Pernand-Vergelesses, Puligny-Montrachet, Saint-Aubin, Saint-Romain, Santenay, and Savigny-lès-Beaune. A grower is not allowed to make Côte de Beaune-Villages from his Pinots in Aloxe-Corton, Beaune, Pommard or Volnay, the four best red wine villages of the Côte de Beaune.

It is a complicated piece of AC legislation, designed to give growers every possible chance of selling wines which have tended to stick. The same red wine could be sold, to take one example, either as Auxey-Duresses, or as Côte de Beaune-Villages, or as Auxey-Côte de Beaune. A grower must choose a name at harvest time, but may change his or her mind later. Yes, of course this can be reconciled with the concepts of the sanctity of original Burgundian *terroirs*, it just needs to be taken slowly.

No doubt to keep us concentrating on our studies, and to foil anyone who might think he or she had talked, read and tasted sufficiently broadly in Burgundy to have got clear the individuality and quality levels of those three AC groups, the authorities have thrown in a fourth, a wine called Côte de Beaune, which is allowed to be white as well as red. This, however, is a specific, tiny *appellation*, details of which may be found in the chapter on Beaune.

There is little point trying to establish a production area for Côte de Beaune-Villages, for this would be the sum of all the red vineyard land, at village *appellation* level, in the sixteen communes. The five-year average production (1988–92) for Côte de Beaune-Villages (to arrive at it Auxey-Côte de Beaune, Blagny-Côte de Beaune etc. have all been added together) was 24,000 cases of red wine.

Côte de Beaune-Villages growers

For growers making Côte de Beaune-Villages, reference may be made to the individual communes producing the village *appellations* listed above.

THE RENAISSANCE OF THE HAUTES CÔTES

Leave the valley of the Saône behind you, break up through the Côte, and you find yourself in a constantly changing countryside of small hills, plateaux and streams. It is an area which has come to life again over the last twenty years, producing fine wine. There are about 350 wine growers, in over forty communes, cultivating over 1,000 hectares of vineyard by 1990. Approximately a quarter belong to the Cooperative des Hautes Côtes, its premises based on the Pommard road out of Beaune. Many growers still combine wine-making with the growing of *petits fruits* – raspberries and blackcurrants – and some still keep a cow or a pig, a horse or a flock of sheep.

It is on average 100 metres higher than the Côte de Beaune or Nuits, and cold air moves quickly through these little valleys, so only those slopes facing between south-east and south-west are worth planting to vineyards. But geologically it can be identical to the more famous Côtes. The exact rock strata of the hill of Corton may be found in the Hautes Côtes de Nuits, and its subsoils are made up of fossil-rich Jurassic limestone, where may be seen petrified corals, sea-urchins, algae and oysters. The same clays and fine sands mingle with the eroded limestones.

A century ago there was five times the area of vineyards, then gradually the hillsides were taken over by thorn and bramble. After the phylloxera, replanting had been done with Gamay, or Franco-American hybrids; both produced wines which were little more than ordinary. Mechanization was difficult, and the wines were undercut in price by higher-strength *ordinaires* from the Midi and Algeria. Many families had been ruined by the costs of reconstituting the vineyards, and scarcely had the means to fight mildew or oidium. One man in ten never returned from the Great War. As J.-F. Bazin recounted,[1] in one commune of the Hautes Côtes de Nuits, Arcenant, the area under vines dropped from 360 hectares in 1880, to 230 by 1913 to 40 in 1957.

Vines have been recorded in the Hautes Côtes since AD 761, when a vineyard in Meuilley was given to the Church, according to Dr Lavalle. The Ducal Accounts of 1381 record that Philip the Bold had cellars in Beaune, Pommard, Volnay, Monthelie – and Meloisey, in the Hautes Côtes. Meloisey's wine had been served at the Coronation of Philip-Augustus in 1180.

In August 1961 the Hautes Côtes were granted the right to the *appellations* Bourgogne Hautes Côtes de Nuits or Beaune, and planting proceeded, above all with Pinot Noir. With hindsight, this can be seen as perhaps an error, for the Pinot has difficulty ripening here, where the Chardonnay ripens more successfully. High-vine, lyre-training systems were permitted, which are much cheaper to install.

Hautes Côtes de Nuits

Bourgogne Hautes Côtes de Nuits is produced in eighteen Côte d'Or communes. The law obliges growers to put the word Bour-gogne in front, the marketing experts at INAO having no doubt decided (if they consider these matters) that forcing consumers and foreigners to say five French words to buy a bottle of simple wine would be a good idea, and might even help establish the fame and success of this struggling little area.

The area planted to Hautes Côtes de Nuits in 1991 was 434.36 ha. (red), and 75.42 ha. (white), the five-year average production (1988–92) having been respectively 169,100 and 24,100 cases.

1 *Le Vignoble des Hautes Côtes de Nuits et de Beaune*, Les Cahiers de Vergy, 1973.

Hautes Côtes de Nuits growers

YVES CHALEY   12 ha. (100 per cent)

Hautes Côtes de Nuits (*rouge*) 7.5 ha., (*blanc*) 2 ha., Pinot Beurot 0.25 ha., Aligoté 2.5 ha., Passe-Tout-Grains 1 ha.
  Chaley also has a *négoçiant* licence enabling him to buy grapes and vinify.
Yves Chaley, Curtil-Vergy, 21220 Gevrey-Chambertin

DOMAINE CORNU   16 ha. (60 per cent)

Corton 0.63 ha., Côte de Nuits-Villages 2 ha., Savigny-lès-Beaune 0.25 ha., Pernand-Vergelesses 0.39 ha., Ladoix 0.93 ha., Hautes Côtes de Nuits (*rouge*) 4 ha., (*blanc*) 0.53 ha., Hautes Côtes de Beaune (*rouge*) 2 ha., (*blanc*) 0.6 ha., Passe-Tout-Grains, Aligoté, Crémant de Bourgogne.
  This has become a more dependable cellar than in the past, but I have found the fine *appellations* – Côte de Nuits-Villages, Ladoix and Corton – significantly more worthwhile than the minor ones.
Claude Cornu, Magny-lès-Villers, 21700 Nuits-Saint-Georges

DOMAINE FRIBOURG MARCEL ET BERNARD   18 ha. (70 per cent)

Côte de Nuits-Villages 1.57 ha., Bourgogne Hautes Côtes de Nuits (*rouge*) 8.77 ha., (*blanc*) 1.33 ha., Bourgogne Passe-Tout-Grains and Aligoté
Marcel et Bernard Fribourg, Villers-la-Faye, 21700 Nuits-Saint-Georges

BERNARD HUDELOT-VERDEL   17 ha. (100 per cent)
DOMAINE DE MONTMAIN

Hautes Côtes de Nuits Les Genevrières (*rouge*) 6 ha., Le Rouard (*blanc*) 3.5 ha., Bourgognes Hautes Côtes de Nuits
  Bernard Hudelot is an oenologist, and one of the most dynamic Hautes Côtes wine-makers. New wood is much in evidence for his best wines, which appear with their individual site-names.
Bernard Hudelot-Verdel, Villars-Fontaine, 21700 Nuits Saint-Georges

DOMAINE PATRICK HUDELOT   24 ha. (80 per cent)
HENRY HUDELOT

Nuits-Saint-Georges Bousselots 0.19 ha., Hautes Côtes de Nuits Les Genevrières 4 ha., Les Roncières 1.75 ha., Hautes Côtes de Nuits (*blanc*) 5.5 ha., Aligoté

Hudelot cultivates vineyards and makes wine for Michel Feuillat, Dijon University's Oenology Professor, so there are often experimental *cuvées* here. His single-vineyard Genevrières is a magnificent hillside site, giving rich, firm wine of good length.

Patrick Hudelot, 21700 Villars-Fontaine.

ROBERT JAYER-GILLES   11 ha. (100 per cent)

Echézeaux 0.54 ha., Nuits-Saint-Georges Hauts Poirets 0.3 ha., Damodes 0.11 ha., Côte de Nuits-Villages 1.31 ha., Hautes Côtes de Nuits (*rouge*) 2.37 ha., (*blanc*) 1.33 ha., Hautes Côtes de Beaune (*rouge*) 1.02 ha., (*blanc*) 1.01 ha., Passe-Tout-Grains and Aligoté

Jayer-Gilles delivers a powerfully rich mouthful of flavours, in which new oak plays a vast part – too much for my taste, in Côte de Nuits-Villages and the *appellations* downwards in the pyramid from it.

New oaking can be a highly profitable route to take. In 1993 a new barrel was costing 2,300 fr., resaleable two years later for approximately 1,300 fr. The difference, 1,000 fr. (tax deductible, spread over two years) might represent less than 2 fr. per bottle, but could add 15 fr. per bottle, or more, to a selling price – and immensely speed the sale (to customers hooked on oak-juice compounds). I know these wines have given, and still give, pleasure to many people, but I cannot believe the fashion for this amount of oakiness in minor *appellations* will last.

Robert et Gilles Jayer-Gilles, Magny-lès-Villers, 21700 Nuits-Saint-Georges

HENRI NAUDIN-FERRAND   15.11 ha. (100 per cent)

Ladoix *Premier Cru* La Corvée 0.35 ha., Côte de Nuits-Villages 1.45 ha., Hautes Côtes de Nuits 1.28 ha., Hautes Côtes de Beaune (*rouge*) 4.84 ha., (*blanc*) 0.85 ha., Aligoté 4.54 ha., Passe-Tout-Grains 1.03 ha., Bourgogne (*rosé*) 0.47 ha.

This is one of the best sources in the Hautes Côtes for carefully made, charming wines. Both of Henri Naudin's daughters are qualified oenologists, in addition Claire being an agronomical, and Anne an agricultural engineer (with experience at Sonoma Cutrer). New oak is used judiciously and subtly. An excellent source of Côte de Nuits-Villages and First Growth Ladoix (though this is rare).

Henri, Anne et Claire Naudin, Magny-lès-Villers, 21700 Nuits-Saint-Georges

SIMON FILS   14 ha. (90 per cent)

Bourgogne Hautes Cotes de Nuits (*rouge*) 7 ha., (*blanc*) 1.5 ha., Bourgogne Les Dames Huguettes (Pinot Noir) 2 ha.

Guy et Paul Simon, Marey-lès-Fussey, 21700 Nuits-Saint-Georges

DOMAINE THÉVENOT LE BRUN ET FILS   26.5 ha. (90 per cent)

Bourgogne Hautes Côtes de Nuits Clos du Vignon Monopole (*rouge*) 5.1 ha., (*blanc*) 1.15 ha., Hautes Côtes de Nuits (*rouge*) 5 ha., (*blanc*) 3.05 ha., Hautes Côtes de Beaune (*rouge*) 1.8 ha., Passe-Tout-Grains 3.6 ha., Aligoté Perles d'Or 3.8 ha., Cassis 6.5 ha.

An unusually high 40 per cent of this estate's production is white, including some Pinot Beurot in the Clos du Vignon, which has almost the body of a red wine, though less finesse than Chardonnay. Since 1970 they offer an Aligoté *perlant*, with double the normal carbon dioxide dissolved in it, after bottling directly from the lees. It keeps its youthfulness really well. Weather permitting, using well-tried methods, they make lovely wines here, of real interest every year. Their Cassis is excellent, and they do Framboise too.

Maurice et Jean et Daniel Thévenot, Marey-lès-Fussey, 21700 Nuits Saint Georges

ALAIN VERDET   8 ha. (100 per cent)

Bourgogne Hautes Côtes de Nuits (*rouge* and *rosé*) 6.2 ha., Bourgogne (*blanc*) Chardonnay 1.5 ha., Bourgogne Aligoté 0.3 ha.

'If you have a headache from my wines I give you your money back' says Verdet, who has tended his vines and wines organically since 1971 – without chemical or synthetic products, weedkillers or pesticides. He clips his vineyards, and bottles his wines, under a waning moon, and makes all treatments with rain-water. He draws his new oak staves from five sources: Fontainebleau, Tronçais, Saint-Palais, Vosges and Bourgogne. He seems to have entirely mastered the tricky work of fine, organic wine-making in the Hautes Côtes, and I find his wines deliciously full of life and character, particularly the reds.

Alain Verdet, Arcenant, 21700 Nuits-Saint-Georges

VIGOT-BATTAULT, THIERRY   3.5 ha. (100 per cent)

Echézeaux 0.4 ha., Vosne-Romanée Les Gaudichots 0.2 ha., Nuits-Saint-Georges 0.23 ha., Hautes Côtes de Nuits (*rouge*) 1.38 ha., (*blanc*) 0.5 ha., Passe-Tout-Grains and Aligoté

This estate dates from 1987, and Remington Norman thinks Vigot should be encouraged. Alternatively, early encouragement went to his head, when he was praised (by no means immoderately) by Clive Coates in *The Vine* no. 62 (March 1990). The immediate result was a firming-up of his prices to levels which only a foreigner, with not much time but a frantic wish to go home having latched on to a flavour-of-the-month, would be pleased to pay. Enthusiasm by journalists keen to make a splash can sometimes be counter-productive to the wine-drinker's interest. If writers make discoveries, then trumpet them over the heads of the traders whose job it is to agree the value and risk the cash to distribute the stocks, they, the writers, can unwittingly fire up prices.

Thierry Vigot, Grande Rue, 21220 Messanges

Hautes Côtes de Beaune

Bourgogne Hautes-Côtes de Beaune is produced in twenty-two Côte d'Or and seven Saône-et-Loire communes. The law obliges growers to put the word Bourgogne in front, the fledgling marketing department at INAO having perhaps concluded that sales of wines with the simple mention Bourgogne on them had become so startlingly successful world-wide (to the extent that any wine thus labelled positively flew off the shelf without an assistant even having to point at it) that they could do no better than to portmanteau it into the new high-hillside concept, thus immeasurably speeding the return to prosperity of this struggling, scattered area.

The area planted to Hautes Côtes de Beaune in 1991 was 322.8 ha. (red), and 48.6 ha. (white), the five-year average production (1988–92) having been respectively 147,400 and 21,800 cases.

Hautes Côtes de Beaune growers

JEAN-NOEL BAZIN   9 ha. (30 per cent)

Chassagne-Montrachet La Maltroie 0.13 ha., Meursault 1 ha., Auxey-Duresses (*rouge*) 0.56 ha., (*blanc*) 0.41 ha., Hautes Côtes de Beaune (*rouge*) 2.5 ha., (*blanc*) 1 ha., Aligoté
   Much of the Bazin's land at La Rochepot is light, limestone soil, so more appropriate for Chardonnay than Pinot.
Jean-Noël Bazin, rte de Saint-Aubin, 21340 La Rochepot

DOMAINE BOULEY   10 ha. (100 per cent)

Bourgogne Hautes Côtes de Beaune (*rouge*) 8 ha., (*blanc*) 0.5 ha., Bourgogne Passe-Tout-Grains 0.5 ha., Aligoté 0.5 ha., Crémant de Bourgogne 0.5 ha.
Jean-Claude Bouley, Change, 21340 Nolay

DENIS CARRÉ   11 ha. (95 per cent)

Meursault Tillets 0.6 ha., Pommard *Premier Cru* 0.3 ha., Pommard 0.8 ha., Auxey-Duresses 0.55 ha., Saint-Romain 0.48 ha., Bourgogne Hautes Côtes de Beaune 3.5 ha., Bourgogne Chardonnay 0.3 ha., Passe-Tout-Grains and Aligoté
   One of the largest and most dynamic Hautes Côtes estates.
Denis Carré, rue du Puits Bouret, Meloisey, 21190 Meursault

FRANÇOIS CHARLES   11 ha. (90 per cent)

Volnay Frémiets 0.6 ha., Clos de la Cave des Ducs (Monopole) 0.4 ha., Beaune Epenottes 0.55 ha., Pommard 1 ha., Bourgogne Hautes Côtes de Beaune (*rouge*) 5 ha., (*blanc*) 0.45 ha., Passe-Tout-Grains 2 ha.
   The Volnay Monopole is not a *Premier Cru*, but is uphill from the D'Angerville Clos des Ducs, properly surrounded by 2-metre walls. France, Germany and Holland are the main customers here.
François Charles et Fils, Nantoux, 21190 Meursault

DOMAINE DU CHÂTEAU DE MANDELOT   15.22 ha.

Bourgogne Hautes Côtes de Beaune 5.06 ha., Bourgogne Passe-Tout-Grains 8.42 ha., Bourgogne Aligoté 1.74 ha.

The owner, Mme P. Dromard, is related to the Bouchard family, and Bouchard Père et Fils is responsible for the vineyards and wine-making at the château.

PAUL & EMMANUEL GILBOULOT
DOMAINE DES CHENES   6.3 ha. (50 per cent)

Beaune Lulune 0.38 ha., Côte de Beaune La Grande Châtelaine (*blanc*) 2.3 ha., Hautes Côtes de Nuits (*rouge*) 2.2 ha., (*blanc*) 1 ha., Rully (*blanc*) 0.23 ha.

Emmanuel Giboulot is a conscientious bio-dynamist, associated with two other organic wine growers: Jean-Claude Rateau (q.v.) in Beaune and Marcel & Thierry Guyot in Saint-Romain.
Emmanuel Giboulot, Combertault, 21200 Beaune

LES CAVES DES HAUTES CÔTES   348.5 ha. (75 per cent)

Chambertin 0.05 ha., Mazis-Chambertin 0.04 ha., Charmes-Chambertin 0.23 ha., Gevrey-Chambertin Les Cherbaudes 0.22 ha., Les Corbeaux 0.09 ha., Clos du Chapitre (Monopole) 0.97 ha., Gevrey-Chambertin 0.8 ha., Nuits-Saint-Georges Les Pruliers 0.52 ha., Les Procès 0.54 ha., Les Thoreys 0.34 ha., Les Vignes Rondes 0.35 ha., Pommard Pézerolles 0.25 ha., Petit Epenots 0.9 ha., Charmots 0.2 ha., Saint Aubin En Remilly 0.53 ha. Bourgogne Hautes Côtes de Beaune and Nuits, Bourgogne (*rouge* and *blanc*), Aligoté, Passe-Tout-Grains

The main activity here is of course the wines of the Hautes Côtes, but in addition they vinify an astonishing range of *appellations* for a co-operative.

This cellar is the largest vinification unit in the Côte d'Or, handling the production of 5 per cent of its vineyards. Here have been grouped the Caves Coopératives of Pommard, Gevrey-Chambertin, Orches and the Hautes Côtes.[2]

At any moment they have wines ageing in 2,000 barrels (a quar-

---

2 There are other Côte d'Or *coopératives*: Nuits-Saint-Georges, which sells its grapes to Boisset, I believe, and two small ones in Morey-Saint-Denis.

ter are bought anew each year), and a million bottles in stock. To vinify this large volume, they have built a line of vats which are connected to 'de-ballasting' vats, at a lower level. Instead of punching down, the must runs out by gravity, and the hat of grape skins is broken up as it falls through fixed cables in the top third of each vat. The fermenting juice is then sprinkled back over the grape skins, extracting colour and aroma as it trickles through it. I do not know of this system being used elsewhere in Burgundy, but something similar happens at Château Lynch-Bages, for instance, where the must may be run underground, then back up and over. They also have automatic vinification (Vinimatic) vats, half of their red wines being made by each method.

They have equipped themselves with the gentlest of wine-pumps, such as are used by fish breeders for moving their fry harmlessly, from one fish-tank to another.

Evidently, they are well equipped to handle large quantities of wine, but the red wines can have an extractive character, and a tannic finish verging on coarseness. The less ambitious Hautes Côtes *cuvées* can be excellent, inexpensive buys.
Jean-Louis Giraud, Groupement de Propriétaires-Récoltants, route de Pommard, 21220 Beaune

DOMAINE LUCIEN JACOB   13 ha. (60 per cent)

Savigny-lès-Beaune Vergelesses 0.75 ha., Savigny-lès-Beaune 4 ha., Pernand-Vergelesses 0.25 ha., Bourgogne Hautes Côtes de Beaune 7 ha., Bourgogne Aligoté 1 ha., Cassis Noir de Bourgogne 22 ha.
Lucien, Chantal et Jean-Michel Jacob, Echevronne, 21420 Savigny-lès-Beaune

JEAN-BAPTISTE JOANNET

The Hautes Côtes are famous for their fruits, and many wine-growers grow blackcurrants and raspberries as well as grapes. In most cases they have a specialist, such as Joannet, to turn them into *crèmes* and liqueurs. Here may be found a liqueur from the fruit of the little peach trees that used to be so common in the vineyards of both Côtes (most have been torn out to allow tractor turning space), liqueurs from raspberry, apricot and sloe, from tomato, wild rose hip, cassis of course, strawberry and blackberry (the last particularly wonderful). There are also cherries in alcohol. Sloe liqueur (*prunelle*) may last well for four years, wild rose for two, raspberry and cassis for twelve months but the blackberry (*liqueur de mûre*) needs to be drunk when fresh in bottle or within nine or ten months.

Jean-Baptiste et Gilles Joannet, Liqueurs, 21700 Arcenant

DOMAINE JEAN JOLIOT & FILS   10.5 ha. (60 per cent)

Pommard 1.25 ha., Beaune Boucherottes 0.50 ha., Hautes Côtes de Beaune (*rouge*) 5 ha., (*blanc*) 0.5 ha., Meursault 2.25 ha., Crémant, Aligoté, Passe-Tout-Grains

This is one of Frank Schoonmaker's original domaines, now making Hautes Côtes Pinot Noir of great purity and fine, youthful fruit which also ages well.

Jean-Baptiste Joliot, Nantoux, 21190 Meursault

MAZILLY PÈRE ET FILS   13 ha. (90 per cent)

Pommard les Poutures 0.8 ha., Pommard (Noisons) 0.95 ha., Beaune Vignes Franches 0.3 ha., Les Montrevenots 0.45 ha., Cent Vignes 0.2 ha., Volnay 0.1 ha., Savigny-lès-Beaune Narbantons 0.25 ha., Meursault 0.8 ha., Monthelie 0.1 ha., Hautes Côtes de Beaune Clos du Bois Prévot (Monopole) (*rouge*) 2.2 ha., (*blanc*) 0.2 ha., Le Clou 0.75 ha., Hautes Côtes de Beaune (*rouge*) 4.25 ha., Hautes Côtes de Beaune La Perrière (*blanc*) 0.85 ha., Pinot Beurot 0.3 ha., Passe-Tout-Grains 1.2 ha.

Mazilly is a dynamic figure in the Hautes Côtes, but not always successful in drawing charms from hillsides.

Frédéric Mazilly, Meloisey, 21190 Meursault

DIDIER MONTCHOVET   6 ha. (70 per cent)

Beaune Aux Couchérias 0.33 ha., Vignes Franches 0.2 ha., Pommard 0.75 ha., Hautes Côtes de Beaune (*rouge*) 1.5 ha., (*blanc*) 0.2 ha., Aligoté 1 ha., Passe-Tout-Grains 0.2 ha.

Didier Montchovet's estate has been cultivated organically and bio-dynamically since 1984, he and Jean-Claude Rateau in Beaune being the first Côte d'Or growers to choose this route. Montchovet has been a consultant oenologist to the BIVB, and still teaches wine-

tasting at the Lycée Viticole in Beaune. A further 3 hectares of lyre-trained Hautes Côtes de Beaune (red and white) are coming into production. This looks set to become one of Burgundy's leading green estates.
Christine et Didier Montchovet, Nantoux, 21190 Meursault

DOMAINE CLAUDE NOUVEAU   14.25 ha. (75 per cent)

Santenay Grand Clos Rousseau 1.1 ha., Clos Rousseau 0.64 ha., Les Charmes Dessus 0.9 ha., Santenay (*rouge*) 2.3 ha., (*blanc*) 1 ha., Maranges La Fussière and Côte de Beaune-Villages 1.5 ha., Bourgogne Hautes Côtes de Beaune 4.5 ha., Bourgogne Pinot Noir 1.5 ha., Bourgogne Aligoté 0.8 ha.

This carefully-run estate is off the beaten track, and has determined and conscientious owners, though regrettably with a surname which can divert consumers' thoughts towards new Beaujolais – with which there is absolutely no connection. The trip to Marchezeuil-Change (a Burgundy village of which many are unaware) is definitely worth making. It is just a few minutes beyond Santenay.
Claude et Mireille Nouveau, Marchezeuil-Change, 21340 Nolay

MICHEL SERVEAU   8.5 ha. (40 per cent)

Chassagne-Montrachet (*rouge*) 0.54 ha., (*blanc*) 0.2 ha., Saint-Aubin (*rouge*) 0.5 ha., Hautes Côtes de Beaune (*rouge*) 3 ha., Passe-Tout-Grains 1.5 ha., Aligoté 2 ha.

A Hautes Côtes grower of whom I have heard good things, where I hope one day to pay a visit and taste.
Michel Serveau, La Rochepot, 21340 Nolay

Of course, some of the largest estates in the Hautes Côtes are owned by growers and merchants from the Côte. Bouchard Père of Beaune controls the Château de Mandelot with its vines, as mentioned above; Domaine Jean Gros has vineyards at Chevrey near Arcenant; Méo-Camuzet has recently planted Chardonnay; Bertagna has vineyards above Nuits-Saint-Georges; Dominique Guyon of Savigny has 20 hectares in a single block on the south-facing Myon hillside in Meuilley. I understand this took some assembling, for there were 350 individual plots and seventy owners, who had to be seen one by one.

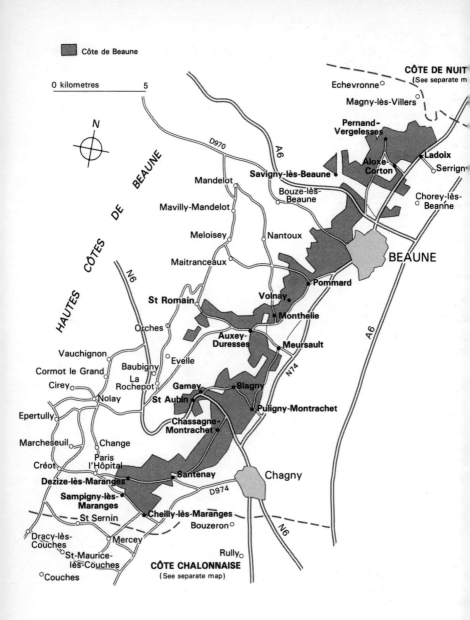

Echevronne

Magny-lès-Villers

Pernand-
Vergelesses

Aloxe-
Corton

Ladoix

Serrign

Chorey-lès-
Beanne

BEAUNE

Savigny-lès-Beaune

Mandelot

Bouze-lès-
Beaune

Mavilly-Mandelot

Meloisey

Nantoux

Maitranceaux

Pommard

St Romain

Volnay

Monthelie

Orches

Auxey-
Duresses

Meursault

Vauchignon

Evelle

Baubigny

La
Rochepot

Gamay

Blagny

St Aubin

Cormot le Grand

Cirey

Nolay

Puligny-Montrachet

Chassagne-
Montrachet

Epertully

Marcheseuil

Change

Paris
l'Hôpital

Créot

Dezize-lès-Maranges

Santenay

Chagny

Sampigny-lès-
Maranges

St Sernin

Cheilly-lès-Maranges

Bouzeron

Dracy-lès-
Couches

Mercey

St-Maurice-
lès-Couches

Rully

Couches

CÔTE CHALONNAISE
(See separate map)

Côte de Beaune

0 kilometres 5

N

D970

A6

HAUTES CÔTES DE BEAUNE

N6

N74

A6

D974

N6

Côte de Beaune and Hautes Côtes de Beaune

19

The Côte de Beaune: Ladoix, Pernand-Vergelesses and Aloxe-Corton

―――

LADOIX

Dozens of the best wines from this village used to be sold as Côte de Beaune-Villages, and assembled into blends. This is changing, but the *appellation* Ladoix still has virtually no reputation. If one is open-mindedly looking for good value Pinot Noir in Burgundy, this can be a terrific source. The Ladoix growers like to claim that their commune gives some of the best First Growth Aloxe-Cortons, and there is some truth in it, given that the best hillside of Aloxe itself is classified *Grand Cru* Corton.

The following have right to the appellation Ladoix *Premier Cru*:

Bois Roussot
Clou d'Orge, Le
Corvée, La
Joyeuses, Les
Micaude, La
Mourottes, Basses
Mourottes, Hautes

First Growth and commune red Ladoix vines covered 82.97 ha. in 1991, with a further 10.22 ha. being planted to Chardonnay. The five-year average production (1988–92) was 35,400 cases of red wine, and 4,700 cases of white.

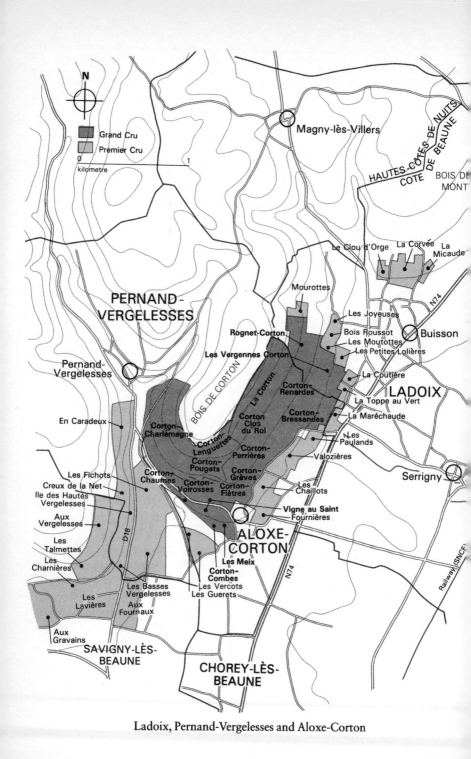

Ladoix, Pernand-Vergelesses and Aloxe-Corton

Main Ladoix growers and merchants

DOMAINE CACHAT-OCQUIDANT ET FILS   7.5 ha. (40 per cent)

Corton Clos des Vergennes 1.5 ha., Aloxe-Corton Les Maréchaudes 0.16 ha., Aloxe-Corton 0.4 ha., Ladoix 0.7 ha., Pernand-Vergelesses (*rouge*) 0.35 ha., (*blanc*) 0.23 ha., Bourgogne Hautes Côtes de Nuits 0.65 ha., Côte de Beaune-Villages 0.64 ha., Bourgogne 1 ha.
Maurice et Jean-Marc Cachat-Ocquidant, place du Souvenir, 21550 Ladoix-Serrigny

CAPITAIN GAGNEROT   (1802)
FRANÇOIS CAPITAIN ET FILS   13.5 ha.

Clos de Vougeot 0.17 ha., Corton Les Renardes 0.33 ha., Corton 1.89 ha., Corton-Charlemagne 0.34 ha., Aloxe-Corton Les Moutottes 0.66 ha., Ladoix La Micaude 1.36 ha., Aloxe-Corton 1.28 ha., Cote de Nuits-Villages 0.67 ha., Pernand-Vergelesses 0.23 ha., Chorey-lès-Beaune 0.66 ha., Ladoix Blanc 0.85 ha.
Maison Capitain Gagnerot, 21550 Ladoix-Serrigny (Tel. 80.26.41.36)

CHEVALIER PÈRE ET FILS   11 ha. (100 per cent)

Corton-Charlemagne 0.34 ha., Corton Le Rognet 0.85 ha., Corton-Lolières 0.45 ha., Aloxe-Corton 1.4 ha., Ladoix Les Corvées 1.5 ha., Clou d'Orge 0.19 ha., Ladoix (*rouge*) 3.14 ha., Les Grechons (*blanc*) 0.6 ha., Passe-Tout-Grains and Aligoté
  Claude Chevalier's father Georges first bottled an entire harvest back in 1959; the family has done so every year since 1969. Although supplying some of Burgundy's, and France's, grandest restaurants, the Chevaliers stay close to the land, with no concessions to elegant dressing just because foreign clients might be coming. If the weather is hot, it may well be bathing trunks.
Claude Chevalier, Buisson, 21550 Ladoix-Serrigny

EDMOND CORNU ET FILS   13 ha. (80 per cent)
PIERRE CORNU

Corton-Bressandes 0.57 ha., Aloxe-Corton Moutottes 0.5 ha., Toppe-au-Vert, Ladoix Les Corvées 0.36 ha., Aloxe-Corton 2.02 ha., Savigny-lès-Beaune 0.83 ha., Ladoix (*rouge*) 3.68 ha., Chorey-lès-Beaune (*rouge*) 1.69 ha., (*blanc*) 0.24 ha., Bourgogne (*rouge*) 2.04 ha., Aligoté

I have tasted rich red wines at this address, particularly the Ladoix *rouge*.

Edmond et Pierre Cornu, Le Meix Gobillon, 21550 Ladoix-Serrigny

PRINCE FLORENT DE MÉRODE   11.38 ha. (50 per cent)
DOMAINE DE SERRIGNY

Corton-Bressandes 1.19 ha., Clos du Roi 0.57 ha., Maréchaudes 1.53 ha., Renardes 0.51 ha., Aloxe-Corton *Premier Cru* 0.69 ha., Pommard Clos de la Platière 3.73 ha., Ladoix Hautes Mourottes (*blanc*) 0.31 ha., Ladoix Côte de Beaune 2.84 ha.

The Prince de Mérode is of Belgian origin; the property has been in his family since 1700. He lives in a moated castle (the moat used to protect a vassal of the Duke of Burgundy) in the plain opposite his Corton vineyards. There are family connections with Château d'Yquem, his wife coming from the de Lur Saluces family.

I suspect that the shy owners have responded to Robert Parker's perceptive critique in his book *Burgundy*. There has apparently been no filtration here since 1989, and they have changed wine-maker, moving to the oenologist Chapelle in Beaune for advice. A conveyor-belt table for grape-sorting has been recently installed.

Estate-bottling dates from 1960, when Robert Haas came to buy, accompanied by the Marquis d'Angerville. At the time, says the Prince, the American market required filtered wines, but now the fashion has changed.

I found their 1992s impressively rich and varied, with good potential. The wines are made in a spacious, converted fifteenth-century cowshed (the cows must have been lodged magnificently) and fine underground cellars, all now temperature-controlled.

Princes Florent et Roger de Mérode, 21550 Ladoix-Serrigny

MICHEL MALLARD ET FILS   13 ha. (95 per cent)

Corton-Renardes 0.65 ha., Corton-Maréchaudes 0.35 ha., Aloxe-Corton *Premier Cru* 1 ha., Savigny-lès-Beaune Serpentières 1.1 ha., Ladoix Les Joyeuses 1 ha., Aloxe-Corton 2.5 ha., Ladoix (*blanc*) 0.72 ha., Côte de Nuits-Villages 1.5 ha., Bourgogne
Michel et Patrick Mallard, route nationale 74, 21550 Ladoix-Serrigny

DOMAINE MAURICE MARATRAY   12.7 ha. (60 per cent)

Corton-Charlemagne 0.33 ha., Corton-Bressandes 0.73 ha., Corton Grandes Lolières 0.09 ha., Aloxe-Corton *Premier Cru* 0.66 ha., Aloxe-Corton 0.84 ha., Ladoix (*rouge*) 3.7 ha., (*blanc*) 1.02 ha., Chorey-lès-Beaune 2.29 ha., Bourgogne (*rouge*) 1.29 ha., (*blanc*) 0.22 ha., Aligoté
    Monsieur Maratray married one of Pierre Dubreuil's daughters, who brought some Corton-Charlemagne with her. This is one of those low-profile Côte d'Or domaines, with a range of well-made minor *appellations*, which gives the lie to those who say you cannot find fairly-priced wine in Burgundy.
Maurice Maratray, place du Souvenir, 21550 Ladoix-Serrigny

DOMAINE ANDRÉ NUDANT ET FILS   13.58 ha. (80 per cent)

Corton-Bressandes 0.6 ha., Corton-Charlemagne 0.15 ha., Aloxe-Corton Les Coutières La Toppe au Vert 0.95 ha., Aloxe-Corton 0.86 ha., Ladoix *Premier Cru* 1.11 ha., Ladoix (*rouge*) 4.13 ha., (*blanc*) 0.62 ha., Savigny-lès-Beaune 0.53 ha., Chorey-lès-Beaune 0.85 ha.
M. et Mme Jean-René Nudant, Cidex 24 No. 4, 21550 Ladoix-Serrigny

GASTON ET PIERRE RAVAUT   12.6 ha. (90 per cent)

Corton-Bressandes 0.42 ha., Corton Hautes Mourottes 0.57 ha., Aloxe-Corton *Premier Cru* 0.4 ha., Aloxe-Corton 2.13 ha., Ladoix Les Corvées 1.66 ha.
Gaston Ravaut, Buisson, 21550 Ladoix-Serrigny

PERNAND-VERGELESSES

This is such a pretty spot, on the main Côte, yet sheltered from its hurly-burly. The established Pernand growers seem a bit sleepy, a bit comfortable. Pernand needs someone to produce exciting red wine with intensity and bite, to give the wealthy *négociants* on the Corton hill a real run for their money, but I have not met him or her yet. Perhaps Christine Dubreuil or Vincent Rapet – if one looks no further than the two major estates – will raise the stakes.

In this village the *crus* are down towards the valley, and the Aligotés (what is left of them) up on the hills, in contrast to one's normal expectations.

The following are classified as *Premiers Crus*:

Caradeux, En
Creux de la Net
Fichots, Les
Ile des Hautes Vergelesses
Vergelesses, Les Basses

First Growth and commune Pernand-Vergelesses covered 83.01 ha. (reds), and 30.09 ha (whites) in 1991. The five-year average production (1988–92) was 37,000 cases of red wines, and 15,000 cases of white.

Main Pernand growers

DOMAINE BONNEAU DU MARTRAY   11.09 ha. (100 per cent)

Corton-Charlemagne 8.7 ha., Corton 2.4 ha.

This property has two extraordinary links with Burgundy's history. Its owner (until his death in 1969) was René Bonneau du Martray, a direct descendant of Nicolas Rolin who caused the Hôtel Dieu to be built in Beaune in 1443. And it would seem that this estate on the borders of Pernand and Aloxe corresponds exactly to the site of the vineyards owned by the Emperor Charlemagne, before he presented them to the Collegiate Church of Saulieu in 775.

Today the estate is managed by Mme du Martray's nephew, Jean le Bault de la Morinière. It has been one of the few top white Burgundy estates fermenting a proportion of its Chardonnays in stainless steel vat (which is the tradition in Pouilly-Fuissé, but not really here), a proportion in barrel. A new more spacious vat-house has been constructed. I have found the Corton-Charlemagnes excellent, the red Cortons less so.

Jean le Bault de la Morinière, Pernand-Vergelesses, 21420 Savigny-lès-Beaune

DOMAINE MARIUS DELARCHE 8.3 ha. (80 per cent)

Corton-Renardes 1.6 ha., Le Corton 0.08 ha., Corton-Charlemagne 1.2 ha., Pernand Ile des Vergelesses 0.35 ha., Les Vergelesses 0.78 ha., Pernand-Vergelesses (*rouge*) 2.25 ha., (*blanc*) 1.2 ha.

Philippe Delarche, 21420 Pernand-Vergelesses

DOMAINE P. DUBREUIL-FONTAINE PÈRE ET FILS 20 ha (80 per cent)
DOMAINE VIRGINIE PILLET

Corton Clos du Roi 1 ha., Corton-Bressandes 0.75 ha., Corton-Perrières 0.5 ha., Corton-Charlemagne 0.75 ha., Pernand Ile des Vergelesses 0.66 ha., Savigny-lès-Beaune Vergelesses 3.5 ha., Pommard Epenots 0.33 ha., Pernand-Vergelesses Clos Berthet (Monopole) (*blanc*) 1 ha., (*rouge*) 0.5 ha.

I have had one or two disappointing bottles of Corton-Charlemagne from here, but also some very sound reds, ageing well, and good white Pernand Clos Berthet.

Like Domaine Jean Trapet in Gevrey, this is an established estate where decision-making is slowly shifting from one generation to the next. Following oenologist Christine Dubreuil's marriage in 1993 to Nicolas Gruère, who makes a neat Bourgogne *rouge* Les Bourgeots from 1.08 ha. of land in Savigny, the pace of change may quicken.

Christine's grandfather, Pierre Dubreuil, put words to the flavours of red Burgundy, for many, when he would say appreciatively of a bottle: '*Ça sent les tripes de poulet*' (that smells of chickens' innards). Today, those aromas (due less to *terroir* than to contact with lees, the wrong sorts of dead yeasts, or sulphide residues) are rarely met with, and not so widely admired. I hasten to add that they are in no way a problem in the finely fruity Dubreuil wines.

Bernard et Christine Dubreuil, 21420 Pernand-Vergelesses

LALEURE-PIOT PÈRE ET FILS   9.5 ha. (100 per cent)

Corton (*rouge*) 0.53 ha., Corton-Charlemagne 0.28 ha., Pernand Ile des Vergelesses 0.5 ha., Les Vergelesses 1.7 ha., Pernand-Vergelesses *Premier Cru* (*blanc*) 0.84 ha., Savigny-lès-Beaune Vergelesses 0.33 ha., Pernand-Vergelesses (*rouge* and *blanc*), Chorey-lès-Beaune, Côte de Nuits-Villages
Jean-Marie et Frédéric Laleure, 21420 Pernand-Vergelesses

DOMAINE RÉGIS PAVELOT ET FILS   7.41 ha. (50 per cent)

Corton 0.28 ha., Corton-Charlemagne 0.58 ha., Pernand-Vergelesses *Premier Cru* (*rouge*) 3.1 ha., Pernand-Vergelesses (*rouge*) 1.23 ha., (*blanc*) 0.54 ha., Aloxe-Corton 0.3 ha.

The place to come to see an almost extinct tradition – picking into wicker baskets, carried on the shoulder. Only used eight days a year, these ones have lasted 40 years, and are still in good condition. In a ripe year you may lose some juice, but you can be sure of not putting much water in the vats, if picking in the rain, for it runs straight through the wicker. A tombstone in the church appears to show there were Pavelots here in AD 1111. The label may be terrible, but the wines, like the family, are interesting.
Régis et Luc Pavelot, 21420 Pernand-Vergelesses

RAPET PÈRE ET FILS   19 ha. (65 per cent)

Corton 1.25 ha., Corton-Charlemagne 2.5 ha., Beaune Clos du Roy 1 ha., Pernand Ile des Vergelesses and Vergelesses 2 ha., Aloxe-Corton 3 ha., Savigny-lès-Beaune 1.25 ha., Pernand-Vergelesses (*rouge*) 1.5 ha., (*blanc*) 2 ha., Côte de Beaune-Villages 1.5 ha., Bourgogne (*rouge*) 1 ha., Bourgogne Aligoté 2 ha.

The family's connection with wine here goes back at least two centuries. I remember the late Robert Rapet pulling out his massive family *tastevin* (inscribed L. Rapet D. Pernand 1792), clapping it between his hands, saying it was built to withstand the pressures of heated conversation.

They make lean white wines which need bottle age. The Aligoté can be lovely, but I have found the reds more patchy.
Roland et Vincent Rapet, 21420 Pernand-Vergelesses

ROLLIN PÈRE ET FILS   12 ha. (70 per cent)

Corton-Charlemagne 0.7 ha., Pernand-Vergelesses (*blanc*) 0.6 ha., (*rouge*) 3 ha., Pernand Ile des Vergelesses 0.7 ha., Aloxe-Corton 0.6 ha., Savigny-lès-Beaune 0.3 ha., Chorey-lès- Beaune 0.3 ha., Hautes Côtes de Beaune (*rouge*)

One of the village's lesser-known but, I think, dependable addresses for both white and red.

Maurice et Rémi Rollin, Pernand-Vergelesses, 21420 Savigny-lès-Beaune

GÉRARD THIÉLY   7.4 ha. (80 per cent)

Corton-Charlemagne 0.35 ha., Corton 0.32 ha., Aloxe-Corton 0.15 ha., Savigny-lès-Beaune 0.5 ha., Pernard-Vergelesses (*blanc*) 0.59 ha., Côte de Beaune-Villages 3.27 ha., Bourgogne and Aligoté
Gérard Thiély, rue de Vergy, 21420 Pernand-Vergelesses

ALOXE-CORTON

On the territory of Aloxe begins the Côte de Beaune, according to Dr Lavalle. The eastern slope of the hill of Corton constitutes one of the most extensive swathes of vineyard of the Côte.

It has been planted with vines since at least AD 858, when the Bishop of Autun, Modoin, donated his Aloxe vines to the cathedral. The Dukes of Burgundy owned vineyards here, as did the Knights Templar and the Kings of France; in 1534 Charlotte Dumay, wife of Gauldry, *garde de la Monnaie* in Dijon, gave a hundred *ouvrées* of vineyard to the Hôtel Dieu in Beaune, which still has them. Surely Charlemagne drank wine from this hillside, before giving his vines to the Collégiale of Saulieu, in 775.

There are two *Grands Crus*, both of which extend on to the adjoining communes of Ladoix and Pernand:

1. Corton, which constitutes the largest *Grand Cru* in Burgundy. In 1991, 99.69 ha. was in production for red wines, with 1.2 ha. for white. The five-year average production (1988–92) for red Corton was 37,560 cases, for white 620 cases. About a quarter of the red total is simply called Corton, but the balance has an individual site-name hyphenated or added on, the eight largest, in descending order

of size, being Corton-Bressandes, Corton-Renardes, Corton Clos du Roi, Corton-Perrières, Corton-Pougets, Corton Le Corton, Corton-Maréchaudes, Corton Le Rognet & Corton, and Corton Clos des Cortons-Faiveley. For the record, the following other additions exist: Clos de la Vigne aù Saint, Les Grèves, Les Languettes, Clos des Meix, Les Vergennes, Hautes Mourottes, Les Combes, La Vigne au Saint, Les Grandes Lolières, Les Chaumes, and finally the smallest: Corton Les Carrières (0.23 ha.), which is a Burgundian *Grand Cru* appellation I only came across in 1993, and which I have yet to taste.

With so large a production (in *Grand Cru* terms) styles are varied, and red Corton goes from fast-softening, solidly fruity wines through to powerfully structured, richly tannic ones which need twelve or more years to soften and can improve for thirty.

2. Corton-Charlemagne, which is the largest white *Grand Cru* in Burgundy. In 1991, 49.9 ha. were in production, the five-year average production (1988–92) for Corton-Charlemagne having been 21,970 cases (four times the volume of Bâtard-Montrachet, which is the next largest white *Grand Cru*). Corton-Charlemagne can be astonishingly rich and full of flavours for a dry white wine.

The following are entitled to the *appellation* Aloxe-Corton *Premier Cru*:

Commune of Aloxe-Corton:
Chaillots, Les
Clos des Maréchaudes
Fournières, Les
Guerets, Les
Maréchaudes, Les
Meix, Les (Clos du Chapitre)
Paulands, Les
Valozières, Les
Vercots, Les

Commune of Ladoix-Serrigny:
Clos des Maréchaudes
Coutière, La
Lolières, Les Petites
Maréchaude, La
Moutottes, Les
Toppe au Vert, La

First Growth and commune Aloxe-Corton represented in 1991: 118.13 ha., the five-year average production (1988–92) for reds having been 57,850 cases, for whites, 270 cases.

Main growers and merchants

PIERRE ANDRÉ (1923) 38 ha.
LA REINE PÉDAUQUE

The Domaines Pierre André are: Domaine de la Juvinière and the Domaine des Terres Vineuses: Clos de Vougeot 1.09 ha., Corton Château Corton André 0.33 ha., Clos du Roi 0.95 ha., Pougets 1.38 ha., Les Combes 0.6 ha., Hautes Mourottes 0.62 ha., Corton-Charlemagne 2.5 ha., Aloxe-Corton *Premier Cru* 2.20 ha., Savigny-lès-Beaune Clos des Guettes 2.35 ha., Ladoix Clos des Chagnots (Monopole) 2.5 ha., Gevrey-Chambertin 1 ha., Aloxe-Corton 2.95 ha., Savigny-lès-Beaune 1.6 ha., Côte de Nuits-Villages Clos des Langres (Monopole) 3.5 ha.

An enormous company, which brutalized one of the entrances to the little village of Aloxe-Corton with its highly visible, jarring warehouse and office block. I have found their wines four-square and burly, as if they saw a vocation in buying keenly-priced lots, for judicious assembly, with the object of pleasing the inexperienced. However, they now have large domaines, and some of their recent bottlings have been confusingly beautiful, with rich fruit and potential, quite shattering my prejudices. I have tended to keep my hand in my pocket when I saw Reine Pédauque bottles, but am now struggling for a much more open mind.

Their 'Exhibition Cellars' are the first the tourist sees when arriving from the north, at Beaune's boulevards. Four million people have been through since they opened, so the firm must certainly have spread a lot of happiness.

Château de Corton-André, Aloxe-Corton, 21420 Savigny-lès-Beaune

MAURICE CHAPUIS 10 ha. (50 per cent)

Corton-Perrières 1.1 ha., Corton-Languettes 0.85 ha., Corton 1.75 ha., Corton-Charlemagne 0.66 ha., Aloxe-Corton *Premier Cru* 1.5 ha.

Claude Chapuis is the author of *Corton* in the Jacques Legrand series, and *Aloxe-Corton: histoire du village et de son vignoble* (Dijon, 1988). I expect the family wines to be good if not spectacular.
Maurice et Claude Chapuis, 21420 Aloxe-Corton

MAX QUENOT FILS ET MEUNEVEAUX   5.6 ha. (50 per cent)

Corton-Bressandes 1 ha., Corton-Perrières 0.66 ha., Corton-Chaumes 0.3 ha., Aloxe-Corton 3.64 ha.
Jean Meuneveaux, Aloxe-Corton, 21420 Savigny-lès-Beaune

DOMAINE COMTE DANIEL SENARD   9.08 ha. (90 per cent)

Corton Clos du Roi 0.64 ha., Corton-Bressandes 0.63 ha., Corton en Charlemagne (*rouge*) 0.4 ha., Corton Clos des Meix (Monopole) 2.12 ha., Corton 0.83 ha., Aloxe-Corton Valozières 0.7 ha., Aloxe-Corton (*rouge*) 2.39 ha., (*blanc*) 0.21 ha., Beaune *Premier Cru* 0.28 ha., Chorey-lès-Beaune 0.51 ha.
With the objective of 'drawing out the maximum of aromas' Philippe Senard (who is a wine-broker as well as an owner) hired oenologist Guy Accad to advise and supervise here, from the 1988 vintage onwards. Low-temperature maceration before the fermentation brings deep colour, with aromas of blackcurrant, and other red fruits, which can be disconcerting, indeed off-putting, to those happy with traditional Pinot aromas. One must add that open-minded consumers often love such wines (until they are told they are 'not classic'). Senard is modifying the Accad approach each year, he says, and soon there will be conclusions to draw from mature bottles of the first vintages.
Philippe Senard, 21420 Aloxe-Corton

DOMAINE DES TERREGELESSES   6.85 ha. (60 per cent)

Corton-Charlemagne 0.35 ha., Savigny-lès-Beaune Vergelesses (*rouge*) 1.09 ha., (*blanc*) 0.55 ha., Chorey-lès-Beaune (*rouge*) 2.31 ha., (*blanc*) 0.23 ha., Beaune 1.22 ha., Savigny-lès-Beaune 1.11 ha.
You would really have to be absorbed in the French language to choose a domaine-name like this, to help sell Savigny-lès-Beaune

Premier Cru Les Vergelesses. The wines are vinified by Philippe Senard, using the methods of his own domaine.
Domaine des Terregelesses, 21420 Aloxe-Corton

MICHEL VOARICK   9 ha. (100 per cent)

Romanée-Saint-Vivant 0.26 ha., Corton Clos du Roi 0.51 ha., Corton-Bressandes 0.6 ha., Corton-Renardes 0.46 ha., Corton-Languettes 0.6 ha., Corton-Charlemagne 1.19 ha., Aloxe-Corton 2.5 ha., Pernand-Vergelesses (*rouge*) 2.5 ha., (*blanc*) 0.42 ha.

I see that Corton-Languettes 1991 from here came fifth in the Gault & Millau Pinot Noir Wine Olympiad No. VIII at Vinexpo in Bordeaux in June 1993, but that the wine 'had a tendency to lightly oxidize in the glass after half-an-hour'. Lightly oxidize? One would have thought this might set the judges' alarm bells ringing.

My experiences of bottles from this cellar – apparently very cold, with the wines infrequently racked – have been more often disappointing than elating, but others rate it very highly as a source for long-ageing Cortons).
Michel Voarick, 21420 Aloxe-Corton

20

Savigny-lès-Beaune and Chorey-lès-Beaune

___

SAVIGNY-LÈS-BEAUNE

Savigny comes third, after Beaune and Santenay, and just ahead of Pommard, as regards quantity of red wine produced on the Côte de Beaune. It is situated at the mouth of the Rhoin, its vines being found on two hillsides, differently orientated. The wines from the Vergelesses Côte, facing south-east and south, are fine and perfumed; those from the east-facing Marconnets slope towards Beaune are more structured.

Savigny lays claim to having seen the invention in 1863 of the first *tracteur-enjambeur*, for cultivating vines by straddling the rows. It was horse-drawn and had wooden wheels and can apparently be seen at the Ferme de Chenôve.

There are fifteen or more wall-inscriptions in Savigny, ranging from the unfashionable *Travailler est un devoir indispensable à l'homme, riche ou pauvre, puissant ou faible, tout citoyen oisif est un fripon*, through the expedient *Il ne faut pas donner son appât au goujon quand on peut espérer prendre une carpe*, to the calm *Malgré les imposteurs, traîtres et jaloux, l'homme patient viendra à bout de tout*. They were inscribed between the seventeenth and nineteenth centuries, no one knows why or by whom.

The following have right to the *appellation* Savigny-lès-Beaune *Premier Cru* or Savigny *Premier Cru*:

Champ Chevrey (Aux Fournaux)
Charnières, Les
Clos la Bataillère (Aux Vergelesses)
Clous, Aux
Dominode, La (Les Jarrons)

Fournaux, Aux
Godeaux, Petits
Gravains, Aux
Guettes, Aux
Jarrons, Hauts
Jarrons, Les
Lavières, Les
Marconnets, Bas
Marconnets, Les Hauts
Narbantons, Les
Peuillets, Les
Redrescut
Rouvrettes, Les
Serpentières, Aux
Talmettes, Les
Vergelesses, Aux (Les Vergelesses)
Vergelesses, Basses

First Growth and commune Savigny-lès-Beaune covered vineyard areas of 315.52 ha. (for red wines), and 23.47 ha. (for whites), in 1991. The five-year average production (1988–92) was 146,600 cases of red wine, and 9,400 cases of white.

Concerning Savigny *blanc*, and Bourgogne *blanc* in the commune, some growers have been making small experimental plantings, with the blessing of the authorities, of other vines than Chardonnay. Several thought they had planted Pinot Blanc (Pavelot, Guillemot, Maurice Ecard, Bize) or Beurot (Bize); however, the Pinots Blancs delivered appear to be Chardonnays, so that particular experiment has gone awry. The Beurot appears to be genuine, but its produce seems better as part of a blend than kept in its pure state (when it can be rich, but lacking a fresh, long finish).

Main Savigny-lès-Beaune growers and merchants

PIERRE BITOUZET   42 ha. (100 per cent)
DOMAINE VINCENT

This newly created, vast estate stretches from Chablis to Mercurey, and includes vines in Aloxe-Corton and Pommard rented on a

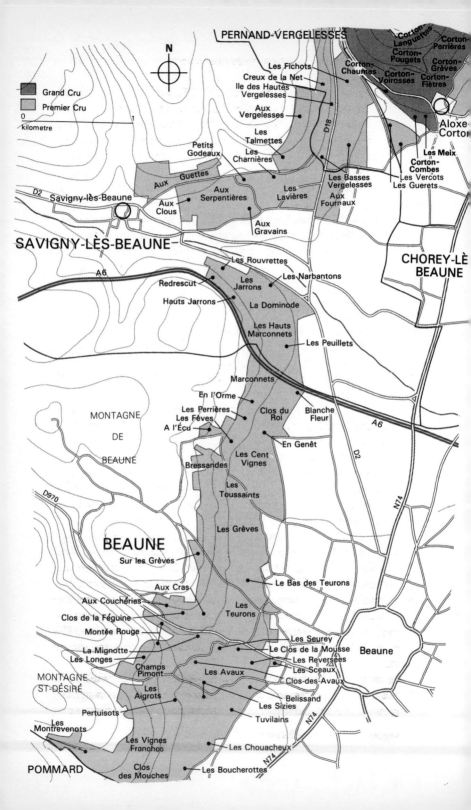

share-cropping basis from the Prince de Mérode family, for whom Pierre Bitouzet used to be manager. I have not yet tried the wines:

Corton-Maréchaudes 1.53 ha., Corton-Charlemagne 0.54 ha., Nuits-Saint-Georges *Premier Cru* 1.32 ha., Volnay-Santenots 0.35 ha., Pommard Clos de la Platière 3.73 ha., Aloxe-Corton Maréchaudes 0.68 ha., Valozières 0.34 ha., Savigny-lès-Beaune *Premier Cru* (*rouge*) 1.34 ha., (*blanc*) 0.31 ha., Ladoix Les Chaillots 2.84 ha., Côte de Nuits-Villages 2.28 ha., Savigny-lès-Beaune (*rouge*) 1.1 ha., (*blanc*) 0.35 ha., Ladoix (*blanc*) 1 ha., Mercurey (*rouge*) 4.1 ha., Chablis Beauroy 5 ha., Montmains 0.35 ha., Chablis 15 ha.
Pierre Bitouzet, 13 rue de Cîteaux, 21420 Savigny-lès-Beaune

DOMAINE SIMON BIZE ET FILS 22 ha. (100 per cent)

Savigny-lès-Beaune Aux Vergelesses 2.31 ha., Marconnets 0.64 ha., Guettes 0.51 ha., Fournaux 1.07 ha., Talmettes 0.77 ha., Serpentières 0.33 ha., Grands Liards 1.5 ha., Savigny-lès-Beaune (*rouge*) 6.63 ha., (*blanc*) 0.75 ha., Aloxe-Corton Le Suchot (Monopole) 1 ha., Bourgogne Perrières (*rouge*) 2.14 ha., (*blanc*) 2.05 ha., Bourgogne Champlains (*blanc*) 2 ha.

If you are obsessed by wine-making, always tasting and talking in your cellar with friends, and back in theirs, you develop little improvements, little habits, which may save time (or consume it), or make work easier, and eventually all add up to creating an estate's unique identity. In Domaine Simon Bize's cramped cellars, they ran out of space, in 1982, to stack all the barrels. Newly-planted Pinot Noir and Chardonnay vineyards, above Savigny on the stony, sloping plateaux of Perrières, were coming on stream. The barrels had to be ranged in the aisles, so when it came to lees-stirring for the Chardonnays, a gentle kick would roll first one, then the whole row, through the quarter-turn needed to tumble the yeasts through the musts, and gently reactivate the fermentations. Less aerating than stirring-up, less muddifying, sufficiently effective – this accidentally-discovered process is now part of white-wine-making here. Bize does not beat his whites, he rolls them, and this partly accounts for their taking time in bottle to mature, so he thinks.

Bize always stacks his new oak barrels on the top, the third, level. Malolactics start faster in new wood, so it is easy to run a syphon down to barrels in the middle or bottom row, to help them start.

Initially, all will have been stacked with wooden bungs, but these are replaced with plastic bungs when the malos begin; two days later these will pop out, identifying which ones are bubbling, saving time and analysis costs.

The Bourgogne Champlains here may be made from Pinot Beurot, Pinot Blanc (so they thought, but it proved to be a Chardonnay clone) and Chardonnay, blended together. This is one of the few domaines to be rescuing Pinot Beurot (the Pinot Gris) from obscurity and neglect in Burgundy. It was one of the first to buy and weather its own split oak staves, in the garden behind the house.

'Ninety-five per cent of the quality here comes from the bunch of grapes – the other five is journalistic bullshit', says Bize, his tongue just half in his cheek.

I cannot imagine anything but a smiling welcome here, whether you wish to buy twelve bottles or half a barrel, and whichever member of the family you meet. Even the dog is trained to invite you in. I must declare an interest, having regularly tasted, bought, sold and drunk wine from here.

Patrick et Simon Bize, 12 rue Chanoine Donin, 21420 Savigny-lès-Beaune

ROGER BONNOT   8 ha. (30 per cent)
DOMAINE BONNOT-LAMBLOT

Savigny-lès-Beaune Dominode 0.45 ha., Vergelesses 0.3 ha., Fournaux 0.3 ha., Savigny-lès-Beaune (*rouge*) 4.5 ha., (*blanc*) 0.5 ha., Aloxe-Corton Valozières 0.3 ha., Aloxe Corton 1 ha.

The garden path takes you past where cheerful, tousle-haired Roger Bonnot grows his vine-grafts, amongst the parsley and vegetables, past the brand new cellar-warehouse, to the rabbit-hutches and chicken-yard, and the cellars under the pigeon loft. Here are the contrasts of Burgundian domaine-bottling, in black and white: a new cellar (financed by the Crédit Agricole, at a fixed 4 per cent, with obligatory repayments over 15 years – highly attractive, given inflation well above that rate), with the old one still preserved, and very much still in use. The wine-stained, rusting old Cherveau vats, with years of grape-pips still adhering to the metal, are as weathered and distressed as a Richard Serra sculpture. You taste what can be achieved without benefit of new oak barrels, to the sound of the

cock crowing and the pigeons cooing. Bottling is straight off the finings, no filter, through a two-beaked tap.
Roger Bonnot, 4 rue de Chorey, 21420 Savigny-lès-Beaune

LUCIEN CAMUS-BRUCHON   6 ha. (50 per cent)

Beaune Clos du Roi 0.19 ha., Savigny-lès-Beaune Gravains 0.38 ha., Lavières 0.32 ha., Narbantons 0.47 ha., Savigny-lès-Beaune 3.5 ha.
Luc Camus-Bruchon, 16 rue de Chorey, 21420 Savigny-lès-Beaune

NICOLE ET JEAN-MARIE CAPRON-MANIEUX   4.5 ha. (70 per cent)

Savigny-lès-Beaune Lavières 0.17 ha., Peuillets 0.26 ha., Savigny-lès-Beaune (*rouge*) 1.18 ha., (*blanc*) 0.44 ha., Pernand-Vergelesses (*blanc*) 0.38 ha., Bourgogne Hautes Côtes de Beaune (*rouge*) 0.18 ha., Bourgogne Aligoté 1.38 ha.
   Tiny quantities of most things here, but very delicious.
Nicole et Jean-Marie Capron-Manieux, 48 rue de Bourgogne, 21420 Savigny-lès-Beaune

DOMAINE CHANDON DE BRIAILLES   13 ha. (100 per cent)

Corton-Bressandes 1.71 ha., Corton Clos du Roi 0.44 ha., Corton-Maréchaudes 0.39 ha., Corton-Charlemagne 0.11 ha., Corton *blanc* 0.32 ha., Aloxe-Corton Valozières 0.28 ha., Savigny-lès-Beaune Lavières 2.6 ha., Fournaux, Pernand Ile des Vergelesses (*rouge* and *blanc*) 3.78 ha., Savigny-lès-Beaune (three-quarters *Premier Cru*) 2.1 ha., Pernand-Vergelesses (*rouge*: three-quarters *Premier Cru*) 1.22 ha., (*blanc*) 0.21 ha.
   This estate has been utterly transformed since Madame de Nicolay's decision, in the late 1980s, to come to live in Savigny, and, with her daughter Claude, take daily responsibility for all matters in vineyard and cellar. 'Burgundy cellars have greatly opened up, thanks to the young', she says, but spring chickens like her are equally responsible for the up-swinging of trap-doors, the out-blowing of cobwebs, and the mutually inquisitive tasting of *vin-maqueurs* (as the French tend to pronounce the word 'wine-makers'). Gone from here are the early-ageing bottles and the

occasional whiffs of volatile acidity, which used to mar wines from this great estate. By the 1989 vintage, there was exceptionally fine extraction of ripe, succulent roundness of fruit. Here are quantities of Cortons with depth of flavour, but also unexpected charm. Here is a prime source of Pernand's best red wine, the Ile des Vergelesses – obscure, hard to pronounce, often a bargain. Here they eye carefully Hubert de Montille's skill on the tight-rope of minimal, or non-existent, chaptalization, adapting and refining their approach to Savigny Lavières (where they own a large chunk) or straight Savigny, with each vintage. Patrick Bize had better look out – but you may find him here. Top growers are in and out of each others' cellars these days, as if they were part of the family.

Nicolay is pronounced Nicolaï, incidentally: the way it used to be spelt (and the way Claude's sister, who creates perfumes, spells her name). Claude has vinified in Oregon, and made two Pinot Noir vintages in 1994, the first in Martinborough, New Zealand, the second six months later in Savigny.

Here also I declare an interest, having recently bought and sold these wines.

Mme Nadine, Mlle Claude et François de Nicolay, rue Soeur Goby, 21420 Savigny-lès-Beaune

DOUDET-NAUDIN   (1849) 5 ha.

Beaune Clos du Roi 0.5 ha., Savigny Aux Guettes 1 ha., Redrescuts (*blanc*) 0.8 ha., Corton-Maréchaudes 1 ha., Aloxe-Corton Les Boutières 1 ha., Pernand-Vergelesses Les Fichots 0.6 ha.

This is a company with a number of very loyal customers. There are two in Switzerland, for instance, and there is Berry Bros & Rudd in London.

I once asked Yves Doudet whether he had noticed any changes in the style of red Burgundies being shipped abroad. He replied, *Je ne changerai pas un iota. La maison Berry aime bien nos vins ... tant que nos vins plaisent à Berry ... Berry, c'est notre meilleur publicité. On a les mêmes notions de tradition. On est flatté et honorifié ...* (I would not change one iota. Berry Bros likes our wines ... and while our wines please Berry ... Berry is our best reference. We have the same traditional ideas – we are flattered and honoured.) What did Yves Doudet think of other people's wines? *Chacun son style. Si les gens aiment les vins jeunes, je les envoie chez les vignerons. Je ne compare pas. Je n'aime pas que les gens comparent nos vins.* (Each to his own style. If people like young wines, I send them round to see growers. I do not compare. I do not like people to compare our wines.)

Robert Parker compares, and has likened these wines, for long-term ageing, to those of Leroy, Lafon and Hubert de Montille, which surprised me mightily.

In fact, Doudet appears to be changing, and I think he must have been comparing. His domaine wine 1990s seem markedly full of characterful Pinot Noir fruit and supple richness, reminding me strongly of the geographical origins named on the labels: Savigny Guettes, and Corton-Maréchaudes. If Parker throws his hands up in horror at this new style, he can ask to taste the old-fashioned Aloxe-Corton Les Maréchaudes 1985, or the Pommard Rugiens 1974, for instance, or any number of 'ancient-method' creations which still await shipping orders.

This merchant was locked in a time-warp, I think, until about 1990. Anyone wishing to understand why consumers – and some writers – can be confused about the taste of red Burgundy could hurry here to buy up what remains.

Yves Doudet, 21420 Savigny-lès-Beaune

MAURICE ECARD PÈRE ET FILS   11.5 ha. (80 per cent)

Savigny-lès-Beaune Serpentières 3 ha., Narbantons 2 ha., Jarrons 2 ha., Peuillets 2 ha., *Premier Cru (blanc)* 0.5 ha., Savigny-lès-Beaune 1.5 ha.

This estate (previously Louis Ecard-Guyot) has for long had a sound reputation, and Maurice Ecard makes excellent Serpentières from his large holding in the vineyard. Marie-Hélène Landrieu-Lussigny[1] believes that snakes in the vines gave a name to this spot, like badgers to Les Tessons in Meursault (the patois is *tasson*), a fox to Le Reniard in Gevrey, and a rat migration to Ratausses and Ratosses (respectively in Savigny and Chorey). Likewise, ant-hills (*fourmillères*) may account for Les Fremières in Chambolle and Morey. However, another explanation is that the name Serpentières

[1] *Les Lieux-dits dans le vignoble bourguignon*, Editions Jeanne Laffitte, Marseilles, 1983.

comes from the snakings of the boundaries between the many holdings.

Maurice et Michel Ecard, 11 rue Chanson-Maldant, 21420 Savigny-lès-Beaune

MAURICE ET JEAN-MICHEL GIBOULOT   10.5 ha. (75 per cent)

Savigny-lès-Beaune Aux Fourneaux 1.3 ha., Aux Serpentières 1 ha., Gravains 0.25 ha., Savigny-lès-Beaune (*rouge*) 5.5 ha., (*blanc*) 1.5 ha., Hautes Côtes de Beaune (*blanc*) 0.5 ha., Bourgogne (*rouge*) 0.25 ha., Aligoté

Jean-Michel Giboulot took over in 1993 as President of Burgundy's Young Professionals of the Vine, one of the first groups to put together within Burgundy itself a well-organized blind, comparative tasting of New World Pinot Noir versus red Burgundy (in March 1992). The local wines came out excellently, though Joseph Drouhin's Oregon Pinot Noir proved to be a striking competition winner.

Giboulot's Savignys are not in the light and supple mould, but rather deep-coloured, quite tannic, designed to age. He also makes an excellent white.

Jean-Michel Giboulot, 27 rue Général Leclerc, 21420 Savigny-lès-Beaune

DOMAINE JACOB-GIRARD ET FILS   10 ha. (60 per cent)

Savigny-lès-Beaune Les Marconnets 1 ha., Les Gravains 1.5 ha., Les Hauts Jarrons 0.38 ha., Savigny-lès-Beaune (*rouge*) 5 ha., (*blanc*) 0.35 ha., Pernand-Vergelesses 1 ha.

Pierre et Patrick Jacob, 2 rue de Cîteaux, 21420 Savigny-lès-Beaune

GIRARD-VOLLOT ET FILS   15 ha. (60 per cent)

Savigny-lès-Beaune Les Peuillets 0.46 ha., Les Rouvrettes 0.46 ha., Les Narbantons 0.4 ha., *Premier Cru* 0.29 ha., Pernand Les Vergelesses 0.42 ha., Savigny-lès-Beaune (*rouge*) 7.68 ha., (*blanc*) 0.25 ha., Aloxe-Corton 0.39 ha., Bourgogne Rouge Les Perrières 2.15 ha.

This is one of Savigny's best estates, the family stretching back thirteen generations to Jean Girard, who was tending Savigny vines in 1614.

Jean-Jacques Girard, 16 rue de Cîteaux, 21420 Savigny-lès-Beaune

DOMAINE PIERRE GUILLEMOT   7.7 ha. (70 per cent)

Savigny-lès-Beaune Serpentières 1.72 ha., Jarrons 0.28 ha., Narbantons 0.33 ha., Savigny-lès-Beaune (*rouge*) 3.13 ha., (*blanc*) 1.39 ha., Côte de Beaune-Villages 0.12 ha., Bourgogne

Jean-Pierre Guillemot, 1 rue Boulanger et Vallée, 21420 Savigny-lès-Beaune

DOMAINES ANTONIN GUYON   50 ha. (100 per cent)
DOMAINE DOMINIQUE GUYON

Corton-Charlemagne 0.75 ha., Corton Clos du Roy 0.75 ha., Corton-Bressandes 1 ha., Corton-Renardes 0.25 ha., Corton 0.25 ha., Aloxe-Corton *Premier Cru* Les Fournières and Les Vercots 2.5 ha., Volnay Clos des Chênes *Premier Cru* 1 ha., Chambolle-Musigny and Chambolle-Musigny Clos du Village 3.5 ha., Gevrey-Chambertin 2.5 ha., Charmes-Chambertin 0.1 ha., Meursault-Charmes 0.75 ha., Savigny-lès-Beaune 2.25 ha., Beaune and Beaune Clos de la Chaume Gaufriot 2 ha., Pernand Les Vergelesses and Les Fichots 1.5 ha., Pernand-Vergelesses (*blanc* and *rouge*) 2 ha., Chorey-lès-Beaune 1 ha., Bourgogne Hautes Cotes de Nuits 23 ha.

An enormous estate, but I have found the red wines disappointing, as if the yields were highish, and then the vattings long, to extract the maximum available – at the expense of texture and silkiness, and without achieving real intensity of fruit. Some whites are fine, and the red Hautes Côtes de Nuits Cuvée des Dames de Vergy – where they are one of the largest owners – can be balanced, fresh and delicious, for youthful drinking. A string of top French restaurants carry these wines. Although Michel Guyon is an old friend I have not visited the domaine for years.

Michel et Dominique Guyon, 21420 Savigny-lès-Beaune

DOMAINE DU PRIEURÉ   11 ha. (80 per cent)
JEAN-MICHEL MAURICE

Savigny-lès-Beaune Les Lavières 0.87 ha., Les Hauts Jarrons 0.3 ha., Savigny-lès-Beaune (*rouge*) 4.54 ha., (*blanc*) 1 ha., Hautes Côtes de Beaune 3 ha.
Jean-Michel Maurice, BP 9, 21420 Savigny-lès-Beaune

CHÂTEAU DE SAVIGNY   44.07 ha. (60 per cent)
MICHEL PONT, CELLIER VOLNAYSIEN

Pommard Rugiens 0.7 ha., Pommard 1 ha., Volney Caillerets 0.5 ha., Volnay Clos des Chênes 0.2 ha., Volnay 4 ha., Beaune Cent-Vignes 0.48 ha., Savigny-lès-Beaune Les Vergelesses 1 ha., Savigny-lès-Beaune 5 ha., Monthelie Champfulliots 1.6 ha., Monthelie 10.7 ha., Auxey-Duresses Le Val 1.3 ha., Auxey-Duresses 1.5 ha., Bourgogne Clos du Roi 3.3 ha., Clos du Château 3.3 ha., Clos du Chapitre 2.8 ha., Meursault Genevrières 1 ha., Meursault 1 ha.

This estate has from 1994 been contracted to, and part-managed by, Labouré-Roi.
Michel Pont, Cellier Volnaysien, Château de Savigny-lès-Beaune

JEAN-MARC PAVELOT   9.9 ha. (80 per cent)

Savigny-lès-Beaune La Dominode 1.55 ha., Aux Guettes 1.42 ha., Narbantons 0.35 ha., Peuillets 0.44 ha., Savigny-lès-Beaune (*rouge*) 4.73 ha., (*blanc*) 0.71 ha., Pernand Les Vergelesses 0.61 ha.

These wines are widely liked and highly respected, and the Dominode can be something special. But I wonder if there is not half a degree, or a degree, of over-chaptalization to help them to their youthful popularity.
M. et Mme Jean-Marc Pavelot, 1 chemin des Guettottes, 21420 Savigny-lès-Beaune

MAISON SEGUIN MANUEL   (1842) 3.1 ha.

Savigny-lès-Beaune Lavières 1 ha., Savigny-lès-Beaune
This firm's *cuverie* bears a famous inscription, which can be translated, 'If my memory serves me right there are five reasons for

drinking: the arrival of a guest, present and future thirst, the quality of the wines and any other reason you like (1772).'
Pierre Seguin, rue Paul Maldant, 21420 Savigny-lès-Beaune

HENRI DE VILLAMONT, SA   9 ha.

Grands Echézeaux 0.5 ha., Chambolle-Musigny *Premier Cru* 2 ha., Savigny-lès-Beaune Clos des Guettes 2 ha., Savigny-lès-Beaune 4.5 ha.

Swiss-owned, this incorporates François Martenot, and is one of Burgundy's half-dozen largest companies.
BP 3, 21420 Savigny-lès-Beaune

CHOREY-LÈS-BEAUNE

Almost all the appropriate village vineyard land is planted with Pinot Noir: in 1991, 125.88 ha., with 0.76 ha. of Chardonnay. The five-year average production (1988–92) for red wine was 69,300 cases, with 360 cases of white. Some of the red goes, quite properly, to form part of Côte de Beaune-Villages blends.

There are no First Growths in Chorey; although there are some inclines, most of the land is pretty flat. Some vineyard land was recently reclassified downwards, from Chorey to Bourgogne *rouge*, as it lay in a sort of basin – a surprising, and encouraging, thing to see.

As broker Tim Marshall has put it, you can get a nice fruity, chocolatey character from a good red Chorey.

Main Chorey-lès-Beaune growers and merchants

ARNOUX PÈRE ET FILS   24.26 ha. (75 per cent)

Corton Le Rognet 0.33 ha., Beaune Cent Vignes 0.5 ha., En Genet and Bas des Teurons 1.35 ha., Savigny-lès-Beaune Aux Guettes 0.4 ha., Vergelesses 0.3 ha., Savigny-lès-Beaune (*rouge*) 3.84 ha., (*blanc*) 0.37 ha., Aloxe-Corton 1 ha., Beaune 0.47 ha., Chorey-lès-Beaune 10 ha., Côte de Beaune-Villages, Pernand-Vergelesses (*blanc*) 0.43 ha., Hautes Côtes de Beaune 1.36 ha., Bourgogne (*rouge*) 0.62 ha., Passe-Tout-Grains and Aligoté

To make a *grand vin*, says Monsieur Arnoux, you must have 13°
– and they seem to chaptalize their village wines, like the First
Growths, accordingly. I have preferred the whites, even though
from young vines as yet.
Michel et Rémi Arnoux, rue des Brenots, 21200 Chorey-lès-Beaune

DOMAINE JEAN-LUC DUBOIS   7.5 ha. (60 per cent)
PAUL DUBOIS-GOUJON
VERONIQUE MILLET-DUBOIS

Beaune Bressandes 0.77 ha., Cent Vignes 0.22 ha., Savigny-lès-
Beaune 1.09 ha., Ladoix Côte de Beaune 0.84, Aloxe-Corton 0.42
ha., Chorey-lès-Beaune (*rouge*) 2.9 ha., (*blanc*) 0.61 ha., Bourgogne
This is one of Chorey's old-established, dependable bottlers.
Jean-Luc Dubois, 7 rue des Brenots, 21200 Chorey-lès-Beaune

DOMAINE JACQUES GERMAIN   16 ha. (100 per cent)
CHÂTEAU DE CHOREY

Beaune Teurons 2 ha., Les Cras 1.5 ha., Les Vignes Franches 1 ha.,
Boucherottes 1 ha., Cent Vignes 0.5 ha., Château de Chorey-lès-
Beaune 5 ha., Bourgogne Château Germain (*rouge* and *blanc*) 2 ha.,
Pernand-Vergelesses (*blanc*) 3 ha.
    Red Chorey-lès-Beaune under the Château label from here
should demonstrate clearly the character of the village wines.
Instead, this one can taste like a jumped-up Bourgogne *rouge*, with
oakiness on the nose, round and alcoholic – a sort-of grower's
answer to *négociant* Burgundy, priced pretentiously, warming and
smooth. The Germain family can surely do better than this with
their Chorey-lès-Beaune. Their First Growth Beaunes like Teurons
and Les Cras can be absolutely splendid, as bright as lighthouses on
a dark night.
François Germain, Château de Chorey-lès-Beaune, 21200 Beaune

DOMAINE GOUD DE BEAUPUIS   12 ha. (70 per cent)

Pommard Epenots 0.25 ha., La Chanière 0.5 ha., Beaune Clos des
Vignes Franches 1.66 ha., Grèves 1.5 ha., Clos Sainte Anne (Sur les
Grèves) 0.33 ha., Savigny-lès-Beaune Vergelesses 0.33 ha., Aloxe-
Corton 0.5 ha., Aloxe-Corton Les Valozières 0.25 ha., Ladoix Les

Hautes Mourottes 0.25 ha., Chorey-lès-Beaune 1.75 ha., Bourgogne Château des Moutots, Aligoté
Emmanuel Goud de Beaupuis, Château des Moutots, 21200 Chorey-lès-Beaune

MAILLARD PÈRE ET FILS   17 ha. (80 per cent)

Corton-Renardes 1.5 ha., Corton 0.2 ha., Aloxe-Corton Grandes Lolières 0.5 ha., Beaune Grèves 0.4 ha., Aloxe-Corton 1.5 ha., Beaune 1.4 ha., Savigny-lès-Beaune 2 ha., Chorey-lès-Beaune 5 ha., Côte de Beaune-Villages 2 ha., Ladoix Côte de Beaune 0.5 ha.

Here is a source of genuine Côte de Beaune wines which possibly (since Chorey is somewhat off the beaten track) will be keenly-priced.
Daniel, Pascal et Alain Maillard, Chorey-lès-Beaune, 21200 Beaune

DOMAINE JEAN-ERNEST MALDANT   10 ha. (30 per cent)

Corton-Grèves 0.44 ha., Corton-Renardes 0.33 ha., Corton-Charlemagne 0.3 ha., Aloxe-Corton Les Valozières 1.14 ha., Aloxe-Corton 1.53 ha., Savigny-lès-Beaune Gravains (*rouge*) 0.8 ha., (*blanc*) 0.45 ha., Ladoix Côte de Beaune 1.55 ha., Chorey Côte de Beaune 1.94 ha.

Sylvain Pitiot is the map-making co-author, with Pierre Poupon, of the beautifully-produced *Atlas des grands vignobles de Bourgogne*, which is a valuable reference work for any serious Burgundy-watcher. He is responsible for wine-making and tending here, believing that nothing should be hurried, not the start of fermentation, not the malolactics, and not the bottling, either.

In his own right Pitiot owns a Monopole: Aloxe-Corton Clos de la Boulotte 1.13 ha., which is presently sold under contract each year for bottling by Antonin Rodet in Mercurey.
Françoise Maldant et Sylvain Pitiot (Consultant), 21200 Chorey-lès-Beaune

DOMAINE TOLLOT-BEAUT ET FILS   20.23 ha. (100 per cent)

Corton-Charlemagne 0.24 ha., Corton-Bressandes 0.91 ha., Corton Les Combes 0.6 ha., Aloxe-Corton Les Fournières 0.71 ha., Les Vercots 0.79 ha., Beaune Les Grèves 0.59 ha., Clos du Roi 1.09 ha., Savigny-lès-Beaune Les Lavières 1.32 ha., Champ Chevrey (Monopole) 1.47 ha., Aloxe-Corton 1.38 ha., Savigny-lès-Beaune 0.45 ha., Chorey-lès-Beaune 11.16 ha., Bourgogne (*rouge* and *blanc*), Aligoté

This has been an extremely dependable estate over at least two decades, though occasionally I have found myself wishing that new-oakiness was less apparent. The wines are clean, balanced, reliably delicious and often magnificent when mature.

Nathalie Tollot, rue Alexandre Tollot, 21200 Chorey-lès-Beaune

21

Beaune

═══════

At the heart of the vineyards of the province, famed for its cellars and the wines of its Côte, a centre for viticulture and oenological teaching, its wine-trade radiating across the globe, animated by fairs and fêtes, adorned with remarkable monuments, Beaune is the wine capital of Burgundy.

So runs a sign in its Wine Museum (the translation is mine) and nobody disputes it. Every visitor to Burgundy goes to Beaune and its Hospices, and quite right too.

This is the hub of western Europe's main motorways, so reaching it has become fast and easy. There are over a hundred restaurants, and since 1991 a new Congress Centre. Because so many of Beaune's mediaeval towers and walls have been used for wine ageing down the centuries they have been saved from destruction or ruin. The moats are gardens, and it is possible to walk round many of the battlements.

This was where the Dukes of Burgundy resided until their move to Dijon in the fourteenth century, and their palace can still be seen. So can many fine houses in its old streets, with quiet interior courtyards, like the Renaissance no. 18 rue de Lorraine, dedicated to the Muses, in an attic of which this book began.

It is a town of greedy eaters, the Saturday-morning market yielding Cîteaux cheeses, corn-coloured Bresse chickens, perhaps a haunch of young wild boar (the blood supplied separately, no extra charge, in a jam jar). The inhabitants will tell you how to choose your butcher, this one for pork, that one for veal, another for chickens. In Beaune, the weather is predicted by feeling the bread: *Le pain est mou; il va pleuvoir.*

Turning to its wine, the commune of Beaune has almost as much vineyard land in production (400 ha. for the 1991 vintage) as Gevrey-Chambertin, which, with 405 ha. and its *Grands Crus* to count in addition, is the Côte d'Or's biggest. The character of red Beaune wine is difficult to define. It does not have the lightness and perfume of Savigny, nor the structure and power of Pommard or Aloxe, nor the superfine balance of Volnay. A good one is harmonious, broad yet not rough, supple when young, improving for a decade.

First Growth and commune Beaune covered a vineyard area of 375.87 ha. (for reds) and 24.98 ha. (for whites) in 1991. The five-year average production (1988–92) for red Beaune was 163,200 cases, for white Beaune 10,700 cases.

The following are classified as *Premiers Crus*, though not all are in use. For the 1991 vintage for instance, 34 were used, where this list extends to ten additional names. It is more practical for some owners to vinify several First Growths together:

Aigrots, Les	Ecu, A l'
Avaux, Les	Epenotes, Les
Beaux Fougets, Les	Fèves, Les
Bélissand	Genêt, En
Blanche Fleur	Grèves, Les
Boucherottes, Les	Grèves, Sur les
Bressandes, Les	Longes, Les
Cents Vignes, Les	Marconnets, Les
Champs Pimont	Mignotte, La
Chouacheux, Les	Montée Rouge
Clos de l'Ecu	Montrevenots, Les
Clos de la Mousse, Le	Orme, En l'
Clos des Avaux	Perrières, Les
Clos des Mouches, Le	Pertuisots
Clos des Ursules (Vignes Franches)	Reversées, Les
Clos du Roi	Seurey, Les
Clos Landry (Clos Saint-Landry)	Sizies, Les
Clos Sainte-Anne (Sur les Grèves)	Teurons, Le Bas des
	Teurons, Les
Couchérias, Aux	Toussaints, Les
Couchérias, Aux (Clos de la Féguine)	Tuvilains, Les
	Vigne de l'Enfant Jésus, La (Grèves)
Cras, Aux	Vignes Franches, Les

Of the vineyard land in production in Beaune for the 1991 vintage, over 75 per cent was First Growth (which sounds a little exaggerated). The word Beaune on its own is rather bland, where Beaune Premier Cru has a more valuable ring to it. I imagine the *appellation* inspectors may have been gently lent on by Beaune's corkscrew *bourgeoisie*, for that 75 per cent to have been achieved.

Much of the vineyard land is owned by Beaune *négociants*, some of whose wine-making philosophy seems to be that Beaune wines be designed principally never to offend anyone.

Given that the wines sell with some difficulty, it is a pity the owners do little to encourage us up into the vineyards, which are beautiful and picturesque, but confusing. Is it right to take Chemin des Vaches to go up past Theurons and Grèves, and does Chemin de Bouche de Lièvre lead to Les Toussaints? Chemin des Mariages is easy, where Beaunois used to stroll in the evening no doubt with heady results, but where exactly is the Vigne de l'Enfant Jésus, and Jadot's excellent Clos des Ursules? Couldn't we be tastefully shown the way?

One thoroughly confusing *appellation* to be found in this commune is Côte de Beaune. This is quite different from Côte de Beaune-Villages, a portmanteau *appellation* which may be applied to red wine from fourteen different *appellations* north and south of Beaune.[1] Côte de Beaune, in contrast, relates to vineyard land on the commune of Beaune which was judged not good enough to be called Beaune; it is generally higher, so ripens later. There are no First Growths, but these *lieux-dits* may be met with: La Grande Châtelaine, Les Topes-Bizot, Les Pierres Blanches, Les Mondes Rondes, Les Monsnières. The five-year average production (1988–92) for Côte de Beaune red was 9,600 cases, with 2,700 cases for the white. Production figures for Côte de Beaune-Villages may be found in the chapter 'Côtes Frontierland'.

At times Beaune seems overrun by tourism, but the town and the boulevards are softened by spectacular displays of flowers. At Hospices auction time, there are chrysanthemums, the colour of crushed raspberries and cream, tumbling like waterfalls from the dormers of the old Market Hall, where the sale takes place. This has a steeply pitched roof, its tiles rusty brown or the colour of red

1 Auxey-Duresses, Blagny, Chassagne-Montrachet, Chorey-lès Beaune, Ladoix, Maranges, Meursault, Monthelie, Pernand-Vergelesses, Puligny-Montrachet, Saint-Aubin, Saint-Romain, Santenay and Savigny-lès-Beaune.

wine lees, all streaked with dark greens from the moss, and silvered with lichens.

It is possible to look at Beaune anew, from unlikely directions. Air Escargot or Ballons de Bourgogne organize balloon flights over the vineyards and villages of the Côte; Beaune Autrement has walks round ramparts and courtyards, a tour of terraced First Growths, or a visit to the American Camp (this I have not yet done), where in 1918 thousands of American soldiers camped beyond the railroad tracks, on their way home from the war. Such tours quite rightly end, of course, with tastings.

Beaune has my favourite brasserie for a beer and a quick meal during wine-buying: Le Gourmandin, place Carnot. Thierry, the manager, serves an imaginative range of wines by the glass from all over France, to accompany fresh leaves of salad from owner-chef Jean Crotet's vegetable garden at nearby Hostellerie de Levernois, or the pick of the remnants of a great Burgundian banquet of the night before. For Jean Crotet, with Joël Perreaut of Les Gourmets in Marsannay, may have done the excellent catering for the Paulée de Meursault, or a Saint-Vincent Tournante.

The second last time I went to Le Gourmandin Thierry served me a red wine blind, obviously Pinot, which proved to be Château Talbot. More recently, it was a deep-coloured, well-oaked young red, certainly Cabernet, which proved to be Beaune, from a Pommard-based grower I had never heard of, Jean-Luc Joillot. It was evidently time to turn this book in, and go back to tasting in the Haut-Médoc; to return to Bordeaux after a three-year absence on Burgundian research. Someone else would be able to check out Joillot . . .

Main merchants and growers

DOMAINE BESANCENOT   10.5 ha. (75 per cent)

Corton-Charlemagne 0.2 ha., Beaune *Premiers Crus* Cent Vignes 3.26 ha., Theurons 1.24 ha., Bressandes 0.92 ha., Toussaints 0.58 ha., Clos du Roi 0.47 ha., Grèves 0.22 ha., A l'Ecu 0.19 ha., Aloxe-Corton 0.19 ha., Beaune 0.32 ha., Pernand-Vergelesses (*rouge*) 1.58 ha., (*blanc*) 0.37 ha., Chorey-lès- Beaune (*blanc*) 0.3 ha.

Stocks of First Growth Beaune going back ten or more vintages have accumulated here – true, Beaune is difficult to sell, but some-

thing must be not quite right. Besancenot does not have a reputation for high yields, so perhaps the problem has been bottling too
late.
Bernard Besancenot, 78 fauborg Saint-Nicolas, 21200 Beaune

ALBERT BICHOT ET CIE, SA (1831)

This dynamic, large firm is a major exporter. It distributes the
Chablis of Domaines Long-Depaquit and La Moutonne (see
Chablis), and the wines of the Domaine du Clos Frantin, 13 ha.,
which once belonged to Général Legrand, *Maréchal de Camp* of the
Emperor Napoleon:
 Corton-Charlemagne 0.66 ha., Chambertin 0.33 ha., Richebourg
0.07 ha., Clos de Vougeot 0.6 ha. (1/3 top, Grand Maupertuis, 2/3
bottom) Vosne-Romanée Aux Malconsorts 1.75 ha., Clos Frantin
(Monopole) 0.1 ha., Grands Echézeaux 0.25 ha., Echézeaux 1 ha.,
Corton-Languettes 0.5 ha., Gevrey-Chambertin, Vosne-Romanée,
Nuits-Saint-Georges. It is also creating a Côte de Beaune estate,
under the label Domaine du Clos du Pavillon (presently 5.93 ha.):
Corton-Charlemagne 0.4 ha., Pommard Clos du Pavillon
(Monopole) 3.93 ha., Aloxe-Corton Les Fournières 0.6 ha., Beaune
Epenottes 1 ha.
 What will the next Bichot generation make of the firm's present
reputation, I wonder? In the past, discouraging regional and village
bottles have sometimes come off the high-tech Bichot bottling-line
in Beaune. The estate red wines can taste magnificent from barrel in
Vosne-Romanée, less so after bottling in Beaune. The firm has a
smaller line for low-volume bottling, and even sometimes bottles
Chambertin or Richebourg straight from the barrel without filtration, I gather. Today, young Albéric Bichot holds the reins, and is
certainly not above tasting blind alongside the Côte d'Or's young
growers, which augurs well.
Albéric Bichot, Bd. Jacques Copeau, 21200 Beaune

DOMAINE GASTON BOISSEAUX 7 ha. (100 per cent)

Beaune Montée Rouge 3 ha., Savigny Les Peuillets 0.5 ha., Chorey-
lès-Beaune 2.5 ha.
Eric Boisseaux, Clos Champagne Saint-Nicolas, 21200 Beaune

BOUCHARD AÎNÉ ET FILS (1750)

Ownership of this old firm, which stems from the same family as Bouchard Père et Fils, passed to Jean-Claude Boisset in early 1993. Bernard Repolt took over as manager, then uncorked and poured down the sink 90,000 bottles of his company's wine . . . because it was not good enough, so I read. Bottling was soon transferred to Nuits-Saint-Georges. See Jaffelin Frères, below.

BOUCHARD PÈRE ET FILS, SA (1731)

With over 93 ha. of vineyards, of which 71 ha. are *Grands* or *Premiers Crus*, this company owns by far the largest estate on the Côte de Beaune:

Corton Le Corton 3.94 ha., Corton-Charlemagne 3.09 ha., Savigny-lès-Beaune Lavières 3.9 ha., Beaune Teurons 2.41 ha., Grèves 1.81 ha., Grèves Vigne de l'Enfant Jésus (Monopole) 3.92 ha., Marconnets 2.32 ha., Clos de la Mousse (Monopole) 3.36 ha., Clos-Landry (*blanc*, Monopole) 1.98 ha.

Beaune du Château is a non-vintage wine coming from 30 ha. of Beaune First Growths: Aigrots 8.19 ha., Sizies 2.92 ha., Pertuisots 0.45 ha., Avaux 4.44 ha., Seurey 0.4 ha., Clos du Roi 0.83 ha., Cent Vignes 2.21 ha., En Genêt 1.26 ha., Bressandes 0.18 ha., Toussaints 0.6 ha., Sur les Grèves 1.16 ha., Champs Pimonts 0.72 ha., Tuvillains 4.03 ha., Bellissands 1.58 ha., Le Bas des Teurons 1.46 ha., A l'Ecu 0.54 ha., Les Teurons 0.15 ha., Les Reversées 0.22 ha., Les Beaux Fougets 0.33 ha.

The estate also includes Pommard Les Rugiens 0.42 ha., Les Combes 0.75 ha., Volnay Caillerets (Ancienne Cuvée Carnot) 3.72 ha., En Chevret 0.27 ha., Taille-Pieds 1.1 ha., Chanlin 0.44 ha., Fremiets Clos de la Rougeotte (Monopole) 1.52 ha., Chambertin 0.15 ha., Chevalier-Montrachet 2.32 ha., Meursault Les Genevrières 1.39 ha., Beaune du Château *blanc* 4 ha. (principally grown in Les Aigrots and Les Sizies), Chambolle-Musigny 0.71 ha., Aloxe-Corton Les Paulands 0.25 ha., Ladoix Côte de Beaune Clos Royer 0.81 ha., Beaune 1.9 ha., Bourgogne Aligoté de Bouzeron 5.61 ha.

The company also distributes the wines of the Château de Vosne-Romanée (see p. 328) and the Château de Mandelot in the Hautes Côtes de Beaune, details of which are to be found on p. 362. They handle exclusively the Domaine du Clos Saint-Marc: Nuits-Saint-

Georges Clos Saint-Marc (Monopole) 0.93 ha., Les Argillières 1.04 ha. The wines of the last two estates are Bouchard-bottled in Beaune.

For years Bouchard Père was spoken of with reverence, being seen as one of Beaune's finest sources. It stood somewhat still during the 1970s and 1980s, when several less grand *négociants* and growers were open-mindedly tasting together, evolving, developing – and overtaking old Bouchard. Tasting fruitless red Burgundies from this address, which seem to have spent too long in wood, or been racked until they were skeletons, has often been depressing. These cellars have some wonderful old bottles in them, both red and white, but they are also filled with many missed opportunities.

In fact Bouchard Père has been evolving since the mid-1980s, and now buys large quantities of grapes for vinifying under its control – a reversal of the old policy of buying made wine. After a major fire in 1989 the firm re-equipped its vinification plant and changed its methods.

Red wine is made using three types of stainless steel, closed vat, all equipped with refrigerating jackets: a revolving Vaslin vat, set at an angle, containing a spiral screw; a cylindrical Rotomatic vat, with narrow screw around its walls (as is used, in part, by Louis Jadot); and a rectangular, fixed Fabbri vat, which is the most expensive, most complicated – and the favourite. What look like bicycle chains inside a giant steel box revolve around its sides, carrying a steel rake gently through the solid mass of grapes and stalks, breaking it up. The same rake efficiently sweeps out all solid matter, once the fermentation is over and the wine has been run off, emptying the vat automatically. A steel grating at the bottom of the vat allows the wine to be run off. One computer-aided person can control the workings of these vats, which form an impressive construction with metal walkways and gantries.

I have tasted a limited range of wines made by the new methods, and they certainly have deeper colour, more extracted fruit character, and better concentration. But I wonder how much the characteristically succulent red Burgundy mouth-feel will become apparent?

For red Burgundy to be great it must not only be an expression of its territorial origin, but also, surely, reflect the personality of whoever makes it. Wine-making here seems gripped by its high technology; I cannot see the wine-maker's personality being anything but drowned. These methods may well be perfectly appropriate for Hautes Côtes de Beaune and Bourgogne *rouges* (goodness knows, we need someone to bring high-tech white heat to the rescue of some of those sad Cinderellas) or indeed for large volumes of Beaune du Château, but is it really the right answer for Volnay Taillepieds or Chevret, for Pommard Rugiens or Beaune Vigne de l'Enfant Jésus? How on earth does one vinify the grapes from 0.15 ha. of Chambertin, if the yield is low, in vats this size? Probably all their old-fashioned, open-topped wooden vats perished in the inferno. I bet Christophe Bouchard misses them sometimes.

They are much more successful with white wines, many of which are excellent. They also do admirable things with good value bottles: Pinot and Chardonnay La Vignée, and Bouzeron Aligoté, where they have been the main pioneers (with Aubert de Villaine).

The firm was unlucky to be caught out vinifying with both tartaric acid and sugar during the tricky-to-make 1987 vintage. Many, many Burgundians must have thought, 'There, but for the grace of God, go I', for such practices, though illegal, are not uncommon. It is much easier to escape detection if one is small. The offence seemed minor, and yet the fine, and the brouhaha, were considerable. Just as with Pierre Coste in Bordeaux, where a sensitive taster and well-intentioned wine-maker was caught out by the authorities, I cannot be alone in wishing real villains would be pursued, instead of standard-bearers who may occasionally stumble.

Jean-François et Christophe Bouchard, Au Château, 21202 Beaune Cedex

CHAMPY PÈRE ET CIE (1720)

This is acknowledged to be the oldest *négociant-éleveur* in Burgundy, the firm possessing its original 1720 price-lists, featuring many First Growth Nuits. These wines would have been loaded on to the back of a cart, for sale in Belgian market-places. Louis Pasteur wrote to the company when experimenting with must-heating. His letters were preserved, and for long Champy's vinification methods (in double-walled copper cauldrons) owed something to his experiments.

For much of the twentieth century M. Mérat – an autograph collector, polo player and cavalry colonel – was at the head of

Champy, ensuring that an old-world leisured air survived in its Second Empire offices and cellars. Champy virtually disappeared from sight, but on his death, the firm was bought by Jadot, who kept the vineyards, added some of the cellars (containing historic old vintage reserves) to its own, and sold the firm on to the Meurgey family – Henry Meurgey *père* being a long-established Beaune broker, his son Pierre having responsibility for rebuilding Champy's fortunes.

The firm believes in fining, but not filtering, its *Grands Crus*. Village wines rarely clarify as well as *Grands Crus*, so filtering can be essential, depending on how they were pressed.

It would be unfair not to mention what I think are exciting developments at Champy since 1990, but I must declare an interest – the Meurgeys being good friends and suppliers. I find the wines frank and open-faced, their characters varied and interesting. At the same address is an export-broking company called DIVA, handling domaine-bottled Burgundies from 200 estates, where customers are in very safe hands.

Henri et Pierre Meurgey, 3 & 5 rue du Grenier à Sel, 21200 Beaune

CHANSON PÈRE ET FILS   (1750) 42 ha.

Beaune Clos des Fèves 3.75 ha., Les Bressandes 1.33 ha., Les Grèves 2.2 ha., Les Clos des Mouches 4.33 ha., Les Marconnets 3.75 ha., Clos du Roi 2.66 ha., Champs Pimont 3 ha., Les Teurons 3.8 ha., Les Blanches Fleurs 1.25 ha., Savigny La Dominode 1.75 ha., Les Marconnets 2.2 ha., Pernand Les Vergelesses 5.5 ha.

With Jadot, Drouhin, Bouchard Père and Louis Latour, Chanson makes up the five-strong 'most distinguished' club of grand old Beaune shippers. During the 1970s and 1980s the wines seemed amateurishly made to me, possibly from over-cropping vineyards, or short vattings, or aged too long in wood. I kept thinking that if Voltaire (who was a Chanson customer) had still been alive he would have shifted supplier. But change may be in the air, so I shall taste young vintages with new attention.

Francois et Philippe Marion, 10 rue Paul Chanson, 21200 Beaune

MAURICE CHENU (1978)

Like Armand Cottin of Labouré-Roi, Maurice Chenu was in the oil business before setting up a wine firm, and, in the space of a dozen years, building estates totalling 28 ha.:

Domaine de la Créa: Beaune Montrevenots 0.5 ha., Pommard 0.5 ha., Auxey-Duresses (*rouge*) 0.5 ha., (*blanc*) 0.5 ha., Saint-Romain (*rouge*) 3 ha., (*blanc*) 3 ha.

Domaine de la Perrière: Beaune Cent Vignes 0.5 ha., Nuits-Saint-Georges 0.6 ha., Mercurey 3 ha., Savigny-lès-Beaune (*rouge*) 3 ha., (*blanc*) 0.5 ha., Chorey-lès-Beaune 2 ha., Bourgogne Clos de la Perrière (*rouge*) 2 ha., (*blanc*) 2 ha.

Domaine des Beaumont: Charmes-Chambertin 0.4 ha., Gevrey-Chambertin *Premier Cru* 0.54 ha., Morey-Saint-Denis *Premier Cru* 0.75 ha., Gevrey-Chambertin 0.85 ha., Morey-Saint-Denis 1 ha.

These wines have been bottled by Chenu, but from the 1993 vintage will all be bottled at the domaines. At a time when *négociants* have been falling like ninepins here is a new one, who recently acquired Maison Raoul Clerget of Saint-Aubin.

Maurice et Cécile Chenu, 21200 Montagny-lès-Beaune

DOMAINE CAUVARD 15.4 ha. (80 per cent)
CAUVARD PÈRE ET FILS

Beaune Teurons 0.52 ha., Bressandes 0.29 ha., Cent Vignes 0.2 ha., Beaune Clos de la Maladière (*rouge*) 1.09 ha., (*blanc*) 0.42 ha., Beaune 0.29 ha., Aloxe-Corton 2.76 ha., Chorey-lès-Beaune 2.2 ha., Pommard 0.8 ha., Volnay 0.3 ha., Bourgogne Les Monts Battois (*rouge*) 1.6 ha., (*blanc*) 0.26 ha., Côte de Beaune Blanc Les Monts Battois 1.35 ha., Corton-Charlemagne 0.24 ha.

Henri et Jacqueline Cauvard, 18 rue de Savigny, 21200 Beaune

PAUL CHAPELLE ET FILLES 4.2 ha. (100 per cent)

Puligny-Montrachet Champs Gains 1.25 ha., Hameau de Blagny 0.25 ha., Santenay Gravières 1.16 ha., Puligny-Montrachet 0.5 ha., Meursault 0.35 ha., Bourgogne *blanc*

Paul Chapelle runs one of Burgundy's most respected private sector wine laboratories, numbering Michel Lafarge, Prince de Mérode, Pousse d'Or, and the Hospices de Beaune among his regular or occasional clients. He is also the consultant wine-maker of a Chinese Cabernet *rosé* which is made from vineyards near and to the east of Beijing, having travelled to China to make wine more than ten times since 1990.

Paul Chapelle et Christine Beck, Le Poil, 21200 Montagny-lès-Beaune

LA COMPAGNIE DES VINS D'AUTREFOIS (1981)

This looks an interesting firm, set up to supply the obvious demand for authentic domaine-bottlings. Jean Pierre Nié is a *négociant*, but he supervises the tending and bottling of his chosen wines *at the property*. They are then dressed in labels which reflect the individual villages or districts whence they come. Some look traditional, some modern, but his range breaks the mould of visual uniformity we usually get from *négociant* bottlings. He distributes Santenay Clos des Mouches (Pierre Lavirotte à Change), Chablis Fourchaume, Montmains and Mont de Milieu (Domaine Jean Goulley à La Chapelle), Meursault Perrières (Paulette Boyer), and many other growers' wines.

Jean-Pierre Nié, 9 rue Céler, 21200 Beaune

CORON PÈRE ET FILS (1879)
DOMAINE DES HÉRITIERS BERNARD CORON   6.2 ha.

Corton 0.5 ha., Beaune Clos du Roi 1 ha., Cent Vignes 1 ha., Champs Pimont 1 ha., Grèves 0.5 ha., Clos des Mouches 0.2 ha., Beaune 2 ha.

Philippe et Jean Marc Dufouleur, 8 blvd Bretonnière, 21200 Beaune

YVES DARVIOT   3 ha. (100 per cent)

Beaune Clos des Mouches (*rouge* and *blanc*) 1 ha., Grèves 0.75 ha., Beaune 1 ha., Bourgogne (*rouge*)

The fashion for Chardonnay meant that Darviot – clinging, no doubt, on to the coat-tails of Joseph Drouhin – could ask, in 1993, nearly twice the price for his white Clos des Mouches as for his red. I think these wine-making skills have been inconsistent, but matters could change. Darviot also holds a *négociant* card.

Yves Darviot, 2 place Morimont, 21200 Beaune

JOSEPH DROUHIN, SA   62 ha. (1880)

In 1880 Joseph Drouhin bought an old Beaune merchant, founded in 1756, to sell wine under his own name. Soon afterwards he acquired the cellars of the Dukes of Burgundy, the Kings of France, and the Collégiale of Beaune. Under his son Maurice Drouhin the firm expanded after the First World War, buying vineyards on the Côte de Beaune.

Maurice Drouhin's nephew and adopted son Robert Jousset-Drouhin took control in 1957 at the age of twenty-three. He foresaw that demand for Burgundies would rise while supply remained stable, and adopted a policy of extension of his estate on the Côte de Nuits – now, thanks to tractors, close enough to Beaune for cultivation. He also took steps to guarantee the authenticity of his wines by allowing none foreign to Burgundy and Beaujolais into his cellars. This meant no Châteauneuf du Pape, no Côtes du Rhône, and no *ordinaire* wines at all. This idealism cannot have endeared him to some in the Burgundy trade at the time, but the stand has been subtly influential and pervasive.

The 62 ha. estate now consists of:

Côte d'Or: Chambertin Clos de Bèze 0.13 ha., Griotte-Chambertin 0.53 ha., Bonnes Mares 0.23 ha., Musigny 0.67 ha., Chambolle-Musigny Les Amoureuses 0.6 ha., *Premier Cru* 1.4 ha., Clos de Vougeot 0.86 ha., Grands Echézeaux 0.48 ha., Echézeaux 0.46 ha., Corton-Bressandes 0.25 ha., Corton-Charlemagne 0.34 ha., Beaune Clos des Mouches (*rouge* and *blanc*) 14 ha., Beaune Grèves 0.81 ha., *Premier Cru* 2.4 ha., Volnay Clos des Chênes 0.27 ha., Chorey-lès-Beaune 2.5 ha., Bâtard-Montrachet 0.1 ha.

Yonne: Chablis Vaudésir 1.41 ha., Les Clos 1.25 ha., Bougros 0.34 ha., Preuses 0.24 ha., Chablis *Premiers Crus* Vaillons, Séchets, Montmains, Roncières and Mont de Milieu 6.9 ha., Chablis 25.9 ha.

The firm also distributes the following domaines exclusively: Domaine Marquis de Laguiche (details in Chassagne-Montrachet) and Domaine du Moulin de Vaudon (Chablis). At Domaine Drouhin in Oregon, USA, the family has pioneered the close planting of *pinots noirs*, in the Burgundian manner, initial results being extremely good. Women wine-makers head up the technical side: Véronique Drouhin in Oregon, Laurence Jobard and Patricia Girault in Beaune.

Robert Drouhin's concern for authenticity and evident conviction that the Burgundy wine-trade is about exceptional bottles have
always been appealing. I think reliability is a high priority here,
which is precious, given the price of the rarest Burgundy.
Robert Jousset-Drouhin, BP 29, 7 rue d'Enfer, 21201 Beaune Cedex

CAMILLE GIROUD, SA

There is something surprising to me about certain old vintages of
these wines: where does the polished, rich middle fruit come from?
The Giroud brothers speak of ageing their wines three years in
barrel, of minimal purchases in light years, and of selecting full,
robust wines, designed to last. I do not share Clive Coates's enthusiasm for the old wines, but plan to taste the younger vintages with
interest as they mature. They have started to rebuild a domaine of
vines with Beaune *Premier Cru* Les Cras 0.32 ha.
Bernard et François Giroud, 3 rue Pierre Joigneaux, 21200 Beaune

HOSPICES DE BEAUNE

The 58 hectares of vines belonging to the Hospices de Beaune are
situated on almost every hillside of Beaune's Côte. But rather than
being sold under their village and vineyard names like other Burgundies, the wines from one village which complement each other
are blended to form different *cuvées*. This system is designed to
produce well-balanced wines, and incidentally means that Hospices
wines cannot be directly compared with non-Hospices wines; you
must take them or leave them. It also simplifies labelling, and estab-
lishes little brand-names, enabling continuity to be ensured; for if
one part of a *cuvée* gets hailed on, or needs replanting, the remaining vineyards keep the joint flag flying.

The wines are always sold by auction on the third Sunday of
November each year.[2] It is the central event of Burgundy's *Trois
Glorieuses* weekend, the other two being a Clos de Vougeot dinner
and the Paulée lunch in Meursault. At the auction, each wine
always used to carry the name of the vigneron who made it, until in

2 Except once, when General de Gaulle called a referendum that day, so they put
the sale back to December. But fewer people came, as habits had been broken,
and the auction did not go well.

1899 it was decided to use instead the names of the Hospices's major benefactors. Nicolas Rolin and Guigone de Salins had founded it; the Dames Hospitalières care for its sick. Others now posthumously famous on wine-bottle labels donated its 600 hectares of woodland or 800 hectares of farmland. Some, of course, gave vines. The first to do this, with a vineyard in the *climat* of 'En le Faye' was a Beaune baker's family in 1459. One of the most recent was Thomas Collignon, an inhabitant of Gevrey-Chambertin with no heirs, who gave a large plot of Mazis-Chambertin, the Hospices's first vineyard on the Côte de Nuits. The *cuvée* was named after his mother, Madeleine Collignon, and auctioned for the first time in 1977. The next gifts were two *cuvées*, a Beaune and a Pommard, from M. and Mme Cyrot-Chaudron.

Recent additions to the Hospices estate have been Bâtard-Montrachet in 1989, and Clos de la Roche in 1990. The first was acquired by an astute exchange of Beaune vineyards (of which they had 22 ha., making the estate over-weighted with Beaunes) for 0.3 ha. Bâtard-Montrachet in the hands of the SAFER. This is a government organization involved in re-grouping scattered landholdings, but which also has a social role to play, favouring young vignerons, many of whom today have difficulty acquiring vineyard land, given its high value. Beaune vineyards were swopped for the Bâtard, giving the Hospices another white *Grand Cru*. The *cuvée* is named Dames de Flandres after the first nuns Nicolas Rolin had brought to the Hôtel Dieu from Flanders, probably from Valenciennes.

The Clos de la Roche (0.43 ha.) was bought with money left by a Mme Kritter, a friend of André Boisseaux of Patriarche. The wine was to be sold as Cuvée Georges Kritter, which cleverly ensures that the name of Patriarche's sparkling wine is not forgotten on auction day, being, indeed, subtly associated with a *Grand Cru* of the Côte de Nuits (all in a very good cause). The Cyrot-Chaudron couple, already benefactors, bought the next-door parcel of Clos de la Roche, and the two wines are vinified together.

There have been some organizational changes at the Hospices since the arrival of M. Antoine Jacquet as director in 1988, and his speedy appointment, in time for the 1988 harvest, of M. Roger Coussy as manager. The management was keen to dispel the impression that the vignerons working the Hospices vineyards (many of whom also looked after their own vines) were free to do what they wished, when they wished – for instance, harvesting for the Hospices on a day of the vigneron's choosing. It became the manager's responsibility to fix treatments, quantities, picking dates, etc. Subcontracting was banned; the work had to be done by the contracted vigneron him- or herself.

The management was right that customers of the Hospices had been concerned, and many of them tasted round in mid-November (in the dark) chomping at the bit in frustration. Virtually the whole estate is either First Growth or Great Growth, but you would never have guessed it from the tasting. The wines appeared to be vinified to be presentable in time for their pre-auction assessment: fine in some vintages, but virtually impossible to achieve in others. Fine if we were talking about Beaujolais Nouveau – but we were not.

Everything was put into new barrels – less, one felt, because the wine's structure and character called every year for 100 per cent new wood, than because this policy simplified the work of the Hospices management. No need to worry about keeping barrels in good condition from one year to the next, one's hands could be washed of that problem.

On reflection, however, the Hospices management may have been smarter than I give it credit for being. Here is Mel Knox on new barrels and Pinot Noir: 'A great rich Pinot will improve for up to 15 to 18 months in new wood, while a lighter vintage will be improved by a new barrel, but for a much shorter period, as little as three months.'[3] Buyers at the auction are obliged to take their purchases away, in their new barrels (for which they are invoiced extra) by the 15th January following the harvest, so if Knox is correct the Hospices could indeed be doing consumers a favour with its 100 per cent new barrel policy.

It is well known that André Porcheret was lured away from the Hospices, in the late 1980s, to be wine-maker at Domaine Leroy in Vosne-Romanée, partly because the pay was poor. The management tried to get him back (as it openly admitted) by offering more money, but was unable to. For several years nothing seemed to have been learned from this event, but prices at the November auction had entered an ineluctable slump. Matters cracked after the 1993 vintage, when the quality of the wines was widely and publicly

3 *Flavours and Chemistry of Wine Barrels*, Knox-Fax Industrial Publications, San Francisco, 1992.

criticized. It had become evident that Hospices wines were lacking in personality precisely because the management had not hired a sufficiently well-qualified, determined, ambitious team to make and tend the wines. Coussy went, and Porcheret was tempted back, in January 1994.

To Coussy's credit, he had been supervising the construction of an ambitious new winery. The Hospices had dug an enormous hole next to its modern Hospital outside the walls of Beaune, and was building (no expense spared) a vat-house and cellar. This was to be functional, not for impressing visitors, with enough stainless steel vats for vatting times to be of optimum length (hmm . . . that begs a question about what had been happening), with wrap-around temperature-control for the vats, pneumatic pumping-down, and humidity and temperature control in the cellars. Apparently the management had taken advice from Louis Jadot and Joseph Drouhin, which all sounded very much to the good.

The Hospices must have had in mind that if André Boisseaux of Patriarche ever decided not to support the auction with his customary passion, or, indeed, if a *pipette* from the sky finally drew him to eternity, the prices in November might crumble. With new and spacious premises estate-bottling could be envisaged, but the wine-making would have to be pretty faultless, if it went that route.

Hospices auction weekend is of far-from-negligible importance for the town of Beaune, indeed for the whole of Burgundy's tourist and wine trade. Something new – the wine of the year – is born and shown in November, at a sombre time of fogs and rain, as winter approaches. This is an annually amazing event with which one cannot afford to tinker. Do so, and the magic could evaporate, that irrational magic which causes people to bid from around the globe at the Hospices de Beaune charity wine auction. Of course the wines might be better if they were made for judging and auction the following spring, as is the case at the Hospices de Nuits, but moving the sale is unthinkable.

Sometimes it has held back stock from auction (it was the case in 1991). I suspect this was partly because, had the whole Hospices production hit the plunging market that year, buyers could not have absorbed it at respectable price levels. That retained stock will have either been bottled for Hospices reserves, or trickled out quietly into the trade. But in future, what is to stop buyers being invited to taste two vintages from barrel when they come to Beaune in November? They could taste appropriate *cuvées* of the young wine, and 12 month-older *cuvées*. These, from the previous vintage, would have been witheld from public tasting because their malolactic fermentations were under way or their sugars were unfinished. Or it might be because their richly fruity, tannic structures (a Pommard here, a Corton there, or a *Grand Cru* from the Côte de Nuits, for instance) – achieved by vinifications specifically appropriate to their *terroirs* – made it inappropriate for them to be assessed and sold six weeks after picking.

On his appointment, André Porcheret spoke out immediately on the need to reduce Hospices yields, saying, according to a report in the *Wine Spectator,* that 'a prestigious domaine such as Hospices should average around 30 hectolitres per hectare (2.2 tons per acre).' Three months later, in April 1994, he told me, '35 hl/ha. – that is my wish, with the agreement of the director. One must not go beyond it. Quality is made in the vineyard.' With great red Burgundy it *always* comes back to yields, and that is where he will no doubt be battling. He will also aim for longer vatting times, with many berries left uncrushed. The vat-house was operational in time for the 1994 vintage, when a helicopter was used to drive water off rain-soaked vineyards, prior to picking. Also for the first time, Porcheret marshalled 30 sorters to eliminate rotten or under-ripe fruit, by sifting through the grape-bunches.

The Hospices vineyards are now planted with a high proportion of old vines, the percentages of different ages having varied as shown in Table 6 over the last twenty-five years.

At present the Hospices de Beaune *cuvées* comprise:

Red wines:
Charlotte Dumay: Corton-Renardes 2 ha., Bressandes 1 ha., Clos du Roi 0.4 ha.

Table 6 Ages of vines in Hospices de Beaune vineyards

| | Percentages | | |
	1968	1977	1993
Fallow land	3	2	1
Vines less than 4 years old	7	5	0
Vines 4–15 years old	28	27	25
Vines 16–30 years old	45	35	23
Vines over 30 years old	17	31	51

Docteur Peste: Corton-Bressandes 1 ha., Chaumes et Voirosses 1 ha., Clos du Roi 0.5 ha., Fiètre 0.4 ha., Grèves 0.1 ha.

Rameau-Lamarosse: Pernand Les Basses-Vergelesses 0.65 ha.

Forneret: Savigny-lès-Beaune Vergelesses 1 ha., Gravains 0.65 ha.

Fouquerand: Savigny-lès-Beaune Basses Vergelesses 1 ha., Talmettes 0.65 ha., Aux Gravains 0.33 ha., Aux Serpentières 0.14 ha.

Arthur Girard: Savigny-lès-Beaune Peuillets 1 ha., Marconnets 0.8 ha.

Nicolas Rolin: Beaune Cent Vignes 1.4 ha., Grèves 0.33 ha., En Genêt 0.2 ha., Teurons 0.5 ha., Bressandes 0.14 ha.

Guigone de Salins: Beaune Bressandes 1.2 ha., Les Seurey 0.8 ha., Champs Pimont 0.6 ha.

Clos des Avaux: Beaune Les Avaux 2 ha.

Brunet: Beaune Les Teurons 0.5 ha., Bressandes 0.5 ha., Cent Vignes 0.5 ha.

Maurice Drouhin: Beaune Les Avaux 1 ha., Boucherottes 0.65 ha., Champs Pimont 0.6 ha., Grèves 0.25 ha.

Hugues et Louis Bétault: Beaune Grèves 1.1 ha., La Mignotte 0.54 ha., Aigrots 0.4 ha., Clos des Mouches 0.33 ha.

Rousseau-Deslandes: Beaune Cent Vignes 1 ha., Montrevenots 0.65 ha., La Mignotte 0.4 ha.

Dames-Hospitalières: Beaune Bressandes 1 ha., La Mignotte 1.13 ha., Teurons 0.5 ha.

Dames de la Charité: Pommard Petits Epenots 0.4 ha., Rugiens 0.33 ha., Noizons 0.25 ha., Refêne 0.35 ha., Combes Dessus 0.2 ha.

Billardet: Pommard Petits Epenots 0.65 ha., Noizons 0.5 ha., Arvelets 0.4 ha., Rugiens 0.35 ha.

Blondeau: Volnay Champans 0.6 ha., Taille Pieds 0.6 ha., Ronceret 0.35 ha., En l'Ormeau 0.25 ha.

Général Muteau: Volnay le Village 0.8 ha., Carelle sous la Chapelle 0.35 ha., Cailleret Dessus 0.2 ha., Fremiet 0.2 ha., Taille Pieds 0.2 ha.

Jehan de Massol: Volnay-Santenots Les Santenots 1.25 ha., Les Plures 0.25 ha.

Gauvain: Volnay-Santenots Les Santenots 0.65 ha., Les Plures 0.75 ha.

Lebelin: Monthelie Les Duresses 0.88 ha.

Boillot: Auxey-Duresses Les Duresses 0.5 ha.
Madeleine Collignon: Mazis-Chambertin 1.75 ha.
Cyrot-Chaudron: Beaune Montrevenots 1 ha.
Raymond Cyrot: Pommard *Premier Cru* 0.64 ha., Pommard 1.01 ha.
Suzanne Chaudron: Pommard 1.37 ha.
Cyrot-Chaudron et Georges Kritter: Clos de la Roche 0.4 ha.

White wines:
Françoise de Salins: Corton-Charlemagne 0.4 ha.
Baudot: Meursault Genevrières Dessus 0.65 ha., Dessous 0.75 ha.
Philippe le Bon: Meursault Genevrières Dessus 0.13 ha., Dessous 0.4 ha.
de Bahèzre de Lanlay: Meursault Charmes Dessus 0.5 ha., Dessous 0.4 ha.
Albert Grivault: Meursault Charmes Dessus 0.5 ha.
Jehan Humblot: Meursault Poruzot 0.5 ha., Grands Charrons 0.1 ha.
Loppin: Meursault Les Criots 0.5 ha., Les Cras 0.2 ha.
Goureau: Meursault Poruzot 0.35 ha., Les Peutes Vignes 0.2 ha.
Paul Chanson: Corton-Vergennes 0.35 ha.
Dames de Flandres: Bâtard-Montrachet 0.35 ha.

Antoine Jacquet (director) et André Porcheret (wine maker), Hôtel Dieu, 21200 Beaune

JABOULET-VERCHERRE, SA   13 ha. (1834)

Corton-Bressandes 0.5 ha., Pommard Clos de la Commaraine (Monopole) 3.9 ha., Petits Noizons 0.4 ha., Beaune Clos de l'Ecu (Monopole) 2.8 ha., Bressandes (*blanc*) 1 ha., Volnay Caillerets 0.25 ha., Puligny-Montrachet Les Folatières 0.8 ha., Savigny-lès-Beaune (*rouge*) 0.35 ha., (*blanc*) 0.15 ha., Bourgogne
This firm has a fine estate and a prominent modern warehouse in easy view from the Beaune *autoroute*. Its wines are closer to old-style *négociant* than to 'new generation' wines.
Michel Jaboulet-Vercherre, 5 rue Colbert, 21200 Beaune

LOUIS JADOT (1859)

The company makes wine from some outstanding red wine sites (and a few whites) from four domaines, totalling 42.25 ha. One of the following domaine names will appear on the labels: Domaine Louis Jadot, Domaine des Héritiers Louis Jadot, Domaine André Gagey, Domaine Robert Tourlière:

Chambertin Clos de Bèze 0.42 ha., Chapelle-Chambertin 0.39 ha., Clos Saint-Denis 0.17 ha., Bonnes Mares 0.27 ha., Musigny 0.17 ha., Clos de Vougeot 3.22 ha., Corton-Pougets 1.54 ha., Corton-Charlemagne 1.88 ha., Chevalier-Montrachet Les Demoiselles 0.51 ha., Gevrey-Chambertin Clos Saint-Jacques 1 ha., Cazetiers 0.12 ha., Combe aux Moines 0.17 ha., Lavaut Saint-Jacques 0.22 ha., Estournelles-Saint-Jacques 0.38 ha., Poissenots 0.19 ha., Chambolle-Musigny Les Amoureuses 0.12 ha., Les Baudes 0.27 ha., Nuits-Saint-Georges Boudots 0.5 ha., Savigny-lès-Beaune La Dominode 2.01 ha., Beaune Clos des Ursules (Vignes Franches) (Monopole) 2.74 ha., Grèves (rouge) 0.65 ha., (blanc) 0.97 ha., Les Theurons 1.41 ha., Bressandes 1.03 ha., Les Vignes Franches 0.5 ha., Les Boucherottes 2.57 ha., Clos des Couchereaux 1.93 ha., Les Avaux 1.43 ha., Les Chouacheux 1.06 ha., Toussaints 0.89 ha., Tuvillains 0.56 ha., Cent Vignes 0.42 ha., Pernand-Vergelesses en Caradeux Clos de la Croix de Pierre (Monopole) 1.5 ha., Puligny-Montrachet Folatières 0.21 ha., Marsannay (rouge) 2.78 ha., (blanc) 0.56 ha., (rosé) 2.38 ha., Chambolle-Musigny 0.44 ha., Santenay Clos de Malte (Monopole) (rouge and blanc) 6.83 ha.

The company's strength on the Côte de Nuits dates from the purchase in 1986 of part of the Clair-Daü family domaine (then caught up in family squabbles).

In addition, they vinify, tend and distribute four-fifths of the wines from the Domaine du Duc de Magenta: Chassagne-Montrachet Abbaye de Morgeot Clos de la Chapelle Monopole 4.5 ha. (two-thirds red, one-third white), Puligny-Montrachet Clos de La Garenne (Monopole) 1.8 ha., Meursault 0.75 ha., Auxey-Duresses Les Bretterins 1 ha.

There was some dismay in Beaune when it was learned, in the mid-1980s, that Louis Jadot was being sold to the Koch family, owners of its American distributor, Kobrand. American owners – or English, for that matter – in Bordeaux had indeed sometimes been disastrous, and one could fear the worst. But the purchase seems to have been highly beneficial to Burgundy. American capital has permitted an imaginative, idealistic *négociant-éleveur* to extend its domaines, build new wine-making facilities, and finance stocks. The Gagey family (André, and now his son Pierre-Henry) who have run Louis Jadot for over thirty years appear to enjoy independence and support. Wine-making is in the hands of the talented and passionate Jacques Lardière, who has been with Jadot since 1970, at the heart of their establishing a coherent policy of grape purchase, and their bringing together of modern and traditional practices.

Burgundy is not rich in English-speaking, hands-on, technically qualified wine-makers to take overseas the message that vinification by instinct, guesswork and inherited intuition is now seriously in decline on both Côtes, and it is tempting to think that Monsieur Lardière might carry that torch, but it could be a mistake to translate *Le vin est une histoire de vibrations* in McMinnville or Martinborough. Faced with a spurting pipette in Beaune such a theory seems perfectly reasonable, and the evidence is before me to prove it. Perhaps the Burgundian wine culture can only be properly absorbed on the spot.

Jadot owns (and used to work in) one of the most extraordinary buildings in Beaune not open to the tourists: the 1470 Couvent des Jacobins, which was built thirty years after the famous Hospices, in the same style. It has a magnificient vaulted roof which is carved with gargoyles and monsters' heads like the Salle des Pauvres, but in this case left unpainted.

It seems to me that this company has gone right to the top of the Burgundian *négociant-éleveur* tree, alongside Faiveley and Joseph Drouhin. It delivers important quantities of fine red wines, right across the range, though the rich, subtly-oaked style is perhaps as much market- as *terroir*-driven. The white wines are also very interesting, for it is not uncommon for their malic acid fermentations to have been partially blocked. This gives them different aromas, and sometimes a harder finish, than is common in Burgundy. Their quality can be superb, and some age magnificently.
André et Pierre-Henry Gagey, 5 rue Samuel Legay, 21200 Beaune

MAISON JAFFELIN (1816)

This firm's base was for years the ancient Caves du Chapitre, situated within the Gallo-Roman Castrum which was Beaune's first settlement. For long majority-owned by the Jousset family (Robert Jousset-Drouhin being at the head of Joseph Drouhin), it was sold to Jean-Claude Boisset in the early 1990s, having probably plunged too deeply into the wines of the expensive 1989 vintage.

Can Jaffelin wines retain their personalities within the enormous Boisset group, I wonder? Trained in the Drouhin school, its manager Bernard Repolt has been an imaginative buyer, for instance launching Les Villages de Jaffelin, a fine range of well-priced bottles from lesser-known communes. Burgundy is for enjoyment, and few, if any, new generation *négoçiants* have been more skilful at putting across this message than Repolt. He now also has responsibility for reviving Bouchard Aîné et Fils. If he can retain some buying and tending independence, he will surely receive immense customer support.
Bernard Repolt, rue Sainte-Marguerite, 21220 Beaune

DOMAINE JOLIETTE   2.26 ha. (100 per cent)

Côte de Beaune Les Pierres Blanches (Monopole) (*rouge* and *blanc*) 1 ha., Les Mondes Rondes (Monopole) 1.1 ha.
Maurice Joliette, 22 rue Richard, 21200 Beaune

MAISON LOUIS LATOUR, SARL   (1797)

Most of the Louis Latour domaine dates from the phylloxera crisis, when the Comte de Grancey, who lived in Paris, lost confidence in the future of wine-making and sold his estate at Aloxe-Corton. Since then it has been extended north to Chambertin and south to Chevalier-Montrachet. The estate consists of about 45 ha. and accounts for just over 10 per cent of the firm's turnover.

Chambertin 0.8 ha., Romanée-Saint-Vivant Quatre Journaux 1 ha., Corton 15 ha. (mainly sold as Château Corton-Grancey), Corton Clos de la Vigne au Saint (Monopole) 2.66 ha., Corton-Charlemagne 9 ha., Aloxe-Corton Les Chaillots 2.5 ha., Les Fournières 1.8 ha., Pernand Ile des Vergelesses 0.75 ha., Beaune Vignes Franches 2.25 ha., Les Perrières 1.33 ha., Clos du Roi 1 ha., Les Grèves 0.5 ha., Pommard Les Epenots 0.5 ha., Chevalier-Montrachet Les Demoiselles 0.5 ha., Volnay, Aloxe-Corton

At this firm the faithful customer is more important than the Burgundian producer – a rare attitude in the Côte d'Or. This dynamic, still independent company is no mindless follower of the *terroir* heresy (as Louis Latour senior might see it). They look far beyond the region's borders, and indeed embraced early twentieth-century technology with the fervour of a Californian frontiersman.

Louis Latour's red wines have been pasteurized for most of this century (being heated to 70°C), after relatively rapid vatting. In style they are early maturing, high in alcohol, and very round – not my idea of fine Burgundy. It may be argued that this physical process of stabilization is preferable to adding chemicals, but I believe the process has an effect on the taste, and is behind the firm's red wine house style. The wines change as they age; they are not stopped rigid in their maturation paths, but they are different from naturally handled red Burgundies. There is no need, these days, to use pasteurization for stabilization purposes. If Latour retain it, presumably it is because of the flavours and textures that come with it, and for the predictability of their wines when exported; their customers are used to it, and must like it. Without doubt these wines have given pleasure on hundreds of thousands of occasions, so why carp? Because I look to red Burgundies for greater excitement, indeed love their unpredictable characters. I find Latour's white wines, which are handled according to recent, regional Chardonnay traditions, in contrast often absolutely splendid, and exactly what one hopes for.

Latour has been a pioneer of successful Chardonnay plantings in the Ardèche hills, west of the river Rhône, way south of Burgundy, and there are Pinot plantings coming on stream in Provence, I understand.

I see from publicity in the *Wine Spectator* (June 1993) that the different Louis Latours, since the appearance of the family in the world of wine, are now being referred to as Louis III, Louis VI (the present one) – sounding like the Kings of France. The *Wine Spectator*'s advertisement tells me that it was Louis III who planted Chardonnay on the Corton hillside, thus creating Corton-Charlemagne – and all this time I had imagined it was the Emperor Charlemagne himself. Instead, we have Louis III to thank. The history books of Burgundian anecdote must obviously be rewritten, now that we know.

More seriously, I gather that Louis VI is researching a book about red Burgundy wine-making down the centuries, which I genuinely look forward to reading.

Louis et Louis-Fabrice Latour, 18 rue des Tonneliers, 21200 Beaune

LYCÉE AGRICOLE ET VITICOLE DE BEAUNE   19 ha. (85 per cent)

Beaune Champs Pimont 0.53 ha., Montée Rouge 1.64 ha., Bressandes 0.76 ha., Perrières 0.77 ha., *Premier Cru* 2.93 ha., Beaune (*rouge*) 2.96 ha., (*blanc*) 1.36 ha., Côte de Beaune 0.7 ha., Bourgogne Hautes Côtes de Beaune (*rouge*) 2.27 ha., (*blanc*) 1.03 ha., Puligny- Montrachet 1 ha.

At any one time 450 students of vines and wine-making are based here, drawn from forty French *départements*. The Lycée has recently become more outward-looking, and in 1990 set up contact with schools and colleges in eleven European countries (including Hungary and Romania) to foster exchanges. Is there a whiff, I wonder, of Europe against the Rest of the World? There is a cooper's workshop (20 students in 1991), possibly unique in France. A much-needed extension to the vat-house was opened in 1991.

M. Vincent, 16 av. Charles Jaffelin, 21200 Beaune

HENRI MOINE   1.3 ha. (100 per cent)

Beaune Grèves 1.3 ha.

M. et Mme Henri Moine, 7 blvd Clémenceau, 21200 Beaune

ALBERT MOROT   7 ha. (1820)

Beaune Bressandes 1.27 ha., Cent Vignes 1.28 ha., Grèves 0.13 ha., Teurons 1 ha., Toussaints 0.77 ha., Marconnets 0.67 ha., Savigny-lès-Beaune Vergelesses Clos La Bataillère (Monopole) 1.82 ha.

Old vines, classic methods, and low yields – with the owner, Mademoiselle Choppin, present at every stage, and herself (*Elle va aux vignes*) working in the vines, I gather. It is a simple formula for success.

Mlle Françoise Choppin, Château de la Creusotte, 21200 Beaune

PATRIARCHE PÈRE ET FILS   (1780)

Until its purchase by M. André Boisseaux after the Second World War this company was one of the quieter traditional shippers. Since then, dynamic marketing turned it, and its associate sparkling wine sister company Kriter, into the largest wine firm in town. Many of the best sites in Beaune for tourist tasting are part of this group, for instance Couvent des Cordeliers and Marché aux Vins, both a few steps from the Hôtel Dieu. The firm has regularly been the prime buyer at the Hospices de Beaune wine auction.

Properties owned, controlled or distributed include a dozen or so hectares of Beaune, the Château de Meursault, the Château de Marsannay (a costly neo-mediaeval construction between Marsannay and Couchey), and the vineyards of the Hospices de Dijon. The firm declined to confirm exact holdings, so I am indebted to the detailed research of Matt Kramer[4] and Jean-François Bazin[5] for much of what follows, the vineyards being held under several names:

Comptoir Vinicole d'Achat: Beaune Grèves 2.2 ha., Toussaints 1.44 ha., Cent Vignes 0.91 ha., Fèves 0.61 ha., Avaux 0.29 ha., Bressandes 0.16 ha.

Château de Meursault: Meursault Charmes 3.04 ha., Perrières 1.77 ha., Volnay Clos des Chênes 2.63 ha., Pommard Epenots 3.64 ha., Fremiers 0.31 ha., Charmots 0.15 ha., Bourgogne Clos du Château

André, Jacques et Pierre Boisseaux: Beaune Clos du Roi 0.26 ha.

Caves du Couvent des Cordeliers: Beaune Aigrots 0.23 ha.

Château de Marsannay: Chambertin 0.1 ha., Ruchottes-Chambertin 0.1 ha., Clos de Vougeot 0.21 ha., Marsannay (*rouge, rosé* and *blanc*) 11 ha., Fixin 2 ha., Gevrey-Chambertin *Premier Cru* 0.6 ha., Gevrey-Chambertin 2 ha., Bourgogne Montre-Cul 2 ha.

André Boisseaux et Gérard Couvert, Société de Diffusion Viticole, BP 10, 21201 Beaune Cedex

PIERRETTE ET JEAN-CLAUDE RATEAU   8 ha. (100 per cent)

Beaune Bressandes 1.1 ha., Reversées 1 ha., Clos des Mariages (Monopole) 0.6 ha., Mariages 0.4 ha., Couchérias (*blanc*) 0.6 ha., Puligny-Montrachet 0.3 ha., Beaune 0.8 ha., Côte de Beaune (*blanc*) 0.18 ha., (*rouge*) 0.35 ha., Hautes Côtes de Beaune (*rouge*) 0.4 ha., (*blanc*) 1.9 ha.

This estate was one of the first in Burgundy (in 1979) to cultivate organically, being affiliated to Nature et Progrès since 1982, and

4 *Making Sense of Burgundy*, William Morrow, New York, 1990.
5 *Chambertin, La Côte de Nuits de Dijon à Chambolle-Musigny*, Jacques Legrand, Paris, 1991.

Demeter since 1992. It has been 100 per cent bio-dynamic since 1981. In due course it will add Pommard *Premier Cru* and Gevrey-Chambertin to the range.

Observation under the microscope of the roots of his vines, around which no herbicides have been sprayed for so long, enables Rateau to see a mushroom growth, called *mycorhize*, whose filaments extend for up to 12 cm out from the roots, with which it is associated by symbiosis. This enables phosphorus to be assimilated naturally from the soil (without it having been applied). The volume of earth explored by these extensions of the roots is multiplied by a factor of 200. If there is water shortage, the filaments shrink back.

He is moving towards greater use of cordon pruning, and raising the levels of the foliage, so as to be able one day, perhaps, to leaf-pluck around the bunches, thus aerating them. Where it is legal in the Hautes Côtes, his vines are formed into a lyre canopy, which keeps the leaves dryer and warmer. If he could lyre prune in Beaune Mariages (which is low, and can be damp) he would do so, but old-fashioned INAO attitudes do not at present permit such experimentation. Thus may Burgundy's fondness for the recent past also impede its progress.

Whenever possible vineyard work tends towards prevention of disease or damage, so as to avoid the need to treat. His methods evolve every month, according to weather conditions and the health of each section of vineyard. I found the wines interesting and excellent, and hope to taste and drink them again.

Pierrette et Jean-Claude Rateau, chemin des Mariages, 21200 Beaune

REMOISSENET PÈRE ET FILS (1879)

This company has a small estate of 2.5 ha. in the Marconnets, Grèves, Toussaints, Bressandes and En Genêt vineyards of Beaune. It believes that a larger domaine would be a disadvantage, for one is tempted to find one's own wines good and call them by famous names when they should be declassed. M. Roland Remoissenet's speciality is combining the roles of *courtier* and merchant.

The advantage of buying from a *négociant-éleveur* is to a large extent having a choice of mature, or aged, stocks. I have tended to find Remoissenet red Burgundies more alcoholically rich than I

really like, sometimes rather florid. I imagine they age in barrel longer, and are racked more often, than is the case with the best growers. The purple-red turns to brown more quickly after bottling, and aromas of aged wine are present when they are dispatched. If one likes this sort of Burgundy, fine, and there are certainly fewer of the uncertainties or disappointments which relate to wines going through a dull period (between young fruitiness, and bottle-aged maturity) than are seen with many growers' wines.
Roland H. Remoissenet, 21200 Beaune

In Bligny-lès-Beaune:

CHÂTEAU DE BLIGNY-LÈS-BEAUNE   20.5 ha. (100 per cent)

Echézeaux 0.34 ha., Vosne-Romanée Au Dessus des Malconsorts 0.57 ha., Vosne-Romanée 1.11 ha., Nuits-Saint-Georges Les Pruliers 1.56 ha., Nuits-Saint-Georges *Premier Cru* 0.84 ha., Corton-Vergennes and Rognets (*rouge*) 0.76 ha., Corton-Vergennes (*blanc*) 0.27 ha., Beaune Clos des Aigrots 2.41 ha., Pertuisots 0.51 ha., Les Grèves 0.42 ha., Clos Saint Desiré 3.06 ha., Beaune 0.33 ha., Pommard Clos de la Chanière 0.67 ha., Les Arvelets 0.31 ha., Clos Blanc 0.2 ha., *Premier Cru* 0.58 ha., Pommard 4.32 ha., Volnay Clos Martin 0.38 ha., Puligny-Montrachet 1.75 ha.

This insurance-company-owned estate has spectacular vineyard holdings, but I have not yet seen evidence of wine-making sensitivity.
Bernard Canonica, Bligny-lès-Beaune, 21200 Beaune

CLAUDE MARÉCHAL   9 ha. (60 per cent)

Savigny-lès-Beaune *Premier Cru* 0.24 ha., Pommard 1.39 ha., Auxey-Duresses (*rouge*) 2.04 ha., (*blanc*) 0.88 ha., Savigny-lès-Beaune 1.5 ha., Ladois Côte de Beaune 0.64 ha., Bourgogne (*rouge*) 1.34 ha., (*blanc*) 0.27 ha., Passe-Tout-Grains and Aligoté

Bligny-lès-Beaune is off the Côte's beaten track, but there is fine wine to be had from here.
Claude Maréchal, 6 route de Chalon, 21200 Bligny-lès-Beaune

In Sainte-Marie la Blanche:

DOMAINE JEAN ALLEXANT   16.5 ha. (50 per cent)

Corton-Vergennes 0.4 ha., Beaune Grèves 0.35 ha., Couchereaux 0.96 ha., Beaune 2.05 ha., Pommard 0.18 ha., Santenay 0.99 ha., Côte de Beaune (*rouge*) 0.85 ha., (*blanc*) 0.31 ha.
Jean et Jérome Allexant, Sainte-Marie la Blanche, 21200 Beaune

DOMAINE ROGER ET JOËL RÉMY   14 ha. (70 per cent)

Aloxe-Corton 0.5 ha., Beaune *Premier Cru* 0.5 ha., Beaune 0.3 ha., Savigny-lès-Beaune 1.5 ha., Chorey-lès-Beaune 2.5 ha., Côte de Beaune-Villages, Bourgogne (*blanc*) 0.5 ha., (*rouge*) 5 ha., Passe-Tout-Grains 0.5 ha., Crémant 1 ha., Aligoté 1.5 ha.
Roger et Joël Rémy, Sainte-Marie la Blanche, 21200 Beaune

22

Pommard

The wines of Pommard have an old reputation for ageing and travelling well. They are described as solid, well-constructed wines of deep colour, comparable to good Cortons or Gevrey-Chambertins in their need to be laid away to soften up.

It is therefore particularly interesting that Claude Bourguignon of LAMS (Laboratory for the Analysis of the Microbiology of Soils), should be well advanced in explaining some of the reasons behind this. It appears to relate to the internal surface layers of the clays in Pommard's soils.

Clays are constructed like the leaves of a book. The calcium (which is positively charged) found naturally on Pommard's limestone hills is the catalyst which ensures the fusion between two negatively charged elements: clay and humus, to give fertile soil. Claude Bourguignon finds that the internal surface areas of Pommard's clays have points in common with the clays of the villages of the Côte de Nuits.

The sound of the name Pommard corresponds to most people's idea of what Burgundy should be. It is not just easy to pronounce, it has a full-bodied, generous ring to it. This has been a mixed blessing, for the wine has had an easier sale than other Burgundies, lulling growers into a false sense of security. If a wine will sell on its name, the pressure to make something of interest is diminished. There are, however, a number of marvellous domaines in this village, as will be seen.

The following are classified as *Premiers Crus*:

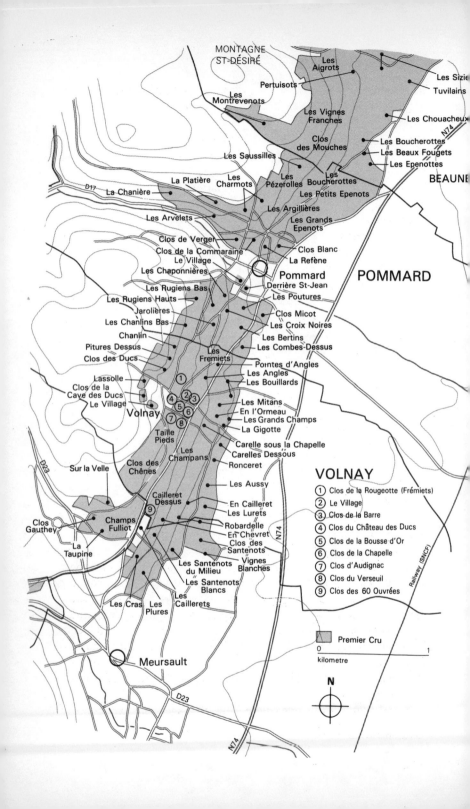

Arvelets, Les
Bertins, Les
Boucherottes, Les
Chanière, La
Chanlins-Bas, Les
Chaponnières, Les
Charmots, Les
Clos Blanc
Clos de la Commaraine
Clos de Verger
Clos des Epeneaux
Clos Micot
Combes-Dessus, Les
Croix Noires, Les

Epenots, Les Grands
Epenots, Les Petits
Fremiers, Les
Jarolières, Les
Largillière, En (Les Argillières)
Pezerolles, Les
Platière, La
Poutures, Les
Refène, La
Rugiens-Bas, Les
Rugiens-Hauts, Les
Saint-Jean, Derrière
Saussilles, Les
Village

First Growth and commune Pommard covered 311.17 ha. in 1991 (there is no such thing as white Pommard). The five-year average production (1988–92) was 144,200 cases.

Main Pommard growers and merchants

COMTE ARMAND   4.6 ha. (90 per cent)
DOMAINE DU CLOS DES EPENEAUX

Pommard *Premier Cru* Clos des Epeneaux (Monopole) 4.6 ha.

This top estate is easy to find: it is opposite the fountain, by Pommard's church. The wines are cellared off an irregular court-yard with worn stone staircases, an open gallery, and mossy old roof-tiles settling in waves over sagging roof-beams.

The wine-maker is a brilliant young Canadian, who each year vinifies three or four separate *cuvées* of his Monopole Clos (which straddles Grands and Petits Epenots, and has vines aged from six to 55 years old), only making a final *assemblage* at bottling time. He has not been fining recent vintages, and does not filter, which seems eminently reasonable given the intensely concentrated, deep-coloured wines he is producing, from low yields. His wines must go to patient owners, with the best possible cellarage. They are not designed for pleasurable early drinking and will need careful decanting.

Pascal Marchand is one of the Côte d'Or's leading exponents of organic cultivation, his walled Monopole vineyard being an ideal site in which to reduce chemical treatments. Eight different Maria Thunn preparations may be applied, particularly in winter, to encourage humus creation. Cow dung may be spread in spring, and silica at flowering and harvest times, to encourage the plant's vigour. But in 1993 he did not hesitate to treat with sulphur and copper sprays, to avoid mildew and other diseases.

He is an observer of nature and plants, and with other growers[1] has pooled his resources to share the costs of a compost spreader, for instance. His compost may be composed of shredded ash bark and wood, cow and horse dung, landscape gardener's refuse, some grapeskins and pips, some straw, with a Maria Thunn homoeopathic composition incorporated in the mixture. 'In many vineyards', says Marchand, 'the soil is doing nothing. It is not working to restore natural elements to the plant.' He aims to reverse this fact of life (or, you might say, death).

Pascal Marchand, Régisseur, place de l'Eglise, 21630 Pommard

DOMAINE BILLARD-GONNET 12 ha. (80 per cent)

Pommard Rugiens 0.3 ha., Clos de Verger 1.48 ha., Chaponnières 1.49 ha., Pezerolles 0.62 ha., Charmots 0.43 ha., Poutures 0.33 ha., Jarollières 0.7 ha., Bertins 0.4 ha., Pommard 3.2 ha., Beaune 0.96 ha.

There is nothing rustic or aggressive about these wines, they are smooth and regularly dependable, behind their civilized labels.

Pierre et Philippe Billard, 21630 Pommard

JEAN-MARC BOILLOT 10.2 ha. (100 per cent)

White: Bâtard-Montrachet 0.18 ha., Puligny-Montrachet Champ Canet 0.6 ha., Referts 0.6 ha., Combettes 0.48 ha., Truffière 0.24 ha., Puligny-Montrachet 1.6 ha., Chassagne-Montrachet 0.25 ha., Meursault 0.23 ha., Aligoté

Red: Pommard Jarollières 1.31 ha., Saucilles 0.4 ha., Rugiens 0.15 ha., Volnay Carelle sous la Chapelle 0.28 ha., Ronceret 0.32 ha., Pitures 0.45 ha., Beaune *Premier Cru* 0.75 ha., Volnay 1.25 ha., Pommard 0.4 ha., Bourgogne (*rouge*) 0.45 ha.

---

1 See Appendix D for list of members.

Jean-Marc Boillot was the first wine-maker at Olivier Leflaive Frères, preceding Franck Grux, and is experienced and capable. He caused anguish to Sauzet-lovers by insisting on his rightful share of the family vineyards (his father having married Etienne Sauzet's daughter). Domaine Sauzet (q.v.) was reduced in size, then leapt clear of its proprietor-shackles to adopt merchant status, enabling its wine-maker, Gérard Boudot, to buy in must or grapes, to bring his production back to pre-split levels.

Jean-Marc Boillot's share of the Domaine Sauzet vineyards formed the basis of his estate, to which he has now added. His first wines seemed a bit high on the alcohol and oak fronts to me, but this domaine should go from strength to strength. He too has merchant status, so can buy in grapes to vinify.

Jean-Marc Boillot, La Pommardière, 21630 Pommard

DOMAINE COSTE-CAUMARTIN   12 ha. (100 per cent)

Pommard Clos des Boucherottes (Monopole) 1.8 ha., Les Fremiers 1.3 ha., Pommard 3.7 ha., Saint-Romain (*blanc*) 3 ha., Bourgogne (*rouge*) 0.77 ha., (*blanc*) 0.55 ha., Passe-Tout-Grains

These wines age under wonderfully dilapidated seventeenth-century buildings. There is a courtyard with an old well, where puppies and children play happily in the dust. The same family has owned the vines since 1780.

In 1992 the *Wine Spectator* decided that Pommard Clos des Boucherottes was the 26th greatest wine in the world. The Sordets (who until 1990 might sell three-quarters of their harvest in barrel) must have been quite surprised. Their heads do not appear swollen.

This is a good Burgundy cellar, which has installed air conditioning for its ground-floor storage, but one certainly needs to taste carefully before making a choice.

Jérome Sordet, rue du Parc, 21630 Pommard

DOMAINE DE COURCEL   8 ha. (90 per cent)

Pommard Rugiens 1 ha., Grand Clos des Epenots 5 ha., Fremiers 0.65 ha., Croix Noires 0.58 ha., Pommard 0.4 ha.

These wines may be compared with the best in the village; I have found them models of harmony.

Gilles de Courcel et Yves Tavant (Manager), 21630 Pommard

DOMAINE MICHEL GAUNOUX   10 ha. (100 per cent)

Pommard Grands Epenots 2.92 ha., Rugiens 0.69 ha., *Premier Cru* (Arvelets, Charmots and Combes) 0.77 ha., Corton-Renardes 1.23 ha., Beaune 3.11 ha., Bourgogne (*rouge*) 0.69 ha.

This domaine venerates its ancestors. It is an immaculate, working museum, dedicated to traditions. Everything is spacious, polished, and well-ordered.

It has exceptional depth of stock, offering wines from the seven or eight most recent vintages, and small amounts from the previous thirty. Yes, thirty. Once the wines are twenty-five years old or so the bottles are inspected for low levels, or seeping corks. If necessary, they are topped up with identical wine, and re-closed with new corks.

The late Michel Gaunoux's grandfather was in the ivory billiard-ball business, until his marriage to a local girl after a chance Volnay wedding meeting.

Very unusually for Burgundy, there is no sampling from the barrel here. 'That way clients only taste what they receive', says Madame Gaunoux, perfectly reasonably. There are two years in barrel (new oak does not enjoy high status), plus two in bottle before release. However, it is then essential to age these wines; drinking them young would completely miss the point.

My personal taste is normally for wines which are lighter in alcohol than these; however, Domaine Michel Gaunoux bottles can work a special magic, and I have quickly found myself bewitched.

Mme Veuve Michel Gaunoux, rue Notre Dame, 21630 Pommard

HÉRITIERS ARMAND GIRARDIN   6.5 ha. (90 per cent)
ALETH LE ROYER-GIRARDIN

Pommard Rugiens 0.36 ha., Epenots 0.54 ha., Charmots 0.57 ha., Refène 0.4 ha., Beaune Clos des Mouches 0.36 ha., Montrevenots 0.42 ha., Meursault Poruzots 0.26 ha., Pommard 1.5 ha., Bourgogne (*rouge*) 1.82 ha., Aligoté

I have heard excellent reports of these wines.

Mme Aleth Le Royer-Girardin, route d'Autun, 21630 Pommard

DOMAINE A.-F. GROS   4.03 ha. (100 per cent)

Richebourg 0.2 ha., Echézeaux 0.26 ha., Vosne-Romanée Aux Réas 0.7 ha., Maizières 0.28 ha., Chalandins 0.33 ha., Bourgogne Hautes Côtes de Nuits 2.02 ha.

With the exception of the Richebourg, these wines are vinified and tended in Pommard by François Parent, who married Anne-Françoise Gros. None of the single-vineyard Vosnes is a First Growth, but they are normally vinified and offered separately. Because of the small production, the Richebourg is made and bottled by Michel Gros, Anne-Françoise's brother, in Vosne-Romanée, which is an admirably sensible arrangement. If only more growers with small *Grands Crus* holdings would pool their resources in this way, instead of trying to vinify tiny quantities independently (or giving up, chucking the grapes in with something else, then calling one wine by two names of origin – one thinks particularly of growers in Clos de Vougeot) the consumer would more often be a winner.

Mme Anne-Françoise Parent-Gros, La Garelle, 21630 Pommard

LAHAYE PÈRE ET FILS   20 ha. (80 per cent)

Corton-Renardes 0.3 ha., Pommard Les Arvelets 1.5 ha., Volnay-Santenots 0.4 ha., Beaune Montrevenots 0.2 ha., Pommard 4 ha., Beaune 0.4 ha., Côte de Beaune 0.3 ha., Meursault Perrières 0.3 ha., Charmes 0.2 ha., Meursault 3 ha., Bourgogne (*blanc*) 3 ha., (*rouge*) 4 ha.

Serge Lahaye and his sons Michel, Dominique and Vincent, place de l'Eglise, 21630 Pommard

DOMAINE RAYMOND LAUNAY   11 ha. (90 per cent)

Chambertin 0.14 ha., Latricières-Chambertin 0.2 ha., Pommard Chaponnières 0.6 ha., Clos Blanc 0.2 ha., Rugiens 0.1 ha., Pommard (Les Perrières) 2.5 ha. Santenay Clos de Gatsulard (Monopole) 3 ha., Ladoix (*blanc*) Clou d'Orge 1.84 ha.

Raymond Launay, 21630 Pommard

DOMAINE LEJEUNE   7 ha. (100 per cent)

Pommard Rugiens 0.25 ha., En l'Argillières 1.3 ha., Les Poutures 1 ha., Trois Follots 0.8 ha., Bourgogne *rouge, blanc* and Aligoté

There is no de-stemmer and no crusher here, grape bunches being placed whole in the vats, then squashed by foot. It may take a week to tread a vat, one-quarter at a time, the work proceeding as if cutting a camembert into four pieces. Must will be pumped over during the first week, to bring the vat temperature up to 30°. If this drops, workers climb back in to reactivate the vats. There is no refrigeration plant. Here is a Burgundian individualist by whose wines it is impossible not to be charmed.

François Jullien de Pommerol, La Confrérie, 21630 Pommard

HÉRITIERS RAOUL LENEUF   4 ha. (50 per cent)

Pommard and Beaune

M. Leneuf's tasting-room is simple and attractive. Built of old stone, it is triangular, with a large open fireplace in one of the walls. This is a family domaine, mainly supplying French and European private homes.

Louis Leneuf, 21630 Pommard

DOMAINE ANDRÉ MUSSY   6 ha. (100 per cent)

Pommard Epenots 0.75 ha., *Premier Cru* 1 ha., Pommard 1 ha., Beaune Epenottes 1 ha., Montremenots 1.25 ha., Volnay 0.25 ha., Bourgogne Pinot Noir 0.5 ha.

Impossible to meet this lean, fit septuagenarian without warming to his enthusiasm and sparkling eye. Clive Coates has been instrumental, I understand, in persuading Mussy to do partial ageing in new oak from the 1989 vintage onwards. The wines of the mid-1980s could be very unapproachable while maturing, never passing through an attractive youthful stage in bottle.

Like Henri Magnien in Gevrey-Chambertin (another septuagenarian) I feel Mussy must have altered his methods in the 1980s. Having made concentrated wines for the long haul for so long, did they both perhaps change their objectives, reasoning that they would make wines they would have a good chance of personally enjoying? It seems perfectly reasonable, and to some extent their private clients will have been ageing with them, so welcoming such an evolution. His daughter having re-married, I understand Mussy's son-in-law is now working with him.

André Mussy, 21630 Pommard

DOMAINE PARENT, SA   11.57 ha. (100 per cent)

Corton-Renardes 0.28 ha., Corton 0.3 ha., Pommard Chaponnières 0.59 ha., Epenots 0.58 ha., Pézerolles 0.34 ha., Chanlins 0.35 ha., Arvelets 0.31 ha., Argillières 0.3 ha., *Premier Cru* 0.22 ha., Beaune Epenottes 1.75 ha., Boucherottes 0.3 ha., *Premier Cru* 0.26 ha., Ladoix La Corvée 0.39 ha., Ladoix 0.37 ha., Pommard 0.63 ha., Bourgogne (*rouge*) 4.35 ha.

The Parent family is a direct descendant of the Burgundian, Etienne Parent, who guided Thomas Jeffferson on his visit to the Côte d'Or in March 1787, and subsequently supplied him with Burgundy for the White House. Jefferson once wrote to Parent, 'I place myself in your hands – quality first, and then the price.' How perceptive.

In order to control the Parent name, some twenty years ago Jacques Parent formed a *négociant* business to buy the grapes of his relation Jean Parent (who had vines in Pommard Rugiens, Volnay Clos des Chênes and Fremiets and the Monopole Monthelie Clos Gauthey). Until 1992, Jacques and his son François also bought grapes and made the wine from a second Monopole, Pommard Clos Micault.

For many years this was a good source of Pommard, but then I came to wish the wines were less chaptalized, particularly the Bourgogne *rouge*, which seemed to be trying to pass for Pommard. What had been *haute couture* wine-making went off-the-peg, giving solidly constructed, powerful wines, which no doubt travelled and aged soundly. Matters evolve fast, however, and I believe this domaine is climbing back up from its period of playing safe, and that we may see fireworks.

M. et Mme François Parent, place de l'Eglise, 21630 Pommard

CHATEAU DE POMMARD   20 ha. (100 per cent)

Owner Jean-Louis Laplanche is a psychoanalyst and Sorbonne professor (responsible for editing the new French translation of Freud) who was stung by the derogatory piece about his vineyard, which is situated almost in the plain, between village and road, in the first edition of this book. He wrote:

> There is no need to listen to Pommard gossips to learn the geographical situation of my domaine. What matters, and I'm proud of it, is the quality of its wine. Plenty of Pommard inhabitants (at least those who are jealous or narrow-minded), prefer to sit back comfortably on the eternal reputation of their *Premiers Crus*. This allows them to believe that quality, being a divine right, may be had without effort or care.
>
> How can I ennumerate my efforts? Old vines, clonal selection, short pruning, very low yields (in 1987: 24 hl/ha. – just ask my neighbours . . .). Hand sorting of the grapes first in the rows then on a table in the vat-house. Long vatting, with *pigeage* thrice a day. Two years ageing in new wood. Elimination of all the *cuvées* of mediocre quality, and bottling only of those *cuvées* which are worthy (sometimes a quarter of the harvest). Those are the elements I would prefer you to mention, rather than architectural anecdotes about the château.
>
> Would you accept the need to distance yourself from ready-made appraisals based on land classification? In Bordeaux, they know how to evaluate and reward continuous efforts . . . It is not the soil which has changed, but the men who now know how to make the most of it. But to convince you, I shall only do it glass in hand . . .

So with trepidation I turned up at the château, to be struck by the magnificent out-buildings (dating from the eighteenth century), but also by his harvesting policy: each picker has two differently coloured baskets, one for perfect bunches, one for imperfect grapes needing to be sorted. Mechanical harvesting? Never – how could he sort the harvest? In the vat-house, eighteen sorters round a stainless steel table clip out rotten grapes.

This is an enormous property, the largest Clos in single ownership in Burgundy, so how does he find his pickers? Each year gypsy caravans roll up, the Romany arriving like snails, their houses on their backs. He negotiates terms with the chiefs of the five tribes.

In 1979 he doubled the number of his fermentation vessels, so he would not have to run off the wine early in years of plentiful yield.

So what about the wine? It is very impressive, and I bought some.

Fifteen thousand visitors pass through his gate each year, and I am sure they go away delighted, as did I.

Jean-Louis Laplanche, au Château de Pommard, 21630 Pommard

DOMAINE POTHIER-RIEUSSET   7 ha. (100 per cent)

Pommard Rugiens 0.3 ha., Epenots 0.15 ha., Clos de Verger 0.35 ha., *Premier Cru* 0.2 ha., Beaune Boucherottes 0.24 ha., Pommard 1.35 ha., Bourgogne (*rouge*) 2 ha., Meursault Caillerets (rouge) 0.26 ha., Bourgogne (*rouge*) 1.96 ha., (*blanc*) 0.46 ha.

One of my first and best experiences of aged red Burgundy, at once gamey and spicy, was Les Rugiens off-years in this stone cellar, 1946 and 1938, tasted in the late 1960s. Let no one say Burgundy cannot age wonderfully.

Mme Marie-Christine Pothier et Virgile Pothier, route d'Ivry, 21630 Pommard

23
Volnay

───────

The village of Volnay sits high up on its hillside, as befits a place whose wines have long been reputed the finest of the Côte de Beaune. Today it has some outstanding estates, setting the highest possible standards.

The names of many of the individual vineyards have been unchanged for 700 years. In the thirteenth century, the Order of Malta owned six *ouvrées* of En Cailleret, and the Priory of Saint-Etienne in Beaune had vines in En Verseux, Les Angles and Carelle. The dukes owned part of Taille Pieds and Chevrey, and in 1250 constructed a château, for the view was so varied, the air so good, and the wines and water so excellent. In 1509 the king owned parts of En Cailleret, Champans, En l'Ormeau and Taille Pieds. On the collapse of Valois Burgundy with Charles the Bold's death, one of Louis XI's first actions was to have the 1477 Volnay harvest brought to his château at Plessis-lès-Tours. Louis XIV is said to have preferred Volnay to all wines and Volnay was served at the royal table for the coronation of Louis XV.

It occurred to the Prince de Condé to have Pinot vines transplanted from Volnay to Chantilly, but the wine they gave did not come up to expectations. The prince complained, so Monsieur Brunet, of Beaune, replied, 'Monseigneur, you should also have taken the soil and the sun.'

The following are classified as *Premiers Crus*:

Angles, Les
Aussy, Les
Barre, La (Clos de la Barre)
Brouillards, Les
Cailleret Dessus (Clos des 60 Ouvrées)
Cailleret, En
Cailleret, Les
Carelle sous la Chapelle
Carelles Dessous
Champans, En
Chanlin
Chevret, En
Clos de l'Audignac
Clos de la Bousse d'Or
Clos de la Cave des Ducs
Clos de la Chapelle
Clos des Chânes
Clos des Ducs
Clos du Château des Ducs
Fremiets
Fremiets (Clos de la Rougeotte)
Gigotte, La
Grands Champs, Les
Lassolle
Lurets, Les
Mitans, Les
Ormeau, En l'
Pitures Dessus
Pointes d'Angles
Robardelle
Ronceret, Le
Taille Pieds
Verseuil, En (Clos du Verseuil)
Village, Le

In the commune of Meursault, the following have right to the *Premier Cru appellation* Volnay-Santenots (which is obligatorily a red wine):

Clos des Santenots
Plures, Les (Les Petures)
Santenots Blancs, Les
Santenots-Dessous, Les
Santenots du Milieu, Les
Vignes Blanches, Les

First Growth and commune Volnay covered an area of 218.03 ha. in 1991 (as in Pommard, there is no white wine). The five-year average production (1988–92) was 98,700 cases.

Main Volnay growers

D'ANGERVILLE, DOMAINE DU MARQUIS   15 ha. (100 per cent)

Volnay Clos des Ducs (Monopole) 2.4 ha., Champans 3.98 ha., Fremiets 1.57 ha., Caillerets 0.45 ha., Taille Pieds 1.7 ha.,

L'Ormeau 0.65 ha., Les Angles 0.53 ha., Pitures 0.31 ha., Pommard
Les Combes 0.38 ha., Meursault-Santenots 1.5 ha.

'I have never asked someone to get into a vat stark naked', says
the owner, and his wine-making does not include any punching-
down. Fermenting must is pumped over twice daily, and the vats
covered by sail-cloth, plastic-sealed for cleanliness, held taut within
metal circles bigger than the vat's diameter. This reduces alcohol
loss, and retains inert gas above the cap. In the period 1979–81
d'Angerville wines may have gone through a light phase, but now I
think they are some of the most harmoniously superb of the Côte de
Beaune.

Wood for new barrels comes from oak forests in the Haute
Marne, the Aube, the Haute Saône, and the Vosges, particularly a
forest 500 metres above sea-level, between Colmar and Gérardmer,
uncut for forty years after the First World War, which gives the
finest, tight-grained staves. It had been a four-year battlefield, and if
you felled the trees, remnants of exploded shells would break the
saws, so the oaks, for many years, were just allowed to grow.

Reflecting on his vineyards, the Marquis d'Angerville has written,

All these place-names, facing towards the south-east, lie upon
marly-limestone deposits. The rocky soil retains the sun's heat,
reflecting it back towards the grapes, quickening their maturation. The slope, often quite steep, prevents excessive dampness
and permits proper drainage. These natural advantages ensure
the wine's structure, and confer its aroma and fine bouquet,
while the weather determines its ability to age.

He is a minimalist, in the league of interventionist wine-makers.
The key to his quality, I think, is low yield.

In the early days of the *appellation contrôlée* laws the present
marquis's father waged unceasing war against dishonest practices.
Consequently, the local commerce closed against him, and he was
forced to bottle his own wine and sell direct.

That is all a long time ago, but his son used to recall the time
when Beaune railway station was probably Burgundy's largest producer. The wines arrived from the south to be rebaptized and dispatched without leaving their trains. As well as combating fraud,
the late marquis undertook the most rigorous selection of quality
producing vines, which became known as Pinots d'Angerville. They
are still to be found on this famous estate, of course, and current

clonal research in his old Taille Pieds vineyard may well result in its plant material being multiplied for wider use.
Jacques d'Angerville, Volnay, 21190 Meursault

DOMAINE BITOUZET-PRIEUR   9 ha. (60 per cent)

Volnay Clos des Chênes 0.35 ha., Taille Pieds 0.35 ha., Pitures 0.75 ha., *Premier Cru* 0.5 ha., Volnay 2 ha., Meursault Perrières 0.27 ha., Charmes 0.3 ha., Clos du Cromin 0.75 ha., Meursault 1 ha.

This is an interesting estate, whose wines are well worth buying when spotted.
Vincent Bitouzet, rue de la Combe, 21190 Volnay

DOMAINE JEAN BOILLOT ET FILS   13.5 ha. (100 per cent)

Nuits-Saint-Georges Les Cailles 1.07 ha., Savigny-lès-Beaune Vergelesses 0.69 ha., Lavières 0.73 ha., Beaune Clos du Roi 0.7 ha., Epenottes 0.64 ha., Volnay Chevrets 2.06 ha., Fremiets 1.31 ha., Caillerets 0.72 ha., Meursault Genevrières 0.16 ha., Puligny-Montrachet Clos de la Mouchère (Monopole) 3.92 ha., Pucelles 0.53 ha., Puligny-Montrachet 0.64 ha.

This domaine has wonderful vineyard sites – Nuits Cailles, Volnay Chevrets and Fremiets, and nearly four hectares of a Monopole First Growth Puligny – but has not always made the most of them. 'A lot of new oak, superb wines – even more perfectionist than Jean-Marc', says one Beaune broker now, however, comparing this Boillot to his brother in Pommard.
Henri Boillot, rue des Angles, 21190 Volnay

JEAN-MARC BOULEY   12 ha. (90 per cent)

Volnay Clos des Chênes 0.5 ha., Carelle sous la Chapelle 0.38 ha., Roncerets 0.3 ha., Caillerets 0.2 ha., Pommard Fremiers 0.5 ha., Rugiens 0.3 ha., Pézerolles 0.3 ha., Beaune Reversées 0.6 ha., Volnay 3.5 ha., Pommard 0.5 ha., Hautes Côtes de Beaune 1.2 ha., Bourgogne (*blanc*) and (*rouge*)

Bouley is from an old Volnay vigneron family, but only since 1986 has he been bottling a high proportion of his production, of which I hear excellent reports.
Jean-Marc Bouley, chemin de la Cave, 21190 Volnay

DOMAINE YVON CLERGET   5.5 ha. (100 per cent)

Clos de Vougeot 0.34 ha., Volnay Caillerets 0.31 ha., Clos du Verseuil (Monopole) 0.68 ha., Santenots 0.68 ha., Carelle sous la Chapelle 0.31 ha., *Premier Cru* 0.47 ha., Volnay 1.08 ha., Pommard Rugiens 0.85 ha., Meursault 0.37 ha., Bourgogne (*rouge*) 0.35 ha.

These wines have seemed to me over-chaptalized, and to lack the exquisitely supple yet dense fruit which characterizes the best Volnay. This is one of Europe's oldest family businesses, for Clergets have been vignerons continuously since 1268, I understand. In the statute book of the Société d'Entraide des Vignerons de Volnay are to be seen the names of the founder members, and their date of settling in Volnay (*Clerget venue à Volnay en 1268*), and on a wall of the meeting room of the *mairie* of Volnay may be found the names of the all the provosts, aldermen and mayors, with the dates when they took up their responsibilities (*Jacques Clerget 1300*).

Yvon Clerget, rue de la Combe, 21190 Volnay

BERNARD ET LOUIS GLANTENAY   8.5 ha. (40 per cent)

Volnay Brouillards 1.17 ha., Santenots 0.67 ha., Clos des Chênes 0.5 ha., Caillerets 0.18 ha., Pommard Saussilles 1.15 ha., Rugiens 0.22 ha., Volnay 2 ha., Pommard 0.22 ha.

A valuable address if one is seeking a dependable bottle at a reasonable price.

Bernard Glantenay, rue de Vaut, 21190 Volnay

GEORGES GLANTENAY ET FILS   9 ha. (60 per cent)

Volnay Brouillard 1.11 ha., Santenots 0.52 ha., Pommard Rugiens 0.22 ha., Volnay 2.35 ha., Pommard 0.43 ha., Bourgogne (*rouge*) 1.36 ha., (*blanc*) 1.25 ha., Passe-Tout-Grains and Aligoté

Bernard Glantenay's brother, whose wines I do not know.

Pierre Glantenay, chemin de la Cave, 21190 Volnay

DOMAINE MICHEL LAFARGE   10.06 ha. (100 per cent)

Volnay Clos des Chênes 0.9 ha., Clos du Château des Ducs (Monopole) 0.57 ha., *Premier Cru* 0.42 ha., Volnay 2.61 ha., Pommard Pézerolles 0.14 ha., Beaune Grèves 0.38 ha., Beaune Teurons 0.2 ha., Côte de Beaune-Villages 0.28 ha., Meursault 1.02 ha., Bourgogne (*rouge*) 1.21 ha., Passe-Tout-Grains and Aligoté

'Vinification is observation', said Lafarge (this was 1988):

> The skills get passed down the generations from mouth to ear, while vinifying. The type of wine made varies greatly with the actual weather during the harvest – take 1959 and 1976. Both were very hot years, but the first had a hot harvest, the second a cold one, and this was responsible for the slow pace at which the 1976 evolved.
>
> Pinot Noir does not like great heats. Very hot years in Burgundy are not the best years. Volnay's luck is that, even when the wines are young you can make the most of them, while a wine from a great year may age almost as well as a growth with a reputation for long life.

It was true: the proof from 1978 and 1945 had been in our glasses.

I have often bought and sold Lafarge wines, which helps me know them well, and does not stop me, I think, being able to assess them objectively.

When Robert Parker wrote, 'Lafarge can be a distressingly inconsistent winemaker'[1] it was like a flash of lightning illuminating the wine-writing scene, at the same time splitting its tallest tree down the middle. Lafarge inconsistent – how could a writer on Burgundy pen that? Could it be that Parker's need to appear authoritative was a higher priority than his concern for knowledge, for accuracy? Surely not. Or was it simply that his confusion over how red Burgundy matures (the 'window of drinkability', discussed in the chapter on tasting) had led him astray? Surely he was not simply floating a controversial opinion to keep his subscribers dangling on hooks – even though that ignoble thought used to recur to me regularly as, at breakneck pace, he assessed, reassessed, downgraded and upgraded young wines as they evolved in their barrels, tanks or bottles. This is the writer with a paragon palate, says *Time*. They might add one day: 'Parker could be a distressingly inconsistent wine-writer, when it came to Burgundy.' But perhaps all is due to

---

1 *Burgundy: a Comprehensive Guide to the Producers, Appellations and Wines*, Simon & Schuster, New York, 1990.

change, if he sticks to his intention, stated in 1992, of no longer providing tasting notes on Burgundies before the wines are bottled. Michel et Frédéric Lafarge, Volnay, 21190 Meursault

HUBERT DE MONTILLE   7.5 ha. (100 per cent)

Volnay Taille Pieds 0.78 ha., Champans 0.55 ha., Mitans 0.73 ha., *Premier Cru* 0.7 ha., Pommard Rugiens 1.1 ha., Pézerolles 1.09 ha., Grands Epenots 0.25 ha., Puligny-Montrachet Le Cailleret 0.51 ha., Bourgogne 0.75 ha.

A small estate, but greatly loved by those who know its mature bottles. As with d'Angerville, I think there was a blip around 1979–81, at a time when red Burgundy looked very expensive (before claret prices began to boom), but, since then, there has rarely been risk of disappointment, so long as the wines were not judged when immature.

Maître Hubert de Montille is a Dijon lawyer (threatening retirement), often deeply involved in wine-related Burgundy litigation; there can be few lawyers who understand the issues better.

A vigneron cultivates the vineyards, but he – aided by his son Etienne, or daughter Alix – supervises the vinification. During the 1959 vintage (his tenth) he made a mistake in calculating the amount of sugar to be used for chaptalizing, with the result that a wine of only 11.5 of alcohol was produced. To his great surprise this developed better in bottle than any of his other 1959s. As a result, very little chaptalization has since taken place on this estate. Punching down features mightily. Yields are low.

For me, that accident had consequences as radical and happiness-enhancing as the expected Turkish attack on the old Hungarian castle of Tokaji, which, legend says, caused the overseer to delay the vintage, resulting in the discovery of noble mould, *botrytis cinerea*, on the grapes. The wine made from their shrivelled, softened skins, was the most luscious anyone had ever tasted, as Hugh Johnson recounts.[2]

It is taking time for other growers to dare to follow him down to more moderate alcohol levels, just as it is taking time for consumers

---

2 *The Story of Wine.* If true, says Johnson, this would pre-date a similar legend in Germany by 120 years, and also considerably pre-date the first dessert wines in Sauternes.

to be prepared to age red Burgundy as long as they sometimes age claret, in order for it to mature correctly.

Not all bottles need cool, humid storage. Some vintages can be wonderful when fresh into bottle, and for two years or so (particularly the Volnays); others need six to ten years to open and soften, then may improve for another ten or twenty (particularly the Pommards). These wines can be a bit strict or severe when immature maybe, but they have no extra fat on them, and no noticeable make-up. They can be brilliant and fascinating like diamonds.

In 1993 the estate acquired 12 *ouvrées* of Puligny-Montrachet Le Cailleret, its first white wine.

Hubert de Montille and family, 21190 Volnay

DOMAINE DE LA POUSSE D'OR   13 ha. (100 per cent)

Volnay Clos de la Bousse d'Or (Monopole) 2.14 ha., Volnay Caillerets Clos de 60 Ouvrées (Monopole) 2.39 ha., Volnay en Caillerets 2.27 ha., Volnay Clos d'Audignac (Monopole) 1 ha., Pommard Les Jarollières 1.05 ha., Santenay Les Gravières 1.87 ha., Santenay Clos Tavannes 2.1 ha.

These vineyards formed part of the 133 hectare estate of Jacques-Marie Duvault-Blochet 'at the time the latter crowned his vineyard empire in his 80th year by acquiring the Romanée-Conti in 1869' (as Richard Olney puts it). The house is cut into a hillside overlooking some of Volnay's best vineyard sites. With its terrace of tulip and catalpa trees it is one of the finest spots on the Côte.

The domaine is the largest proprietor of Volnay Caillerets, owning a third of this vineyard, and is sole owner of the Clos de la Bousse d'Or, which lies at the heart of the hill, in the centre of the village of Volnay.

Within five years of coming to Volnay (his first harvest was 1964) from farming in the Aisne, its director Gérard Potel had earned the respect of some of the most critical wine-makers on the Côte. He was a pioneer of picking out rotten grapes or bunches in poor years, enabling him to bottle all his wines every year.

The estate is owned by a syndicate put together by the late Jean Ferté, a French gastronome who belonged to the Académie des Vins de France, the Académie des Gastronomes and the Club des Cent. With the departure recently of one minority shareholder, his interest was acquired by a group of West Australian wine enthusiasts, and this connection stimulated Gérard Potel into a joint vineyard venture, planting Pinot Noir in Pemberton (Western Australia), which will certainly cause waves when the vines and wines mature.

The estate must always have had an exceptional *entrée*, through M. Ferté and his friends, to the greatest French restaurants and Burgundy lovers, and this clientele must have influenced the style of wine being made. Some commentators are disappointed, perhaps wishing to find noticeable new oakiness, powerfully extracted tannic fruitiness, and those other elements which might cause the bottles to shine when tasted in a line-up. Potel's first vintage produced extremely tannic, long-lasting wines, but he did not aim to repeat that characteristic willy-nilly; on the contrary he tries to respect the style of the year.

He is one of several growers (Tollot-Beaut, Régis Rossignol in Volnay, and Cave de Buxy are others, I understand) experimenting with a Durafroid machine which evaporates excess water, thus reducing the need to chaptalize. This is important research, conducted within an official framework, which may have long-term regional ramifications. It is not a vinification method, he states, but a palliative. Tasting 1992 Caillerets (evaporated) against a traditionally-made Caillerets (chaptalized), the first had obvious merits, when nine months old.

Pousse d'Or for long had a good market in the USA until one day it met with an accident at the hands of Parker Demolitions (Ink) since when its wines have largely gone in other directions.

My most exciting bottles of Volnay have been from other domaines (to which I happened to be closer), but a tasting here of recent vintages in 1993 left me with excellent impressions.

Gérard Potel, 21190 Volnay

RÉGIS ROSSIGNOL-CHANGARNIER   7 ha. (80 per cent)

Volnay *Premier Cru* 0.9 ha., Volnay 1.6 ha., Beaune Les Theurons 0.61 ha., Pommard 0.5 ha., Savigny-lès-Beaune 0.25 ha., Meursault 0.14 ha., Bourgogne (*rouge*) 1 ha., (*blanc*) 0.28 ha., Passe-Tout-Grains and Aligoté

Concentration (by Durafroid machine) gives better structured wines, finds the enthusiastic Rossignol, after three trial vintages.

M. et Mme Régis Rossignol-Changarnier, rue d'Amour, 21190 Volnay

ROSSIGNOL-FÈVRIER PÈRE ET FILS   7.7 ha. (100 per cent)

Volnay Robardelle 0.42 ha., *Premier Cru* 0.85 ha., Pommard 1.34 ha., Bourgogne (*rouge* and *blanc*), Aligoté
Marcel et Frédéric Rossignol, rue du Mont, 21230 Volnay

BERNARD VAUDOISEY-MUTIN   10 ha. (80 per cent)
DOMAINE CHRISTOPHE VAUDOISEY

Volnay (including Cailleret and Clos des Chênes) 4 ha., Pommard (including Chanlins) 1 ha., Meursault (including Vireuils) 1 ha., Bourgogne 4 ha.

Here two generations vinify together (but sell separately). The younger seems an unyielding character, like his wine. He de-stalks it, but still ends up with something rather abrupt.
Bernard et Christophe Vaudoisey, 21190 Volnay

JOSEPH VOILLOT   10 ha. (80 per cent)

Volnay Champans 1.07 ha., Fremiets 0.7 ha., Cailleret 0.2 ha., Volnay 2.2 ha., Pommard Rugiens 0.3 ha., Pézerolles and Epenots 0.6 ha., Pommard Clos Micault 0.15 ha., Pommard 2 ha., Bourgogne 2.3 ha., Meursault Cras 0.2 ha., Meursault 0.2 ha.

Voillot has experimented with the Durafroid evaporation machine (owned in tandem with Michel Lafarge and Régis Rossignol) since the 1990 vintage, typically gaining 0.4°. It seems an improvement on bleeding the vats, for only water is removed, leaving acidity, tannins, sugars and other elements to enrich the must. One may expect to taste well-concentrated wines from this address, both supple and fine.
Joseph Voillot, Volnay, 21190 Meursault

24

Monthelie, Saint-Romain and Auxey-Duresses

MONTHELIE

In 1855 Dr Lavalle recorded that the wines of Monthelie were worth three-quarters those of Volnay; if Volnay was offered at 400 francs *la queue* (456 litres), Monthelie would be offered at 300 francs. The relationship today, over a hundred years later, is almost identical. In terms of fruit richness and harmony, Monthelie wines are to Volnays as Listracs are to Saint-Juliens: set back from the prime sites, they need a ripe vintage, skilful wine-making and bottle age, to show their fine paces.

Vines were recorded at Monthelie as early as the ninth century, when Count Adalhard gave a *finage* to the church of Saint-Nazaire d'Autun. No stream crosses the commune, and there is no arable land; it is dedicated to wine-producing, but relatively little is made – not enough for the name to have become well known.

Some growers spell the village 'Monthélie', but it is generally pronounced Monthelie, the middle 'e' hardly sounded. This is the spelling adopted.

The following are classified as *Premiers Crus*:

Cas Rougeot, Le
Champs Fulliot, Les
Château Gaillard, Le
Clos Gauthey, Le
Duresses, Les
Meix Bataille, Le
Riottes, Les
Taupine, La
Velle, Sur la

Vignes Rondes, Les
Village de Monthelie, Le

First Growth and commune Monthelie are planted on 107.49 ha. (red wines), and 4.31 ha. (whites). The five-year average production (1988–92) was 49,000 cases of red, and 2,300 cases of white.

Main Monthelie growers

J. BOIGELOT   (8 ha. (50 per cent)
ERIC BOIGELOT

Volnay-Santenots 0.15 ha., Taille Pieds 0.19 ha., Monthelie Champs Fulliots 0.39 ha., Sur la Velle 0.24 ha., Pommard 0.33 ha., Volnay 0.18 ha., Monthelie 3.5 ha., Meursault 0.68 ha., Bourgogne (*blanc*) 0.69 ha.
Jacques et Eric Boigelot, 21190 Monthelie

DOMAINE DENIS BOUSSEY   10.9 ha. (55 per cent)

Red: Monthelie Champs Fulliots and Sur la Velle 0.67 ha., Monthelie Hauts-Brins 1.17 ha., Monthelie 2.2 ha., Volnay *Premier Cru* 0.17 ha., Volnay 0.61 ha., Pommard 0.55 ha., Aloxe-Corton 0.24 ha., Savigny-lès-Beaune 0.25 ha., Bourgogne (*rouge*) 0.3 ha.
White: Meursault Charmes 0.2 ha., Meursault 2.2 ha., Monthelie Champs Fulliot 0.2 ha., Monthelie 0.72 ha., Bourgogne Chardonnay 1.38 ha.
   This cellar has a long history of successful bottling.
Denis Boussey, Grande Rue, Monthelie, 21190 Meursault

XAVIER BOUZERAND   7 ha. (100 per cent)

Monthelie *Premier Cru* 0.97 ha., Monthelie (*rouge*) 2.89 ha., (*blanc*) 0.34 ha., Beaune 0.3 ha., Meursault 0.43 ha., Auxey-Duresses (*blanc*) 0.41 Bourgogne Aligoté and Passe-Tout-Grains
Xavier Bouzerand et Ulrich Dujardin, 21190 Monthelie

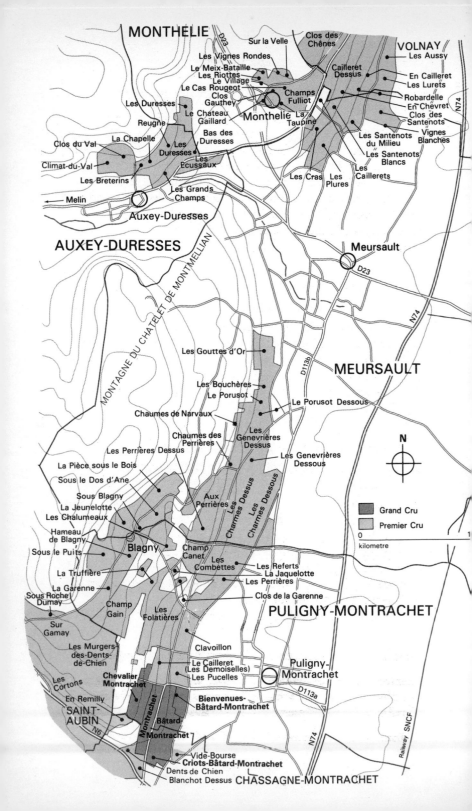

DOMAINE DARVIOT-PERRIN   8.5 ha. (50 per cent)

Volnay La Gigotte (Monopole) 0.3 ha., Volnay-Santenots 0.55 ha., Beaune Bélissands 0.55 ha., Meursault Charmes 0.3 ha., Chassagne-Montrachet Les Bondues (*rouge*) 0.4 ha., Blanchots Dessus (*blanc*) 0.4 ha., Volnay 1 ha., Beaune 0.15 ha., Monthelie 0.18 ha., Chassagne-Montrachet (*blanc*) 0.5 ha., Meursault 1.5 ha.

An estate which makes very little Monthelie, even though based there. I expect to find excellent bottles at this address.

Didier Darviot, Grande Rue, 21190 Monthelie

PAUL GARAUDET   9 ha. (85 per cent)
GEORGES GARAUDET

Monthelie Les Duresses 0.9 ha., Meix-Bataille 0.4 ha., Clos-Gauthey 1.1 ha., Monthelie (*rouge*) 2 ha., (*blanc*) 0.9 ha., Volnay Ronceret 0.19 ha., Volnay 0.37 ha., Pommard 0.3 ha., Puligny-Montrachet 0.14 ha., Meursault 2 ha., Bourgogne (*blanc*) 0.7 ha., (*rouge*) 0.18 ha.

Neat wines here, the red Monthelies needing time to open up.

Paul Garaudet, Monthelie, 21190 Meursault

CHÂTEAU DE MONTHELIE   8.85 ha. (100 per cent)

Monthelie *Premier Cru* Sur La Velle 3.1 ha., Monthelie 2.95 ha., Rully *Premier Cru* (*blanc*) 1.36 ha., (*rouge*) 1.4 ha.

Parts of this wonderful manor house, with glazed coloured tiles, date back to the fourteenth century. De Suremain believes in relatively short vattings – eight days, at highish temperature – and a faint proportion of new oak, perhaps 10–15 per cent. This does not sound like a recipe for transatlantic export, and sure enough his sales are all in Europe. Much effort is going into vineyard care here, and the wines are worth following.

Eric de Suremain, Monthelie, 21190 Meursault

DOMAINE MONTHELIE-DOUHAIRET   6 ha. (100 per cent)

Monthelie Le Meix Bataille, 0.42 ha., Les Duresses (*rouge*) 0.25 ha., (*blanc*) 0.23 ha., Volnay Champans 0.89 ha., Pommard Les Chanlins 0.27 ha., Pommard Les Fremiers 0.19 ha., Volnay 0.14

ha., Monthelie (*rouge*) 2.18 ha., (*blanc*) 0.22 ha., Meursault Les Santenots 0.3 ha., Meursault 0.18 ha.

The origins of this domaine go back 200 years to the building of Mlle Douhairet's house and *cuverie*. The latter was constructed round a massive wooden press, worked by a 'squirrel wheel' which can still be seen.

To correspond with Mlle Douhairet is to be wafted back in time with *fin-de-siècle* courtesy. She signs her letter thus: *A l'aurore de cette année nouvelle, je me fais un plaisir de vous présenter mes voeux les meilleurs et les plus chaleureux. Que l'année vous épargne les soucis de santé et vous dispense une large part de bonheur. En attendant la joie de vous recevoir au domaine* . . .

One does not expect technical perfection if one chooses to buy wines from an estate like this; instead, one takes a small risk, and may be rewarded by wines of real character and interest. With the involvement of André Porcheret, now at the Hospices de Beaune, the element of chance has been reduced.

Mlle Armande Douhairet, Monthelie, 21190 Meursault

POTINET-AMPEAU   7 ha. (75 per cent)

Pommard les Pézerolles 0.5 ha., Volnay Clos des Chênes 0.66 ha., Auxey-Duresses Les Duresses 0.25 ha., Monthelie Champs Fulliot 0.33 ha., Monthelie 2 ha., Meursault Perrières 0.33 ha., Charmes 0.5 ha., Meursault 2 ha., Puligny-Montrachet 0.25 ha.

Stepping down into this Monthelie cellar brings back my earliest Burgundian memories: the damp, mushroomy smell from rows of dark, well-kept barrels – a total contrast to the showy bank of creamy-white new ones, giving off vanilla and fresh wood smells, which is now more common. Much of the stock is kept below the Ampeau courtyard in Meursault – divided in two, when the family split the inheritance, by a low wall. Potinet is an interventionist, and one may find the alcohol, or acidity, levels intrusive (like the wall). There are rare stocks of old bottles, but careful choosing is needed.

Henri Potinet-Ampeau et Mme Pascal Durrieu-Potinet, Monthelie, 21190 Meursault

SAINT-ROMAIN

Saint-Romain is a steep little village, surrounded by precipices, really part of the Hautes Côtes, yet attached to the Côte de Beaune. It has a barrel-maker, François Frères, who supplies the Domaine de la Romanée-Conti, Henri Jayer, the Hospices de Beaune, Domaine Leflaive and many of the best Californian and Oregonian estates. Looking back downhill from Saint-Romain-le-Haut, substantial stocks of François oak staves can be seen weathering. This is perhaps the single most significant factor setting one cooper apart from another: how much wood do they weather and how much do they buy in (more or less green) when they receive orders for barrels?

There are no First Growths in Saint-Romain (it is usually a week later to ripen than the main Côte, owing to its altitude). Of commune Saint-Romain, 42.51 ha. were planted to Pinot Noir in 1991, with 33.61 ha. to Chardonnay. The principal sites are: Poillange, Sous-le-Château, Sous-Roche, Sous-la-Velle, Jarron and Combe-Bazin. The five-year average production (1988–92) was 21,700 cases of red wine and 17,700 cases of white.

This village can be an excellent source of fine white Burgundy after a hot summer and autumn, when overripe wines from the main Côte can lack acidity, balance and staying power. However, there are few good domaine-bottlers, indeed I believe that the *Revue du Vin de France* has concluded that most of the best white Saint-Romains are to be had from *négociants-éleveurs*, such as Joseph Drouhin and Jean Germain in Meursault.

Main Saint-Romain growers and merchants

DOMAINE D'AUVENAY 3.26 ha. (100 per cent)

Bonnes Mares 0.26 ha., Criots-Bâtard-Montrachet 0.06 ha., Puligny-Montrachet Folatières 0.51 ha., Meursault Narvaux 0.73 ha., Chaumes des Perrières 0.08 ha., Pré de Manche 0.1 ha., Auxey-Duresses (*blanc*) 1.2 ha., Aligoté

Like the Domaine Leroy in Vosne-Romanée, this estate has been cultivated bio-dynamically since the end of 1988. The objectives are no chemical treatments, weed-killers, pesticides or synthesized fertilizers, and the reintroduction of 'the knowledge of the cosmic rhythms essential for the regeneration of the soil, the work of the earth and the attentions necessary for the vines throughout the year'.

It is distributed directly by its owner, independently of Maison Leroy in Auxey-Duresses, so I understand. I have not tasted these wines, but methods and aims being the same as those in Vosne, am sure they will be excellent. Bonnes Mares is the most recent addition.

Mme Bize-Leroy, Saint-Romain, 21190 Meursault

DOMAINE HENRI ET GILLES BUISSON   12 ha. (80 per cent)

Saint-Romain (*rouge*) 4.35 ha., (*blanc*) 1.35 ha., Corton 0.33 ha., Volnay 0.2 ha., Pommard 0.15 ha., Meursault 0.31 ha.

Gilles Buisson, Saint-Romain, 21190 Meursault

BERNARD FÈVRE   10.5 ha. (70 per cent)

Saint-Romain (*blanc*) 1.7 ha., (*rouge*) 1.4 ha., Auxey-Duresses (*rouge*) 1.2 ha., Pommard Epenots 0.6 ha., Beaune Montremenots 1.1 ha., Pommard 0.9 ha., Savigny-lès-Beaune 0.43 ha.

Fèvre cultivates part of his uncle André Mussy's estate in Pommard, and until 1987 they used to tend and bottle their wines in the same cellar. From 1987 the Fèvre wines have gone into bottle earlier, to retain their fruit, so Mme Fèvre says. From 1993 all vinification takes place in Saint-Romain; I wonder if this will become a dependable source.

Bernard Fèvre, Saint-Romain, 21190 Meursault

GAEC GERMAIN PÈRE ET FILS   2 ha. (35 per cent)

Beaune Montremenots 0.2 ha., Pommard 0.8 ha., Beaune 0.7 ha., Saint-Romain Côte de Beaune (*rouge*) 5 ha., (*blanc*) 1.5 ha., Hautes Côtes de Beaune 1 ha.

Bernard et Patrick Germain, Saint-Romain, 21190 Meursault

ALAIN GRAS 7.7 ha. (90 per cent)
RENÉ GRAS-BOISSON

Saint-Romain (*blanc*) 3 ha., (*rouge*) 2.5 ha., Meursault 0.5 ha., Auxey-Duresses (*blanc*) 0.4 ha., (*rouge*) 1.34 ha.

From recent, small beginnings this has become one of the best cellars in the village, quality being dependable since the late 1980s. 'Saint-Romain always has enough acidity', says Alain Gras. His white Saint-Romain is vinified in tank, his red sees a bit of new wood; he aims for tender, fresh fruitiness.

Alain Gras, Saint Romain, 21190 Meursault

PIERRE TAUPENOT PÈRE ET FILS 9.04 ha. (60 per cent)

Saint Romain Côte de Beaune (*rouge*) 2.58 ha., (*blanc*) 1.12 ha., Auxey-Duresses *Premier Cru* (*rouge*) 0.8 ha., Auxey-Duresses (*rouge*) 1.9 ha., (*blanc*) 0.77 ha., Passe-Tout-Grains and Aligoté

Over a hundred thousand bottles lie ageing here, stretching back ten vintages, for the assiduous sifter with time to taste carefully.

Pierre Taupenot, rue du Chevrotin, 21190 Saint-Romain

AUXEY-DURESSES

The best vineyards of this village are south or south-east facing, situated in the small valley which runs back from the Côte towards La Rochepot. The reds were sold as Pommard or Volnay before the arrival of AC legislation, the whites as Meursault. Some of the latter are indeed finer than lesser Meursaults.

The following are classified as *Premiers Crus*:

Breterins, Les
Chapelle, La
Climat du Val
Clos du Val
Duresses, Bas des
Duresses, Les
Ecussaux, Les
Grands-Champs, Les
Reugne

First Growth and commune Auxey-Duresses covered, in 1991, an area of 99.18 ha. (reds) and 34.01 ha. (whites). The five-year average production (1988–92) for Auxey-Duresses was 42,200 cases (reds), and 16,300 cases (whites).

Main Auxey-Duresses growers and merchants

ALAIN CREUSEFOND   12 ha. (40 per cent)

Auxey-Duresses Le Val 2 ha., Les Duresses 0.4 ha., Auxey-Duresses (*blanc*) 1.4 ha., (*rouge*) 1.7 ha., Meursault Poruzots 0.43 ha., Meursault 1 ha., Volnay 0.4 ha., Monthelie 0.4 ha., Bourgogne (*blanc* and *rouge*)

Gérard Creusefond *père* married a Mlle Prunier, from one of the traditional vigneron families of Auxey. Well-tried old methods bring dependable results here.

Gérard et Alain Creusefond, Auxey-Duresses, 21190 Meursault

JEAN-PIERRE DICONNE   6.9 ha. (60 per cent)

Auxey-Duresses *Premier Cru* 0.64 ha., Meursault Narvaux 0.77 ha., Luchets 0.57 ha., Meursault 0.24 ha., Auxey-Duresses (*rouge*) 1.45 ha., (*blanc*) 1.13 ha., Bourgogne *rouge*, *blanc*, Passe-Tout-Grains and Aligoté

The reds here can be rustic and mouth-coating, the opposite of youthful fruity Pinot for early drinking; but this is Auxey, so no harm in that. The whites can be splendid.

Diconne is a grower who is passionately preoccupied and involved in what he is doing in vineyard and cellar, without perhaps fully mastering the processes involved. The quality ranges from unsuccessful to inspiring. If I were a Côte d'Or-based *négociant* I would consider early buying in barrel and speedy collection from this source, if a consumer I would be hopeful, but circumspect, with the domaine-bottlings. You may be sure, I believe, of a warm and characterful Burgundian welcome.

Jean-Pierre Diconne, rue de la Velle, 21190 Auxey-Duresses

DOMAINE ANDRÉ ET BERNARD LABRY   12 ha. (100 per cent)

Auxey-Duresses Côte de Beaune 4.48 ha., Monthelie 0.44 ha., Bourgogne Hautes Côtes de Beaune (*rouge* and *blanc*) 3.3 ha., Passe-Tout-Grains 1 ha., Meursault 0.4 ha., Bourgogne Aligoté 0.8 ha., Crémant de Bourgogne 1.5 ha.

This estate in a hamlet up the valley from Auxey makes good wine, and has experimented successfully, I understand, with high vines.

Bernard Labry, à Melin, Auxey-Duresses, 21190 Meursault

ETABLISSEMENTS LEROY   (1868)

This is a family business, where the boss – Mme Bize-Leroy, who entered her father's firm in 1955 – is the buyer. Several million bottles of Burgundy's oldest and finest vintages lie ageing in its underground stone cellars. The firm has a well-deserved, exceptional reputation for purchasing top quality wines in the best vintages, and for tending, bottling and maturing them immaculately.

The company distributes an estate of 22.42 ha., the Domaine Leroy in Vosne-Romanée (where details may be found). Mme Bize-Leroy also owns another estate, the 3 hectare Domaine d'Auvenay, details being shown in the chapter on Saint-Romain, whence it is directly distributed.

I have always resisted doing business here because of an early glimpse of the profit margin (which left a scar on my appreciation of the lady who runs the place). It was the early 1970s; as an inexperienced buyer, I had just spent a day in Chablis where First Growth Chablis was costing, at that time, around 10 fr. per bottle at the grower. As I was tasting Côte d'Or wines later the same week with Mme Bize-Leroy in Auxey, she enthused about a recent purchase of Montée de Tonnerre – would I taste it? It was indeed excellent, then I learned the price she was asking – 27 fr. per bottle, I think it was – which seemed an outlandish mark-up. This might be the best Montée de Tonnerre of its vintage, and thrill every consumer, but there appeared to be no room for a merchant to make a margin on it. That, of course, was a trader's reaction, and if one remembered that the price of fine Burgundy was principally set by demand (as it still is), the only response had to be good luck to the lady in her pursuit of customers prepared to pay her price.

Until 1 January 1992 this firm distributed the wines of the Domaine de la Romanée-Conti in all markets except the USA and UK. The Leroy family has owned half of that domaine, since the purchase by Henri Leroy of Jacques Chambon's half-share in the estate under the Occupation, in 1942.

Mme Lalou Bize-Leroy, Auxey-Duresses, 21190 Meursault

JEAN-PIERRE ET LAURENT PRUNIER   8 ha. (50 per cent)

Auxey-Duresses Les Duresses 0.54 ha., Le Val 0.5 ha., Monthelie *Premier Cru* 0.2 ha., Auxey-Duresses (*blanc*) 3 ha., (*rouge*) 1 ha., Pommard 0.4 ha., Beaune 0.45 ha., Monthelie 0.35 ha., Meursault 0.4 ha., Saint-Romain (*blanc*) 1 ha., (*rouge*) 0.5 ha.

Mme Jean-Pierre et Laurent Prunier, rue Traversière, 21190 Auxey-Duresses

MICHEL PRUNIER   10 ha. (80 per cent)

Volnay Caillerets 0.3 ha., Beaune Les Sizies 0.25 ha., Auxey-Duresses Clos du Val 0.48 ha., *Premier Cru* 0.75 ha., Auxey-Duresses (*rouge*) 1.75 ha., (*blanc*) 1 ha., Meursault 0.35 ha., Bourgogne (*blanc*) 0.7 ha., Crémant de Bourgogne 0.5 ha.

This is an excellent address, which has recently added Bourgogne Chardonnay to its range, so as to offer an inexpensive bottle alongside more famous names.

Michel Prunier, route nationale, Auxey-Duresses, 21190 Meursault

PASCAL PRUNIER   4.75 ha. (75 per cent)

Auxey-Duresses Les Duresses 0.47 ha., Monthelie Les Vignes Rondes 0.49 ha., Beaune Les Reversées 0.13 ha., Les Sizies 0.32 ha., Beaune 0.34 ha., Pommard 0.17 ha., Auxey-Duresses (*blanc*) 1.19 ha., (*rouge*) 0.38 ha., Saint-Romain (*blanc*) 0.92 ha., (*rouge*) 0.35 ha.

There are many Pruniers in Auxey, good wines being found here as at Pascal's parents' and brother's estate, Jean-Pierre et Laurent Prunier.

The white Auxey-Duresses comes from the hillside leading to

Saint-Romain, and is less buttery, more mineral, than those from land which touches Meursault. He makes deep-coloured reds which require bottle-age.

Pascal Prunier, rue Traversière, Auxey-Duresses, 21190 Meursault

PHILIPPE PRUNIER-DAMY   14 ha. (60 per cent)

Auxey-Duresses Clos du Val 0.4 ha., Monthelie Les Duresses 0.42 ha., Pommard 1 ha., Beaune 0.6 ha., Volnay 0.25 ha., Auxey-Duresses (*rouge*) 3 ha., (*blanc*) 2.4 ha., Monthelie 1.25 ha., Meursault 0.6 ha., Hautes Côtes de Beaune 2 ha.

Philippe Prunier-Damy, 21190 Auxey-Duresses

DOMAINE ROY   11 ha. (60 per cent)

Volnay-Santenots 0.85 ha., Auxey-Duresses Les Duresses 0.86 ha., Le Val 2.47 ha., Auxey-Duresses (*blanc*) 0.46 ha., Auxey-Duresses Côte de Beaune 2.49 ha., Bourgogne Clos Saint Christophe 2.25 ha.

Bernard Roy is a major owner in the First Growth Clos du Val; I have had excellent wine from here, though have not retasted recently.

He was one of the first exponents, in the early 1960s, of *vignes hautes et larges* pruning, now adapted to a variable lyre-training system. His vines are planted at intervals of 1.2 m and 3.3 m (three times the normal span between rows) and allowed to grow to shoulder height. One-third as many vines produces three times as many grapes per vine, so the overall yield remains stable, but both frost damage and rot are reduced by the greater distance between foliage and soil. The lyre shape may be opened to allow the leaves to catch the sun, then closed for harvesting and winter vineyard work. He did it to protect his soils from erosion, but one of the biggest advantages proved to be the cutting of labour costs in working the vineyard.

The larger space between the rows enables him to use a harvest transporter of his own invention. This de-stalks and crushes, or presses (depending on the grape-colour), immediately after picking. It is the closest anyone has come to the oenologist's ideal of pressing white grapes immediately, to ensure maximum freshness. The must is stored under CO_2 pressure until it reaches the vats. Manpower is saved here also, since the transporter only needs emptying at midday and in the evening.

In 1988 Bernard Roy summarized three main advantages to be had from wide planting and high training: total absence of erosion; excellent resistance to winter and spring frosts; less likelihood of rot, so healthier grapes producing better wines. Most of his Burgundian neighbours have remained unconvinced, preferring the traditional methods of planting and training; however Henri Latour in the village also trains high, there are two other growers in Melun, and of course many in the Hautes Côtes. Anyone studying Bertrand Devillard's experiments with lyre-training at the Château de Mercey as a means of reducing production costs will also find valuable data at this address.

Vincent et Dominique Roy, Auxey-Duresses, 21190 Meursault

25

Meursault and Blagny

More white wines are grown in this commune than in any other of the Côte d'Or, and they have made its reputation. They are less vigorous and racy than Puligny-Montrachet, less stylishly opulent than Chassagne-Montrachet, but have an ample, enveloping richness which makes them highly approachable. Pierre Bréjoux points out (and it is worth reading between his lines) that the tint of Meursault is a beautiful green-gold, and that the wines keep their bouquet, freshness and flavour perfectly when their development in hogshead allows a fairly early bottling.

The first mention of vineyards is in 1102 when Duke Odo II of Burgundy gave vines to Cîteaux. The vineyard of Santenot is mentioned in 1218, and that of Charmes in 1366. Les Santenots today is of course a red wine vineyard. It stands on the border with Volnay, and is sold under its neighbour's name.

The hamlet of Blagny is uphill from Meursault's finest vineyard Les Perrières. The Blagny vines straddle the commune boundary with Puligny, well-sheltered and perfectly orientated. P. Bréjoux finds Meursault-Blagny *un grand vin très franc de goût. C'est lui qui se rapproche le plus du Montrachet et du Chevalier-Montrachet.*

The following are classified as *Premiers Crus*:

Blagny, Sous
Bouchères, Les
Caillerets, Les
Charmes-Dessous, Les
Charmes-Dessus, Les
Chaumes de Narvaux, Les
Chaumes des Perrières, Les
Clos des Perrières
Clos Richemont (Cras)
Cras, Les
Dos d'Ane, Sous le
Genevrières-Dessous, Les
Genevrières-Dessus, Les
Gouttes d'Or, Les
Jeunelotte, La
Perrieres, Aux
Perrières-Dessous, Les
Perrières-Dessus, Les
Pièce sous le Bois, La
Plures, Les
Porusot, Le
Porusot-Dessus, Le
Porusots-Dessous, Les
Santenots Blancs, Les
Santenots du Milieu, Les

The following wines have right to the *Premier Cru appellation* Meursault-Blagny (which is obligatorily white):

Blagny, Sous
Dos d'Ane, Sous le
Jeunelotte, La
Pièce sous le Bois, La

The following wines have right to the *appellation* Blagny *Premier Cru* (obligatorily red):

Blagny, Hameau de
Blagny, Sous
Dos d'Ane, Sous le
Garenne, La
Jeunelotte, La
Pièce sous le Bois, La
Puits, Sous le

First Growth and commune Meursault in 1991 covered 352.88 ha. (whites) and 20.02 ha. (reds). The five-year average production (1988–92) for white Meursault was 188,600 cases, for red 10,400 cases. First Growth and commune Blagny *rouge* covered 7.94 ha., giving a five-year average production (1988–92) of 2,580 cases.

The proprietors of the Clos des Perrières, Héritiers Albert Grivault, are applying for this 1 hectare Monopole to be promoted from *Premier Cru* to *Grand Cru* status. This seems logical in one way, for it is recognized that a top Perrières, particularly one from the Perrières-Dessous strip, can be the most intensely complete wine of Meursault. But some growers (J.-F. Coche-Dury, for instance) make wonderful Perrières from Perrières-Dessus – better than some in what is thought to be the finer band of vineyard. If Clos des Perrières gets promotion, why not at least the rest of that part of the

First Growth sharing identical soil and subsoil? Will there be proper soil analyses?

And what to call it? Perrières on its own is rather neutral, and this vineyard name appears in many other villages. Les Perrières, maybe. You cannot have Meursault Perrières covering both a *Grand Cru* and a *Premier Cru*. Extend Clos des Perrières outside its walled site (if the Grivault heirs would countenance it)? Clos Saint-Denis and Clos de la Roche have no defining walls, so why not? It looks a knotty problem for INAO to resolve.

It is perhaps unwise to encourage this discussion by airing it, for the end result, from the consumer's point of view, is that the price will go up. No doubt we will be told that Burgundy's previously slightly muddled, hazy hierarchy has been clarified (but will it have been?), that a price increase can be justified, and that it is a due recompense.

Meursault is of course the scene of the Paulée de Meursault each November. Much closer to the soil, and to the growers themselves, than the more formal Clos de Vougeot Tastevins banquets, this is an astonishingly warm celebration, and the greatest Burgundian banquet of them all. It lasts for hours, but there are none of the interminable *longueurs* of a Clos de Vougeot dinner, thanks to the procession of lively, rare, and curious bottles. People are not ashamed of admitting their responsibilities here, the bottles have proper labels, with the names of the grower and *négociant* being happily, proudly shown. It means the wines are really good in Meursault; at the Clos de Vougeot they can be very dull indeed.

Main Meursault growers and merchants

ROBERT AMPEAU ET FILS   10 ha. (100 per cent)

White: Puligny-Montrachet Les Combettes 0.66 ha., Meursault Les Perrières 1 ha., Les Charmes 0.5 ha., La Pièce sous le Bois 0.75 ha., Meursault.
Red: Blagny La Pièce sous le Bois 0.75 ha., Auxey-Duresses Les Ecusseaux 1 ha., Volnay Les Santenots 1.5 ha., Pommard 1 ha., Beaune Clos du Roi 0.5 ha., Savigny Les Lavières 0.66 ha.

Stocks stretch back – some of them really great – through twenty vintages, but calm the excitement, for there are all sorts of hoops to be jumped through before you are offered the bottle of your dreams. Do not aspire simply to buy white wines: you must take an equal quantity of red. Nor imagine you can buy from the best vintages: they may not be on release. Will lesser years be attractively priced? They may be, but it would be naïve to assume it. If they are, taste with care, for we may be sure the Ampeaus know the value of their stocks better than we do.

Robert et Michel Ampeau, 6 rue du Cromin, 21190 Meursault

DOMAINE RAYMOND BALLOT-MILLOT ET FILS 14 ha. (75 per cent)
PH. BALLOT-DANCER
VEUVE CHARLES DANCER-LOCHARDET

Meursault Perrières 0.7 ha., Genevrières 0.5 ha., Charmes 0.35 ha., Les Criots 0.65 ha., Chassagne-Montrachet La Romanée 0.45 ha., Morgeot (*blanc*) 0.6 ha., (*rouge*) 0.34 ha., Volnay-Santenots 0.52 ha., Taille Pieds 0.35 ha., Pommard Rugiens 0.42 ha., Péze-rolles 0.6 ha., Charmots 0.2 ha., Beaune Epenottes 0.45 ha., Pom-mard 2 ha., Beaune 0.4 ha., Chassagne-Montrachet (*blanc*) 0.42 ha., (*rouge*) 0.34 ha., Meursault (*blanc*) 2.25 ha., (*rouge*) 0.3 ha., Bourgogne (*rouge*) 0.25 ha., Aligoté and Passe-Tout-Grains

Ten generations have built up this estate, which has a wide spread of top vineyards in four of the best villages of the southern Côte de Beaune. Reports can be contradictory: that the whites tend to over-richness – or alternatively, are unflattering when young.

I hear good things about the reds, and two white *cuvées* for insiders (Meursault Les Criots, and Chassagne La Romanée), but have yet to enter the cellar.

Philippe Ballot, 9 rue de la Goutte d'Or, 21190 Meursault

DOMAINE DE BLAGNY 10.95 ha. (15 per cent)
COMTESSE P. DE MONTLIVAULT

Meursault Blagny La Genelotte (Monopole) *blanc* and *rouge* 3 ha., La Pièce sous le Bois 2 ha., Sous le Dos d'Ane 2 ha., Blagny 1 ha., Puligny-Montrachet Les Chalumeaux 0.4 ha., Hameau de Blagny 2 ha.

From this hamlet up the slope between Meursault and Puligny it is said that all the clocks of the Côte can be heard to strike. The

monks of Maizières were the first to plant vines here. They built a farm and the fifteenth-century chapel.
Famille de Montlivault, Blagny, 21190 Meursault

DOMAINE GUY BOCARD   8.5 ha. (80 per cent)

Meursault Charmes 0.67 ha., Genevrières 0.18 ha., Grands Charrons, sous la Velle, Narvaux, Limozin 4.5 ha., Auxey-Duresses *Premier Cru* 0.19 ha., Monthelie 0.12 ha., Bourgogne (*blanc* and *rouge*) and Aligoté
A young grower of whom good things are expected.
Guy Bocard, 4 rue de Mazeray, 21190 Meursault

PIERRE BOILLOT   2.5 ha. (100 per cent)

Meursault Charmes 0.5 ha., Goutte d'Or 0.2 ha., Volnay-Santenots 0.5 ha., Pommard 0.5 ha., Bourgogne (*rouge*) 0.55 ha.
A thousand private customers, built up over three decades, account for these wines each year, so I doubt whether M. Boillot is looking to export. There is such pleasure to be had from receiving consumers, and seeing them pay for the stock they carry away with them, that charming overseas buyers who prove to be late payers completely lose their appeal for him.
Any traveller through Burgundy with greenbacks or rather buffbacks seeking bottles of good wine could do much worse than rendezvous here.
Pierre Boillot, 3 rue de Leignon, 21190 Meursault

BERNARD BOISSON-VADOT   7 ha. (75 per cent)

Puligny-Montrachet Folatières 0.42 ha., Meursault Genevrières 0.13 ha., Meursault Grands Charrons 0.65 ha., Chevalières 0.4 ha., Meursault 3 ha., Monthelie 0.2 ha., Bourgogne (*rouge*) 1 ha., (*blanc*) 0.8 ha., Passe-Tout-Grains and Aligoté
'These wines have personality, but are straightforward, like the man who makes them. Not enormous wines with feathers coming out in all directions, but as simple as a piece of country bread on a table. His Bourgogne *rouge*, for instance' – thus a broker, Patrick Saulnier Blache, of wines I do not know.
Bernard Boisson-Vadot, 1 rue du Moulin-Landin, 21190 Meursault

HUBERT BOUZEREAU-GRUÈRE   12 ha. (50 per cent)

Red: Corton-Bressandes 0.15 ha., Chassagne-Montrachet 2 ha., Santenay 0.25 ha., Meursault 0.13 ha., Bourgogne (*rouge*) 0.8 ha., Passe-Tout-Grains
White: Meursault Charmes 1 ha., Genevrières 0.2 ha., Chassagne-Montrachet Les Chaumées 0.55 ha., Saint-Aubin Les Cortons 0.28 ha., Le Charmois 0.3 ha., Meursault Grands Charrons 0.9 ha., Tillets 0.75 ha., Limozin 0.55 ha., Puligny-Montrachet 0.5 ha., Chassagne-Montrachet 0.25 ha., Meursault 0.3 ha., Bourgogne (*blanc*) 0.65 ha., Aligoté

I expect to find the reds satisfactory here, but the whites below par – perhaps due to over-comfortable yields.

Hubert Bouzereau-Gruère, 22A rue de la Velle, 21190 Meursault

MICHEL BOUZEREAU   11 ha. (100 per cent)

Meursault Genevrières 0.52 ha., Charmes 0.22 ha., Perrières 0.05 ha., Blagny 0.55 ha., Les Tessons 0.5 ha., Grands Charrons 1.3 ha., Puligny-Montrachet Champs Gains 0.3 ha., Champs Canet 0.13 ha., Meursault 2.2 ha., Beaune Les Vignes Franches 0.5 ha., Epenottes 0.55 ha., Pommard 0.5 ha., Volnay 0.4 ha., Bourgogne (*rouge*) 0.8 ha., (*blanc*) 0.7 ha., Aligoté 1.8 ha.

Thanks to the pneumatic press it is now possible to vinify separately the produce of even so small a plot as 0.05 ha. of Perrières, and ferment a barrel's worth.

Michel Bouzereau has taken over from Bernard Michelot the role of presenting Meursault's face to the world, as president of its grower's union, which he does with a lively smile. This is maybe the best Bouzereau cellar in the village (there are half a dozen wine-making relations).

Michel et Jean-Baptiste Bouzereau, 3 rue de la Planche Meunière, 21190 Meursault

PHILIPPE BOUZEREAU   10 ha. (80 per cent)

Meursault Charmes 0.25 ha., Genevrières 0.1 ha., Puligny-Montrachet Champs Gains 0.65 ha., Chassagne-Montrachet Pasquelles 0.2 ha., Beaune Teurons 0.5 ha., Corton-Bressandes 0.15 ha., Meur-

sault *blanc* and *rouge* 4 ha., Chassagne-Montrachet and Santenay *blanc* and *rouge* 1 ha.
Philippe Bouzereau, 15 place de l'Europe, 21190 Meursault

PIERRE BOUZEREAU-EMONIN   12 ha. (80 per cent)
VINCENT BOUZEREAU
JEAN-MARIE BOUZEREAU

Puligny-Montrachet Folatières 0.29 ha., Meursault Charmes 0.43 ha., Goutte d'Or 0.22 ha., Narvaux 1.02 ha., Meursault (*blanc*) 2.8 ha., (*rouge*) 0.44 ha., Beaune Pertuisots 0.86 ha., Volnay Champans 0.77 ha., Santenots 0.36 ha., Pommard Chanlins 0.33 ha., Auxey-Duresses Les Duresses 0.15 ha., Monthelie (*rouge*) 0.44 ha.
   This family has experimented with new wood, and recognizes how easy it is to overdo matters.
Pierre, Vincent et Jean-Marie Bouzereau, 7 rue Labbé, 21190 Meursault

YVES BOYER-MARTENOT   8.5 ha. (70 per cent)

Meursault Perrières 0.63 ha., Charmes 0.67 ha., Genevrières 0.19 ha., Narvaux 1.23 ha., L'Ormeau 0.64 ha., Meursault (*blanc*) 0.22 ha., (*rouge*) 0.24 ha., Pommard 0.54 ha., Auxey-Duresses Les Ecusseaux 0.51 ha., Bourgogne (*blanc*) 0.5 ha., (*rouge*) 0.33 ha., Aligoté
M. et Mme Yves Boyer, 17 place de l'Europe, 21190 Meursault

ANDRÉ BRUNET   7 ha. (25–50 per cent)

Meursault Charmes 1.5 ha., Genevrières 0.15 ha., Volnay-Santenots 0.3 ha., Meursault Les Cras (*rouge*) 0.75 ha., Meursault (*rouge*) 0.45 ha., Meursault, Bourgogne
   An immaculate looking cellar, fine reds and whites which show their origins clearly.
André Brunet, 27 rue de Cîteaux, 21190 Meursault

CHATEAU DE MEURSAULT

(See Patriarche Père et Fils, Beaune)

CLAUDE ET HUBERT CHAVY-CHOUET   5 ha. (100 per cent)

Puligny-Montrachet Hameau de Blagny 0.25 ha., Pommard Chanlins 0.5 ha., Puligny-Montrachet 1 ha., Bourgogne (*blanc*) 0.5 ha., (*rouge*) 0.5 ha., Aligoté
Claude et Hubert Chavy-Chouet, 29 rue de Mazeray, 21190 Meursault

ALAIN COCHE-BIZOUARD   8.5 ha. (95 per cent)

Meursault Charmes 0.23 ha., Goutte d'Or 0.19 ha., Chevalières 0.3 ha., Le Limozin 0.2 ha., L'Ormeau 0.36 ha., Meursault (*blanc*) 0.99 ha., (*rouge*) 0.39 ha., Auxey-Duresses (*blanc*) 0.21 ha., (*rouge*) 0.39 ha., Pommard Platière 0.26 ha., Monthelie Les Duresses 0.3 ha., Monthelie 0.23 ha., Bourgogne (*blanc*) 0.82 ha., (*rouge*) 1.38 ha., Passe-Tout-Grains and Aligoté
    This estate is the successor to that of Julien Coche-Debord, Alain Coche's late father.
Alain Coche, 5 rue de Mazeray, 21190 Meursault

J.-F. COCHE-DURY   9 ha. (70 per cent)

Corton-Charlemagne 0.3 ha., Meursault Perrières 0.5 ha., Meursault (*blanc*) 3.5 ha., (*rouge*) 0.3 ha., Volnay *Premier Cru* (Clos des Chênes and Taille Pieds) 0.3 ha., Auxey-Duresses (*rouge*) 0.5 ha., (*blanc*) 0.25 ha., Monthelie (*rouge*) 0.25 ha., Bourgogne (*rouge*) 1.5 ha., (*blanc*) 1 ha., Bourgogne Aligoté 0.3 ha.
    There is as much competition between buyers for allocations here as in any Burgundy cellar, the white wines being particularly creamy, subtle and delicious. Monsieur Coche-Dury is not remotely affected, setting normal prices for his immaculate bottles. No aesthetics here, the new-wine cellar is a functional bunker.
    He pays enormous attention to his sparing use of new oak, its age and origins, buying fresh-felled staves in March, for outdoor ageing two years before assembly into barrels. Tronçais, Vosges, Jura, Cher, and Allier are all past, or present, sources, often reviewed.
    He filters neither whites nor reds, and when asked what advice he gives, therefore, to his customers, concerning storage, replies, 'A good cellar, and do not move the bottles about. The best wine is that which is set down, and only picked up once, when you want to

drink it. The more you move it (particularly when it is old) the more you massacre it.' He supplies many top restaurants and specialist merchants (whose pleasant job it is to ensure that the bottles are properly cellared), and a lucky bunch of private customers.
Jean-François Coche-Dury, 9 rue Charles Giraud, 21190 Meursault

DOMAINE DARNAT   3.5 ha. (100 per cent)

Meursault Les Cras Clos Richemont (Monopole) 0.75 ha., Meursault Gouttes d'Or 0.12 ha., Meursault 1.5 ha., Bourgogne Blanc and Aligoté 0.40 ha.
Vincent et Henri Darnat, 20 rue des Forges, 21190 Meursault

BERNARD DELAGRANGE ET FILS   23 ha. (100 per cent)

Volnay Caillerets 0.4 ha., Champans 0.4 ha., Taille Pieds 0.3 ha., Clos du Village (Monopole) 1.2 ha., Pommard Les Chanlins Bas 0.4 ha., Beaune Les Boucherottes 0.42 ha., Meursault Charmes 0.25 ha., Beaune 4.5 ha., Meursault (*blanc*) 1 ha., (*rouge*) 0.3 ha., Auxey-Duresses (*rouge*) 1 ha., (*blanc*) 0.4 ha., Savigny-lès-Beaune (*rouge*) 0.3 ha., (*blanc*) 0.5 ha., Saint-Romain (*blanc*) 0.55 ha., Bourgogne
Bernard et Philippe Delagrange, 10 rue du 11 novembre, 21190 Meursault

SYLVAIN DUSSORT   4.5 ha. (95 per cent)

Meursault 0.5 ha., Bourgogne Chardonnay 2 ha., Beaune Blanches Fleurs 0.25 ha., Chorey-lès-Beaune 0.3 ha., Bourgogne Pinot Noir 0.65 ha., Aligoté 1 ha.
   This can be a source of rich white Burgundy, not from glamorous vineyard origins, but full of life and quality.
Sylvain Dussort, 2 rue de la Gare, 21190 Meursault

DUVERGEY-TABOUREAU   (1868)

An old Meursault company which is resurfacing, with Antonin Rodet backing, to offer a range of domaine-bottled wines. There is Mâcon-Azé (*blanc*) Domaine de la Garenne, owned by Georges Blanc's *sommelier* in Vonnas (doing a rather better job, from young vines, than Blanc himself at the Domaine d'Azenay), on the plus side. Not so brilliant are the current offerings from Château de Mercey, but this property is due for a shake-up, following Rodet's purchase of 50 per cent of the vineyards.

Grouping domaine stocks at one address seems a good idea, but the selection of domaines must be really rigorous. Here may also be found Jean-Ernest Maldant of Chorey, with several Cortons, and Bernard Bellicard of Puligny, with First Growths from the Côte de Meursault, plus growers from Rully, Côte de Brouilly etc.

Philippe Ochin, 6 rue des Santenots, 21190 Meursault

JEAN-PHILIPPE FICHET 5 ha. (100 per cent)

Meursault Perrières 0.46 ha., Tillets, Tessons and Charrons 0.4 ha., Chassagne-Montrachet Les Chênes 0.9 ha., Monthelie 0.8 ha., Bourgogne (blanc) 0.42 ha., (rouge) 0.79 ha., Aligoté 1 ha.

A new, highly spoken-of name among domaine-bottlers in the village, whose wines I do not yet know.

Jean-Philippe Fichet, 2 rue Sudot, 21190 Meursault

DOMAINE FRANÇOIS GAUNOUX 9.5 ha. (80 per cent)

Meursault Goutte d'Or 0.64 ha., Meursault Clos de Tavaux (Monopole) 0.94 ha., Volnay Clos des Chênes 0.86 ha., Pommard Grands Epenots 1.28 ha., Epenots 0.94 ha., Rugiens (hauts) 0.43 ha., Beaune Clos des Mouches 0.77 ha., Corton-Renardes 0.64 ha., Pommard 1.5 ha., Bourgogne Château Gaunoux (blanc) 0.64 ha., (rouge) 0.77 ha.

It is a mistake to telephone here for the number of François Gaunoux's son Jean-Michel (who makes wine independently of his father, as is often, and quite normally, the case) for his stepmother may reply that she does not know it, and that it is nothing to do with her. She is more forthcoming about details of the estate when she hears it relates to the update of a book, and precise that between the two estates (suddenly her memory has cleared) the wines of the better vineyard sites are to be found under her roof. Yes, they do call their Bourgogne blanc Château Gaunoux. It is ages since I tasted these wines, but I hesitate to be a further trouble to Mme Gaunoux.

François Gaunoux, 23 rue du 11 novembre, 21190 Meursault

JEAN-MICHEL GAUNOUX   6 ha. (60 per cent)

Meursault Perrières 0.57 ha., Goutte d'Or 0.3 ha., Corton-Renardes 0.33 ha., Volnay Clos des Chênes 0.3 ha., Pommard 1.5 ha., Meursault 1.5 ha., Bourgogne (*blanc*) 0.21 ha., (*rouge*) 0.55 ha.

Jean-Michel Gaunoux broke away from Domaine François Gaunoux to make wine on his own account with effect from the 1990 vintage. The family's roots were Pommard, and red-wine-making is in his blood.

Jean-Michel Gaunoux, 1 rue de Leignon, 21190 Meursault

CHÂTEAU GÉNOT-BOULANGER   19.08 ha. (30 per cent)
CHARLES H. GÉNOT

Meursault Clos du Cromin 1.42 ha., Chassagne-Montrachet (*blanc*) Chenevottes 0.3 ha., Vergers 0.21 ha., Clos Saint-Jean 0.06 ha., Beaune Grèves 1.03 ha., Volnay Les Aussy 0.4 ha., Volnay 1.21 ha., Pommard Clos Blanc 0.33 ha., Pommard 2.21 ha., Mercurey (*rouge*) Les Sazenay 1.73 ha., Mercurey (*rouge*) 7.18 ha., (*blanc*) 2.62 ha.

A big estate with some great vineyard holdings, but I have often found the red wines disappointing. Is it that the vat installations, at different levels, draw the wine-maker into more pumpings than is ideal, or that these particular Pinots give wine which lacks concentration? No doubt many factors are involved.

Mme Delady-Génot and Claude Enjalbert (oenologist and manager), 25 rue de Cîteaux, 21190 Meursault

DOMAINE HENRY GERMAIN ET FILS   5.16 ha. (60 per cent)

Chassagne-Montrachet Morgeot (*blanc*) 0.57 ha., Meursault Charmes 0.64 ha., Limozin 0.26 ha., Chevalières 0.23 ha., Clos du Cromin 0.28 ha., Beaune Bressandes 1.24 ha., Chassagne-Montrachet (*rouge*) 0.54 ha., Meursault 0.41 ha., Bourgogne (*rouge*) 0.22 ha., (*blanc*) 0.16 ha., Aligoté and Passe-Tout-Grains

Henri Germain is a brother of François Germain, and learnt his craft at the family estate, Château de Chorey-lès-Beaune, setting up independently in 1973. This is a low-profile estate where scrupulously-made wines, which are highly unlikely to disappoint, may be found.

M. et Mme Henri, et Jean-François Germain, rue des Forges, 21190 Meursault

MAISON JEAN GERMAIN   1.61 ha. (100 per cent)

Saint-Romain Clos sous le Château 0.85 ha., Puligny-Montrachet Les Grands Champs 0.28 ha., Corvée des Vignes 0.13 ha., Meursault Meix Chavaux 0.28 ha., La Barre 0.07 ha.

A small merchant business, which for twenty years until Jean Germain's ill health in 1993 bought grapes or must, selected and tended wines, and bottled the produce of Jean Germain's own vines. The wines have been dependable and good; however the future direction of the business was, in early 1994, unclear.

Jean Germain et Joseph de Bucy, 9 rue de la Barre, 21190 Meursault

DOMAINE ALBERT GRIVAULT   5 ha. (35 per cent)

Meursault Clos des Perrières (Monopole) 1 ha., Meursault Perrières 1.5 ha., Meursault 1.5 ha., Pommard Clos Blanc (*rouge*) 1 ha.

With the arrival of a younger generation, there has been a big jump in quality here. Juice is still sold straight from the press to serious specialists like Louis Jadot, but the tending of the domaine-bottlings has been transformed by enthusiastic amateurs. These are some of the greatest vineyard sites in the village.

Michel Bardet et Mlle Marguerite Bardet, 7 place du Murger, 21190 Meursault

PATRICK JAVILLIER   8.6 ha. (100 per cent)

Meursault Les Tillets 1.5 ha., Clos du Cromin 1 ha., Cloux 0.36 ha., Casse-Tête 0.14 ha., Narvaux 0.24 ha., Puligny-Montrachet 0.18 ha., Savigny-lès-Beaune (*blanc*) 0.71 ha., Bourgogne (*blanc*) 2.65 ha., Pommard 0.2 ha., Savigny-lès-Beaune Serpentières 0.7 ha., Grands Liards 0.54 ha., Bourgogne (*rouge*) 0.34 ha.

Since finishing oenological studies in Dijon in 1974 Patrick Javillier has expanded the estate which his father, Raymond, handed over in 1976. A small merchant's business, Guyot-Javillier, has been run in tandem with the domaine, buying in First Growth Meursault, Puligny and Chassagne, so that clients might have a wide choice.

I have had some wonderfully fresh Meursault from his hands, less balanced Bourgogne *blanc;* but wrestling with the problem of the oakiness, weight and clarity of the region's most simple AC is one of the wine-maker's greatest challenges. The results are worth monitoring annually here.

Patrick Javillier, 7 impasse des Acacias, 21190 Meursault

FRANÇOIS JOBARD   4.5 ha. (95 per cent)

Meursault Genevrières 0.53 ha., Poruzot 0.59 ha., Charmes 0.16 ha., Meursault Blagny 0.21 ha., Meursault 1.87 ha., Blagny La Pièce sous le Bois (*rouge*) 0.28 ha.

Absolutely no exaggeration in the use of new oak, indeed those flavours are imperceptible in these wines. It is a deep cellar, and the wines age their full course in wood, sometimes over two years, before bottling. Lean, not opulent, extremely fine, slow-maturing, understated in youth – these bottles are for those who have access to cool cellarage to bring them to perfection.

François Jobard, 2 rue de Leignon, 21190 Meursault

DOMAINE DES COMTES LAFON   12.6 ha. (100 per cent)

Montrachet 0.33 ha., Meursault Charmes 1.71 ha., Genevrières 0.55 ha., Perrières 0.8 ha., Goutte d'Or 0.39 ha., Désirée 0.46 ha., Clos de la Barre (Monopole) 2.1 ha., Meursault 0.6 ha., Volnay-Santenots du Milieu 3.78 ha., Champans 0.52 ha., Clos des Chênes 0.39 ha., Monthelie Les Duresses 1 ha.

This estate's name is inextricably linked to Meursault's most famous feast, the Paulée – deriving from *poêlée* (literally a casserole) according to some, from *épaule à épaule* (shoulder to shoulder) according to others, from *paulier* (the tithe-collector) according to J.-F. Bazin – which has taken place on Monday lunchtime, after the Hospices de Beaune Auction weekend, each November since 1933. The idea dates from Jules Lafon (Dominique's grandfather) inviting his vignerons and friends to a harvest celebration in 1923. Jacques Prieur, with his vignerons and friends, joined the party the following year. Jules Lafon was one of the founders of the Chevaliers du Tastevin in the 1930s, which in the early days revolved (inevitably, on the Côte de Nuits) around red wines. 'What is to be done about our whites?' mused the Meursault growers, and came up with the idea of a literary prize – 100 bottles of Meursault – and the widening of the guest-list of their elbow-to-elbow celebration, where the hosts, the growers of Meursault, bring their finest, rarest and oldest bottles to the feast.

Between 1987 and 1994 this estate has been taking back those vineyards which until then had been on a crop-sharing basis. Although this has meant that admirable growers such as Pierre Morey, who had farmed Lafon land, have lost their access to certain vineyards, the Lafon skills and commitment are so high, and the results so fine, that it is impossible to express regret.

The white wines here often surpass, in complexity, potential and deliciousness, *Grands Crus* from lesser wine-makers in Chassagne or Puligny. The cellar is the deepest in the village, fermentations are unhurried, bottling takes place with minimal treatment. And in recent years Dominique Lafon has greatly improved the red wine quality, though he new-woods his Volnays a bit more strongly than this consumer really likes.

It is often disastrous if a grower reads, year in, year out, that he or she makes great wines, but so far Dominique Lafon's head seems firmly attached to his shoulders, and of perfectly recognizable size. He carries a brilliant banner for Meursault. May he long retain that easy contact with his peers which was so evident when he started as a young broker.

Dominique Lafon, Clos de la Barre, 21190 Meursault

DOMAINE LATOUR GIRAUD   10 ha. (100 per cent)

Meursault Genevrières 2.39 ha., Perrières 0.15 ha., Charmes 0.45 ha., Meursault 3.25 ha., Puligny-Montrachet Champ Canet 0.34 ha., Bourgogne (*blanc*) 1.32 ha., Pommard Refène 0.25 ha., Volnay Clos des Chênes 0.25 ha., Meursault Caillerets (*rouge*) 0.18 ha., Maranges La Fussière (*Premier Cru*) 1.5 ha.

Pierre Latour was for many years a broker of Côte de Meursault white wines to the local trade, and until 1982 most of his own wine was sold in bulk. After studying viticulture and oenology, his son Jean-Pierre has now joined him.

This is one of the few Côte de Meursault estates to use metal vats for *Premier Cru* wine-making. Approximately half the fermentation takes place thus in bulk, at a controlled temperature of 18°, after which the wines are run into barrels of different ages to complete it.

Clive Coates roundly criticized some of the Latour Giraud Genevrières of the mid-1980s in *The Vine* (August 1989) – quite rightly in my view – to the owner's indignation. Alternative opinions should be sought, the record should be put straight. Robert Parker, in his *Burgundy: a Comprehensive Guide*, a year later, said that he had consistently enjoyed this domaine's wines, both red and white.

The unusual white-wine-making method for Meursault – fermentation starting in vat, then racking into barrel – may be partly responsible for problems. At one time they spent a lot of money installing vats, and are no doubt attached to them, but maybe they could use them to allow the musts to fall bright, and to unify their *cuvées*, rather than for fermentations. Perhaps a fining and filtration policy needs perfecting, or air conditioning and humidity-control considering.

They have a wonderful Genevrières holding. Meursault is so full of lively young growers exchanging ideas and experiences that solutions here cannot be far away.

Jean-Pierre Latour, 8 av. E. de Moucheron, 21190 Meursault

DOMAINE JOSEPH MATROT   18.2 ha. (100 per cent)
DOMAINE PIERRE MATROT
THIERRY ET PASCALE MATROT

Meursault Perrières 0.53 ha., Meursault Charmes 1.12 ha., Meursault Blagny 1.8 ha., Meursault 4.7 ha., Puligny-Montrachet Les Chalumeaux 1.32 ha., Les Combettes 0.31 ha., Volnay-Santenots 1.4 ha., Blagny La Pièce sous le Bois 2.35 ha., Auxey-Duresses 0.57 ha., Bourgogne Chardonnay 2.26 ha., Bourgogne Aligoté 1.72 ha.

Thierry Matrot is an iconoclastic and imaginative wine-maker. 'It is an enormous error to identify new wood with quality – it's face-paint', he says, and determinedly aims to use no new oak at all on his best white wines.

The first vintage he made solo was 1983, having worked alongside his father Pierre for the 1981, then with him for the 1982, when – as he puts it – they discovered that vintage time is not the moment to stop for discussions about what to do next. You cannot have two people deciding matters in the vat-house, one person has to act.

He knows the flavours and characters of his slices of touching hillside – Charmes, Perrières, Blagny, Combettes, Chalumeaux – intimately, describing them with insight and love. The fleshy attack of a Meursault Charmes, always unctuous and round (if sometimes flabby); the elegance and harmony of Perrières, the firm, hard, mineral character of Meursault Blagny, like a Chablis *Premier* or *Grand Cru*. Blagny whites go so well with shellfish, and light summer dishes cooked in their own juices, flavoured with dill, where a Meursault Charmes needs richer fare – white meat, or turbot, with a cream sauce, or *purées* of autumn vegetables, celery, mushrooms. Puligny Combettes is a rich and opulent wine for the armchair in front of the fire, after an autumn expedition mushroom-picking, where Chalumeaux demands your attention with its life, its floral aromas; perhaps a bit tarty, but wonderful with simply steamed fish, black pepper and herbs, and all the flavours of the sea.

On the red-wine-making front this estate is equally original, for it practises *remontage* not *pigeage* (see glossary), which is unusual in Burgundy. The fermenting must is pumped over twice a day, aerating it for the first few days of fermentation, the object being each time to pump over half of each vat's juice (this may take 7 to 15 minutes per vat). Thierry Matrot uses a narrow-gauge pipe, so the strong jet may turn the cap of grape skins over, dampening it. So he practises *pigeage*, but with a juice-jet. His red wines are whenever possible completely unchaptalized, but naturally rich. They have an individual mouth-feel, appealing and structured yet without hardness, and the best age famously.

For some years this estate had exclusive agency arrangements in several countries. It has now started opening doors to new customers, which seems a good idea, for it probably needs several knowledgeable enthusiasts to get the Matrot message across, given that many of our palates have been half-deadened by too much oaky Chardonnay, not to mention juicy-fruity young Pinots, which these decidedly are not.

Pierre et Thierry Matrot, 21190 Meursault

DOMAINE MICHELOT   23 ha. (100 per cent)

Meursault Perrières 0.21 ha., Genevrières 1.48 ha., Charmes 1.54 ha., Poruzot 0.1 ha., Puligny-Montrachet Folatières 0.13 ha., Garenne 0.1 ha., Meursault *lieux-dits* Clos Saint-Félix 0.75 ha., Narvaux 1.23 ha., Grands Charrons 0.79 ha., Clos du Cromin 0.92 ha., Limozin 0.67 ha., Tillets 0.88 ha., sous la Velle 2 ha., Puligny-Montrachet 0.29 ha., Meursault 2 ha., Bourgogne (*blanc*) 6 ha., Santenay Gravières 0.38 ha., Commes 0.35 ha., Pommard 0.13 ha., Bourgogne (*rouge*) 1.08 ha.

I love the entry route to Bernard Michelot's cellars. It is like finding one's way down the twirls of a giant Burgundian snail-shell: round one corner, down a bit, turn right, back on your tracks until a light-bulb, half obscured by dusty bottles, comes into sight, above a cobwebby tasting table. A final turn left and his wide, low cellar opens out before you on all sides, double-stacked with new oak barrels. Bernard Michelot's smile and open hospitality must have made literally thousands of friends for Meursault.

There have been times when the Michelot message has been one-dimensional, the new-oaky flavour dominating his fruit. Sometimes, tasting round in the late 1980s, I found myself thinking that Michelot was to Meursault what Leflaive had become to Puligny: a greatly-loved estate, but one where the yields had gone a whisker or three too high. But his bottles have given immense pleasure to countless people. In an oaky, Chardonnay wine-world where well-made, dependable Meursault is still the exception not the rule, criticism is rather irrelevant. And one can always find delicious *cuvées* here – maybe a Bourgogne *blanc*, a Limozin, or a Genevrières. New oak is much less evident than it used to be, and there are additional, spacious new cellars.

Jean-François Mestre (from Santenay), Bernard Michelot's son-in-law, co-runs the estate. He looks the part of a Michelot, with a Burgundian accent to match a rich, village vocabulary they did not teach me in school. We may not understand every word, but we never have problems getting the sense, and in his hands the domaine looks set to go from strength to strength. Individual family names also appear on Domaine Michelot bottles: Michelot-Buisson, Chantal Michelot, Geneviève Michelot and Mestre-Michelot.
Bernard Michelot et Jean-François Mestre, 31 rue de la Velle, 21190 Meursault

FRANÇOIS MIKULSKI   6 ha. (100 per cent)

Meursault Genevrières 0.5 ha., Charmes 0.25 ha., Poruzots 0.6 ha., Meursault 1.14 ha., Volnay-Santenots 0.4 ha., Meursault Caillerets (*rouge*) 0.15 ha., Meursault (*rouge*) 0.15 ha., Bougogne (*blanc*) 0.4 ha., Aligoté and Passe-Tout-Grains

A quarter of this estate is cultivated ecologically. Mikulski is a nephew and neighbour of Pierre Boillot, and has taken over some of his vines. He puts a sparkle into 1,500 bottles of his Aligoté, and I bet this is not the only departure from tradition. Along with Patriarche, Fichet, Dussort, etc. Mikulski is part of the next generation of Meursault *vin-maqueurs* snapping at the heels of the establishment (Lafon, Roulot, Matrot and Co.)

François Mikulski, 5 rue de Leignon, 21190 Meursault

DOMAINE BERNARD MILLOT   8.5 ha. (30 per cent)

Meursault Perrières 0.13 ha., Goutte d'Or 0.25 ha., Beaune Les Sizies 0.45 ha., Puligny-Montrachet 0.46 ha., Meursault (*blanc*) 2 ha., Les Criots (*rouge*) 0.48 ha., Bourgogne (*rouge*) 0.69 ha., (*blanc*) 0.72 ha.

Bernard Millot, 27 rue de Mazeray, 21190 Meursault

DOMAINE MILLOT-BATTAULT   8 ha. (70 per cent)

Meursault Charmes 1.5 ha., Volnay-Santenots 0.3 ha., Beaune Epenottes 0.22 ha., Pommard Rugiens 0.33 ha., Meursault 3 ha., Bourgogne

Quite a high proportion of new oak is put to these Côte de Beaune reds: half the barrels for Volnay and Beaune, nearly two-thirds for the Pommard.

Pierre Millot, 7 rue Charles Giraud, 21190 Meursault

DOMAINE MONCEAU-BOCH   4 ha. (100 per cent)
MME LOUIS GUIDOT

Volnay Champans 1.07 ha., Santenots 0.35 ha., Auxey-Duresses Les Grands Champs 0.41 ha., Derrièr Le Four 0.7 ha., Meursault Goutte d'Or 0.1 ha., Les Luraules 0.9 ha., Les Chevalières 0.41 ha.

Les Luraules is a wedge of vines between Goutte d'Or and

Grands Charrons. There are plans for Monsieur Guidot's son François to manage this estate directly in future, with the addition of Aloxe- Corton (1.6 ha.) and some Pernand-Vergelesses (*rouge*).
Hubert Guidot, 2 rue du moulin Judas, 21190 Meursault

DOMAINE JEAN MONNIER ET FILS   17 ha. (100 per cent)

Pommard Grands Epenots Clos de Cîteaux (Monopole) 3 ha., Les Argillières 0.7 ha., Les Fremiers 0.4 ha., Beaune Les Montrevenots 1 ha., Meursault Genevrières 0.4 ha., Charmes 0.9 ha., Meursault Clos du Cromin 1.7 ha., La Barre 1.3 ha., Chevalières 0.8 ha., Puligny-Montrachet 1 ha., Volnay 0.4 ha., Meursault (*rouge*) 1.2 ha., Bourgogne (*rouge*) 3.6 ha., (*blanc*) 0.6 ha., Aligoté

Jean-Claude Monnier does not tire of saying that this is 'one of the rare domaines in Burgundy to make both white and red wines of quality'; I am not sure where he has been looking, there seem to be plenty if you taste about. I think we are safer, here, with the reds than the whites. The red wine of the historic Grands Epenots Clos de Cîteaux – given by Odo, Duke of Burgundy to the Abbey in 1207 – can be splendid.
Jean-Claude Monnier, 20 rue du 11 novembre, 21190 Meursault

DOMAINE RENÉ MONNIER   16 ha. (80 per cent)

Meursault Charmes 1.2 ha., Les Chevalières 2.5 ha., Le Limozin 1 ha., Puligny-Montrachet Folatières 0.85 ha., Puligny-Montrachet 0.23 ha., Maranges La Fussière 1.3 ha., Santenay Commes Dessus 0.2 ha., Charmes 0.25 ha., Monthelie 1 ha., Volnay Clos des Chênes 0.8 ha., Beaune Cent Vignes 2 ha., Toussaints 0.8 ha., Pommard Les Vignots 0.76 ha., Bourgogne (*rouge*) 1.5 ha., (*blanc*) 1.5 ha.

This estate used to be run by the late René Monnier's son-in-law Hubert Monnot, then the latter's widow. She is now married to Jean-Louis Bouillot, who is reported to have thrown himself into the estate's affairs with enthusiasm, to be aided perhaps by a step-son completing his wine studies.

On a recent visit California wine-maker David Ramey (no mean Chardonnay stirrer himself) might have had some reservations about the origins of the barrel staves but had none about the enthusiasm of Monsieur Bouillot, who showed interest in how

things are done in Sonoma Valley, in stark contrast to several other Côte de Beaune growers, to whom it would never occur that, just conceivably, Chardonnay wine-makers working on different continents might learn something from each other.
M. et Mme Jean-Louis Bouillot-Monnier et Xavier Monnot, 6 rue du Dr Rolland, 21190 Meursault

PIERRE MOREY   8.24 ha. (95 per cent)

Bâtard-Montrachet 0.48 ha., Meursault Perrières 0.52 ha., Meursault (*blanc*) 0.98 ha., (*rouge*) 0.27 ha., Pommard Epenots 0.43 ha., Monthelie 0.78 ha., Bourgogne (*blanc*) 1.24 ha., (*rouge*) 0.71 ha., Passe-Tout-Grains and Aligoté
    For many years one of Comte Lafon's vine-tenders on the half-fruit system, Pierre Morey used to make Montrachet and Meursault Charmes from Lafon vines. Now manager at Domaine Leflaive, he also looks after, with exemplary skill, his own family holdings. He is a superb wine-maker, and given his experience at Leflaive, is bound to be bringing the best of organic methods to his land. He can still offer Montrachet, having taken merchant status to be able to buy in grapes.
Pierre Morey, 9 rue Comte Lafon, 21190 Meursault

ALAIN ET CHRISTIANE PATRIARCHE   12 ha. (60 per cent)

Meursault Blagny La Pièce sous le Bois 0.22 ha., Genevrières 0.2 ha., Poruzots 0.18 ha., Meursault 4 ha., Blagny (*rouge*) 0.22 ha., Bourgogne (*blanc*) 3 ha., (*rouge*) 2 ha.
Alain et Christiane Patriarche, 12 rue des Forges, 21190 Meursault

DOMAINE JACQUES PRIEUR   14 ha. (100 per cent)

Chambertin 1 ha., Musigny 1 ha., Clos de Vougeot 1.25 ha. (bottom), Beaune Aux Cras Clos de la Féguine (Monopole) 2 ha., Volnay Champans 0.33 ha., Clos des Santenots (Monopole) 1 ha., Les Santenots 0.75 ha., Meursault Clos de Mazeray *rouge* and *noir* (Monopole) 3 ha., Les Perrières 0.33 ha., Puligny-Montrachet Les Combettes 1.5 ha., Montrachet 0.66 ha., Chevalier-Montrachet 0.2 ha.
    With Lafon, this estate has the most wonderful array of vineyards

– in this case extending up both Côtes – of any domaine in the village. For years they threw insufficient enthusiasm (to put it mildly) into the wine-making; however, since the involvement of Bertrand Devillard with his friends (see Antonin Rodet, Mercurey), coinciding with a Prieur generation-change – Martin Prieur picking up the pipette – matters are greatly improving.

Jean et Martin Prieur, et Bertrand Devillard, Château des Herbeux, 2 rue des Santenots, 21190 Meursault

ROPITEAU FRÈRES (1848)

Exclusive Distributions: Domaine de la Fourchaume (Chablis), Château de Lescure (Beaujolais), Domaine Begon (Meursault).

This firm was for long part of the Taillan group (whose other wine interests include Chantovent, Ginestet and Château Chasse-Spleen, in Moulis). The late Bernadette Villars brought exceptional drive and skill to the autonomy she must have enjoyed as wine-maker at Château Chasse-Spleen. Could the Meursault team of François Mariotte and Philippe Girard make a similar success of Ropiteau? They vinified and barrel-aged sizeable quantities of Meursault de Ropiteau each year, as well as all the village's First Growths, and a general range of Burgundy's reds. In 1994, however, Taillan sold Ropiteau to J.-C. Boisset. It will be interesting to see how much autonomy will in future be permitted.

François Mariotte, 13 rue 11 novembre, 21190 Meursault

DOMAINE ROUGEOT 14 ha. (100 per cent)

Meursault Charmes 0.5 ha., Meursault 3 ha., Bourgogne Chardonnay 2 ha., Pommard 1 ha., Ladoix Côte de Beaune 3 ha., Volnay-Santenots *Premier Cru* 1 ha.

Marc Rougeot, 6 rue André Ropiteau, 21190 Meursault

DOMAINE GUY ROULOT 12 ha. (100 per cent)

Meursault Charmes 0.25 ha., Perrières 0.25 ha., Meursault Tessons Clos de Mon Plaisir (Monopole) 0.8 ha., Les Luchets 1 ha., Les Vireuils 0.7 ha., Les Meix Chavaux 2 ha., Les Tillets 0.5 ha., Bourgogne Chardonnay 1 ha., Auxey-Duresses (*rouge*) 1.5 ha., Monthelie (*rouge*) 0.3 ha, Bourgogne Pinot Noir 2 ha., Aligoté, Marc de Chardonnay

> I've got five children, but I can't be sure they're all mine, not really sure, do you get me? But my wine – it was I who made it, I know. There are no direct vines (ungrafted vines) in my vineyards, no Noahs, no Otellos or 5455s as they all planted after the war. Put this down as you're taking notes: you must never drink wines at room temperature – let a wine warm in the glass by all means, but serve it fresh. You ask how methods have changed over the years – well, we're cleaner than we used to be.

That was the late Paul Roulot talking, Jean-Marc Roulot's grandfather, in the late 1960s. He was a self-styled *brande-vinier* (patois for distiller). He was a member of the Brotherhood of the Knights of the Tasting-Cup, a Commander of the Bresse Chicken and the Blue Ribbon, a Knight of the Fir-Cone and the Fish-Stew, his walls being hung with the arms of these outlandish gastronomic brotherhoods.

His vines were mostly straight Meursault, with a little Perrières and Charmes. Distilling was his hobby: for instance, a light plum brandy to fill that awkward gap after the fish-course when he felt a pause was indicated and that digestion should be helped. Also ratafia made from *fine*, not *marc*, and *pernod* (or was it real *absinthe*?): limpid green and pungent from the steeping of fennel and wormwood leaf, liquorice root and artemisia. In his *cuverie* I saw the pressed skins and pips waiting for distillation. They looked like sultanas and smelt damply of fresh fruit.

His son Guy Roulot was a first-rate white-wine-maker, but died tragically in the prime of life in 1982. He had expanded the family's range of well-placed hillside vineyard sites, all labelled individually, and was also a famous distiller, known for his aged, smooth, Chardonnay *marcs*, and his rare *eau-de-vie de poire*. The 1982 and 1983 vintages were made by the American Ted Lemon, who subsequently went to Château Woltner in California, the years from 1984 to 1988 by the Roulots' cousin Franck Grux, who then went to Olivier Leflaive, inspiring French commentators to liken top winemakers to football stars, Grux being dubbed Maradonna; the transfer fees, however, are not comparable.

From 1989 Guy's son Jean-Marc returned to Meursault to make the wines, while maintaining his career as an actor (so long as it does not cut into vintage time). He aims to match oak-stave origins and ages more carefully with his different vineyards each year, and is gently reducing chaptalization levels for the reds. One day, maybe, he will restart distilling *poire*.

This is a fine cellar to visit, with three old transversal galleries in one direction, and four wide, practical, barrel-filled vaults at right angles. There is plenty of room to stand straight, walk about and talk, with a very open welcome. You ask a straight question, and the answer is batted straight back. The wines are just as clear, well-defined and memorable.

Jean-Marc Roulot, 1 rue Charles Giraud, 21190 Meursault

JACQUES THEVENOT-MACHAL   6 ha. (80 per cent)

Meursault Poruzot 1.13 ha., Charmes 0.24 ha., Meursault (*blanc*) 0.52 ha., (*rouge*) 0.48 ha., Puligny- Montrachet Folatières 0.43 ha., Charmes 0.49 ha., Puligny-Montrachet 0.83 ha., Volnay-Santenots 0.47 ha., Pommard 0.3 ha.

I have had good red wines from this address, and gather that the whites now do not lag far behind.

Jacques Thevenot-Machal, 13 rue des Forges, 21190 Meursault

26

Puligny-Montrachet

No village in Burgundy is more associated with its great white wines (indeed a whole book has recently been devoted to it, its residents and the tiniest details of their lives[1]). Puligny added Montrachet to its name in 1879. The village is of Gallo-Roman origin, first recorded as Puliniacus in a *diplôme* of Pope Urbain II in 1095. There are four *Grands Crus* on the territory:

1. Montrachet (7.68 ha. The five-year average production (1988–92) for Montrachet was 4,520 cases.) Montrachet is something of a *parvenu* amongst *Grands Crus*, Courtépée stating that it was not *en réputation* at the beginning of the seventeenth century, when twenty-four *ouvrées* were acquired for a mere 750 *livres*. It was first mentioned in 1482, already much divided according to Dr Lavalle. But nobody disputes its place today as potentially the greatest white wine of Burgundy.

This is the one white Burgundy one should never touch until it has had serious bottle-ageing (at least eight years, even in a light vintage – when it can be particularly well balanced). Given its expense and rarity, it is a real pity to drink it immature.

2. Chevalier-Montrachet (7.22 ha. The five-year average production (1988–92) for Chevalier-Montrachet was 3,010 cases). This *Grand Cru*, famous for finesse and elegance, is situated uphill from Montrachet, and rated only just behind it.

3. Bâtard-Montrachet (12.37 ha. The five-year average production (1988–92) for Bâtard-Montrachet was 5,490 cases). Almost always

1 Simon Loftus, *Puligny-Montrachet: Journal of a Wine Village in Burgundy*, Ebury Press, London, 1992.

a richer, fatter wine than Chevalier this can be magnificent, and hard to resist, when youthful.

4. Bienvenues-Bâtard-Montrachet (3.53 ha. The five-year average production (1988–92) for Bienvenues-Bâtard-Montrachet was 2,030 cases). The wine is often less weighty than a top Bâtard, but succulently long-flavoured.

Approximately half of both Montrachet and Bâtard-Montrachet are situated in the commune of Chassagne-Montrachet, but the total surface areas and productions have been shown above. Chevalier and Bienvenues are entirely in Puligny.

The following are classified as *Premiers Crus*:

Blagny, Hameau de	Demoiselles, Les (Cailleret)
Cailleret, Le	Folatières, Ez
Chalumeaux, Les	Folatières, Les
Champ Canet	Garenne, La
Champ Gain	Jaquelotte, La
Chaniot, Au	Perrières, Les
Clavoillon	Peux Bois
Clos de la Garenne	Pucelles, Les
Clos de la Mouchère (Perrières)	Puits, Sous le
Clos des Meix	Referts, Les
Combettes, Les	Richarde, En la
Courthil, Sous le	Truffière, La

First Growth and commune Puligny-Montrachet in 1991 covered 204.31 ha., the five-year average production (1988–92) having been 116,800 cases for white wines, and 1,500 cases for reds.

Towards the end of the 1980s yields reached high levels in some Puligny cellars. The village's production has averaged 10,000 hl over the last ten years, and at least 2,000 hl are sold as must at harvest time. The grower does not see this wine, does not have it tasted in his cellar, does not have to defend its quality once it is made (though some buyers build incentives, or minimum stipulations, into their contracts).

Puligny gives wines which are drinkable more quickly than the whites of Chassagne-Montrachet or Meursault, attributable no doubt to subtle combinations of site and microclimate, but also perhaps to there being no proper cellars here. The water table is so high they cannot dig, and storing wine at ground level probably speeds its evolution. Top estates (Sauzet and Leflaive were the first, I think) have now installed temperature control, so it will be interesting to see if Puligny's tendency to mature more quickly than its neighbours is affected.

The village has my favourite hotel for wine-trading – Le Montrachet, place des Marronniers – which often buzzes with wine gossip, and has the enormous advantage of bath-water which runs extremely hot and fast. If I am late back from tasting (as inevitably I am) a quick dip can always be managed. There is also an impassioned *chef-sommelier*, Jean-Claude Wallerand, who offers warm hospitality – not that common from wine-waiters.

Main Puligny-Montrachet growers and merchants

LOUIS CARILLON ET FILS   11 ha. (50 per cent)

Bienvenues-Bâtard-Montrachet 0.12 ha., Puligny-Montrachet Les Combettes 0.5 ha., Les Champs Gains 0.25 ha., Les Champs Canet 0.75 ha., Les Perrières 0.75 ha., Les Referts 0.25 ha., Puligny-Montrachet 5.5 ha., Chassagne-Montrachet Les Macherelles (*blanc*) 0.5 ha., Chassagne-Montrachet (*rouge*) 0.5 ha., Saint-Aubin Les Pitangerets (*rouge*) 1 ha., Mercurey Les Champs Martin 0.5 ha.

There have been Carillons at Puligny since 1632. Their *cuverie* is situated in a house built with stones from the old château. They claim that Saracen influence may show in the pointed arches of the vat-room, and perhaps in the entry down a corridor. The *curé* of Puligny hid himself here during the Revolution; his makeshift confessional and escape-route at the back can still be seen.

Carillon Puligny-Montrachets may be understated, may not show the strongest personalities, but I have often been highly delighted to find these dependable wines in my glass, both domaine- and merchant-bottled.

Jacques Carillon et famille, rue Drouhin, Puligny-Montrachet, 21190 Meursault

CHARTRON ET TRÉBUCHET, SA   (1984)

Nearly three-quarters of the activity of this firm (which incorporates the Dupard Aîné company, founded in 1860) is white Burgundies, its flagship wines being those of the 9 hectare Domaine Jean Chartron in Puligny:

Chevalier-Montrachet 1 ha., Puligny-Montrachet Clos du Cailleret 2.45 ha. (*blanc* 1.72 ha. and *rouge* 0.73 ha.), Les Folatières 1.75 ha., Clos de la Pucelle (Monopole) 1.16 ha., Saint-Aubin Dents du Chien 0.5 ha., Bourgogne *blanc* and *rouge*

This estate has wonderful vineyard sites, but the resulting bottles have sometimes been disappointing, in my experience. As a customer of Olivier Leflaive, Chartron's neighbour and competitor, it is not easy for me to write about Chartron wines objectively, but I am trying. The company was formed in 1984, when Beaune politician Louis Trébuchet joined forces with Puligny grower and merchant Jean-Louis Chartron. In the early years the wines often seemed too squeaky-clean for comfort. Aromas of Chardonnay would be present, but when tasted the wines could seem emaciated, as if over-handled or over-filtered. Visiting the premises in 1994 I did not notice temperature control for the domaine wine storage, which could be a cause of problems when vinifying at ground floor level in Puligny. Some sumptuous bottles of the 1989 vintage were delivered, however: Clos du Cailleret, for instance. The firm has machine-harvested, but found it unsatisfactory, I gather.

To settle inheritance matters with his sister, in 1993 Jean-René Chartron sold, to the Saiers, just over a third of a hectare of Puligny-Montrachet Le Cailleret, and just over half a hectare of the Clos du Cailleret itself (to Domaine de Montille); so what used to be a Monopole Clos is broken up. Quite a chunk of his production was being sold as grapes at the 1992 harvest, leading one to believe that demand for his wines under his own label might be less than insistent. To be fair, this was a moment of world recession, and he was not the only Côte de Meursault grower to be feeling its effects. Jean-René Chartron et Louis Trébuchet, 13 Grande Rue, Puligny-Montrachet, 21190 Meursault

GÉRARD CHAVY ET FILS   11.5 ha. (75 per cent)

Puligny-Montrachet Les Folatières 2.3 ha., Les Clavoillons 0.79 ha., Les Perrières 0.37 ha., Beaune Cent Vignes 0.33 ha., Puligny-Montrachet 4.94 ha., Bourgogne (*blanc*) 0.87 ha., (*rouge*) 0.65 ha., Aligoté 0.64 ha.

Gérard Chavy, 12 rue du Château, 21190 Puligny-Montrachet

DOMAINE HENRI CLERC ET FILS 25.73 ha. (85 per cent)

Chevalier-Montrachet 0.15 ha., Bienvenues-Bâtard-Montrachet 0.64 ha., Bâtard-Montrachet 0.18 ha., Puligny-Montrachet Pucelles 0.08 ha., Combettes 0.62 ha., Folatières 1.61 ha., Champs Gains 0.32 ha., Puligny-Montrachet (*blanc* and *rouge*) 2.33 ha., Meursault Sous le Dos d'Ane 0.55 ha., Clos de Vougeot 0.31 ha., Echézeaux 0.33 ha., Blagny Sous le Dos d'Ane (*rouge*) 0.93 ha., Beaune (*blanc* and *rouge*) 0.44 ha., Santenay 0.69 ha., Bourgogne (*blanc*) 6.33 ha., (*rouge*) 5.18 ha., Passe-Tout-Grains and Aligoté

Results can be irregular from this cellar, which dispatches 15,000 cases each year – occasionally delicious, at other times tarty and florid. New-oak tannins may dominate, perhaps from the practice of sometimes fermenting in tank, then racking into new wood for ageing; or it may be due to experimentation with oak chips, which would be perfectly legal (but surprising). Once when I was there, Monsieur Clerc had been painting his barrels with linseed oil, giving a strange look and smell to the cellar. At times his wines have had a remarkable aroma of smoked ham – as if, had he been using them, he had over-toasted the oak-chips before dunking them. Some tasters lap up smoky bacon flavours in white Burgundy, so probably there was a ready market. Now his daughter is helping him.

Bernard Clerc, place des Marronniers, Puligny-Montrachet, 21190 Meursault

GUILLEMARD-CLERC 1.6 ha. (100 per cent)

Bienvenues-Bâtard-Montrachet 0.18 ha., Beaune Clos des Couchérias 0.71 ha., Puligny-Montrachet 0.2 ha., Bourgogne (*blanc*) 0.44 ha.

Bernard Clerc's daughter has been building a domaine here with her husband since 1990, the first reports being encouraging.

Corinne et Franck Guillemard, 2 Hameau de Blagny, 21190 Puligny-Montrachet

DOMAINE LEFLAIVE 21 ha. (100 per cent)

Montrachet 0.08 ha., Chevalier-Montrachet 1.91 ha., Bâtard-Montrachet 2 ha., Bienvenues-Bâtard-Montrachet 1.15 ha.,

Puligny- Montrachet Les Pucelles 3.05 ha., Les Combettes 0.73 ha., Clavoillon 4.79 ha., Folatières and Chalumeaux 0.45 ha., Puligny-Montrachet 3.73 ha., Blagny *Premier Cru (rouge)* 1.62 ha., Bourgogne (blanc) 1.74 ha.

This domaine borders a peaceful grassy square with triple rows of chestnut trees, stone benches and a *boules* pitch.

Some Burgundy watchers (Tim Atkin,[2] for instance) have voiced concern that standards slipped at this famous estate during the mid- to late 1980s. It coincided with the last years of *régisseur* Jean Virot's stewardship, and the hand-over by one generation, Vincent Leflaive, to his daughter and nephew, Anne-Claude and Olivier. Vincent Leflaive was a much-loved *bon viveur*, who embodied the spirit of the domaine – indeed, for many, the spirit of Puligny – for many years. He died in 1993.

These wines have often been reliable and delicious, and when few Burgundian domaines could be really depended on, this was rare and precious. With a global reputation, as here, it must become much more difficult to take risks. There must be enormous pressure to deliver the expected goods, every vintage. I think yields and chaptalization levels crept up, so that any natural balance a light year might have could become skewed (as happened with some of the 1987s, for instance). With people queuing for allocations Jean Virot sometimes played for safety, I think.

The new *régisseur* is the modest, smiling Pierre Morey, a brilliant wine-maker from Meursault. He can only work with the fruit he receives, of course, but, while respecting traditions, I think he may bring greater individuality to the wines.

On the technical side, one unusual practice is the ageing of the whites for ten months in barrel, then blending them and holding them in stainless steel a further eight months before bottling. This must contribute to their exceptional harmony.

Since 1990, the estate has been experimenting with bio-dynamic methods, inspired by Rudolf Steiner, which associate natural and homoeopathic treatments with the seasons and with planet move-ments. Of the domaine's 21 hectares, three are currently treated in this way (village wines, *Premiers Crus* and *Grands Crus*, including 0.5 ha. of Chevalier-Montrachet). Some initial incredulity amongst vineyard workers at the unusual practices has given way to accept-

2 *Chardonnay*, Viking Penguin, London, 1992.

ance. After all, Jean Virot used to say that work should stop if the moon was russet, and it is often observed that atmospheric pressure affects barrel-lees, and the clarity and condition of wines before bottling.

Results looked broadly positive after two years, and in due course analysis of the microbial soil flora by Claude Bourguignon, vineyard observation, and like-with-like comparative tasting of the wines will allow Anne-Claude Leflaive-Jacques and her co-owners to decide whether the methods should be extended to the whole domaine.

They have halted the use of herbicides and synthesized chemicals, reverting to ploughing, and pruning at a later date. Moving between the two systems is the difficult period, until the natural predators have re-established themselves, so traditional anti-red spider insecticide may still be used in emergency. The domaine is beginning to make its own compost (sheep and cow dung), which will contribute to revitalizing, and rebalancing, its soils.

Anne-Claude Leflaive-Jacques et Olivier Leflaive, 21190 Puligny-Montrachet

OLIVIER LEFLAIVE, SEVIB SA (1984)

This *négociant* firm is separate from Domaine Leflaive, though the man whose name it bears is involved in both. It came into existence because demand for the domaine's wines was regularly outstripping supply, and the obvious solution was to buy grapes from other growers to vinify, tend and mature. It also owns or distributes the produce of 8.5 ha. of vineyards: Meursault Poruzots 0.41 ha., Chassagne-Montrachet Les Chaumées 0.15 ha., Puligny-Montrachet 0.99 ha., Chassagne-Montrachet (*blanc*) 0.41 ha., (*rouge*) 1.12 ha., Bourgogne (*blanc*) 0.72 ha., (*rouge*) 1.63 ha., Aligoté 2.82 ha.

Objectivity for me here is impossible, for I have been regularly between the four-high stacks of these barrels, trying to buy and trade good *cuvées*. What was attractive about a *négociant* supplier to a London importer known, until the mid-1980s, for domaine-bottled Burgundies? Principally it was longer length of stock of wines, so we could re-buy the wine selected, instead of having to restart the whole process, as soon as we were successful; also, a *négociant* could pass on the price advantage of bulk buying from Burgundy growers unable, or unwilling, to bottle themselves. The price in barrel drops significantly, if wine-consuming markets weaken. And Olivier was a grower before he hung up his *négoçiant* sign – still is – so operates with something of a grower's cast of mind. The name Leflaive helped, of course, it must be added.

Franck Grux made wine at Domaine Guy Roulot in Meursault before coming here. He is as open-minded as any wine-maker in the district, with a widely-travelled palate. He has a Burgundian overview of Chardonnay, from the Châlonnais up to Charlemagne (fuelled by annual grape-buying) which is uncommon, and is respectful, though not fanatical, when it comes to the *terroir* religion.

If one is being critical, one may say that they can make their Mercurey *blanc* taste almost like Meursault here, when it ought to know its place, of course, and taste like no such thing. Consumers, however, relish decent-tasting white Burgundy which transcends its modest origins.

Olivier Leflaive et Franck Grux, place du Monument, 21190 Puligny-Montrachet

STÉPHAN MAROSLAVAC-TRÉMEAU 15.5 ha. (15 per cent)

Puligny-Montrachet Champs Gains 2.7 ha., Referts 0.44 ha., Folatières 0.27 ha., Pucelles 0.17 ha., Clos du Vieux Château 0.72 ha., Meursault Blagny 0.5 ha., Puligny-Montrachet 2 ha., Santenay 0.65 ha., Bourgogne

I warmly recommend Simon Loftus's perceptive portrait of how three generations of this Croatian immigrant family have woven themselves into Puligny's vineyard and village life.[3] The grandson of the original Stéphan has his own, separate domaine: Roland Maroslavac-Léger.

Stéphan Maroslavac-Trémeau, 5 Grande Rue, 21190 Puligny-Montrachet

CHÂTEAU DE PULIGNY-MONTRACHET 22 ha. (100 per cent)

Montrachet 0.04 ha., Chevalier-Montrachet 0.25 ha., Bâtard-Montrachet 0.04 ha., Puligny-Montrachet Folatières 0.52 ha.,

---

3 *Puligny-Montrachet: Journal of a Village in Burgundy.*

Chalumeaux 0.3 ha., Garenne 0.14 ha., Meursault Perrières 0.45 ha., Porusot 0.72 ha., Pommard Pézerolles 0.27 ha., Saint-Aubin En Remilly (*blanc*) 1.03 ha., (*rouge*) 0.26 ha., Puligny-Montrachet 1.5 ha., Chassagne-Montrachet 0.9 ha., Meursault 0.7 ha., Monthelie Les Duresses 0.27 ha., Monthelie (*rouge*) 3 ha., (*blanc*) 0.47 ha., Pommard 0.11 ha., Saint-Romain (*blanc*) 0.47 ha., Côte de Nuits-Villages (*rouge*) 3.5 ha., (*blanc*) 0.67 ha., Bourgogne (*blanc*) Clos du Château 2.86 ha., Bourgogne (*rouge*) 2.81 ha.

The Crédit Foncier de France bought this property, then 15 ha. of vineyard, from the Laroche family of Chablis in April 1989. A new winery and storage area have been built (temperature- and humidity-controlled), and vineyards added, the most recent being a few rows of Montrachet and Bâtard-Montrachet – enough to make half a barrel of each. This estate evidently has the potential to make some of the finest wines in the village.

Jacques Montagnon, Domaine du Château, 21190 Puligny-Montrachet

DOMAINE JEAN PASCAL ET FILS   15 ha. (80 per cent)

Puligny-Montrachet Les Folatières 0.62 ha., Les Chalumeaux 0.85 ha., Hameau de Blagny 0.27 ha., Les Champs Gains 0.47 ha., Puligny-Montrachet 3.87 ha., Volnay Caillerets 0.18 ha., Volnay 0.21 ha., Pommard 0.76 ha., Puligny-Montrachet (*rouge*) 0.36 ha., Blagny (*rouge*) 0.18 ha., Auxey-Duresses 0.24 ha., Meursault 0.26 ha., Bourgogne (*blanc*) 2.8 ha., (*rouge*) 1.45 ha.

Jean Pascal and his son Jean-Luc were active vine nurserymen during the expansive years of the 1980s. With the block on vineyard extensions since 1991 this work is much curtailed, no doubt giving the son welcome extra time for his own vines and wines.

Jean-Luc Pascal, 20 Grande Rue, 21190 Puligny-Montrachet

PAUL PERNOT ET SES FILS   19 ha. (20 per cent)

Bâtard-Montrachet 0.6 ha., Bienvenues-Bâtard-Montrachet 0.38 ha., Puligny-Montrachet Pucelles 0.28 ha., Folatières 2.88 ha., Champ Canet 0.34 ha., Clos de la Garenne 0.67 ha., Chalumeaux 0.55 ha., Puligny-Montrachet 5 ha., Meursault Blagny *Premier Cru* 0.31 ha., Blagny La Pièce sous le Bois 0.34 ha., Volnay Carelles 0.25 ha., Pommard (Noizons) 0.27 ha., Beaune Teurons 0.22 ha.,

Clos de dessus des Marconnets 0.43 ha., Reversées 0.33 ha., Beaune 0.72 ha., Santenay (*rouge*) 2.3 ha., Bourgogne (*blanc*) 1.5 ha., (*rouge*) 0.8 ha.

Given the good (for the growers) prices paid for top white Burgundies immediately after the harvest, this estate has regularly sold many of its wines to Joseph Drouhin; there they may be tasted (sometimes to be assembled with others, sometimes not), prior to tending, ageing and distribution. Vineyard acquisitions by the domaine in recent years mean that there are increasing quantities available for passing enthusiasts.

Paul, Paul-Marc et Michel Pernot, 7 place du Monument, 21190 Puligny-Montrachet

ETIENNE SAUZET, SA   8 ha. (100 per cent)

Bâtard-Montrachet 0.2 ha., Bienvenues-Bâtard-Montrachet 0.15 ha., Puligny-Montrachet Les Combettes, 1.1 ha., Champ Canet 1.2 ha., Les Perrières 0.55 ha., Les Referts 0.75 ha., Puligny-Montrachet 3 ha., Chassagne-Montrachet 0.5 ha., Bourgogne *blanc* 0.55 ha.

Etienne Sauzet used to describe himself as the son of a *petit vigneron*. He brought his estate to prominence, during the years 1930–70, from virtually nothing. He died in 1975, leaving one daughter, Madame Colette Boillot-Sauzet. The estate is run by her son-in-law, Gérard Boudot, who is one of the most dazzling white-wine-makers in Burgundy. The moment to taste with him, if you possibly can, is twelve to eighteen months after the harvest, when his wines are ready for bottling. They brim over with life, like thoroughbreds barely restrainable in the paddock before a Classic. Failing this insider-track privilege, his bottles are excellently distributed by top-end wine stockists.

After the 1990 harvest, one of Boudot's wife's brothers (Jean-Marc Boillot) exercised his right to cultivate his one-third share of the inheritance, so Domaine Etienne Sauzet was shorn of a third of its vineyards. Boudot responded by creating a family company, Etienne Sauzet, SA, which buys grapes from the domaine and vinifies them, together with additional grapes or must bought in from other growers; so they can continue to offer similar quantities of stock to their clients. They also buy grapes from some Puligny *Premiers Crus* which the domaine never owned, like Folatières and

La Garenne. From the 1991 vintage onwards, all wines are sold by the company, and since domaine-grapes and bought-in grapes are made together there is currently no way of making a distinction. However, there is no need for alarm, Boudot's wine-making hand being as steady as ever (even if sometimes, perhaps, a little heavy with the new oak).

Gérard Boudot, Puligny-Montrachet, 21190 Meursault

27

Saint-Aubin and Gamay

─────────

These villages stand in a fold of the hills behind the Côte, their vineyards facing a variety of directions, south-east to south-west. Gamay, a hamlet of Saint-Aubin, is the where the vine that bears its name, and now gives such deliciously fruity, soft red wine when grown in the Beaujolais, was probably first discovered. Easier to cultivate than the Pinot and higher-yielding, it often brought a better income to north Burgundy's growers in the days before the Pinot Noir was recognized for the noble plant it is.

Only a decade ago in Saint-Aubin twice as much red as white wine was being made, but the valley, so close to Puligny and Chassagne, is now seen as a fine source of whites, fetching higher prices than Pernand or Auxey *blancs*. A lot of the red wine used to be sold – some still is – as Côte de Beaune-Villages.

The following are classified as *Premiers Crus*:

Castets, Les	Murgers des Dents de Chien, Les
Champlots, Les	Perrières, Les
Champs, Es	Pitangeret
Charmois, Le	Puits, Le
Chatenière, La	Ranche, En la
Combes au Sud, Les	Remilly, En
Cortons, Les	Roche Dumay, Sous
Créot, En	Sentier du Clou, Sur le
Echaille	Tour, Derrière la
Edouard, Derrière Chez	Travers de Marinot, Les
Frionnes, Les	Vermarain à l'Est, Bas de
Gamay a l'Est, Le Bas de	Vignes Moingeon
Gamay, Sur	Village, Le
Marinot	Vollon à l'Est, En
Montceau, En	

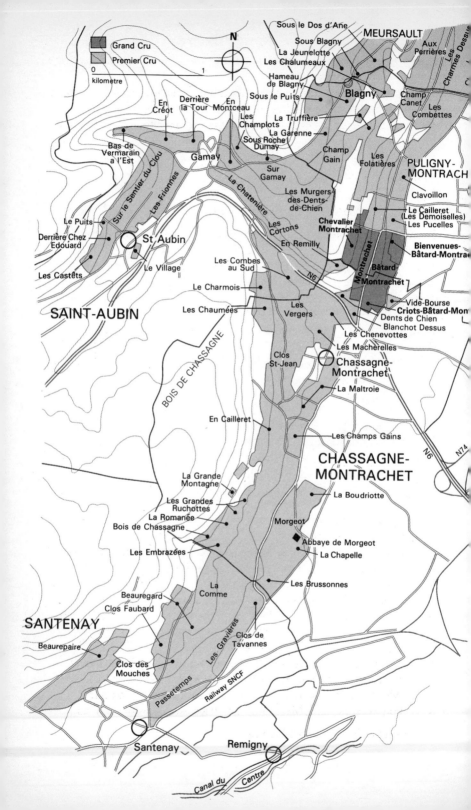

First Growth and commune Saint-Aubin covered areas of 66.27 ha. (reds) and 61.1 ha (whites) in 1991. The five-year average production (1988–92) was 32,800 cases of red wine, and 27,900 cases of white.

Main Saint-Aubin growers and merchants

GILLES BOUTON   10 ha. (80 per cent)

Puligny-Montrachet La Garenne 0.76 ha., Hameau de Blagny 0.4 ha., Sous le Puits 0.68 ha., Meursault Blagny La Jeunelote 0.9 ha., Saint-Aubin (*blanc*) en Remilly 1.4 ha., Champlots 0.21 ha., Murgers des Dents de Chien 0.23 ha., (*rouge*) En Créot 0.99 ha., Champlots 0.44 ha., Chassagne-Montrachet (*blanc*) 0.7 ha., (*rouge*) 0.86 ha., Puligny-Montrachet 0.33 ha., Blagny Sous le Puits 0.47 ha., Blagny 0.11 ha., Bourgogne (*blanc*) 0.21 ha., (*rouge*) 0.25 ha., Aligoté
Gilles Bouton, Gamay, 21190 Saint-Aubin

DOMAINE MARC COLIN   16 ha. (75 per cent)

Montrachet 0.11 ha., Chassagne-Montrachet Caillerets 0.9 ha., Champs Gains 0.45 ha., Chassagne-Montrachet (*blanc*) 1.2 ha., (*rouge*) 2.1 ha., Puligny-Montrachet La Garenne 0.25 ha., Saint-Aubin (*blanc*) Chatenière 0.9 ha., Combes 0.5 ha., Remilly 1.1 ha., Les Cortons 0.5 ha., Charmoy 0.35 ha., en Montceau 0.7 ha., *Premier Cru* (*rouge*) 1.2 ha., Puligny-Montrachet 0.35 ha., Saint-Aubin (*rouge*) 1.9 ha., Santenay 1.1 ha., Bourgogne (*rouge*) and Aligoté
   This is a excellent address, Marc Colin now being aided by two sons: Pierre-Yves (who worked the 1993 vintage at Chalk Hill, Sonoma) and Joseph.
Marc, Pierre-Yves et Joseph Colin, Gamay, 21190 Saint-Aubin

DOMAINE DU CHÂTEAU SAINT-AUBIN   8 ha. (100 per cent)

White: Meursault La Pièce sous le Bois 0.8 ha., Puligny-Montrachet sous La Garenne 0.29 ha., Saint-Aubin *Premier Cru* 0.42 ha., Chassagne-Montrachet 0.09 ha., Criots-Bâtard-Montrachet 0.05 ha.
Red: Volnay 0.29 ha., Meursault La Pièce sous le Bois 0.9 ha.,

◁ Saint-Aubin and Chassagne-Montrachet

Puligny-Montrachet 0.22 ha., Saint-Aubin *Premier Cru* 0.61 ha., Côte de Beaune-Villages

Some fine vineyard sites here, and each bottle carries the family crest, dating back to 1581 – but this is really not enough. The wine-makers cannot be highly qualified, or else they are unaware of the many recent technical advances on the Côte de Beaune, or else they are just coasting along.

A family split must have occurred at some stage, for there are at least two Blondeau-Danne labels; the other, after brief acquaint-ance, seemed no better than this one.

Charles et Denis Blondeau-Danne, Au Château, 21190 Saint-Aubin

HUBERT LAMY-MONNOT   13 ha. (100 per cent)

Criots-Bâtard-Montrachet 0.05 ha., Saint-Aubin *Premier Cru* Les Frionnes (*blanc*) 2.67 ha., Chassagne-Montrachet *Premier Cru* 0.13 ha., Saint-Aubin *Premier Cru* Les Castets (*rouge*) 1.6 ha., Puligny-Montrachet 0.9 ha., Chassagne-Montrachet (*rouge*) 1.9 ha., Saint-Aubin (*blanc*) 0.65 ha., Santenay 0.6 ha., Côte de Beaune-Villages 2.3 ha., Hautes Côtes de Beaune 1.4 ha.

Jean Lamy *père* was one of Saint-Aubin's original domaine-bot-tlers; his two sons, Hubert here, and René, who moved to smarter Chassagne, continue the traditions. This can be an honest source, though the reds were sometimes a bit rugged, and irregular, during the 1980s. Lamy has a purpose-built winery, with plenty of space, a rare advantage in Burgundy's tight-packed villages. I often find myself thinking the wines should be better than they are.

M. et Mme Hubert Lamy, Saint-Aubin, 21190 Meursault

DOMAINE LARUE   13 ha. (60 per cent)

Puligny-Montrachet *Premier Cru* 1.5 ha., Chassagne-Montrachet *Premier Cru* (*rouge*) 0.3 ha., Saint-Aubin *Premier Cru* (*blanc*) 2.5 ha., (rouge) 2.5 ha., Blagny *Premier Cru* 0.3 ha., Puligny-Montra-chet (*blanc*) 1 ha., (*rouge*) 0.5 ha., Chassagne-Montrachet (blanc) 0.3 ha., (*rouge*) 2 ha., Bourgogne (*blanc*) 0.3 ha., Aligoté

One of these brothers is married to a Rapet daughter from Per-nand, neatly joining two of the best-value white villages of the Côte de Beaune.

Didier et Denis Larue, 21190 Saint-Aubin

ANDRÉ MOINGEON ET FILS   6.68 ha. (40 per cent)

Saint-Aubin *Premier Cru* 0.95 ha., Puligny-Montrachet La Garenne 0.42 ha., Puligny-Montrachet 1.6 ha., Chassagne-Montrachet 0.31 ha., Saint-Aubin Cote de Beaune (*rouge*) 2.68 ha., Blagny Cote de Beaune (*rouge*) 0.36 ha.
André, Michel et Gérard Moingeon, Gamay-Saint-Aubin, 21190 Meursault

HENRI PRUDHON ET FILS   10 ha. (70 per cent)

Saint-Aubin (*rouge*) Frionnes 1.5 ha., Sur le Sentier du Clou 1.5 ha., (*blanc*) Les Perrières 1 ha., Saint-Aubin (blanc) 1 ha., (*rouge*) 3 ha., Chassagne-Montrachet (*rouge*) 0.8 ha., Puligny-Montrachet, Bourgogne
Henri et Gérard Prudhon, Saint-Aubin, 21190 Meursault

ROUX PÈRE ET FILS   25 ha. (100 per cent)

Red: Santenay *Premier Cru* 2 ha., Chassagne-Montrachet Clos Saint-Jean 0.75 ha., Chassagne-Montrachet 1 ha., Saint-Aubin 4.5 ha., Bourgogne Les Grands Charmeaux 4.75 ha.
White: Saint-Aubin *Premier Cru* La Chatenière 2 ha., La Pucelle 3.75 ha., Puligny-Montrachet Les Enseignères 0.35 ha., Meursault Clos des Poruzots 0.25 ha.

When Marcel Roux inherited this estate in 1960 there were four hectares of vines, two horses and some cows. The wines were normally sold in barrel, but frost in 1956 followed by hail in 1957 meant that the cellar was virtually empty. He borrowed money, rented vines, and bought a tractor. With three sons joining him, the domaine had to expand, and now it's a sizeable business, the results uneven.
Marcel, Christian et Régis Roux, Saint-Aubin, 21190 Meursault

GÉRARD THOMAS   9.5 ha. (50 per cent)

Puligny-Montrachet La Garenne 1.12 ha., Meursault Blagny 1 ha., Saint-Aubin *Premier Cru* (*blanc*) 3 ha., (*rouge*) 1.5 ha.

This is a fine, long-established Saint-Aubin source, particularly good for whites.

Gérard Thomas, Saint-Aubin 21190, Meursault

28

Chassagne-Montrachet

―――――

In this village and in Santenay reappear the strata of oolitic Bathonian limestone which are partly responsible for the characteristics of the great red wines of the Côte de Nuits. Good reds of Chassagne and Santenay may not show the dense fruit, allied to complex length of flavour, of the best *Premiers* or *Grands Crus* of that Côte, but they have their own splendid qualities, benefit from ageing, and can be terrific value.

The place has long been occupied, for a text of AD 1007 mentions a villa in the *climat* of La Romanée, presumably a Roman farm. There is some quarrying of pink, beige and veined limestone, which polishes well. In the hillside may be seen quarries, some abandoned, whence the villagers no doubt extracted stone for their homes and the altars and altar-steps of nearby fourteenth- and fifteenth-century churches.

About half each of the total surfaces of Montrachet and Bâtard-Montrachet lie in the commune of Chassagne (details were given in the chapter devoted to Puligny-Montrachet).

In addition, Chassagne has one *Grand Cru* entirely to itself: Criots-Bâtard-Montrachet (1.68 ha. The five-year average production (1988–92) for Criots-Bâtard-Montrachet was 790 cases.)

This is Burgundy's smallest white *Grand Cru*. What is its specific character? Richard Fontaine, who makes it, and can also compare it with various Montrachets and Bâtard-Montrachets in the family cellars, finds the aroma very hard to define – perhaps lightly musky.

First Growth and commune Chassagne-Montrachet represent 290 ha., the five-year average production (1988–92) having been 86,000 cases of white wine and 74,300 cases of red. White Chassagne has been selling for 50 per cent more than the red, so many growers have pulled up Pinot from land well suited to them (for instance, in Clos Saint-Jean) to replace them with Chardonnay, reversing the position of twelve years ago, when red Chassagne outsold the white.

There is a record number of *Premier Cru* vineyard names (fifty-one) in Chassagne-Montrachet, but the obscurer sites have the right to alternatives (twenty to Morgeot, three to Clos Saint-Jean, three to Cailleret; full details may be found in Pitiot and Poupon's *Atlas*, pp. 164–5):

Abbaye de Morgeot	Embrazées, Les
Baudines, Les	Fairendes, Les
Blanchot Dessus	Fairendes, Les Petites
Boirettes, Les	Francemont
Bois de Chassagne	Guerchère
Bondues, Les	Jendreau, Champ
Borne, La Grande	Macherelles, Les
Boudriotte, La	Maltroie, La
Brussonnes, Les	Montagne, La Grande
Cailleret, En	Morgeot
Cardeuse, La	Murées, Les
Champs Gains, Les	Pasquelles, Les
Chapelle, La	Petingeret
Chaumées, Les	Places, Les
Chaumes, Les	Rebichets, Les
Chenevottes, Les	Remilly, En
Clos Chareau	Romanée, La
Clos Pitois	Roquemaure, La
Clos Saint-Jean	Ruchottes, Les Grandes
Clos, Les Grands	Tête du Clos
Clos, Les Petits	Tonton Marcel
Combards, Les	Vergers, Les
Commes, Les	Vide Bourse
Crets, Ez	Vigne Blanche
Crottes, Ez	Vigne Derrière
Dent de Chien	Virondot, En

The *Cordon de Royat* type of pruning has for long been established in Chassagne-Montrachet and Santenay for Pinot Noir, which is giving the growers here a head start, when they replant in the 1990s. In other villages of both Côtes, growers are having to relearn their pruning skills to cope correctly with the higher-yielding clones of Pinot Noir now widely used, for which *Cordon de Royat* (not the traditional Guyot) is the almost essential pruning system.

Chassagne-Montrachet white wines have often, recently, been more subtle, more complex, and more interesting than the whites from Puligny, where there have been a lot of high yields and over-oaking. But they really need bottle age, where Pulignys can be utterly delicious when youthful. There is a *caveau* in the village where many growers' wines may be tasted and compared, and this is a good place to start if passing through Burgundy without having had time to arrange introductions.

Main Chassagne-Montrachet growers and merchants

DOMAINE AMIOT-BONFILS   8 ha. (90 per cent)

White: Montrachet 0.1 ha., Chassagne-Montrachet Les Caillerets 0.6 ha., Les Vergers 0.5 ha., Macherelles 0.5 ha., Les Champs Gains 0.4 ha., Clos Saint-Jean 0.25 ha., Puligny-Montrachet Les Demoiselles 0.3 ha., Saint-Aubin en Remilly 0.15 ha., Chassagne-Montrachet 0.5 ha., Bourgogne (*blanc*) 0.3 ha., Aligoté
Red: Chassagne-Montrachet Clos Saint-Jean 0.25 ha., La Maltroie 0.2 ha., Les Vergers 0.15 ha., Chassagne-Montrachet 2.60 ha.

The aim here is to bottle red wines, and the *Grand Cru*, without filtration.

Guy et Thierry Amiot, rue du Grand Puits, 21190 Chassagne-Montrachet

DOMAINE BACHELET-RAMONET PÈRE ET FILS   12 ha. (40 per cent)

White: Bâtard-Montrachet 0.4 ha., Bienvenues-Bâtard-Montrachet 0.16 ha., Chassagne-Montrachet Les Ruchottes 0.39 ha., La Romanée 0.25 ha., La Grande Montagne 0.49 ha. (with 1.5 ha. to be planted), Cailleret 0.56 ha., Morgeot 0.36 ha., Chassagne-Montrachet 1.89 ha.
Red: Chassagne-Montrachet Clos de la Boudriotte 1.03 ha., Clos Saint-Jean 0.74 ha., Morgeot 0.31 ha., Chassagne-Montrachet 1.53 ha.

A famous name, but not wines I have been able to depend on. I wonder if problems are in the past, and if we may look forward regularly to top bottles under this label, Monsieur Bachelet now being helped by his son-in-law.

Jean Bachelet et Alain Bonnefoy, 21190 Chassagne-Montrachet

BLAIN-GAGNARD 7.7 ha. (80 per cent)

Bâtard-Montrachet 0.34 ha., Criots-Bâtard-Montrachet 0.21 ha., Chassagne-Montrachet Caillerets 0.56 ha., Boudriotte 0.46 ha., Morgeot 0.86 ha., Clos Saint-Jean 0.22 ha., Chassagne-Montrachet (*blanc*) 0.57 ha., (*rouge*) 1 ha., Pommard 0.52 ha., Volnay 0.37 ha., Chassagne-Montrachet Clos Saint-Jean (*rouge*) 0.22 ha.

'Red Chassagnes have rather wild flavours,' says Blain, 'so I do not put them in new wood.' As elsewhere in this family, the wine-making is thoughtful and conscientious, avoiding the showy. The Montrachet juice is identical to that for Gagnard-Delagrange, the grapes being pressed in a small, old-fashioned vertical press, then divided. The straight Chassagne white is made as the ancestors used to do it: two different village origins, with two or three First Growths in the blend. In those days there was no fixation on *terroir* and First Growth names of origin, instead the wines were offered as different *cuvées*: *Ceci plus fin, ceci plus corsé.*

Jean-Marc Blain-Gagnard, 15 route de Santenay, 21190 Chassagne-Montrachet

CHÂTEAU DE CHASSAGNE-MONTRACHET 14 ha. (50 per cent)
DOMAINE DU PIMONT
DOMAINE CLERGET

Saint-Aubin Charmois (*blanc*) 5 ha., (*rouge*) 3 ha., Frionnes (*rouge*) 0.5 ha., Pitangerets (*blanc*) 0.5 ha., (*rouge*) 0.5 ha., Chassagne-Montrachet (*blanc*) 4 ha., Chaumées (*rouge*) 0.5 ha.

Château de Chassagne-Montrachet is a grand address from which to sell Burgundy, but not yet a good one. I suspect that work needs to be done in the vineyards, so that an appropriate volume of ripe fruit may be harvested. The commune owns a residential wing of the château, which is being restored.

Patrick Clerget, 5 chemin du Château, 21190 Chassagne-Montrachet

MICHEL COLIN-DELÉGER ET FILS   19.4 ha. (90 per cent)
MADAME FRANÇOIS COLIN
DOMAINE SAINT-ABDON

Chevalier-Montrachet 0.16 ha., Puligny-Montrachet Les Demoiselles 0.26 ha., La Truffière 0.5 ha., Chassagne-Montrachet Chaumées 1.5 ha., Chenevottes 0.75 ha., La Maltroie (*blanc*) 0.42 ha., (*rouge*) 0.15 ha., Morgeot (*blanc*) 0.65 ha., (*rouge*) 0.24 ha., Remilly 0.7 ha., Vergers 1 ha., Clos Saint-Jean 0.05 ha., Chaumées Clos Saint-Abdon (Monopole) 0.44 ha., Chassagne-Montrachet (*blanc*) 1.5 ha., (*rouge*) 5.05 ha., Saint-Aubin Charmois 0.34 ha., Combes 0.2 ha., Santenay Gravières 0.9 ha., Maranges *Premier Cru* 0.9 ha., Santenay 1.4 ha., Côte de Beaune-Villages 0.4 ha., Bourgogne *rouge* and *blanc*, Aligoté and Crémant

What mouth-watering *appellations*! Les Demoiselles is contiguous with Montrachet and Chevalier-Montrachet, and La Truffière one of the rarest and most intriguing First Growths of Puligny.

This used to be Domaine François Colin, Michel's father, and it also incorporates the vineyards whose wines were previously offered under the label Georges Deléger-Niéllon. I have had excellent bottles.

Michel Colin, 3 impasse des Crêts, 21190 Chassagne-Montrachet

DELAGRANGE-BACHELET   1 ha. (100 per cent)

Montrachet 0.07 ha., Bâtard-Montrachet 0.13 ha., Chassagne-Montrachet (*blanc*) Caillerets 0.37 ha., Chassagne-Montrachet

These wines are made and tended in the Blain-Gagnard cellar. Grandfathers in this family tend to keep active for years beyond the normal, Edmond Delagrange (born 1910) being well on the way to catching up Père Joseph Bachelet, a charming old vigneron, born 1873, who survived until he was 97. I once asked him whether post-phylloxera wines equalled the pre-louse products and he was sure they did. 'When you graft a pear tree on to a quince root you don't harvest quinces. In any case, one didn't make only good wine in the old days.' Part of the longevity secret must be family togetherness; Monsieur Delagrange has a grand-daughter living either side of him, with his daughter not far away in the same village. Lunching in each household once a week must do wonders for keeping up the spirits.

Edmond Delagrange, 17 route de Santenay, 21190 Chassagne-Montrachet.

FONTAINE-GAGNARD   7 ha. (100 per cent)

Bâtard-Montrachet 0.3 ha., Criots-Bâtard-Montrachet 0.33 ha., Chassagne-Montrachet (*blanc*) Les Caillerets 0.56 ha., Morgeot 0.23 ha., Les Vergers 0.34 ha., La Maltroie 0.57 ha., Chenevottes 0.07 ha., Morgeot (*rouge*) 0.31 ha., Clos Saint-Jean (*rouge*) 0.29 ha., Chassagne-Montrachet (*blanc*) 0.97 ha., (*rouge*) 1.05 ha., Volnay Clos de Chênes 0.36 ha., Pommard Rugiens 0.21 ha., Bourgogne (*rouge*) 0.46 ha., Passe-Tout-Grains

Fontaine was a Mirage 3 jet engine technician before switching careers to Chassagne, making his first wines in 1985. Like many growers, he prefers to imprison the fruit of his white wines before it might be too late. 'One does not need new wood for Chassagne whites', he says; 'it does not marry well'. He goes on, 'It is rare to do the same thing twice. One must observe.' Perhaps his wines have become more approachable, more outgoing, in recent years. Both colours can be excellent.

Richard Fontaine-Gagnard, 19 route de Santenay, 21190 Chassagne-Montrachet

GAGNARD-DELAGRANGE   4 ha. (95 per cent)

Montrachet 0.08 ha., Bâtard-Montrachet 0.26 ha., Chassagne-Montrachet (*blanc*) La Boudriotte 1.13 ha., Morgeot 0.75 ha., (*rouge*) *Premier Cru* 0.98 ha., Volnay Champans 0.36 ha.

Impossible for me to be objective here, Gagnard (who is as solid as a block of Chassagne marble) has sometimes sold me Montrachet, and it can take years to source good Montrachet. Here is a grower who may offer a price drop before the buyer gets round to suggesting it. There are a few new oak barrels, but not enough to leave a taste.

No point trying to drop in here, the channels must be used. Some writers (if they go unannounced) find Jacques Gagnard crusty, but he has never been dependent on the media for customers, and treats everyone pretty much alike, I suspect.

Not that I have never had a disappointment. I remember returning with a bottle of Boudriotte once, which had a strange geranium odour. Gagnard smelt it. *Il a un nez de réduit* (the nose is suffering from lack of oxygen), he said, and stuffed the cork back in. All I had to do was oxygenate the wine: tell the customers to shake air into it (he demonstrated, pumping the bottle up and down). We had tried this, and it had had no effect on the smell at all, so I had hoped the owner might have it analysed, tell me the cause of the fault, or talk about how other customers were handling the problem – but no. He handed me my bottle back, so that I could carry on shaking it, presumably, and I departed, chastened. It was a lesson in taking the rough with the smooth, I guess (what farmers have to do all the time). On the next visit he was as frank and open as ever, the wines splendid. I never spoke about geraniums again, nor did he.

To talk about wine-making faults to a Burgundian grower can be like calling attention to a child's birthmark. It is the one area that makes doing business with them sometimes difficult. One may think that the customer is always right, but one also needs to take a long view.

Jacques Gagnard-Delagrange, 21190 Chassagne-Montrachet

JEAN-NOËL GAGNARD   8.5 ha. (75 per cent)

Bâtard-Montrachet 0.37 ha., Chassagne-Montrachet (*blanc*) Les Caillerets 1 ha., Morgeot 0.8 ha., *Premier Cru* 1.2 ha., Chassagne-Montrachet (*rouge*) Clos Saint-Jean 0.33 ha., Clos de la Maltroye 0.33 ha., Morgeot 0.77 ha., Chassagne-Montrachet (*blanc* and *rouge*) 2 ha., Santenay Clos de Tavannes (*rouge*) 0.3 ha.

This has been a prime source of great white Burgundy for many years (I do not know the reds so well) offered with deference and modesty. If the quality is going to be maintained (there is no reason to believe it will not) demand will stay as firm as ever.

M. et Mme Jean-Noël, et Caroline Gagnard, Chassagne-Montrachet, 21190 Meursault

MARQUIS DE LAGUICHE ET SES FILS   4.75 ha.

Montrachet 2 ha., Chassagne-Montrachet Morgeot (*blanc*) 1.75 ha., (*rouge*) 1 ha., Chassagne-Montrachet (*blanc*)

This estate, which owns the largest slice of Montrachet, sells its must under contract to Joseph Drouhin (q.v.), who vinifies, tends and bottles the wines in Beaune. In my limited experience, the results have been excellent. The simple Chassagne, for instance, can taste as good as a First Growth.

DOMAINE LAMY-PILLOT   17 ha. (60 per cent)

Red: Chassagne-Montrachet 4 ha., Morgeot 0.5 ha., Clos Saint-Jean 0.5 ha., La Boudriotte 0.5 ha., Santenay Les Charrons 0.7 ha., Blagny La Pièce sous le Bois 0.5 ha., Saint Aubin Les Castets 1 ha., Saint Aubin 2 ha., Bourgogne 2 ha.
White: Montrachet 0.05 ha., Chassagne-Montrachet Morgeot 0.5 ha., *Premier Cru* 1 ha., Saint-Aubin Les Pucelles 0.8 ha., Saint-Aubin, Bourgogne, Crémant de Bourgogne

'Punching-down with the feet is really essential, and one person does this job several times a day. It is indispensable for disuniting the colour from the skins, into the juice – just as women need to rub the cuffs and collars of shirts, to get the dirt out. Ageing in oak barrels is important, and wood origins bring different nuances of flavour; the drying of the wood – good, or not – may bring agreeable, or really disagreeable, tastes. After fifteen years wine-making without de-stalking I changed to two-thirds de-stalking, and longer time in vat.'

René Lamy is a brusque, direct talker, as burly as his brother Hubert in Saint-Aubin. 'I share-crop a little slice of Montrachet, and will have 300 bottles of wine next year! [This was in 1989] It's a great reward for a *petit vigneron*.'

René Lamy-Pillot, route de Santenay, 21190 Chassagne-Montrachet

DOMAINE DU DUC DE MAGENTA   12 ha. (20 per cent)

Chassagne-Montrachet Abbaye de Morgeot Clos de la Chapelle (Monopole) 4.5 ha. (two-thirds white, one-third red), Puligny-Montrachet Clos de La Garenne (Monopole) 1.8 ha., Puligny-Montrachet 0.75 ha., Meursault 0.75 ha., Auxey-Duresses (*blanc*) 2 ha., (*rouge*) 1 ha., Bourgogne (*blanc*) 1 ha.

At harvest-time, the grapes or must are split at this estate, 80 per cent going under contract to Beaune, where the wines are ably made, and subsequently marketed, by Louis Jadot. The balance is vinified at the Abbaye de Morgeot, and offered domaine-bottled. A new wine-maker, Gérard de Gonneville, was appointed in 1993,

and the duchess, who is a Scot, is pursuing studies at the Beaune Lycée Viticole. The estate is set to expand, I understand.
Abbaye de Morgeot, Chassagne-Montrachet

CHÂTEAU DE LA MALTROYE   16 ha. (85 per cent)

Bâtard-Montrachet 0.33 ha., Chassagne-Montrachet Clos du Château de la Maltroye (Monopole) (*blanc* and *rouge*) 2.5 ha., Grandes Ruchottes 0.5 ha., Vigne Blanche 1.5 ha., Clos Saint-Jean 0.33 ha., Morgeot (*blanc* and *rouge*), Boudriottes, Chenevottes, Romanée, Santenay La Comme 2 ha.
André et Monique Cournut, Chassagne-Montrachet, 21190 Meursault

DOMAINE BERNARD MOREAU   9.5 ha. (80 per cent)

Red: Chassagne-Montrachet Morgeot La Cardeuse (Monopole) 0.66 ha., Chassagne-Montrachet 3.52 ha., Bourgogne (*rouge*) 1.36 ha.
White: Chassagne-Montrachet Grandes Ruchottes 0.35 ha., Morgeot 0.33 ha., La Maltroie 0.66 ha., Les Chenevottes 0.2 ha., Saint-Aubin En Remilly 0.28 ha., Chassagne-Montrachet 1.21 ha., Aligoté
Bernard Moreau, route de Chagny, 21190 Chassagne-Montrachet

ALBERT MOREY   1.3 ha. (100 per cent)

Bâtard-Montrachet 0.15 ha., Chassagne-Montrachet (*blanc*) 0.84 ha., (*rouge*) 0.32 ha.
Albert Morey, Chassagne-Montrachet, 21190 Meursault

BERNARD MOREY   9.3 ha. (100 per cent)

Chassagne-Montrachet Les Embrazées 1.04 ha., Les Baudines 0.36 ha., Morgeot 0.64 ha., Caillerets 0.31 ha., Saint Aubin Les Charmois 0.33 ha., Beaune Grèves 0.65 ha., Santenay Grand Clos Rousseau 0.4 ha., Chassagne-Montrachet (*rouge*) 3.05 ha., (*blanc*) 0.28 ha.

This is one of Albert Morey's sons, and a highly reputed cellar whose wines I wish I knew better.

M. et Mme Bernard Morey, Chassagne-Montrachet, 21190 Meursault

JEAN-MARC MOREY   8 ha. (100 per cent)

Chassagne-Montrachet Caillerets 0.7 ha., Chaumées 0.4 ha., Chenevottes 0.1 ha., Champs Gains (*blanc*) 0.5 ha., (*rouge*) 0.65 ha., Clos Saint-Jean (*rouge*) 0.2 ha., Chassagne-Montrachet (*blanc*) 1 ha., (*rouge*) 2 ha., Saint-Aubin Les Charmois 0.2 ha., Santenay Grand Clos Rousseau 0.4 ha., Santenay 0.35 ha., Beaune Grèves 0.7 ha.

Brother of Bernard Morey, Jean-Marc also makes splendid wines, both white and red.

Jean-Marc et Anne-Marie Morey, Chassagne-Montrachet, 21190 Meursault

DOMAINE MARC MOREY ET FILS   9.3 ha. (100 per cent)

White: Bâtard-Montrachet 0.13 ha., Chassagne-Montrachet Chenevottes 1.8 ha., Virondot 0.6 ha., Caillerets 0.3 ha., Morgeot 0.25 ha., Puligny-Montrachet Les Pucelles 0.4 ha., Saint-Aubin Les Charmois 0.25 ha. Chassagne-Montrachet 0.7 ha.

Red: Chassagne-Montrachet Caillerets 0.6 ha., Morgeot 0.55 ha., Chassagne-Montrachet 2.2 ha., Beaune 0.5 ha.

Morey's son-in-law Bernard Mollard now vinifies here, and is one of those hoisting up quality in Chassagne, so Jean-Claude Wallerand, *sommelier* at Le Montrachet, informs us in his book,[1] which I have found particularly helpful in these white wine villages.

Marc Morey et Bernard Mollard, Chassagne-Montrachet, 21190 Meursault.

MICHEL MOREY-COFFINET   7.8 ha. (80 per cent)

Chassagne-Montrachet (*blanc*) La Romanée 0.8 ha., Caillerets 0.75 ha., En Remilly 0.3 ha., (*rouge*) Morgeot 0.4 ha., Chassagne-Montrachet (*blanc*) 1.5 ha., (*rouge*) 1 ha., Bourgogne (*rouge*) 1.5 ha., (*blanc*) 0.5 ha.

---

1 Jean-Claude Wallerand and Christian Coulais, *Bourgogne, guide des vins Gilbert & Gaillard*, Editions Solar, Lonrai, France, 1992.

Michel Morey is Marc's son, cousin of Jean-Marc and Bernard, and has been estate bottling since 1990.

Michel Morey, 6 place du Grand Four, 21190 Chassagne-Montrachet

MICHEL NIÉLLON   5 ha. (100 per cent of the whites)

Chevalier-Montrachet 0.22 ha., Bâtard-Montrachet 0.12 ha., Chassagne-Montrachet Clos de la Maltroie (*blanc*) 0.34 ha., (*rouge*) 0.6 ha., Vergers (*blanc*) 0.4 ha., Champs Gains (*blanc*) 0.5 ha.,Chenevottes (*blanc*) 0.1 ha., Clos Saint-Jean (*rouge*) 0.15 ha., (*blanc*) 0.15 ha., Chassagne-Montrachet (*blanc*) 1.1 ha., (*rouge*) 1.3 ha.

Monsieur Niéllon's is a smiling, friendly face, but working conditions in this little cellar are very tight. I think he is lucky that chunks of Chevalier and Bâtard are powerful magnets to draw in buyers, for I have not found that his more modest wines exert so powerful an attraction.

M. et Mme Michel Niéllon, Chassagne-Montrachet, 21190 Meursault

FERNAND ET LAURENT PILLOT   8 ha. (80 per cent)

White: Chassagne-Montrachet Les Vergers 0.88 ha., Morgeot 0.36 ha., Grandes Ruchottes 0.37 ha., Chassagne-Montrachet Vide-Bourse 0.45 ha., Chassagne-Montrachet 0.63 ha., Puligny-Montrachet 0.49 ha..

Red: Chassagne-Montrachet Clos Saint-Jean 0.11 ha., *Premier Cru* 0.7 ha., Chassagne-Montrachet (Morgeot and Champs Gains) 1.5 ha., Saint-Aubin *Premier Cru* 0.42 ha., Santenay

A carefully-tended cellar under a neat modern house, where the village meets the vines. These white Pillot wines have an open style of fruitiness; one might wish for more grip or structure, but they can be very appealing. I think they could make more of their reds.

After Laurent Pillot's marriage to one of the four daughters of the late Jean-Claude Pothier-Emonin (brother of Virgile Pothier-Rieusset) of Pommard, a further 5 ha. of red vineyards joined this estate, representing half of the old Domaine Pothier-Rieusset: Pommard Rugiens 0.28 ha., Clos de Vergers 0.42 ha., Charmots 0.31 ha., Refène 0.22 ha., Beaune Boucherottes 0.23 ha., Volnay *Premier Cru* 0.23 ha., Pommard 0.96 ha., Volnay 0.48 ha., Bourgogne (*rouge*) 0.77 ha., (*blanc*) 1.13 ha. So red wine-making is bound to get more attention.

Fernand et Laurent Pillot, Chassagne-Montrachet, 21190 Meursault

JEAN PILLOT ET FILS   10 HA. (70 PER CENT)

White: Chassagne-Montrachet Morgeot 0.5 ha., Champs Gains 0.3 ha., Chenevottes 0.3 ha., Caillerets 0.2 ha., Puligny-Montrachet 0.5 ha., Chassagne-Montrachet
Red: Chassagne-Montrachet Les Macherelles 0.5 ha., Morgeot 0.5 ha., Chassagne-Montrachet 4.5 ha., Santenay 1.3 ha., Bourgogne (*rouge*)

Jean-Marc Pillot studied three years at the Beaune Lycée Viticole, and is an oenologist.

Jean-Marc et Jean Pillot, 1 rue Combard, 21190 Chassagne-Montrachet

DOMAINE PAUL PILLOT   12 ha. (65 per cent)

Chassagne-Montrachet (*blanc*) La Romanée 0.5 ha., Caillerets 0.5 ha., Champs Gains, Chassagne-Montrachet Clos Saint-Jean (*rouge*) 2.5 ha., Chassagne-Montrachet (*blanc*) 1 ha., (rouge) 1 ha., Saint Aubin Les Charmois, Bourgogne (*rouge*)

If I were looking for a top bottle of Chassagne La Romanée I would certainly come here. He is perhaps more regularly successful with his whites than his reds.

Paul Pillot, rue du Clos Saint-Jean, 21190 Chassagne-Montrachet

DOMAINE RAMONET   18 ha. (90 per cent)

Montrachet 0.25 ha., Bâtard-Montrachet 0.7 ha., Bienvenues-Bâtard-Montrachet 0.33 ha, Chassagne-Montrachet Les Grandes Ruchottes 1.06 ha., Clos de la Boudriotte (*rouge*) 1 ha., La Boudriotte (*blanc*) 1 ha., Morgeot (*rouge*) 0.5 ha., (*blanc*) 3.5 ha., Caillerets 0.5 ha., Les Vergers 0.4 ha., Clos Saint Jean 0.75 ha., Les Chaumées 0.25 ha., Puligny-Montrachet Champs Canet 0.4 ha., Saint Aubin Les Charmois 0.25 ha., Chassagne-Montrachet (*rouge*) 2.25 ha., (*blanc*) 0.75 ha., Puligny-Montrachet (0.8 ha. from 1998), Bourgogne (*rouge*), Aligoté and Passe-Tout-Grains

Wines from this domaine have in the past been offered under the labels of Ramonet-Prudhon and André Ramonet, respectively grandfather and father of Jean-Claude and Noël Ramonet who now run it. Jean-Claude is the quiet one, Noël bursts with energy.

For any domaine-bottled Burgundy enthusiast this is a place of pilgrimage. Here the late Pierre Ramonet's Chassagne-Montrachet Grandes Ruchottes 1934 was reserved by Raymond Baudoin, of *Revue du vin de France*, for Frank Schoonmaker, American importer. The wine reached the USA before the war, but could not be paid for until it ended. It launched Pierre Ramonet-Prudhon on an international market, a forerunner for literally hundreds of exporting domaines.

Within living memory, this family's origins were lowly. Pierre (whose father was a joiner) was a vigneron at the Château de la Maltroye, his wife, née Mlle Prudhon, a vigneronne at the Abbaye de Morgeot. Ramonets are fantastic workers, and they must have saved their *sous* to buy vines.

These wines are as full of fruit as a coiled spring, held under tension, is full of energy. In the past, Ramonet bottles were sometimes of uneven quality. People used to buy in barrel, and have the bottling done elsewhere. But things have completely changed – there is now extraordinary consistency in the wines, which are explosions of fresh, characterful fruit when they are youthful, and after ageing in a cold, damp cellar – well, just do it . . .

My best experiences have been Bâtard, Bienvenues, and the *Premiers Crus*. In a cellar which only makes a tiny quantity of Le Montrachet, have there been years when their gregarious enthusiasm has led them to allow just too many visitors a few mouthfuls (another de-bunging, another tiny barrel aeration)? That Montrachet gets 100 per cent new wood, which oaks its flavours like no other wine in this cellar, light vintage or rich.

Their red wines are supple but concentrated, the products of ten-day vatting, without excess tannins. A good vintage may stay the course for thirty years, all done by balance, and finesse.

These people work by instinct and handed-on experience, not their technical training, so if you seek 100 per cent security, go elsewhere.

Jean-Claude et Noël Ramonet, 21190 Chassagne-Montrachet

29
Santenay

———

Santenay is the most southerly village of the Côte d'Or devoted to wine-making. It stands on a small river, the Dheune, and possesses, as H. Delonguy and Claude Sauvageot wrote in *Notice sur Santenay* in 1884, everything that can be expected of the countryside: woods, meadows and springs.

It is very different from the three tightly packed, great white wine villages due north, being set back from main roads and the traffic of the route nationale 74, the Côte swinging westwards, at the foot of rearing, stepped hillsides, with birds singing in the spacious gardens and a fountain playing on the main square. The waters of Santenay are extremely salty, and prescribed for gout and rheumatism; its wines can be deep-coloured and stoutly constructed, longer-lived than some Côte de Beaunes. This is the second most important village, after Beaune, for the volume of red wines produced on this Côte.

As in Chassagne, limestone strata have reappeared here which are also found on the Côte de Nuits, which probably accounts for the solid structure of red Santenays. They may not have the finesse of the wines of the best villages of the Côte de Beaune, but many have an appealing, earthy chewiness and fruit. They can be excellent value, and age well.

The following are classified as *Premiers Crus*:

Beauregard
Chainey, Le (Grand Clos Rousseau)
Clos de Tavannes
Clos des Mouches
Clos Faubard
Clos Rousseau, Grand

Clos Rousseau, Petit
Comme Dessus
Comme, La
Fourneaux, Les
Gravières, Les
Maladière, La
Passetemps

First Growth and commune Santenay in 1991 covered areas of
350 ha. (red wines) and 11.75 ha. (whites). The five-year average
production (1988–92) was 148,200 cases of red wine, and 6,600
cases of white.

Main Santenay growers and merchants

ADRIEN BELLAND   11 ha. (40 per cent)
JEAN-CLAUDE BELLAND

Chambertin 0.41 ha., Corton Clos de la Vigne au Saint 0.49 ha.,
Corton-Grèves 0.55 ha., Corton-Perrières 0.69 ha., Corton-
Charlemagne 0.35 ha., Aloxe-Corton Clos du Chapitre 1 ha., Chassagne-Montrachet Morgeot 0.49 ha., Santenay Clos des Gravières
1.22 ha., La Comme 1.17 ha., Aloxe-Corton 0.59 ha., Puligny-
Montrachet 0.45 ha., Santenay 3.62 ha., Côte de Beaune-Villages
   Wine-making takes place in constricted conditions here, in the
centre of town, and has been evolved by M. Belland *père*, one feels,
to fit around the available vats, barrels, spaces and corners – as is
often the case in Burgundy. Good wines may certainly be found by
careful combers.
Adrien et Jean-Claude Belland, place du Jet d'Eau, 21590 Santenay

DOMAINE JOSEPH BELLAND   20 ha. (90 per cent)
DOMAINE DE LA CHAPELLE

Santenay Beauregard 3 ha., Commes 3 ha., Gravières 1.5 ha., Chas-
sagne-Montrachet Clos Pitois (Monopole) 3 ha., Pommard Les
Cras 1 ha., Criots-Bâtard-Montrachet 0.64 ha., Puligny-
Montrachet Champs Gains 0.6 ha.
Joseph Belland, BP 10, rue de la Chapelle, 21590 Santenay

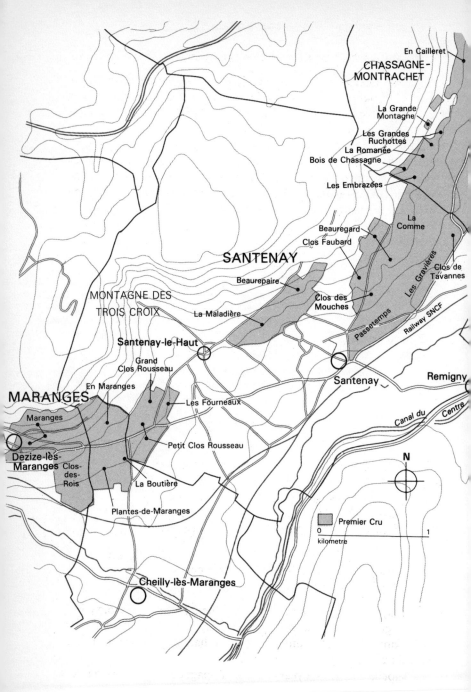

En Cailleret

CHASSAGNE-
MONTRACHET

La Grande
Montagne

Les Grandes
Ruchottes

La Romanée

Bois de Chassagne

Les Embrazées

La
Comme

Beauregard

Clos Faubard

Les Gravières

Clos de
Tavannes

SANTENAY

Beaurepaire

MONTAGNE DES
TROIS CROIX

La Maladière

Clos des
Mouches

Passetemps

Railway SNCF

Santenay-le-Haut

Santenay

Remigny

Grand
Clos Rousseau

Canal du

Centre

MARANGES

En Maranges

Les Fourneaux

Maranges

Petit Clos Rousseau

N

Dezize-lès-
Maranges

Clos-des-
Rois

La Boutière

Plantes-de-Maranges

Premier Cru

0   1
kilometre

Cheilly-lès-Maranges

Santenay and Maranges

DOMAINE BORGEOT 16 ha. (60 per cent)

Santenay Gravières (*rouge*) 1 ha., (*blanc*) 0.16 ha., Beauregard 0.6 ha., Comme 0.26 ha., Chassagne-Montrachet Morgeot (*blanc*) 0.12 ha., Santenay 2 ha., Bourgogne Aligoté 5 ha., Bourgogne (*rouge*) 4 ha., (*blanc*) 2 ha., Crémant de Bourgogne

Bargees on the Canal du Centre, which passes less than 50 metres from this estate, might make a note of these cellars, which lie just east of Santenay. The red wines ferment without de-stemming, and are carefully bottled by the owners themselves, after a light filtration. Remigny has an old reputation for its Aligotés, and the Chardonnays here are also fine.

Pascal et Laurent Borgeot, route de Chassey-le-Camp, 71150 Remigny

DOMAINE BRENOT 7.5 ha.

Montrachet 0.05 ha., Bâtard-Montrachet 0.3 ha., Chassagne-Montrachet Remilly 0.15 ha., Puligny-Montrachet Les Enseignères 0.3 ha., Santenay Blanc Le Clos Genêt 0.25 ha., Santenay Passetemps 1 ha., Santenay 0.9 ha., Maranges 1.1 ha.

Philippe Brenot, BP 12, 21590 Santenay

DOMAINE DE LA BUISSIÈRE 9 ha. (50 per cent)
JEAN MOREAU

Santenay Clos des Mouches 1 ha., Clos Rousseau 0.4 ha., Beaurepaire 1 ha., *Premier Cru* (*blanc*) 0.2 ha., Santenay 3 ha., Pommard 0.3 ha., Cote de Beaune-Villages 0.55 ha., Santenay (*blanc*) 0.2 ha.

Mme Jean Moreau, 4 rue de la Busaière, 21590 Santenay

PH. CHAPELLE ET FILS 18 ha. (100 per cent)
DOMAINE DES HAUTES-CORNIÈRES

Santenay Gravières 2 ha., Commes 1 ha., *Premier Cru* 0.75 ha., Chassagne-Montrachet Morgeot (*rouge*) 1.75 ha., (*blanc*) 0.85 ha., Santenay (*rouge* and *blanc*) 9.25 ha., Aloxe-Corton 1 ha., Ladoix 1 ha.

Chapelle worked six years with Champagne Deutz before returning to run this family estate. Around his wines some hours or days of wine tourism may agreeably be spun, for, unusually, there is space here for fifty people to sit and taste comfortably. Thanks to an association with other domaines (Coste-Caumartin in Pommard and Gilles Remoriquet in Nuits) a wide variety of *appellations* may be tasted.

His white wines are unusually-made for the Côte de Beaune. The Santenay *blanc* is fermented in vat, initially without sulphur, then briefly barrel-aged for early bottling. The Chassagne Morgeot ferments only a short time on its lees, until the second fermentation is over, after which it is racked and sulphured and returned to barrel. These sound like recipes for one-dimensionalism, and indeed I found the wines good, yet simple. On similarly limited acquaintance I found the reds sound, though somehow lacking spark. If more overseas buyers or commentators engaged in open tasting·and discussion here the traditional family styles, which go to 7,000 contented French consumers, might evolve into something more spectacular, but who is to say if that would increase the sum of human happiness?
Jean-François Chapelle, 21590 Santenay-le-Haut

MICHEL CLAIR   11 ha. (75 per cent)

Santenay Gravières 1.13 ha., Clos de la Comme 0.47 ha., Clos du Beaurepaire 0.31 ha., Clos de Tavanne 0.21 ha., Santenay 7.92 ha., Santenay (*blanc*) 0.21 ha.
Michel Clair, 21590 Santenay

DOMAINE DU CLOS DE MALTE   7.5 ha. (30 per cent)
L. E. JOLY PÈRE ET FILS

Santenay Clos de Malte 6.83 ha., Sous la Fée 0.5 ha.
  For these wines, see Louis Jadot in Beaune.
Henry Joly, 21590 Santenay

DOMAINE FLEUROT-LAROSE   11 ha. (60 per cent)
RENÉ FLEUROT ET FILS

Chassagne-Montrachet Abbaye de Morgeot (*rouge*) 3.5 ha., (*blanc*) 3 ha., Clos de la Roquemaure (Monopole) (*blanc*) 0.65 ha., Santenay Clos du Passetemps (Monopole) (*rouge*) 1.9 ha., (*blanc*) 0.6 ha., Bourgogne

Over the years it has been possible to drink excellent bottles from this estate, but I wonder if they do not make them more by luck than really good management. They have top vineyards (though their last rows of Montrachet and Bâtard-Montrachet were sold to the Château de Puligny-Montrachet in April 1994), and one of the largest cellars, with two floors underground, in Burgundy, where the wines of Duvault-Blochet's great nineteenth-century estate used to age. But success is very unpredictable in difficult years. Do they occasionally trade in an ancient barrel for some new ones, I wonder? Progress here has been slow.

René et Nicolas Fleurot-Larose, Château du Passetemps, 21590 Santenay

JACQUES GIRARDIN   6.5 ha. (50 per cent)

Santenay Beauregard 1 ha., Clos Rousseau 1.5 ha., Maladière 0.5 ha., Santenay 1.5 ha., Chassagne-Montrachet Morgeot (*blanc*) 0.2 ha., Savigny-lès-Beaune Les Gollardes 0.45 ha., Maranges 0.5 ha.

Switzerland and Germany are important markets for these wines, which can age well.

Jacques Girardin, 13 rue de Narrosse, 21590 Santenay

DOMAINE VINCENT GIRARDIN   11 ha. (100 per cent)

Santenay La Maladière 1 ha., Les Gravières 0.4 ha., Clos de la Confrérie (Le Haut Village) (Monopole) 1.19 ha., Les Charmes 0.5 ha., Savigny-lès-Beaune Les Gollardes (*rouge*) 0.7 ha., Les Vermots Dessus (*blanc*) 0.5 ha., Chassagne-Montrachet Morgeot (*rouge*) 0.3 ha., (*blanc*) 0.3 ha., Maranges Clos des Loyères 1 ha., Côte de Beaune-Villages 0.7 ha.

This has been an expanding estate, which by the early 1990s was claiming to be Santenay's leading exhibition prize-winner. The wines are very attractive when youthful, and are changing consumer perceptions of the village's wines.

Vincent Girardin, Château de la Charrière, 21590 Santenay

YVES GIRARDIN   11 ha. (30 per cent)

Santenay Maladière 1.3 ha., Clos Rousseau 1.35 ha., Passe-Temps 0.46 ha., Grand Clos Rousseau 0.36 ha., Santenay (*rouge*) 2.7 ha., (*blanc*) 2.8 ha., Chassagne-Montrachet (*blanc*) Clos Saint-Jean 0.45 ha., Maranges 0.75 ha., Hautes Côtes de Beaune 0.6 ha., Bourgogne (*rouge*) 0.23 ha.

   For the present, Yves and Jacques Girardin continue to vinify at the Château de la Charrière, where there are many variations on similar themes, the vineyards being split between members of the family. The results are generally dependable.
Yves Girardin, route de Dezize, 21590 Santenay

JESSIAUME PÈRE ET FILS   14 ha. (90 per cent)

Santenay Gravières (*rouge*) 5 ha., (*blanc*) 0.5 ha., Beaune Cent Vignes 1.16 ha., Volnay Brouillards 0.34 ha., Auxey-Duresses Ecusseaux (*rouge*) 0.5 ha., (*blanc*) 0.5 ha., Santenay 2.5 ha., Bourgogne, Aligoté
Bernard, Marc et Pascal Jessiaume, rue de la Gare, 21590 Santenay

DOMAINE LOUIS LEQUIN   7 ha. (50 per cent)

Red: Corton-Languettes 0.09 ha., Santenay La Comme 1 ha., Le Passe-Temps 0.6 ha., Chassagne-Montrachet Morgeot 0.32 ha., Santenay 3.16 ha., Pommard 0.14 ha., Nuits-Saint-Georges 0.15 ha., Maranges 0.18 ha., Bourgogne (*rouge*)
White: Bâtard-Montrachet 0.12 ha., Corton-Charlemagne 0.09 ha., Chassagne-Montrachet Morgeot 0.29 ha., Santenay Clos Rousseau 0.29 ha.

   The late Jean Lequin (father of René – see below – and Louis) used to compare the modern vigneron to a country doctor, knowing a little about a lot, relying on experience and observation and only needing to call in a specialist (the oenologist) when affairs got out of control. He was really describing himself – most aptly too. One of his proudest possessions was a hand-written notebook inscribed, *J'appartien à Antoine Lequin, vigneron à Santenay 1783*. His two sons, while working together, extended the estate with purchases in Pommard and Nuits-Saint-Georges, though I am not sure they completely mastered the extraction of earthy warmth and mouth-filling fruit from their Santenay grapes (while staying the right side of roughness).

From 1993 the estate has being split between them, so while long-living bottles bearing the name Domaine Lequin-Roussot will no doubt continue to give pleasure for many years, new vintages will appear under the names of the two brothers. Concerning Louis Lequin, a quarter of the red grapes will be going into the vats uncrushed, with the object of achieving rich fruitiness. Louis was the wine-making brother, and close to the vines, in the old partnership. He is interested in family history, like his father, telling how the family's fortunes partly came from a great-grandfather who made money collecting snails in the vineyards, for supply to Algiers and Paris restaurants, and by mining silica (when the vines were dormant in winter) up in the hills, the extracted sand going to the glass factories of Châlons.

Louis et Cécile Lequin, 1 rue du Pasquier de Pont, 21590 Santenay

DOMAINE RENÉ LEQUIN-COLIN   8.16 ha. (70 per cent)

Red: Corton-Languettes 0.09 ha., Santenay La Comme 0.89 ha., Le Passe-Temps 0.6 ha., Chassagne-Montrachet Morgeot 0.31 ha., Pommard 0.14 ha., Nuits-Saint-Georges 0.15 ha., Chassagne-Montrachet 0.37 ha., Santenay 3.55 ha., Bourgogne (*rouge*) 0.5 ha..

White: Bâtard-Montrachet 0.12 ha., Corton-Charlemagne 0.09 ha., Chassagne-Montrachet Morgeot 0.29 ha., Caillerets 0.16 ha., Vergers 0.45 ha., Chassagne-Montrachet 0.17 ha., Santenay 0.27 ha.

The Lequin white wines used to lag behind the reds, but with input and new vineyards (Vergers, Caillerets) from the Chassagne-based Colin family, into which René married, one may surely expect well-balanced bottles. 'For both red and white wines certain little secrets allow us to mark our wines with a personal touch', says René, mysteriously.

René et Josette Lequin-Colin, 21590 Santenay

PROSPER MAUFOUX, SA   (1860)

This firm's wines have a big following in the United Kingdom, but I have not found them dependably interesting.

Pierre et Vincent Maufoux, 1 Place de Jet d'Eau, 21590 Santenay

MESTRE PÈRE ET FILS   19.5 ha. (35 per cent)

Red: Santenay La Comme 2.5 ha., Gravières 2 ha., Passe-temps 1.5 ha., Clos Faubard 1.5 ha., Santenay 2.5 ha., Chassagne-Montrachet Morgeot 0.18 ha, Chassagne-Montrachet 0.5 ha., Ladoix 1.2 ha., Maranges 1 ha., Aloxe-Corton 1.2 ha., Corton 0.37 ha.
White: Santenay Passe-Temps 0.5 ha., Beaurepaire 1 ha., Chassagne-Montrachet Tonton Marcel (Monopole) 0.25 ha., Ladoix Clou d'Orge 0.6 ha., Santenay 0.5 ha.

This estate has vintages going back six to nine years, most of their bottle sales being made in France. It can be a good source for aged red Santenay.

Gérard, Michel et Philippe Mestre, place du Jet d'Eau, 21590 Santenay

LUCIEN MUZARD ET FILS   20 ha. (25 per cent)
DOMAINE DE L'ABBAYE DE SANTENAY

Santenay Clos Tavannes 1 ha., Maladière 4.5 ha., Gravières 0.71 ha., Clos Faubard 1.45 ha., Beauregard 0.17 ha., Pommard 0.31 ha., Chassagne-Montrachet (*rouge*) 0.12 ha., Santenay (*rouge*) 4.5 ha., (*blanc*) 0.3 ha., Bourgogne and Aligoté

Lucien Muzard started in the vines aged fourteen, being taught by Louis Clair and his wife, whose Abbaye de Santenay vineyards they now partly sharecrop. No de-stemming here, giving wines of deep colour, individuality and potential.

Lucien, Claude et Hervé Muzard, 21590 Santenay

OLIVIER PÈRE ET FILS   8.4 ha. (80 per cent)

Santenay Beaurepaire 1.8 ha., Santenay (*rouge*) 3.5 ha., (*blanc*) 0.6 ha., Pommard 0.4 ha., Savigny-lès-Beaune Les Peuillets 1.1 ha., Bourgogne (*rouge*) 0.9 ha.

Hervé Olivier et Valérie Girardin-Olivier, rue Gaudin, 21590 Santenay

DOMAINE PRIEUR BRUNET   18 ha. (100 per cent)

G. Prieur (1804) distributes this fine domaine: Bâtard-Montrachet 0.15 ha., Meursault Charmes 1.5 ha., Santenay Maladière 5.3 ha.,

Clos Rousseau 0.25 ha., Comme 0.35 ha., Santenay (*rouge*) 3 ha., (*blanc*) 0.55 ha., Volnay-Santenots 0.4 ha., Pommard Platières 0.25 ha., Beaune Clos du Roy 0.4 ha., Chassagne-Montrachet Morgeot (*rouge*) 0.75 ha., Embrazées (*blanc*) 0.15 ha., Meursault 5 ha.

Rather old-fashioned labels, but excellent wines here, and dependable through the range. If one seeks an example of elegant, harmonious Santenay this Maladière can be lovely – and there are 30,000 bottles each vintage.

Guy Prieur et Claude Uny, Château Perruchot, 21590 Santenay-le-Haut

CHÂTEAU PHILIPPE-LE-HARDI   88 ha. (80 per cent)

Mercurey *Premier Cru* 7 ha., Mercurey (*rouge*) 59.5 ha., (*blanc*) 5.5 ha., Aloxe-Corton 2.2 ha., Beaune Clos du Roi 0.9 ha., Saint-Aubin (*blanc*) 0.9 ha., Hautes Côtes de Beaune (*blanc*) 12 ha.

The Château de Santenay stands above the village; it was one of Philippe le Hardi's fortresses. In its grounds are two magnificent plane trees, claimed to be the oldest in France. Here the whole red harvest ferments in rotating vats, and, on occasions, only one *cuvée* of Mercurey has been made each vintage, giving half a million bottles of one wine. A lot of these Mercurey vineyards have difficulty ripening their fruit, being situated on a north-facing windswept plateau whose classification as village Mercurey may perhaps, one day, be reviewed. If some sections of Chorey-lès-Beaune merited downgrading to Bourgogne because they lay in a dip (as I saw happen in the late 1980s – to the credit of those responsible) surely plateau Mercurey – not to mention alluvial Mercurey – also merits scrutiny.

In 1988 this property was sold for 94m fr. to the Beaujolais shippers Aujoux & Cie (part of the Swiss wine group Amann Vins, SA), and five years later was changing hands again.

Château de Santenay, 21590 Santenay

30

Maranges and Couchois

THE NEW *APPELLATION* MARANGES

Let us first consider the wines of Maranges, which come from the hillside which extends beyond Santenay, and are the last wines of the Côte de Beaune proper, going south.

They are grown over the Côte d'Or's boundary with the Saône-et-Loire, in the three communes of Dezize-lès-Maranges, Sampigny-lès-Maranges and Cheilly-lès-Maranges. The three communes had all tacked on the words ' –lès-Maranges', in reference to the shared hillside making their best wine, erroneously believing this would help the wines to sell. The decision was reversed in 1989, since when there has been this simpler, one-word *appellation*.

The best Maranges used to be medicine wines, going into Côte de Beaune-Villages blends to beef up lighter, or defective, elements. This hillside gives strong-flavoured wines of substantial colour and fruit, but bringing a supple mouth-feel into the equation is not so easy.

First Growth and commune Maranges covered an area of 155 ha. (for red wines) and 1.9 ha. (for whites) in 1992. The five-year average production (1988–92) was 86,500 cases (for reds) and 950 cases (for whites, in respect of the 1991 and 1992 vintages averaged).

Main Maranges growers

BERNARD BACHELET ET SES FILS 37.5 ha. (50 per cent)

Chassagne-Montrachet Morgeot 0.3 ha., Puligny-Montrachet Grands Champs 0.65 ha., Meursault Charmes 0.1 ha., Narvaux

0.75 ha., Chassagne-Montrachet (*blanc*) 1.7 ha., (*rouge*) 3.5 ha., Pommard Chanlins 0.8 ha., Gevrey-Chambertin 0.9 ha., Santenay Clos des Mouches 0.5 ha., Santenay 3.5 ha., Saint-Aubin *Premier Cru* (*rouge*) 2.5 ha., Maranges La Fussière 6 ha., Clos Roussots 2 ha., Maranges 4 ha., Hautes Côtes de Beaune, Bourgogne (*rouge* and *blanc*), Aligoté, Passe-Tout-Grains

During the 1980s I thought that too much sulphur was some-times used on these wines, yields seemed too high, and quality was irregular.

Progress has been made. They now vinify everything in Chas-sagne-Montrachet, in the old de Marcilly premises on the low road out towards Santenay. The bottles are then mainly cellared in Dezize, where the estate began, and where they must be the largest owners of First Growth Maranges. The Bachelet brothers look hard workers, and more fine surprises may be on the way.

Jean-François, Vincent et Jean-Louis Bachelet, 71150 Dezize-lès-Maranges

YVON ET CHANTAL CONTAT-GRANGÉ   6.5 ha. (60 per cent)

Maranges La Fussière 0.4 ha., Clos Roussots 0.35 ha., Santenay (*rouge*) 0.8 ha., (*blanc*) 0.35 ha., Maranges (*rouge*) 1 ha., (*blanc*) 0.5 ha., Hautes Côtes de Beaune 1.5 ha., Bourgogne and Aligoté

This couple has been making Burgundy (entirely from rented vines) for a mere dozen years, having originated in Annecy, Haute Savoie.

Yvon et Chantal Contat-Grangé, 71150 Dezize-lès-Maranges

DOMAINE DU CHÂTEAU DE MERCEY   44 ha.

Santenay *rouge* 1 ha., Mercurey (*rouge* and *blanc*) 15 ha., Bour-gogne Hautes Côtes de Beaune (*rouge* and *blanc*) 25 ha., Bour-gogne Aligoté 3 ha.

Half-ownership of these vineyards (and there is more to plant) went in 1989 to Antonin Rodet of Mercurey. Many are situated at an altitude of 250–90 metres, similar to those of the Côte de Beaune. Plans are laid to turn the Hautes Côtes vines over to lyre-shaped canopies and high-training methods to reduce costs and improve results. The old vines will be left in place, but two rows out of three pulled up, giving 3,333 vines per hectare, instead of

10,000. There will be mechanical pre-pruning (a revolutionary Burgundian concept), and the sowing of grass between the rows.

This is set to become one of Burgundy's most interesting experimental vineyard projects. There is plenty of room to improve the quality of the wines, and I am sure that will happen fast.

The INAO still sets its face against non-traditional vine-training methods in Bourgogne AC, and the region's village *appellations*, but I suspect that this has more to do with bureaucrats preferring not to leave their specially-built, hexagonally-shaped offices and taste abroad, than that they seriously believe that current productions of Bourgogne AC and village ACs cannot be improved, nor growers' incomes conceivably augmented.

Bertrand Devillard et Jacques et Michel Berger, 71150 Cheilly-lès-Maranges

DOMAINE MAURICE CHARLEUX   10 ha. (30 per cent)

Santenay 2 ha., Maranges 7 ha., Bourgogne (rouge) 1 ha.
Maurice Charleux, 71150 Dezize-lès-Maranges

DOMAINE CHEVROT   12.5 ha. (80 per cent)

Santenay Clos Rousseau 1.6 ha., Maranges (*rouge*) 2.5 ha., (*blanc*) 0.7 ha., Hautes Côtes de Beaune (*rouge*) 3.5 ha., (*blanc*) 0.7 ha., Bourgogne (*rouge* and *rosé*) 1 ha., Aligoté 1.5 ha., Crémant de Bourgogne 1 ha.

These wines age under a beautiful, barely restored, ochre-stoned late-eighteenth-century house built by a Dijon lawyer, with arched cellars running its whole length. It is one of the first places to come to taste Maranges, both white and red. The Chevrots have been bottling since 1970, export to half-a-dozen countries, and are a fine source of modestly-priced wines, for drinking relatively young – though the First Growth Santenay can need cellaring.

One may be sure of a friendly, smiling welcome, with none of the petty jealousies sometimes seen in more famous villages: 'If you are going to Sampigny, have you tasted at the Duchemins, Jean-Louis or Eric? In Dezize, Bernard Bachelet of course, and do you know Contat-Grangé?' Good Maranges growers are happy to encourage the spreading of the name.

Catherine et Fernand Chevrot, 71150 Cheilly-lès-Maranges

DOMAINE LAURENCE   4 ha. (40 per cent)

Maranges Clos Roussots 4 ha.

Laurence's estate has shrunk in size; he is also a local wine-broker.

Jean-Paul Laurence, 71150 Dezize-lès-Maranges

THE WINES OF THE COUCHOIS

This is a mini-district of vineyards, which is a physical prolongation of the Côte de Beaune, but has never been part of it. It lies north-west of the Côte Chalonnaise, and might logically seem attachable to that Côte, but Couchois growers have not shown enthusiasm for the idea. The landscape more resembles Hautes Côtes – 90 per cent of the vineyards being on hillsides – and perhaps it will one day be joined to the Hautes Côtes de Beaune. For the present, the BIVB links the Couchois with the Côte Chalonnaise.

It is not much more than a ten-minute drive from Santenay, but the prettiest way to approach it is from Mercurey, on the main Chalon-Autun road, which brings one to the ravishing Château at Couches. Old, golden-grey stones, a great square tower-gate, four rectangular buttresses holding up a chapel on the edge of a precipitous drop to the valley, this is the castle of Marguerite de Bourgogne, so-called from the belief (as the *Blue Guide* puts it) that the repudiated wife of Louis X did not die before the king's remarriage in 1315, as the official histories have it, but spent the rest of her life here as the secret prisoner of her cousin's family. There is a vestige of the duchess in Puligny-Montrachet, where the Sentier de Couches, perhaps originally a Roman road, separates the *Premiers Crus* from the village *appellation* of Puligny. This was the route, so Simon Loftus[1] tells us, which linked Couches with the duchess's spiritual home, the Cistercian abbey of Maizières in the plain to the east.

The wines of the Couchois are mainly red, Pinot Noir covering 245 ha. and Gamay 95 ha., making respectively Bourgogne *rouge* and Bourgogne Passe-Tout-Grains. Aligoté is grown on 14 ha., Chardonnay on 6 ha. Much of this wine goes to make André Delorme's delicious Crémants.

1 *Puligny-Montrachet: Journal of a Wine Village*, Ebury Press, London 1992.

Pinocchio in the Couchois

The Priory of Couches in the Middle Ages belonged to the bailiwick of Beaune, and had its own press. There are 1,000 years of wine-making history here, but the phylloxera almost completely destroyed it. Two-thirds of the wine-growers went to work for the Schneider company in nearby Le Creusot, the industrial centre (using locally-mined coal) to which Louis XVI had moved the royal glass-works, from Sèvres, in the 1780s. The Schneider company, as the *Blue Guide* tells us, produced France's earliest steam loco-motives, armaments, cranes, and bridges, and the Couchois hill-sides were replanted with hybrids to supply the workers' *vin de table*. Hybrid vines covered these hills from 1900 to 1960.

One or two families nevertheless planted Pinots, notably Edou-ard Dessendre, father and grandfather of Roger and Jean-Claude Dessendre, now leading domaine-bottlers in the Couchois. Dessen-dre *grand'père* became known as Pinocchio for his laughable deter-mination not to give up on Pinot.

This is not mono-culture land; there are Charolais herds in the valley, wheat and barley on the plateaux, many springs, and walnut trees in the hedges. As vineyard land it is interesting, for Pinot and Chardonnay grow on hillsides, red marls and clay-limestone. Aligoté and Gamay are planted where the limestone strata hit the granite and sandstone platform beneath. This is frontier territory, like Bussières, Serrières and Pierreclos in the Mâconnais.

There are three main wine-growing villages: Saint-Sernin above its vines, Saint-Maurice below its vines, and Dracy beside the vines. Couches itself is a succession of low slopes, but there are only three wine-growers among the cattle-rearers.

I have only visited the Dessendre family (and am indebted to them for much of the above) their details being:

DOMAINE DE LA TOUR BAJOLE   11.5 ha. (75 per cent)
MARIE-ANNE ET JEAN-CLAUDE DESSENDRE
ROGER DESSENDRE

Bourgogne Pinot Noir 6.5 ha., Chardonnay 1.4 ha., Passe-Tout-Grains 2.3 ha., Aligoté 1.3 ha.

This was the first cellar in the district to have a heat-exchanger. There is a pneumatic press, and an adjustable, precise stemmer-crusher. Equally significant, there are plenty of old vines. Some wines are still made for the blending market: a super-purple Gamay, intensely fruity (no carbonic maceration for this one) will do wonders for someone's Passe-Tout-Grains blend, but you could hardly drink it on its own. The Pinots are another matter, and these are the wines they bottle. Very ripely fruity, in the good vintages, they need five or more years in bottle to soften (that is the Couchois *terroir*). Roger Dessendre has retired from vineyard work, but not from offering 100,000 bottles of maturing Pinot Couchois, with good stocks going back to 1985 and 1983. Spicy and perfumed, lively and full, these are beautiful wines.

'The Domaine will receive you with pleasure, you will be able to taste its wines and visit the places where they are made and stored, but be prudent and warn us of your arrival, for at the domaine one is at the same time vineyard-worker, wine-maker and salesperson, and the first function implies much attentiveness in the vines.' This thoughtful warning may be born in mind the length and breadth of Burgundy.

Marie-Anne, Jean-Claude et Roger Dessendre, 71490 Saint-Maurice-lès-Couches.

31
The Côte Chalonnaise: Bouzeron and Rully

INTRODUCING THE CÔTE CHALONNAISE

The four historic wines of this area, which used also to be known as the Région de Mercurey, are, from north to south: Rully, Mercurey, Givry and Montagny. Bouzeron is a recent addition, as described below.

As well as these individual commune wines, with their recently revised First Growth hillsides, large volumes of regional *appellation* wines are produced. Production of straight Bourgogne has expanded enormously in the last fifteen years, white wines climbing from 1,000 hl to 4,600 hl, the reds even more steeply, from 4,000 hl to an astonishing 38,000 hl.

Since a decree of 27 February 1990 a specific *appellation* – Bourgogne Côte Chalonnaise – may be applied, if analysis is satisfactory, and tasting tests are passed. The *labélisation* (as it is known) for Bourgogne Côte Chalonnaise is one of the strictest in Burgundy, I believe, as many as 40 per cent of the samples submitted being regularly refused. Rejection does not bring financial disaster on the grower, for the wine will go to market nevertheless as Bourgogne. Bourgogne Côte Chalonnaise, however, is steadily building itself a reputation as something better. Excellent Crémants de Bourgogne are also made from wines grown in this region, for instance those of André Delorme.

Let us look at the five individual village wines of the Côte Chalonnaise – in some cases, with their *Premiers Crus* – starting from the north.

BOUZERON

In March 1979 there appeared a new *appellation* on the Côte Chalonnaise: Bourgogne Aligoté de Bouzeron, this being a small Saône-et-Loire village just over the boundary from the Côte d'Or. At its best the wine is medium-weight but piercingly fruity, with a very clean finish, and without excess acidity.

It is the only village in Burgundy having a commune *appellation* for its Aligotés, which are grown on both sides of the little valley. Regional Bourgogne Aligoté may contain up to 15 per cent of Chardonnay; however in Bouzeron the wine must be 100 per cent Aligoté grape, and the maximum yield is lower too, 55 hl/ha., compared with 60 hl/ha.

The tiny *appellation* has prospered, plantations climbing by 40 per cent from 29 hectares in 1984 to 45 hectares in 1987. Aubert de Villaine writes: 'This increase is explained by the success of Aligoté de Bouzeron, thanks to the efforts of the growers and Maison Bouchard Père et Fils, which owns vines in Bouzeron, purchases 30–40 per cent of the wines produced, and distributes throughout the world.' A major role has also been played by Aubert and Pamela de Villaine who bought their property in Bouzeron in 1973, and rapidly saw the potential of the wines. The five-year average production (1988–92) for Aligoté de Bouzeron was 18,700 cases.

The name is due to change, to Bouzeron, without mention of its grape, in the same way that Sauvignon de Saint-Bris is due to become Saint-Bris. Bouzeron will still have to be made from 100 per cent Aligoté. Although the Bouchard Père, Delorme and Chanzy wines can be very good it takes a lot to beat the de Villaine bottles.

DOMAINE CHANZY FRÈRES   36.2 ha. (85 per cent)
DOMAINE DE L'HERMITAGE

Bourgogne Aligoté Bouzeron Clos de la Fortune 10.54 ha., Bourgogne Clos de la Fortune (*blanc*) 2.52 ha., (*rouge*) 2.59 ha., Rully (*blanc*) 4.17 ha., (*rouge*) 8.08 ha., Mercurey Clos du Roy (*rouge*) 1.73 ha., (*blanc*) 0.29 ha., Santenay Beaurepaire (*rouge*) 0.33 ha., (*blanc*) 0.1 ha., Mercurey (*rouge*) 4.36 ha., (*blanc*) 0.46 ha., Vosne-Romanée 0.34 ha., Puligny-Montrachet 0.6 ha.

As can be seen, this is a very big estate, and recent acquisitions

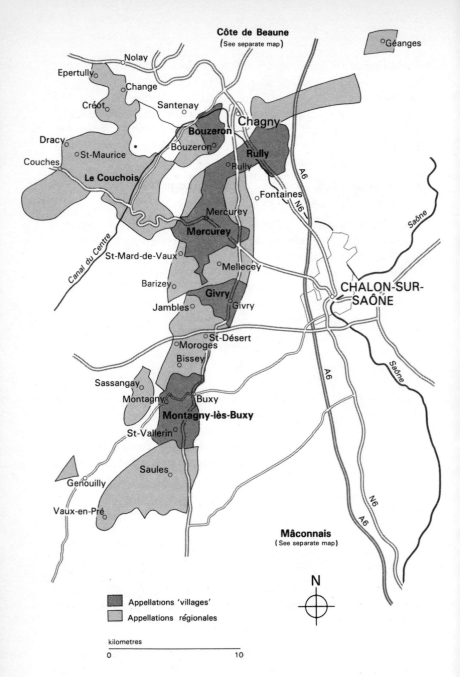

Côte Chalonnaise and Couchois

mean that it has a foothold on all three Côtes. It delivered honest, though for me rarely outstanding wines, during the 1980s. From the early 1990s the domaine has had its own bottling line, instead of relying on a contract bottler, and the vines are of course older; surely, we may look for more exciting bottles.

Daniel Chanzy, Domaine de l'Hermitage, Bouzeron, 71150 Chagny

CHEMORIN PÈRE ET FILS 12.6 ha. (20 per cent)
DOMAINE DES CORCELLES

Rully (*blanc*) 4.5 ha., (*rouge*) 0.5 ha., Maranges 0.6 ha., Bourgogne Aligoté de Bouzeron 6.5 ha., Bourgogne (*rouge*) 0.5 ha.
Julien et Michel Chemorin, Bouzeron, 71150 Chagny

PIERRE COGNY 9.6 ha. (35 per cent)

Rully Grésigny 0.54 ha., Rully (*blanc*) 0.23 ha., (*rouge*) 0.37 ha., Bourgogne Aligoté de Bouzeron 5.25 ha., Bourgogne (*rouge*) 2.2 ha., (*blanc*) 0.8 ha.
Pierre Cogny, 71150 Bouzeron

A. ET P. DE VILLAINE 19.5 ha. (80 per cent)

Bourgogne Aligoté de Bouzeron 8.7 ha., Mercurey (*rouge*) 1 ha., Rully Les Saint Jacques (*blanc*) 1.5 ha., Bourgogne Côte Chalonnaise Les Cloux (*blanc*) 3 ha., Bourgogne Côte Chalonnaise La Digoine (*rouge*) 5.5 ha.

This estate belongs to one of the co-directors of the Domaine de la Romanée-Conti, Aubert de Villaine and his American wife Pamela. His international friendships and contacts ensured that Bourgogne Aligoté de Bouzeron (which *appellation* only dates from March 1979) rapidly started rubbing shoulders with long-established fine Burgundies on specialist wine-merchants' shelves.

Here the tending of the vines is 'more-or-less biological, manure being solely organic with trace-elements, treatments being made with copper sulphate, sulphur and plant essences'.

De Villaine has found that where his Bourgogne *blanc* gains from being partially fermented in small barrels, the Bouzeron Aligoté is best when vinified in vat. Twenty years' specialization in the vinification of Aligoté have turned him into a master, indeed procedures have been established which he finds valuable every year. Fine, healthy Aligoté vine-plants are, of course, the first essential, to be goblet-pruned (not Guyot), to restrict the yields to a carefully targeted 50–55 hl/ha. A pneumatic press gives juice as clear as if it had been allowed to settle, which is lightly sulphured, then fermented in vats of around 35 hl, using the natural, local yeasts. A must-aeration early on should get round mercaptan smells. The fermentation temperatures are pegged to those of his Chardonnays bubbling in small barrels, so they follow the natural curves of the vintage.

His reds are made for drinking 'either very young, from six months after the bottling, to take advantage of their fruit, or after waiting three years, when the hollow period (which is standard with all Pinots Noirs) has ended. With red meats, Reblochon . . .' Here also the yields are carefully targeted – 35 hl/ha. for Pinot Noir being a limit to be breached at the gravest peril. Chaptalization is non-existent, or minimal. The wines are beautiful, and excellent value.

Mercurey and Rully *blanc* are new *appellations* for this estate. Aubert et Pamela de Villaine, Bouzeron, 71150 Chagny

RULLY

Until the arrival of Bouzeron, Rully was the first village *appellation* of the Côte Chalonnaise, or Région de Mercurey. It is said to take its name from a wealthy Gallo-Roman owner, Rubilium. A legacy of vines to the Abbey of Saint-Marcel was made in the eleventh century; in the seventeenth a gift of 22 *feuilletes de vin clairet très exquis* was made by the inhabitants of Chalons to Louis XIII.

The name of Rully was for long chiefly associated with the manufacture of sparkling wine, some by the Champagne method, some from outside the Burgundy area; the village's own still wines were hardly known.

The foundation of this sparkling wine industry in Rully dates from 1822. After discussion with the mayor of Avize, a Chalons businessman, Fortune-Joseph Petiot-Groffier invited the eighteen-year-old François-Basile Hubert, a cooper's son, to apply Champagne methods to the wines of the Chalonnais. Hubert later founded his own company, which prospered thanks to contracts with Marseille shipowners to supply the soldiers during the Crimean War, and the Italian army on campaign. Pierre Goujon states that he made large dispatches of what were called 'Vins de Champagne' to America during its Civil War.[1]

A hundred years ago there were 600 hectares of vines in Rully, but by the late 1940s a mere forty hectares were left producing AC wine. There was much replanting in the 1980s, and now plantations are back up to 300 hectares. The five-year average production (1988–92) for white Rully was 81,500 cases, for red 54,400 cases. Production looks like settling down at around 70 per cent white wine, 30 per cent red. With so many young, high-yielding vines about, grape maturity is not always satisfactory.

The following vineyards of Rully are *Premiers Crus*:

Agneux	Meix-Caillet
Bressande, La	Molesme
Champ-Clou	Mont-Palais
Chapitre	Pieres, Les
Clos du Chaigne	Pillot
Clos Saint-Jacques	Préau
Cloux	Pucelle, La
Ecloseaux	Rabourcé
Fosse, La	Raclot
Grésigny	Renarde, La
Margoté	Vauvry
Marissou	

Pitiot and Servant's *Les Vins de Bourgogne*[2] has red Rully as being all elegance and finesse, with odours of lilac, violet, raspberry and cherry. I do not think most growers are making wine like that at all. Instead of going for delicious, yummy fruitiness they are often producing wines which do not have Mercurey's structure, but have picked up some of its astringency. Perhaps I have not been tasting enough red Rullys.

White Rully, on the other hand, can be a very beautiful wine, and one of the best value white Burgundies available.

And this by tradition is the place to come for Burgundy's best

---

1 *Le Vignoble de Saône et Loire au XIXème siècle*, Université Lyon II, Lyon, 1973.
2 Presses Universitaires de France, Paris, 1992.

Crémants. Where Crémants from the Yonne may be dry, sometimes lacking ripeness of aroma, and Mâconnais Crémants will tend to be heavily based on Chardonnay, these Chalonnais Crémants should provide the richest harmonies.

Main Rully growers and merchants

DOMAINE BELLEVILLE   30 ha. (100 per cent)

Rully (*blanc* and *rouge*) Les Cloux, Chapitre, Rabourcé, Raclot, La Fosse, La Pucelle, 10 ha., Rully (*blanc* and *rouge*) 10 ha., Mercurey (*blanc*) 0.4 ha., (*rouge*) 0.3 ha., Côte de Beaune-Villages 1.5 ha., Hautes Côtes de Beaune 1.5 ha., Crémant de Bourgogne

This family successfully grows large quantities of fruit, but the resulting wines can show vegetal, stalky characteristics, presumably from unripe, machine-picked grapes. These white Rullys can taste like basic Mâcons, and the reds lack fruitiness and length. There are also, however, *cuvées* which show good balance, and offer value.

Christian Belleville, rue de la Loppe, 71150 Rully

RAYMOND BÊTES   10 ha. (25 per cent)

Rully La Pucelle 0.5 ha., Rully (*blanc*) 6 ha., (*rouge*) 2 ha., Bourgogne (*blanc*) 1 ha., Aligoté

A younger generation grower to whom we can look for some of the best bottles of the *appellation*.

Raymond Bêtes, Agneux, 71150 Rully

DOMAINE BRELIERÈ   7.31 ha. (100 per cent)
JEAN-CLAUDE BRELIÈRE

Rully (*rouge*) Les Montpalais 0.6 ha., Le Pria 2.35 ha., (*blanc*) Les Margotey 2.25 ha., Les Champs Cloux 0.5 ha., Rully (*blanc*) 1.25 ha., Aligoté 0.36 ha.

After a period when this estate was drifting somewhat Brelière *fils* has picked up the reins, from the mid-1980s. His prior studies were foreign languages and their literatures: Spanish and English (from both sides of the Atlantic). German-speakers need not hold back from visiting, either. He must hold some sort of Burgundian domaine record for language skills, and the wines are well worth tasting too.

Jean-Claude Brelière, place de l'Eglise, 71150 Chagny

DOMAINE MICHEL BRIDAY   10 ha. (100 per cent)

Rully (*blanc*) Grésigny 0.72 ha., La Bergerie 1.6 ha., La Pucelle 0.5 ha., (*rouge*) Les Chailloux 1 ha., Champs Cloux 0.62 ha., Rully (*rouge*) 1 ha., Mercurey Clos Marcilly 0.9 ha., Mercurey 0.45 ha., Bourgogne (*rouge*) 1.7 ha., Aligoté

A first impression that disorderly scruffiness reigns is not contradicted by vat and bottle tastings, which show wines of wildly varying potentials for ageing and giving pleasure. Briday senior is president of the local grower's union. The son tells me that his American importer, Mr Rosenthal, has been asking for unfiltered wines since 1987, and that the family has followed him down that route, affixing an explanatory back-label. I would have thought there were other, more pressing, priorities to be sorted out first, but perhaps unfiltered wine from a dedicated artisan (Mr Rosenthal's words) sells so automatically in the USA that there is no cause for anxiety.

Michel et Stéphan Briday, 89 Grande Rue, 71150 Rully

EMILE CHANDESAIS   (1933)

This company distributes a 10 ha. estate: Rully Clos Saint-Jacques (*blanc*) 2 ha., Bourgogne Champs Perdrix (*rouge*) 4.8 ha., (*blanc*) 3 ha., part of which, on a hillside opposite their premises in Fontaines, has been a site for Pinot Noir and Chardonnay clonal selection experiments. It handles the Château de Nety (Beaujolais-Villages) and Domaine Gouffier (Mercurey and Bourgogne). The firm is now part of the Picard group in Chagny, but retains its stock-holding and wine-tending independence, I understand.

Emile Chandesais et Dominique Clemandot, BP 1, Fontaines, 71150 Chagny

JEAN DAUX, DOMAINE DE L'ECETTE   9.2 ha. (65 per cent)

Rully (*blanc*) 2.6 ha., (*rouge*) 1.95 ha., Bourgogne (*blanc*) 2.45 ha.
Jean Daux, Rue de Geley, 71150 Rully

ANDRÉ DELORME, SA   68.7 ha. (100 per cent)

This firm distributes the wines of Jean-François Delorme's Domaine de la Renarde, which has been built up to over 60 ha. (partly wholly-owned vineyard, partly farmed) over the last thirty years. As well as the Monopole Rully Varot (*blanc*) 7.7 ha., and (*rouge*) 10.13 ha., there are holdings in the white Rully *Premier Crus* Grésigny 0.8 ha, and Les Cloux 0.3 ha., the red Champs Cloux 0.32 ha., and both red and white Marissou 0.56 ha., Molesme 0.91 ha., and La Fosse 0.71 ha. There are a further 27.8 ha. of red and white Rully, also Mercurey Clos du Roy 0.5 ha., Les Crêts 0.57 ha., Les Velées 0.29 ha., Mercurey 3.49 ha., Givry Clos du Cellier aux Moines 4.41 ha., Bourgogne Aligoté de Bouzeron 1.7 ha., Montagny L'Epaule 1.77 ha., and Crémant de Bourgogne 4.82 ha.

This is one of the most dependable and dynamic companies on the Côte Chalonnaise, whose sparkling wines and white wines I often admire and enjoy, but about whose red Rullys I am not so sure. Red Rully can be the essence of red Burgundian vinous fruitiness, a sort of young Volnay for those on a budget. When Delorme makes red Côte Chalonnaise he likes to leave in up to 70 per cent of the stalks (pumping over, but not punching down) to achieve a wine with a certain tannic structure – a contender to be taken seriously in the red Burgundy hierarchy, it seems.

Jean-François Delorme, rue de la République, 71150 Rully

JEAN-YVES DEVEVEY   4.5 ha. (80 per cent)
DOMAINE DU BOIS-GUILLAUME

Hautes Côtes de Nuits (*blanc*) 1.5 ha., (*rouge*) 1 ha., Bourgogne (*rouge*) 1 ha., Aligoté 0.3 ha., Passe-Tout-Grains 0.2 ha.

The owner was an export broker and merchant for five years before taking on his father's vineyards. Barrel-fermented white Hautes Côtes is a speciality, and most of his wines are exported.

Jean-Yves Devevey, rue du Breuil, Demigny, 71150 Chagny

RAYMOND DUREUIL-JANTHIAL   7 ha. (100 per cent)

Puligny-Montrachet Champs Gains 0.19 ha., Rully Meix Cadot 0.44 ha., Les Cloux 0.08 ha., Mercurey 0.88 ha., Rully (*blanc*) 0.52

ha., (*rouge*) 2.04 ha., Bourgogne (*blanc*) 0.53 ha., (*rouge*) 0.56 ha., Passe-Tout-Grains and Aligoté

These reds are vinified with the stalks left in, in the old French manner, stamped morning and eve, then aged underground. I look forward to trying them.

Raymond et Raymonde Dureuil-Janthial, rue de la Buisserolle, 71150 Rully

DUVERNAY PÈRE ET FILS   16 ha. (40 per cent)

Rully (*blanc*) Les Cloux 1.5 ha., Raclots 1.5 ha., Rabourcé 4.4 ha., (*rouge*) Cloux 0.8 ha., Champs Cloux 2.5 ha., Rully Le Meix de Pellerey (Monopole) 1.4 ha., Mercurey (*rouge*) 1.2 ha., (*blanc*) 0.3 ha.

The Duvernays farm the vines of the Domaine Saint-Michel, and have moved to an old farm and larger premises on flat land east of the village. These white wines would be much better if the premises were temperature-controlled, as M. Duvernay recognizes; but markets having turned down, it is hard to invest. I suspect that the best way to buy here is to stand under the pneumatic press with a clean vat on wheels, taking first-run juice away promptly. Over the years it might easily become a top source for bottled wines as well.

Georges Duvernay, rue de l'Hôpital, 71150 Rully

DOMAINE DE LA FOLIE   18 ha. (80 per cent)

Rully (*rouge*) Clos de Bellecroix (Monopole) 5 ha., En Chaponnière 1 ha., Rully (*blanc*) Clos Saint-Jacques (Monopole) 1.8 ha., Clos du Chaigne (Monopole) 3.5 ha., Rully *blanc* 6 ha., Bourgogne Aligoté 0.5 ha.

The drive up to this property has more of a Provençal than a Burgundian feel to it. A spacious house surrounded by pine and oak is approached through broad hillsides of vineyard.

Jérôme took over (mercifully) from his brother Xavier from the 1989 vintage, and the red-wine-making now aims for greater fruit and flavour, with longer vatting times. Their white Rully can be unusually fine and lemony in vat or barrel, but may lose these qualities during handling. He is experimenting with plastic racks of grilled oak staves (previously used for barrels) submerged in his red wine vats – authorized, he says, and worth trying, given the high price of barrels (*not* oak-chips, he stresses). A local oenologist is on hand with advice when needed. Jérôme Noël-Bouton (whose father worked in the oil industry, as President of Primagaz) is an open-minded, Paris-based commercial lawyer during the week, coming to La Folie at weekends. He appears resolved to take the property up to its full quality potential (which has not recently been realized). Jérôme Noël-Bouton, La Folie, route de Rully, 71150 Chagny

DOMAINE GUYOT-VERPIOT   8 ha. (95 per cent)

Rully *blanc* Les Cloux 0.31 ha., Rully (*blanc*) 4.3 ha., (*rouge*) 2.5 ha., Bourgogne Aligoté 1 ha.

We may be luckier here with whites than reds.
Hubert Guyot et Françoise Guyot-Verpiot, rue du Château, 71150 Chagny

HENRI ET PAUL JACQUESON   10.4 ha. (80 per cent)

Rully Les Clouds (*blanc*) 1.25 ha., Grésigny 2.3 ha., La Pucelle 2.4 ha., Rully Chaponnières (*rouge*) 1.15 ha., Mercurey Naugues 0.65 ha., Mercurey 0.7 ha., Aligoté 0.8 ha. Passe-Tout-Grains 0.6 ha.

This place is spotless, and is run with skill and passion. It has been temperature-controlled since 1989. Jacqueson does a lot of work with barrels (buying his staves directly from a splitter in the Cher, weathering them in his garden) and there are subtle gradings of fruit and oak in both red and white wines, from all four Burgundy grapes. Rully is a big, straggly village; aim uphill, above the church. You may almost buy with your eyes closed, but if you do you will miss the photographs of smiling, slim-legged, lightly-dressed girl workers treading down his solid Pinot skins, pips and stalks – which are an unexpected extra attraction.
Paul Jacqueson, En Chevremont, 71150 Chagny

DOMAINE ANDRÉ LHÉRITIER   4 ha. (70 per cent)

Rully Clos Roch (*blanc*) 0.35 ha., (*rouge*) 0.65 ha., Aligoté de Bouzeron 0.4 ha., Bourgogne (*rouge*) 1.2 ha., (*blanc*) 1 ha.

If staying or eating in Chagny at Lameloise or near it, but pushed for time, one can take a brief walk round the back into an authentic grower's cellar, full of blackened barrels and lively, stony-flavoured green-gold wine with Rully's characteristic bite.

M. et Mme André Lhéritier, 4 blvd de la Liberté, 71150 Chagny

H. NIEPCE   5 ha. (50 per cent)
DOMAINE DU CHAPITRE

Rully (*blanc*) Les Cloux 1.03 ha, Rabourcé 0.35 ha., Mont-Palais 1.24 ha., (*rouge*) Clos du Chapitre (Monopole) 1.23 ha., Les Préaux 0.27 ha.

This family descends directly from a grandfather Niepce, brother of Nicéphore, one of the inventors of photography. The first cameras are in the museum of Châlons-sur-Saône, but some of Nicéphore's papers may be seen at this house.

This is old France, and an authentic source of rustic Rully, simply made. No barrels are used, and the wines – all First Growths – bottled by contractor. The reds ferment with their stalks, giving a more tannic Rully than most. It could benefit immensely from younger generational input, and of course investment.

Henriette Niepce, Clos du Chapitre, rue des Buis, 71150 Rully

DOMAINE PIERRE-MARIE NINOT   10 ha. (100 per cent)
DOMAINE RENÉ NINOT-RIGAUD

Rully *blanc* Grésigny 1 ha., Rabourcé 0.5 ha., Chaponnières 1 ha., Le Meix Guillaume (Monopole) (*rouge*) 1.5 ha., (*blanc*) 0.55 ha., Clos de la Bergerie (Monopole) (*rouge*) 0.5 ha., (*blanc*) 2.5 ha., Mercurey *rouge* Les Crêts 0.5 ha.

This vineyards are farmed, and the wines made and bottled, by Jean-François Delorme.

Pierre-Marie Ninot, Cellier Meix Guillaume, 71150 Chagny

CHÂTEAU DE RULLY   45 ha.

Rully (*blanc*), partly *Premier Cru*, 35 ha., (*rouge*) 10 ha.

Only a few years back just three productive vineyard hectares depended from this big, partly twelfth-century mediaeval hillside château. The dynamism of Bertrand Devillard of Antonin Rodet in Mercurey is turning this label into one of the best, and most highly valued, of the *appellation*. Details may be found with those for Rodet, in Mercurey.

The Comtes de Ternay own an unusual sixteenth-century wine glass, large enough to hold three litres or four bottles of wine. Tradition has it that an ancestor, Charles de Saint-Ligier, used to drain it in one, though this seems impossible, for the rim is so wide that the wine pours past the sides of one's mouth.

Comtes Charles et Christian d'Aviau de Ternay, au Château, 71150 Rully

32

Mercurey

The reputation of Mercurey's wines goes back to charters of AD 557 and 885, the name recalling a Roman temple to Mercury, later replaced by a windmill. The wines are harvested in the communes of Mercurey and Saint-Martin-sous-Montaigu. This is the most important *appellation* of the Côte Chalonnaise.

It is very easy to drive to Mercurey from Beaune, visit growers on the main street, then return to the Côte d'Or having seen little but flat vineyards and fields of maize on the lowlands. But if one takes the main Chalon–Autun road westwards out of Mercurey, immediately a striking, shovel-shaped wedge of vineyard may be seen on the flank of the hills, edged by pine trees, with succeeding swathes of hillside vines lining the road whenever the contours and the orientation permit. These are not even the First Growths, but they make strikingly beautiful country. Mercurey growers claim their wines are undervalued, but if they encouraged tourists to picnic up in their woods, and to walk the forest edges, more might make Mercurey their chosen halt.

After the last war the annual production was scarcely 50,000 cases, however the five-year average production (1988–92) for red Mercurey was 274,100 cases, and for white 26,800 cases. There are several merchants in the area to help sales (Antonin Rodet, Protheau, Chandesais), and the Côte d'Or families of Faiveley and Bouchard Aîné both have large vineyard holdings (see pp. 337 and 546), the former a record number of Monopoles (see Appendix A).

There has been a recent reclassification of Mercurey's *Premiers Crus*, taking the First Growth area from around 15 ha. to over 100 ha. Three of the original five (Clos du Roi, Clos Voyen or Les Voyens, Clos Marcilly, Clos des Fourneaux, Clos des Montaigus) were historic Monopoles. The following vineyards were added with effect from the 1989 vintage:

Les Croichots
La Cailloute
Les Combins
Champs Martins
Clos des Barraults
Clos des Myglands
Clos l'Evêque
Grand Clos Fortoul
Les Naugues
Les Crêts
Clos Tonnerre
Les Vasées
Les Byots
Sazenay
La Bondue
Le Levrière
La Mission
Griffères
Les Velley
Clos Château de Montaigu
La Chassière
Les Ruelles Clos de Paradis

Hydraulic works and land regrouping

The broad, sweeping flanks of the Mercurey vineyard catch great quantities of water in a heavy storm. Before the little retaining walls, the hedges and the peach trees were removed to allow in vine-straddling tractors, this water was often harmlessly channelled and absorbed, but a great storm in 1981 caused serious flooding. There were two metres of muddy water in some cellars, and one domaine needed 400 man-hours to clean it all up. Earth and silt poured into the main street.

After this flood, funds were obtained from regional, departmental and village sources to undertake one of France's most ambitious vineyard hydraulic schemes, linked with a regrouping of scattered holdings. The slopes have been cut with channels to slow the water.

Bands of concrete stop the flows, canalizing them into drains down towards settlement tanks, where the precious surface soil is deposited, the water being allowed to run down into the valley. By 1993 almost all the major vineyard amphitheatres (Champs Martins/Combins, Sazenays, Les Velley) had been protected. This co-operative venture, touching every vigneron in the village, is bound to have had beneficial effects far beyond its basic hydraulic *raison d'être*.

Red Mercurey is usually well coloured and structured, and with good potential for ageing, rather than youthful charm. White Mercurey can often, in my experience, be disappointing, turning yellow-brown, taking on aromas of straw, and losing freshness without gaining finesse or aged qualities. This is primarily an area for red-wine-makers, and Chardonnay has sometimes been planted more because a grower wished to have white in his cellar than because the land was appropriate – or alternatively because a bit of pebbly soil was unsuitable for red. There are few pneumatic presses, and white wine savvy runs fairly shallow.

Detailed soil analyses in Mercurey might result in certain plots being downgraded to Bourgogne *rouge* (as has happened in Chorey-lès-Beaune), and to others being identified specifically for whites, which would be welcome.

There is a lot of indifferent wine from vineyards on land demonstrably less well placed than the best, which must partly account for the variability seen in the Château Philippe-le-Hardi wines, and some bottles under Picard labels.

Consumers are often confused and disappointed by Mercurey (the most expensive *appellation* of the Côte Chalonnaise) because of these quality variations. Too much land near the alluvial valley floor has Mercurey *appellation* when it should be Bourgogne. Above all, the north-wind-swept plateau above the First Growths of Combins and Champs Martins often fails to ripen properly, but this too may be called Mercurey.

The growers and local merchants need to find ways of eliminating the halt, the lame and the blind, or perhaps outsiders should do more blind tastings of Mercureys, carefully comparing like with like, publishing the results, warts and all. More growers need to start shouldering their responsibilities.

En route for Mercurey

If one drives from Beaune to Mercurey through the back hills, by the pretty route via Remigny and Chassey-le-Camp, one goes past a dozen neat, domaine-bottling estates. These mainly sell to passing French tourists in search of bargains – but if some of the enthusiasts for New World Pinot Noir extend their interests to the French version who knows what the effects might be? This could be a rich hunting ground. Here are limestone-rooted, mature, fine Pinots, whose potential for deliciousness is not yet fully realized.

DOMAINE MAURICE BERTRAND ET FRANÇOISE JUILLOT 13.04 ha. (100 per cent)

Montagny Les Coères 3.87 ha., *Premier Cru* 6.43 ha., Bourgogne (*rouge*) 1.75 ha., Aligoté 1.01 ha.

One of Michel Juillot's daughters, Françoise, associated herself in 1989 with a Montagny grower in his early fifties owning fine vineyards, but with no heirs: Maurice Bertrand. He looks after the vines, while she and her husband make the wines. The Juillot family thus has a solid foot in the southernmost *appellation* of the Côte Chalonnaise; only Bouzeron presently escapes them. Well-equipped, capable and committed, this estate looks poised to produce some of the best Montagnys around. The *Premier Cru* wine may see no wood at all, the Les Coères will ferment in 15–20 per cent new oak.

Mme Françoise Feuillat-Juillot, BP 10, Grande Rue, 71640 Mercurey

DOMAINE BORDEAUX-MONTRIEUX 4.48 ha. (90 per cent)

Mercurey Grand Clos Fortoul *Premier Cru* (Monopole) 2.5 ha., Clos l'Evêque 0.15 ha., Clos Fortoul (Monopole) 1.85 ha.

This family also owns Domaine Thénard in Givry, where improvements are under way. The two Monopoles are surrounded by their original fifteenth-century walls, 1.5 metres thick at the base, 4 metres high.

M. Bordeaux-Montrieux, Jamproye, 71640 Mercurey

DOMAINE BRINTET   9.7 ha. (70 per cent)

Mercurey La Charmée 1.5 ha., La Levrière (Monopole) 1.3 ha., La Corvée 1.2 ha., La Vigne d'Orge 1 ha., Les Byots 0.38 ha., Mercurey (*blanc*) 1 ha., (*rouge*) 1 ha., Bourgogne *rouge* and *blanc*

Be sure to give the large, black watch-dog a wide berth; apart from that, few worries here. There is a fine new vat-house, the reds being made in open metal vats, the whites seeing no wood at all.
Luc Brintet, Grande Rue, 71640 Mercurey

DOMAINE DE LA CROIX JACQUELET

(See Maison J. Faiveley, Nuits-Saint-George)

LOUIS DESFONTAINE   13.5 ha. (100 per cent)
DOMAINE DU CHÂTEAU DE CHAMIREY

Mercurey (*rouge*) 3.11 ha., (*blanc*) 0.45 ha., Bourgogne Cote Chalonnaise (*rouge*) 6.5 ha., (*blanc*) 0.8 ha., Passe-Tout-Grains 1.7 ha., Aligote 1.5 ha.

Barely moderate wine-making skills here, I have suspected, with a tendency to leave wines too long in wood, giving caramelized aromas, and fruitiness which dries out with bottle-age.

However, I am told this impression is completely off-beam, the owner being a talented individualist who simply holds back his excellent youthful *cuvées* until older stocks are sold, and young vintages can be released. Obviously this needs investigating.

There is a 2.4 ha. Monopole 'Clos de la Perrière', but it was not being vinified separately in 1992.
Louis Desfontaine, Le Château, Chamilly, 71510 Mercurey

P.-J. GRANGER PÈRE ET FILS   10 ha. (65 per cent)
DOMAINE DE LA MONETTE

Mercurey *Premier Cru* Les Montaigus 1 ha., Les Velay (*rouge*) 1 ha., (*blanc*) 0.5 ha., Mercurey Vieilles Vignes 6.5 ha.

A generation-change is under way here, smoothly if my tasting of fine and interesting wines, both white and red, is any guide. 'I buy new barrels when I need to replace the wood, not for flavouring purposes', states the son, Pierre-Emmanuel. There is a new vat-house, and dusty old cellars where the wines age under great oak beams running across the room at chest height. Could the wines be improved? If lively sales permit investment in temperature control for the barrel store and ground-floor cellars, perhaps.

Paul-Jean et Pierre-Emmanuel Granger, Chamirey, 71640 Mercurey

JEANNIN-NALTET PÈRE ET FILS 8 ha. (100 per cent)

Mercurey *Premier Cru* Clos des Grands Voyens (Monopole) 5 ha., Clos L'Evêque 1 ha., Naugues 1 ha., Mercurey (*rouge*) 0.5 ha., (*blanc*) 0.5 ha.

This is a long-established, helpful, welcoming bottler, the owner of one of the historic Monopole First Growths. For me the wines fall between two stools – neither fruity and supple nor structured for long-term ageing, they vaguely please at various stages.

Thierry Jeannin-Naltet, rue de Jamproyes, 71640 Mercurey

DOMAINE EMILE JUILLOT 8.5 ha. (65 per cent)

Mercurey *Premiers Crus* La Cailloute (Monopole) (*rouge*) 1.45 ha., (*blanc*) 0.25 ha., Les Combins 1 ha., Champs Martins (*rouge*) 0.9 ha., (*blanc*) 0.2 ha., Les Croichots 0.5 ha., Mercurey (*rouge*) 2 ha., (*blanc*) 1.35 ha., Bourgogne (*rouge*) 0.42 ha., (*blanc*) 0.4 ha.

I think quality here could be transformed with some fine tuning. The lightly-coloured wines I saw tasted fine from barrel, but markedly less well after bottling.

Jean-Claude et Nathalie Theulot, Clos Laurent, 71640 Mercurey

DOMAINE MICHEL JUILLOT 32 ha. (100 per cent)

Mercurey (*rouge*) Clos des Barraults 2.5 ha., Clos Tonnerre (Monopole) 2.7 ha., Clos du Roi 0.5 ha., Les Champs Martins (*rouge*) 1 ha., (*blanc*) 0.5 ha., Mercurey (*rouge*) 13 ha., (*blanc*) 3 ha., Aloxe-Corton 0.5 ha., Corton-Perrières 1.2 ha., Corton-Charlemagne 0.8 ha.

This is the most dynamic estate in the village, and has been for two decades, since Michel Juillot demolished five houses to purpose-build an airy space for wine-making and barrel-ageing (his parents thought he was crazy). The domaine has tripled in size, and spawned family offshoots with vineyards in neighbouring villages:

Domaine Laborbe-Juillot for Givry and Rully, Domaine Bertrand-Juillot for Montagny.

Its size causes them concern, for, as Michel Juillot says, in Burgundy you must pick when the grapes are ripe. If you are an old-fashioned family unit with 3 or 4 hectares this can be done over Friday to Monday, with friends and relations. 'Why have small domaines in Burgundy always done so well, and big estates never? Because of the harvest length', says Juillot. 'Look at 1991 – too ripe, and picked too late. Look at 1992 – the last five days, it was too late. (Of course, you *could* blame the bureaucrats for choosing the wrong starting date.) In Bordeaux they can handle big properties, picking Merlot before the late-ripening Cabernet, in California you can pick different grapes week by week. But Burgundy needs little vat-houses.'

Thanks to their skills and hard work, Michel and his son Laurent Juillot earn high prices for their Mercureys. They are some of the surest values in the whole of Burgundy, and can be bought, drunk or cellared with confidence. The Juillot men are great exaggerators (Madame Michel Juillot being a counter-weight of level-headed common sense), and at times blow their trumpets a bit stridently, but you have to blow trumpets loudly in Mercurey, if you want to get the news out. Ask an average Pommard or Gevrey grower where Mercurey is, and he could not even find it on the map. He certainly would not go there to taste, but then, he has no need to, does he?

Michel et Laurent Juillot, BP 10, Grande Rue, 71640 Mercurey

DOMAINE LORENZON   5 ha. (100 per cent)

Mercurey Champs Martins 2.7 ha., Croichots (*blanc*) 0.2 ha., Mercurey (*rouge*) 2.3 ha.

Bruno Lorenzon travels widely on behalf of the cooperage Tonnellerie de Mercurey (which is owned by an Aube-based stave-splitter), and this has allowed him rare opportunities to forge friendships and exchanges of views with ex-hexagonal Pinot Noir growers, particularly New Zealanders such as Clive Paton and Larry McKenna. He has vinified there three times (Corbans, Neudorf), and in South Africa (KWV's experimental domaine). 'It helps me to lose the small-town mentality which can be met with in

France', he says. His father Alfred still does most of the vineyard work, Bruno having been wine-making since 1987.
Bruno Lorenzon, rue du Reu, 71640 Mercurey

DOMAINE LA MARCHE   24 ha.

Mercurey *Premier Cru* Les Vasées 1 ha., Clos La Marche (Monopole) 3 ha., Mercurey (*rouge*) 17 ha., (*blanc*) 3 ha.

This estate, owned by the Bouchard Aîné family, came up for sale in 1993, after the sale of the company to J.-C. Boisset. The family also owns Beaune Les Sceaux 1 ha.
Paul Bouchard, Société Civile La Marche, 71640 Mercurey

YVES DE LAUNAY   18 ha. (50 per cent)
DOMAINE DU MEIX-FOULOT

Mercurey Clos du Château de Montaigu (Monopole) 2 ha., Les Velleys 1.5 ha., Les Byots 0.75 ha., Mercurey (*rouge*) 9.25 ha., (*blanc*) 1.6 ha.

An unusual vein of light soil crops up here, which has given the name of Meix-Foulot or 'Mad-house' to the place. Half a hectare of white grapes are grown on it.

There have been six generations of de Launay, and as they say, 'When you come to Mercurey if you wish to call on us at Meix-Foulot you had better ask the way, as the estate is hidden among hilly vineyards away from anything.' Better to be hard to find than sacrifice privacy by putting up a sign. They are deeply rooted in the locality, drawing oak from Burgundian forests, using a local cooper to make them up.

Slightly eccentric wine-making, I feel, by a gifted, experienced, well-intentioned amateur, the contract-bottled results being hit or miss. But I am sure customers are rarely unhappy, particularly if they have visited this beautiful spot, and can age the reds long enough. 'I am very lucky', says de Launay, 'to live surrounded by my vines and with a pretty view – across a dip to the tower of the church of Touches. Imagine, when it is under the snow, lit up at night . . .'
Paul de Launay, route de Chamirey, Touches, 71640 Mercurey

JEAN MARÉCHAL   10 ha. (100 per cent)

Mercurey *Premier Cru* 4 ha. (Clos l'Evêque 1 ha., Clos Barrault 0.7 ha., Les Naugues 1 ha., Champs Martins 0.5 ha.), Mercurey (*rouge*) 4 ha., (*blanc*) 0.5 ha.

Married in 1949, Jean Maréchal started bottling in 1950, and now has 3,000 private French customers. These are not red Burgundies according to the perceived *goût français* (light, early-maturing), but rather long-lived Mercureys, some of which may be enjoyed when young. Anyone interested in wine-trading (whether as buyer or seller) may learn from watching and listening to this distinguished wine-maker as he calmly directs a taster to his wine's best points, past any temporary short-coming, adding value to his by-no-means-expensive wines with each word. It is a pleasure to buy here, easy to park opposite, and you will not be let down.
Jean Maréchal et Jean-Marc Bovagne, Grande Rue, 71640 Mercurey

DOMAINE JEAN-PIERRE MEULIEN   9 ha. (98 per cent)

Mercurey La Cray 0.9 ha., Mercurey (*rouge*) 4 ha., (*blanc*) 0.7 ha., Bourgogne *rouge* 3 ha., Aligoté 0.3 ha.
   This can be a good source, I have found.
Jean-Pierre Meulien, rue du Clos l'Evêque, 71640 Mercurey

ROGER ET MICHÈLE NARJOUX   14.5 ha. (50 per cent)
DOMAINE DU CRAY

Mercurey *Premier Cru* Clos des Montaigu (*rouge*) 2 ha., (*blanc*) 0.5 ha., Clos de Paradis 0.5 ha., Givry Les Servoisines (rouge) 1.5 ha., (*blanc*) 0.5 ha., Mercurey (*rouge*) 4.5 ha., Bourgogne Côte Chalonnaise 5 ha., Aligoté
   'We drink wine here, we don't drink oak', said the bustling Madame Narjoux, who had 120 knitters and seamstresses under her orders until she gave up that career to be wine-maker, while her husband supervised his grape-pickers. I tasted a ripely splendid Bourgogne *rouge* 1992 (20 per cent new oak) which was surely not expensive, and there are many grander growths. Clos des Montaigus from a good vintage can take ten years here to reach its delicious peak.

Mme Roger Narjoux, Domaine du Cray, 71640 Saint-Martin-sous-Montaigu

FRANÇOIS PROTHEAU ET FILS, SA

This firm distributes the 59 ha. Domaine Maurice Protheau et Fils, the name Domaine des Fromanges being used for the Rullys, and the name Domaine de la Corvée when the wines are sold through supermarket sectors: Mercurey Clos l'Eveque 7 ha., Les Champs Martins 0.5 ha., Clos des Corvées 6 ha., La Fauconnière 6.35 ha., Les Velley 1.5 ha., Les Ormeaux (*blanc*) 3 ha., Mercurey (*rouge*) 15 ha., Rully Les Fromanges (Monopole) (*blanc*) 7 ha., La Chatalienne (*blanc*) 3.5 ha., (*rouge*) 2 ha., Bourgogne (*rouge*) 5 ha., Aligoté 2 ha.

Since 1990, a new stainless steel vat-house, with robotized pneumatic punching-down, has been in operation, run by Philippe Protheau's oenologist sister Mme Martine Cibin-Protheau. Most of this family-owned firm's sales are in France, but it aims to make more structured, deeper-coloured wines than in the past, and to expand exports. This has been a sleeping giant amongst Mercurey domaines. I have rarely come across the wines, but the domaine's potential is self-evident.

Philippe Protheau, Le Clos l'Eveque, 71640 Mercurey

JEAN RAQUILLET   8 ha. (80 per cent)

Mercurey *Premier Cru* Naugues 0.5 ha., *Premier Cru* 1 ha., Mercurey (*rouge*) 5.5 ha., Les Velées (*blanc*) 0.5 ha., Bourgogne (*rouge*) 0.5 ha., Aligoté

A new, temperature-controlled vat-house went up here in 1991, and this control extends also to cellar storage. François Raquillet has his own bottling line, bought in partnership with a friend, so bottling is not left to chance. These are vivacious wines, ripe and harmonious.

François et Jean Raquillet, BP 16, rue de Jamproyes, 71640 Mercurey

ANTONIN RODET, SA (1875)

This firm (partly owned by Champagne Laurent Perrier, since 1991) has recently made enormous strides, and now owns or controls an exceptional number of fine vineyards, stretching from Mercurey up to Gevrey-Chambertin:

Château de Chamirey

The estate consists of 35 hectares of Mercurey (two-thirds red, one-third white), the most notable vineyards being the First Growths: Clos du Roi, La Mission, Clos l'Evêque, en Sazenay and Les Ruelles. The red wines are vinified partly in stainless steel horizontal vats with automatic, slowly turning blades which improve, so they say, on the results obtained from stirring up skins and must in the traditional manner with the legs and feet. It is a leading source of Mercurey *blanc*.

Château de Rully

Since 1986 Rodet has been responsible for the running (and extension by planting) of this estate, its wine-making and distribution. A year later it also took on responsibility for the Domaine du Prieuré of Armand Monassier in Rully, the two estates now totalling 45 ha., all being sold (quite properly) under the label Château de Rully. It was in full production by 1991, 80 per cent being white, 20 per cent red.

Domaine Jacques Prieur

In 1988 a 50 per cent holding of this famous estate (see Meursault) was acquired by A. Rodet and a group of mainly Burgundian investors: Financière Clayeux, Groupe Poch, Financière Labruyère Eberlé, and Famille Neyrat. The Devillard influence, aided by a conscientious Martin Prieur, was felt without delay. Domaine Jacques Prieur wine-making had been half-hearted for many years, and some of their bottles very miserable offerings, but transformations are under way.

Domaine Rodet

Rodet has half-owned the Domaine du Château de Mercey since 1989, where experimental vine canopy management, and low density planting are being installed (details may be found in the Maranges section).

From reading an interview with one of Rodet's wine-makers,

Mme Nadine Gublin, in the BIVB's *Vinification: l'expérience bour-guignonne*, it is obvious that much new thought is also going into their wine-making. She writes of the need to react to each vintage rapidly and specifically, refusing to be a spectator, or to submit. Sorting of grapes for ripeness and health, bleeding-off of juice, and greater use of yeast cultures and pneumatic presses are all now crucial to success.

Rodet's director Bertrand Devillard is a Burgundian prepared to admit that criticisms are still voiced:

> One sometimes hears that, because of Burgundy's success, we have become arrogant, and that our red wines, besides, are heavy, our whites tiring, that they are all expensive – and so complicated to understand.
>
> Heavy? Only if people do not know the fruity, delicate elegance of Pinot Noir, when it has been well tended, and bottled when still fresh. Tiring? Our wines have fruit and elegance, the opposite ... The days of sulphured, oxidized wines are over. Expensive? Without doubt, but the message has been heard ... We promise, you will have great wines at reasonable prices. Complicated? To be sure, for after a thousand years of history and work on our hillsides, whose sites are so varied ... their personalities impinge on us. They are our masters, and we endeavour to serve them.

Bertrand Devillard has had the boldness to give his domaine wine-makers their heads, and their own bottling-lines, letting them make the finest wines they can, even if it does show up the shortcomings of one or two basic Rodet *négociant* blends – the Pommard, or the Bourgogne *rouge*, for instance. I suspect that, once he is on top of lyre-training in the Hautes Côtes, he will waste no time turning his attention to the basic Pommard.

Bertrand Devillard, 71640 Mercurey

DOMAINE SAIER 21.8 ha. (100 per cent)

Mercurey *Premier Cru* Champs Martins (*rouge*) 3 ha., (*blanc*) 0.28 ha., Mercurey (*rouge*) 8 ha., (*blanc*) 4 ha., Bourgogne Clos du Prieuré (*rouge*) 6.5 ha.

Hand-harvesting is the policy here, with fermentation in open, stainless steel vats, and punching-down, to produce fruity, relatively supple Mercureys, for bottling sooner rather than later. They can be long flavoured and succulently delicious.

Domaine Saier also owns superb vineyards in the Côte d'Or, details of which may be found where they are vinified, at the Clos des Lambrays, in Morey-Saint-Denis.

Fabien et Louis Saier (owners) et Thierry Brouin (manager), Le Closeau, 71640 Mercurey

DOMAINE DE SUREMAIN   25 ha. (50 per cent)

Mercurey Clos l'Evêque 3.5 ha., Sazenay (*rouge*) 1.5 ha., (*blanc*) 1.1 ha., Bondue 2.18 ha., Clos Voyen 2 ha., Croichots 1.5 ha., Les Crets 1 ha., *Premier Cru* (*blanc*) 0.5 ha., Mercurey (*rouge*) 11.5 ha.

This estate seemed as disorganized in 1993 as on my first visit twenty years previously, and made me think about the inconsistencies of Brussels. The most hygienic and punctilious farm cheese-maker is forced to invest in all manner of sparkling new buildings and equipment to avoid closure, yet a wine-maker does not even have to own a broom, duster or paintbrush (let alone use them) while handling food products. These wines come from top Mercurey sites, and could be outstanding. Many I found disappointing, albeit difficult to judge given the uncontrolled high temperatures at which they were being stored and served.

Hugues et Yves de Suremain, Grande Rue, 71640 Mercurey

EMILE VOARICK, SCV   60 ha.

Corton Clos des Fiètres 0.7 ha., Mercurey (*rouge*) Clos du Roy 1.16 ha., Clos Paradis (*rouge*) 2.5 ha., (*blanc*) 0.5 ha., Mercurey (*rouge*) 16.5 ha., (*blanc*) 2 ha., Beaune Montée *rouge* 0.95 ha., Givry (*rouge*) 2 ha., (*blanc*) 0.2 ha., Bourgogne (*rouge*) 17.3 ha., (*blanc*) 1 ha., Passe-Tout-Grains 7.2 ha., Aligoté 1.5 ha.

Michel Picard, of the Chagny-based *négociant* Picard Père et Fils owns this domaine, the wines being made and bottled at the estate.

M. Nicot, Saint-Martin-sous-Montaigu, 71640 Givry

33

Givry and Montagny

———

GIVRY

Givry growers would have it that in the Middle Ages their wines were on an equal footing with those of Beaune. Certainly they paid the same taxes, for an *ordonnance* of 1349 states, *Tonnel de vin de Beaune . . . et de Givry paiera six sous d'entrée à Paris*. In 1390 Philippe le Hardi's wife Marguerite de Flandres stocked her cellars at the Château de Germolles with ten *queues* of Beaune and forty-five *queues* of *Givry et environs* according to P. Bréjoux.

Like the other villages of this region, Givry has seen much replanting (particularly with Pinot Noir, which has more than doubled its surface in ten years). The five-year average production (1988–92) for red Givry is 81,500 cases, for white 11,600 cases. It is harvested in the communes of Givry, Dracy-le-Fort and Jambles.

Its price remains very approachable, and those cellars known for domaine-bottling have been finding demand buoyant. This can cause quality problems, for everything sometimes gets bottled, where in the past the lesser *cuvées* might be sold in bulk, with just the best being domaine-bottled. And the wines? Red Givry is richly fruity Pinot Noir which is not strongly marked by origin, often quite supple, with a cherry aroma. To tell the whites apart from Montagny? Not easy.

First Growths classified, and then again

In the summer of 1993, an opportunity seems to have been missed by the INAO (not for the first time) to take into account the interests of consumers.

An initial classification (in the early 1990s) had elevated a number of well-placed historic Clos, and the classic hillside west of the town, to First Growth status. But there were illogical, inexplicable gaps, to the dismay of the owners. These well-placed sites have now also been consecrated First Growth. Where the INAO let consumers down was in bowing to grower pressure, allowing a multiplication of totally obscure new names. Indifferent qualities are likely to find shelter behind unheard-of sites (as often in Burgundy). The INAO lives in a producers' world of its own creation.

Two dozen Givry First Growth names means that some domaines have quasi-monopoly of their sites. The danger is that they will tell us that, whatever the character or the quality, *c'est le terroir*, with the implication: this is what the wine *is*, and if you do not rate it you must be ignorant or inexperienced.

Consumers, and their servants, can of course subvert this cosy arrangement by tasting a bunch of Givry First Growths blind alongside each other – like, as much as possible, with like. Accordingly I list all Givry First Growths from north to south as a crow might fly, were it weaving overhead:

Clos Jus. This east-facing slope has been planted recently (around 1989), having been abandoned. It is the first fine Givry slope uphill from the road as the visitor's car approaches from the north. Clos Charlé faces south-east, then the hillside swings so that Clos de la Servoisine and Clos du Cellier aux Moines face south. Another swing brings the slope back to east-facing for the main vineyards alongside, then south of, the town: Petit Marole, Vaux, Marole, Bois Chevaux, Petits Prétants, Clos Saint-Pierre, Clos Saint-Paul, Clos Salomon, Grands Prétants, Clos de la Barraude, En Vignes Rouges, Bois Gauthier, Le Vigron, Les Grandes Vignes, Clos Marceaux, Clos du Vernoy, Les Berges, Clos du Cras Long.

There are fine hillsides between Givry and Montagny – Saint-Désert, for instance – which do not qualify for either commune *appellation* but produce excellent Bourgogne *rouge*. One has only to taste bottles from Goubard or Derain to recognize their quality and value.

Givry growers

RENÉ BOURGEON   8.5 ha. (100 per cent)

Givry (*rouge*) 4.5 ha., Clos de la Brûlée (Monopole) (*blanc*) 2 ha., Bourgogne Côte Chalonnaise 2 ha.

'I am against sulphur', says Bourgeon (who told me he had had more media coverage than any grower in Burgundy, and who had obviously loved it), and: 'I am against racking – air oxidizes our wines.' He claims to take advice from Michel Rolland in Libourne, Michel Bouchard in Beaune and Guy Accad in Nuits-Saint-Georges (he cold-macerates at just above freezing point – for 11 days in 1990, at 2°C), and also to rub shoulders with Michel Feuillat. I found the wines pretty odd.

René Bourgeon, Jambles, 71640 Givry

DOMAINE CHOFFLET-VALDENAIRE   10 ha. (40 per cent)

Givry *Premier Cru* Clos Jus 1 ha., Givry (*rouge*) 7.5 ha., (*blanc*) 1 ha., Passe-Tout-Grains 1.3 ha., Aligoté 0.4 ha.

Jean Chofflet et Denis Valdenaire, Russilly, 71640 Givry

MICHEL DERAIN (in Saint-Désert)   6 ha. (20 per cent)

Givry (*blanc*) 0.5 ha., Bourgogne *rouge* Clos Saint-Pierre 1.5 ha., Bourgogne *rouge* 2.5 ha., Passe-Tout-Grains 1 ha., Aligoté 0.5 ha.

Here are excellent examples of regional Bourgogne *rouge*, demonstrating how well it can age and improve over three to four years. Derain is not keen on wood, but likes wines which will hold their qualities. He is a conscientious (others might say maniacal) enthusiast, who has been bottling small quantities for passing devotees for thirty years.

Michel Derain, Saint-Désert, 71390 Buxy

DESVIGNES, PROPRIÉTÉ   11.5 ha. (80 per cent)

Givry Clos du Vernoy 0.7 ha., Clos Charlé 0.5 ha., Givry (*rouge*) 8 ha., (*blanc*) 1.3 ha., Aligoté and Passe-Tout-Grains

One of Givry's original estate-bottlers, since the mid-1950s.

René et Eric Desvignes, 36 rue de Jambles, Poncey, 71640 Givry

DU GARDIN   7 ha. (100 per cent)

Givry Clos Salomon *rouge* (Monopole) 7 ha.

This is a wonderful, curious, hillside site, with a story to take us back to the time of the Crusades. The Clos takes its name from the Salomon family which held land in Givry in the thirteenth century. It is recorded that in 1375 Hugues Salomon sold wine to the Pope.

I have found the wine soft and fruity, but habitually lacking concentration, as if the yields were too high, and the wine consequently too much in need of sugaring. Or perhaps the resources for appropriate vinification are not yet in place, or reconstituted vines not yet sufficiently deep-rooted. The historic, flagship wine Givry Clos Salomon could surely come much better than this.

Mme J. du Gardin, Clos Salomon, 71640 Givry

MICHEL GOUBARD (in Saint-Désert)   22 ha. (80 per cent)

Bourgogne Côte Chalonnaise Mont Avril (*rouge*) 12 ha., (*blanc*) 1.9 ha., Bourgogne Côte Chalonnaise (*rouge*) 3 ha., (*blanc*) 4 ha., Passe-Tout-Grains 1 ha., Aligoté 0.5 ha.

Goubard first bottled his whole production as long ago as 1979, and hopes to achieve this again soon. Mont Avril faces full southeast. I have had splendid bottles from here.

Michel et Pierre-François Goubard, Bassevelle, 71390 Saint-Désert

DOMAINE JEAN-MARC JOBLOT   13 ha. (100 per cent)

Givry Clos du Cellier aux Moines 2.5 ha., Clos des Bois Chevaux 1.2 ha., Clos Grand Marolle 1.2 ha., Clos de la Servoisine (*rouge*) 2.3 ha., (*blanc*) 1.2 ha., En Veau (*rouge*) 2.2 ha., (*blanc*) 0.7 ha., Givry (*rouge*) 1.3 ha., (*blanc*) 0.7 ha.

'The vineyards have been put in an iron collar', says Joblot,[1] who is Givry's most radical grower. He has three hectares of vines trained high, planted between 1965 and 1974 when erosion, grey rot and the cost of labour gave cause for concern. Unless current legislation is modified he will be obliged to uproot them by the year 2000 (or lose the right to his Givry *appellation*). Yet these vines are in balance, unstressed by crowding, yielding correct quantities.

---

1 *On met le vignoble dans un carcan.*

There has been no fertilizing here since 1978 (it took five or six years for the vines to settle down to the new regime).

Eighty per cent of his red wines are made in horizontal, stainless steel cylindrical vats containing an endless screw to tumble the skins when required. These Magyar vats were made in Dole, and have sieves in the lower surfaces allowing muddy impurities to fall out of suspension and not be stirred around while fruit and colour are being extracted. His wine-making objectives are to operate initially with minimum oxygen and sulphur, racking into new barrels each year, where the wines come into balance with oxygen through the wood's pores. He aims for 12°4 to 12°7 of alcohol; his wines are kieselguhr-filtered.

'I love the odour of new wood. If I had not been a vigneron I would have been a carpenter. It gives pleasure to our clients', says Joblot, tongue only slightly in cheek. 'Don't make the Côte Chalonnaise into a ghetto – let us aim to make great wines if we can. There are fifteen years of reflection in these wines, which are stable and solid in constitution. This is a *Grand Vin* culture, heart and soul.' It most certainly is, the whites being ripe and opulent, the deep-coloured red wines being spicily fruity and richly flavoured.

Jean-Marc et Vincent Joblot, 4 rue Pasteur, 71640 Givry

DOMAINE LABORBE-JUILLOT 10.6 ha. (100 per cent)

Givry Clos Marceaux (Monopole) 3 ha., Le Vernoy (*blanc*) 0.3 ha., Santenay Clos Genêt 0.52 ha., Rully La Chatalienne (*rouge*) 1.5 ha., Les Saint-Jacques (*blanc*) 4.2 ha., Montagny La Crée 1 ha.

Some red Givry can be a bit weedy, but not this one, which has ample fruit and colour. I believe this couple (whose cellars are now in Mercurey) will continue to make good progress with their wines, as experience is gained and their young white Rully vines put down roots.

Jean et Pascale Laborbe-Juillot, Clos Marceaux, 71640 Givry

THIERRY LESPINASSE 2.5 ha. (50 per cent)

Givry en Choué (*rouge*) 0.2 ha., (*blanc*) 0.3 ha., Bourgogne Clos du Champ-Martin (Monopole) 2 ha., Crémant de Bourgogne

Thierry Lespinasse, à Rosey, 71390 Givry

VINCENT LUMPP   6.95 ha. (80 per cent)

Givry Clos du Cras Long 0.65 ha., La Grande Berge (*rouge*) 1.2 ha., (*blanc*) 0.4 ha., Cras Long 0.3 ha., Givry (*rouge*) 2.2 ha., (*blanc*) 0.7 ha., Aligoté and Passe-Tout-Grains

The whites ferment in tank at low temperature here, and see no wood.

Vincent Lumpp, Poncey, 45 rue de Jambles, 71640 Givry

FRANÇOIS LUMPP   5.6 ha. (100 per cent)

Givry Clos du Cras Long 0.65 ha., Clos Jus 0.5 ha., Petit Marole (*rouge*) 0.56 ha., (*blanc*) 0.24 ha., Le Pied du Clou (Monopole) (*rouge*) 0.89 ha., Givry (*rouge*) 1.7 ha., (*blanc*) 1 ha.

The Lumpp brothers used to vinify together, but have gone separate ways since the 1990 harvest. François has had temperature-controlled premises on the main road through Givry since the 1991 harvest. A quarter of his crop is white, higher than is usual for Givry.

François Lumpp, 71640 Givry

GÉRARD MOUTON   10 ha. (80 per cent)

Givry Clos Jus 2.05 ha., Clos Charlé 2 ha., La Grande Berge 1.5 ha., Givry (*rouge*) 2.5 ha., Champ Pourot (*blanc*) 1.03 ha., Aligoté and Passe-Tout-Grains

M. et Mme Gérard Mouton, 1 rue du Four, Poncey, 71640 Givry

DOMAINE RAGOT   7.5 ha. (100 per cent)

Givry Clos Jus 1 ha., (*rouge*) 4 ha., Champ Pourot (*blanc*) 2 ha., Aligoté and Passe-Tout-Grains 0.5 ha.

An established source of domaine-bottled Givry, with sound wines, if without striking individuality.

Jean-Paul Ragot, 4 rue de l'Ecole, Poncey, 71640 Givry

MICHEL SARRAZIN ET FILS   24 ha. (80 per cent)

Givry Les Grands Prétants 1.5 ha., Givry (rouge) 8.5 ha., (blanc) 2 ha., Maranges (rouge) 2 ha., Bourgogne Côte Chalonnaise (rouge) 3 ha., Passe-Tout-Grains, Aligoté and Crémant de Bourgogne

Guy Sarrazin and Jean-Marc Joblot are the two principal new-oak enthusiasts in Givry. This property is up on the hill above Poncey, with plenty of working space and dependably good bottles.

Guy Sarrazin, Charnailles près Jambles, Poncey, 71640 Givry

DOMAINE THÉNARD   22 ha. (60 per cent)

Montrachet 1.83 ha., Grands Echézeaux 0.54 ha., Corton Clos du Roi 0.9 ha., Pernand Ile des Vergelesses 0.85 ha., Chassagne-Montrachet Clos Saint-Jean (blanc) 0.17 ha., Givry Clos Saint-Pierre (Monopole) 2.12 ha., Le Cellier aux Moines 3.22 ha., Les Bois Chevaux 7.66 ha., Givry (rouge) 1.83 ha., (blanc) 2.34 ha.

The family has owned its Givrys here since 1760, and its Montrachet since 1872. It is very faithful to Remoissenet, Bordeaux-Montrieux Sr. saying, 'We let Remoissenet take exactly what he wishes. And we bottle what is left.' This is quite the opposite of what most growers claim – and of course one cannot always believe them, for local négociants-éleveurs, with a broker on the spot to help choose and take delivery of the best cuvées, can be first in the buying field, offering payment immediately after the harvest.

I have drunk some rather dull Remoissenet-shipped Thénard Givrys; however the quality at the domaine seems on an upward curve, and they now have a richer palette of Grand Cru appellations than in the past. Is their heart in their Givrys, I wonder, or more in the grander appellations to the north? Over twenty-five years they have been taking their Givry vineyards back up the hillsides, so the owner states. In the past the flatter land was much planted. There is a machine and forty people to do the harvesting.

The Montrachet is vinified here, and then uplifted by Remoissenet to age in Beaune (though it may be possible to taste from barrels with a Louis Latour chalk-mark on them, for some of his Montrachets have been sourced here).

The wines age in a wonderful, late-eighteenth-century, tall, single-arched cellar, the Givrys in great tuns.

M. Bordeaux-Montrieux, 7 rue de l'Hôtel de Ville, 71640 Givry

MONTAGNY

Montagny is a name which applies only to white wines, from the Chardonnay grape. The vines grow in a spectacular horseshoe of hillsides a few minutes outside Buxy, around the village of Montagny, and on nearby slopes in the the the communes of Jully-lès-Buxy and Saint-Vallerin. The five-year average production (1988–92) for Montagny was 103,000 cases – nearly four times the figure of fifteen years ago, and likely to rise further. It seems set to become an increasingly good source of economically priced white Burgundy, if so far without the individuality of the best white Rullys. But this may be a matter of wine-making habits, and young vines. The local reds are Bourgogne Côte Chalonnaise and Passe-Tout-Grains.

In the last fifteen years vineyard plantations have gone from 160 hectares to over 800 hectares, entirely with clonal stocks. Hydraulic works have been undertaken to prevent erosion and aid drainage, and appropriate soils chosen for Pinot Noir, Chardonnay or Aligoté. During this period the co-operative financed a Montpellier-trained soil and vine technician to oversee this work. At present many vines are of course young, but by the year 2000 this will be a very important, mature vineyard.

Montagny is the southernmost village *appellation* of the Côte Chalonnaise. The name is a relatively recent one, for previously the wines, both white and red, were sold as Côte de Buxy. Here may be found the wall-inscription: *Ne laeseris vinum* (Do no harm to wine). The co-operative is excellent, and has the lion's share of production.

For many years the words *Premier Cru* could appear on a label of Montagny, irrespective of the precise vineyard land it came from, if the wine had a minimum alcoholic content of 11.5° before the grapes were picked. (That, at any rate, was the theory.) Now, the best 53 hillside plots have been identified, and these are the registered *Premiers Crus*. Montcuchot and Les Coères are two which seem pre-eminent – I am not listing them all. Hopefully a simplification will follow, and some portmanteau names be chosen in due course, as in Chablis, to cover specific sites.

Montagny growers

CAVE DES VIGNERONS DE BUXY   750 ha. (60 per cent)

Montagny Les Coères 11 ha., Mont-Cuchot 12 ha., Les Chagnots 6 ha., Montagny 51 ha., Rully (*blanc*) 1 ha., (*rouge*) 1 ha., Mercurey 6 ha., Givry 6 ha., Bourgogne Côte Châlonnaise (*blanc*) 38 ha., (*rouge*) 125 ha., Bourgogne Clos de Chenôves (*blanc*) 3 ha., (*rouge*) 5 ha., Bourgogne (*blanc*) 12 ha., (*rouge*) 11 ha., Mâcon-Villages 21 ha., Mâcon Supérieur (*rouge*) 42 ha., Bourgogne Aligoté 132 ha., Passe-Tout-Grains 113 ha., Crémant de Bourgogne (Chardonnay) 17 ha., (Pinot) 21 ha.

Since 1982 a revolutionary punching-down procedure for Pinots Noirs has been developed here, in place since the 1988 vintage. It has been jointly patented by the Cave de Buxy and Constructions Soudées du Côteau, the vat-maker who built it. A single, piston-operated hydraulic jack, whose angle may be varied towards the edges or centre of the vat, punches the cap of grape skins down, over and round. It moves on rollers from the top of one open vat to the next, as needed. Before its installation, the co-operative could pump its Pinot juice over, but could not punch down.

The oenologists here are convinced that pip-control is one of the keys to seductive mouth-feel in Pinot Noir, so difficult to achieve. Punching down liberates the pips from the grapes early on in vinification. They seek to remove them from the floating cap of grape skins, where the temperature is higher than elsewhere in the vat, and yeasts may work on the tannins in the pips. The pips fall to the bottom of the vat (which is not achieved by simply spraying juice over), whence they hope to develop a system of extracting them, or isolating them from the fermenting must.

Buxy achieves good extraction of spicy, rich Pinot Noir flavours, with supple, soft tannins, without jamminess or bitterness. They have a large, temperature-controlled warehouse for small-barrel ageing (20 per cent being renewed each year), where their Bourgognes *rouges* are tended and stored until bottling.

Chardonnays ferment here mainly in stainless steel vats, but will in future be partly aged in monster (250 hl) oak tuns. They have found that if they try to blend Chardonnay fermented and aged in stainless steel (protected from oxidation) with barrel-aged Chardonnay (which will have been absorbing air all the time) the blend is unsatisfactory. Old-fashioned wooden tuns should help to obtain a more harmonious blend.

This is one of Burgundy's show-places, with a continuing programme of investment in new equipment, research and development. During the 1992 vintage, for instance, they experimented with the Entropie system of vacuum concentration (developed for desalination in the Persian Gulf) and are currently comparing the results obtained with those of the cheaper Durafroid system, and traditional chaptalization practices.

Dozens of New World wine-makers have come to see it – many more New Worlders than local major operators, which is not surprising if one asks oneself the questions, 'What could a Côte d'Or wine-maker *conceivably* learn from visiting the Coopérative at Buxy? Where is Buxy, anyway?' I understand, however, that the system has been installed at the Château de Meursault – if Patriarche were not so secretive it might be possible to applaud it – and may be on stream for the new vat-house at the Hospices de Beaune.

Grape pips are valued in at least one way in Buxy: they yield the oil used in the hydraulic punching-down piston, so that, if an accident ever occurs, they will easily be able to eliminate this vegetable oil by centrifuge.

Their Bourgogne Clos de Chenôves has no connection with the village near Dijon; it is an old Clos, once connected with the Abbey of Cluny, close to Buxy.

Roger Rageot, Les Vignes de la Croix, 71390 Buxy

CHATEAU DE DAVENAY 31 ha.

Montagny *Premier Cru* 17 ha., Rully *Premier Cru (blanc)* Meix-Cadot and La Bergerie 2.5 ha., Rabourcé 0.5 ha., *(rouge)* Meix-Cadot 0.4 ha., Hautes Côtes de Beaune 2 ha., Bourgogne *(rouge)* 3.5 ha., Aligoté 2.8 ha.

Like Domaine Emile Voarick in Mercurey, this is owned by Michel Picard of Picard Père et Fils of Chagny, making him one of the largest Côte Chalonnaise owners.

Château de Davenay, 71390 Montagny-Buxy

BERNARD MICHEL   10 ha. (100 per cent)

Montagny Les Coères 0.5 ha., *Premier Cru* 2 ha., Montagny 1.5 ha., Bourgogne Côte Chalonnaise 4 ha., Aligoté

With the 1993 vintage, Monsieur Michel handed over to his daughter and her husband, having been bottling all his crop since 1970. Both apparently did three years' study at Beaune's Lycée Viticole. I found the white wines fine, but that they need to get a grip on the reds.

Bernard Michel, Philippe et Arlette Andreotti, Les Guignottes, Saint-Vallerin, 71390 Buxy

CHÂTEAU DE LA SAULE   11 ha. (70 per cent)
DOMAINE ALAIN ROY
ALAIN ROY-THÉVENIN

Montagny Mont-Cuchot 0.31 ha., Les Burnins 1.3 ha., Les Vignes sur le Cloux 3.25 ha., Montagny 4.23 ha., Passe-Tout-Grains and Aligoté

One of Montagny's most dependable properties, making flowery, ripe, well-balanced wines.

Alain Roy, Montagny-lès-Buxy, 71390 Buxy

VEUVE STEINMAIER ET FILS   17 ha. (80 per cent)

Givry *Premier Cru* Bois Gauthier 4.2 ha., Clos de la Barraude (Monopole) 2.4 ha., Givry (*rouge*) 2 ha., (*blanc*) 3.11 ha., Montagny *Premier Cru* Mont-Cuchot 1.4 ha., Les Coères 1.9 ha., Passe-Tout-Grains and Aligoté

This is one of Montagny's finest old properties. In January 1992 the Cave de Buxy bought the domaine buildings here, and rented the vineyards, intending to continue to vinify at the estate – an imaginative co-operative departure.

Jean Steinmaier, Montagny-lès-Buxy, 71390 Buxy

JEAN VACHET   7.65 ha. (90 per cent)

Montagny Les Coères, 1.78 ha., Montagny 1.53 ha., Bourgogne
(*rouge*) 2.02 ha., (*blanc*) 0.49 ha., Passe-Tout-Grains 0.92 ha., Aligoté 0.91 ha.
Jean Vachet, Saint-Vallerin, 71390 Buxy

34

The Mâconnais: Mâcon, Saint-Véran
and the Pouillys

The reputation of the wines of the Mâconnais dates back to a mention by the Latin poet Ausonius, but it was not until the eleventh and twelfth century that vineyards were widely cultivated, the monks of the Abbey of Cluny, founded on the western edge of the vineyard area, being responsible for the extension.

In the seventeenth century, southern Mâconnais wines went to Paris. The French markets were partitioned by customs barriers under the *ancien régime*, Dijon and Chalons obstructing the sale of Mâcon wines in Franche Comté and Alsace, the Lyon market being virtually closed to all wines not harvested in the *gouvernement du Lyonnais*. Although heavy transport charges were incurred in reaching Paris these were incidental if the wine was of high quality. During the Revolution and under the Empire the wines were exported to Belgium, the Low Countries and Germany, at the expense of Bordeaux, whose deliveries were disrupted by the British blockade of coastal shipping.

Getting the wines to Paris was never easy. As Pierre Goujon describes,[1] in summer the Saône or the Canal du Centre were often too low for navigation, while in winter ice might halt all movement. It became usual to make two dispatches to Paris, one in October after the harvest, and one in the spring. There were numerous trans-shipments, from the Saône to the Canal du Centre, from the latter to the Loire or another canal. Navigating the sandbanks of the Loire was tricky, and those living on the banks were used to digging out passing boats. Losses were important, and two *tonneaux* of wine had to be allowed for the personal consumption of the boat-

1 *Le Vignoble de Saône-et-Loire au XIXème siècle*, Université Lyon II, Lyon, 1973.

men. Sometimes the autumn convoys became blocked, not reaching Paris till the spring. Pierre Goujon quotes from family papers assembled by A. Bernard: 'Here I am at last arrived on the banks of the Loire; I had much trouble with my wines. We have already lost ten hogsheads from breakages, yawning staves, worm-holes in the wood; generally there has been much seepage. From our three boats we are loading on to eight.'

In 1854 the arrival of the railway changed everything. Nine years later Guigue de Champvans wrote in *Le Vignoble mâconnais*:

> Not long ago the wine merchant, whose deliveries took place regularly twice a year, made his purchases twice, in spring and autumn. The railway has thrown the trade in completely new directions. Today he buys constantly, at any season, depending on what he sells and requires. The ease and speed of transport removes the need to store unless for speculative or blending purposes. His central warehouse is the vineyard itself.

The Mâconnais is a region of chains of small hills, mostly running north–south, parallel to the river Saône. Shaped like a trapezium on its end, it is about 35 km long by 10–15 km wide, limited to the east (its longest side) by the plain of the Saône, to the west by the foothills of the Morvan and Charolais.

The bedrock is a continuation of the Jurassic strata we met in the Côte d'Or. A lifting of the south of the Mâconnais resulted in the erosion of the limestone and the emergence of the Hercynian bedrock, which is where the Beaujolais begins. Particularly resistant Jurassic strata have survived, forming the startling rock crests of Solutré and Vergisson which characterize the Pouilly-Fuissé countryside.

The Mâconnais is less dominated by its vineyards than the Beaujolais. It is a countryside of undulating wood-capped hills with rounded summits, 400–500 metres high, less densely populated and poorer than the Beaujolais. Vineyards alternate with meadows, divided by spinneys of sweet chestnut and acacia. Cherry trees and walnuts stand in the fields, and parallel to the rows of vines one may see rows of potatoes, both in flower together. As one drives down the roads light-brown kids, their horn-stumps just visible, disappear into the grass verge like baby roe-deer. There is plenty of room for extension of the vineyard area if the current popularity of Chardonnay lasts, and if white Mâcon can establish itself in consumers' minds as a Chardonnay of quality.

The climate in the Mâconnais is a temperate but uncertain one, with extremes of cold in February, and heat in July and August. Frost is feared until the Foire de Mâcon is past – which usually corresponds to the Ice Saints in the calendar. The average annual rainfall is about 800 mm. The instability of the climate accounts for the importance of soil, orientation and altitude of the vineyards; and it is responsible for many farms cultivating more than one crop or also raising animals. Many have cows or goats and make their own cheese.

The role of the wife is very important, indeed R. Boidron[2] has shown that only 7 per cent of vineyard concerns are run by bachelors. Tending vineyards is time-consuming, and the wife's contribution vital at certain times: for the bending and tying of the shoots, the trimming of excess leaves, the attaching, the chopping back of vegetation, the harvest. The careful arching and firm attachment of the two fruit-bearing Chardonnay shoots in the Mâconnais is a delicate task, demanding dexterity and skills she often acquired as a child in her parents' vines. It should be done on humid days, never when there is a dry wind from the north or east. In certain vineyards it is perfectly executed and a beautiful, symmetrical sight they make.

The *appellations* that are specific to the Mâconnais, with their average annual production over the five years 1988–92 are shown in Table 7.[3] If one compares the average harvest with a five-year average from the mid-1970s (1972–6), one sees that the production of white Mâcon has gone up by 60 per cent, and that of Saint-Véran has more than doubled. The Pouillys have increased by ten to twenty per cent (most of the good land had already been planted up). Red Mâcons have marginally fallen back.

The Mâconnais has about 6,000 hectares of AC vineyard; a hundred years ago there was over three times that area under vines, for Mâcon wines were known as the Grands Ordinaires de France, the most widely-planted vine being the Gamay. Today the Chardonnay has taken over, and it covers nearly 60 per cent of the vineyard

2 *Le Mâconnais viticole*, CETA Viticole du Mâconnais, Chambre d'Agriculture de Saône-et-Loire (undated).
3 *Source*: Fédération Viticole de Saône-et-Loire and Fédération des Caves Coopératives de Bourgogne.

area, the Gamay accounting for one-third, the Pinot Noir one-tenth. Co-operative cellars handle nearly 80 per cent of white Mâcons, and nearly 65 per cent of the red; altogether there are sixteen of them.

Table 7 Mâconnais *appellations* with their average production 1988–92

	Average total harvest (hectolitres)	Percentage produced by co-operatives
WHITE WINES		
Mâcon (*blanc*), Mâcon-Villages, Mâcon plus specific village	171,155	77
Saint-Véran	27,770	43
Pouilly-Vinzelles and Pouilly-Loché	4,290	80
Pouilly-Fuissé	41,799	14
Average annual total	245,014	
RED WINES		
Mâcon (*rouge* and *rosé*) Mâcon Supérieur Mâcon plus specific village	57,708	64
Average annual total	57,708	
Average annual production (white and red)	302,722	

The co-operative movement in the Mâconnais dates from the 1920s when the storage capacity of the growers was stretched to its limit, prices were on the floor, yet still the wines failed to sell. Many wines, it must be admitted, were made from hybrid vines, and frequently the growers did not possess proper vinification equipment. Contact was made with co-operatives in the Midi to obtain advice, and the first *cave* built in the Mâconnais at Saint-Gengoux de Scissé, in 1926. It was followed by Lugny a year later, then seventeen others before 1934.

Viticulture today has become highly mechanized, with more and more growers using selective weed-killers, reducing the number of ploughings and hoeings and harvesting by machine.

Plantations of vines in wide rows, trained high, have been tried but generally proved unsuccessful. The advantages of the system are that it requires fewer vines per hectare, that cultivation does not call for an expensive *tracteur-enjambeur*, and that fewer man-hours are required. But ten years of experiments in the Saône-et-Loire[4] revealed that yields were regularly lower with high vines, allied, in the case of the Chardonnay, to lower natural sugar production. Acidities were always greater, for high vines do not benefit from heat reflected off the ground. Comparative tastings favoured the traditionally-trained vine in the case of the Aligoté and the Chardonnay. They were inconclusive for the Pinot Noir, and the high vines in this case proved the more resistant to grey rot. Comparable quality could only be obtained from *Pinots Noirs* trained high if a quarter to a third of the normally-expected yield was sacrificed – which more or less eliminated the benefits gained from lower-cost plantation and cultivation.

As might be expected, a fair proportion of Burgundy's regional *appellations* are produced in the Saône-et-Loire, the *département* which lies between the Côte d'Or and the Rhône *département*, where Beaujolais is produced. It includes the wine areas of Côte Chalonnaise and the Mâconnais, but also (illogically, as these are *crus* Beaujolais, so by rights should be in the Rhône *département*) Saint-Amour and parts of Chénas and Moulin-à-Vent. Here are to be found a quarter of the Bourgogne *blanc* and the base wine for Crémant de Bourgogne, and just under half the Bourgogne Aligoté, the Bourgogne Passe-Tout-Grains and Bourgogne Grand Ordinaire. Those Pinot Noirs not forming part of Crémant or Passe-Tout-Grains blends are sold as Bourgogne *rouge*.

THE MÂCONNAIS, BIRTHPLACE OF CHARDONNAY?

This is possibly the origin of the Chardonnay grape, for there is a village called Chardonnay south-west of Tournus. No one, however, can establish whether the village was named after the grape, or vice versa.

The Mâconnais could be the Chardonnay crucible, where France

---

4 R. Boidron, *Vignes hautes et larges*, L'Exploitant Agricole, Saône-et-Loire, March 1978.

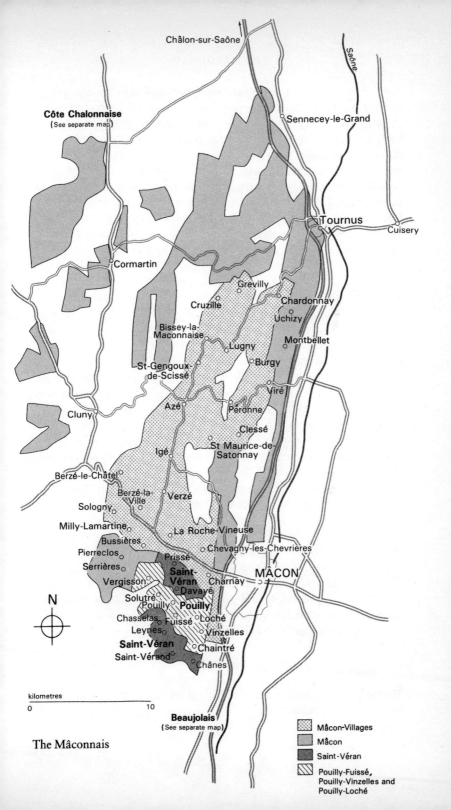

Châlon-sur-Saône

Saône

Côte Chalonnaise
(See separate map)

Sennecey-le-Grand

Tournus

Cuisery

Cormartin

Grevilly

Cruzille

Chardonnay

Bissey-la-
Maconnaise

Uchizy

Montbellet

Lugny

St-Gengoux-
de-Scissé

Burgy

Viré

Azé

Péronne

Cluny

Clessé

Igé

St Maurice-de-
Satonnay

Berzé-le-Châtel

Berzé-la-
Ville

Verzé

Sologny

Milly-Lamartine

La Roche-Vineuse

Bussières

Chevagny-les-Chevrieres

Pierreclos

Prissé

Serrières

**Saint-
Véran**

MÂCON

Vergisson

Charnay

Solutré

Davayé

Pouilly

Pouilly

Chasselas

Fuissé

Loché

Leynes

Vinzelles

Saint-Véran

Chaintré

Saint-Vérand

Chânes

N

kilometres

0   10

Beaujolais
(See separate map)

The Mâconnais

Mâcon-Villages

Mâcon

Saint-Véran

Pouilly-Fuissé,
Pouilly-Vinzelles and
Pouilly-Loché

might forge strong answers to competing, in-roading Chardonnays from around the world, from Australia, Eastern Europe, California, New Zealand, Chile, Oregon, not to mention the Midi of France itself – everywhere the grape is planted. It is a melting pot of Chardonnay wine-making methods, but as yet unfocused, still operating perilously near survival levels.

Half the time they are making Chardonnay with one hand tied behind their backs, for there is obsession with what is seen as the local way of doing it: high grape-yields and fermentation in tank. Few New World Chardonnay growers are so hidebound, which undoubtedly accounts for many of their successes.

Mâcon co-operatives

The big Mâcon co-operatives can be good sources for the supply of regular styles in volume, often at prices near the floor. Economies of scale and cheap finance mean they can offer cheap Chardonnays. But visiting them, there is often a feeling of self-satisfaction amongst the growers and their administrators, and a lack of curiosity about overseas consumers. Members are happiest when people come to visit them, but little concerned with what foreigners might actually drink in their homes. They travel abroad, but to find new customers, I suspect, rather than to talk to existing ones. Of course, if they do travel, it will be on the strict condition that the trip be tied in with watching a rugby match.

If only more co-operative managers would declare, 'We are not just going to process our members' grapes, we are going to make some of the world's best Chardonnays.' Economies of scale and cheap finance would mean they could offer fine value, as well as satisfying the town-dweller's yearnings for authenticity, and for links with a historic countryside. Some already do – for instance Prissé or Lugny, while Chardonnay is re-equipping itself. Others sit back, offering cheapness and a name, rarely pursuing top quality with determination. Small growers almost always beat such co-operatives for technical mastery, quality and value.

Mâcon tasting and visiting

Normally in the Mâconnais you taste the older vintage in the cellar before the new wine, which is so aromatic, fresh and vivacious. If you taste the other way round, the older wine may seem dull and flat, and to have lost its fruit. And you often taste the reds before the whites.

One may visit Burgundy for nearly thirty years, tasting and buying, and think one knows the prettiest corners – and then one goes up the valley west of Serrières, towards the Col du Grand Vent, at the foot of the highest peak in the district, the Mère Boittier, and discovers a completely unexpected Burgundian countryside. This is the source of Mâcon's best reds: a golden triangle of sandy, granite-based soils, its points being Pierreclos, Bussières and Serrières. The red grape is the Gamay, but its wines are nothing like the meagre, hard red Mâcons produced from limestone soils by careless co-operatives further north. These are Gamays grown on sandy granite, rich and structured, dense and supple, not so different from the Saint-Amours or Juliénas they resemble.

This is a do-it-yourself district; in Serrières, for instance, there are twenty or more private growers averaging four hectares of vineyard each, and not a co-operative wine-making facility in sight. Most sell their wine in bulk.

This is where famous Nuits-Saint-Georges exporters used to buy their blends in the bad old days (pre–1973) before *appellation contrôlée* was enforced in the United Kingdom. One shipper who I could name, for instance, bought 800 hectos per year from these corners. If New York or London consumers still hanker after 'old-style' Burgundy, they might consider tasting wines from here, and may then discover that what they loved was not Pinot Noir Burgundies, but granite Mâcon Gamays. The bonus is that these wines are available very economically.

POUILLY-FUISSÉ

For years I made the mistake of approaching Pouilly-Fuissé from the flat plain, through the western suburbs of Mâcon. This is a breeding-ground for expressways and roundabouts, where one is constantly going under or over the high-speed train, the old railway-line or the *autoroute*, and there are no proper signs to lead one to south Burgundy's finest white *crus*, nor to the prehistoric Solutré rock. In any case, what is there to discover, but a white Burgundy which sells primarily on its name?

This was the wrong approach. I needed to come in from behind, from the hills (and, of course, with a more open mind). From Pierreclos, follow the signs to Vergisson, climbing up sparse hillsides. You breast a rise, and on a rolling plateau of brown earth and vine rows (this is December) see straight ahead the scrub-covered projection of the rock of Vergisson, vines neatly covering all the slopes capable of cultivation. Breast a second rise and a second rock, Solutré, is straight ahead, where prehistoric man sheltered, gnawing on horse bones. Here there are pastures high up between rock and woods; this is pre-alpine countryside, unlike any other spot in Burgundy.

The hills form amphitheatres around the best villages: the steep-sided corrie up to Vergisson, the rounded circus in which the hamlet of Pouilly shelters, the broader encirclement round the little town of Fuissé. Soils are generally richer in clay in Fuissé, sparser, limey and alkaline in Pouilly, Solutré and Vergisson. Chaintré has the beginnings of sandy granites, with neutral or acid soils giving wines which open up fast, tending to win the young-wine competitions. Certain hillsides, like the broad south-facing sweep at Solutré, are perfectly placed to catch the maximum sun; others face frankly north, and must sometimes give grapes which barely ripen. This, surely, is one explanation for the district's varying quality.

In the United Kingdom prior to 1973 the name Pouilly-Fuissé was much applied to cheap dry white wines of base, sometimes non-Burgundian, origin, and this falsified the consumer's palate. The USA used to absorb half the crop of Pouilly-Fuissé each year – a massive purchase for one country – but that fashion passed, leaving many Americans with unhappy memories of the sulphurous, underripe wines sometimes delivered at the time of that strong demand. The image of Pouilly-Fuissé is still thoroughly tarnished in two of its major export markets.

There might be some benefit in classifying the sites of Pouilly-Fuissé, to establish *Premiers Crus*, and this might advance growers' interests (so long as the drawing of lines was stricter than, for instance, when they decided on the *Premiers Crus* of Beaune). If there were First Growths in Pouilly, where there are indubitably superior sites, it might raise the image of the *appellation* abroad. Currently, consumer's interests are well served by a situation which allows adventurous enthusiasts to pursue the best bottles – what buying Burgundy is all about. The message is inside the bottle, and the price tag often modest.

Many growers and merchants seem more concerned with presenting a simple, commercial product than producing bottles which reflect the individuality and potential of their sites. Sulphur levels are often still carelessly high, and use of small cooperage hit and miss.

Many wines are power-packaged – got up to look expensive – but you look in vain for an imaginative label design. If only a few growers would nip through the Mont Blanc tunnel (now barely three hours' drive away) into Italy, and find themselves an imaginative Milanese or Florentine graphic designer.

These wines must take their places alongside the world's oaked Chardonnays, where the technical competition is very strong. Pouilly-Fuissé sometimes stinks of mercaptan (like some bottles from the Cave de Chaintré) or makes your forehead throb, from its sulphur dioxide content, or shows other vinification or bottling faults. It is no wonder that, while world sales of Chardonnay stay buoyant, in the early 1990s Pouilly-Fuissé growers had cellars full of unsold vats. A famous name is not enough.

Fortunately, there are shining exceptions, and plenty of wines to lift the heart, as you will find amongst the suppliers. And the potential of these hillsides is enormous.

LOCHÉ AND VINZELLES

Loché is a tiny village, its walls and houses built in beautiful creamy, ochre stone. Here, as in Vinzelles, there have been no large properties involved in domaine-bottling, to carry a flag for either *appellation*. Instead, France's inheritance laws have caused the vineyard plots to be split, and split again. Philippe Bérard at the Domaine Saint Philibert aims to fill this gap for Loché; for Vinzelles, the co-operative dominates the name, its wines often dreary.

SAINT-VÉRAN, AND AROUND LEYNES

These are some of the best-value white wines of the Mâconnais, a good Saint-Véran from Davayé or Prissé, for instance, being to my mind at least the equal, at half the price, of many Pouilly-Fuissé from Chaintré. The AC names were allotted haphazardly. Saint-Véran is harvested in the communes of Chânes, Chasselas, Davayé, Leynes, Prissé, Saint-Amour, Saint-Vérand and Solutré.

Received wisdom in Leynes, and in the neighbouring villages which also make Saint Véran in the *appellation*'s southern crescent (the other three are Chânes, Chasselas and Saint-Vérand) is that this sector gives wines which take longer to open, but then repay keeping. I am not so sure. It is an area of mixed subsoil, some limestone, some granite, and estates making both white and red, with habits of selling in bulk. Are the Gamays always on the granite, and the Chardonnays on the limestone? I do not think wine-making expertise is as high as in those villages, deeply imbued with white wine culture, which touch, or see, the prehistoric rocks of Vergisson and Solutré. And they are not really part of a Gamay culture, either. Feet are in both camps, and wine-making sometimes unfocused.

In fact, this is border-country, almost a no-man's land. Administratively, it is part of the four *départements* of Burgundy (Yonne, Côte d'Or, Saône-et-Loire and Nièvre), yet it produces wines with names – Beaujolais-Villages, Beaujolais *blanc* – which belong to the rival region south, the Rhône. Who speaks for these wines, who is concerned about their quality levels? They often fall between two stools.

Main Mâconnais growers, including Pouilly-Fuissé, Pouilly-Loché, Pouilly-Vinzelles and Saint-Véran

AUVIGUE BURRIER REVEL ET CIE

This small, *négociant* specialist makes and tends the wines of several family estates, as well as buying in grapes and wine for vinification and tending. As a customer, I declare an interest. The 4.5 ha. family properties comprise: Les Fils de R. Revel: Pouilly-Fuissé 1.5 ha., Les Chailloux 1 ha., Domaine André Auvigue: Pouilly-Fuissé 0.75 ha., La Frairie 1.25 ha.

Jean-Pierre Auvigue produces wines which are often reticent when young, without an ounce of spare flesh on them; the antithesis of tropical fruity, come-hither Chardonnays from the New World (or the Old apeing the New). Their charms are discreet and varied, and they usually need cellaring.
Jean-Pierre et Michel Auvigue, Le Moulin du Pont, 71850 Charnay-lès-Mâcon

JEAN-PHILIPPE BAPTISTA   10 ha. (25 per cent)
RENÉ DUSSAUGE
DOMAINE DES GIRAUDIÈRES

Mâcon-Villages 3 ha., Mâcon-Bussières (*rouge*) 6.5 ha., Bourgogne (*rouge*) 0.5 ha.
Baptista trained as an architectural designer before he joined his father-in-law M. Dussauge to make wine. This is a conscientious small estate, saving money to graduate to a pneumatic press for its whites, already equipped with a machine-harvester (which doubles as a vine-straddling tractor for the rest of the year).
Anyone despairing of, or despising, red Mâcon for quality or value may do well to check out these bottles.
René Dussauge et J.-P. Baptista, Les Giraudières, 71960 Bussières

DANIEL BARRAUD   6 ha. (70 per cent)

Pouilly-Fuissé La Verchère 1.3 ha., Vieilles Vignes 2 ha., Saint-Véran 1.5 ha., Mâcon-Vergisson La Roche 0.5 ha.
This property makes a new-oaked, old vines blend in the spirit of a 'Grand Chardonnay de Bourgogne', but to my mind its La Verchère is a much more balanced Pouilly-Fuissé. The wines here have good concentration, and need bottle-ageing; this estate could go from strength to strength.
Daniel Barraud, 71960 Vergisson

CHÂTEAU DE BEAUREGARD   34.4 ha. (30 per cent)

Pouilly-Fuissé 18.31 ha., Saint-Véran 5.8 ha., Mâcon-Villages 0.36 ha., Fleurie 5.08 ha., Moulin-à-Vent 1.9 ha., Beaujolais-Villages 2.93 ha.
One of Pouilly's biggest properties, much of the wine going to

Louis Latour. This has not been a property to drop into, unannounced, but with a generation-change to come may evolve towards greater domaine-bottling.
Jacques Burrier, 71960 Fuissé

BÉNAS FRÈRES   16 ha. (40 per cent)

Mâcon-Serrières (*rouge*) 8 ha., Mâcon (*blanc*) 6 ha., Bourgogne (*rouge*) 2 ha.

There is some clay in the sandstone here, but not much lime, so the whites do not have the right to Mâcon-Villages: quite right too, they are best drunk young. The red wine can be fruity and supple, going well with their *mi-chèvre* cheeses (half goat, half cow) from the home herds. From 2,000 bottles in 1970 they are now up to 50,000, destined mainly for France, Belgium and Switzerland, via homing tourists.
Maurice, Daniel et Alain Bénas, Serrières, 71960 Pierreclos

DOMAINE BERNARD-GOUSSU   39 ha. (60 per cent)
CHÂTEAU DE LEYNES
CHÂTEAU DES CORREAUX

Beaujolais-Villages 25 ha., Saint-Véran 12 ha., Beaujolais *blanc* 2 ha.

An imposing château making both red and white, whose bottle sales could surely develop more speedily if there was greater wine-making accuracy.
Jean Bernard-Goussu, au Château, 71570 Leynes

ANDRÉ BESSON   11 ha. (80 per cent)
DOMAINE DE POUILLY

Pouilly-Fuissé (Pouilly and Solutré) 8 ha., Saint-Véran 2 ha., Mâcon-Villages, Mâcon (*rouge*)

There is a modicum of wine-making expertise here, but not enough to take the estate to the top rank – which is where it ought to be, given its sites. Malolactic fermentations are systematically encouraged, but total sulphur levels not deemed crucial.
A. Besson, Pouilly, 71960 Solutré

ANDRÉ BONHOMME   7.5 ha. (100 per cent)

Mâcon-Viré 7.5 ha.

This is the grand-daddy of Mâcon *blanc* domaine bottlers; he started in 1957. 'I threw down a challenge to my father who was a vigneron' he says; 'he wanted me to be a teacher, but I asked him: Who takes your profit?' At the time it was impossible to make money from vineyards, for *négociants* more or less set their buying prices by calculating back from what the market would stand. By domaine-bottling, Bonhomme *fils* could turn the property into profit. He bought his first stainless steel tank in 1966, and has been master of his fermentation temperatures since 1970. (Stand up the Mâcon Coopérative Président, out there, who can say as much – there are people who would love to meet you.) He has his own bottling-line (with a pre-rinser); picks his grapes manually; and ferments for around four days in tank, then into small barrels (about 20 per cent new). Jean Thévenet, amongst others, had an idea or two from here.

Here is a happy, chatty, patient wine-maker. If the grapes do not ripen early, as in 1987, you leave them on the vine until they do. If the harvest is plentiful, as in 1992, you must tell your pickers to cut only those grapes which are yellow and ripe (you cannot do that if you pick by machine, he did not need to add). It all sounds very simple. To relax on Sundays, he looks after his bees and makes delicious honey, which one may buy at the domaine.

Not surprisingly, one finds his wines in the best French restaurants abroad. Is he valued in the Mâconnais? Most certainly. *C'est un sacré bonhomme* they may say with affection.

André Bonhomme, Cidex 2108, 71260 Viré

GEORGES BURRIER, SARL

Guy Burrier is commissionaire, merchant, grower and mayor of Fuissé, owning 4 ha. of Pouilly-Fuissé.

Guy Burrier, 71960 Fuissé

CAVE COOPÉRATIVE DE CHAINTRÉ   190 ha. 25 per cent)

Pouilly-Fuissé, Pouilly-Vinzelles, Saint-Véran, Mâcon-Villages, Beaujolais (*blanc*), Beaujolais-Villages.

This co-operative accounts for about 15 per cent of the production of Pouilly-Fuissé (not 'nearly 95 per cent' as stated by Parker in his Burgundy book). Georges Duboeuf has the wines from his own vineyards vinified here, the *caviste* proudly explains, though I wonder why. Probably by leaving his wines here Duboeuf can ensure he has first pickings of the *cave*'s vats.

There are some reasonable *cuvées*, but I do not see the complexity, nor the intensity of fruit, to be found in good private cellars, nor much quality difference when moving from lowly wines to taste the Pouilly-Fuissé. They handle a lot of grapes, and have produced a sumptuous, glossy brochure full of poetry hymning the owner of the Roman villa on which the *cave* was built – but on the viticultural front, much needs doing.

Amongst the Pouilly-Fuissé villages, Chaintré is despised – and probably was lucky to find itself name-linked to the best *coteaux* of Solutré, Vergisson & Co. But there are some excellent sites in Chaintré, and it is regrettable that these are not particularly valued. M. Desroches, Caviste, Cave de Chaintré, Cidex 418, 71570 Chaintré

CAVE COOPÉRATIVE DE CHARDONNAY 250 ha. (30 per cent)

Mâcon-Chardonnay, Mâcon-Uchizy and Mâcon-Villages 220 ha., Mâcon (*rouge*) 15 ha., Bourgogne (*rouge*) 15 ha., Crémant de Bourgogne

The village of Chardonnay traces its origins back over 1,000 years to Cardonacum, from the Gaulish Cardo (thistle country), but no proof has yet been found to link the origin of the Chardonnay grape conclusively here.

The co-operative dominates wine-making in the village (claiming 98 per cent of the production), and has above-average quality objectives. Since the 1988 vintage a control committee liaises with growers over yields, ripeness, and vine-age, and temperature control during wine-making is being installed more widely (about time too).

Completely new premises were being built in 1993 on a larger site at the entry to the village from Uchizy; however, their outspoken, dynamic director Gérard Pallot left in a cloud of dust early that year. We must hope that the admirable initiatives get strengthened, not diluted by grower inertia or short-sightedness. Current results may be seen in their best white, the Cuvée du Millénaire, which is drawn from old-vine sites, all harvested the same day, and which can be fruity, clean-flavoured and long. But hard finishes on some of the wines make me suspicious of their sulphuring ambitions.

Alain Gricourt, Président, Cave de Chardonnay, 71700 Chardonnay

DOMAINE CORDIER PÈRE ET FILS   8.6 ha. (85 per cent)

Pouilly-Fuissé Les Vignes Blanches 0.85 ha., Pouilly-Fuissé 5.65 ha., Pouilly-Loché 0.5 ha., Mâcon-Fuissé and Mâcon-Villages 1.5 ha.

This is an impeccably clean cellar, with electronically-controlled stainless steel temperature-control snake pipes installed within the old wooden vats. Thanks to this, they see no need to risk loss of typicity by using outside yeast cultures.

The Pouilly-Loché comes from vines abutting Pouilly-Fuissé. It does not have the richness or length of a top Pouilly-Fuissé, but the price reflects this. Father and son appear equally involved and enthusiastic.

Roger et Christophe Cordier, Fuissé, 71960 Pierreclos

DOMAINE CORSIN   9 HA. (80 PER CENT)

Pouilly-Fuissé 3.7 ha., Saint-Véran 4.5 ha., Mâcon-Villages 0.3 ha.

A single *cuvée* of Pouilly-Fuissé is made here, from a bottling in May or June after the harvest, which ages excellently. There are two bottlings of Saint-Véran (one early, from youngish vines). The family are local brokers, Corsin *père* acting regularly for Loron. The cellar is in Pouilly, the tasting-room being easy to find, and highly recommended, in Davayé.

Gilles Corsin, 'Les Coreaux', 71960 Fuissé

DAVAYÉ, LYCÉE VITICOLE ET AGRICOLE   17 ha.
DOMAINE DES PONCETYS

Saint-Véran 12.5 ha., Pouilly-Fuissé 0.32 ha., Mâcon (*rouge*) 4.2 ha.

The establishment of this Lycée dates from 1963. A law was

passed (when Edgar Pisani was Minister of Agriculture, under General de Gaulle) creating small-scale Lycées and Agricultural Colleges throughout France, always near big towns, to aid the training of country-born young people, and their adaptation to town, and modern, living. The first students here would have been completely swamped at Mâcon's big Lycée; many brought the smell of cowshed, goat and straw with them. They came from isolated villages, from houses without bathroom, or television, and had often never seen the sea.

The vines around the Lycée are part of an estate which dates back three hundred years, when it was owned by the Bishops of Autun. Talleyrand may well have sipped wine from these hillsides on the occasion of his first and last Mass at Autun, following his elevation to the bishopric and its 22,000 *livres* of annual income, in January 1789.

Students at the Lycée today may learn about vineyards, winemaking and also goat-breeding. There are over 30,000 goats in the Saône-et-Loire, one hundred of them on the model farm here in Davayé. These are alpine goats, dark brown, wilder and more rustic than the calm white Saanen goats whose milk makes the neat logs and pyramids of the vast co-operatives of Poitou and Charente which dominate the French goat-cheese industry. (Sancerre and Chavignol is a transition zone, with both alpine and white goats.) Most Saône-et-Loire goat cheeses are made on the farms, and they are smallish cheeses: very concentrated in flavour, however, for it takes two litres of goat's milk to give a Charolais tower, one-third of a litre to make a tiny breeches button (*bouton de culotte*), as the cheeses are called. Many Mâcon wine-makers can sell you goat cheeses, the fresh ones being often deliciously mild and creamy.

The Davayé wines are made under the supervision of the well-meaning Alain Faure, but I have found the whites lacklustre. For an educational establishment they seem rather stuck in their wine-making ruts. Having equipped their old wooden vats with temperature control, they contentedly buy six new small oak barrels per year. There are, however, experiments with a second generation pneumatic press, and it is perhaps no bad thing for students to experience straightforward, traditional practices. Perhaps it is unreasonable to expect a state-run college to preach, let alone practice, risk and adventure.

Alain Faure, Lycée Viticole de Mâcon Davayé, 71960 Davayé

DOMAINE DES DEUX ROCHES   31 ha. (100 per cent)

Saint-Véran Terres Noires 3 ha., Vieilles Vignes 2 ha., Saint-Véran 15 ha., Mâcon-Davayé and Mâcon-Villages 7 ha., Mâcon-Pierre-clos (*rouge*) 2 ha., Mâcon (*rouge*) 2 ha.

This domaine makes some of the best Saint-Vérans, and white Mâcons I know, and has been one of the fastest growing domaine-bottlers of the district. I must declare an interest, having often bought here. It is run by two dynamic brothers-in-law, and is quite a show-case, with an immaculate, steely, tiled winery (in use since 1990), two pneumatic presses, and varying trial batches of barrel-fermented Chardonnay in oaks of differing origins. It demonstrates how excellence can be achieved with machine-harvesting.

The Terres Noires Saint-Véran comes from an unusual site which contains 8 per cent humus (where an average soil might contain 2 per cent). It used to be scrubland, and no doubt dead leaves and twigs accumulated over many centuries in the pebbly, clay-lime soil, darkening its colour.

Jean-Luc Terrier et Christian Collovray, Davayé, 71960 Pierreclos

CORINNE ET THIERRY DROUIN   6.5 ha. (50 per cent)

Pouilly-Fuissé Les Crays 0.18 ha., Pouilly-Fuissé 4 ha., Mâcon Domaine du Vieux Puits (*blanc*) 1.7 ha., (*rouge*) 0.4 ha.

This white Mâcon does not have a Mâcon-Villages *appellation*, but it comes from Bussières land, adjoining Vergisson. An old vines Pouilly-Fuissé is also made, in small quantities.

Corinne et Thierry Drouin, Le Martelet, 71960 Vergisson

JEAN-MICHEL ÉT BEATRICE DROUIN   5.5 ha. (75 per cent)
DOMAINE DES GERBEAUX

Pouilly-Fuissé 4.3 ha. (of which 1.1 ha. is in the hamlet of Pouilly, partly Les Chailloux and en Chanroux, 2.5 ha. in Solutré, partly Les Gerbeaux and La Mûre, and Fuissé Les Longs Poils), Saint-Véran 0.36 ha., Mâcon-Solutré 0.8 ha.

Much progress has been made here since 1988, Jean-Michel Drouin following each of his seventeen separately vinified lots of wine with passionate involvement. Like many Pouilly-Fuissé grow-ers he is well-equipped with snake-pipe temperature control for his

small-vat fermentations. He presses slowly and gently, uses varied yeast cultures, rouses the lees regularly, and makes soft, delightful wines which show extremely well when young.
Jean-Michel Drouin, Solutré-Pouilly, 71960 Pierreclos

ROGER DUBOEUF ET FILS   5 ha. (65 per cent)

Pouilly-Fuissé Les Plessis 2 ha., Verchères de Savy 1.2 ha., Mâcon-Chaintré 1.5 ha., Beaujolais (*blanc*) 0.4 ha.

Roger Duboeuf is elder brother to the more famous Georges (and a third of Roger's production goes in bulk to the Georges Duboeuf merchant business in Romanèche). Historic vats, presses and tools are evidence that the family has been cultivating Chaintré plots since the fifteenth century.
Roger et Philippe Duboeuf, Savy, 71570 Chaintré

J.A. FERRET   15 ha. (40 per cent)

Pouilly-Fuissé Les Menetrières and Le Tournant de Pouilly (Hors Classe) 8 ha., Le Clos (Tête de Cru), Les Perrières, Vergisson (4 ha.)

With its low lighting, stained glass, and polychrome wooden lectern (an eagle astride a snake and globe) this would be a chapel, were it not for the neat rows of barrels. It is not so much the individual sites which are venerated in this hushed vault, but the wines themselves, and, I suspect, the customers. Those wines retained for bottling are harmoniously blended into Hors Classe and Tête de Cru *cuvées* of the highest quality, though these would shine more brightly if less sulphur were sometimes used. They go to Robuchon, Girardet, Alain Chapel, and many other great names abroad, since Robert Parker justifiably spread wider the fame of this domaine.

In July 1992 Mlle Colette Ferret sold her dental surgeon's practice to live in Fuissé, helping her eighty-five-year-old, then still highly active, mother, Madame Jeanne Ferret. Only a tiny proportion of new wood is deemed necessary, and rousing the wines no longer practised. Natural yeasts transform the sugars, after two systematic, day-long, settling periods in vat for the pressed musts. Thus are impurities cleared away, right from the start. The wines often spend two years or more in wood, and do not fear bottle age, as they rightly put it. Madame Jeanne Ferret passed away in 1993.
Mlle Colette Ferret, Le Plan, Fuissé, 71960 Pierreclos

MICHEL FOREST   2.8 ha. (100 per cent)

Pouilly-Fuissé Les Crays 1.2 ha., La Roche 0.4 ha., Pouilly-Fuissé 1.2 ha.

All wine-making is in oak barrel here, with different proportions of new wood being used.

Michel Forest, Les Crays, Vergisson, 71960 Pierreclos

MAURICE GONON PÈRE ET FILS   8.5 ha. (50 per cent)
DOMAINE DES PROVENCHÈRES

Mâcon *rouge*

'You say you make wine – but where?' is how visitors tend to greet Monsieur Gonon, whose home is up a green valley of trees and woods, with not a vine in sight. They started bottling in 1971 (700 bottles), and now regularly deliver 30,000 each year. They also keep cows, Charolais, and thirty goats, whose cheeses accompany the family to the Paris *Caves Particulières* fair each year, and greatly help their fine red Mâcon to be enjoyed.

Maurice et Michel Gonon, Serrières, 71960 Pierreclos

GUFFENS-HEYNEN   3 ha. (80 per cent)

Pouilly-Fuissé Clos des Petits Croux 0.12 ha., La Roche 0.2 ha., Les Croux 0.17 ha., Les Crays 0.15 ha., Pouilly-Fuissé 0.4 ha., Mâcon-Pierreclos en Chavigne (*rouge*) 0.8 ha., (*blanc*) 1.2 ha.

There are three categories of wine in the world, so Guffens will tell us: everyday table-wine, wine for pleasure (this could be a Mâcon-Villages or a Beaujolais, chosen for its simple delights), and wine for reflection. This last will come from low yields, will need age to become good, and may be the snapshot of a civilization, of a time or a place. It will halt you, make you reflect, make you talk.

Jean-Marie Guffens and his wife are Belgian; they arrived in the Mâconnais, when he was 22, in 1976. His studies? Architecture, and Theatre School. Hers? Fine Arts. He is to Pouilly what Joseph Roty is to Gevrey (you can't stop them talking) but I suspect that Guffens is more widely travelled, open-minded and revolutionary. Guffens wines sell as fast, and as expensively, as any grower's south of Chassagne. How has he gone so far, so fast? Because most of the others have not moved.

To make a living in the Mâconnais you really have to fight. Maybe you have to go back into your vines two months after picking, to bring in the bunches the pickers had missed, to keep the fermentations going, and make up your quantities. You discover what benefit comes from long, cold, slow fermenting. It is like discovering *confit de canard*; it happened, surely, on a snowy day, when if the duck was not to be preserved it would have rotted. And when every drop counts, you separate your first pressings from your second, you carefully nurture the lees, the deposit from the musts, rich in yeasts and organic matter.

This estate has been bottling (filtration is eschewed) since 1979; there has been no fertilizing for ten years, and no herbicides either. They aim to aid nature to defend itself. The tiny quantities of wine are fascinating, including a most surprising, intensely flavoured, long and tannic Gamay, 'made according to anti-carbonic-mastur-bation methods', says Guffens. It certainly does not resemble Beau-jolais. In 1991 he formed a *négociant* business, Verget SARL in Sologny, to buy grapes, frequently from the Côte d'Or. So there will be Guffens-made Bâtard, Puligny, Chassagne, Meursault and more. Jean-Marie Guffens et Germaine Heynen, 'En France' Vergisson, 71960 Pierreclos

DOMAINE GUILLEMOT-MICHEL   6.5 ha. (100 per cent)
SCEA DE QUINTAINE

Mâcon-Clessé Quintaine 6.5 ha., Mâcon-Clessé Sélection de Grains Cendrés

Two oenologists under one roof here, working with the minimum of chemical products. And local, not cultured, yeasts for ferment-ing. Local yeasts make wine-making more difficult, for they give lower alcohol levels, and higher volatile acidity, but this couple finds that such wines have more complexity.

There is a yeast culture from the Bordelais which gives an aroma of white peaches, if used in a Mâcon cellar. It appears delightful and interesting, but then you find the same smell at a friend's, some villages away, and realize that the yeast is blotting out the wine's originality. The same thing happens with some cloned vine-types: you may recognize the product of a given clone, blind, in a neigh-bour's cellar.

They do not chaptalize here, and any rotten grapes in the vines will be left there; to pick them would mean increasing the sulphur dose.

In ripe years (1990, 1992) they make a rich, yet delicate, aromatic, dessert wine from nobly-rotten grapes, which they describe as *Sélection de Grains Cendrés*. (The Alsatians having trade-marked *Grains nobles*, the Guillemots coined a cindery derivative of *cinerea botrytis*, the mould which does the noble work.) Like their dry wines, these have great fruit, freshness, length and ageing potential.

All these wines are beautiful – they took my breath away. (I am sure I do not need to say this, but they might not do well in blind tastings. Stronger statements could shout them down. One bottle, two glasses and a friend should be all you need.)

Marc Guillemot et Pierrette Michel, Quintaine, 71260 Clessé

ALAIN GUILLOT   6.5 ha. (100 per cent)
DOMAINE DES VIGNES DU MAYNES

Clos des Vignes du Maynes (Monopole), Bourgogne *blanc* (Chardonnay) 2.5 ha., Bourgogne *rouge* (Pinot Noir) 2.5 ha., Mâcon *rouge* and *rosé* 1.5 ha., Marc and Fine de Bourgogne

This family came to organic viticulture and wine-making because of the late Pierre Guillot's fragile health, following imprisonment in Germany during the Second World War. He was a lawyer from Paris, who bought vineyards here in 1954.

Mâcon wines at that time often had high doses of sulphur dioxide, and were treated with potassium ferro-cyanide (to eliminate traces of iron, commonly found in wine before the arrival of plastic and stainless steel for grape-handling). Such wines gave Guillot headaches and heartburn, so he cultivated his own vineyards with the minimum of chemicals. He was ejected from the local co-operative and denied access to local wine laboratories, and his children found that their school-mates would be obliged to change pavements, when going shopping on Thursday afternoons, so their parents would not have to say *bonjour* to a family of cranks and eccentrics. It cannot have been much fun.

Disparaged by the authorities in the past, biological agriculture was recognized by the French Ministry of Agriculture in 1981, states Alain Guillot, who is now President of the National Agro-Biological Viticultural Committee. He fertilizes with composted humus, straw from untreated cereal crops and dwarf white clover; adds powdered rock to supplement naturally-occurring trace elements; protects his vines by encouraging ladybirds to prey on harmful insects, by copper sulphate, powdered sulphur and pow- dered marine algae sprays, and never uses finings, nor sulphur after the grapes have been picked. No herbicides, no pesticides and no petro-chemical derivatives go into the vineyards (but he does filter with kieselguhr). He says he does not have grey rot problems, nor spider predators.

Since the vines once belonged to the monks of Cluny (Vignes du Maynes is a deformation, which must date from the Revolution, of *vignes des moines*) he affirms '900 years of uninterrupted organic cultivation and wine-making'.

What are the wines like? Pretty odd, if you have been brought up, like me, on chemical classicism. 'You must file away the world of chemists', says Guillot, 'this is a new sensation, something else'. Indeed, tasting these wines, in which sulphur plays so small a part, one may imagine without difficulty that this is how Pinot Noir tasted to the Valois Dukes. From the barrel, they have a lively freshness, and natural light fruit, which is most appealing. But whites and reds evolve far more quickly than the wines we normally see, often developing oxidized aromas, honeyed smells, gamey and *rancio* flavours, while less than two years old.
Alain Guillot, Cruzille, 71260 Lugny

CAVE COOPÉRATIVE D'IGE   265 ha. (25 per cent)

Mâcon-Villages 120 ha., Saint-Véran 5 ha., Bourgogne (*rouge*) 35 ha., Mâcon-Igé (*rouge*) 95 ha., Crémant de Bourgogne 10 ha.

It is perfectly possible to buy, very economically, a wine called Bourgogne *blanc* from a source such as this, Mâcon-Villages being declassified to the alternative name, on demand. A lot of Gamay grows on limestone-clay here, which they pick by machine, and ferment partly by semi-carbonic maceration, partly in traditional open vats. The result is more tannic, less soft by miles, than a Beaujolais, a bit chewy and firm.
Marc Vachet, Cave des Vignerons d'Igé, 71960 Igé

ROGER LASSARAT   9 ha. (100 per cent)

Pouilly-Fuissé Clos de France 0.81 ha., Pouilly-Fuissé 2.23 ha., Saint-Véran 4.17 ha., Mâcon-Vergisson 0.5 ha., Mâcon *rouge* 0.93 ha., Vosne-Romanée *Premier Cru* En l'Orveau 0.38 ha.

Tasting from barrel there are some very fine individual lots of Saint-Véran and Pouilly-Fuissé, but I have been less lucky with finished bottles. Maybe total sulphur levels have been a bit high, or some of the quality diminished by pre-bottling treatments. Monsieur Lassarat now seems to be bringing his new oak into fine balance with the fruitiness.

His holding of First Growth Vosne-Romanée is a surprise (and not easy to cultivate at this distance). He bought the vines by chance, after lunching in Nuits with a stranger who was selling vineyards on behalf of SAFER (a government organization which regroups and distributes much-split vineyard land).

Roger Lassarat, Le Martelet, 71960 Vergisson

DOCTEUR BERNARD LÉGER-PLUMET   8 ha. (90 per cent)
HENRI PLUMET ET HÉRITIERS

Pouilly-Fuissé Le Clos du Chalet, Les Chailloux and La Rochette 5 ha., Saint-Veran Les Cornillaux 2.5 ha., Beaujolais 0.5 ha.

Dr Léger was destined for medical research until the sudden death of his father-in-law Henri Plumet, who had been a Pouilly-Fuissé owner, and for some years director of Auvigue Burrier et Revel. Léger studied oenology for a year in Dijon, then set up a country medical practice in Solutré, where he and his wife look after both the locals and the superbly-placed family vines, high on the Pouilly hamlet hill.

These wines don't exactly smile at you when young, but this has not been Dr Léger's objective, and it does not stop them selling out quickly. Often his malolactics are intentionally blocked, and I suspect one needs to cellar his bottles literally three or four years to drink them at their best.

Docteur Bernard Léger-Plumet, Les Gerbeaux, 71960 Solutré-Pouilly

CAVE COOPÉRATIVE DE LUGNY   1,150 ha. (40 per cent)

Mâcon-Lugny Les Charmes 85 ha., Mâcon-Lugny, Mâcon-Saint-Gengoux, Mâcon-Péronne, Mâcon-Burgy, Mâcon-Villages, Mâcon Supérieur Rouge (Gamay), Bourgogne Pinot Noir, Crémant de Bourgogne

Four-fifths of Lugny's production is Chardonnay, the balance being split between Gamay (Mâcon *rouge* or *rosé*) and Pinot Noir (making Bourgogne *rouge*). This is the largest co-operative in the Mâconnais, and indeed Burgundy. With its recently-expanded facilities it can produce 4 million bottles a year. Its vineyards are spread over a dozen communes, five being devoted exclusively to the vine: Lugny (mainly whites), Saint-Gengoux de Scissé (mainly reds), Bissy-la-Mâconnaise, Cruzille and Péronne.

Lugny merged with its neighbour Saint-Gengoux de Scissé in 1965 when, as in the 1920s, few buyers could be found for the wines in spite of low prices. The two cellars transformed themselves into a Groupement de Producteurs, which gave access to larger funds and was a significant psychological sales aid. For customers, be they foreign importers or passing Frenchmen, prefer the idea of dealing with a group of producers rather than a co-operative. The white wines produced in this northerly section of the Mâconnais seem to have their own originality: less steely, more flowery than, say, a Mâcon-Prissé. To some extent this is due to the presence of Chardonnay musqué vines in the vineyards, small proportions in a blend adding relief to the wines.

Paul Brunet, BP 6, rue des Charmes, 71260 Lugny

DOMAINE ROGER LUQUET   17 ha. (100 per cent)

Pouilly-Fuissé Clos du Bourg (Monopole) 1 ha., En Châtenet 0.46 ha., Pouilly-Fuissé 4.3 ha., Saint-Véran Les Grandes Bruyères 1.4 ha., Saint-Véran 4 ha., Mâcon *blanc* Clos de Condemine 4.5 ha.

The highest-profile domaine in Fuissé is of course Vincent at the Château, but here is another which is dynamic and effective, and it too has some really old vines in its Pouilly-Fuissé vineyards.

Fruitiness of the grape is its motto, though a new-oaked *cuvée*, called Bois Seguin, is made (running against the grain of Monsieur Luquet's wine-making beliefs).

Mâcon La Condemine is a youngish vineyard, laid out for

machine harvesting when planted. They cut the grapes by hand, however, for trials have shown that the flattering (when young) machine-harvested wine tends to turn ochre and maderize too fast for comfort. A small merchant's business, R. Luquet, SARL, runs alongside the estate.

This hard-working, hospitable domaine is open virtually every day of the year, including Sunday mornings and public holidays. Three Luquet families rotate the welcoming duties. A visit is warmly recommended.

Roger Luquet (opposite the church), 71960 Fuissé

DOMAINE MANCIAT-PONCET   13 ha. (80 per cent)
DOMAINE JEANNE PONCET
DOMAINE DES CRAYS

Pouilly-Fuissé Les Crays 1.5 ha., La Roche 0.5 ha., Vergisson 3 ha., Mâcon-Charnay 6 ha., Mâcon-Bussières 2 ha.

Claude Manciat is an experienced and reflective grower-bottler. An American contact, Bobby Kacher, influences him towards overt oakiness (such bottles may be marked *cuvée bois*), but he is too wily to let the fickle US market dominate his thoughts. 'I'm not looking for stardom', he says; 'it's dangerous.'

Hand-harvesting is highly valued, not least for the personal enrichment of meeting, lodging and feeding young French Canadian students each year, or surgeons from Poland, who, to his mild surprise, find Mâcon grape-picking worthwhile.

Claude Manciat et Jacques Nomède, Levigny, 71850 Charnay-lès-Mâcon

DOMAINE MATHIAS   8 ha. (100 per cent)

Pouilly-Fuissé 3.2 ha., Pouilly-Vinzelles 1 ha., Mâcon-Loché and Mâcon-Villages 1 ha., Beaujolais *blanc* 1 ha., Beaujolais-Villages 0.8 ha.

Pouillys from Chaintré can be either a bit rustic, or simple, supple and tender, compared to those from the best sites in other communes. This is an interesting cellar in which to taste Mâcon *blanc*, Beaujolais *blanc* and Pouilly-Vinzelles side by side, the first two coming from thick soils, Vinzelles from more pebbly, limey hillsides (and showing more finesse). The cellar sees little difference between

its Fuissé and its Vinzelles, but vinifies the first in small barrels, so trying to justify the higher price.
Jean et Gilles Mathias, La Bergerie, 71570 Chaintré

OLIVIER MERLIN   6 ha. (100 per cent)
DOMAINE DU VIEUX SAINT-SORLIN

Mâcon La Roche Vineuse (*blanc*) 4 ha., (*rouge*) 0.8 ha., Saint-Véran 0.2 ha., Bourgogne *rouge* 1 ha.

'On the technical front, one should advance with modesty, and at a moderate pace', believes Merlin, who did not omit to gain top qualifications (three years general agricultural diploma, another three at the Beaune Lycée, then two vintages in Napa) before settling on a vinous rock half way between his origins in the Charolais, and his wife's in the Doubs. 'Mâcon wine has a very bad image', he says; 'it is considered a good wine, but no more. The best sites are not yet valued.' Yes, that is true, and the way out is to vinify the plots one by one, taste and compare. No better place than here, where Gamays, Pinots and Chardonnays are all great.
Olivier Merlin, La Roche Vineuse, 71960 Pierreclos

GILLES NOBLET   9 ha. (100 per cent)
DOMAINE DE LA COLLONGE

Pouilly-Fuissé 7.4 ha., Pouilly-Loché 0.28 ha., Saint-Véran 0.7 ha., Mâcon-Fuissé 0.77 ha.

A rare source of Loché – which normally has less stuffing than the Pouilly-Fuissé. These wines may not have the brilliance and depth of flavour of the most expensive Pouilly-Fuissés, but they open up relatively soon.
Gilles Noblet, 71960 Fuissé

JEAN-PAUL PAQUET   9 ha. (100 per cent)
DOMAINE DE FUSSIACUS
DOMAINE LES VIEUX MURS

Pouilly-Fuissé 6.5 ha., Mâcon-Fuissé 2.5 ha.

Les Vieux Murs can be a lively, classic Pouilly, fermented and aged in big, old wooden casks, Domaine de Fussiacus having more pretentions, coming from old vines, gilded with new wood.

(Fussiacus is the name of the Roman settler whose name has evolved into Fuissé.)
Jean-Paul Paquet, Les Mollards, 71960 Fuissé

MICHEL PAQUET   9 ha. (100 per cent)
DOMAINE DES VALANGES

Pouilly-Fuissé (Solutré and Fuissé) 1 ha., Saint-Véran (Davayé) 6 ha., Mâcon-Villages (Davayé and Fuissé) 2 ha.
Michel Paquet, 71960 Davayé

DOMAINE DU PRIEURÉ   17.3 ha. (50 per cent)

Mâcon-Villages 10 ha., Bourgogne (*rouge*) 5 ha., Mâcon (*rouge*) 2 ha., Aligoté 0.3 ha.
  Pierre Janny is an oenologist whose wines may be enjoyed while taking the view from his 580-metre high Mont Saint-Romain inn, above Blanot, where walkers are welcome. The means of getting about are provided for bikers and horse-riders. He also runs the Domaine de la Condemine (4.4 ha.: Mâcon-Péronne 4 ha., Bourgogne (*rouge*) 0.2 ha., Mâcon (rouge) 0.2 ha.).
Pierre Janny, Le Prieuré, 712690 Bissy-la-Mâconnaise

PRISSÉ, GROUPEMENT DE PRODUCTEURS   330 ha. (30 per cent)

Saint-Véran Les Monts 10 ha., Saint-Véran 100 ha., Mâcon-Prissé 10 ha., Mâcon-Chevagny 16 ha., Mâcon La Roche Vineuse 16 ha., Mâcon-Villages 29 ha., Pouilly-Fuissé 3 ha., Mâcon Supérieur *rouge* 100 ha., Bourgogne 35 ha., Bourgogne Aligoté 10 ha.
  When the Prissé co-operative was founded in 1928, 95 per cent of the wines vinified were from the Gamay. Sixty years later, the Chardonnay accounts for nearly three-quarters of the production. I cannot be objective, having often bought wine here (aided by a broker) and been delighted. A great *caviste* (M. Vessot, now retired) and an enlightened president, with some growers who clip off grapes if they are too plentiful, has made a winning co-operative formula.
René Duvert, Président, et Georges Brichon, Caviste, 71960 Prissé

DOMAINE DE ROALLY   3.5 ha. (100 per cent)
HENRI GOYARD

Mâcon-Viré 2 ha., Mâcon-Montbellet 1.5 ha.

No oak barrels here, and no cultured yeasts either. This is a tiny domaine, in a district of monster co-operatives and big estates, and hand-picking is the rule. Goyard believes that quality in the Mâconnais has dropped several points since picking was generally mechanized, in which case, if the bunches are not intact when brought in, heavy dosing with sulphur will result. On quality machine harvested wines can taste beautiful when young, but then they tend to plunge. It is the opposite here: these lively wines need two years in bottle to open up.

Henri Goyard, Le Buc, 71260 Viré

DOMAINE DE RUÈRE   10 ha. (10 per cent)
DOMAINE ELOY

Mâcon-Villages 4.2 ha., Mâcon-Pierreclos (*rouge*) 2 ha., Mâcon-Bussières 2 ha., Bourgogne *rouge* 1.27 ha.

Here one may see the dividing line between the limestone, calcareous soils of northern Mâconnais (where Monsieur Eloy grows his Chardonnays) and the sandy, granite soils on which his Bussières Gamays thrive. Thirty, fifty metres one way or the other, and you have moved from white wine land to red. He also grows old Gamays on a steep, south-facing Pierreclos hillside.

Bottling has been done by an itinerant machine, its operator perhaps over-zealous with the filter pad, filter-cartridge, sulphur dioxide, or gum arabic (all perfectly legal, but too much of any will diminish quality). If the family bottlings were to be expanded by Didier Eloy (Maurice's son) this could no doubt be resolved.

Maurice Eloy, Ruère, 71960 Pierreclos

DOMAINE SAINT-PHILIBERT   6 ha. (35 per cent)
PHILIPPE BÉRARD

Pouilly-Loché Clos des Rocs (Les Mûres)(Monopole) 2.2 ha., Pouilly-Loché 2.3 ha., Mâcon-Loché 1.5 ha.

Until 1985 Philippe Bérard's grapes went to the Vinzelles co-operative. He was then a wine trader, and decided that, unless something was done, the tiny Pouilly-Loché *appellation* might wither away, or be absorbed into Pouilly-Vinzelles, his family vine-yards withering with it. He has been wine-making and bottling since 1986, experimenting (no doubt at times feeling rather isolated) with reduced chaptalization levels, and slowly opening markets beyond the local restaurants.

He has a collector's passion for vineyard, cooperage and wine-making tools, and is installing an imaginative display to bring out the innate beauty of old adzes, secateurs, pruning shears, bill-hooks, cleavers, dibbles, grubbers, home-corkers, frost pots, scald-ing buckets, and much else, above his vat-house.

Philippe Bérard, Domaine St Philibert, Loché, 71680 Vinzelles

DOMAINE RAPHAËL SALLET   7.5 ha. (75 per cent)

Mâcon-Uchizy 7.5 ha.

Raphaël Sallet's father still has his vines within the local co-operative, but they hope that his extra 14 hectares will be added to the son's estate-bottling venture over the years. This is a source of machine-harvested, soft, early-maturing Chardonnay.

Raphaël Sallet, rue du Puits, 71700 Uchizy

ROGER SAUMAIZE   7 ha. (70 per cent)
DOMAINE SAUMAIZE-MICHELIN

Pouilly-Fuissé Clos de la Roche 1.5 ha., Les Ronchevats 0.5 ha., Pouilly-Fuissé 3 ha., Saint-Véran 0.5 ha., Mâcon-Villages 1 ha., Mâcon (*rouge*) 0.5 ha.

Two single-vineyard Pouillys – one from the limestone rock, one from clay-lime – demonstrate the individuality and interest to be found in wines from good Vergisson sites, when the wine-making is well done. The lesser *appellations* are dependable, too.

Roger et Christine Saumaize, Vers la Croix, 71950 Vergisson

DOMAINE TALMARD   31 ha. (100 per cent)

Mâcon-Chardonnay, Mâcon-Uchizy, Mâcon-Plottes 28 ha., Mâcon (*rouge*) 1 ha., Bourgogne Pinot Noir 2 ha.

This is an astonishingly successful large estate, whose efforts have taken the name of Uchizy to many markets round the globe.

The Talmard brothers created their vineyards in 1958, taking the grapes to the Chardonnay co-operative until 1972. In the mid-1970s they started making the wine themselves, and from 1978 have bottled all their production. They had to invest 5 francs per litre to set up their wine-making facility – exactly what they had been paying the co-operative for vinification expenses – so the investment was amortized within twelve months. (No one, however, followed them out of co-op land, at the time. Solidarity feelings must run high.)

This is a mixed farming estate, also growing maize for animal feed, and some wheat, the latter giving a straw side-crop which goes straight back between the vine rows as humus. They believe in high-density planting (9,000 vines per hectare against a more common 7,000), machine harvesting, and minimal ploughing. The Chardonnays are rich, soft and delicious. But watch out for Volga the dog, who looks friendly but had unhappy experiences in puppyhood with stone-throwing visitors. She has strong jaws and regular teeth; stout corduroys are a good idea, for these wines are worth knowing, and a fine demonstration of what can be done with machine harvesting on a large estate.

Paul et Philibert Talmard, Uchizy, 71700 Chardonnay

JEAN THÉVENET   14 ha. (100 per cent)
DOMAINE DE LA BONGRAN
DOMAINE EMILIAN GILLET

Mâcon-Viré 4 ha., Mâcon-Clessé 10 ha.

One of the outstanding domaines of the Mâconnais, which may be depended on for white wines of concentration, richness, balance and length. The vines have an average age of forty years, and yields are significantly lower than is current. Modern chemical insecticides and fungicides are not used, the Chardonnays being protected by 'proven natural compounds' such as *bouillie bordelaise*, by hoeing and tractor work. The picking date is usually later than the average (which means that chaptalization can often be dispensed with) and noble rot is encouraged. When this appears, a remarkable dessert wine is produced.

In May 1989, a newly-built winery here won first prize (ahead of twenty-two rivals) for 'exceptional modern architectural and technical innovation and design (whilst in keeping with and highlighting the image of Burgundy)'.

Jean Thévenet, Quintaine-Clessé, 71260 Clessé

MARCEL VINCENT ET FILS 40 ha. (100 per cent)
CHÂTEAU DE FUISSÉ
DOMAINE DE L'ARILLIÈRE

Pouilly-Fuissé Château Fuissé 19 ha., (of which Le Clos (Monopole) 2.6 ha., and Les Brûlées (Monopole) 1.5 ha.), Saint-Véran 6 ha., Mâcon-Villages 1 ha., Morgon Charmes 7.5 ha., Juliénas 7 ha.

From the immaculate cellars of the old Château de Fuissé Jean-Jacques Vincent has been an unstoppable enthusiast for Pouilly-Fuissé. He will sit down at a table, shoot his cuffs into the air, pick up a corkscrew, and, grinning broadly, proceed to demonstrate that great white Burgundy sources do not dry up south of Chassagne. He brings top agricultural and wine-making qualifications to his family estate and business, which has for years been the *appellation*'s prime standard-bearer.

Wine-making here is temperature-controlled from crush to dispatch, with vat wines held under inert nitrogen to reduce the need for sulphur, and malolactics blocked to retain freshness. The sturdier wines are oak-vinified or oak-aged, as appropriate, and here one may taste the same wine from oaks of different origins, which is always fascinating. A less successful, envious rival might tell you that Vincent makes *vins technologiques*, and I can sometimes see what is meant, in front of a bottle from his *négociant* business. But his Château Fuissé bottlings – particularly the *vieilles vignes* – are usually very special. The Morgon and Juliénas, made by traditional, non-Beaujolais methods ('so as not to gum up the character of their origins') can be really delicious.

In the early 1990s, Jean-Jacques Vincent bought another 4 ha. of Pouilly-Fuissé vines, at a time when small growers had seen prices of their wine fall from 12,000 fr. to 4,000 fr. per barrel (and they could hardly give the liquid away). He has made money, where unsophisticated hill workers are really pushed for cash, by setting his sights really high, and having the technical mastery to deliver top quality even when the weather is unfavourable.

Jean-Jacques Vincent-Source, Au Château, 71960 Fuissé

VIRÉ, CAVE COOPÉRATIVE DE   320 ha. (65 per cent)

Mâcon-Viré and Mâcon-Villages 256 ha., Crémant de Bourgogne 64 ha.

I have had good wines from here, the second largest co-operative in the region, but am sure quality levels could be significantly raised if the determination was there to do so.

Emmanuel Béné, En Vercheron, 71260 Viré

VINZELLES, CAVE DES GRANDS CRUS BLANCS   128 ha. (35 per cent)

Pouilly-Fuissé 5.55 ha., Pouilly-Vinzelles 36.35 ha., Pouilly-Loché 17.98 ha., Saint-Véran 5.3 ha., Mâcon-Vinzelles, Mâcon-Loché, Mâcon-Villages, Beaujolais *blanc*, Saint Amour and regional ACs

This co-operative is completely dominant in its district, accounting for about 80 per cent of the production of both Pouilly-Vinzelles and Pouilly-Loché. Its buildings are conveniently sited for travellers on the main short cut round Mâcon, north-west from the *route nationale* 6, at Crèches, towards the best vineyards of the Mâconnais. It vinifies several fine individual sites, for instance part of Les Mûres in Pouilly-Loché, and the Château de Laye, in Pouilly-Vinzelles, which was visited by Thomas Jefferson in 1788.

It would need quite a shake-up to raise the quality above average levels. Only since 1990 has temperature control during wine-making been significantly installed, and I imagine that three out of four of the oldish presses squeeze inordinate quantities of solids into the musts. On my last visit, I shocked myself rigid by spitting straight back into a vat full of wine. The manhole cover was so rusted and dirty, in a moment of inattention I mistook it for an open drain. Major investment could bring the wine-making plant up to the sparklingly decorative levels seen by tourists in the bottle-shop, and given the precious, historic slopes from which these grapes come, it does not seem too much to ask.

Some of the (mainly machine-harvested) wines are actually very good, particularly while young, before treatment, sulphur addition and bottling. No doubt local merchants collect their bulk selections extremely promptly.

Michel Moreau, Président, Cave de Vinzelles, 71680 Vinzelles

35

The Beaujolais, Its Villages
and Crus

The Beaujolais merits a book, not a chapter. This is merely an introduction, to make the mouth water.

Beaujolais lies beyond the southern border of the official, administrative region of Burgundy (which is made up of the four *départements* of Yonne, Nièvre, Côte d'Or and Saône-et-Loire), the region being centred on the Rhône *département*. It has split itself off from northern Burgundy, electing to go its own, independent way in the marketing and promoting of its red wine (only 2 per cent of the production is white).

Beaujolais, the wine, has often come to be despised. Much of it is made to be drunk immediately as Nouveau, and lacks individuality. It has ceased to express its grapey or territorial origins and is either gimmicky or simplistic. Wine-making technique has ridden roughshod over district variations. The wines can often be delicious and inexpensive, offering good value, but Beaujolais-Villages and the famous *crus*, in many markets, have lost both affection and respect. The Beaujolais Nouveau phenomenon is at the root of the problem, wine for immediate consumption having gone from 10 per cent of the total Beaujolais harvest in 1960, to over 50 per cent of the harvest, by 1986. By the 1992 harvest, a third of all Beaujolais-Villages was sold as Nouveau, as was just under half of the AC Beaujolais.[1]

All may not have been well in Beaujolais, but equally, the story is a complicated one. Each year, around 170 million bottles are produced, so how could it be otherwise? In fact, there are at least

1 *Source: Données d'economie*, UIVB, July 1993.

two Beaujolais wine cultures, as we shall see, and it is as rash to generalize about this area as any other part of vinous Burgundy.

Beaujolais history

The Beaujolais region is part of the Lyonnais. It came into being in the eleventh century, founded by Béraud, first Lord of Beaujeu, its capital, which sits strategically on the shortest passage between the Saône and Loire valleys. It was named as Bellijocum in 1031.

Villefranche has been the commercial and administrative capital of the region since the sixteenth century. It owes its importance to its position as a market town, surrounded by the agricultural lands of Bresse and Beaujolais, on the main north–south trade route. It was granted its charter of freedoms in 1260 by Guichard IV, Sire of Beaujeu.

Only in the last two hundred years has the Beaujolais become dominated by viticulture. Before the Revolution it was one of the most miserable and least populated regions in France, according to Cochard and d'Aigueperse.[2] The sandy soil gave a harvest of rye or barley every three or four years and a few sheep cropped amongst the briars. The transformation took place as a result of the division of the large estates after the Revolution, and thanks to the opening up of new markets in the north of France after the road had been improved from the Saône to the Loire. The suppression of internal customs barriers encouraged the growers to bring more land into cultivation. The population is said to have tripled in sixty years.

In *Jadis en Beaujolais*, Justin Dutraive describes how the completion of the Canal de Briare in 1642 had enabled the Beaujolais growers to take their wines economically to Paris. The first communes entitled to do so were Saint-Lager, Fleurie and Chénas. The land route through Burgundy had been expensive, twenty-nine *pièces* loaded on to three carts and a four-wheeled wagon requiring eighteen horses to pull them. River transport by the Loire and the new canal was longer and slower, but cheaper. There were three routes to the Loire but the most used was from Port de Belleville to Port de Pouilly. Horses were used for the first stage, and Charolais oxen, strong as oil-presses, on the uplands, then horse-drawn carts downhill to the Loire. It was thirsty work and there were as many

2 Quoted in Justin Dutraive, *Jadis en Beaujolais*, M. Lescuyer et Fils, Lyon, 1976.

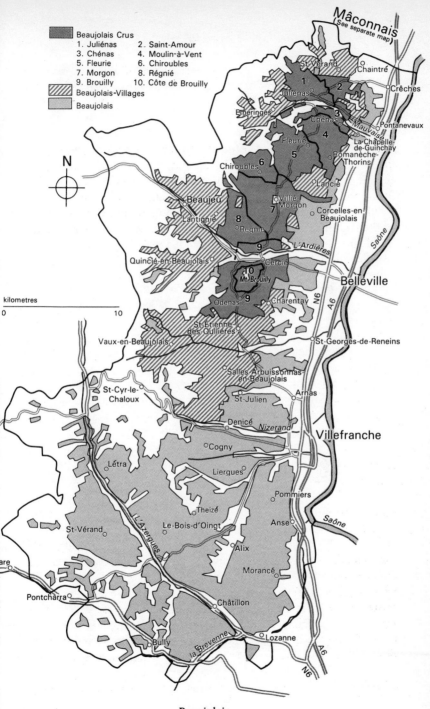

Beaujolais

public houses on the road as there were kilometre-posts. There was no river navigation at night, everything stopped in fog, and there were sixteen tolls, to the profit of local landlords. When Briare was reached, a tasting took place; anything acetic went on down the Loire to the vinegar establishments of Orléans. A month's navigation was required before Port-au-Vin, Paris, was reached.

Beaujolais wine-making

The great secret of the Beaujolais, according to Dr J. Guyot a hundred years ago,[3] is the Gamay grape. It established and maintains its legitimate reputation. Well, yes and no. For the Gamay grape, unless you know how to handle it, produces rather dull wine, with no particular fruitiness or character, as can be seen by tasting Gamays from Savoie, or Saint-Pourçain on the upper Loire, squashed and fermented traditionally. What transforms it is a special vinification.

The real secret of success of these wines lies, I think, in their lack of bitterness, their softness. The Gamay grape has lower natural levels of tannins than any other of the red grapes grown in northerly latitudes – Pinot Noir, Cabernet Franc, Merlot, Malbec – but it has anthocyanin levels (which contribute the rich purple colour) to beat both Pinot Noir and Merlot.[4]

But you have to handle it very specially. For much of what follows, I am indebted to M. Louis Pelletier and to the Sicarex-Beaujolais (the government-backed vine and wine research unit in Villefranche) for their descriptions of the process, as to the UIVB's admirably forthright manual for wine-makers *Terroir + Savoir-Faire = Qualité*.

The first objective is to pick the bunches carefully and bring the grapes whole and unsquashed to the vat-house, and for this small tubs holding no more than 60 kilograms of grapes are required. A harvesting machine cannot be used, nor can a stemmer-crusher (the machine which in most red-wine-making areas squashes the grapes, at the same time removing all or some of the stalks). Nor can pumps, so conveyor-belts are needed to carry the bunches up to their vats.

3 *Etude des vignobles de France*, Paris, 1868.
4 Colloque, BIVB, Nolay, 1990.

Ideally, vinification takes place in a vat no larger than 60 hecto-litres, though most vats in co-operative cellars are over twice that size. Ten to 30 per cent of the vat's contents will quickly become juice, owing to the bunches falling on to one another, and this increases during maceration to reach 40 to 70 per cent in large vats, which is their disadvantage.

Three distinctly different things will be going on in a Beaujolais vat, in the liquid at the bottom, in the intermediary zone where bunches are floating in juice, and on top, where the bunches are surrounded by carbon dioxide gas, which has been produced, quite naturally, by fermentation beginning in the bottom third. Depend-ing on the yield of fruit, on the maturity, on the rottenness or health of the grapes, and on what he or she wishes to achieve, a wine-maker will vary the methods used.

It is very difficult to gauge vineyard yields prior to picking, so vats often need to be bled (anything from 5 to 15 per cent may go down the drain) to increase the proportion of solids. Sulphur diox-ide (an antiseptic) may be added, the temperature may be substan-tially varied, and the liquid may be regularly pumped up, and sprayed over the grape bunches. Chaptalization sugar will be added, and almost certainly, yeast cultures. Books could be written about the different yeasts available to Beaujolais growers, the vary-ing aromas they produce and their action on sugar and acid.

Winemakers in those *crus* (Chénas, Moulin-à-Vent, Juliénas, Morgon, for instance) not aiming to produce wines for immediate drinking may dispense with the top section in the vat, where bun-ches can be surrounded by gas. They may use wooden grids to hold the grapes submerged, and reduce the pumpings-over.

Those making Beaujolais Nouveau need the top third, for here takes place a complicated anaerobic metabolism which reduces the malic acidity in the grapes, and produces, without the action of yeasts at all, 2° of alcohol as well as important by-products.

In the middle section of the vat, the grape skin is a sort of osmotic membrane, through which alcohol from the juice moves to the inside of the unsquashed grape. By spraying the grape-cap a good extraction of colour, tannin and volatile constituents will be achieved.

At the bottom of the vat, yeasts transform the sugar into alcohol and carbon dioxide, and essential volatile constituents. Different yeasts will affect the final acidity levels, the colour, tannins, aromas and flavours.

Temperature control has become more and more important to the making of good Beaujolais, particularly if it is to be drunk immediately. Indeed, new methods (thermo-vinification – see Domaine Paul Cinquin in Regnié) may well significantly transform the quality levels during the late 1990s, if they can be adapted to large volumes.

It also appears possible that the heavy dependence on sugar can be reduced in the near future, by use of the Durafroid method of extracting water by pumping air through must at normal temperatures.[5] Experiments are also under way into methods of drying out grape bunches in a warm-air room, prior to fermenting. The latter might cost an estate 350,000 fr. to install, the former half as much. Such investments are not beyond the reach of the medium-sized domaine, and the investment would be quickly justified by the savings made by not having to buy sugar, partly in a grey market! The quality of juice-dehydrated wines appears, on brief acquaintance, higher than that of sugared wines. As of 1994, this method is still on trial, as yet unauthorized.

Beaujolais wine-making (carbonic semi-maceration) is an adaptation of the classic system of carbonic maceration, which requires no addition of sulphur dioxide and no pumping over of juice, but a saturation of the vat with bottled carbon dioxide gas immediately it is filled, followed by ten to twelve days' maceration. In the Beaujolais, no gas is pumped into the vat. The maceration process takes two to six days, at the end of which the vat may contain half liquids, half solids; the grapes are pressed to extract the rest, and fermentation continues, perhaps after additional sugaring, and a temperature reduction to 16–18°.

Of course, in the *crus*, the vatting-time and methods are adapted, if wines are being made that are not for immediate consumption. One could say that there are two utterly different wine cultures in the Beaujolais; they get merged together, because each helps to sell the products of the other. Some people make agreeably fruity quaffers, while others – like Louis Champagnon and his family in

5 Under development across the Saône from Belleville, due east of Mont-Brouilly, by Durafroid, SA. This is the same method as is currently being tested at Domaines de la Pousse d'Or, Michel Lafarge, Tollot-Beaut and others, in the Côte d'Or.

Chénas, for instance, or Louis-Claude Desvignes in Morgon – make bottles of wine of such richness of fruit and such substantial texture that you have to sit down, take time, and sip them while talking. They are inexpensive, too. I am sure there are dozens of other such wine-makers, for the discovering.

When wine-makers in the *crus* lack skills, or mastery, the taste of the grape stem gets into the wine. This is one of the few wine regions in the world (with a tiny number of exceptions, Château des Jacques in Moulin-à-Vent being one) where all the stems are left in with the fermenting wine. Most red-wine-makers, in France and round the globe, remove at least a proportion of the stems or stalks, for they can give vegetal, or leafy aromas – often, indeed, a woody taste, relating directly to the hardened stalk. I used to think that the special character in the aroma of many northern Beaujolais *crus* related to the old wooden tuns in which many partly age, but now believe that the dusty-woody character, which wipes out their fruitiness when young, generally relates to the grape-stalks. These wines need bottle-age – often a year or two – for this character to melt in with their fruitiness. The deftest wine-makers avoid this fault, no doubt by handling the bunches gently, and by manipulating the must with extreme care.

So, as we see, it is the methods of wine-making, not the Gamay grape alone, which give Beaujolais wines their variety and character. It should be added that the Beaujolais climate suits the grape ideally. To obtain wine of mouth-watering freshness, the grapes are picked just before ripeness. A natural alcoholic degree of 10–11°, allied to six grams of acidity, is a good balance; when a hot year produces natural degrees of 11° 5 and acidities of five grams or less, some growers will acidify the wines with tartaric acid to redress the balance. And of course in years of imperfect ripeness, growers add sugar.

Abuses with over-chaptalization have for long been common in this region. Highish alcoholic content is a great hider of other defects, and until recently it was not uncommon for *négociants* to be frankly uninterested by a Beaujolais-Villages grower wishing to sell wine rating less than 13°. Adherents of certain co-operatives used to drive their trailers up to the cellar, at vintage time, with the sugar bags lying on top of the fruit, ready to be poured straight in; for it was a serious logistical problem for co-operatives to buy in, and stock, sufficient tons of sugar for the harvest, and particularly problematical when the quantities they needed went far beyond what the law allowed. Since the discovery of a way of analysing fraudulent chaptalization (by a method called nuclear resonance) co-operatives and wine-makers have been moving slowly towards the legal lines, dimly aware, no doubt, that one day the inspectors of the fraud squad might loosen their barking, sharp-toothed dogs on them, unless some progress could be seen. We now have *maximum* alcohol levels for all the categories of Beaujolais *appellations*, this being designed to discourage sugar-abusers. Sugar-abuse relates principally to vineyards where the yields have got out of control, for limited chaptalization is so much a part of the Beaujolais formula it would be commercially suicidal to attempt to eliminate it. Gamay and sugar go together like bees and honey.

What happens with sugaring and acidifying, and what is legal, do not yet hang together, but the extremes are getting closer. In the Quality Charter of Sicarex-Beaujolais,[6] no secret is made of the fact that current regulations (which authorize an enrichment of 2° alcohol, while excluding acidification, if sugaring has taken place) are 'unsuitable' (*inadaptée*). 'Discussions under way permit the hope that norms may be established which are in line with technical realities', states the ever-practical Sicarex.

The countryside

The visitor to the Beaujolais discovers a countryside which is very different from northern Burgundy. Water is found in many places, so farms and manor-houses are spread regularly over the countryside, vineyards and people being cheek by jowl. Each village has clusters of hamlets around it. There are islands of woodland in the vines, meadows in the valleys, lollipop trees and red-roofed houses in a story-book landscape; a mixed agricultural economy, with a high population density. It is one immense village submerged in a vast vineyard, cut by countless twisting up-and-down roads, the hand of man evident wherever you look.

Up in the hills above Chiroubles, or in the vast amphitheatre of vines around Vauxrenard, horses still hoe between the rows on the steep slopes. Wild purple lupins grow from rock outcrops and

6 *Terroir + Savoir-Faire = Qualité – La Vinification Beaujolaise, Les Améliorations de la Vendange*, Sheet 10/p. 6, distributed by l'Union Viticole du Beaujolais, UVB, Villefranche-sur-Saône, 1992.

the roadside verges in June. One rounds a corner and comes upon a green woodpecker standing with its beak in the air, or a hoopoe feeding in the long grass. One reaches a hilltop to find oneself fifty feet from a circling black-and-white flecked buzzard; on another crest, a helicopter spraying at eye-level.

'Southern Burgundy is a jigsaw of plains, basins, hills and dissymmetric slopes', wrote Dr J. Guyot in 1868. The vineyards of the Beaujolais are to be found on a wide variety of bedrocks, dating from the primary to the tertiary eras. It can be divided into three parts: the Haut-Beaujolais, the Bas-Beaujolais and the valley of the Saône.

The Haut-Beaujolais is a chain of hills with steep slopes, cut by east–west valleys, running from Saint-Amour in the north to the level of Villefranche in the south. The soil is acid, sandy and made up of permeable schists derived from the granite rock, relatively easy to work. The Bas-Beaujolais begins after the valley of the Nizerand, which flows into the Saône at Villefranche. It is of lower altitude, its soil clay and limestone, richer and deeper. This area used to be known as the Beaujolais-Bâtard, its wines rated below those of the north. The rating is unchanged, but the name is now Beaujolais des Pierres Dorées, from its ochre limestone houses. The third part, the valley of the Saône, has tertiary and quaternary soils. Less rained on and hotter than the hillsides, it is subject to brusque changes of temperature owing to the north–south winds, and is unsuitable for viticulture.

There are, of course, local soil variations in the wine-producing villages. In Odenas (Brouilly AC) or Saint-Etienne-la-Varenne (Beaujolais-Villages AC) one may find granite, in Juliénas schists, in Frontenas (Beaujolais AC) pebbles, in Theizé (Beaujolais AC) pebbles too, but also sandstone and various limestones. The soil plays its part in the vegetative cycle; sandy granite soils, for instance, delay the opening of the buds.

One vine dominates the region, covering 98 per cent of the vineyard area: the Gamay Beaujolais. P. Galet gives its synonyms: Gamay *noir à jus blanc*, Petit Gamai, Gamay *rond*, Bourguignon *noir*. It is a productive vine, all its buds being fertile, giving a satisfactory harvest even after spring frosts, for the shoots come a second time. The bunches are compact and cylindrical and subject to grey rot. It is planted at a density of 9,000 to 10,000 plants per hectare. Short pruning is the classic method in the Beaujolais, with the vine trained to a goblet or fan shape. Each vine has three to five horns, carrying two fruit-bearing eyes per shoot, the maximum permitted total being twelve. Long pruning (Guyot) is permitted for Beaujolais AC, as is a mixed system featuring a long fruit-bearing shoot and one to five shorter canes, each bearing two fertile buds. These tend to speed up the vegetative cycle slightly.

One cannot fully taste of the Beaujolais if one knows nothing about *vigneronnage*, says Georges Duboeuf in his book[7] – and he is surely right. It is similar to *métayage* (crop-sharing) in the Côte d'Or, and a very ancient way of running vineyards, but much more widespread in Beaujolais than in northern Burgundy. The landlord does not work his own land, he has an agreement with a vigneron to cultivate the vines; they make the wine together, then share it fifty-fifty. In a typical *vigneronnage*, the proprietor has to pay for all planting and replanting costs, for wine-making equipment, and a sum towards harvesting costs ('a full day's vintaging for each barrel of wine due back'), the wine due back being half the crop. Worker and landowner prosper, or become impoverished, together. It is very common in big Beaujolais properties to find six, ten or more vignerons vinifying under one roof, with the owner involved, alongside. This is a democratic, co-operative effort, and the pervasive presence of *vigneronnage* throughout the region has undoubtedly contributed to the softening of class structures that one cannot fail to notice, after a period further north, if one spends time in the Beaujolais and observes the way social groups relate.

Vines and clonal selection

Research has been under way since 1960 to discover by clonal selection the most suitable types of Gamay for replanting in the Beaujolais, as we saw in the chapter on vines and viticulture. Sicarex-Beaujolais in Villefranche is responsible, overseeing its own experimental plots at Liergues and Jarnioux, and others spread around the vineyard area on individual domaines. Multiplication of 'satisfactory' clones of Gamay began in 1977, the object being the eventual renewal of the 40,000 hectares (half of it in the Beaujolais) of Gamay vineyards in France. Six clones (Nos. 509, 358, 222, 282,

---

7 Georges Duboeuf and Henri Elwing, *Beaujolais, vin du citoyen*, Jean-Claude Lattès, Poitiers, 1989.

656 and 787) are now likely to account for 80 per cent of the replanting. The early releases included high-yielders, and when these were matched with vigorous root-stocks, such as SO4, the excessive fruit production did nothing to bind consumers to the wines of Beaujolais.

The most important root-stock in the northern Beaujolais is the Vialla, said to be the sole descendant of a Labrusca vine which survived the phylloxera. It has a remarkable affinity with the Gamay, and thrives in granite soils. Other root-stocks are used in the Bas-Beaujolais, most of which we have already met in the Côte d'Or – the all-purpose 3309C, the SO4, the 101–14, and a new one called 420A, a *Berlandieri* × *Riparia* cross, which is suitable for pebbly granite soils above a certain altitude. It is also found above 350 metres on the terraces of Chiroubles, Regnié and Villié-Morgon.

Who makes and trades the wines

Co-operatives vinified a mere 28 per cent of the 1993 harvest in the Beaujolais, so are much less dominant than in the Mâconnais. Seven date back to the period 1929–34: Chiroubles, Liergues, Quincié, Saint-Jean d'Ardières, Fleurie, Gleizé and Chônas, the remainder having been founded between 1954 and 1961: Lachassagne, Sain-Bel, Létra, Saint-Vérand, Saint-Etienne-des-Oullières, Bully, Le Bois d'Oingt, Le Perréon, Saint-Laurent, Juliénas and Theizé. In respect of the 1993 harvest, they produced 37 per cent of the AC Beaujolais, 22 per cent of Beaujolais-Villages and 17 per cent of the *crus*, according to the *Fédération des Caves Coopératives* in Villefranche. Nearly a third of the Beaujolais and Beaujolais-Villages 1993 sold as Nouveau came from them.

Seventy per cent of the Beaujolais region's wines are made by around four thousand medium-sized, family concerns, cultivating 5 to 10 hectares. There is very little foreign investment in vineyards, and the local wine trade, too, is almost entirely in French hands, though the Swiss, who are the most important export customers, have footholds.

The tendency for growers to cut out their local merchants is one that can be observed in every vineyard area of France, but it has not attained proportions in the Beaujolais comparable to those in the Côte d'Or. Beaujolais merchants are more agile than the north

Burgundians. They work on smaller margins, have less obligation to finance stocks, and provide the important service of making reliable styles of wine available in quantity throughout the year.

A well-balanced Beaujolais might be a blend of three wines: something supple and fruity from Saint-Etienne-des-Oullières; a *cuvée* from Marchampt or Beaujeu to bring body and staying power, and a Saint-Julien wine, from the borders of the Beaujolais-Villages, to bring fatness. In the early part of the year the merchant may try to ship his wines from Le Perréon or Blacé, which can make excellent Primeurs; if he is exporting, he may draw stocks from Vauxrenard for their staying power, or Emeringes for their colour. If he must keep within a price he will go to the marginal zones to the south and north, particularly the Beaujolais des Pierres Dorées.

A study by UIVB relating to 1991/2 shows that direct sales between producers and private customers, restaurants or retailers accounted for just under 15 per cent of all Beaujolais wines. Only 9 per cent of Beaujolais AC is sold directly by the growers, and just over 12 per cent Beaujolais-Villages. In Fleurie, where there is an important co-operative and buoyant international demand through the trade, direct sales accounted for less than 14 per cent of the *appellation*. However, the proportion has climbed inexorably in other *crus* over the last fifteen years, Côte de Brouilly now despatching 42 per cent of its harvest directly, Morgon 36 per cent, Chénas and Chiroubles both over a third.

The Villefranche wine show

Each year, the *Concours des deux bouteilles* in Villefranche in early December is a key moment for the young vintage to be assessed by growers and traders, prizes being given in each *appellation* for the finest showings at that time.

No notes are made by tasters, but it is fast, friendly, instructive and effective. Bottles are disguised with a sheet of purple tissue paper, secured by two rubber bands, to be torn off to reveal the winners and losers as soon as the tasters have discussed and pronounced. Three thousand samples are assessed by 900 tasters in a couple of hours: this is a group activity, a working party. In the Beaujolais culture, *négociants* rub shoulders easily with growers, and here everyone tastes together standing up, so no time is wasted. Three lines of bottles get formed, to arrive at a result. Good bottles go in the front line, less good behind, with a third row for dogs. You retaste the ones in front, agree a Number One, then off come the wraps, agreement having been achieved by grunts, whispers and plenty of discussion.

Beaujolais Nouveau

Which are the good years? It is easy to work out, Duboeuf explains in *Beaujolais, vin du citoyen*. You need to know when the vine flowered, to add on a hundred days for the grapes to ripen, plus five days for wine-making, twenty to thirty days to finish the process, and ten days for bottling; so around five months between flowering and the third Thursday of November. If the flowering was late, and the sun slow to do its ripening work during the summer, growers have to pick *before the grapes are ripe*, in order to have something ready on the third Thursday, which means more sugar into the vats than is good for balance.

It sounds as if the release day ought to be pushed back, if the flowering is late, but growers and traders do not like this idea, fearful of missing their sell-by date. Here, surely, is one reason why Beaujolais Nouveau has lost respect.

Here too, yields are the crux

Georges Duboeuf puts his finger down firmly on the page, again and again, with details of excess yields.[8] 'The true danger for Beaujolais is . . . too much indifferent wine', he writes. In Beaujolais, with new clones and over-fertile root-stocks these yields have hit 99 hectolitres per hectare. We can be sure he has tasted vats holding three-figure yields, but is too circumspect, or too tactful, to name the names.

In 1976, he shows us, the average yield was 48.65 hl/ha. Ten years later it was 63.12 hl/ha. Of course, some increase relates quite properly to improved methods of cultivating and protecting the vines. But he comments, 'Clonal selection (which is inestimably beneficial to viticulture) was originally conceived to maintain or improve quality. If stupidly used to increase quantity, will it become a curse?' From the pages of his book he speaks directly to Beau-

8 *Beaujolais, vin du citoyen*, pp. 33, 52, 67, 74, 87, 94, 100, 146.

jolais growers: '*Vigneron beaujolais*, beware the disappointed consumer!'

Cracking the Beaujolais problem

Unless one takes the trouble to scratch below the surface of the Beaujolais it is easy to see nothing but a region dominated by Duboeuf (see below), or by co-operatives, or by *négociants*, and to make a superficial judgement, thinking that beyond these power blocks there is nothing but a mass of disappointing wine. It is true that millions of disappointing bottles get sold each year (though to their credit, they are often cheap and soft). But if one treats the area as a source of fine wine, and is prepared to pay 5 or 10 per cent above base prices, there are millions of other, lovely bottles to be found. The buying job must be done properly, that is all.

SPECIALIST BEAUJOLAIS AND MÂCONNAIS MERCHANTS

LES VINS GABRIEL ALIGNE

Gabriel Aligne et Alain Béraud, La Chevalière, 69430 Beaujeu

AUJOUX

Swiss-owned for many years, and amongst the half dozen largest Beaujolais firms, Aujoux deals mainly with Switzerland, the largest export market for Beaujolais.

PAUL BEAUDET (1869)

This small firm, a stone's throw from Loron and Thorin, is now directed by Etienne Akar, who came into wine trading from Ford Tractor marketing aged forty-seven. It is currently more successful with Beaujolais reds than white Mâcons, I think.

Paul Beaudet, place de la Gare, 71570 Pontanevaux

CELLIER DES SAMSONS

Ten co-operative cellars (previously known as PDVB) have grouped
together near Beaujeu, to pool the services of three oenologists,
with central facilities for storage, bottling, marketing and export.
They cover the Beaujolais from north to south, and include some of
the best co-operatives in the *crus*: Juliénas, Fleurie, Chiroubles,
Saint-Etienne-des-Oullières, Le Perréon, Saint-Julien, Liergues,
Lachassagne, Bois d'Oingt and Bel-Air.
Cellier des Samsons, Pont des Samsons, 69430 Quincié-en-Beaujolais

CHAMPCLOS (1974)

This firm's owner, SDVF of Bordeaux, went into receivership in
1994. Champclos has been built up over two decades as a Beaujolais specialist, handling a full range of domaine-bottled *crus*, as
well as Beaujolais and Beaujolais-Villages bottled with their estate
names.
Robert Félizzato, BP 164, route de Beaujeu, 69823 Belleville

E. CHEVALIER ET FILS, SA

Best known for its sparkling wines, this firm was bought by J.-C.
Boisset in 1994. Here may also be found wines from the family-
owned property Clos des Tournons (Mâcon-Villages 4 ha., Mâcon
rouge 3 ha., Bourgogne Pinot Noir 2 ha.), and these estates: Beau-
jolais-Villages Domaine de l'Ecussol, Château de Thulon, Regnié
Domaine de Chastys, Morgon La Grange Cochard, Moulin-à-Vent,
Domaine des Quatre Filles, Saint-Amour Domaine de Lucie.
Jean Chevalier, 'Les Tournons', 71850 Charnay-lès-Mâcon

COLLIN BOURISSET, SA

This firm distributes the wines of two estates: the Domaine des
Hospices de Romanèche-Thorins (Moulin-à-Vent des Hospices 6.5
ha.) and Domaine Bourisset (Moulin-à-Vent 5 ha.), both being
made for long-term ageing.
Paul Bourisset et Commission Administrative Des Hospices de

Romanèche-Thorins, Collin-Bourisset, Crèches, 71570 Roma-nèche-Thorins

T. DAVID ET L. FOILLARD

A large firm, mainly selling in bulk, whose wines have tended to lack charm for me. They distribute many wines (including the historic Château La Nerthe in Châteauneuf du Pape), three leading Beaujolais estates being Colonel Foillard's Domaine de la Dîme in Juliénas 5 ha., Moulin-à-Vent Domaine de la Pierre 8 ha., and Fleurie Chapelle des Bois 5 ha.

Jean-Louis Foillard, impasse du Moulin, 69830 Saint-Georges-en-Beaujolais

VINS DESSALLE, SA

I found this firm a valuable source for several years, on condition one could obtain early bottlings. Shortage of space meant that much of their stock was left in growers' vats, and wines bottled in or after the summer were rarely the equal of the spring bottlings. They have a 10 ha. estate (Beaujolais and Brouilly) and often show the domaine source of each *cru* on their labels (for instance Michel Tête's Juliénas, certain *cuvées* of which may also be had estate-bottled).

Sylvain Fessy, Les Villards, 69823 Belleville

LES VINS GEORGES DUBOEUF (1964)

In the 1950s, Georges Duboeuf's family were simply vignerons in Chaintré. Thirty years later, his name symbolizes Beaujolais more than any other. You rarely find his wines on supermarket shelves, but in top restaurants and specialist merchants. They often bear the name of the domaine whence they are drawn.

There is a 3 ha. Pouilly-Fuissé estate, and the firm distributes a large, often-changing range of wines exclusively, including: Morgon Jean Descombes, Fleurie Domaine des Quatre Vents, Chiroubles Château de Javernand, Beaujolais-Villages Château des Pierres, Beaujolais Château de Pierreux and Château de Nervers. But its main activity is the full range of Mâcon and Beaujolais *appellations*, cheerfully labelled and unsnobbishly promoted.

Amongst his grower suppliers (and perhaps this is one of the secrets of his success) there is no suspicion of the disdain sometimes shown by many Côte d'Or growers for their *négoçiant* customers. As one Duboeuf grower said to Chantal Lecouty,[9] 'Before Georges Duboeuf, let's be honest, Beaujolais growers often went hungry. He's not only promoted Beaujolais, he's also made us live.'

In June 1993 he inaugurated a spectacular wine theme-park (*Le Hameau du Vin*) in buildings adjoining his business, opposite Romanèche railway station. It is a wine museum, revamped with a touch of Disney, and features an electronic theatre, superb colour film of the Beaujolais fermentation process, and exhibits to take visitors through every phase of vine-growing and wine-tending. Wine may be tasted and bought at the end – books, and T-shirts too.

Growers know Georges Duboeuf is up at 5.30 a.m., and they can telephone him in his office by six. An unknown American importer is coming to taste at their domaine, does Duboeuf know anything about him? He finds out, letting the grower know if he is a slow payer, or thought to be sound, for instance.

As we have seen, many large properties are looked after on the *vigneronnage* principle, as at Château de Raousset, or Château de la Chaise. At vintage time, the many growers, along with the landowner, all vinify together in the same vat-house (known as a *cuvage* in the Beaujolais). They have tended their vines and grapes differently; now, being bound by how the estate is equipped (no cooling at the Institut Pasteur's Château Les Ravatys in Saint-Lager, for instance, or well set-up, as at the Château de Juliénas) the growers will make varying successes of the wine-making.

The trade buyer who rises before dawn and is walking up and down these rows of vats chatting, watching and sniffing, taking an option here, making a suggestion there, will be able to reserve some of the best wines in mid-fermentation. This is the key, I believe, to Duboeuf's success: good buying, regularly reviewed and revised. Others can do it, but no one does it better. He is Burgundy's greatest *négoçiant* buyer, indeed arguably the whole region's greatest *négoçiant*, if one considers how he consistently adds value to what he buys and sells, while encouraging and educating the producers to take their own decisions, fly their own colours, bask in some glory and reinvest. He is a *négoçiant* with a difference, in that he only

9 *Revue Vinicole Internationale*, February 1989.

works with Gamay Noir and Chardonnay from around Mâcon, not touching Pinot Noir, of course. But to stick to what one knows and is good at (like Etablissements Jean-Pierre Moueix of Libourne, for instance, which touches no white Bordeaux wine whatsoever, but is a master of the reds) is a recipe for success.

Duboeuf has woven his company into the fabric of the Beaujolais – into its restaurants, its co-operatives, its domaines, its homes – so that you find the threads wherever you go. And in the process, after modest beginnings as a contract bottler and wine-broker, he has in thirty years built up the region's largest wine firm. The turnover of the business was around 500m fr. by 1990 and 1991 (over double that of Loron and Mommessin, then running second and third in the Beaujolais). Kriter-Patriarche was the only Burgundy business with larger volume sales (but Kriter is not a Burgundy, we should remember).

Georges Duboeuf is a master at getting his message to those who will repeat it or act on it. The Beaujolais message and the Duboeuf message are so intimately entwined that often he seems to be speaking simply for all the south Burgundians. He was born in 1933, his son Franck in 1960. When the generation change moves into gear – there is no sign of it yet – I am sure there will be a smooth transition, for Franck has shadowed his father through growers' homes and cellars from an early age, and must be surrounded by their goodwill.

Les Vins Georges Duboeuf, BP 12, 71570 Romanèche-Thorins

PIERRE DUPOND, SA (1860)

The family estate extends over 30 hectares, the vineyards being Beaujolais Domaine des Communes, Beaujolais-Villages Domaine de Boischampt, Brouilly Côtes de Nervers, Juliénas Domaine de Boischampt.

Hervé Dupond, 339 rue de Thizy, 69653 Villefranche

EVENTAIL DE VIGNERONS PRODUCTEURS

A different sort of co-operative, in that the growers make their wines at home, but have pooled their resources so that treatment, storage, bottling and dispatch take place from a central spot. Growers do not necessarily send all their best wines to Corcelles – some

are held back for domaine-bottling – but (I declare an interest, having often bought wine here) this can be an excellent-value source.
Eric Berthaud, Corcelles, 69220 Belleville

PIERRE FERRAUD ET FILS, SA

This small firm has a fine reputation amongst cognoscenti, but for me has never quite lived up to it when the wines have been tasted alongside its peers. Perhaps they are not trying to be best, but simply balanced and delicious, at which they certainly succeed. They own 15 ha. of vineyard, and handle many domaines exclusively, particularly: Fleurie, Clos des Garands and Château de Grand Pyre, Moulin-à-Vent GFA des Marquisats, Morgon Domaine de l'Evêque, Côte de Brouilly Domaine des Pavés Bleus and Brouilly Domaine Rolland.
Yves-Dominique Ferraud, 31 rue Maréchal Foch, 69220 Belleville

LORON ET FILS, ETABLISSEMENTS (1821)

Saint-Amour Domaine des Billards 14 ha., Juliénas Domaine de la Vieille Eglise 9 ha., Château de Fleurie 10 ha., Moulin-à-Vent Domaine Lémonon 9 ha.

The most influential (after Georges Duboeuf) company in the district, and a major buyer from many more leading estates than the family-controlled ones listed. Loron is a valuable – arguably the finest – link between volume buyers and the growers of Beaujolais and Mâconnais. They have done it for decades, back to when Etablissements Nicolas in Paris was a fine wine force to be seriously reckoned with, and Loron their Mâcon-Beaujolais broker. They have been an invisible giant, however, and are still often content to let leading Burgundian firms – Louis Jadot, for instance – draw away much of their finest stock. Whether it is Beaujolais Nouveau, the full range of *crus*, Pontanevaux-vinified *vin de table*, or top-sited Pouilly-Fuissé, Loron can source it, in large, dependable volumes.
Xavier Barbet et Jean-Marie Loron, Pontanevaux, 71570 La Chapelle-de-Guinchay

MOMMESSIN ET THORIN, SA

The Mommessin family firm was for long the third largest Beaujolais-Mâconnais shipper, after Duboeuf and Loron, and like them can be a very dependable source. With its 1994 absorption of Thorin (whose previous owner, the German firm Racke, retains a 35 per cent shareholding) it will have moved to second place. The Thorin premises are due to close, but the separate brands to be retained. Mommessin distributes the family estates Pouilly-Fuissé Domaine Bellenand à Solutré (3 ha.) and Moulin-à-Vent Domaine de Champ de Cour (7 ha., 'aged in new oak'). Thorin's best-known wine is the interesting Moulin-à-Vent Château des Jacques (q.v.). In the Côte de'Or, the Mommessins are exclusive owners of the *Grand Cru* Clos de Tart (see Morey-Saint-Denis).

Didier Mommessin et Patrice Noyelle, La Grange Saint-Pierre, 71850 Charnay-lès-Mâcon

JOSEPH PELLERIN (1912)

This is one of the largest Beaujolais firms after Duboeuf, Mommessin and Loron, and has been owned (along with Dourthe and Kressman of Bordeaux) by Bols Liqueurs, since 1990. 'Our role is as bottlers', it says, and does not subcontract this vital activity.

Franck Mignot et Philippe Dry, SNJP, BP 8, 69830 Saint-Georges de Reneins

PIAT, ETABLISSEMENTS
INTERNATIONAL DISTILLERS AND VINTNERS, FRANCE

This is Grand Metropolitan's main French wine-bottling base, now much associated with table wines. They handle hundreds of thousands of bottles of Piat d'Or, along with Beaujolais, other south Burgundy *appellations*, Rhône, and Bordeaux, for export to 80 countries. They have reduced their exclusive Beaujolais *crus* activity, but still handle Beaujolais-Villages Château Varennes on a sole basis.

Etablissement Piat, BP 10, 71570 La Chapelle de Guinchay

PAUL SAPIN
SAPIN-BROUSSELOUX, ETABLISSEMENTS

A small Beaujolais merchant whose estate consists of 12 ha. in the following *appellations*: Morgon Lathevalle and Ruyère, Regnié Les Futs and Le Cérisier, and various plots of Beaujolais-Villages and Beaujolais.
M. Emile Brousseloux, BP 1, 69821 Lancié-en-Beaujolais

SAVOUR CLUB (1964)

Europe's largest mail order fine wine distributor, this firm stocks wine from throughout France in its spacious Lancié cellars, dispatching a million cases a year to Belgian, German, Swiss and French consumers. Sixty per cent of what it sells is bottled in Lancié, where pallets are stacked eight high. Beaujolais represents 8 per cent of its trade, Burgundy a further 5 per cent.
Alain Richard, 69821 Lancié-en-Beaujolais

SOBEMAB

This stands for SOciété d'embouteillage BEaujolais MAconnais Bourgogne, Burgundy's largest contract bottler. An enormous quantity of wine bottles (30 million per year in Chânes, a further 10 million at the domaines) are filled by this company. It is strategically placed astride the Mâcon and Beaujolais districts, but their three mobile bottling plants (soon to be four, with the commissioning of a high-tech, computerized vehicle in 1994) are active in domaine courtyards all over Burgundy. The business began in 1968, with one mobile bottling lorry, settling in 71570 Chânes in 1973 (the postal code is significant, being sometimes the only clue to reveal the whereabouts of a bottling bearing a famous brand).

This firm is for people who prefer not to put their fingers in the glue, say those domaine-bottlers who would not dream of subcontracting such crucial links in the quality chain as stabilizing, filtering and bottling. But the service can sometimes be excellent, no doubt depending on what instructions are given to SOBEMAB, and to supervision on the day. It is now used by 75 Burgundian merchants, a dozen of them exclusively. Sarrau, Chanut, Jacques Dépagneux, Gobet, Vernaison, Compagnie des Vins d'Autrefois,

Piat for some *crus*, Champclos exclusively from January 1994 – these are just a few of the names who need SOBEMAB (see SVGC, below). Top growers also find the firm valuable – for instance Vincent and Luquet in Fuissé, when they expand beyond their own vineyard productions, and need storage, bottling and dispatch services for the wines they buy in from other growers.

Jean-Michel Roux, SOBEMAB, Cidex 514, 71570 Chânes

SVGC

The Société de Vente des Grands Crus was formed in 1992, grouping like-minded companies wishing to share administrative expenses and use SOBEMAB's 'modern, efficient hi-tech establishment'. The firms are Chanut Frères, Jacques Dépagneux, Gobet SA and Robert Sarrau, distributing family-owned domaines such as Chiroubles Château de Javernand 25 ha., Juliénas Château des Capitans 7 ha., Mâcon-Viré Clos du Chapitre 3 ha., and Beaujolais-Villages Domaine de la Chapelle de Vatre 8.5 ha., Jean-Michel Roux's estate: Juliénas Les Mouilles 3 ha., Fleurie Grand Pré 4 ha., and Morgon Château Gaillard 2 ha., and also a full range of Beaujolais *crus* and wines.

Jean Dépagneux, Les Chers, 69840 Juliénas

LES VINS LOUIS TÊTE

For me these wines have often missed the mark, seeming rather pale in colour and short-vatted, lacking the intensity of fruit which low yields would give. However, they are well thought of locally, so it is probably more a question of taste than quality. North Europeans need something more warming than do Mediterraneans. The firm distributes Beaujolais-Villages Château des Alouettes, and owns a 10 ha. domaine: Beaujolais-Villages (Lantigné), Regnié and Moulin-à-Vent.

Jean Tête, 69430 Saint-Didier-sur-Beaujeu

TRENEL FILS SA, ETABLISSEMENT

As well as holding fine Beaujolais and Mâconnais wine stocks, this small firm makes *liqueurs de petits fruits* (Crème de Cassis, de Framboise, etc.) and ages Marc de Bourgogne.

H. de Boissieu, Le Voisinet, BP 49, 71850 Charnay les Mâcon

The Villages, the Districts, and Some Growers of Beaujolais

SAINT-AMOUR

In 1991, there were 304 ha. of vineyard in production. Over the five vintages 1987–91 the average harvest was 16,500 hl.

Saint-Amour is a wine which holds up well in bottle, while often being highly drinkable when youthful. The price can sometimes be high, for the name is appealing and the production small. Some tasters detect odours of peach and raspberry on the nose.

A selection of Saint-Amour growers

DOMAINE DES DUC   27 ha. (65 per cent)

Saint-Amour 9.5 ha., Chénas 9.3 ha., Pouilly-Loché 0.58 ha., Beaujolais-Villages (*rouge*) 7.5 ha., (*blanc*) 0.4 ha., Beaujolais 0.6 ha.

There is a 40 per cent difference in the price between Chénas and Saint-Amour, relating not to quality but to renown. This estate may appear scruffy, but I have had good bottles from here.
Marie-Jo, Jacques, Claude et Laurent Duc, et Lucien Blanchard, La Piat, 71570 Saint-Amour-Bellevue

RAYMOND DURAND   3 ha. (70 per cent)

AOC Saint-Amour
Raymond Durand, En Paradis, 71570 Saint-Amour-Bellevue

JACQUES JANIN   8.5 ha. (30 per cent)
DOMAINE DES DARRÈZES

Saint-Amour 5.5 ha., Juliénas, Beaujolais-Villages
Jacques et Madeleine Janin, Le Bourg, 71570 Saint-Amour

DOMAINE DU MOULIN BERGER   10 ha. (10 per cent)

Saint-Amour 6.3 ha., Juliénas 2.7 ha., Beaujolais 1 ha.

Most of these wines have gone in bulk for bottling in Belgium and Switzerland, but taking the top Saint-Amour prize (for a per-

fectly balanced, exceptional wine, I thought) in Villefranche 1993 may encourage more home bottling.
Michel et Pascale Laplace, Le Moulin Berger, 71570 Saint-Amour

MME ANDRÉ POITEVIN   4.5 ha. (65 per cent)

Saint-Amour Clos de la Brosse 1.1 ha., Saint-Amour 3 ha., Beaujolais-Villages 0.32 ha.

This may be the oldest cellar in Saint-Amour, dating from 1399. The house stands on top of a rise, where the mail-coach used to pull in, on its way from Mâcon to Beaujeu. The best *cuvées* here are deep-coloured, well-structured and intensely full of fruitiness.
André Poitevin, La Diligence, 71570 Saint-Amour-Bellevue

PAUL SPAY   20 ha. (80 per cent)
DOMAINE DE LA CAVE LAMARTINE

Saint-Amour 14 ha., Juliénas 3 ha., Beaujolais-Villages Saint-Amour (*blanc*) 3 ha.

The white Saint-Amour is a rarity, but a rather undistinguished, tank-fermented wine, destined for rapid consumption by passing enthusiasts, like the reds, I suspect.
Paul et Bernadette Spay, place de l'Eglise, Le Bourg, 71131 Saint-Amour-Bellevue

JULIÉNAS

In 1991, there were 587 ha. of vineyard in production. Over the five vintages 1987–91 the average harvest was 33,200 hl.

The first Beaujolais is said to have been planted on this spot, and the name to hark back to Julius Caesar. The vineyards are high up on hillsides; like Saint-Amour the wine should be solidly built, and a good one evolves most interestingly with bottle age.

A selection of Juliénas growers

CHÂTEAU DU BOIS DE LA SALLE
CAVE DES PRODUCTEURS DE JULIÉNAS SICA

One of the best *cru* Beaujolais co-operatives, this groups over 250 vignerons, cultivating nearly 350 ha. situated mainly in Juliénas and Beaujolais-Villages, but also making Saint-Amour. About 10 per cent of the crop is bottled at the property.
Paul Audras, 69840 Juliénas

CHÂTEAU DE JULIÉNAS   50 ha.

Château de Juliénas and Les Chers, Les Bessets, La Ville, La Prat
This magnificent property's vines are mainly situated half-way up the Juliénas hillsides, in the centre of the *appellation*. They aim to bottle in May or June (the quantity varies from year to year) and produce wines that will keep.

'A good Beaujolais vat is shaped like an even-sided cube', says Condemine, in his spacious eighteenth-century press house, which used to have seven old presses lined down the middle. Today, each stainless steel vat is temperature controlled. Beneath are wonderful old cellars, whose floors follow the steep slope of the rock, 1745 being carved into the ends of the ashlared stone ribs which hold small barrels off the ground. There is not much small barrel-ageing here now, but that was how the wines used to be stored, no doubt. This is a private home, not a château one may visit, but it is perfectly possible to buy wine at the entrance gateway.

As I tasted a two-year-old Juliénas with Condemine *père*, he said, 'By the time it is ready, there will be none left.' It is hard, indeed, to resist drinking these wines, even though they will improve.
François et Thierry Condemine, au Château, 69840 Juliénas

DOMAINE JACQUES PERRACHON   25 ha. (40 per cent)
DOMAINE DE LA BOTTIÈRE
DOMAINE DES PERELLES
DOMAINE DES MOUILLES

Juliénas 11 ha., Moulin-à-Vent 7 ha., Morgon Les Versauds 2.3 ha., Beaujolais-Villages 4.2 ha.

There are several Perrachons here (and at Château Bonnet in Chénas), who have assembled some prime sites over the years.
Jacques, Laurent et Fabrice Perrachon, 69840 Juliénas

JEAN-MARC MONNET   5.5 ha. (50 per cent)
DOMAINE CHATAIGNIER-DURAND

Juliénas 4.5 ha., Chiroubles 0.5 ha., Saint-Véran 0.5 ha.

Monnet has taken on the vineyards of René Gonon, a much-loved, now-retired Juliénas grower (whose wines were served by Paul Bocuse and many other enthusiasts). Monnet also works land owned by the Château de Juliénas, and many of his wines are made in that fine vat-house. They are then partly aged in cement vat, partly in wooden tun.
Jean-Marc Monnet, Les Chers, 69840 Juliénas

MICHEL TÊTE   10 ha. (75 per cent)
DOMAINE DU CLOS DU FIEF

Juliénas 7 ha., Saint-Amour 1 ha., Beaujolais-Villages 2 ha.

Michel Tête recommends serving his three wines at different temperatures: 12° for Beaujolais-Villages, 14° for Saint-Amour, 17° for the Juliénas, the Cuvée Prestige of the latter (a blend from some of the best sites in the commune) being made for drinking when four to eight years old. Thermo-vinification may be used for the Beaujolais-Villages, traditional methods for the *crus*. I see that Duboeuf in his book raises the question (apropos of this grower) of whether Juliénas can be good with an alcohol level of less than 13–13.5°. If Michel Tête's customers demanded such wines, he could, I am sure, supply such needs.
Michel Tête, Les Gonnards, 69840 Juliénas

CHÉNAS

In 1991, there were 260 ha. of vineyard in production. Over the five vintages 1987–91 the average harvest was 15,000 hl.

As with the eight other original Beaujolais *crus*, at the time of the vintage Chénas wines may be declared (in other words, registered) under the *appellation contrôlée* Bourgogne *rouge*, if the grower so wishes; or later, they may be declassified from Chénas to that name. This has often been extremely useful to the north Burgundians, for well-structured north Beaujolais *crus*, such as Chénas, if blended with a weak-coloured but otherwise fine Pinot Noir, could quite legally bring much-needed fruit and richness to, say, a Bourgogne *rouge* blend. This role bolstering other wines has been detrimental to Chénas making much of a name for itself, and the word Chénas lacks the evocative or come-hither charm of neighbouring *crus*. The co-operative has at times produced weakling, fruitless *cuvées* which have not helped.

Many growers are turning to small oak barrels to bring interest to their bottles, and so long as these are then well-aged, pleasing wines can result. I think I prefer un-new-oaked Chénas like Champagnon's, however.

A selection of Chénas growers

CHÂTEAU BONNET   16 ha. (80 per cent)

Chénas 11 ha., Moulin-à-Vent 2 ha., Juliénas 2 ha., Beaujolais (*blanc*) 0.5 ha.
Pierre et Pierre-Yves Perrachon, Les Paquelets, 71570 La Chapelle de Guinchay

DOMAINE CHAMPAGNON   15 ha. (35 per cent)

Chénas 9.45 ha., Moulin-à-Vent 3 ha., Fleurie 1 ha.
   Three-quarters of the commune of Chénas has right to the *appellation* Moulin-à-Vent, so Chénas is rather the poor relation. This, however, can be a wonderful Chénas source, the wines richly textured.
Louis-Patrick, Jean-Yves et Louis Champagnon, Les Brureaux, Chénas, 69840 Juliénas

FERNAND CHARVET   7 ha. (50 per cent)
DOMAINE DES VIELLES CAVES

Moulin-à-Vent 4.5 ha., Chénas 2.5 ha.
Le Bourg, 69840 Chénas

DOMAINE DESVIGNES 13 ha. (20 per cent)
CHÂTEAU DES JEAN LORON

Chénas 13 ha.

Chénas is like a sheaf of flowers in a velvet basket, so Monsieur Desvignes would have us know. His family have owned this property since 1816.

Gabriel Desvignes, Château des Jean Loron, 71570 La Chapelle de Guinchay

DOMAINE HUBERT LAPIERRE 7.5 ha. (70 per cent)

Chénas 4.1 ha., Moulin à Vent 3.4 ha.

Hubert Lapierre has been bottling since 1977, and doubled the size of his estate in 1989 (by withdrawing vineyards from the cooperative). He uses wooden grids to hold the skins submerged, for each *appellation* making a standard, and an old vines, *cuvée*, with, in addition, a Chénas *cuvée* part-aged in small oak barrels, partly new. Concerning the new-oak wine, 'my clients are split down the middle. Some do not want to hear of it, some like it. It's yes or no.' The wine needs to be four or more years old for harmony to be achieved.

Hubert Lapierre, Les Gandelins, 71570 La Chapelle de Guinchay

SANTÉ PÈRE ET FILS 8 ha. (80 per cent)

Chénas 4 ha., Juliénas 3 ha., Moulin-à-Vent 1 ha.
Bernard et Jean-Louis Santé, 71570 La Chapelle de Guinchay

GEORGES TRICHARD 14 ha. (100 per cent)
DOMAINE DES PIERRES

Saint-Amour Domaine Les Pierres 5.5 ha., Saint-Amour 3.3 ha., Chénas 2.8 ha., Beaujolais-Villages 1.9 ha.

We are in capable hands at this professionally run estate, which includes vineyards previously owned by Prime Minister Balladur. Trichard's son is presently an oenologist at Champagne Perrier-Jouët.

Georges Trichard, route de Juliénas, 71570 La Chapelle de Guinchay

MOULIN-À-VENT

In 1991, there were 644 ha. of vineyard in production. Over the five vintages 1987–91 the average harvest was 35,400 hl.

One should follow the signs from the main road in Romanèche, uphill to the windmill, park, climb up to the little monument, and gaze around. It stands on a hill-prow, in the centre of a broad amphitheatre of vines, quite evidently a wine-making hub.

But the windmill has lost its sails, just as the *appellation* Moulin-à-Vent has lost its pre-eminence. These brown, manganese-rich slopes can produce deep-coloured red wines, both lean and concentrated in their fruitiness. Traditional wine-making methods include a submerging of the hat of grape skins by the use of wooden grids at the top of the vats, accentuating richness of flavour and the tannin-content of the wines. When made this way, Moulin-à-Vent needs several years for the tannins to soften, which in the Nouveau-dominated Beaujolais culture which has held a whip-hand over the region since 1985 few people are prepared to allow. The fashionable, and most expensive, wine has become Fleurie. In spite of the outstanding potential of most of its territory (not everything classified Moulin-à-Vent is of equal quality; there are heavy-cropping lands down towards Romanèche) the wine is misunderstood and often mismade. The truncated body of the windmill is like the stubby body of a rare moth, stripped of its colourful wings.

Moulin-à-Vent was first mentioned as recently as 1757 – and the wine was being exported. Four hogsheads were sold, for dispatch to Namur, Belgium, at a price of 112 francs *la botte*. Export markets, surely, are where its prosperity could lie again, but it would need long-term grower and merchant commitment to re-establish the idea of its originality.

A selection of Moulin-à-Vent growers

CHÂTEAU DU MOULIN-À-VENT   31 ha. (10 per cent)
FAMILLE BLOUD PROPRIÉTAIRE

Moulin-à-Vent 30 ha., Beaujolais-Villages 1.5 ha.

The aim here appears to be tender and fruity wines which will last. More than eight days' vatting would give wines which would be too astringent, the owner feels. A high proportion of the wines are aged in small barrels, with no excesses of new wood, but somehow without achieving outstanding results. Given how little they bottle at the estate, do they stringently select their greatest vats for the château label, or do local buyers carry them off, I wonder? This is fine Gamay Noir, aged in small cooperage, no more no less.

Mme Flornoy, Château du Moulin-à-Vent, 71580 Romanèche-Thorins

DOMAINE BOURISSET   11.5 ha. (100 per cent)
MOULIN-À-VENT DES HOSPICES

Moulin-à-Vent Domaine des Hospices 6.5 ha., Domaine Bourisset 5 ha.

These concentrated Moulin-à-Vents, offered through Colin-Bourrisset in Crèches (q.v.) are well worth seeking out.

Paul Bourisset, Commission Administrative des Hospices de Romanèche-Thorins, 71570 Romanèche-Thorins

DOMAINE DE LA BRUYÈRE   9 ha. (80 per cent)
R. ET M. SIFFERT

Moulin-à-Vent 9 ha.

Raymond et Michel Siffert, La Bruyère, Romanèche-Thorins

DOMAINE DIOCHON   7 ha. (80 per cent)

Moulin-à-Vent Burdelines 0.5 ha., Moulin-à-Vent 5 ha., Fleurie 0.5 ha., Beaujolais-Villages 1 ha.

This estate fines with egg-whites, then bottles without use of filter-pads. Most of the wine is sold in France, but America, England and Ireland account for a proportion.

Bernard Diochon, Le Moulin-à-Vent, 71570 Romanèche-Thorins

PAUL JANIN   10 ha. (90 per cent)
DOMAINE DES VIGNES DU TREMBLAY
DOMAINE DES JUMEAUX

Moulin-à-Vent 6.5 ha., Beaujolais-Villages 3.5 ha.
   Monsieur Janin claims an average age of 60 years for the vines of
his property.
Paul Janin, 'La Chanillière', 71570 Romanèche-Thorins

JACKY JANODET   7.5 ha. (30 per cent)

Moulin-à-Vent 4 ha., Morgon 2.3 ha., Beaujolais-Villages 1 ha.,
Beaujolais *blanc* 0.2 ha.
   Janodet makes sumptuous wines, his Beaujolais-Villages (from
the commune of Romanèche-Thorins) seeming the equal of several
crus – and priced accordingly. If I were choosing to lay down
Moulin-à-Vent, this would be one of my first stops.
Jacky Janodet, Les Garniers, 71570 Romanèche-Thorins

CHÂTEAU PORTIER   29 ha. (70 per cent)
HÉRITIERS MICHEL GAIDON

Moulin-à-Vent Champ de Cours et Clos des Maréchauds 12 ha.,
Fleurie Les Moriers 8 ha., Chiroubles 6 ha., Beaujolais-Villages 1.5
ha., Beaujolais 0.6 ha.
Mme Pahud et Mme Reynier, rue Notre Dame, 21200 Beaune

CHÂTEAU DES JACQUES   50 ha. (80 per cent)

Moulin-à-Vent 40 ha., Grand Clos de Loyse Beaujolais *blanc*
(previously Château de Loyse) 10 ha.
   Jean-Paul Thorin's family claims to have been present at Moulin-
à-Vent for nearly fifteen centuries. Until the mid-1970s they owned
substantial Côte d'Or vineyards, and this may explain why unusual
methods of wine-making pertain here. The Gamay grapes are de-
stalked and squashed, then ferment for 12 days in 130 hl vats (twice
the normal size in Beaujolais). Each vat has a pump for must-
recycling, and a sprinkler to keep the hat of skins damp. The wine is
then aged in wine-rinsed Tronçais small oak casks (half, or more,
renewed each year) for 4–5 months. Some Beaujolais growers tell

you that de-stalking is illegal, but this is true of Beaujolais-Villages, not of the *crus* which, as we have seen, may be declared as, or declassified to, Bourgogne *rouge* AC.

The Beaujolais *blanc* Chardonnays are hand-picked and pneu-matically whole-bunch pressed, then fermented and aged in steel. The ripest wines are estate-bottled, the less ripe being sold in bulk to Switzerland. This is a dependable, balanced white wine which one may confidently buy for drinking as soon as one sees it. The Château des Jacques reds need to be three – better still, four – years past their vintage-dates, when they become rich, harmonious, delicious red Burgundies. There is nothing stalky or grassy about the aromas of these wines.

Jean-Paul Thorin et Michel Sauzey, Château des Jacques, 71570 Romanèche-Thorins

FLEURIE

In 1991, there were 819 ha. of vineyard in production. Over the five vintages 1987–91 the average harvest was 45,100 hl.

Easy to pronounce, attractive to drink yet holding up stoutly in bottle, with one of the largest productions of the nine top growths – Fleurie has many advantages. The wine makes approachable drinking for newcomers, and has a richness and harmony which can entirely satisfy the knowledgeable.

A selection of Fleurie growers

DOMAINE BERROD   22 ha. (70 per cent)

Fleurie La Madone 1.5 ha., Fleurie 6.5 ha., Moulin-à-Vent 7 ha., Beaujolais-Villages 7 ha.

Deeply-coloured, often well-structured wines here, which if served blind to an unwary Burgundian from Pinot country can cause much astonishment and dismay: 'It is not possible you can make wines like this from Gamay.' But it *is*. These vat-rooms are extremely well equipped, temperature-controlled throughout. The Moulin-à-Vent ages in small barrels, and can taste markedly oaky until bottle-aged two or three years.

René, Roland et André Berrod et Christian Ruet, Les Roches du Vivier, 69820 Fleurie

CAVE DES PRODUCTEURS DE FLEURIE 400 ha.

Fleurie, Morgon, Moulin-à-Vent, Regnié, Chiroubles, Beaujolais-Villages, Beaujolais
This is a well respected co-operative, vinifying 30 per cent of the *appellation* Fleurie, selling mostly in bulk to local bottlers.
Cave Coopérative de Fleurie, BP 2, 69820 Fleurie

JEAN-PAUL CHAMPAGNON 10 ha. (50 per cent)

Fleurie Les Roches 0.5 ha., Fleurie 9.5 ha.
Champagnon married a Miss Berrod; this is a label one may regularly see in French restaurants, and order with enthusiasm.
Jean-Paul Champagnon, La Treille, 69820 Fleurie

MICHEL CHIGNARD 8 ha. (100 per cent)

Fleurie Les Moriers, Fleurie
This is a well-established estate-bottler making delicious wines, with overseas customers, decent restaurants and a private clientèle.
Michel Chignard, Le Point du Jour, 69820 Fleurie

M. DARROZE 15 ha. (30 per cent)
CLOS DES QUATRE VENTS
DOMAINE DES QUATRE VENTS

Fleurie Clos des Quatre Vents 10 ha., Domaine des Quatre Vents 5 ha.
M. Darroze has been a two-customer man for 35 years, he says: M. Bujard at Lutry in Switzerland, and Georges Duboeuf.
M. Darroze, 69820 Fleurie

GUY DEPARDON   7.5 ha. (50 per cent)
DOMAINE DU POINT DU JOUR

Fleurie Clos du Point du Jour (Monopole) 1.3 ha., Fleurie 4.2 ha., Brouilly 1.5 ha., Morgon 0.5 ha.

'I've worked with Duboeuf for twenty-seven years', says Depardon, 'without a contract. Word of mouth.' Fleurie no longer comes cheaply, but here we may be sure of a delicious one. These wines are silky, supple, never thin. You clap your tongue around them.
Guy Depardon, Le Point du Jour, 69820 Fleurie

DOMAINE DE LA GRAND' COUR   11 ha. (65 per cent)
SOCIÉTÉ DUTRAIVE

Fleurie Chapelle des Bois 5 ha., Fleurie Champagne 4.5 ha., Brouilly 1.5 ha.
Jean-Louis et Jean Dutraive, 69820 Fleurie

DOMAINE MONROZIER   8.3 ha. (10 per cent)

Fleurie and Moulin-à-Vent
  Most of these wines go for bottling in Switzerland.
Régis Monrozier, Les Moriers, 69820 Fleurie

FERNAND VERPOIX   9 ha. (100 per cent)

Fleurie Clos de la Chapelle des Bois 4 ha., Fleurie Champagne 5 ha.
  These wines do not have Fleurie's most magical succulence, but they are deeply-coloured and taste most impressive in a line-up.
Fernand Verpoix, 69820 Fleurie

CHIROUBLES

In 1991, there were 396 ha. of vineyard in production. Over the five vintages 1987–91 the average harvest was 19,500 hl.
  The area under vines (and consequently the production) of Chiroubles has increased by a quarter over the last fifteen years, so the wine no longer has quite the scarcity value it used to have. For a

time it was always in demand in France, and one of the first communes each year to sell out at grower's level.

Chiroubles, for me, has sometimes been the least satisfactory Beaujolais *cru*. Expensive – owing to rarity – but often rather over-sugared. These terraces are so high, no doubt maturity often comes late (or barely). A good Chiroubles, however, is the very essence of what fine Beaujolais is all about, with an intensity of fruit and a piercing freshness which can be magically revitalizing. The co-operative is often a superb source.

A selection of Chiroubles growers

DOMAINE CHEYSSON   26 ha. (70 per cent)
DOMAINE EMILE CHEYSSON

Chiroubles 26 ha.

This is one of the largest estates in the village, and a leading domaine-bottler, but has not been my favourite source for Chiroubles of intense, bright, concentrated fruitiness.

Jean-Pierre Large, Régisseur, Clos Les Farges, Le Bourg, 69115 Chiroubles

LA MAISON DES VIGNERONS

The village co-operative makes some wonderful wines, and not just Chiroubles. There are also outstanding Morgon, Regnié, Beaujolais-Villages and small quantities of other *crus*.

Cave Coopérative, 69115 Chiroubles

MÉZIAT PÈRE ET FILS   10.5 ha. (80 per cent)
DOMAINE DE LA COMBE AU LOUP

Chiroubles 3 ha., Regnié 3 ha., Morgon 0.5 ha., Beaujolais-Villages Cuvée de l'Oisillon 3.5 ha., Beaujolais 0.5 ha.

There are several Méziat estates; Gérard-Roger's wines are the ones I have found most consistently delicious. His father Albert Méziat was one of the forerunner Beaujolais domaine-bottlers, a member of the Duboeuf-animated growers' marketing group L'Ecrin Mâconnais-Beaujolais in the late 1950s.

The wines today are aromatic, long-flavoured, and light-handedly complex.

Gérard-Roger et David Méziat, 69115 Chiroubles

ALAIN PASSOT   8.5 ha. (80 per cent)
DOMAINE DE LA GROSSE PIERRE

Chiroubles 7 ha., Fleurie 0.7 ha., Beaujolais-Villages 0.7 ha.

This couple used to send their wines to market via Eventail des Vignerons-Producteurs in Corcelles, but increasingly domaine-bottle the best of their production. The wines are intensely fruity, pungent and rich.

M. et Mme Alain Passot, 69115 Chiroubles

CHÂTEAU DE RAOUSSET   38 ha. (30 per cent)
DOMAINE DE RAOUSSET
VIGNERONNAGE DE GRILLE-MIDI

Chiroubles 16 ha., Fleurie 11.5 ha., Morgon 10.5 ha.

One of the major Chiroubles estates, the quality varying according to the way vines and vats are tended by the different vignerons responsible. Jacky Passot's wines from these vineyards can be outstanding.

Gilles Bouillard, Régisseur, Château de Raousset, 69115 Chiroubles

HÉRITIERS COMTE DE RAOUSSET   6 ha. (50 per cent)
CHÂTEAU DE RAOUSSET

Chiroubles 4 ha., Morgon 1.7 ha., Fleurie 0.3 ha.

Since 1989 two of the Raousset heirs have pursued a separate path, the wines being offered from across the road, although all are vinified and bottled at the château, by different vignerons. It adds up to a lot of choices each vintage, under the Raousset name.

Rémy Passot, en face Château de Raousset, 69115 Chiroubles

MORGON

In 1991, there were 1,108 ha. of vineyard in production. Over the five vintages 1987–91 the average harvest was 61,500 hl.

With Brouilly, this is the largest production of the ten growths. Morgon comes from hillside vineyards between Fleurie and Brouilly, giving richer, more structured wines than either. Locals tells us that its particular character comes from the disintegrating schists on which it grows. This is one of the key sources of *cru* Beaujolais, for in any vintage one may choose from around 1,200 different Morgon *cuvées*; each year some seven million bottles are produced, by 250 growers.

When young, the wines may lack the spark and piercing fruit of a top Chiroubles, or the concentrated, mouth-coating firmness of a good Côte de Brouilly. One *may* drink them young, but the best, I think, need a year or so's bottle age. Then they have a texture such as when you run your fingers over the green baize of a billiard cloth, feeling the slate beneath. This is not velvet, nor the opulence of a deep-piled oriental rug, but their palpable texture and complex flavours may be enjoyed without undue expense. There are masses of good growers, who are not obsessed with new oak (unlike some Chénas people).

A selection of Morgon growers

DOMAINE NOËL AUCOEUR   9 ha. (100 per cent)

Morgon 6 ha., Regnié 1.25 ha., Beaujolais-Villages 0.5 ha., Beaujolais 0.75 ha.

This estate has bottled for twenty years, the wines being released twelve months later than from most growers. I have found the results rather patchy.

Noël Aucoeur, Le Rochaud, 69910 Villié-Morgon

GUY BRETON   3 ha. (100 per cent)

Morgon 3 ha.

Breton works closely with Marcel Lapierre, using little or no sulphur dioxide. I have had varied luck with these bottles: on one occasion an intriguing, delicious Morgon 1991 from old vines, on another a wine with strangely camphorous, candied violet aromas. Natural, certainly, but tasting very strange, for Morgon. He made a cracking good Beaujolais Nouveau 1993 (a tricky vintage for Nouveau).

Max Breton, 69910 Villié-Morgon

DOMAINE DE LA CHANAISE   13 ha. (80 per cent)

Morgon 11.5 ha., Regnié 0.58 ha., Beaujolais 0.71 ha.

Pierre et Dominique Piron, 69910 Villié-Morgon

LOUIS-CLAUDE DESVIGNES   13 ha. (33 per cent)

Morgon Côte du Py 1.5 ha., Javernières 2.1 ha., Morgon 9 ha., Beaujolais 0.6 ha.

There are no small barrels here, no old wood tuns, no wooden grids to hold the cap submerged, and no particularly long vattings. Good concentration and rich tannins are achieved, I believe, by low yields, and the dexterity of a straightforward, capable vigneron.

The seventeenth-century Desvignes house has a striking interior courtyard, the wide overhang of roof tiles being suspended in mid-air by beams which run right across the house. This contrasts with the less spectacular Mâconnais building method, where the over-hang is more often held up by pillars rising from a first-floor bal-cony. The overhang protects the walls from rain and snow (and of course growers as they go up and down the outside steps, to and from the cellar).

Unusually in the Beaujolais, Desvignes makes separate *cuvées* from two of his best hillsides: Côte du Py is the more famous Morgon site; its wine can be wonderfully rich. Javernières is for me the more interesting, with a firm, harmonious, complex finish. The right *cru* Beaujolais is worth laying away – here is a prime can-didate.

Louis-Claude Desvignes, La Voûte, Le Bourg, 69910 Villié-Morgon

DOMAINE DUHEN-GAUDET   9 ha. (25 per cent)

Morgon 8 ha., Saint-Amour 0.5 ha., Regnié 0.5 ha.

This Morgon, assembled from several centrally-placed sites, can

age well, and is regularly kept an extra year in the cellar before release.
M. et Mme Jean-Baptiste Duhen-Gaudet, 69910 Morgon

DOMAINE FERNAND GRAVALLON   13 ha. (80 per cent)

Morgon 10 ha., Chiroubles 0.5 ha., Fleurie 0.45 ha., Beaujolais-Villages 2.5 ha.

This is well-balanced Morgon for early to mid-term drinking, which regularly sells out to French clients by the Christmas fifteen months after its vintage.
Fernand Gravallon, Vermont, 69910 Villié-Morgon

MARCEL LAPIERRE   10 ha. (100 per cent)

Morgon 9 ha., Beaujolais 1 ha.

All wines here are made using the natural yeasts found in vine-yard and vat-house, and using no sulphur dioxide. Thereafter, Lapierre handles some of his wines in a modern way – treating, sulphuring and filtering, while others are aged in small oak barrels (no more than 10 per cent new) without sulphur, for bottling without filtration. Storing the latter wines is of course delicate, so a back-label and carton sticker are affixed, warning that, if the wine is stored at over 14°C, it may deteriorate. Perfectly fair – you take your choice, and take responsibility. In the vineyards, no weed-killers, but pesticides are sparingly used, likewise chaptalization sugar if needed. He operates like a human being, not a fanatic.

These wines should be drunk on purchase, or stored in a real cellar, in other words. They may be cloudy, for he cannot keep them more than eight months in wood, if he wishes to retain the fruiti-ness. They can be delicious and light, with a soft, clean aftertaste.

Outside his cellar a sculptor has created a retractable, wooden tasting table, incorporating spitoon and gushing water, which is as original and amusing as his wines.
Marcel Lapierre, 69910 Villié-Morgon

CAVEAU DE MORGON

This was the first *caveau* in the Beaujolais, and can receive up to 360 people at a time, laying on local sausage, goat's cheese, and

plenty of Morgons to taste. Every year 75,000 bottles are sold from this address, and in the summer it is humming with passers-by.
Monsieur G. Berrod et Madame Petit, 69910 Villié-Morgon

JACKY PASSOT   10 ha. (35 per cent)
DOMAINE DE FONTRIANTE

Morgon 5 ha., Chiroubles 3 ha., Fleurie 0.75 ha., Regnié 1 ha., Beaujolais-Villages 0.5 ha.
    Some splendid Morgon *cuvées* may be tasted here, due for assembling together into a harmonious, richly textured whole.
Jacky et Christiane Passot, Fontriante, 69910 Villié-Morgon

DOMAINE DES PILLETS   35 ha. (25 per cent)
GÉRARD BRISSON

Morgon Les Charmes 33.5 ha., Regnié 1.5 ha.
Gérard et Germaine Brisson, Les Pillets, 69910 Villié-Morgon

DOMAINE DE RUYÈRE   12 ha. (50 per cent)

Morgon, including Côteau des Charmes 9.5 ha., Regnié 1 ha., Beaujolais-Villages 1.5 ha.
Paul Collonge, Les Pillets, 69910 Villié-Morgon

PIERRE SAVOYE   14.5 ha. (90 per cent)
DOMAINE SAVOYE

Morgon Côte du Py 10 ha., Morgon 2.5 ha., Chiroubles 0.5 ha., Beaujolais 1.5 ha.
    Morgon has no fear of wrinkles, says Pierre Savoye; with three to four years it develops aromas of cherries, and may start resembling Pinot as it ages. This is a favourite source for many private French customers, with a little exporting being done.
Pierre Savoye, la Côte du Py, route de Belleville, 69910 Villié-Morgon

REGNIÉ

In 1991, there were 518 ha. of vineyard in production. Over the four vintages 1988–91 the average harvest was 35,000 hl.

In 1988, after a nine-year struggle, the growers of Regnié-Durette succeeded in having their wines lifted from *appellation* Beaujolais-Villages into position as the tenth *cru*, named simply Regnié. The wines of the two villages come from a hilly enclave adjoining Brouilly, Chiroubles and Morgon, and had regularly fetched higher prices than was common for their regional *appellation*. In *Beaujolais, vin du citoyen* Georges Duboeuf wrote in 1989 that the Côte de Durette would emerge as a fine source for early-drinking Regnié, with Vernus, Ponchon and Les Braves as sites for more full-bodied styles. From a consumer's point of view, a higher price now has to be paid for these wines, without much greater individuality being delivered than can be found in good Beaujolais-Villages. There are fine exceptions, but as an *appellation*, Regnié has yet to make a distinctive mark.

A selection of Regnié growers

DOMAINE DES HOSPICES DE BEAUJEU   82 ha.

Regnié 47 ha., Morgon 8 ha., Brouilly 8 ha., Beaujolais-Villages 19 ha.

The first donation to the Hospices de Beaujeu dates from 1240, two centuries before the now more famous Hospices de Beaune saw the light of day. It was established by the Lords of Beaujeu, for the poor and sick. As in Beaune, donations of all sorts – forest, vineyard, farmland – enabled it to carry out its charitable works.

Ten hectares are cultivated directly by the Hospices, the balance being looked after by a dozen growers in the Beaujolais manner of *vigneronnage*. The growers keep their share of the wines, selling them under their own names, without mention of the Hospices. The latter disposes of its crop by public auction on the second Sunday of December, the wines going mainly to local *négociants*, and often also to Swiss and Belgians. From the 1993 vintage, domaine-bottling has been available.

The buildings being classified Historic Monuments it was forbidden to build a vat-house extension above ground. So they buried it; all vats have automatic temperature control.

Alain Bellesort Oenologue, Domaine des Hospices de Beaujeu, La Grange Chartron, 69430 Regnié-Durette

PAUL CINQUIN   6.5 ha. (100 per cent)
DOMAINE DES BRAVES

Regnié 6.5 ha.

Cinquin is a vine nurseryman, but also a controversial grower, who has been experimenting with heat fermentation of his harvest since the early 1980s. He may well have perfected something revolutionary, and of wide application, for the Gamays of Beaujolais.

Briefly, his method is to sulphur the grapes with 5–6 gr/hl sulphur dioxide, to pump his vat over once it is full, and then to leave it for twelve hours for the sulphur to act. He then circulates the must into a heating vat, to bring its temperature to 40°C, at which point he runs air through it, to de-sulphur it. He then raises the temperature to 65° (this may take seven hours), holds it there for 12 to 14 hours, then cools the must back down to 20° to 22° (which takes another seven hours). He adds yeast, chaptalizes, then ferments for two to three days, after which he presses, reduces the temperature to 15°, and lets the fermentation finish at this low temperature. The wines take on colour and fruit quickly, while remaining supple.

He made particularly successful 1992s – a tricky Beaujolais vintage, which a year later were looking and tasting youthful and excellent.

I think the method may be highly appropriate to Beaujolais, Beaujolais-Villages, and perhaps some *crus* destined for youthful drinking, but suspect it might gum up the differences between the origins of the best sites. How the wines age long term remains to be seen, but this is pretty academic with the regional *appellations*, of course.

Paul et Franck Cinquin, Les Braves, 69430 Regnié

DOMAINE DE LA GÉRARDE   5.7 ha. (50 per cent)

Regnié
Roland et Gisèle Magrin, Hameau de Vernus, 69430 Regnié-Durette

DOMAINE DE PONCHON   12.5 ha. (35 per cent)
YVES DURAND

Brouilly Pisse-Vieille 2.8 ha., Brouilly 0.7 ha., Regnié 9 ha.
Jean et Yves Durand, Ponchon, 69430 Regnié-Durette

DOMAINE PASSOT LES RAMPEAUX   6 ha. (60 per cent)
DOMAINE DES RAMPEAUX

Morgon Côte du Py 0.45 ha., Morgon 2 ha., Regnié 2.8 ha., Chiroubles 0.6 ha., Fleurie 0.28 ha.

René Passot has been mayor of Regnié, and one of the domaine-bottling movers of the new *cru*. Water drawn from his own well is used for cooling here, the concrete vats having been equipped with internal stainless steel cooling pipes, on all four sides, since the late 1980s – a crucial advantage, encouraging fine aroma development.
Bernard, Rémy et René Passot, 69430 Regnié-Durette

ANDRÉ RAMPON   2.3 ha. (20 per cent)

Regnié 2.3 ha.
Cultivation here takes place 'without chemical products or weed-killers'.
André Rampon, Vernus, 69430 Regnié-Durette

JOEL ROCHETTE   5 ha. (100 per cent)

Regnié 2.25 ha., Brouilly Pisse-Vieille 0.75 ha., Beaujolais-Villages (Lantigné) 2 ha.
This is a good source of robust, well-concentrated Regniés.
Joel Rochette, Le Chalet, 69430 Regnié-Durette

BROUILLY

In 1991, there were 1,217 ha. of vineyard in production. Over the five vintages 1987–91 the average harvest was 72,800 hl.

This is the largest *appellation* of the nine growths, and often the best value for money. At its best it has supple charm, and delightfully aromatic fruit, with a record number (68) of growers offering wine in bottle.

CÔTE DE BROUILLY

In 1991, there were 303 ha. of vineyard in production. Over the five vintages 1987–91 the average harvest was 17,400 hl.

Côte de Brouilly wines are grown on the steep slopes of the prominent Mont-Brouilly. They are usually well-structured and quite firm when young, with good potential, requiring at least six months to a year's bottle age to show their paces.

Many Côte de Brouilly growers have Brouilly vines, and vice versa, so I have grouped the growers together.

A selection of Brouilly and Côte de Brouilly growers

MAURICE BONNETAIN   6.5 ha. (70 per cent)

Côte de Brouilly 5.5 ha., Brouilly 1 ha.

Paris restaurants, and some Swiss, still take wine in barrel from growers such as Bonnetain, who tends part of the large Institut Pasteur estate. This is early-drinking Brouilly, for serving by the pitcher.

Maurice Bonnetain, place du Monument, 69220 Saint-Lager

DOMAINE DU CHÂTEAU DE LA CHAIZE   94 ha. (100 per cent)

A beautiful and historic property, dating from 1676, where the site, the château, the vat-room and the vaulted cellar (at 110 metres the longest in the Beaujolais) are all classified historic monuments. It represents 10 per cent of the Brouilly *appellation*, and is surrounded by the Beaujolais' most extensive woods. Nine or ten different vignerons tend the vineyards and make the wines, so as well as the château's own wines, there are dozens of vignerons' vats to choose from. The château-bottled wine can vary from bottling to bottling but is often fine and delicious. A visit is well worth while, for La Chaize is to Brouilly what Beychevelle is to Saint-Julien.

Owner: Marquise de Roussy de Sales, Manager: Pierre Martray, Odenas, 69460 Saint-Etienne-des-Oullières

DOMAINE CRET DES GARANCHES   9 ha. (50 per cent)
DOMAINE BERNARD DUFAITRE

Brouilly
Bernard et Yvonne Dufaitre, Odenas, 69460 Saint-Etienne-des-Oullières

DOMAINE DELACHANAL   5.2 ha. (50 per cent)

Côte de Brouilly 2.6 ha., Brouilly 2.6 ha.
Martine et Jean-Pierre Charmette, Brouilly, Odenas, 69460 Saint-Etienne-des-Oullières

DOMAINE LAFOND   17 ha. (50 per cent)

Brouilly 3 ha., Côte de Brouilly 1.5 ha., Beaujolais Supérieur 12 ha.
   This cellar is well equipped to thermo-vinify Beaujolais for Primeur drinking, with a powerful underground refrigeration plant to achieve speedy re-cooling with minimum loss of aroma. To make a decent quantity of good Beaujolais Nouveau is not simple. With heat, two days in the classic-sized vats (70 hl) can be enough, and four pressings per day can be made, if you work fast. Pierre Lafond makes neat, award-winning Brouilly too.
Pierre et Thierry Lafond, Bel Air, 69220 Saint-Lager

ANDRÉ LARGE   3.88 ha. (5 per cent)

Côte de Brouilly 3.15 ha., Brouilly 0.73 ha.
   There is a boiler for must-heating, but no means of cooling. Pressing takes place in an antique, arm-operated (now mechanically assisted) wooden basket press, such as must have been universal in the Beaujolais sixty years ago. Each vat takes most of a day to press. Wine is partly stored in an ancient, circular wooden fermentation vessel, the top being sealed each year after the fermentation has finished with planks, some plaster to block the cracks, and a home-run cement of lime and sand, which must be broken up, pre-vintage, each year. André Large's two delicious wines go mostly to

L'Eventail des Vignerons in Corcelles for tending and bottling. In these astonishingly simple conditions, he and his wife make some of Eventail's most dependable, characterful and lively wines.
M. et Mme André Large, Mont-Brouilly, 69460 Odenas

ALAIN MICHAUD   9 ha. (80 per cent)

Brouilly 8 ha., Beaujolais 1 ha.

'If you are called *cru*, you should not taste like Beaujolais-Villages', says Michaud, and sure enough, this is not the place to come for Brouilly Primeur. 'People went too far with yeast experiments, chasing aromas. Red wine is for drinking when eating, you need tannins . . .' When young these wines are firm, resulting from up to twelve days' maceration, the skins held submerged with wooden grids. But they are worth waiting for, and last really well.
Alain et Marc Michaud, Beauvoir, 69220 Saint-Lager

OLIVIER RAVIER   15 ha. (100 per cent)
DOMAINE DE LA PIERRE BLEUE
DOMAINE DES SABLES D'OR   15 ha. (100 per cent)

Côte de Brouilly 3.8 ha., Fleurie La Madone 1 ha., Beaujolais 10 ha.

Ravier is President of l'Union Viticole du Beaujolais, so speaks for every vigneron in the region. He is much involved in the blind-tasting assessments which are necessary for Beaujolais wines to have the rights to their *appellations*. There must be some controversial discussions, I imagine, but as an accomplished wine-maker of *crus* as well as of straight Beaujolais (a third of it being made for Nouveau consumption) he is a well-qualified helmsman. On the Mont-Brouilly hillside, at his Domaine de la Pierre Bleue, he has constructed a spacious tasting-room to seat fourteen in fine conditions for assessment, which can be available to traders, wine-makers and enthusiasts. Through Olivier Ravier SARL he also brokes domaine-bottlings from his friends and family.
Olivier Ravier, Descours, 69220 Belleville

LES ROCHES BLEUES   6 ha. (85 per cent)

Côte de Brouilly 2.8 ha., Brouilly 3.2 ha.

Louis Bassy, Côte de Brouilly, Odenas, 69460 Saint-Etienne-des-Ouillières

DOMAINE DU SOULIER   14 ha.
MANION-MALHERBE

Brouilly 9 ha., Côte de Brouilly 5 ha.

Michel Malherbe et Patrick Monternier, Brouilly-Odenas, 69460 Saint-Etienne-des-Oullières, Cidex, 69220 Saint-Lager

CHÂTEAU THIVIN   20 ha. (80 per cent)

Côte de Brouilly 7 ha., Brouilly 7.7 ha., Beaujolais-Villages Manoir du Pavé 4.5 ha., Beaujolais 1 ha.

A captured spring tumbles perpetually into one of the entry courtyards of this famous, much-loved property. It hugs the Mont-Brouilly hillside, with vat-house and cellars cleverly dove-tailed into one another to take advantage of the fall in the land. All movement of grape bunches takes place by gravity, and the spent skins then fall gently out of their vats for pneumatic pressing. The juice flows on down into underground vats, where it can be lowered in temperature to maintain its aromas. Not a pinch of unnecessary chaptalization sugar ever goes near these wines, I suspect, and the consistency of wine-making is exemplary. Sufficient volume of wine is produced to allow the occasional vat to be eliminated from the final Côte de Brouilly bottlings.

This wine has one of Burgundy's most striking labels, designed by the present owner's great uncle in 1946. On a shield-shaped neck-label a rampant, black lion bursts up through a grating (like those on New York streets from which steam incessantly pours, or over which Marilyn stood, while the hot air billowed her skirts). The shield has a fleur-de-lys and a symbolic castle keep, with beside it an open-doored tower – open to ideas coming either way, no doubt. The wine was bottled at the château, we are told, and this is *L'Eclat de Rire de la Table* – the shout of laughter round a table, though whether that refers to the effect of the label or the wine in the bottle is not made clear. That goes for the neck-label. The body label shows the vineyards, house, trees, garden, and the hill behind, along with the wine's name, place of birth, legal origin, and the name of its maker. The contents – I am thinking of the 1992 – were charming and delicious.

Evelyne et Claude-Vincent Geoffray, Château Thivin, 69460 Odenas

BEAUJOLAIS-VILLAGES

In 1991, there were 5,778 ha. of Gamay Noir vineyard in production, with 35 ha. of Chardonnay. Over the five vintages 1987–91 the average total harvest was 344,300 hl.

Growers in all these villages may, if they wish, replace the word 'Villages' on their main label with the actual name of the village whence the grapes come; thus a Lantigné wine may be sold as Beaujolais-Lantigné, though the small type beneath will announce *Appellation* Beaujolais-Villages *Controlée*, that being the portmanteau name of origin which covers them all.

The wine can be made in forty-odd communes: Juliénas, Jullié, Emeringes, Chénas, Fleurie, Chiroubles, Lancié, Villié-Morgon, Lantigné, Beaujeu, Regnié, Durette, Cercié, Quincié, Saint-Lager, Odenas, Charentay, Saint-Etienne-la-Varenne, Vaux, Le Perréon, Saint-Etienne-des-Oullières, Blacé, Salles-Arbuissonnas, Saint-Julien, Montmelas, Rivolet, Denicé, Les Ardillats, Marchampt and Vauxrenard in the Rhône *département*, and Leynes, Saint-Amour-Bellevue, La Chapelle-de-Guinchay, Romanèche, Pruzilly, Chânes, Saint-Vérand and Saint-Symphorien d'Ancelles in the *département* of Saône-et-Loire.

If one has the buying-time to find it, nothing beats the *appellation* Beaujolais-Villages for French Gamay Noir value and deliciousness. Various villages continue the line of hills southwards from Morgon, and Brouilly – Saint-Etienne-la-Varenne, Vaux, Le Perréon, Salles-Arbuissonnas – which can be superb sources, as can Lantigné, Marchampt and Beaujeu itself, further west. Prices for good ones are not much lower than the minor *crus*, but the welcome can be particularly warm. Most Beaujolais-Villages is judiciously blended by bulk buyers, from sources in the forty different villages, to achieve balance, character and the price-point they desire. For a listing of the specialist Beaujolais and Mâconnais merchants, please see above.

AC BEAUJOLAIS AND AC BEAUJOLAIS SUPÉRIEUR

In 1991, there were 9,957 ha. of Gamay Noir vineyard in production, with 147 ha. of Chardonnay. Over the five vintages 1987–91 the average total harvest was 623,900 hl.

A selection of Beaujolais-Villages and Beaujolais growers

CHATEAU DE BASTY   17 ha. (70 per cent)
DOMAINE DE CHASSANTOUR

Regnié 3 ha., Beaujolais-Villages 14 ha.
Gilles Perroud, Lantigné, 69430 Beaujeu

CHÂTEAU DE BOISFRANC   17 ha. (80 per cent)

Beaujolais Supérieur 17 ha.
  Nine hectares here are cultivated organically, and M. Doat wonders if his unchaptalized *cuvées* are unique in the region, or simply rare.
Robert et Thierry Doat, 69640 Jarnioux

DOMAINE R. BOSSE-PLATIÈRE   3.6 ha. (100 per cent)

An estate which has followed bio-dynamic organic methods since 1972.
M. et Mme René Bosse-Platière, Les Carrières, Lucenay, 69480 Anse

DANIEL BULLIAT   15 ha. (30 per cent)

Chiroubles 2.11 ha., Beaujolais-Villages 12.8 ha.
  A dependable source of well-structured Beaujolais-Villages.
Daniel et Mylène Bulliat, Chavannes, 69430 Beaujeu

BERNARD CHAFFANJON   16 ha. (70 per cent)
DOMAINE DE CLOS SAINT PAUL

Morgon 2.5 ha., Regnié 1.2 ha., Beaujolais 12.5 ha.
The best wine here is the straight Beaujolais, I think. Either a non-chaptalized *cuvée* originally made for the colourfully-pictured Paris bistro on its label, or the lightly chaptalized 11.8° version, which is a satisfying, moderately luxurious wine for every day. The unchaptalized wine tastes close to fresh grape juice, but at 11° may be light for some tastes. It is available at Nouveau time, or from vat into your container thereafter until it runs out.
Bernard Chaffanjon, 69220 Saint Jean d'Ardierès

VIGNOBLE CHARMET   14 ha. (70 per cent)

Beaujolais La Ronze, Masfraise et La Centenaire, Beaujolais (*blanc*) La Goyette d'Or 0.5 ha.
This is not Beaujolais-Villages territory, but right down south, within easy reach of Lyon. An exceptional estate, where the average age of the vines is fifty years, and they grow on an unexpected outcrop of decomposed granite, with clay-silica sands and pebbles, such as one expects to find in *cru* Beaujolais territory. There is even some limestone, used for the Chardonnays. 'We aim for balanced wines of low degree which are close to the fruit', states Lucien. Many top prizes, won consistently over more than thirty years, rightly spotlight their skills.
Lucien et Jean-Marie Charmet, Vignoble du Coteau de la Ronze, 69620 Le Breuil

CLOS DE CREUSE-NOIRE   5 ha. (50 per cent)

Beaujolais-Villages Clos de Creuse-Noire 5 ha.
Leynes is the most northerly village of the Beaujolais-Villages region, its wines being produced on clay-siliceous soil. They never mature early, states M. Giloux, but may last for ten years.
Edmond Giloux, 71570 Leynes

PAUL GAUTHIER   11.3 ha. (15 per cent)
DOMAINE DES GRANGES

Beaujolais-Villages 5 ha., Beaujolais 6.3 ha.
A high proportion of both Beaujolais-Villages and Beaujolais are made for primeur drinking at this estate.
Paul et Denise Gauthier, Les Granges, Blace, 69460 Saint-Etienne-des-Oullières

CHÂTEAU DU GRAND VERNAY   12 ha. (65 per cent)

Beaujolais-Villages 7 ha., Côte de Brouilly 3 ha., Beaujolais Primeur 1.9 ha.
   This is the same family which owns Château Thivin (see Côte de Brouilly) and similar methods apply. The wines are made by Claude Geoffray's sisters: principally Beaujolais-Villages and Beaujolais, but also some Côte de Brouilly from land leased around the chapel.
Béatrice et Isabelle Geoffray, Charentay, 69220 Belleville-sur-Saône

DOMAINE DES GRANDES BRUYÈRES   19 ha. (70 per cent)
DOMAINE DES TEPPES DE CHATENAY

Beaujolais-Villages 10 ha., Macon-Azé, Macon-Villages et Bourgogne (blanc) 9 ha.
   Tesseidre also works as a broker, offering wines from the Beaujolais crus, to complement his regional whites (the Azé vinified in oak) and reds.
Jean-Pierre Teisseidre, Les Grandes Bruyères, 69460 Saint-Etienne-les-Oullières

PIERRE JOMARD   15 ha. (70 per cent)

Beaujolais 6 ha., Coteaux du Lyonnais 9 ha.
Pierre Jomard, 'Le Morillon', Fleurieux-l'Arbresle, 69210 l'Arbresle

CLAUDE ET MICHELLE JOUBERT   13 ha. (70 per cent)

Beaujolais-Villages Lantigné 4.6 ha., Juliénas Les Bessays 6.3 ha., Côte de Brouilly Chavannes 1.1 ha., Regnié La Chapelière 1 ha.
Claude et Michelle Joubert, Lantigné, 69430 Beaujeu

MARIE-THÉRÈSE ET BERNARD MÉRA   6 ha. (60 per cent)

Beaujolais-Villages 3.8 ha., Beaujolais 1.8 ha., Beaujolais *rosé* 0.25 ha.
Marie-Thérèse et Bernard Méra, Le Bourg, 69430 Marchampt

DOMAINE MIOLANE   23 ha. (80 per cent)

Beaujolais-Villages
  A highly dependable supplier of Beaujolais-Villages, René Mio-
lane's home and winery stand opposite a steep hillside which the
family has arm-cultivated for three centuries.
René et Christian Miolane, Le Cellier, Salles-Arbuissonnas, 69460
Saint-Etienne-des-Oullières

H. MONTERNOT ET FILS   11 ha. (90 per cent)

Beaujolais-Villages 7.3 ha., Beaujolais 3.6 ha.
  This estate has been experimenting since 1977 with recom-
mended Gamay clones in 4 hectares of its vineyard.
Jacky Monternot, Les Places, 69460 Blacé

BERNARD NESME   7.3 ha. (30 per cent)

Beaujolais-Villages Lantigné (*rouge*) 6.5 ha., (*blanc*) 0.3 ha., Beaujolais 0.5 ha.
  Selling Beaujolais Nouveau is like selling washing powder, says
Nesme: it is a marketing exercise. A wine which is too aromatic will
not go well with food, he feels, so aims for richness, with a good
finish, which these Lantigné wines often deliver quite naturally.
Bernard Nesme, Les Vergers, Lantigné, 69430 Beaujeu

PAUL PARRIAUD   13 ha. (75 per cent)
CELLIER DE LA MERLATIÈRE

Fleurie 0.23 ha., Morgon 3.5 ha., Beaujolais-Villages 8 ha.
  These relatively soft wines are mainly sold in France.
Paul et Maryse Pariaud, 69220 Lancié

JEAN-CHARLES PIVOT   12 ha. (100 per cent)

Beaujolais-Villages (Domaine La Sorbière, Quincié) 6 ha., (Domaine Le Colombier, Le Perréon) 6 ha.

The owner aims for pleasing wines, with enough substance to last, but not such structure as would detract from their pivotal element: fruit and aroma. He achieves it very successfully by blending wines from his two Beaujolais-Villages sources: Le Perréon, where the vines grow on granite (making delicious early-maturers) and Quincié, where the soil is clay-silica. I have found the wines excellent, if sometimes a little head-spinning.

Jean-Charles Pivot, Montmay, Quincié-en-Beaujolais, 69430 Beaujeu

New World Gamay

It is most surprising that no New World vineyard areas have successfully planted *Gamay Noir à jus blanc*. Beaujolais is commercially so buoyant, one would have thought rival wine-producing countries would have jumped on its band-wagon. Good Gamay is so deliciously drinkable; rare are the Shiraz, the Zinfandel or the Cabernet blends, which can touch it for appealing, soft fruitiness.

Obtaining the right clones of Gamay has no doubt been an obstacle; vinifying Gamay according to the Beaujolais methods, in small vats after hand-picking, has no doubt been another, and finding a name for the results a crucial third. The names of the authentic, original French wines immensely help their ready sale, being pronounceable and sweet-sounding: Beaujolais itself, Fleurie, Saint-Amour, Juliénas. The bald word 'Gamay' is neither evocative nor mellifluous, but all it perhaps needs is a little expanding: Gamay Noir or Gamay *rond* (one of its synonyms), maybe Gamay Granite, Gamay Schist, Gamay Slate or Gamay Sandstone, to celebrate its affinity with the soils on which New Worlders might plant it. This is not to wish the Beaujolais growers ill-fortune, by encouraging competition, but rather to stimulate some rivalry, for Chardonnay and Pinot rivalry has undoubtedly contributed to improved wine-making in the Côte d'Or. A bit of global Gamay planting might reawaken interest in the southern part of Burgundy, as well as expanding consumers' choices.

The two Burgundies

Only one thing stands between the two Burgundies – Beaujolais on the one hand, and everything north of it, on the other – and the established, widespread international respect which they both surely deserve: the rooting out of those second-rate wines which muddy the markets from time to time, devaluing the brilliant bottles, confusing consumers. That respect is there, but it needs to be grasped. Second-rate Beaujolais deserves hissing out of existence, just like second-raters carrying the Côte d'Or's precious, historic *appellations*. The INAO has not seen how to do it, and we cannot expect 100 per cent locally-manned (yes, it is mostly men) tasting panels to shoot themselves in the financial feet, either. But would they be shooting themselves in the feet? So can we?

Envoi

Je voudrais souligner tout d'abord que le goût est une configuration d'une richesse immense. Elle nous vient gratuitement et maintient en éveil notre corps, et nécessairement notre esprit, sur ce chemin de la sensibilité propre à l'homme. Reconnaître l'odeur des fraises sur un marché, découvrir les senteurs de cassis d'un vin, en démasquer le terroir, ce sont des expériences aussi riches que passer dans une galerie de peintures . . .

. . . Je dirai enfin que, si on n'a pas cette culture du goût, on ne peut pas jouer. Alors, la question est de savoir si les gens veulent être des passifs ou des actifs face à leur alimentation. S'ils sont passifs, ils sont exploités; s'ils sont actifs, ils mènent leur vie et s'amusent. Le plaisir est à ce prix.

Jacques Puisais, of Institut Français du Goût, Tours.
Interview with Caroline de Beaurepaire,
published in *Nourritures*, *Revue Autrement*, Paris,
September 1989.

APPENDICES

APPENDIX A

150 Monopoles: Burgundy Vineyards under Single Ownership

———

Commune	Monopole vineyard	Size (in hectares)	Owner or distributor
AUXERRE	Clos de la Chaînette (Bourgogne *blanc* and *rosé*)	4.5	Hôpital Psychiatrique de l'Yonne
CHABLIS	Clos des Hospices (Clos)	2.14	J. Moreau & Fils
	Clos du Château de Fleys	0.86	André Philippon
	Moutonne (Vaudésir and Preuses)	2.35	Domaine de la Moutonne
CHENÔVE	Clos du Chapitre (Bourgogne)	2.8	Michel Pont, Ch. de Savigny-lès-Beaune
FIXIN	Clos de la Perrière	5.18	Domaine de la Perrière
	Clos du Chapitre	4.78	Pierre Gelin
	Clos du Meix-Trouhans	1.8	Camille Crusserey
	Clos Napoléon (Aux Cheusots)	1.8	Pierre Gelin
GEVREY-CHAMBERTIN	Clos de la Justice	2	Pierre Bourée
	Clos de la Brunelle	0.26	Joseph Roty
	La Bossière	0.45	Harmand-Geoffroy

Commune	Monopole vineyard	Size (in hectares)	Owner or distributor
	Clos des Ruchottes-Chambertin	1.06	Domaine Rousseau
	Clos du Couvent	0.5	Domaine des Varoilles (Naigeon-Chauveau)
	Varoilles, Les	5.97	
	Meix de Ouches	1.05	
	Clos Saint-Pierre	0.4	
	La Romanée	1.06	
	Clos du Fonteny	0.67	Bruno Clair
	Clos Tamisot	1.5	Pierre Damoy
	En Motrot	0.5	Denis Mortet
MOREY-SAINT-DENIS	Clos de la Bussière	2.5	Domaine Georges Roumier
	Clos de Tart	7.5	Mommessin
VOUGEOT	Clos Blanc de Vougeot	2.28	Domaine de l'Héritier-Guyot
	Clos Bertagna	0.3	Domaine Bertagna
	Clos de la Perrière	2	Domaine Bertagna
VOSNE-ROMANÉE	Clos des Réas	2.12	Jean Gros
	Clos du Ch. de Vosne-Romanée	1.46	Famille Liger-Belair
	Clos Frantin	0.1	Domaine du Clos Frantin (Bichot)
	Romanée, La	0.85	Ch. de Vosne-Romanée (Bouchard Père)
	Romanée-Conti, La	1.8	Domaine de la Romanée-Conti
	Tâche, La	6.06	Domaine de la Romanée-Conti
	Clos Goillotte	0.55	Prieuré-Roch
NUITS AND PREMEAUX	Château Gris (aux Crots)	2.8	Lupé-Cholet (Bichot)
	Clos de l'Arlot (*rouge* 2 ha. *blanc* 1 ha.)	3	Domaine de l'Arlot

Commune	Monopole vineyard	Size (in hectares)	Owner or distributor
	Clos de la Maréchale	9.55	J. Faiveley
	Clos des Perrières	1	Jouan-Marcillet
	Clos de Thorey	4.11	Moillard
	Clos des Corvées	5	Domaine du Général Gouachon
	Clos des Forêts Saint-Georges	7	Domaine de l'Arlot
	Clos des Grandes Vignes	2.12	Moillard
	Clos des Porrets Saint-Georges	3.5	Henri Gouges
	Clos de Lupé (Bourgogne *rouge*)	2.2	Lupé-Cholet (Bichot)
	Clos Saint-Marc	0.93	Domaine Clos Saint-Marc/ Bouchard Père
	Didiers, Les	2.45	Hospices de Nuits
CÔTE DE NUITS-VILLAGES	Clos des Langres	3.5	Domaine de la Juvinière/P. André
	Clos du Chapeau	1.5	Domaine de l'Arlot
HAUTES CÔTES DE NUITS	Clos du Vignon (*rouge* 5.1 ha. *blanc* 1.15 ha.)	6.25 5.1 1.15	Thévenot-le-Brun
	Clos St Philibert (*blanc*)	3.5	Méo-Camuzet
HAUTES CÔTES DE BEAUNE	Clos on Bois Prévot (*rouge* 2.2 ha. *blanc* 0.2 ha.)	2.4	Mazilly Perè & Fils
LADOIX	Clos les Chagnots	2.5	Domaine Les Terres-Vineuses/ P. André
ALOXE-CORTON	Corton Clos des Cortons-Faiveley	2.97	J. Faiveley
	Corton Clos des Meix	2.12	Daniel Senard

Commune	Monopole vineyard	Size (in hectares)	Owner or distributor
	Corton Clos de Vergennes	2	Distrib. Moillard
	Clos de la Boulotte	1.13	Sylvain Pitiot/ Rodet
	Le Suchot	1	Simon Bize & Fils
PERNAND-VERGELESSES	Clos Berthet (*blanc* 1 ha. *rouge* 0.5 ha.)	1.5	P. Dubreuil-Fontaine & Fils
	Clos de la Croix de Pierre (en Caradeux)	1.5	Louis Jadot
SAVIGNY-LÈS-BEAUNE	Clos la Bataillère (Vergelesses)	1.82	Albert Morot
CHOREY-LÈS-BEAUNE	Champ Chevrey	1.47	Tollot-Beaut
	Château de Chorey	1	Domaine Germain
BEAUNE	Clos de la Féguine (Cras)	2	Jacques Prieur
	Clos de la Mousse	3.36	Bouchard Père & Fils
	Clos de l'Ecu	2.8	Jaboulet-Vercherre
	Clos des Ursules (Vignes Franches)	2.74	Louis Jadot
	Clos Saint-Landry (*blanc*)	1.98	Bouchard Père & Fils
	Vigne de l'Enfant Jésus (Grèves)	3.92	Bouchard Père & Fils
CÔTE DE BEAUNE	Clos des Topes Bizot	4.25	Machard de Gramont
	Les Pierres Blanches (*rouge* & *blanc*)	1	Joliette
	Les Mondes Rondes	1.1	Joliette
POMMARD	Clos de Cîteaux (Grands Epenots)	3	Jean Monnier

Commune	Monopole vineyard	Size (in hectares)	Owner or distributor
	Corton Clos de Vergennes	2	Distrib. Moillard
	Clos de la Boulotte	1.13	Sylvain Pitiot/ Rodet
	Le Suchot	1	Simon Bize & Fils
PERNAND-VERGELESSES	Clos Berthet (*blanc* 1 ha. *rouge* 0.5 ha.)	1.5	P. Dubreuil-Fontaine & Fils
	Clos de la Croix de Pierre (en Caradeux)	1.5	Louis Jadot
SAVIGNY-LÈS-BEAUNE	Clos la Bataillère (Vergelesses)	1.82	Albert Morot
CHOREY-LÈS-BEAUNE	Champ Chevrey	1.47	Tollot-Beaut
	Château de Chorey	1	Domaine Germain
BEAUNE	Clos de la Féguine (Cras)	2	Jacques Prieur
	Clos de la Mousse	3.36	Bouchard Père & Fils
	Clos de l'Ecu	2.8	Jaboulet-Vercherre
	Clos des Ursules (Vignes Franches)	2.74	Louis Jadot
	Clos Saint-Landry (*blanc*)	1.98	Bouchard Père & Fils
	Vigne de l'Enfant Jésus (Grèves)	3.92	Bouchard Père & Fils
CÔTE DE BEAUNE	Clos des Topes Bizot	4.25	Machard de Gramont
	Les Pierres Blanches (*rouge* & *blanc*)	1	Joliette
	Les Mondes Rondes	1.1	Joliette
POMMARD	Clos de Cîteaux (Grands Epenots)	3	Jean Monnier

Commune	Monopole vineyard	Size (in hectares)	Owner or distributor
	Clos de la Maréchale	9.55	J. Faiveley
	Clos des Perrières	1	Jouan-Marcillet
	Clos de Thorey	4.11	Moillard
	Clos des Corvées	5	Domaine du Général Gouachon
	Clos des Forêts Saint-Georges	7	Domaine de l'Arlot
	Clos des Grandes Vignes	2.12	Moillard
	Clos des Porrets Saint-Georges	3.5	Henri Gouges
	Clos de Lupé (Bourgogne *rouge*)	2.2	Lupé-Cholet (Bichot)
	Clos Saint-Marc	0.93	Domaine Clos Saint-Marc/ Bouchard Père
	Didiers, Les	2.45	Hospices de Nuits
CÔTE DE NUITS-VILLAGES	Clos des Langres	3.5	Domaine de la Juvinière/P. André
	Clos du Chapeau	1.5	Domaine de l'Arlot
HAUTES CÔTES DE NUITS	Clos du Vignon (*rouge* 5.1 ha. *blanc* 1.15 ha.)	6.25 5.1 1.15	Thévenot-le-Brun
	Clos St Philibert (*blanc*)	3.5	Méo-Camuzet
HAUTES CÔTES DE BEAUNE	Clos on Bois Prévot (*rouge* 2.2 ha. *blanc* 0.2 ha.)	2.4	Mazilly Perè & Fils
LADOIX	Clos les Chagnots	2.5	Domaine Les Terres-Vineuses/ P. André
ALOXE-CORTON	Corton Clos des Cortons-Faiveley	2.97	J. Faiveley
	Corton Clos des Meix	2.12	Daniel Senard

Commune	Monopole vineyard	Size (in hectares)	Owner or distributor
GIVRY	Clos de la Barraude	2.4	Steinmaier
	Clos Marceaux	3	Laborbe-Juillot
	Clos Saint-Pierre	2.12	Baron Thénard
	Clos Salomon	7	Du Gardin
POUILLY-FUISSÉ	Clos du Bourg (Fuissé)	1	Roger Luquet
	Le Clos (Fuissé)	2.6	Vincent & Fils
	Les Brûlées (Fuissé)	1.5	Vincent & Fils
MÂCON-LOCHÉ	Clos des Rocs (Les Mûres)	2.2	Domaine Saint-Philibert
MÂCON-LUGNY	Clos des Vignes du Maynes (*blanc* 2.5 ha. *rouge* 2.5 ha.)		Alain Guillot

I will be thankful for all suggested corrections or additions to this list. Please fax details directly to me in London: (0) 171 226 4575. All contributions will be gratefully acknowledged.

APPENDIX B

Recent Burgundy Vintages

These are brief overviews of Burgundy vintages. There are thousands and thousands of individual vineyard origins, with their different interpretations, each year, and the real answers now lie, of course, in the individual bottles.

I have been fortunate to have access to the descriptions of recent vintages by the Beaune broker Henri Meurgey of DIVA et Cie and the weather statistics collected by the Service de la Protection des Végétaux, and gratefully acknowledge my debt to them. For more detailed information on Burgundy vintages (back to 1865) reference may be made to *The Great Vintage Wine Book II* by Michael Broadbent.

I have aimed to describe some of the relevant characteristics of the grape-growing season and wine-making conditions, along with how the wines tasted when young, or have developed.

What they are like at a later stage depends completely on how they have been stored. Unless you can be certain of good storage conditions throughout a Burgundy's life my advice is to be wary of buying it when aged; instead, buy Burgundy young, taste it young, then store it properly, if it seems worth keeping. Taste the wines, or discuss them, every couple of years as they age.

1994   The weather during the flowering and up to the end of August was excellent for grape growth and health, however two weeks of wet weather occurred in early September. This halted the ripening process, diluting acidities. Those who harvested early often had to contend with rain, but the week of 23–29 September was finer, benefiting late-pickers.

1993   Mildew was a real problem during the early part of the summer, and the crop a potentially large one. Pinot skins were thicker than in 1992, and the grapes healthier. The red wines generally have more powerful fruit, with excellent colour and potential (if they were not diluted by harvest rain). Many good *crus* Beaujolais were made. The whites (Côte d'Or and Chablis) were late to ripen, it was a large harvest, and most pickers were caught by the rains. When they have concentration, the wines are excellent, but concentration is the problem.

1992   In Chablis they generally picked too late, and yields were at record highs. Many wines had low acidities, and many will be fragile. But if a grower had pruned tight, and possibly green-harvested, respectable natural alcohol levels were achievable. In the Côte d'Or, whites were generally very well-balanced, and often picked in better weather than the reds. These can lack exceptional fruit concentration; often the grapes were large, and the yields higher than in 1991. The reds are tender wines, likely to make rapid or mid-term drinking.

1991   The reds generally came out better than the whites, which, although cleanly fruity, can be short and rather flabby: diluted from the water they took up, and often lacking acidity. Red grape skins were thick and strong, and many excellent wines were made.

The right to pick was given, on the Côte de Beaune, on 25 September – which was to be followed by three days' rain. There was then sunny weather for four days, followed by more rain. This is a year when freedom over the picking date could have really benefited quality. (Burgundy had escaped the severe frost damage of 22 April 1991, which affected Bordeaux, the Loire and many other French vineyards.)

1990   The natural sugar levels were often excellent, where the yields were not over-swollen by some rain at the end of August. Many growers did not need to chaptalize, and did not. Generally healthy, well-balanced wines, both red and white, the best reds being magnificent, with plenty of colour and extract, and excellent potential for ageing.

1989   Growers decided they should mark the bicentenary of the French Revolution with record prices, on the grounds that everyone would want to buy a souvenir – which was a big mistake. The large crop of red wines often lacked the fruit intensity of the previous year. There were fairly high natural sugars, and ripe, appealing fruitiness helped early sales, but both 1990 and 1988 reds look set for rosier futures. Many white 1989s were unbalanced by high alcohol levels, and lowish acidity, but have made sumptuous youthful drinking – though at steep prices. The best white wines are concentrated and superb.

1988   The red wines were healthy, though often not particularly attractive when young. Although often hard, the best have densely concentrated flavours and good potential. Many 1988 whites have structure and acidity, and have been slow to mature. It is difficult – or perhaps simply too early – to generalize about this vintage.

1987 Thankfully the yields were relatively low, for there was generally insufficient natural ripeness when the grapes were picked, in windy, coolish conditions. Many wines were overchaptalized, but those growers who avoided that pitfall produced fruity, fine wines for early and mid-term enjoyment. The white wines are generally inferior to the two vintages on either side.

1986 It is fashionable to say that the whites were generally excellent, but there was some rot around, and high yields. Many whites lack concentration and staying power, and should be drunk sooner rather than later. The reds were much more tricky. It rained on grapes which were reaching maturity, and much water was taken up, so acidities dipped, and sugars were diluted. Even those growers who hand-sorted their grapes to eliminate rot had difficulty making good wine. The pips represented an abnormally high proportion of the mass; this is thought to be partly responsible for the hardness of many wines.

1985 Siberian conditions hit the region in January 1985, causing vine deaths in low-lying vineyards, and in Chablis. The summer was generally favourable, and a large harvest of healthy, richly fruity, well-balanced wines was made. Some lack staying power and concentration, but many made brilliant youthful drinking, and others will age well: they should be tasted, or discussed, at least biennially, however. The best white wines were initially dumb and four-square, but are ageing magnificently.

1984 Rain in August on a smallish potential crop could have caused widespread rot; but September was cold, preventing the spread of rot, but also hindering ripening. Low natural sugar levels and highish acidities however – not a recipe for memorable wines.

1983 Flowering was a little late, but went well. In July and August hailstorms damaged grapes on the Côte de Nuits (Vosne, Vougeot and Chambolle particularly). Rain in early September encouraged outbreaks of rot; however from 12 September hot sun dried, matured and in some cases shrivelled the grapes.

The resulting red wines appeared, when young, to be full of richness and potential, but their fruitiness proved often short-lived, and tannins began to dominate; many browned quickly. The whites were often high in alcohol, but lacked acidity.

1982 Considerable care was needed in selecting Côte d'Or wines as some red vineyards yielded 75 hl/ha. Many whites were delicious when young, but lacked acidity. The good wines have been charming, but not many are still improving.

1981 Some exceptional Chablis and white Burgundy, and the Beaujolais was generally successful. Côte d'Or reds were correct but lacking flesh, finishing rather dry. Some have evolved well. There had been spring frosts, and hail in parts of the Côte de Nuits.

1980 Disappointing weather in the spring and early summer was followed by a finer August and September, but it rained during the late vintage. There was some rot and not all the grapes were ripe; however some surprisingly good wines were made, particularly on the Côte de Nuits.

1979 A large harvest of generally healthy grapes, the wines having less concentration and staying power than the 1978s. Nuits and Vosne hit by hail. White vineyards yielded particularly abundantly.

1978 The flowering was late, and the weather unfavourable – which remained the case until the end of August. September was sunny, with temperatures at summer levels, saving the crop. Although the harvest was late, when ripeness was achieved before the picking the quality was very good for both red and white wines throughout the region.

1977 Abundant production, particularly on the Cote de Nuits. The summer had been wet, requiring many treatments against mildew and rot. Low natural degrees, so heavy chaptalization, the result being *une corpulence assez maigre* and high acidities.

1976 A good quality vintage from an abundant and healthy harvest. Red wines appeared deep-coloured stayers, with structure and stronger-than-normal tannins; however in many cases the fruit had been baked away by the hot summer, and they now lack vivaciousness. Whites generally lacked acidity to balance their richness. Mercurey and Rully were badly affected by hail.

1975 From mid-August the initial high hopes for quality were dashed by rain. A small harvest, losses being due to grey rot. Some Côte de Beaune whites were respectable; most red wines browned early.

1974   Average size harvest, but short, fruitless tannic wines. Low degrees in the Côte de Nuits.

1973   Record production in the Côte d'Or: 388,745 hl, but wines often below minimum legal natural sugar levels and lacking acidity to boot. Red wines flat and uninteresting, some whites respectable. The law of 1893 which defined the relationship between alcohol and dry extract in wine was much flouted by the excessive sugaring.

1972   Abundant quantity, particularly on the Côte de Beaune, after a late flowering and not much sun until 10 September. Red wines healthy with excellent colour, some lacking flesh. Acidities high in red wines and whites, but this has enabled many reds to age extremely well.

1971   June was cold and wet, giving shrivelled berries and not many of them. Picking began 18 September, a ripe and healthy harvest. The year marred by heavy hailstorms in Côte de Beaune and to a lesser extent Côte de Nuits. When free of goût de sec (the 'mousy' taste produced by hail) both reds and whites were exceptionally good.

1970   A very abundant harvest, low natural degrees on the Côte de Nuits particularly. Whites uneven in quality, reds lacking the fruit and concentration of 1971 or 1969.

1969   The grapes ripened well after a rainy flowering. Reds: very good colour, good fruit and tannin, though some did not live up to their youthful promise; whites: well-balanced.

1968   A few respectable white wines were made, but grey rot was widespread and the red wines were pale, thin and early browners.

1967   A year of irregular quality. Spring frosts reduced the yields, the Côte de Beaune whites and Beaune itself being worst hit. Hail in August and rain in September brought grey rot. The whites were better than the reds.

1966   June was good, July and August poorish, but September put things right. Quite a large yield, wines had character and elegance. A sound vintage.

1965   A small yield of poor wines, some of the reds having a 'yellow-brown colour from the beginning which was most distressful to behold'. High acidity and low sugar content throughout the region.

1964   Abundant yield of powerful, aromatic red wines after a very hot summer; the whites were rich and luscious.

1963   A large yield of red wines which generally lacked concentration; the whites were better.

1962   Well-balanced fine wines, an excellent year for reds and particularly whites.

APPENDIX C

Glossary of Wine Terms

BENTONITE: A clay with colloidal properties, used to fine and clarify wines, particularly whites.

BIVB: Bureau Interprofessionnel des Vins de Bourgogne.

CASEIN: This is used for fining wines, particularly whites; it is the principal protein in milk.

CEP: Vine stock.

CEPAGE: Type of vine.

COURTIER EN VINS: Wine broker

CHAPTALIZATION: The addition of sugar to grape-must at the moment of wine-making, in order to increase alcoholic content.

CLIMAT: A specific vineyard site.

CLOS: An enclosed plot of land or vineyard (but not all *clos* are, in fact, surrounded by walls).

CRU: See *Grand Cru, Premier Cru*.

CUVÉE: The contents of a vat (*cuve*) or several vats blended together.

DIATOMACEOUS EARTH: see Kieselguhr.

DOMAINE: A vineyard estate.

EGG-WHITE: Egg albumen, used to clarify wines, particularly reds.

FEUILLETTE: The Chablis barrel, holding 132 litres.

GELATINE: An animal protein derived from animal bone, cartilage or skin, used to fine wines, particularly reds.

GRAND CRU: Great Growth – the highest classification in Burgundy for the best individual vineyards.

HECTARE (ha.): Approximately 2.5 acres.

HECTOLITRE (hl): One hundred litres, approximately 22 gallons.

HOGSHEAD: See *Pièce*.

INAO: Institut National des Appellations d'Origine.

INFUSORIAL EARTH: see Kieselguhr

670

ISINGLASS: Prepared from the dried swim-bladder of certain cartilagenous fish (particularly sturgeon), this is used to fine wines.

KIESELGUHR: A chemically inert siliceous earth, used to aid filtration, when clarifying wines.

LEES: The sediments which fall to the bottom of vat or barrel during and after fermentation (see Racking).

LIEU-DIT: The place-name of a specific vineyard site, often of ancient and obscure meaning.

MARC: The mass of skins, pips and stalks left behind after the wine has been run off. It is is later distilled to produce a spirit, itself called *marc*.

MONOPOLE: The description given by Burgundians to a vineyard under single ownership. Appendix A lists 150 Monopole vineyards.

MUST: The grape-juice before and during fermentation, at the end of which it has become wine.

NÉGOCIANT: Wine-maker stock-holder, tender, shipper and merchant.

ONIVIT: Office National Interprofessionnel des Vins de Table

PIÈCE: The Burgundy barrel, holding 228 litres (approximately 25 dozen bottles). Mâconnais-Beaujolais barrels hold 212–16 litres.

PIGEAGE: The punching-down of the red grape-skins under the surface, while a wine is fermenting in vat (see p. 128).

PIPETTE: Glass or stainless steel tube used to transfer small quantities of wine for tasting or analysis from barrel to glass or sample bottle.

PREMIER CRU: First Growth. One would expect this description to apply to Burgundy's best vineyards but confusingly it means the second best (see *Grand Cru*).

PRIMEUR: Used to describe a wine made to be attractive when drunk young, such as new Beaujolais.

RACKING: Removing wines from one vat or barrel to another, leaving the lees (q.v.) behind, to be discarded.

RECOLTE: The harvest or vintage.

REMONTAGE: The pumping-over of grape-juice or fermenting wine, with or without aeration, to encourage yeast growth and the extraction of colour, aroma and flavours from the grape-skins.

SA: Société Anonyme.

SARL: Société A Responsabilité Limitée.

SULPHUR DIOXIDE (SO_2): Gas formed by burning sulphur in air, which, when dissolved in water, forms sulphurous acid (H_2SO_3). It is added to wine or must as an anti-oxidant and germicide.

TASTEVIN: A shallow tasting receptacle about 2 cm deep by 8 cm across, made of silver or baser metal. Its surface is indented with stripes and dimples to catch the light when tasting hazy young wine.

UIVB: Union Interprofessionnel des Vins de Beaujolais.

VIGNERON: Wine-grower.

VIN DE GARDE: A wine for keeping, i.e. which requires and will benefit from maturation.

APPENDIX D

Organic Wine-Growers in the Côte D'Or

Mme Bize-Leroy,
Domaine d'Auvenay,
21190 Auxey-Duresses

Dominique Derain,
Ancienne Cure,
21190 Saint-Aubin

Domaine Prieuré-Roch,
Philippe Pacalet,
21700 Nuits-Saint-Georges

Emmanuel Giboulot,
21200 Combertault

SCEA Thierry Guyot,
21190 Saint-Romain

Jean et Thierry Javillier,
21190 Meursault

Anne-Claude Leflaive,
21190 Puligny-Montrachet

Pascal Marchand,
Domaine des Epeneaux,
21630 Pommard

François Mikulski,
5 rue de Leignon,
21190 Meursault

Didier Monchovet,
21190 Nantoux

Jean-Claude Rateau,
Chemin des Mariages,
21200 Beaune

Alain Verdet,
21700 Arcenant

APPENDIX E

Useful Addresses

Bureau Interprofessionnel des Vins de Bourgogne
12 blvd Bretonnière,
BP 150, 21204 Beaune Cedex
Tel.: 80 24 70 20   Fax: 80 24 69 36
Contact: Jean-Charles Servant

The BIVB has three regional sub-offices: Chablis, covering the Yonne,
Beaune, covering central Burgundy, and Mâcon for its region, the Saône-et-
Loire (which includes the Côte Chalonnaise), the details being:

BIVB: Chablis
Le Petit Pontigny,
1 rue de Chichée,
BP 31, 89800 Chablis
Tel.: 86 42 42 22   Fax: 86 42 80 16
Contact: Véronique Vallenot

BIVB: Beaune
Rue Henri Dunant,
21204 Beaune
Tel.: 80 22 21 35   Fax: 80 24 15 29
Contact: Dominique Lambry

BIVB: Mâcon
520 av. de Lattre de Tassigny,
71000 Mâcon
Tel.: 85 38 20 15   Fax: 85 38 82 20
Contact: Nelly Blau

L'École du Vin
12 blvd Bretonnière,
BP 150, 21204 Beaune Cedex
Tel.: 80 24 70 20   Fax: 80 24 69 36

A *la carte* tasting courses and seminars, including 'weekend escapes', are available for beginners, enthusiasts and professionals, in English, French and German. Lasting from one hour to five days, in 1994 they cost from 50 to 3250 frs.

Groupe des Jeunes Professionels de la Vigne
24 bis rue du Lieutenant Dupuis
21200 Beaune
Tel.: 80 22 05 12   Fax: 80 24 05 57

The GJPV offers a wide, annual training programme aimed mainly at professionals, particularly its 500 young Burgundian wine-grower members. There are also tasting initiation courses for consumers led by Jean-Pierre Renard.

The Beaujolais is a completely separate area, however, the border of the Saône-et-Loire *département* was inconveniently drawn (from a wine point of view) after the French Revolution. It is viticulturally a few kilometres too far south. Saône-et-Loire, with Yonne, Côte d'Or, and Nièvre are the four *départements* which make up today's administrative Burgundy. The result is that certain parts of the northern *crus* Beaujolais – Saint-Amour, Juliénas, Moulin-à-Vent, Chénas, with chunks of Beaujolais-Villages, Beaujolais Supérieur and Beaujolais are in the Saône-et-Loire *département*. They find themselves cut off from logical inclusion with their brothers in the Rhône *département*, further south, where the bulk of the wines of Beaujolais are made.

For most enquiries relating to the Beaujolais, the best contact is with UIVB:

Union Interprofessionnelle des Vins du Beaujolais
BP 317,
210 blvd Victor Vermorel,
69661 Villefranche
Tel.: 74 02 22 10   Fax: 74 02 22 19
Contact: Michel Rougier and Michel Deflache

However, much Beaujolais *blanc* is made in the Saône-et-Loire, so for that, and the other no-man's-land *appellations*, it may be best to talk to BIVB Mâcon.

Bibliography and Further Reading

NEW LITERATURE

Since the mid-1980s, nearly twenty notable books have appeared on Burgundy, two of the most thought-provoking being by American writers (Kramer and Parker). In addition to general works such as Halliday and Johnson's *The Art and Science of Wine*, Hugh Johnson's *The Story of Wine* and Jancis Robinson's *Vines, Grapes and Wines* (details appear in the main bibliography, below) which range over the globe but are shot through with enlightening references to Burgundy, I have found the following helpful or indispensable:

Jean-François Bazin,
> *Le Clos de Vougeot*, 1987
> *Montrachet*, 1988
> *Chambertin: La Côte de Nuits de Dijon à Chambolle-Musigny*, 1991
> *La Romanée-Conti*, 1994
> Le Grand Bernard des Vins de France, Jacques Legrand, Paris.
> These books are *tours de force* of painstaking research. Full of information about individual growers and estates, they are particularly strong on who bought which row of vines from whose great-aunt, when and why. No Burgundy fanatic will want to be without them, particularly the two most recent. Only Montrachet has, to date, been translated into English, by Longman Group UK, in 1990.

BIVB, *Vinification: l'expérience bourguignonne, résultats d'essais*, Bureau Interprofessionnel des Vins de Bourgogne, Beaune, July 1993.
> This is a valuable summary of wine-making practices, with a discussion of recent tests and trials, aimed at the specialist and wine-maker, particularly relating to Pinot Noir.

Georges Duboeuf and Henri Elwing, *Beaujolais, vin du citoyen*, Jean-Claude Lattès, Poitiers, 1989.
This book now has a slightly dated air, for it was written to coincide with the 200th Anniversary of the French Revolution. It gives an entertaining and valuable behind-the-scenes view of the region – there are few other accounts – partly-ghosted by Elwing, partly written by the master himself. It deserves revision and translation; in the meantime, it is available at Duboeuf's *Le Hameau des vins*, in Romanèche-Thorins.

Nicholas Faith, *Voyage en Bourgogne*, Caisses des Dépôts et Consignations, Paris, 1991.
This is perhaps the funniest, most broad-sweeping introduction to the subject ever written by a foreigner. Privately printed, and only available in French, it is now extremely rare.

Eunice Fried, *Burgundy: the Country, the Wines, the People*, Harper & Row, New York, 1986.
Miss Fried was the first to go behind the scenes to describe oak forests and barrel-makers, or to persuade the Abbey of Cîteaux to allow her an insider's view. Her highly readable book is peopled with lovingly described Burgundians and insights into its wine life.

Gault & Millau Guide, *Le Vin*, Paris, 1992.
This is produced annually, and provides helpful, enthusiastic descriptions of many growers and sources.

Le Guide Hachette des vins 1993, France, 1992.
This appears annually, and in Burgundy the editors have enlisted the help of the BIVB to organize blind tastings. In 1992, 24 tastings took place, covering 3,000 wines, of which just over half were successful. These are professionally run, and perhaps the nearest the French come to Australia's State Wine Shows. Most of the wines judged are young, so it is more useful for choosing early-drinking bottles and crowd-pleasers, than special bottles for long ageing.

Matt Kramer, *Making Sense of Burgundy*, William Morrow, New York, 1990.
The author is *terroir*-smitten, and writes passionately from a traditional French viewpoint. The book is dedicated to Mme Bize-Leroy, and her *négociant-propriétaire* philosophy echoes between the lines of many pages, Matt Kramer being *plus Leroyaliste que Leroy*.
There are some fascinating lists of growers in the best *Grands Crus* and *Premiers Crus*, to be found nowhere else. For anyone with the funds

to consider buying vineyards on the Côte, this book is essential; for anyone seeking to understand how the Burgundian wine-making proprietor's mind works it is extremely valuable.

Simon Loftus, *Puligny-Montrachet: Journal of a Village in Burgundy*, Ebury Press, London, 1992.
Loftus writes evocatively about the place, the history, the wines and the vineyards, and with rare directness about the people. This is for Burgundy enthusiasts: Puligny seen through the cracks in the gloss.

Jake Lorenzo, *Cold Surveillance, the Wine Columns*, Wine Patrol Press, Vineburg USA, 1993.
Lorenzo is a tough-as-nails private eye, but also a wine-writer. This is a dangerous, anarchic book, for adults only.

Remington Norman, *The Great Domaines of Burgundy: a Guide to the Finest Wine Producers of the Côte d'Or*, Kyle Cathie, London, 1992.
A beautifully-produced book with excellent photographs and maps, covering 111 top estates of central Burgundy. The author reports in minute detail what growers have told him about their wine-making methods or objectives, and for some enthusiasts this is engrossing, for others hard to plough through.

Richard Olney, *Romanée-Conti*, Flammarion, Paris 1991.
This was written with the co-operation of the two owning families, and before the split which resulted in Mme Bize-Leroy's departure from co-directorship of the Domaine de la Romanée-Conti, and Olney is sometimes uncritical in his celebration of the achievements of this great estate. That apart, his book is a fastidious and welcome account. Where else are the myths surrounding key Burgundian wine anecdotes so painstakingly evaluated? Where else may one read an explanation of nineteenth-century vineyard layering, written from a modern standpoint, which may well be of relevance in countries (Australia, for instance) where phylloxera is not endemic? Here is not only a description, but also a photograph, of wooden vats being flamed with *eau-de-vie* to disinfect them before use. The book is a feast of loving descriptions, fine photographs, family trees, with many valuable and curious insights, and I hope it will one day appear in English.

Robert M. Parker Jr., *Burgundy, a Comprehensive Guide to the Producers, Appellations and Wines*, Simon & Schuster, New York, 1990.
Nearly 800 pages long, covering the whole region including Beaujolais, this ambitious book describes and assesses the wines, villages and par-

ticularly the growers and merchants who supply the best wines. It describes many little heard-of or undiscovered Burgundian estate bottlers with admirable forthrightness.

Parker's influence on Burgundy drinking has been complex and pervasive. He trained as a lawyer, and he sometimes writes about Burgundy as if he thinks it should be sent to prison. The lawyer's adversarial standpoint is an original one, and it can make for startling diatribes, as he goes for a conviction and heavy sentence, or seeks the acquittal of a plausible felon who has pulled the wool over his eyes in some dingy, underground cell.

The book has been marketed in France as La Bible. Like the sacred book itself, it is part myth, part revelation, part fact, part hearsay. In places full of insights, useful guidance, and valuable records, in others it is merely pretentious. Like an Apostle, Parker can appear to have written up a note some time after the event took place, though this may add drama to the telling. Unless the reader is already an expert I am not sure how he or she can tell the wheat from the chaff.

He is genuinely trying to make sense of Burgundy and its wines, and explain it as best he can to his readers. But he is doing it in a way which is inappropriate, imposing on the region a celebrity system, a star-is-born, Hollywood mentality – to which he no doubt believes Americans will easily be able to relate. American culture puts high values on glamour, wealth and visible public success. His approach constantly lionizes certain individuals, making them particularly suitable for a certain type of American consumption.

But Burgundy is too shattered, by a process dating from the French Revolution, into thousands of small splinters to lend itself to this analysis, or this type of promotion. This may be a path suitable for some Americans, but others, and consumers in other countries, may ask themselves if they want Burgundies to be hijacked into an American mould.

When I read[1] that he seeks to dismiss *The Vintner's Art: How Great Wines are Made*[2] by James Halliday and Hugh Johnson as 'having little to do with the art of fine wine-making' – in my view the book is concerned with little else, and gives a global overview of unquestionable interest and value – I wonder if I detect a whiff of Parker trying to rubbish a competitor? Halliday and Johnson close their book with three pages of closely argued discussion on the subject of filtration, coming to conclusions with which Parker evidently does not concur. But I strongly recommend that everyone interested in fine wine should buy that book,

---

1 In the issue of *The Wine Advocate* devoted to reviewing 1990 red Burgundies from the Côte de Nuits.
2 Published in the United Kingdom as *The Art and Science of Wine*, Mitchell Beazley, London, 1992.

and refer to it regularly, as I do, if ever they feel themselves getting technically out of their depth. One may not agree with everything that Halliday and Johnson write, but it is a mistake to dismiss them.

Parker's 100-point system

After several years' trials in the field, Parker's 100-point system can now be seen to be inappropriate for evaluating fine young Burgundies, whether white or red. Their outward appearances seesaw naturally while they are young, and they can no more be number-rated than the beauty of a butterfly can be caught by photographing its chrysalis. It is time for Parker to consider leaving his automated recording systems behind, or at least only using them when the insects have hatched and dried their wings in the sun.

The 100-point system has introduced many new drinkers to Burgundy, wealthy, reasonably-off and impoverished, and it allows some of the best bottles to be distributed down channels where those handling the wines need have no knowledge of the product whatsoever. The system seeks to simplify the buying job, and Parker has made it work, in his fashion.

Today's true wine enthusiast needs to question the value of point systems, and understand their pseudo-scientific (to use Hugh Johnson's phrase), superficial nature. 100-point systems are an effective way of communicating judgements of wines to be drunk young, but for *Grands Crus* they are a blind alley, from which writers should consider turning back.

The best numbers to attach to any individually-evaluated fine wine are a fax number, a telephone number, and its price, with a good address of where to find it.

Sylvain Pitiot and Pierre Poupon, *Atlas des grands vignobles de Bourgogne* (2 vols.), Jacques Legrand, Paris, 1985.
This is a luxury reference atlas with superb maps of the vineyards from Fixin to Maranges, in pleasing-to-handle book format. The owners and producers in these central Burgundian villages are listed in minute detail, in respect of the 1984 vintage, and details of the finest sites are given. *Terroir* is discussed, and there is a history of how the Côte's vineyards have been mapped since 1728.

Sylvain Pitiot and Jean-Charles Servant, *Les Vins de Bourgogne*, Presses Universitaire de France, Paris, 1992 (translated as *The Wines of Burgundy*, Paris, 1994).
This is the successor to Poupon and Forgeot's guide of the same title, which provided essential Burgundian facts and figures through ten editions from 1952 to 1985. There are no people in this book, it often

describes ideals rather than realities, and it lacks a decent index, but there is always a well-thumbed copy within reach of my work-bench.

Serena Sutcliffe's Guide to the Wines of Burgundy, revised and updated by Serena Sutcliffe and Michael Schuster (originally published as *Serena Sutcliffe's Pocket Guide to the Wines of Burgundy*), Mitchell Beazley, London, 1992.
There is no question of where Ms Sutcliffe stands in relation to Hugh Johnson's already-quoted statement, 'Burgundy is either pure or it is nothing'. She has no time for wines which do not reflect their origins with clarity, and this makes her book an accurate indicator of the best addresses. It is a valuable, pocket-sized reference book for the whole region.

Jean-Claude Wallerand and Christian Coulais, *Bourgogne, guide des vins Gilbert & Gaillard*, Editions Solar, Lonrai, France, 1992.
This gives many helpful details on over 300 domaines from Chablis to the Maconnais, but ignores the Beaujolais. The reader sometimes has to work hard to identify which proprietors are really admired by the authors, who tend to say subtly polite things about everyone. But I found the book particularly valuable for the southern Côte de Beaune, Wallerand's heartland.

MAGAZINES AND SUBSCRIPTION NEWSLETTERS

Michel Bettane, *La Revue du vin de France*, Paris (subscription, 9 issues per year), 18–20 rue Guynemer, 92441 Issy-lès-Moulineaux.
This magazine often includes tastings of Burgundies on a like-with-like basis, professionally conducted by teams of mainly French tasters. Michel Bettane is the principal Burgundy correspondent. French wine writers can be muted in their criticisms, perhaps sensing that ostracism or worse may await those seeming to be unpatriotic. While it is evident that Bettane knows much more than he sometimes feels able to put on paper, he can be splendidly outspoken and constructive.

Clive Coates MW, *The Vine*, London (monthly subscription).
The Vine has contained some of the best regular commentary and news on the top growers of the Côtes de Beaune and Nuits, from the vintages of the late 1980s and early 1990s. I have often used it, while always wishing Coates would taste more of his wine ranges blind, and publish his tasting notes, marks and assessments, exactly as he wrote them *when the wines were blind*. It would make such interesting reading. Of course,

if he did this, some growers might never invite him back, but would that matter? There is no shortage of good growers these days.

To my mind, this has become more valuable, as the long tasting notes have partly given way to domaine assessments, and information gathered on the spot. There are still plenty of tasting notes, which many people find useful. Quality assessments are more dependable, and often better informed, than Parker's. Coates concentrates on the central Côte d'Or, and this is his strength.

Decanter Magazine (monthly subscription), Priory House, 8 Battersea Park Road, London SW8, and
Wine Magazine (monthly subscription), Publishing House, 652 Victoria Road, South Ruislip, Middlesex HA4 0SX.
During the early 1990s many English wine-writers have had extended love affairs with the wines of France's rival, English-speaking producer countries, which in the UK market have often been seen to beat France for value, novelty and excitement. Although few Pinots Noirs from outside France can equal the quality and deliciousness of Burgundy's village wines – let alone those from top sites – red Burgundy has tended to be neglected. *Wine*, however, has had a strong pair of strikers (Robert Joseph and Charles Metcalfe) when they have run with the Burgundy ball, and sparks often fly from the *Decanter* letters page (for instance, in October 1991, when John Livingstone-Learmonth wrote an open letter to Robert Parker on The Peril of Points, and Parker replied at length).

The Wine Advocate, Robert M. Parker Jr., PO Box 311, Monkton, Maryland 21111, USA (bi-monthly subscription).
For Parker's Burgundy writings, see above.

Wine Spectator (fortnightly or monthly subscription), M. Shanken Communications, 387 Park Avenue South, New York, NY 10016.
If there was a story to be had about wine-making rivalries in Vosne-Romanée in the early 1990s, the chances are the news first broke in the pages of *Wine Spectator*.

The Underground Wine Journal, Wine Journal Enterprises Inc., Pasadena, 1994 (bi-monthly subscription)
This covers Burgundy at enormous length, giving wine-grower assessments and many tasting notes, which appear to have been written by groups of friends or committees; as a simple reader, it is hard to know. If only it were tautly edited it could be more influential.

Other American subscription journals which cover Burgundies include Stephen Tanzer's *The New York Wine Cellar* and Claude Kolm's *The*

Fine Wine Review (2443 Fillmore Street, PO Box 455, San Francisco, California, 94115). Both cover producers in depth, with precise analysis and well-reasoned, provocative tasting notes.

FURTHER READING

Académie de Dijon, *Géologie de la Côte d'Or*, Centre Régional de Documentation Pédagogique, Dijon, 1967.

Akar, Etienne, 'Fair Play? French Tasting Panels', *Wine Magazine*, London, February 1987.

Agnel, H., *Guide des plantations de vignes*, ITV, Paris, 1964.

Anon., *Détails historiques et statistiques sur le département de la Côte d'Or*, Dijon Imprimerie Carion, chez Gaulard-Marin, November 1818.

Arlott, John and Fielden, Christopher, *Burgundy Vines and Wines*, Davis-Poynter, London, 1976.

Arnoux, Claude, *Dissertation sur la situation de Bourgogne, London, 1728* (facsimile edn. Daniel Morcrette, Luzarches, November 1978).

Asher, Gerald, 'Pinot Noir: Back to the Future' (April 1988),' A Trip to Burgundy' (April 1989), 'Chardonnay: Buds, Twigs and Clones' (May 1990), 'Burgundy's Best' (October 1993), in *Gourmet Magazine*.

Asher, Gerald, *On Wine*, Jill Norman and Hobhouse, London, 1983.

Atkin, Tim, *Chardonnay*, Viking Penguin, London, 1992.

Audin, M., *Le Musée folklorique de Beaujeu*, Les Editions de Cuvier, Villefranche, 1945.

Aulas, Michel, *Anthologie du Beaujolais*, Gougenheim, Lyon.

Barr, Andrew, *Pinot Noir*, Viking Penguin, London, 1992.

Barr, Andrew, *Wine Snobbery*, Faber and Faber, London, 1988.

Bastien, Bruno, *Principaux types de grands vins rouges de la Côte d'Or*, Mémoire d'études ENSSAA, Beaune, 1970.

Baticle, Yves *et al.*, *La Bourgogne, espace et société: civilisations populaires régionales*, Editions Horvath, Roanne, 1987.

Bazin, Jean-François, *Bourgogne*, Editions Arthaud, Paris, 1990.

Bazin, Jean-François, *Bourgogne de 1975 à 1985*. Informations et Conjoncture, Paris, 1976.

Bazin, Jean-François, *Les Grands Vins de Fixin*, Editions de Saint-Seine-l'Abbaye, 1984. 21440 Saint-Seine-l'Abbeye.

Bazin, Jean-François, *Le Vignoble des Hautes Côtes de Nuits et de Beaune*, Les Cahiers de Vergy, 1973.

Bazin, Jean-François, *Le Vin de Bourgogne ou l'ivresse du succès*, Reproduction de texte de l'enquête parue dans *Les Depêches*, Dijon, CIB, Beaune, 1971.

Beeston, Fiona, *The Wine Men*, Sinclair-Stevenson, London, 1991.

Bernard, Albert, *La Vigne et le vin en Mâconnais septentrional 1800–1921*, Librairie M. Renaudier, Mâcon, 1933.

Bernard, Raymond *et al.*, *Le Vin de Bourgogne*, Editions Montalba, Lausanne, 1976.

Bertall, *La Vigne: voyage autour des vins de France*, Plon, Paris, 1878.

Berthelier, Bernard, *L'Evolution et l'avenir de l'Aligoté*, Fédération Interprofessionnelle des Vins de Bourgogne, Beaune, 1978.

Bihaut, Dr Sylvain, *Le Vin authentique: ecologie et oenologie*, Editions Sang de la terre, Paris, 1993.

Bisson, Jean, *Pinots – origine, variations et technologie*, Station d'expérimentation viticole, 58 Cosne-sur-Loire (undated).

Blanchet, Suzanne, *Les Vins de Bourgogne*, Editions Jéma, Marmonde, 1985.

Boidron, R., *Le Mâconnais viticole*, CETA Viticole du Mâconnais, Chambre d'Agriculture de Saône et Loire (undated).

Boidron, R., *La Sélection clonale en Saône-et-Loire*, L'Exploitant Agricole, 1977.

Boidron, R., *Vignes hautes et larges*, L'Exploitant Agricole, Saône-et-Loire, 1978.

Boidron, R., Leguay, M. *et al.*, *La Sélection clonale en Bourgogne et Franche-Comté*, Groupement régional d'amélioration et de prémultiplication de la vigne du centre-est, Mâcon, 1988.

Boisset, Pierre, *Millésimes et campagnes: les carnets d'un acheteur de vins*, Robert Laffont, Paris, 1989.

Bourguignon, Claude, *Le Sol, la terre et les champs*, Editions Sang de la terre, Paris, 1989.

Bourguignon, Claude, *Vers une approche physique, chimique et biologique des terroirs de vigne*, LAMS, Is-sur-Tille, 1990.

Bourguignon, Claude, *Vers une nouvelle approche de la fertilisation des sols agricoles*, LAMS, Is-sur-Tille, 1991.

Bréjoux, Pierre, *Les Vins de Bourgogne*, Société Française d'Editions Vinicoles, Paris, 1967.

Bro, Louis, *Chablis, porte d'or de la Bourgogne*, Paris, 1959.

Broadbent, Michael, *The Great Vintage Wine Book II*, Mitchell Beazley, London, 1991.

The Bureau Interprofessionnel des Vins de Bourgogne (BIVB) in Beaune (succeeding the Féderation des Interprofessions des Vins de la Grande Bourgogne), publishes regular summaries of research findings, with accounts of wine-related symposia, to which which I have often referred, making reference to individual authors by footnotes in the text. The main reports used, in order of publication, are:

Commission Recherche Progrès et Qualité, Activity Reports, FIVB, March 1986, May 1988, June 1989.

Ier Colloque professionnel des vins de Bourgogne: la qualité et la typicité des vins de Bourgogne (Santenay, BIVB, January 1989*)*.

IIème Colloque professionnel des vins de Bourgogne: réussir et protéger la qualité (Nolay, BIVB, January 1990).

Ier Forum-Débat: Marché et communication des vins de Bourgogne (Puligny-Montrachet, BIVB, January 1991).

Qualité hygiénique des vins et environnement: nouvelles perspectives, Mâcon, BIVB, April 1991.

IIIème Colloque professionnel des vins de Bourgogne: nutrition, fertilisation, qualité (Vosne-Romanée, BIVB, January 1992).

Etude de la maturation: 10 ans de résultats en Bourgogne, BIVB, July 1992.

La maîtrise des rendements, BIVB, Mâcon, March 1993.

Vinification: l'expérience bourguignonne, résultats d'essais, BIVB, Beaune, July 1993.

IVème Colloque professionnel des vins de Bourgogne: techniques de qualité et approches économiques: acquis et perspectives (Beaune, April 1994).

BIVB has also collaborated in the publication of *Bourgogne, la revue du vin* by Société d'Edition et de Publication de Bourgogne, Dijon, of which reference has been made to the issues of November and December 1991, January, February, March, April, May, July, August/September, October, November, December 1992, and January 1993.

Cannard, Henri, *Balades en Bourgogne guide des vignobles de Chablis et de l'Auxerrois*, vol. I, Dijon, 1983.

Cannard, Henri, *Balades en Bourgogne: guide des vignobles de la Côte d'Or*, Henri Cannard, Imprimerie, Dijon, 1988.

Cannard, Henri, *Marsannay et ses vignobles*, Collection de la Vinothèque, Henri Cannard, Dijon-Lac, 1991.

Capus, J., *L'Evolution de la législation sur les appellations d'origine*, Louis Larmat, Paris, 1947.

Caspar, P., *Le Climat de Dijon et de ses environs*, RGL, 1949.

Chapuis, Claude, *Aloxe-Corton: histoire du village et de son vignoble*, Imprimerie Pornon, Dijon, 1988.

Chapuis, Claude, *Corton*, Jacques Legrand, Paris, 1989.

Chapuis, Louis, *Vigneron en Bourgogne*, Robert Laffont, Paris, 1980.

Chauvet, Marcel et Reynier, Alain, *Manuel de viticulture*, Editions J. B. Baillière, Paris, 1975.

Cavalloro, Prof Raffaele (ed.), *Integrated Pest Control in Viticulture*, (EC Experts Group, Portoferraio, September 1985), A. A. Balkema, PO Box 1675, 3000 BR Rotterdam, Netherlands, 1987.

Chidgey, Graham, *Guide to the Wines of Burgundy*, Pitman, 1977

Clos-Jouve, Henry and Benoit, Félix, *Le Beaujolais secret et gourmand*, Solarama, 1973.

Colette, *En Bourgogne dans les vignes du Seigneur*, Chauvenet-Léon Damour, Paris.

Colombet, Albert, *L'Action tutélaire du Parlement de Bourgogne vis-à-vis des vignes et des vins de notre province*, Bulletin de la Société d'Archéologie de Beaune, Congrès des Sociétés Savantes, Beaune, 1951.

Colombier, Jean, *Les Vins d'appellation d'origine contrôlée* (Application Côte d'Or), Memoires d'études ENSSAA, Beaune, 1971.

Commeaux, Charles, *Histoire des Bourguignons* (parts 1 and 2), Fernand Nathan, Paris, 1980.

Coste, Pierre, *Les Révolutions du Palais, histoire sensible des vins*, J.-C. Lattès, January 1988.

Courtépée, M. (Prêtre) and Béguillet, M. (Avocat), *Description générale et particulière du Duché de Bourgogne*, 7 vols, 1775-85.

Dahl, Roald, 'Romanée-Conti and the Wine Maiden', 1980s American Magazine article.

Danguy, M. R. and Aubertin, M. Ch., *Les Grands Vins de Bourgogne: la Côte d'Or*, H. Armand, Dijon, 1892.

Delissey, M., *Beaune, ses vins fins et le commerce du vin*, 1961.

Denman, James L., *Wine and its Counterfeits*, London, 1876.

Derognat, Donnot and Defer-Lagoutte, *Beaujolais Mâconnais: ecologie, archéologie et oenologie*, CRDP, Académie de Lyon, 1975.

Des Ombiaux, *Petit Manuel de l'amateur de Bourgogne*, 1908.

Dion, Prof. Roger, *Histoire de la vigne et du vin en France des origines au XIXème siècle*, Paris, 1959.

Doutrelant, P. M., *Les Bons Vins et les autres*, Editions du Seuil, Paris, 1976.

Dulau, L., *Géologie de la Côte d'Or*, 1961.

Dumay, Raymond, *La Mort du vin*, Editions Stock, Paris, 1976.

Dumay, Raymond (ed.), *Le Vin de Bourgogne*, Editions Montalba, Lausanne, June 1976.

Durand, E. and Guicherd, J., *La Culture de la vigne en Côte d'Or*, Arthur Batault, Beaune, 1896.

Dutraive, Justin, *Jadis en Beaujolais*, M. Lescuyer et Fils, Lyon, 1976.

Editions du Cuvier, *Almanach du Beaujolais*, Jean Guillermet, Villefranche, 1933, 1937, 1941, 1945, 1948, 1955, 1956, 1957, 1958, 1960.

Engel, René, *Propos sur l'art du bien boire*, Filiber, Nuits-Saint-Georges, 1971.

Eyres, Harry, *Wine Dynasties of Europe (Grivot of Vosne-Romanée)*, Lennard Publishing, Oxford, 1990 .

Faith, Nicholas, *Voyage en Bourgogne*, Caisses des Dépôts et Consignations, Paris, 1991.

Ferré, L., *Traité d'oenologie bourguignonne*, INAO, Paris, 1958.

Fielden, Christopher, *White Burgundy*, Christopher Helm, London, 1988.

Foillard L. and David, T., *Le pays et le vin Beaujolais*, J. Guillemet, Ville-franche.

Forgeot, Pierre, *Guide de l'amateur de Bourgogne*, Presses Universitaires de France, Paris, 1967.

Forgeot, Pierre, *Origines du vignoble bourguignon*, Presses Universitaires de France, Paris, 1972.

France, Benoît (Maps): *Vignobles de Bourgogne: Côte de Beaune; Côte de Nuits; Pommard; Volnay; Meursault; Chablis, Auxerrois, Tonnerrois*, Editions Provicart, 115 rue Monge, 75005 Paris.

Fromageot, L., Marion, Maurice, Colombet, Albert, Perraux, Lucien, *Bulletin de la Société d'Archéologie de Beaune*, 25–7 May 1951.

Gadille, Rolande, *Le Vignoble de la Côte bourguignonne*, Les Belles Lettres, Publications de l'Université de Dijon, Paris, 1967.

Galet, P., *Cépages et vignobles de France*, vol. II, Paul Dehan, Montpellier, 1958.

Gardien, Jacques, *Le Vin dans la chanson populaire bourguignonne*, L'Arche d'Or, Dijon, 1967.

George, Rosemary, *The Wines of Chablis*, Sotheby Publications, London, 1984.

Ginestet, Bernard, *La Bouillie bordelaise*, Flammarion, Paris, 1975.

Ginestet, Bernard, *Chablis*, Jacques Legrand, Nathan, Paris, 1986.

Goujon, Pierre, *Le Vignoble de Saône-et-Loire au XIXème siècle*, Université Lyon II, Lyon, 1973.

Grivot, Françoise, *Le Commerce des vins de Bourgogne*, SABRI, Paris, 1962.

Guimberteau, G. (ed.), *Le Bois et la qualité des vins et eaux-de- vie*, Vigne et vin publications internationales, Martillac, 1992.

Guyou, Aline and Parel, Jean-Luc, *Vigne, sol, sous-sol en Beaujolais*, Mémoire de fins d'étude 5ème Promotion des Elèves Ingénieurs, Institut Supérieur d'Agriculture Rhône Alpes (ISARA), Lyon, 1976.

Guyot, J., *Etude des vignobles de France*, Paris, 1868.

Hallgarten, Fritz, *Wine Scandal*, Weidenfield & Nicolson, London, 1986.

Halliday, James, 'Pinot Noir', lecture given to Institute of Masters of Wine student seminar, Sydney, January 1992.

Halliday, James, *Wine Atlas of Australia and New Zealand (Climatic Change and the Greenhouse Effect)*, HarperCollins, London, 1991.

Halliday, James and Johnson, Hugh, *The Art and Science of Wine*, Mitchell Beazley, London, 1992.

Hugonnet, Huguette and Burgin, Albert, *Meursault autrefois . . .* , Société d'Histoire et d'Archéologie de Beaune, vol. LXIV, 1983.

Hyams, Edward, *Dionysus: a Social History of the Wine Vine*, Sidgwick & Jackson, London, 1987.

Jacquemont, Guy, *De la mise en bouteilles obligatoire dans la région de production Bourgogne*, Mémoire d'études ESA Purpan, Toulouse, 1970.

Jackson, David, and Schuster, Danny, *The Production of Grapes and Wine in Cool Climates*, Gypsum Press, Christchurch, 1994.

Jeffs, Julian, *The Wines of Europe*, Faber and Faber, London, 1971.

Johnson, Hugh, *The Story of Wine*, Mitchell Beazley, London, 1989.

Johnson, Hugh, *The World Atlas of Wine*, 4th edn, Mitchell Beazley, London, 1994.

Johnson, Hugh, *Wine Companion*, 2nd edn, Mitchell Beazley, London 1987.

Jullien, A., *Topographie de tous les vignobles connus*, de Lacroix et Baudry, Paris, 1832.

Kempf, Michel, 'Rapport de Stage', Centre de formation permanente pour adultes, Section 'Techniques et Métiers de la Vigne et du Vin', Lycée Agricole de Mâcon-Davayé, 1977/8.

Knox, Mel, *Futsing around in the Forests of France*, International Oak Symposium, San Francisco State University, June 1993.

Knox, Mel (contributor of articles on oak and barrels), *The Oxford Companion to Wine* (ed. Jancis Robinson), Oxford University Press, Oxford, 1994.

Knox, Mel, *Flavours and Chemistry of Wine Barrels*, Knox-Fax Industrial Publications, San Francisco, 1992.

Kramer, Jane, 'Letter from Europe (Armande Douhairet of Monthelie)', *New Yorker*, January 1990.

Lagrange, André, *Catalogue du Musée du vin de Bourgogne à Beaune*, G.-P. Maisonneuve et Larose, Paris, 1974.

Landrieu-Lussigny, Marie-Hélène, *Les Lieux-dits dans le vignoble bourguignon*, Editions Jeanne Laffitte, Marseille, 1983.

Laurent, Robert, *Les Vignerons de la Côte d'Or au XIXème siècle*, Les Belles Lettres, Paris, 1958.

Lavalle, Dr Jean, *Histoire et statistique de la vigne et des grands vins de la Côte d'Or*, 1855 (facsimile edn Fondation Geisweiler, Nuits-Saint-Georges, 1972).

Lebeau, Frère Marcel, *Essai sur les vignes de Cîteaux des origines à 1789*, Bibliothèque Municipale de Dijon, 1986.

Lee, Terry H. (ed.), 'Aspects of Grapevine Improvement in Australia, Clonal Selection of Pinot Noir and Chardonnay in France', seminar proceedings, Australian Wine Research Institute, Urrbrae, South Australia, November 1986.

Léglise, Max, 'L'Evolution de la vinification des vins de Bourgogne depuis le début du siècle', Congrès des sociétés savantes, Beaune, 1972.

Léglise, Max, 'La Vinification en rouge en Bourgogne – méthode classique et recherches nouvelles', INRA, Station Oenologique, Beaune.

Léglise, Max, *Une Initiation à la dégustation des grands vins*, DIVO, Lausanne, 1976.

Léglise, Max, Naudin, R. and Prévost, J., 'Essais de traitement de raisins rouges entiers par la vapeur d'eau avant vinification', Extrait de Progrès Agricole et Viticole, 84 Année Tome CLXVII.

Leneuf, Noel, Lautel, Robert and Rat, Pierre, *Terroirs et vins de France* (Bourgogne-Beaujolais), ed. Charles Pomerol, Total-Edition-Presse, Paris, 1984–6.

Lichine, Alexis, *Encyclopaedia of Wines and Spirits*, 5th edn, Cassell, London, 1982.

Lynch, Kermit, *Adventures on the Wine Route*, Farrar, Straus & Giroux, New York, 1988.

Loubère, Leo A., *The Wine Revolution in France, the Twentieth Century*, Princeton University Press, Oxford, 1990.

Marilier, Jean, *Histoire de l'Eglise en Bourgogne*, Editions du Bien Public, Dijon, 1991.

Marrison, L. W., *Wines and Spirits*, Penguin Books 1958.

Masters of Wine, Institute of, *Journal of Wine Research* vol. 1 no. 3 (Organic wine production); vol. 3 no. 1 (Resvératrol); vol. 3 no. 2 (Organic wine overview); vol. 3 no. 3 (Climate variability); vol. 4 no. 2 (Resvératrol).

Matthews, Patrick (ed.) *Christie's Wine Companion No. 2*, Christie's Wine Publications, London, 1983.

Matthews, Patrick (ed.) *Christie's Wine Companion*, Webb & Bower/ Michael Joseph, London, 1987.

Méras, Mathieu, *Le Beaujolais au moyen âge*, Edition du Cuvier, Villefranche, 1956.

Mitchell, Charlotte and Wright, Iain, *The Organic Wine Guide*, Mainstream Publishing, Edinburgh, 1987.

Morelot, Dr, *Statistique de la vigne dans le département de la Côte d'Or*, Dijon, Paris, 1831.

Morris, Jasper, *The White Wines of Burgundy*, Octopus Books, London, 1988.

Morris, Jasper (contributor, many Burgundy sections), *The Oxford Companion to Wine*, ed. Jancis Robinson, Oxford University Press, Oxford, 1994.

Morton Shand, P., *A Book of French Wines*, revised and edited by Cyril Ray, Penguin Books, Harmondsworth, 1968.

Naudin, René, *L'Elevage des vins de Bourgogne en fûts neufs de chêne (résultats d'expérimentation)*, ITV, Beaune, 1989.

Ordish, George, *The Great Wine Blight*, Sidgwick & Jackson, London, 1987.

Orizet, Louis, *Mon Beaujolais*, Editions de là Grisière, Mâcon, 1976.

Ousby, Ian, *Blue Guide Burgundy*, A. & C. Black, London, 1992.

Pacottet, P., *Viticulture*, Paris, 1905.

Parker, Robert M., Jr., *Wine Buyer's Guide*, Simon & Schuster, New York, 1987.

Perriaux, Lucien, *Histoire de Beaune et du pays beaunois*, Presses Universitaires de France, Paris, 1974.

Peynaud, Emile, *Connaissance et travail du vin*, Dunod, Paris, 1981.

Peynaud, Emile, *The Taste of Wine: the Art and Science of Wine Appreciation*, translated by Michael Schuster, Macdonald Orbis, London, 1987.

Piat, Hubert, *Le Beaujolais*, Editions France Empire, Hubert Piat, Paris, 1977.

Piat, Hubert, *Mon Beaujolais quotidien: mythe et réalités*, Charnay-lès-Mâcon, 1991.

Poulain, R. and Jacquelin, L., *Vignes et vins de France*, Flammarion, Paris, 1960.

Poulet, Philibert, *Grand Livre du vin – 1747*, Poulet, Père et Fils & Jean Dupin, Beaune, 1960.

Poupon, Pierre, *Nouvelles Pensées d'un dégustateur*, Confrérie des Chevaliers du Tastevin, Nuits-Saint-Georges, 1975.

Poupon, Pierre, *Plaisirs de la dégustation*, Presses Universitaires de France, Paris, 1973.

Poupon, Pierre, *Toute la Bourgogne, portrait d'une province*, Presses Universitaires de France, Paris, 1970.

Poupon, Pierre, *Vignes et jours, carnet d'un Bourguigon*, Jean Dupin, Beaune, 1963.

Poupon, Pierre and Forgeot, Pierre, *Les Vins de Bourgogne*, 8th edn, Presses Universitaires de France, Paris, 1977.

Practical Winery & Vineyard and The International Wine Academy, *International Oak Symposium Proceedings*, San Francisco State University, June, 1993.

Prial, Frank and Edwards, Michael, *The Companion to Wine*, Prentice Hall, New York, 1992.

Puisais, Jacques, 'Le Goût, sens des sens, propos recueillis par Caroline de Beaurepaire', *Nourriture*, in *Revue autrement*, no. 108, September 1989.

Quittanson, Charles and Aulnoyes, François des, *L'Elite des vins de France*, Centre Nationale de Coordination, Paris, 1969.

Quittanson, Charles and Vanhoutte, R., *La Protection des Appellations d'Origine et le commerce des vins et eaux de vie*, La Journée Vinicole, Montpellier, 1970.

Rat, Pierre, *Bourgogne Morvan*, Guides Géologiques Régionaux, Masson & Cie, Paris, 1972.

Réal, Antony, *Les Grands Vins, curiosités historiques*, 1887.

Redding, Cyrus, *A History and Description of Modern Wines*, Whittaker, Treacher & Arnot, London, 1833.

Richard, Jean (ed.), *Histoire de la Bourgogne*, Editions Privat, Toulouse, 1988.

Richardot, Jean-Pierre, *Papa Bréchard, vigneron du Beaujolais*, Editions Stock, Paris, 1977.

Rodier, Camille, *Le Clos de Vougeot*, Librairie L. Venot, Dijon, 1949.

Rodier, Camille, *Le Vin de Bourgogne*, L. Damidot, Dijon, 1948.

Robinson, Jancis (ed.), *The Oxford Companion to Wine*, Oxford University Press, Oxford, 1994.

Robinson, Jancis, *Vines, Grapes and Wines*, Mitchell Beazley, London, 1986.

Rose, Anthony, *Harrods Book of Fine Wine edited by Joanna Simon (Jean-Marie Raveneau of Chablis)*, Mitchell Beazley, London, 1990.

Rozet, Georges, *La Bourgogne, tastevin en main*, Horizons de France, Paris, 1949.

Sadrin, Paul et Anny, *Meursault*, Jacques Legrand, Paris, 1994.

Saintsbury, George, *Notes on a Cellar-Book*, Macmillan, London, 1927.

Sauvage, Didier, *et al.*, *Compte rendu des travaux 1991 de la service viticole de la Chambre d'Agriculture de Saône-et-Loire*, Chambre d'Agriculture de Mâcon, 1992 .

Savage, Mark (contributor), *The Oxford Companion to Wine*, ed. Jancis Robinson, Oxford University Press, Oxford, 1994.

Savage, Mark, *The Red Wines of Burgundy*, Octopus Books, London, 1988.

Schuster, Michael, *Understanding Wine: a Guide to Winetasting and Wine Appreciation*, Mitchell Beazley, London, 1992.

Seward, Desmond, *Monks and Wine*, Mitchell Beazley, London, 1979.

Siloret, G., *Le Vin*, Hachette, Paris.

Silvy-Leligois, Hubert, *La Vigne Fossile de Bernouil*, Auxerre, December 1988.

Simon, André L., *Bottlescrew Days*, Duckworth, London 1926.

Simon André L., *The History of the Wine Trade in England*, facsimile edn, The Holland Press, London, 1964.

Spurrier, Steven, *The Académie du Vin Concise Guide to French Country Wines,* Putnam Publishing, New York, 1983.

Taransaud, Jean, *Le Livre de la tonnellerie*, La Roue à Livres, Paris, 1976.

Union Interprofessionnelle des Vins du Beaujolais, *La Vente Directe, 1975 à 1977*, Villefranche, 1978.

Union Viticole du Beaujolais, *Terroir + Savoir Faire = Qualité – Lutte raisonnée, vinification, fertilisation*, UVB, Villefranche-sur-Saône, 1992.

Vaughan, Richard, *Valois Burgundy*, Allen Lane, Penguin Books, London, 1975.

Vedel, A., Charle, G., Charnay, P. and Tourmeau, J., *Essai sur la dégustation des vins*, INAO, Mâcon, 1972.

Vermorel, M. V. and Danguy, M. R., *Les vins du Beaujolais, du Mâconnais et Châlonnais*, Dijon, 1894 (réimpression avec préface d'André Vedel, Jeanne Laffitte, Marseille, 1982).

Vinceneux, Jacques, *Beaunois de jadis: population, métiers, quartiers, comportements 1690–1789*, Centre Beaunois d'Etudes Historiques, Beaune, 1984.

Wallace, Dr Peigi, 'Geology of Wine', 24th International Geological Congress, Section 6, London, 1972.

Warner Allen, H., *A History of Wine*, Faber and Faber, London, 1961.

Waugh, Auberon, *Waugh on Wine*, Fourth Estate, London, 1986.

Young, Alan, *Chardonnay, the World's Most Popular Grape,* Sidgwick & Jackson, London, 1988

Younger, William, *Gods, Men and Wine*, The Wine and Food Society/ Michael Joseph, London, 1966.

Yoxall, H. W., *The Wines of Burgundy*, The International Wine and Food Society/ Michael Joseph, London, 1968.

Index

Main references to Burgundy suppliers in Part 2 are in bold. Numbers in italic denote maps, diagrams and figures.

Individual vineyards are shown under the village name in which the vineyard is found, except in the case of *Grands Crus* which have their own entries.

Most vineyards and *lieux-dits* are spelt in a variety of ways by their Burgundian owners and I have tried within the text to respect these individual spellings, as they appear on wine labels. For ease of reference in the Index, however, page numbers are grouped beside the most common spelling, each vineyard appearing within its relevant commune.

Goubard, Michel 555
Goud de Beaupuis, Domaine 392–3
Gouges, Domaine Henri 339–40
Gouges, Henri 173, 176
Goyard, Henri 592
grafting 45, 78–81
Gramont, Domaine Machard de 342–5
Gramont, Bertrand Machard de 343
Grand' Cour, Domaine de la 630
Grande Rue, La 310, 318; Grands Crus
(Great Growths) 6, 142, 144,
160–1, 185
Grand Vernay, Château du 647
Grandes Bruyères, Domaine des 647
Grands Crus 6
Grands Echézeaux 313, 315, 318, 322,
324, 328, 391, 399, 406, 558
Granger, P.-J. 543–4
Granges, Domaine des 647
Gras, Alain 451
Gras-Boisson, René 451
grass sowing 95–6
Gravallon, Domaine Fernand 635
great growths *see Grands Crus*
grey rot 48, 64, 82–3, 95, 98–101, 106,
107, 110, 130, 133, 134, 153, 181,
140–1
Griffe, Joël 244
Grille-Midi, Vigneronnage de 632
Griotte-Chambertin 262, 268, 269,
270, 273, 277, 288, 406
Grivault, Domaine Albert 468
Grivot, Domaine Jean 315
Grivot, Etienne 127
Groffier, Robert 286
Gros, Domaine A.-F. 429
Gros, Domaine Anne et François 316
Gros, Domaine Jean 316–17
Gros, Domaine Michel 316–17
Gros Frère et Soeur 315
Grosse Pierre, Domaine de la 632
Grossot, Corinne et Jean-Pierre 220
growers 160–4, 195–7, 3–233 *passim*;
organic 671–2
Guffens-Heynen 583–4
Guidot, Mme Louis 474–5
Guillemard-Clerc 484
Guillemot, Domaine Pierre 389
Guillemot-Michel, Domaine 584–5
Guillot, Alain 585–6
Guyard, Jean-Pierre 255
Guyon, Domaine Dominique 389
Guyon, Domaines Antonin 389

Guyot, J. *quoted* 62
Guyot-Verpiot, Domaine 536

Haegelen-Jayer, Domaine 317
Halliday, James 52–3, 120, 150;
quoted 114, 119, 136, 150, 151,
156
Hameau de Blagny 404
Harmand-Geoffroy, Domaine 271
harvesting: date 116–18; dealing with
a bad harvest 140–2
harvesting machines 101–2, 209
Hautes-Cornières, Domaine des
513–514
Hautes Côtes, Les Caves des 362–3
Hautes Côtes de Beaune (map) 366
Hautes Côtes de Beaune 6, 300–01,
341, 342, 346, 361, 362, 363, 364,
365, 385, 390, 391, 418, 437, 450,
453, 455, 494, 516, 521, 532, 561;
(*blanc*) 348, 356, 357, 360, 361,
363, 388, 419, 519, 522; (*rouge*)
357, 358, 359, 361, 364, 365, 376,
420, 524; Clos du Bois Prévot 363;
La Perrière (*blanc*) 363; Le Clou 364
Hautes Côtes de Nuits (map) 351
Hautes Côtes de Nuits 294, 305, 314,
315, 316, 323, 332, 337, 338,
355–7, 357, 359, 369, 389, 429;
(*blanc*) 345, 346, 349, 358, 359,
362, 534; (*rouge*) 345, 346, 356,
357, 358, 362, 525; Clos du Vignon
(Monopole) 359; Les Chaumes 335;
Clos Saint-Philibert (Monopole)
(*blanc*) 320; Les Genevrières (*rouge*)
356
hectare; conversion table 197, 669
hectolitre; conversion table 197, 669
histamine 157
Heresztyn, Domaine 271
L'Héritier-Guyot 307–8
L'Hermitage, Domaine de 527–8
Histoire et Statistique de la Vigne
(1855) 31
Hospices de Beaune 407–13
Hospices de Nuits-Saint-Georges 339
Hudelot, Domaine Patrick 358
Hudelot-Noëllat, Alain 308
Hudelot-Verdel, Bernard 357–8
Huguenot, Domaine 255
humidity 51

d'Igé, Cave Coopérative 586–7

Monopoles (single ownership
vineyards) 655–63
Monrozier, Domaine 630
Montagny 11, 337, 559–60, 562, 563;
La Crée 556; L'Epaule 534; Les
Burnins 662; Les Chagnors 560;
Les Coères 542, 560, 562, 563; Les
Vignes sur le Cloux 562; Mont-
Cuchot 560, 562, 563; Premier Cru
544, 563, 564
Montchovet, Didier 364
Monternot, H. 648
Monthelie, Château de 447
Monthelie-Douhairet, Domaine 447–8
Monthelie (map) 446
Monthelie 364, 390, 444, 445, 447,
448, 453, 454, 455, 456, 466, 475,
476, 489; (rouge) 445, 447, 448,
463, 464, 478, 488; Champs-
Fulliots 390, 445, 448; Clos-Gauthey
447; Hauts-Brins 445; Les Duresses
413, 447, 455, 464, 470, 489;
(blanc) 447; (rouge) 447; Les Vignes
Rondes 454; Meix-Bataille 447;
Premier Cru 445, 454
Monthelie Sur la Velle 445, 447
Montille, Hubert de 119, 120, 440–1
Montlivault, Comtesse P. de 460–1
Montmain, Domaine de 357–8
Montrachet 324, 469, 477, 480, 485,
488, 493, 499, 501, 502, 504, 508,
513, 558
Moreau, J. 224
Moreau, Jean 513
Morey, Albert 505
Morey, Bernard 505–6
Morey, Domaine Marc 506
Morey, Jean-Marc 506
Morey, Pierre 476
Morey-Coffinet, Michel 506–7
Morey-Saint-Denis (map) 284
Morey-Saint-Denis 266, 267, 270, 271,
273, 281–2, 283, 286, 287, 288,
289, 291, 307, 313, 323, 324, 344,
404; (blanc) 285; (rouge) 285; Aux
Charmes 283; Clos Baulet 287; Clos
de la Bussière (Monopole) 295;
Clos des Ormes 287; Clos Sorbès
291; en la Rue de Vergy (blanc) 252;
(rouge) 252; Faconnières 287;
Gruenchers 287; La Riotte 288; Les
Charrières 344; Les Chenevery 283;
Les Millandes 271, 273, 283, 289;

Les Ruchots 283; Les Sentiers 286;
Les Sorbets 289; Monts Luisants
287; (blanc) 288; (rouge) 324;
Premier Cru 285, 286, 287, 288,
404; Rue de Vergy 277, 279, 288
Morgeot (blanc) 461; (rouge) 461
Morgon 7, 627, 629, 630, 631, 632,
633, 634, 635, 636, 637, 639, 646,
648; Caveau de 635–6; Charmes
595; Côte du Py 634, 636, 639;
Javernières 634; Jean Descombes
612; La Grange Cochard 611;
Lathevalle 617; Les Versauds 621;
Ruyère 617
Morot, Albert 418
Mortet, Denis 274
Mortet, Thierry 274
Mothe, Guy 215
Mouilles, Domaine des 621–2
Moulin-à-Vent 577, 621, 623, 624,
625, 626, 627, 628, 629; Burdelines
626; Champ de Cours 627; Château
des Jacques 616; Clos des
Maréchauds 627; Domaine des
Hospices 626; Domaine Lémonon
615
Moulin-à-Vent, Château du 625–6
Moulin-à-Vent, des Hospices 626
Moulin Berger, Domaine du 619–20
Mouton, Gérard 557
Moutonne, Domaine de la 225–6
Mugneret, Denis 323
Mugneret, Domaine Georges 322
Mugneret, Domaine Gérard 321–2
Mugneret-Gibourg, Domaine 322–3
Mugnier, Jacques-Frédéric 295
Muscadet 92
Musée de Vin, Beaune 102
Musigny 5, 292, 294, 295, 296, 318,
332, 337, 406, 414, 476; (blanc)
296
Musigny, Domaine des 296–7
Mussy, Domaine André 430–1
Muzard, Lucien 518

Naddef, Philippe 255
Naigeon-Chauveau et Fils 274–5
Nallet, Henri 235
Narjoux, Roger et Michèle 547–8
Naudin, René 145, 146, 148
Naudin-Ferrand, Henri 358–8
négociants 9, 12, 28, 115–16, 140,

qualities in wine 16; age 9; after-taste
25; aroma 9, 21, 23, 24–5, 27, 127,
133–6, 142, 145–9, 150–2, 155,
186, 210; balance 24, 29, 64;
bouquet 25, 29, 151, 152; colour 9,
23, 24, 29; flavour 9–10, 23, 25, 29,